EUROPE IN THE TWENTIETH CENTURY
source studies on contemporary
issues and problems

THE DORSEY SERIES IN EUROPEAN HISTORY

EDITOR THEODORE S. HAMEROW *University of Wisconsin*

STROMBERG *A History of Western Civilization*

BLACK *Posture of Europe, 1815–1940:*
Readings in European Intellectual History

WHITE *Medieval History: A Source Book*

SENN *Readings in Russian Political and*
Diplomatic History, Volumes I and II

GOOCH *Interpreting European History,*
Volumes I and II

FUNK *Europe in the Twentieth Century:*
Source Studies on Contemporary
Issues and Problems

EUROPE IN THE TWENTIETH CENTURY

source studies on contemporary issues and problems

Edited by

ARTHUR LAYTON FUNK

University of Florida

1968

THE DORSEY PRESS, Homewood, Illinois

IRWIN–DORSEY LIMITED, Nobleton, Ontario

First Printing, May, 1968

Library of Congress Catalog Card No. 68–19504

Printed in the United States of America

INTRODUCTION

WHAT THE PROBLEMS ARE   The 14 case studies in this volume constitute a collection of source materials bearing on some of the more significant historical episodes that have occurred since the close of the First World War. While the collection emphasizes European political history, several of the studies, such as those of the Manchurian and Suez crises, deal with modern history in a worldwide framework. In all cases an attempt has been made to include primary source material, and in only a few instances will there be found interpretations of events by others than those who participated directly in them. If an interpretive statement has from time to time been included, this has been done either to clarify a point that otherwise would remain obscure, or because the person quoted has an unusual claim to the privilege of interpreting the events of his era.

WHAT THE PROBLEMS ARE NOT   This volume makes no pretense of being a collection of documents in the sense of comprising a *complete* set of sources for any particular historical problem. It is rather a *sampling of representative materials*. Consider, for example, the documents relevant to the origins of the Second World War. Those published in the series *Documents on German Foreign Policy* and *British Foreign Policy* alone provide thousands of pages of information bearing on the subject. The case studies given here can use only a sampling, a suggestion of what a volume contains rather than an exhaustive employment of it.

Nor are many documents quoted in full. Desirable as it may be to study complete texts, the editor had to choose between presenting a few complete texts, with much extraneous material, or a larger number of short excerpts, each one relevant to the question under consideration. Similarly, where a choice existed between a conventional official communication and the more revealing remarks of a participant, the latter frequently has been selected. Many of the formal diplomatic notes exchanged between heads of governments, which form the bulk of many a "white book," have been neglected when greater insight into the negotiations could be obtained from contemporary memoirs or from data not made public at the time. Complete texts of treaties and diplomatic exchanges must be sought elsewhere; the documents in this volume more closely approximate the excerpts in a historian's notes ready for use in the writing of history.

CONSTRUCTION OF THE PROBLEMS   Each problem is constructed as if it comprised the materials gathered by a historian during his own research. This assumes that a historian proceeds through certain steps:

1. He reads through the mass of available documents.
2. He selects those, or parts of those, which he finds relevant.
3. He analyzes these:
   a) in terms of their origins, authorship, and general frame of reference;
   b) in terms of internal consistency and logic;
   c) in comparison with other reliable sources of information.
4. He draws his conclusions with regard to the historical episode he has under consideration.

It must be assumed, however, that the average undergraduate would be unable to apply this process. Accordingly, this collection may be considered as carrying out steps (1), (2), and part of (3). In general, except where the setting is quite obvious, a brief introduction establishing the frame of reference for each document has been provided, but the analysis suggested in (3*b*) has been left largely to the student. Limitations of space have rendered comparison of sources difficult; this would have been possible only by sacrificing something of the scope of each problem, and as the aim of the collection is primarily historical rather than historiographical, it was felt to be more valuable to present broader problems at the expense of providing a great deal of comparative material. Point 4 is of course left entirely to the student.

FOR WHOM INTENDED   The case studies have been designed as a supplement for textbooks in the junior and senior courses in 20th-century history and in contemporary international relations. It is assumed that a student will study the problems in conjunction with a text or with other works in history and international relations. While introductions have been written to supply the documents' settings and to establish a continuity to the groups of selections as a whole, these have been kept to a minimum with the idea of letting the sources speak as much as possible for themselves.

HOW THEY MAY BE USED   The editor envisages at least three uses to which the collections may be put. First, simply as collateral reading. There are 14 studies, convenient for use in a one-semester course, and each one averages a length sufficient to provide a reasonable amount of weekly supplementary reading.

Second, to serve as a basis for term papers. Using only the documents supplied and attempting to answer the questions "For Consideration," the student could so exercise his powers of judgment, analysis, and interpretation that his paper, based on these excerpts as substantiation, could very possibly turn out to be a better piece of historical exposition than a paper written from the secondary sources habitually employed by students.

The third use is simply an extension of the second, for advanced students. In this case the student would use the collection as a point of departure, as a bibliography or calendar of papers. The sources from which quotations have been taken are referred to in the footnotes. Learning from the excerpts essentially what can be found in the original work, the student would seek out the actual volumes for further data; he would check information against encyclopedias and reference books; and he would examine the best secondary works to compare and contrast various schools of interpretation. Obviously, work of this sort begins to approximate research at the graduate level, but it should by no means be too difficult for a superior student who has access to an adequate library.

SELECTION OF PROBLEMS   The aim has been to present problems of major historical significance, yet narrow enough in scope to permit a reasonably intensive scrutiny. The Paris Peace Conference, for example, is too vast a subject to permit in limited space profitable examination of all its aspects. Consequently a single issue at the conference was selected as representative of the questions under consideration. The issue of the Saar was chosen because the conference so nearly collapsed at the time Wilson and Clemenceau were debating it. The Balfour Declaration provides a fine example of idealism in politics, the consequences of which led to one of the gravest conflicts of mid-century. The Suez case, later in the volume, presents a dramatic sequel and demonstrates, in its remarkable parallels with the Manchurian crisis of 1931, how inextricably great powers are enmeshed in the ambitions and aggression of have-not nations.

The Locarno Era suggests a halcyon period of good will in the 1920's; it is worth a close examination to see whether the seeds of renewed conflict were not present. The Manchurian crisis demands consideration for two compelling reasons: it exemplified the first major aggression since 1918, and it demonstrated *par excellence* the well-intentioned and fruitless efforts of the League of Nations to apply the principles of collective security. Locarno and Manchuria, occurring almost contemporaneously, emphasize both the hope and the despair of the 20th century.

It was felt desirable to include at least one study each on questions associated with socialism, communism, democracy, fascism, and colonialism. Hence the studies on the Labour Party in Great Britain, the rise of Stalin in Russia, the 1934 riots in France, Nazi aggression in central Europe, and the withdrawal of France from Vietnam. For a problem that would illustrate political and diplomatic maneuverings in wartime, that of Poland was chosen because it received more attention at Yalta than any other question, and because it became a very important element in the genesis of the Cold War. The growing tension between the Soviet Union and the West is further illustrated by a study of the conflicts in Germany which led to the Berlin blockade. The postwar period has been dominated by a shift in the world power structure and by the everpresent threat of nuclear war. The conflict between Russia and China represents this shift, while the effort of de Gaulle to bring France into that atomic club concerns the other.

A casual perusal of this list reveals that the great majority of problems deal with war, with threats of war, with attempts to avoid war, or with the settlement of wars. Does this reflect a bias on the part of the compiler, or does it mean simply that the most vital concerns of our time are the questions of security and of violence in political life? It may be that future historians will find another *leitmotif* for the contemporary era, but at the mid-point of the 20th century the result of our *machtpolitik* heritage strikes us wherever we look. We cannot escape it.

VALUE OF THE CASE STUDY APPROACH   The approach used in this book is based on the assumption that knowledge of primary sources and a certain minimum of detailed information are necessary before a historian dare attempt an interpretation of history. It is maintained that only the historian who has achieved a respect for detail and who has studied a variety of source materials is equipped to make generalizations and to comprehend the "why" of historical causality. Furthermore, this collection of problems is presented in the belief that working with sources, criticizing, analyzing, and interpreting them, constitutes a valuable intellectual discipline in itself. Just as mathematics develops skills in integration and deduction, so historical analysis should develop powers of reasoning that constitute a good in themselves, and more pragmatically, should assist a student to comprehend the complex structure of contemporary society.

Gainesville, Florida   ARTHUR L. FUNK
April, 1968

TABLE OF CONTENTS

SECTION I

The Settlement after the First World War

THE SAAR QUESTION

A representative dispute at the peace conference, 1917-19

Of the many complex and controversial problems associated with the Paris Peace Conference, few emphasize the fundamental antagonisms prevailing there so well as the question of the Saar. While relatively minor compared to the questions of the Rhineland and reparations, of which it formed a part, the Saar question neverthe-less generated tensions out of all proportion to its significance. It proved to be, in a sense, sympto-matic of the differences between Clemenceau and Wilson, and it came close to bringing to a pre-mature end all the conversations among the Big Four.

The French claims on the Saar Basin are established in the fol-lowing documents. The memoran-dum of March, 1919, was drawn up by André Tardieu, able French statesman who was one of Clem-enceau's principal advisers during the conference. In writing the me-morial he leaned heavily, accord-ing to his own testimony, on pre-liminary researches made by a French committee formed to study problems affecting the peace settlement.

Le Bienvenu

FOR CONSIDERATION   The agreement with Russia, while secret, was revealed in 1917 after the Czarist government had been overthrown. No public claims in regard to the Saar had been made by France before the conference opened. Is the historic argument for restitution, based on 22 years of possession during the Napoleonic era, a valid one? Is the argument for reparations more valid?

French Premier Briand to the French Ambassador to England, Cambon, January 12, 1917

You rightly pointed out to Lord Grey that not only can there be no question about the recovery of Alsace-Lorraine, but that this should not be regarded as a gain or as an accession of new territory. . . . It must likewise be understood that Alsace and Lorraine must be restored to us not in the mutilated condition in which they were left by the treaty of 1815, but with the frontiers as they existed before 1790. We shall thus have the geographic and mineral basin of the Saar, the possession of which is essential to our industries, and the memory of the successive mutilations of our frontier must be obliterated.[1]

Russian Foreign Minister Pokrovsky to the French Ambassador to Russia, February 14, 1917

In your note of today's date your Excellency was good enough to inform the Imperial Government that the Government of the Republic was contemplating the inclusion in the Terms of Peace to be offered to Germany the following demands and guarantees of a territorial nature:

1. Alsace-Lorraine to be restored to France.

2. The frontiers are to be extended at least up to the limits of the former principality of Lorraine, and are to be drawn up at the discretion of the French Government, so as to provide for the strategical needs and for the inclusion in French territory of the entire iron district of Lorraine and of the entire coal district of the Saar Valley.

.   .   .   .   .

. . . I have the honour . . . to inform your Excellency . . . that the Government of the Republic may rely upon the support of the Imperial Government for the carrying out of its plans as set out above.[2]

Memorandum Presented by the French Delegation to the Committee of Four (Clemenceau, Lloyd George, Orlando, Wilson), March, 1919

I. Restitution

Landau was ceded to France in 1648. Sarrelouis was built by Louis XIV. . . . All the rest of the Sarre Basin became French between 1792 and 1795. . . .

It was force alone that separated these regions from France. The Treaty of Paris, May 13, 1814, had not attempted this separation, which was effected only at the request of Prussia in 1815, without reference to the wishes of the population. . . .

Two objections have been offered. The separation, though violent and unjust, dates back a century. Is it possible to blot out one hundred years of history? Besides, must we not take into consideration the

---

[1]*British Blue Book*, Cmd. 2169 (London: His Majesty's Stationery Office, 1924), p. 2. Quoted by permission of the Controller of Her Britannic Majesty's Stationery Office.

[2]*Ibid.*, p. 7.

great German immigration, systematically carried on through half a century, which has profoundly modified the population?

To the first objection it may be answered that in the opinion of the Conference time does not suffice to eliminate righteous claims. Poland is revived after more than a century, and Bohemia after more than four centuries. To the second objective, the French Government can also oppose some of the most justifiable decisions of the Conference. The systematical colonization of a country conquered by force is not an excuse for the outrage to which it has been subjected. . . .

II. Reparation

. . . . .

It is notorious that the industrial destruction committed by Germany in France was especially directed against the coal and industrial zone of the departments of the Nord and the Pas-de-Calais. Two-thirds of the surface, as well as of the production of this zone, have been systematically destroyed by the invader. . . . This destruction was not the result of chance or of war operations. It was an integral part of the economic plan of the German Staff. . . . The results . . . are as follows: Two hundred shafts rendered useless for several years. All plants in existence at that date entirely destroyed. A production of over 20,000,000 tons, or 50 per cent, of the national production, withdrawn from the country. . . . The labour population of 100,000 workmen, thrown out of work and their families reduced to want. In all, a material damage of at least 2,000,000,000 francs gold (price of 1912) to which should be added loss of production during the ten years required for reconstruction. . . .

France needs this basin, not only to furnish coal to Alsace and Lorraine, which consume 7,000,000 tons more than they produce, but for herself also. Before the war, France imported annually 23,000,000 tons. With the added needs of Alsace and Lorraine, she would therefore without the Sarre coal be obliged to import even after the re-establishment of her mines in the North, 30,000,000 tons, and, until this re-establishment, 50,000,000 out of a total consumption of 75,000,000. . . . In other words, France would be economically tributary to Germany, who, through coal, would control the prices of all our steel and iron in the east and thus dominate our policies. . . . Such a situation would mean imposing upon France defeat in peace after victory in war. . . .

This necessary reparation is an easy reparation. The Sarre Mines belong almost in their entirety to the Prussian and Bavarian Treasuries. . . . The cession from State to State presents no difficulty; the few private mines that exist would be repurchased by the German State from their owners and ceded to the French State. . . .

As special reparation for the destruction of her mines, as well as a necessary element in the total reparation, France is justified in claiming the Sarre Basin.[3]

---

[3]André Tardieu, The Truth about the Treaty (Indianapolis, Ind.: The Bobbs-Merrill Co., Inc., 1921), pp. 251–62. Copyright 1921, 1949, used by special permission of the publishers, The Bobbs-Merrill Company, Inc.

G reat Britain was represented at the Peace Conference by its Prime Minister, David Lloyd George. In many instances Lloyd George, along with Wilson, opposed the French Premier; but on the Saar question, Britain was not unwilling to compromise.

FOR CONSIDERATION   Lloyd George's memoirs, from which one of these excerpts is taken, were published in 1938. He has very little to say about the Saar question, very little on the meetings of April, 1919, from which Wilson in discouragement almost returned home early. Tardieu, on the other hand, devotes many pages to the problem in his memoirs. May this suggest something of the relative interests of France and England?

Comments of David Lloyd George

The two issues which created the greatest trouble between France, on the one hand, and Britain and the United States of America on the other, were the fixation of the Western boundaries of Germany (this included the highly controverted questions of the Rhine frontier and the future destiny of the Saar coalfields); and the extortionate demand put forward by French ministers for reparations from Germany. It was fortunate for the Conference that France was represented by an exceptionally strong and courageous man, otherwise the Peace Conference would either have been shattered on these passionately controverted topics, or it would have anticipated the process with which we are so familiar in international conferences of to-day, of postponing difficulties to the point of futility and impotence. For his failure to insist upon the extreme French claims on these various issues against all obstacles and opposition, M. Clemenceau was criticized by a formidable junta of Right-Wing and Centre leaders. He met all his critics with the steadiness and the cunning of the best swordsman in France.[4]

British Memorandum on Frontiers, February 4, 1919

. . . The French claim for a revision of the frontier in this district [the Saar Valley] appears to us to deserve support, but it might well be laid down that the assignment of any portion of the Saar coalfield to France should be specifically included as part of the indemnity payable to France. If this principle is accepted, the new frontier should be one which gives to France either the whole or, at any rate, the larger part of the coal-field and should be drawn in such a way as to give her full security in the possession of it. . . .[5]

[4]David Lloyd George, *Memoirs of the Peace Conference* (New Haven, Conn.: Yale University Press, 1939), Vol. I, pp. 578–79. Quoted by permission of the publishers.
[5]David Hunter Miller, *My Diary at the Conference of Paris* (New York: Appeal Printing Co., 1924), Vol. V, pp. 31–32.

President Wilson set forth his proposals for a peace settlement in the Fourteen Points. Later, at the conference, American experts drew up proposals which appeared to be in contradiction to Point 8, especially as clarified in the Lippmann-Cobb interpretation which had been approved by Wilson.

FOR CONSIDERATION   Notice that later President Wilson stood virtually alone in his opposition to the French position. Is it clear on what grounds he made his stand? Is it likely that the appeal of the Saar inhabitants influenced him?

Point Eight of Wilson's Fourteen
Points (January 8, 1918) and Com-
mentary of Walter Lippmann and
Frank Cobb, October 30, 1918

All French territory should be freed
and the invaded portions restored, and
the wrong done to France by Prussia in
1871 in the matter of Alsace-Lorraine,
which has unsettled the peace of the
world for nearly fifty years, should be
righted in order that peace may once
more be made secure in the interest of all.
    Commentary. . . . Attention is called
to the strong current of French opinion
which claims the "boundaries of 1814"
rather than of 1871. The territory claimed
is the valley of the Saar with its coalfields.
No claim on grounds of nationality can
be established, but the argument leans on
the possibility of taking this territory in
lieu of indemnity; it would seem to be a
clear violation of the President's proposal.[6]

Report Prepared by the Intelligence
Section of the American Delegation
for the President, January 21, 1919

It is recommended that in addition,
territory in the basin of the Saar forming
a part of Lorraine in 1814 be also restored
to France, equitable compensation being
made to those Germans who wish to sell
their property to repatriate themselves. . . .

[6]*Papers Relating to the Foreign Relations of
the United States, 1918, Supplement I, The
World War* (Washington, D.C.: U.S. Government Printing Office, 1933), Vol. I, pp. 409–10.

This recommendation is made because
the change from ┴he 1814 to the 1815 line
was the first of the series of Prussian encroachments on French territory. . . . The
restoration of the line of 1814 in Lorraine
may also be viewed as an indemnity for
the damage inflicted by Germany to the
French coal mines of Lens and Valenci-
ennes.[7]

Petition Presented to President Wilson
by the Inhabitants of Saarbrücken,
December, 1918

. . . We are German as regards race,
history, language and sentiment. We desire to remain united with our German
brethren even in this time of trouble and
misfortune. For more than 900 years the
Saarbrücken country was an independent
German principality. In 1807, at the time
of the French Revolution, it was annexed
to France, but was restored to Germany
by the Second Peace of Paris in 1815, as
a part of the Prussian Rhine provinz.
. . . The annexation of the region of
Saarbrücken to France for the second
time would be inconsistent with the principles of peace settlement laid down by
President Wilson, and accepted not only
by Germany but by her opponents as
the basis for establishing the terms of
peace. . . .[8]

[7]Miller, *op. cit.,* Vol. IV, p. 213.
[8]Sidney Osborne, *The Saar Question* (London: George Allen & Unwin, Ltd., 1923), p.
361. Quoted by permission of the publishers,
George Allen & Unwin, Ltd., London.

On January 18, 1919, the Peace Conference opened at Paris. The first two
months of the sessions, in which the relatively clumsy Council of Ten
dominated the proceedings, brought no clear-cut decisions on the northern
boundaries of France. In March the Big Four—Clemenceau, Lloyd George,
Orlando, and Wilson—quietly determined to work out major decisions by
themselves. At these Council of Four meetings, starting on March 17, 1919,
heated discussions on the Rhineland and on reparations began. On March
28, Tardieu presented to the Council the French claims on the Saar, basing

his arguments on the memorandum he had drawn up earlier. Lloyd George appeared receptive to the French position, but Wilson completely rejected the proposal. The following documents suggest something of the controversy between Clemenceau and Wilson at this time.

Notes of the Meeting of the Council of Four, March 28, 1919, Afternoon

WILSON: . . . I am ready to set forth a plan (1) to assure to France compensation in kind during the period of recuperation in the French mines; (2) to assure the integrity of industrial unity in the Saar. Both can be done without annexation and without violation of our principles. One must not forget that these principles bind us to Germany, to whom we have made, since the armistice, a definite commitment. If we do not want to put ourselves in the wrong and go back on our word, we must not interpret our own principles too broadly for our own benefit. . . . There is no nation more intelligent than the French nation. If you will let me express to you frankly my way of looking at it, I have no fear of her judgment. Undoubtedly, if they saw that we were not applying the same principles everywhere, the French people would not accept a solution which seemed unfavorable to them; but if we show them that we are doing our best to act justly in all places where comparable problems exist, the sense of justice which is in the heart of the French people will rise up and tell me: "You are right." I have so high an opinion of the ideals of the French nation that I believe she will always accept a principle founded on justice and applied with equality.

The annexation to France of these regions does not have an adequate historical basis. One part of these territories was French for only twenty-two years; the rest have been separated from France for more than a hundred years. I know the map of Europe is covered with ancient injustices and they cannot possibly all be rectified.

What is just is to assure to France compensation which is owing to her for the loss of her own coal mines, and to give the entire Saar area those guarantees she needs for the use of her own coal. If we do that, we will be doing all that one could reasonably require.

CLEMENCEAU: I take note of President Wilson's words and of his excellent intentions. He leaves out feeling and memory: and in that area I have some reservations about what he has said. The President of the United States does not comprehend the basis of human nature. The fact of war cannot be forgotten. During the first three years of this war, America did not see it at first-hand; during that period we lost 1,500,000 men. We have no more manual labor. Our English friends, who have lost fewer than we, but enough to have also suffered very much, will understand me. . . .

I respect your feelings, which are very honorable. Your role is a great one. But you go counter to your objective. You do not sow hate, but you will encounter bitterness and regret. That is why one must bring about a justice which is not mathematical, but which takes feeling into account.

You are prepared to accord us justice from an economic point of view. For that I thank you. But economic needs are not everything. The history of the United States is a glorious history, but a short one. For you one hundred years is a very long period; for us it is not much. I have known men who saw Napoleon with their own eyes. We have our own concept of history and it cannot possibly be the same as yours.

I simply ask you, when you are alone, to think about what I have just said and

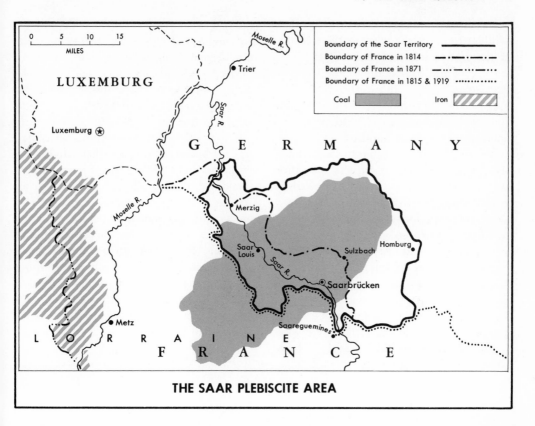

THE SAAR PLEBISCITE AREA

to ask yourself whether in all conscience it does not contain a grain of truth.[9]

Comments of David Lloyd George

There never was a greater contrast, mental or spiritual, than that which existed between these two notable men. Wilson with his high but narrow brow, his fine head with its elevated crown and his dreamy but untrustful eye—the make-up of the idealist who is also something of an egoist; Clemenceau, with a powerful head and the square brow of the logician—the head conspicuously flat topped, with no upper storey in which to lodge the humanities, the ever vigilant and fierce eye of the animal who has hunted and been hunted all his life. The idealist amused him so long as he did not insist

on incorporating his dreams in a Treaty which Clemenceau had to sign. It was part of the real joy of these Conferences to observe Clemenceau's attitude towards Wilson during the first five weeks of the Conference. He listened with eyes and ears lest Wilson should by a phrase commit the Conference to some proposition which weakened the settlement from the French stand-point. If Wilson ended his allocution without doing any perceptible harm, Clemenceau's stern face temporarily relaxed, and he expressed his relief with a deep sigh. But if the President took a flight beyond the azure main, as he was occasionally inclined to do without regard to relevance, Clemenceau would open his great eyes in twinkling wonder, and turn them on me as much as to say: "Here he is off again!"

. . . . .

There was a memorable meeting where President Wilson's homiletic style pro-

---

[9]Paul Mantoux (ed.), *Les délibérations du Conseil des Quatre* (Paris: Centre National de la Recherche Scientifique, 1955), Vol. 1, pp. 68–71.

voked from Clemenceau one of his most brilliant replies. It arose over the question of the restoration to France of the 1814 frontier of the Saar Valley. . . . Clemenceau pleaded for the restoration of a frontier thus accorded to France in the hour of complete defeat. President Wilson retorted "that was a hundred years ago— a hundred years is a very long time." "Yes," said Clemenceau, "a very long time in the history of the Etats-Unis." Wilson then diverged into his usual rhapsody about the superiority of right to might: he referred to those great French idealists—Lafayette and Rochambeau—whose names were held in immortal honour in the United States; and he ended an eloquent appeal to Clemenceau by quoting Napoleon's saying on his deathbed that "in the end right always triumphed over might." Clemenceau did not reply in English, of which he had a considerable mastery, but as was his invariable practice when he had something to say to which he attached importance, sent for an interpreter and then replied in French. He said: "President Wilson has quoted Napoleon as having said that in the end might was beaten by right. He says that he uttered this sentiment on his deathbed. Had it been true it was rather late for him to have discovered it. But it was not true. President Wilson alluded in glowing language to those idealistic young Frenchmen who helped to liberate America. However exalted the ideals of Lafayette and Rochambeau, they would never have achieved them without force. Force brought the United States into being and force again prevented it from falling to pieces." The President acknowledged the cogency of the reply.[10]

---

[10]Lloyd George, op. cit., Vol. I, pp. 223–25.

On the evening of March 28, Clemenceau and Tardieu discussed the American opposition to their claims. As Wilson appeared most concerned about a violation of the principle of self-determination, next day they presented the French claims with a different emphasis.

French Note on the Saar Question, March 29, 1919

It is true that . . . the majority of the population is German owing to immigration. We recognize this fact by not claiming annexation. On the other hand we insist on a solution which would recognize in part at least France's unquestionable claim on a country consecrated French by the will of its inhabitants.

. . . The question of sovereignty of this region should not be settled immediately. For the time being it will not be placed under the sovereignty either of Germany or of France, but under the protection of the League of Nations. . . .

France will receive from the League of Nations a double mandate:

(1) Military occupation
(2) Right of visa or veto on the local administration . . .

French nationality will be conferred individually and after investigation upon those who ask for it. . . .

At the end of fifteen years the inhabitants who have not already manifested their choice must be given an opportunity to do so. . . .[11]

---

[11]Tardieu, op. cit., pp. 267–68.

By March 31, Wilson was ready to concede that French use of the Saar mines was justified as reparation for the destruction of French mines by the Germans. A special committee of experts, André Tardieu for France, Charles H. Haskins for the United States, and Headlam-Morley for England, was directed to examine the social and economic problems associated with such a transfer. Two days later the report was ready. It dealt with technical matters, but included no recommendations as to the kind of administration that might be required to implement the suggestions. Consequently, Tardieu persuaded his colleagues to add the following conclusion to the report. This implied that the committee felt it necessary to go farther than Wilson was prepared to go, for he had not agreed to French control of the area in which the mines were located.

Annex to Committee of Three Report, April 5, 1919

The undersigned are agreed in the opinion that if the above articles which appear to be necessary from the social and economic point of view were to be applied without the establishment of a special administrative and political regime, serious difficulties and conflicts would invariably arise.[12]

---

[12]*Ibid.*, p. 270.

Wilson's reaction to the way the conference was proceeding is indicated in the following documents.

FOR CONSIDERATION   Several factors must be borne in mind: first, the Saar was not the only problem under discussion at this time. All the aspects of the Left Bank of the Rhine and reparations problems were being considered simultaneously. Second, the delegates, anxious to complete the preliminary draft by May, were under severe pressure. Third, President Wilson had influenza, which confined him to his room from April 3 to 7. During this period Colonel House represented him at the council table and reported developments. The ship *George Washington* was at President Wilson's disposal for his transportation to and from Europe. In spite of his request for the ship to be placed in readiness for his departure, he did not carry out his inclination to leave at this time.

Excerpts from the Diary of Colonel House

March 28, 1919. I asked the President to bring his position on the French [Saar] boundary proposals in harmony with the British. The British and ourselves are practically in agreement, therefore it would be a tactical mistake to have the United States take a stand in which she was not supported by Great Britain. I advised yielding a little in order to secure harmony, so that the accusation could not be made that we were unreasonable. He promised to do this.

April 2, 1919. The President tried to get me to admit that the solution which our experts have proposed and which Clemenceau might be willing to take as to the Saar Valley was inconsistent with the Fourteen Points. I replied that there were many who thought otherwise.

April 6, 1919. . . . the President telephoned he would like to see me at four o'clock. He had our fellow Commissioners there and we discussed at great length the best possible means of speeding up the Peace Conference. It was determined that if nothing happened within the next few days, the President would say to the Prime Ministers that unless peace was made according to their promises, which were to conform to the principles of the Fourteen Points, he would either have to go home or he would insist upon having the conferences in the open.[13]

Admiral Benson to Navy Department, April 7, 1919

What is earliest possible date U.S.S. *George Washington* can sail for Brest, France, and what is probable earliest date of arrival Brest? President desires movement this vessel expedited. Carefully conceal fact that any communication on this subject has been received. . . .[14]

Comments of Isaiah Bowman, Chief Territorial Adviser of U.S. Peace Commission

On a certain day three of us were asked to call at the President's house, and on the following morning at eleven o'clock we arrived. President Wilson welcomed us in a very cordial manner. . . . He remarked:

Gentlemen, I am in trouble and I have sent for you to help me out. The matter is this: the French want the whole Left Bank of the Rhine. I told M. Clemenceau that I could not consent to such a solution of the problem. He became very much excited and then demanded ownership of the Saar Basin. I told him I could not agree to that either because it would mean giving 300,000 Germans to France.

Whereupon President Wilson further said:

I do not know whether I shall see M. Clemenceau again. I do not know whether he will return to the meeting this afternoon. In fact, I do not know whether the Peace Conference will continue. M. Clemenceau called me pro-German and abruptly left the room. I want you to assist me in working out a solution true to the principles we are standing for and to do justice to France, and I can only hope that France will ultimately accept a reasonable solution. I want to be fair to M. Clemenceau and to France, but I cannot consent to the outright transference to France of 300,000 Germans.[15]

Comments of General Mordacq, Clemenceau's *Chef de Cabinet*

At the afternoon session, a dramatic episode. Mr. Wilson again took his place. He declared once more that he could not accept the French proposals, even though they were agreed to by England.

The discussion between the two leaders [Wilson and Clemenceau] then became extremely sharp and bitter. Neither one could understand the other. Each rested on his position. Mr. Wilson in particular declared flatly that he would not give in, regardless of the consequences resulting

[13]Charles Seymour (ed.), *The Intimate Papers of Colonel House* (Boston: Houghton Mifflin Co., 1928), Vol IV, pp. 412–17.

[14]*Ibid.,* pp. 417–18.

[15]E. M. House and C. Seymour (eds.), *What Really Happened at Paris,* by American delegates (New York: Charles Scribner's Sons, 1921), pp. 464–65. Quoted by permission of the publishers, Charles Scribner's Sons.

from his attitude. This was serious, as it was purely and simply a break in the negotiations.

That evening, M. Clemenceau told me categorically that he could not continue like that, "that Mr. Wilson was desperately set on placing obstacles in our path," and that he had decided he might as well break off negotiations next day.

In spite of the concessions made by M. Clemenceau, in spite of the modifications in the text which he had continually accepted at Mr. Wilson's request, the latter, at the last moment, would always bring up a new objection. "This is all the more exasperating," added the Premier, "in that each time Mr. Wilson is absent, for some reason or other every-thing goes along fine; when he is there, nothing goes at all. There is definitely nothing to be done with him. In any case, we must finish. We will draw up the treaty with England and Italy. America can do what she likes. After all, she is not absolutely obliged to make peace at the same time as we and under the same conditions."

"And what is Mr. Lloyd George's attitude right now?"

"Very good. He too is absolutely exasperated and will go along with us."[16]

---

[16]General Mordacq, *Le Ministère Clemenceau* (Paris: Librairie Plon, 1931), Vol. III, pp. 216–17. Quoted by permission of the publishers, Librairie Plon, Paris; all rights reserved.

W ilson directed his legal counselor, David Hunter Miller, to draft a proposal which would supplement the technical proposals of the Committee of Three and, in his view, answer the objections that there were inadequate administrative provisions. This proposal was made by Wilson on April 8, and was categorically rejected by Clemenceau, who set forth his objections the next day in a formal note.

President Wilson's Note on the Saar, April 7, 1919

Nothing in these articles shall be deemed to impair the political or civil rights of German subjects, and subject to the provisions of these articles the sovereignty of Germany over the said territories is recognized as continuing.

A permanent Commission of Arbitration shall be appointed to decide all questions and differences which may arise in regard to these articles. . . . France and Germany agree that any dispute whatsoever, not only arising under these articles but any dispute the decision of which may be affected by the terms of these articles, shall be referred to the said Arbitration Commission. . . .[17]

---

[17]Miller, *op. cit.*, Vol. VIII, pp. 22–23.

Notes of a Meeting of the Council of Four, April 8, 1918

. . . . .

Mr. Lloyd George said that the report prepared by M. Tardieu, Dr. Haskins, and Mr. Headlam-Morley on the Saar Valley was to the effect that no really workable scheme could be drawn up on the basis that they had been given.

He thought therefore that it would be necessary to adopt some other scheme. He then read extracts from three alternative schemes which had been submitted to him at an earlier stage by Mr. Headlam-Morley. The scheme which attracted him most was scheme C, which would create a new state in the Saar Valley, somewhat larger than had hitherto been proposed, in customs union with

France and for which France would have a mandate from the League of Nations. He handed copies of these schemes to M. Clemenceau (who undertook to consult M. Tardieu about it) and Col. House.[18]

Clemenceau's Reply to President Wilson's Note, April 9, 1919

. . . . .

According to the terms suggested by President Wilson the consequences would be as follows:

(1) The inhabitants would be represented in the Reichstag where incidents could be artificially provoked.

[18]*Papers Relating to the Foreign Relations of the United States. The Paris Peace Conference, 1919* (Washington, D.C.: U.S. Government Printing Office, 1946), Vol. V, pp. 60-61.

(2) The whole German and Prussian administrative system that has oppressed the region for one hundred years would be continued.

(3) Every economic measure however indispensable taken by the French Government would be indefinitely held up by the German authorities who, to this end, would have only to bring an action before the Court of Arbitration.

(4) If the 72,000 workmen placed under French labour laws started a strike, what legislation could be applied to the basin?

Franco-German friction would thus be multiplied in this region and would be reflected in all the relations between the two countries. No special and local Tribunal would be able to repair the damage done in this way.[19]

[19]Tardieu, *op. cit.,* pp. 274–76.

The conference had now reached a deadlock over the Saar question. There was concern that Wilson would take an unceremonious departure on the *George Washington*. But at the afternoon session of April 9, the President brought out a compromise proposal that included some of the suggestions already made. The new scheme was vigorously debated, and ultimately turned over to the Committee of Experts.

Notes of the Meeting of the Council of Four, April 9, 1919, Afternoon Session

WILSON: I propose that Germany leave this area for fifteen years under the administration of a Commission named by and responsible to the League of Nations. The population would retain its laws, its present institutions, with the Commission having power to carry out modifications required by the special economic system which the treaty will establish. I would give to this Commission both the functions of an arbitration court to settle cases under the treaty, and legislative and executive power in the entire area.

Fundamental regulations would guarantee religious freedom, respect for academic institutions, etc. Finally, Germany's sovereignty would be suspended for fifteen years and, at the end of this period, the population would itself decide its fate by plebiscite.

All the other proposals remove the country from German sovereignty without placing it under French sovereignty, at the same time giving it a French governor named by the League of Nations. I prefer the arrangement I have just described, which puts the country under a provisional rule until the results of the plebiscite are known.

LLOYD GEORGE: It seems to me that this meets M. Tardieu's objections . . . .

CLEMENCEAU: I understand that German sovereignty would be suspended and the administration turned over to the League of Nations. But in that case, why should not the League of Nations give France a mandate ?

LLOYD GEORGE: I must point out that the entire economic life of the country would already be in French hands.

WILSON: I am looking with all my strength for a solution which will satisfy you and satisfy me: I don't see anything acceptable which abolishes German sovereignty. The declarations we have made, the commitments I have made, promise France a reparation of the wrongs done to her in 1871. Perhaps I should have said: "The wrongs done to France in Alsace Lorraine," or some other formula which would have included the violation of French rights in 1815. But we have spoken only of the Treaty of Frankfort and we are bound by what we have said.

I cannot return to the United States and say to the American people: "Upon examination we have found it expedient to go back on our word." They would tell me that we are committed by the armistice terms and by the statements made at the time it was signed.

I am asking you to find a road in your direction. I have taken many steps in order to meet you; don't make it impossible for me to give you as much help as I can.[20]

---

[20]Mantoux, op. cit., Vol. I, pp. 203–04.

Notes of the Meeting of the Council of Four, April 10, 1919, Morning Session

CLEMENCEAU: In Article I, I read that sovereignty remains with Germany. I should like to substitute for this sentence another which would indicate that sovereignty is transferred to the League of Nations. . . .

LLOYD GEORGE: The easiest way, as I said yesterday, is not to use the word "sovereignty" at all, but simply to write: "Germany relinquishes the administration of this region to the Allied Powers, as trustees of the League of Nations."

WILSON: I must point out that the Allied Powers do not constitute a person under the law, while the League of Nations does. I would prefer to write that Germany renounces the administration of this region in favor of the League of Nations.

CLEMENCEAU: Would this not seem to leave the sovereignty to Germany?

LLOYD GEORGE: It seems to me that the formula is satisfactory.

CLEMENCEAU: Not for me.

ORLANDO: It's a question of words. The word "administration," in French and Italian, has a very narrow sense, like the German "Verwaltung." If we wish to avoid an ambiguity, which M. Clemenceau fears, we should replace "administration" with "government."

This proposal was adopted.[21]

---

[21]Ibid., pp. 209–10.

During the discussions Lloyd George in general supported the French view and, as a compromise, suggested that the Saar become independent with French ownership of the mines. Around this proposal and the French and American proposals, a compromise was worked out in which France would get the mines, the Saar Basin would be administered by the League of Nations, and a plebiscite would in 15 years determine the ultimate disposition of the region. A draft of this compromise was approved on April 13. The first draft of the treaty was submitted to the German delegation on May 7. As the section on the Saar underwent but few changes, the final version, as incorporated in the Treaty of Versailles, is given here.

**Excerpts from Part III, Section IV
(Saar Basin) and Annex to Section IV,
Treaty of Versailles, June 28, 1919**

Art. 45. As compensation for the destruction of the coal-mines in the north of France and as part payment towards the total reparation due from Germany for the damage resulting from the war, Germany cedes to France in full and absolute possession, with exclusive rights of exploitation, unencumbered and free from all debts and charges of any kind, the coal-mines situated in the Saar Basin. . . .

.   .   .   .   .

Art. 48. [Defines boundaries of the Saar Basin.]

Art. 49. Germany renounces in favour of the League of Nations, in the capacity of trustee, the government of the territory defined above.

At the end of fifteen years from the coming into force of the present Treaty the inhabitants of the said territory shall be called upon to indicate the sovereignty under which they desire to be placed.

.   .   .   .   .

Annex

1. From the date of the coming into force of the present Treaty, all the deposits of coal situated within the Saar Basin . . . become the complete and absolute property of the French State. . . .

3. As far as concerns the mines which are being worked, the transfer of the ownership to the French State will apply to all the accessories and subsidiaries of the said mines, in particular to their plant and equipment both on and below the surface. . . .

5. The value of the property thus ceded to the French State will be determined by the Reparation Commission. . . .

This value shall be credited to Germany in part payment of the amount due for reparation. . . .

14. The French State shall always have the right of establishing and maintaining, as incidental to the mines, primary or technical schools for its employees and their children, and of causing instruction therein to be given in the French language, in accordance with such curriculum and by such teachers as it may select. . . .

16. The Government of the territory of the Saar Basin shall be entrusted to a Commission representing the League of Nations. This Commission shall sit in the territory of the Saar Basin.

17. The Governing Commission provided for by paragraph 16 shall consist of five members chosen by the Council of the League of Nations, and will include one citizen of France, one native inhabitant of the Saar Basin not a citizen of France, and three members belonging to three countries other than France or Germany.

The members of the Governing Commission shall be appointed for one year and may be reappointed. . . .

18. The Chairman of the Governing Commission shall be appointed for one year from among the members of the Commission by the Council of the League of Nations and may be reappointed. The Chairman will act as the executive of the Commission.

19. Within the territory of the Saar Basin the Governing Commission shall have all the powers of government hitherto belonging to the German Empire, Prussia, or Bavaria, including the appointment and dismissal of officials, and the creation of such administrative and representative bodies as it may deem necessary. It shall have full powers to administer and operate the railways, canals and the different public services. Its decisions shall be taken by a majority. . . .

21. It will be the duty of the Governing Commission to ensure, by such means and under such conditions as it may deem suitable, the protection abroad of the interests of the inhabitants of the territory of the Saar Basin. . . .

27. The present stipulations will not affect the existing nationality of the inhabitants of the territory of the Saar Basin. . . .

28. Under the control of the Governing Commission the inhabitants will retain their local assemblies, their religious liberties, their schools and their language. The right of voting will not be exercised for any assemblies other than the local assemblies, and will belong to every inhabitant over the age of twenty years, without distinction of sex. . . .

30. There will be no military service, whether compulsory or voluntary, in the territory of the Saar Basin, and the construction of fortifications therein is forbidden. Only a local gendarmerie for the maintenance of order may be established. It will be the duty of the Governing Commission to provide in all cases for the protection of persons and property in the Saar Basin. . . .

34. At the termination of a period of fifteen years from the coming into force of the present Treaty, the population of the territory of the Saar Basin will be called upon to indicate their desires in the following manner: A vote will take place by communes or districts, on the three following alternatives: (a) maintenance of the régime established by the present Treaty and by this Annex; (b) union with France; (c) union with Germany. All persons without distinction of sex, more than twenty years old at the date of the voting, resident in the territory at the date of the signature of the present Treaty, will have the right to vote. The other conditions, methods and the date of the voting shall be fixed by the Council of the League of Nations in such a way as to secure the freedom, secrecy and trustworthiness of the voting.

35. The League of Nations shall decide on the sovereignty under which the territory is to be placed, taking into account the wishes of the inhabitants as expressed by the voting: . . .

36. If the League of Nations decides in favour of the union of the whole or part of the territory of the Saar Basin with Germany, France's rights of ownership in the mines situated in such part of the territory will be repurchased by Germany in their entirety at a price payable in gold. The price to be paid will be fixed by three experts, one nominated by Germany, one by France, and one, who shall be neither a Frenchman nor a German, by the Council of the League of Nations; the decision of the experts will be given by a majority. . . .[22]

---

[22]*Papers Relating to the Foreign Relations of the United States. The Paris Peace Conference, 1919,* Vol. XIII, p. 162–82.

Aﬀ ter the German delegation completed its study of the May 7 draft of the proposed treaty, it brought forth several long protests. One of these protests and two reactions are given here.

Proposal of German Experts, May 16, 1919

According to Article 45 of the Peace Treaty, the chief object of the measures proposed in Part III, Section IV, concerning the Saar Basin, is to furnish compensation for the destroyed coal mines in the North of France and to make good in part the war-damages caused by Germany. . . .

The point at issue is therefore to satisfy and safeguard economic interests of France. . . .

Having in view the necessity of adequately supplying France with coal, it

Simplicissimus, *Munich,* 1929

"The only proper foundation for the League of Nations. Upon these conditions, Germany may enter the League!"

A German View of the Peace Treaty of 1919

does not seem advisable to treat the question of the Saar territory without having regard to the coal supplies to France and some of her Allies, . . .

We are prepared immediately to ascertain to what extent we are capable of supplying the required quantities and for this purpose to draw up a plan of delivery. . . .

The object of the measures provided for . . . concerning the Saar territory is, just as that of the occupation of the territory to the left of the Rhine and of the bridge-heads, to ensure the fulfilment of the obligation which will be undertaken by Germany. . . .

The desired guarantees for regularity of production and of delivery may be given in the following way:

a. By the participation of French concerns which is to be realized to an extent ensuring to them a considerable influence upon the administration of the German concerns in question.

b. By the grant of a right of precedence as to the surplus of the entire Ger-

man output in coal over and above the home-requirements.[23]

Clemenceau's Reply to German Proposals, May 24, 1919

. . . concerning the Saar Basin, I must explain that the Allied and Associated Governments have chosen this particular form of reparation because it was felt that the destruction of the mines in the North of France was an act of such a nature that a definite and exemplary retribution should be exacted; this object would not be attained by the mere supply of a specified or unspecified amount of coal. This scheme therefore in its general provisions must be maintained, and to this the Allied and Associated Powers are not prepared to agree to any alternative.

For this reason the suggestion you make . . . for some other means of making good the deficiency of coal, . . . cannot be accepted. In particular, I would point out that no arrangement of the kind put forward could give to France the security and certainty which she would receive from the full exploitation and free ownership of the mines of the Saar.

Similarly, the proposed handing over of shares in German coal mines situated in German territory and subject to German exploitation would be of doubtful value to French holders, and would create a confusion of French and German interests which, under present circumstances, could not be contemplated. The complete and immediate transfer to France of mines adjacent to the French frontier constitutes a more prompt, secure and businesslike method of compensation for the destruction of the French coal mines; at the same time, by securing that the value of the mines should be credited to the reparation account due from Germany, it makes full use of them as a means of payment on the general account of reparation.[24]

---

[23]*Ibid.,* Vol. V, pp. 820–22.
[24]*Ibid.,* pp. 915–17.

General Jan Smuts of South Africa to President Wilson, May 30, 1919

The German answer to our draft peace terms seems to me to strike the fundamental note which is most dangerous to us, and which we are bound to consider most carefully. They say in effect that we are under solemn obligation to them to make a Wilson Peace, a peace in accordance with your Fourteen Points and other Principles enunciated in 1918. To my mind there is absolutely no doubt that this is so. . . .

The question becomes, therefore, most important whether there are important provisions of the Treaty which conflict with or are not covered by, but go beyond, your Points and Principles. I notice a tendency to put the whole responsibility for deciding this question on you, and to say that, after all, President Wilson agrees to the Treaty and he knows best what the Points and Principles mean. This is most unfair to you, and I think we should all give the gravest consideration to the question whether our Peace Treaty is within the four corners of your speeches of 1918.

Frankly I do not think this is so, and I think the Germans make out a good case in regard to a number of provisions. All the one-sided provisions, which exclude reciprocity or equality, and all the pinpricks, with which the Treaty teems, seem to me to be both against the letter and the spirit of your Points. I cannot find anything in the Points or the Principles which would cover, for instance, the one-sided internationalization of German rivers, and the utterly bad and one-sided administration arranged in respect of them. Reparation by way of coal cannot cover the arrangements made in respect of the Saar Basin and its people. I even doubt whether the occupation of the Rhine for fifteen years could be squared either with the letter or the spirit of your Points and Principles.[25]

[25]W. K. Hancock and Jean van der Poel (eds.), *Selections from the Smuts Papers* (New York: Cambridge University Press, 1966), Vol. IV, pp. 208–09.

Although the Treaty of Versailles was signed on June 18, 1919, it was eight months before the Governing Commission was finally appointed. Chairman of the five-man commission was the French member, M. Victor Rault, who was frequently charged with partisanship toward French interests. During the first few years of its functioning, the commission, supported by French troops, ruled autocratically. The following document represents the point of view of the Saar citizens.

Memorial of the Political Parties of the Saar Basin to the League of Nations, 1922

The undersigned political parties which, excepting the very small Communist party, represent the entire population of the Saar Basin, beg to submit, most respectfully, the following to the League of Nations. . . .

We protest most emphatically against the Government's attribution of its great difficulties in the administration of the Saar Basin, as officially reported to Geneva, to a disloyal opposition of the leading sections of the population. We declare that this discordance is due solely to the autocratic actions and methods of the Government.

. . . The people are convinced that the Government does not live up to the task set for it by the League of Nations "to know no other duty and have no other interest than the welfare of the inhabitants of the Saar Basin," and that the measures it has been taking have been principally dictated by interests which are outside the limits of the Saar Basin. This general conviction of the people has been further strengthened by the fact that the most influential and the politically most important positions in the Government have not been filled by inhabitants of the territory but—as in a Colonial system—by foreigners, to wit, in this case by Frenchmen.

According to the Peace Treaty of Versailles . . . the Governing Commission is bound to hear the elected representatives of the people before altering existing laws and ordinances and to ask their opinion before imposing new taxes. We can only interpret this stipulation as signifying that the views of said representatives of the people shall be taken into consideration. These representatives have, however, often declared that it is of no use whatever for them to give their opinion upon bills placed before them by the Government because their views are always absolutely ignored.

. . . . . .

On April 12, 1921, without the consent of the people's representatives, the Government introduced a new rate for direct taxes resulting in an important change in the tax laws.

. . . . . .

If the Saar Basin, the country ruled by the League of Nations, is not to be economically ruined within a short time, if the population is to be freed from severe oppression and be able to breathe freely again, then affairs must be remedied without further delay. In our distress we respectfully beg the League of Nations:

1. To examine all laws and changes of laws which have been promulgated against and without the consent of the elected representatives of the people.

2. To order an early withdrawal of the French military forces and of the French police.

3. To comply with a most ardent desire of the population and appoint the Saar Member of the Governing Commission only upon his nomination or selection by the Saar inhabitants.

4. To select as President of the Governing Commission a man who is able to understand and employ our spoken and written language.

5. To choose, as soon as new elections take place, such members for the Governing Commission who shall exercise a neutral administration devoted exclusively to the interests and welfare of the inhabitants of the Saar Basin.[26]

---

[26]Osborne, op. cit., pp. 367–72.

Although there were many criticisms launched against the League administration of the Saar, the years between the signing of the Versailles Treaty and the plebiscite in 1935 were relatively quiet. The following document suggests something about French and German attitudes in the 1930's.

Report of the Saar Governing Commission to the League of Nations, September 30, 1933

The National Socialist Party is carrying on more or less unscrupulous activities in all spheres of public and private life in the Saar, waging an incessant campaign of threats, denunciations and disguised boycotting against inhabitants of the Territory suspected of not sharing its political ideas. Reckless in its choice of the methods of imposing its will, the National Socialist Party never hesitates to make it clear that any persons who oppose it will be made to pay heavily for their present attitude after the plebiscite, and has succeeded in creating an atmosphere of intense excitement in the Saar, which has aroused the opposition of other political parties that refused to submit; the result has been an increase in acts of violence and terrorism.

.   .   .   .   .

In the circumstances, the Governing Commission is likely to be placed in an intolerable position if this state of affairs is not remedied without delay. In order to carry out its mission, it must preserve its authority intact without the latter being weakened by illegal pressure brought to bear on Saar opinion by a political party. The Governing Commission, for its part, cannot engage in party politics; it is fully conscious that it owes protection to all inhabitants of the Territory without distinction of origin, opinion, religion or nationality; and it does not forget that the plebiscite provided for at the termination of the present regime must be held under conditions of perfect independence. It therefore considers that the present position calls for the adoption of exceptional measures without delay, and this view is borne out by all the symptoms cited above.[27]

[27]League of Nations, *Official Journal*, January, 1934.

After 1934, Nazi campaigns were organized to obtain a decisive German vote in the coming plebiscite. The League of Nations, placing the plebiscite problem on its agenda as early as January, 1934, determined that the vote should be administered impartially and fairly. On June 16, 1934, a Plebiscite Commission was appointed, which, arriving in the Saar shortly afterward, began preparation of voting lists. On January 13, 1935, the voting took place with the following results.

Statistics of the Plebiscite, January 13, 1935

Registered voters	539,541
Votes cast	528,105
For union with Germany	477,119
For the *status quo*	46,613
For union with France	2,124
Invalid ballots	905
Blank ballots	1,292[28]

With the plebiscite clearly showing the inhabitants' disposition to return to Germany, there remained only the technical matter concerned with German purchase of the mines. At Basel, on February 11, 1935, the experts concluded that of the total value of the mines (900,000,000 French francs), there remained 611,200,000 francs to be paid. This was to be paid in coal deliveries and was almost complete when war broke out in 1939.

The following document summarizes the role of the League as an administrator. Miss Wambaugh, an American specialist on plebiscites, was a deputy member of the League Commission.

[28]*Ibid.*, February, 1935.

Comments of Sarah Wambaugh, Deputy Member of the Saar Plebiscite Commission

The League achieved in the Saar an admirable record of success. For fifteen years its Governing Commission gave the inhabitants an excellent administration, fulfilling its more than thankless task with skill and devotion. It is undeniable that during that most difficult period which followed the World War, and including four years of world depression, the Saar Territory was well and conscientiously governed, order was maintained, the officials were well paid, the roads repaired, the school system was excellent, with training for every vocation, the taxes were lower than those of either neighbor, and with all this the Territory was left with cash in the treasury and no public debt. The most valid criticism at the time was that it was not a parliamentary government but a dictatorship. The advent of the totalitarian dictatorship in Germany made that reproach less forceful. In any case the Catholic Saarlanders enjoyed under the League Commission a degree of religious equality and tolerance unknown in the past and undreamed of today. Thanks to the fact that the limits of their activity were laid down in a clear and precise charter, the international government by five men without ties of race, patriotism,

creed, education, profession, or general outlook, was accomplished with surprising ease and harmony. That the German government and the Saarlanders themselves should often have felt discontent and that this should have brought criticism on the Governing Commission and on the League of Nations was, in the political circumstances, inevitable. It is a question whether the Saar experiment was necessary, although possibly it was the best solution to be found at the time for a difficult problem; it is certain, however, that history will declare it to have given us a model of international government.

With the plebiscite at the end of the fifteen years the League Council scored a second success, for at a most difficult moment in the world's history it administered a vote in a manner so impartial and so scientific as to wipe the Saar problem, which had threatened to lead the Continent into a war, off the international docket. Certainly if any future plebiscite regarding sovereignty is to enjoy to the full the prestige of a free and convincing expression of the popular will, it must be held under the highest international auspices.[29]

---

[29]Sarah Wambaugh, *The Saar Plebiscite* (Cambridge, Mass.: Harvard University Press, 1940), pp. 321–22. Quoted by permission of Harvard University Press.

POSTSCRIPT   During World War II, the Saar suffered heavily from Allied bombing. By 1945, 43 percent of Saarbrücken had been destroyed, and only two blast furnaces continued to operate. After the war, the Saar fell into the French zone, and a series of conventions enabled France to monopolize coal production and to develop profitable economic relations between Lorraine and the Saar. In 1954, an agreement was reached between France and West Germany whereby the area should become "Europeanized," the first territory to come under administration of the West European Union. But the Saarlanders would have none of this, and in a plebiscite of October 23, 1955 rejected the scheme by a 2 to 1 vote. Paris and Bonn thereupon accepted incorporation of the Saar into West Germany (with advantageous economic concessions to France) and the Saar returned to the Fatherland once more on January 1, 1957.

BIBLIOGRAPHY

SOURCES USED IN THIS PROBLEM

1. Collections and Official Documents

British Blue Book, Cmd. 2169. London: His Majesty's Stationery Office, 1924.

Official Journal, League of Nations.

Papers Relating to the Foreign Relations of the United States, 1918. Supplement I, *The World War.* 2 vols. Washington, D.C.: U.S. Government Printing Office, 1933.

Papers Relating to the Foreign Relations of the United States: The Paris Peace Conference, 1919. 13 vols. Washington, D.C.: U.S. Government Printing Office, 1942–47.

2. Others

HANCOCK, W. K., and VAN DER POEL, JEAN (eds.). *Selections from the Smuts Papers.* 4 vols. New York: Cambridge University Press, 1966.

HOUSE, E. M., and SEYMOUR, C. (eds.). *What Really Happened at Paris,* by American delegates. New York: Scribner's, 1921.

LLOYD GEORGE, DAVID. *Memoirs of the Peace Conference.* 2 vols. New Haven, Conn.: Yale University Press, 1939.

MANTOUX, PAUL (ed.). *Les délibérations du Conseil des Quatre.* 2 vols. Paris: Centre National de la Recherche Scientifique, 1955.

MILLER, DAVID HUNTER. *My Diary at the Conference of Paris.* 21 vols. New York: Appeal Printing Co., 1924.

MORDACQ, GENERAL. *Le Ministère Clemenceau.* Paris: Librairie Plon, 1931.

OSBORNE, SIDNEY. *The Saar Question.* London: Allen & Unwin, 1923.

SEYMOUR, CHARLES (ed.). *The Intimate Papers of Colonel House.* 4 vols. Boston: Houghton Mifflin Co., 1926–28.

TARDIEU, ANDRÉ. *The Truth about the Treaty.* Indianapolis, Ind.: Bobbs-Merrill, 1921.

WAMBAUGH, SARAH. *The Saar Plebiscite.* Cambridge, Mass.: Harvard University Press, 1940.

SELECT LIST OF BOOKS RECOMMENDED FOR FURTHER READING

BAKER, RAY STANNARD. *Woodrow Wilson and World Settlement.* Garden City, N.Y.: Doubleday, 1922.

BIRDSALL, PAUL. *Versailles Twenty Years after.* New York: Reynal & Hitchcock, 1941.

BRUUN, GEOFFREY. *Clemenceau.* Cambridge, Mass.: Harvard University Press, 1943.

BURNETT, PHILIP M. *Reparation at the Paris Peace Conference.* New York: Columbia University Press, 1940.

COWAN, LAING GRAY. *France and the Saar, 1640–1948.* New York: Columbia University Press, 1950.

CRAIG, GORDON A., and GILBERT, FELIX (eds.). *The Diplomats 1919–1939.* Princeton, N.J.: Princeton University Press, 1953.

FLORINSKY, MICHAEL T. *The Saar Struggle.* New York: Macmillan, 1934.

FREYMOND, JACQUES. *The Saar Conflict.* New York: Carnegie Endowment for International Peace, 1960.

The Future Position of the Saar. Appendix to the Report of the Committee on General Affairs. Council of Europe. Strasbourg, 1954.

GELFAND, LAWRENCE E. *The Inquiry: American Preparations for Peace, 1917–1919.* New Haven, Conn.: Yale University Press, 1963.

HASKINS, C. H., and LORD, R. H. *Some Problems of the Peace Conference.* Cambridge, Mass.: Harvard University Press, 1920.

LEDERER, IVO J. (ed.). *The Versailles Settlement: Was It Foredoomed to Failure?* Boston: D. C. Heath, 1960.

LINK, ARTHUR S. *Wilson the Diplomatist: A Look at His Major Foreign Policies.* Baltimore: Johns Hopkins Press, 1957.

LUCKAU, ALMA M. *The German Delegation at the Paris Peace Conference.* New York: Columbia University Press, 1941.

MANTOUX, ETIENNE. *The Carthaginian Peace, or, The Economic Consequences of Mr. Keynes.* Pittsburgh: University of Pittsburgh Press, 1952.

NICOLSON, HAROLD G. *Peacemaking, 1919.* New York: Houghton Mifflin, 1933.

RUSSELL, FRANK M. *The Saar: Battleground and Pawn.* Stanford, Calif.: Stanford University Press, 1951.

SEYMOUR, CHARLES. *Geography, Justice, and Politics at the Paris Conference of 1919.* Washington, D.C.: American Geographical Society, 1951.

SHOTWELL, JAMES T. *At the Paris Peace Conference.* New York: Macmillan, 1937.

TEMPERLEY, HAROLD W. V. *A History of the Peace Conference of Paris.* 6 vols. London: Oxford University Press, 1921–24.

THOMPSON, MALCOLM. *David Lloyd George: the Official Biography.* London: Hutchinson, 1948.

THE BALFOUR DECLARATION

Great Britain and the beginnings of

the Palestine Mandate, 1914-22

When Great Britain and France declared war on Turkey on November 5, 1914, the partition of the Turkish Empire, of which Palestine was a part, became a definite possibility. One of the first members of the British Cabinet to consider the future of Palestine was Viscount Herbert Samuel, an able Jew who held the post of president of the Local Government Board of the Asquith government. His account of his efforts to interest the Cabinet follows.

FOR CONSIDERATION   Compare this account with other data regarding influences on the government. Would Viscount Samuel wish to give himself as much credit as possible for his role? To what extent do the documents he cites corroborate his comments? A comparison of Samuel's *Memoirs* with Weizmann's *Trial and Error* is interesting, as one finds differing emphases of personal influence. Keep in mind, however, that both memoirs were written long after the events in question, Samuel's in 1945 and Weizmann's in 1949.

Comments of Viscount Samuel

The moment Turkey entered the war the position was entirely changed. If Palestine was to be given a new destiny, Great Britain, with her important strategic interests in the Middle East, was directly concerned. The question who was to succeed the Turk in controlling the country that bordered on the Suez Canal was one to which our Government would have to give serious consideration. For myself the matter had an additional and special interest. The first member of the Jewish community ever to sit in a British Cabinet (Disraeli having, when a child, been withdrawn from the community by his father) it was incumbent upon me at least to learn what the Zionist movement was and what it was doing. I got in touch with Dr. Weizmann, who was already one of the principal leaders of the Zionist Organization, obtained its publications and read them with care. . . .

My conclusions soon became definite enough for me to go to the Foreign Secretary and talk them over. A note of the conversations, dated November 9th, 1914, was as follows:

I spoke to Sir Edward Grey to-day about the future of Palestine. In the course of our talk I said that now that Turkey had thrown herself into the European War and that it was probable that her empire would be broken up, the question of the future control of Palestine was likely to arise. The jealousies of the great European Powers would make it difficult to allot the country to any one of them. Perhaps the opportunity might arise for the fulfilment of the ancient aspiration of the Jewish people and the restoration there of a Jewish State. . . .

I said that I myself had never been a Zionist, because the prospects of any practical outcome had seemed so remote that I had not been willing to take a part in the movement. But now the conditions are profoundly altered. If a Jewish State were established in Palestine it might become the centre of a new culture. The Jewish brain is rather a remarkable thing, and under national auspices, the state might become a fountain of enlightenment and a source of a great literature and art and development of science. . . .

I thought that British influence ought to play a considerable part in the formation of such a state, because the geographical situation of Palestine, and especially its proximity to Egypt, would render its goodwill to England a matter of importance to the British Empire. . . .

Grey said that the idea had always had a strong sentimental attraction for him. The historical appeal was very strong. He was quite favourable to the proposal and would be prepared to work for it if the opportunity arose. . . .

A few weeks later I had formulated the ideas I had expressed to Grey in a draft memorandum for the Cabinet. After giving an outline of the facts, I examined the possible alternatives for the future of Palestine, and concluded that annexation to the British Empire, together with active encouragement of Jewish colonization and cultural development, would be the best solution. . . .

In March [1915] I circulated the memorandum in a revised form, expanding some paragraphs, condensing others, and leaving out the rhetoric. The possible alternatives for Palestine were discussed under five heads: (a) annexation by France; (b) remaining Turkish; (c) internationalization; (d) the establishment of an autonomous Jewish State; (e) a British Protectorate, with encouragement for Jewish settlement. The last was advocated.[1]

---

[1]Viscount Samuel, *Grooves of Change: A Book of Memoirs* (London: Cresset Press, 1945), pp. 139–42. Copyright 1946 by Viscount Samuel. Reprinted by permission of the author.

For a long while Jewish people had been attempting to obtain a national refuge in Palestine. The Zionist Organization, founded in 1897, had for years under the leadership of Theodor Herzl negotiated in vain with Turkey for concessions. But the entry of Turkey into the war on the side of the Central Powers suggested to Zionists the possibility of gaining English support for their cause. One of the ablest Zionists in England was Dr. Chaim Weizmann, a Russian-born chemist who was a lecturer at Manchester University and vice president of the English Zionist Federation. He had met C. P. Scott, editor of the *Manchester Guardian*, through whom he was able to reach members of the government. In December, 1914, Tshlenov and Nahum Sokolow, of the World Executive of the Zionist Organization, joined Weizmann in putting the Zionist case before such

British leaders as Lloyd George, Arthur Balfour, and Herbert Samuel. The following letter reflects Weizmann's thoughts at this time.

Letter of Chaim Weizmann to C. P. Scott, March, 1915

The British cabinet is not only sympathetic toward the Palestinian aspirations of the Jews, but would like to see these aspirations realized. I understand Great Britain would be willing even to be the initiator of a proposal to that effect at the peace conference. But at the same time Great Britain would not like to be involved in any responsibilities. In other words, they would leave the organization of the Jewish commonwealth as an independent political unit entirely to the care of the Jews. At the same time there is a view prevalent that it is not desirable that Palestine should belong to any great power.

These two views are in contradiction. If Great Britain does not wish anyone else to have Palestine, this means that it will have to watch it and stop any penetration of another power. Surely, a course like that involves as much responsibility as would be involved by a British protectorate over Palestine, with the sole difference that watching is a much less effective preventative than an actual protectorate. I therefore thought that the middle course could be adopted . . . viz.; the Jews take over the country; the whole burden of organization falls on them, but for the next ten or fifteen years they work under a temporary British protectorate. . . .

A strong Jewish community on the Egyptian flank is an efficient barrier for any danger likely to come from the north. . . .

England . . . would have in the Jews the best possible friends, who would be the best national interpreters of ideas in the Eastern countries and would serve as a bridge between the two civilizations. That again is not a material argument, but certainly it ought to carry great weight with any politician who likes to look fifty years ahead.[2]

[2]Chaim Weizmann, *Trial and Error* (New York: Harper & Row, 1949), pp. 177–78. Copyright 1949, by The Weizmann Foundation.

At the same time that some members of the British government were interesting themselves in Zionist aspirations, Great Britain was negotiating for Arab aid against Turkey and promising eventual independence of Arab states, to be guaranteed by Britain, France, Russia, and Italy. What the terms of this independence should be was the subject of secret correspondence between the British High Commissioner in Cairo, Sir Henry McMahon, and Sherif Hussein of Mecca. Excerpts from two of these letters are given here, with other comments which help throw light on the correspondence.

FOR CONSIDERATION   These letters were not published until 1939, when they were used to strengthen the Arab case against the Jews. Was Palestine included in the McMahon guarantee? McMahon excludes Syria and the "Holy Places." Did this exclude Palestine? What is the significance to the historian of Sir Henry's statement made 22 years later?

Sherif of Mecca Hussein to British High Commissioner Sir Henry McMahon, July 14, 1915

Whereas the whole of the Arab nation without any exception have decided in these last years to live, and to accomplish their freedom, and grasp the reins of their administration both in theory and practice; and whereas they have found and felt that it is to the interest of the Government of Great Britain to support them and aid them to the attainment of their firm and lawful intentions (which are based upon the maintenance of the honour and dignity of their life) without any ulterior motives whatsoever unconnected with this object . . .

For these reasons the Arab nation see fit to limit themselves, as time is short, to asking the Government of Great Britain, if it should think fit, for the approval, through her deputy or representative, of the following fundamental propositions, leaving out all things considered secondary in comparison with these, so that it may prepare all means necessary for attaining this noble purpose, until such time as it finds occasion for making the actual negotiations:

Firstly. England to acknowledge the independence of the Arab countries, bounded on the north by Mersina and Adana up to the 37° of latitude, on which degree fall Birijik, Urfa, Mardin, Midiat, Jezirat (Ibn 'Umar), Amadia, up to the border of Persia; on the east by the borders of Persia up to the Gulf of Basra; on the south by the Indian Ocean, with the exception of the position of Aden to remain as it is; on the west by the Red Sea, the Mediterranean Sea up to Mersina. England to approve of the proclamation of an Arab Khalifate of Islam.[3]

---

[3] *British White Paper*, Cmd. 5957 (London: His Majesty's Stationery Office, 1939), p. 3. Quoted by permission of the Controller of Her Britannic Majesty's Stationery Office.

Sir Henry McMahon to Sherif Hussein, October 24, 1915

.   .   .   .   .

The two districts of Mersina and Alexandretta and portions of Syria lying to the west of the districts of Damascus, Homs, Hama and Aleppo cannot be said to be purely Arab, and should be excluded from the limits demanded.

With the above modification, and without prejudice to our existing treaties with Arab chiefs, we accept those limits.

As for those regions lying within those frontiers wherein Great Britain is free to act without detriment to the interests of her ally, France, I am empowered in the name of the Government of Great Britain to give the following assurances and make the following reply to your letter:

(1) Subject to the above modifications, Great Britain is prepared to recognise and support the independence of the Arabs in all the regions within the limits demanded by the Sherif of Mecca.

(2) Great Britain will guarantee the Holy Places against all external aggression and will recognise their inviolability.

(3) When the situation admits, Great Britain will give to the Arabs her advice and will assist them to establish what may appear to be the most suitable forms of government in those various territories.

(4) On the other hand, it is understood that the Arabs have decided to seek the advice and guidance of Great Britain only, and that such European advisers and officials as may be required for the formation of a sound form of administration will be British.

(5) With regard to the *vilayets* of Bagdad and Basra, the Arabs will recognise that the established position and interests of Great Britain necessitate special administrative arrangements in order to secure these territories from foreign aggression, to promote

the welfare of the local populations and to safeguard our mutual economic interests. . . .[4]

Comments of Sir Henry McMahon

Sir,—Many references have been made in the Palestine Royal Commission Report and in the course of the recent debates in both Houses of Parliament to the "McMahon Pledge," especially to that portion of the pledge which concerns Palestine and of which one interpretation has been claimed by the Jews and another by the Arabs.

.   .   .   .   .

I feel it my duty to state, and I do so definitely and emphatically, that it was not intended by me in giving this pledge to King Hussein to include Palestine in the area in which Arab independence was promised.

I also had every reason to believe at the time that the fact that Palestine was not

4*Ibid.*, pp. 7–8.

included in my pledge was well understood by King Hussein.[5]

Comments of Colonel C. E. Vickery

Sir,—Since it has been decided to publish the letter addressed by Sir Henry McMahon to Sherif Hussein in 1915 it may be of interest to record my impressions of the interview that I had with the late King Hussein in 1920 under instructions from Cairo to read personally the original copy of this letter held by the King.

.   .   .   .   .

I can say most definitely that the whole of the King's demands were centred round Syria and only round Syria. Time after time he referred to that vineyard, to the exclusion of any other claim or interest. He stated most emphatically that he did not concern himself at all with Palestine and had no desire to have suzerainty over it for himself or his successors. . . .[6]

5Letter to the London *Times,* July 23, 1937, Quoted through the courtesy of *The Times,* London.
6Letter to the London *Times,* February 21, 1939. Quoted through the courtesy of *The Times,* London.

As the Hussein-McMahon negotiations concerned an area in which France had certain interests, the British Foreign Office designated Sir Mark Sykes, an expert on the Near East, to negotiate with a French representative for a tentative partition of the Turkish Empire. Sykes and the French official, Georges Picot, reached the understanding explained in the accompanying map by February, 1916. Further negotiations were carried on with Russia and Italy, but they did not affect the Palestine area.

FOR CONSIDERATION   Keep in mind the fact that the Sykes-Picot conversations were secret and unknown to the Zionists, who, however, maintained frequent relations with Sir Mark Sykes. What effect did the agreement have on Zionist aspirations? After the Czarist regime was overthrown in 1917, the terms of the Sykes-Picot Agreement were made public by the revolutionary government.

During 1915 and early 1916, because of its concern with the Arabs and

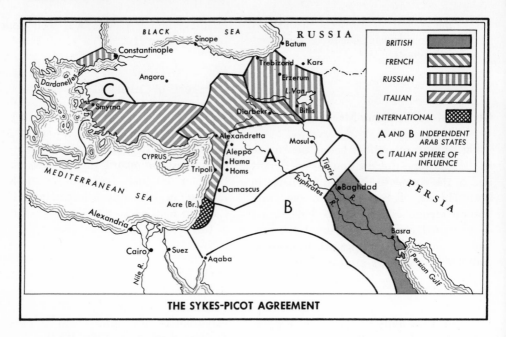

THE SYKES-PICOT AGREEMENT

its relations with the other Entente powers, Great Britain did not carry on active negotiations with the Zionists. But the matter of a Jewish settlement in Palestine was not forgotten, either by the press or by the government, as the following documents indicate.

The *Manchester Guardian* editorial was written by Herbert Sidebotham, who perceived the close relationship of British imperialist strategy with Zionist aims. He was instrumental in forming the British Palestine Committee, whose organ *Palestine* was influential in propagandizing the Zionist case.

Excerpt from Editorial in the
Manchester Guardian,
November 22, 1915

. . . In the long run there can be no satisfactory defence of Egypt or the Suez Canal so long as Palestine is in the occupation of a hostile or possibly hostile Power. . . .

A couple of thousand years before the Suez Canal was built, the rulers of Egypt were perplexed with the problems of the defence of their land frontier, and what helped them to solve it was the existence in the old Jewish nation of powerful buff-er States against the great military Empires of the north. . . . If Palestine were now a buffer State between Egypt and the north, inhabited as it used to be by an intensely patriotic race, friendly as it was in the past to Egypt because that Power was less aggressive as a rule than the great military Empires of the north, the problem of Egypt in this war would be a very light one. It is to this condition that we ought to work. Palestine must either be a part of Egypt (which it is not, neither geographically nor racially), or it must be a buffer State which is prevented from becoming hostile to Egypt. On the realisation of that condition depends the whole future of the British Empire as a sea Empire.[7]

Aide-Memoire from the British Embassy in Russia to Russian Foreign Minister Sazonov, March 13, 1916

. . . Although as is known, many Jews are indifferent to the idea of Zionism, yet a numerous, and the most influential, part of Jewry in all the countries would very much appreciate an offer of agreement concerning Palestine which would com-

pletely satisfy the aspiration of the Jews.

If the above view is correct, then it is clear that by utilizing the Zionist idea, important political results can be achieved. Among them will be the conversion, in favour of the Allies, of Jewish elements in the Orient, in the United States, and in other places, elements whose attitude at the present time is to a considerable extent opposed to the Allies' cause.

. . . The only purpose of H. M. Government is to find some arrangement, sufficiently attractive to the majority of the Jews, which might facilitate the conclusion of an agreement ensuring the Jewish support. . . .[8]

[7]*The Manchester Guardian*, November 22, 1915. Quoted through the courtesy of *The Manchester Guardian*.

[8]E. Adamow (ed.), *Die Aufteilung der asiatischen Türkei* (Dresden: Ministeriums für Auswärtige Angelegenheiten, 1932), pp. 64–65.

In the fall of 1916 the British government revived its interest in the Jewish projects for Palestine. The president of the Armenian National Committee in London, James A. Malcolm, played a significant role in persuading Sir Mark Sykes of the value of Jewish support, particularly in the United States. The following selection, while not a primary source in the usual sense, is presented because it contains interesting references to source material.

FOR CONSIDERATION   In the light of Thomson's statement, does it appear that the effect of Zionist propaganda on the British government has perhaps been overemphasized? Why was Great Britain so anxious at this time to obtain American sympathies? Why should President Wilson have been suspicious of the Sykes-Picot Agreement?

Comments of Malcolm Thomson, English Biographer

In his monumental history of Zionism, *Die Zionistische Bewegung* (Vol. I, p. 656), Dr. Adolf Boehm says that when the U.S.A. had turned down the Sykes-Picot proposals for partitioning the Near East, Mr. Malcolm, President of the Armenian National Committee in London, advised Sir

Mark Sykes to influence Wilson through Brandeis, and to guarantee Palestine forthwith to the Jews, in order to gain their support. . . .

I myself, when writing the biography of the late Earl Lloyd George, studied the mass of documents dealing with the affair, and independently reached the same conclusion. In brief summary I noted how, when earlier efforts of Dr. Weizmann and his friends had failed to influence the Government to support their Zionist programme, Mr. James A. Malcolm suggested and initiated, on the ground of Zionism's potential value to the Allied war effort, a fresh approach to Sir Mark Sykes, the Under-Secretary to the War Cabinet; put him in touch with Dr. Weizmann and his associates; and was a member of the deputation that visited the Quai d'Orsay to win over the French to the proposal, after it had found favour with the new Coalition Cabinet under Lloyd George and the Foreign Office had sent word to Brandeis and through him had worked on Wilson, in Washington.

Curiously, in the account which Dr. Weizmann gives of the Balfour Declaration in chapters XV–XVI of his autobiography [*Trial and Error*] he makes no mention of Mr. Malcolm's vitally impor-tant intervention, and attributes his own introduction to Sykes to the late Dr. Gaster. I have communicated with Mr. Malcolm, who informs me that Dr. Gaster was only brought in some months after the negotiations had commenced, in February, 1917. . . . Dr. Weizmann's omission is the more surprizing, because he wrote to Mr. Malcolm on 5th March, 1941, saying:

You will be interested to hear that some time ago I had occasion to write to Mr. Lloyd George about your useful and timely initiative in 1916 to bring about the negotiations between myself and my Zionist colleagues and Sir Mark Sykes and others about Palestine and Zionist support of the Allied cause in America and elsewhere.[9]

---

[9]Letter to the *London Times Literary Supplement*, July 22, 1949, p. 473. Quoted through the courtesy of *The Times*, London.

In the fall of 1916, the Zionists endeavored to resolve their internal differences and to draw up a formulation of their aspirations in Palestine which could be submitted to the government. The following excerpt summarizes the main points of a memorandum drawn up for this purpose.

FOR CONSIDERATION   Do the terms used definitely envisage the establishment of a Jewish state?

Summary of the "Outline of a Programme for a New Administration of Palestine and for a Jewish Resettlement of Palestine in Accordance with the Aspirations of the Zionist Movement, October, 1916"

1. The recognition of a separate Jewish nationality or national unit in Palestine.
2. The participation of the Jewish population of Palestine in local self-government insofar as it affects all the inhabitants without distinction.

3. The protection of the rights of minority nationalities.
4. Autonomy in exclusively Jewish matters, such as Jewish education, religious and communal organization.
5. The recognition and legalization of the existing Jewish institutions for the colonization of Palestine.
6. The establishment of a Jewish chartered company for the resettlement of Palestine by Jewish settlers.[10]

---

[10]*Report of the Executive of the Zionist Organization to the XIIth Zionist Congress* (London: National Labour Press, 1921), Part IV, p. 71.

As a result of conversations of Sir Mark Sykes with Weizmann and Sokolow it was agreed that the government should enter into formal negotiations with the Zionists. These are here described in Sokolow's words.

FOR CONSIDERATION   Did Sokolow's discussions with the French imply a revision or renunciation of the Sykes-Picot Agreement?

Comments of Nahum Sokolow

The 7th of February, 1917, constitutes a turning-point in the history [of Zionism]. Shortly before this date Lieut. Colonel Sir Mark Sykes, Bart., M.P., had communicated with Dr. Weizmann and the author on the question of the treatment of the Zionist problem. Sir Mark Sykes, who is a distinguished authority on oriental matters and who had earlier given attention to the Arab question, was entrusted with the study of the Zionist problem. In conjunction with a representative of the French Government, M. Georges Picot, he had devoted great attention to the question, and both had had first conversations with Dr. Moses Gaster. At the commencement of the year 1917 Sir Mark Sykes entered into closer relations with Dr. Weizmann and the author, and the discussions held with the latter led to the meeting of February 7th, 1917, which marks the commencement of official negotiations. Besides Sir Mark Sykes, the following took part in this meeting: Lord Rothschild, Mr. Herbert Bentwich, Mr. Joseph Cowen, Dr. M. Gaster (at whose house the meeting took place), Mr. James *de* Rothschild, Mr. Harry Sacher, Right Hon. Herbert Samuel, M.P., Dr. Chaim Weizmann, and the author. The deliberations yielded a favourable result, and it was resolved to continue the work. For further regular consultations with Sir Mark Sykes and M. Georges Picot, the author was chosen. Discussions on questions connected with the Zionist programme took place. In consequence of these negotiations and of the great importance of the Zionist question to all the Governments of the Entente Powers, the author was called to Paris in March, 1917, by the French Government. On the 22nd of March he was received at the Ministry of Foreign Affairs in Paris, where he outlined the principles of the Zionist programme. He received the assurance that the French Government regarded the programme very favourably, and was authorzied to inform the Zionist Organization of Russia and America of this result by telegraph.[11]

---

[11]Nahum Sokolow, *History of Zionism, 1600–1918* (London: Longmans, Green and Company, 1919), Vol. II, p. 52. Quoted through the courtesy of the Zionist Organization, London.

In May, 1917, Arthur Balfour (who had succeeded Grey as Foreign Minister when Lloyd George became Prime Minister in December, 1916) visited the United States and received assurances, through Justice Louis Brandeis, that President Wilson was in sympathy with the idea of a British protectorate in Palestine as well as with Zionist aims. In June, Balfour suggested to the Zionists that they formulate a statement which might be considered by the Cabinet. The draft of July 18 was the result.

FOR CONSIDERATION   Notice that the proposal does not explicity use the term "Jewish State." The omission of the term was a compromise to avoid criticism on the part of the government and non-Zionist Jews.

Zionist Proposal for a Declaration by the British Government, Submitted to British Foreign Minister Balfour on July 18, 1917

His Majesty's Government, after considering the aims of the Zionist Organization, accept the principle of recognizing Palestine as the National Home of the Jewish people and the right of the Jewish people to build up its national life in Palestine under a protection to be established at the conclusion of peace, following upon the successful issue of the war.

His Majesty's Government regard as essential for the realization of this principle the grant of internal autonomy to the Jewish nationality in Palestine, freedom of immigration for Jews, and the establishment of a Jewish National Colonizing Corporation for the re-establishment and economic development of the country.

The conditions and forms of the internal autonomy and a Charter for the Jewish National Colonizing Corporation should, in the view of His Majesty's Government, be elaborated in detail and determined with the representatives of the Zionist Organization.[12]

_____

[12]*Report to the XIIth Zionist Congress,* Part IV, pp. 71–72.

The Zionist formula was scrutinized carefully by the British War Cabinet, one of whose members, Edwin Montagu, Secretary of State for India, and an anti-Zionist Jew, severely criticized it as compromising the position of Jews outside Palestine. Other anti-Zionist Jews attacked the formula, and certain modifications were suggested by American Zionists when the draft was forwarded to President Wilson. Finally the Cabinet approved the version which follows and which became known as the Balfour Declaration.

FOR CONSIDERATION   Is it completely clear what is meant by the expression "national home for the Jewish people"? What difference was made by the substitution of "*a* national home" for "*the* national home"? Did the declaration envisage the ultimate establishment of a Jewish state?

The Balfour Declaration, November 2, 1917

His Majesty's Government view with favour the establishment in Palestine of a national home for the Jewish people, and will use their best endeavours to facilitate the achievement of this object, it being clearly understood that nothing shall be done which may prejudice the civil and religious rights of existing non-Jewish communities in Palestine, or the rights and political status enjoyed by Jews in any other country.[13]

_____

[13]*Ibid.*

The motivation which prompted the British government and Balfour in particular to sponsor the Zionist cause can scarcely, because of its complexity, be explained with complete satisfaction. Leonard Stein has devoted an entire volume to the question,[14] but the wealth of detail he produced makes the problem more complicated than ever. Was Balfour merely an idealist or a hard-headed master of *Realpolitik*? The two documents which follow give support to both interpretations.

Comments of Arthur Balfour in the House of Lords, June 21, 1922

My noble friend told us in his speech, and I believe him absolutely, that he has no prejudice against the Jews. I think I may say that I have no prejudice in their favour. But their position and their history, their connection with world religion and with world politics, is absolutely unique. There is no parallel to it, there is nothing approaching to a parallel to it, in any other branch of human history. . . . Nobody who knows what he is talking about will deny that they have at least—and I am putting it more moderately than I could do—rowed all their weight in the boat of scientific, intellectual and artistic progress, and they are doing so to this day. You will find them in every University, in every centre of learning; and at the very moment when they were being persecuted, when some of them, at all events, were being persecuted by the Church, their philosophers were developing thoughts which the great doctors of the Church embodied in their religious system. As it was in the Middle Ages, as it was in earlier times, so it is now. And yet, is there anyone here who feels content with the position of the Jews? They have been able, by this extraordinary tenacity of their race, to maintain this continuity, and they have maintained it without having any Jewish Home.

What has been the result? The result has been that they have been described as parasites on every civilisation in whose affairs they have mixed themselves—very useful parasites at times I venture to say. But however that may be, do not your Lordships think that if Christendom, not oblivious of all the wrong it has done, can give a chance, without injury to others, to this race of showing whether it can organise a culture in a Home where it will be secured from oppression, that it is not well to say, if we can do it, that we will do it. . . . I could defend—I have endeavoured, and I hope not unsuccessfully, to defend—this scheme of the Palestine Mandate from the most material economic view, and from that point of view it is capable of defence. I have endeavoured to defend it from the point of view of the existing population, and I have shown—I hope with some effect—that their prosperity also is intimately bound up with the success of Zionism. But having endeavoured to the best of my ability to maintain those two propositions, I should, indeed, give an inadequate view to your Lordships of my opinions if I sat down without insisting to the utmost of my ability that, beyond and above all this, there is this great ideal at which those who think with me are aiming, and which, I believe, it is within their power to reach.[15]

---

[14]Leonard Stein, *The Balfour Declaration* (New York: Simon and Schuster, Inc., 1961).

[15]*Parliamentary Debates, Lords* (London: His Majesty's Stationery Office, 1922), Vol. 50, Cols. 1016–18. Quoted by permission of the Controller of Her Britannic Majesty's Stationery Office.

Excerpts from a Memorandum of Arthur Balfour, August 11, 1919

This brings into clear relief what I fear is the unhappy truth, namely, that France, England, and America have got themselves into a position over the Syrian problem so inextricably confused that no really neat and satisfactory issue is now possible for any of them.

The situation is affected by five documents, beginning with our promise to the ruler of the Hedjaz in 1915; going on to the Sykes-Picot Agreement with France of September 1916; followed by the Anglo-French declaration of November 1918; and concluding with the Covenant of the League of Nations of 1919; and the directions given to the Commission sent out to examine the Arab problem on the spot—directions which, it must be observed, were accepted by France, Britain, and America, though the Commission itself was, in the end, purely American in composition. These documents are not consistent with each other; they represent no clear-cut policy. . . .

These difficulties are well illustrated by the Sykes-Picot Agreement of 1916. What its authors aimed at was the creation of two clearly-defined areas, one carved out of Syria and the other out of Mesopotamia—the first which should be French, as Tunis is French, the other English, as Egypt is English. Between them was to lie a huge tract occupied in part by nomad Bedouins, in part by a sedentary Arab-speaking population, urban and agricultural, who should be independent in the sense that they would live their own life in their own way, but who would be under the patronage, and for certain purposes under the control, either of France or of England. . . . As I read history, such an overlordship is not alien to the immemorial customs and traditions of this portion of the Eastern world.

On the other hand, the scheme does seem to me quite alien to those modern notions of nationality which are enshrined in the Covenant and proclaimed in the declaration. These documents proceed on the assumption that, if we supply an aggregate of human beings, more or less homogeneous in language and religion, with a little assistance and a good deal of advice, if we protect them from external aggression and discourage internal violence, they will speedily and spontaneously organise themselves into a democratic state on modern lines. They will, in language borrowed from the declaration, establish "a national government," and enjoy "an administration deriving its authority from the initiative and free choice of the native population."

If by this is meant, as I think it is, that when the Turkish tyranny is wholly past the Arabs will desire to use their new-found freedom to set up representative institutions, with secret voting, responsible government, and national frontiers, I fear we are in error. They will certainly do nothing of the sort. The language of the Covenant may suit the longitude of Washington, Paris, or Prague. But in the longitude of Damascus it will probably get us into trouble, unless, indeed, we can agree to treat it with a very wide latitude of interpretation.

. . . . . .

The language of the Covenant assumes or asserts that in the regions we are discussing, as in other portions of the Turkish Empire, there are in the advanced chrysalis state "independent nations" sufficiently "developed" to demand "provisional recognition," each of which is to be supplied by the Powers with a mandatory till it is able to stand alone. Where and what are these "independent nations"? Are they by chance identical with Syria, Mesopotamia, and Palestine? If so, the coincidence with the Sikes-Picot arrangement is truly amazing, for no such idea was present to the minds of those who framed it. . . .

The contradiction between the letter

of the Covenant and the policy of the Allies is even more flagrant in the case of the "independent nation" of Palestine than in that of the "independent nation" of Syria. For in Palestine we do not propose even to go through the form of consulting the wishes of the present inhabitants of the country, though the American Commission has been going through the form of asking what they are. The four Great Powers are committed to Zionism. And Zionism, be it right or wrong, good or bad, is rooted in age-long traditions, in present needs, in future hopes, of far profounder import than the desires and prejudices of the 700,000 Arabs who now inhabit that ancient land.

In my opinion that is right. What I have never been able to understand is how it can be harmonised with the declaration, the Covenant, or the instructions to the Commission of Enquiry.

I do not think that Zionism will hurt the Arabs; but they will never say they want it. Whatever be the future of Palestine it is not now an "independent nation," nor is it yet on the way to become one. Whatever deference should be paid to the views of those who live there, the Powers in their selection of a mandatory do not propose, as I understand the matter, to consult them. In short, so far as Palestine is concerned, the Powers have made no statement of fact which is not admittedly wrong, and no declaration of policy which, at least in the letter, they have not always intended to violate.

.   .   .   .   .

Since the literal fulfilment of all our declarations is impossible, partly because they are incompatible with each other and partly because they are incompatible with facts, we ought, I presume, to do the next best thing. And the next best thing may, perhaps, be attained if we can frame a scheme which shall, as far as possible, further not merely the material interests but the hopes and habits of the native population; which shall take into account the legitimate aspirations of other peoples and races, in particular, of the French, the British, and the Jews; and which shall embody, as completely as may be, the essential spirit of the various international pronouncements, whose literal provisions it seems impossible in all cases to fulfil. . . .

If Zionism is to influence the Jewish problem throughout the world Palestine must be made available for the largest number of Jewish immigrants. It is therefore eminently desirable that it should obtain the command of the water-power which naturally belongs to it, whether by extending its borders to the north, or by treaty with the mandatory of Syria, to whom the southward flowing waters of Hamon could not in any event be of much value.

For the same reason Palestine should extend into the lands lying east of the Jordan. It should not, however, be allowed to include the Hedjaz Railway, which is too distinctly bound up with exclusively Arab interests.[16]

_____

[16]*Documents on British Foreign Policy 1919–1939*, First Series (London: Her Majesty's Stationery Office, 1952), Vol. IV, pp. 342–47. Quoted by permission of the Controller of Her Britannic Majesty's Stationery Office.

T he following documents are presented to throw additional light on the question of motives behind the formulation of the Balfour Declaration.

FOR CONSIDERATION   Lloyd George's statement to the effect that he was indebted to Weizmann for his contribution to the war effort in developing a process for the production of acetone, needed to manufacture the high explosive cordite, has largely influenced historians. Is it likely that it is accurate? Lloyd George's testimony before the Peel Commission was published in 1937 and his memoirs in 1933. Does his interpretation hold up in the light of the comments of Weizmann (1949) and Samuel (1945)? Why should Lloyd George have wished to belittle his own role in the negotiations?

Statement on Testimony of Lloyd George on the Balfour Declaration, Given to the Peel Commission

In the evidence he gave before us, Mr. Lloyd George, who was Prime Minister at that time, stated that, while the Zionist cause had been widely supported in Britain and America before November 1917, the launching of the Balfour Declaration at that time was "due to propagandist reasons"; and he outlined the serious position in which the Allied and Associated Powers then were. The Rumanians had been crushed. The Russian Army was demoralized. The French Army was unable at the moment to take the offensive on a large scale. The Italians had sustained a great defeat at Caporetto. Millions of tons of British shipping had been sunk by German submarines. No American divisions were yet available in the trenches. In this critical situation it was believed that Jewish sympathy or the reverse would make a substantial difference one way or the other to the Allied cause. In particular Jewish sympathy would confirm the support of the American Jewry, and would make it more difficult for Germany to reduce her military commitments and improve her economic position on the Eastern front. . . .

The idea was, and this was the interpretation put upon it at the time, that a Jewish State was not to be set up immediately by the Peace Treaty without reference to the wishes of the majority of the inhabitants. On the other hand, it was contemplated that when the time arrived for according representative institutions to Palestine, if the Jews had meanwhile responded to the opportunity afforded them by the idea of a national home and had become a definite majority of the inhabitants, then Palestine would thus become a Jewish Commonwealth.[17]

Comments of David Lloyd George

When our difficulties [of producing acetone] were solved through Dr. Weizmann's genius I said to him: "You have rendered great service to the State, and I should like to ask the Prime Minister to recommend you to His Majesty for some honour." He said: "There is nothing I want for myself." "But is there nothing we can do as a recognition of your valuable assistance to the country?" I asked. He replied, "Yes, I would like you to do something for my people." He then explained his aspirations as to the repatriation of the Jews to the sacred land they had made famous. That was the fount and origin of the famous declaration about the National Home for Jews in Palestine. As soon as I became Prime Minister I talked the whole matter over with Mr. Balfour, who was then Foreign Secretary. As a scientist he was immensely interested when I told him of Dr. Weizmann's achievement. We were anxious at that time to enlist Jewish support in neutral countries, notably in America. Dr. Weizmann was brought into direct contact with the Foreign Secretary. This was the beginning of an association,

---

[17]Palestine Royal Commission, *Report* (London: His Majesty's Stationery Office, 1937; reprinted 1946), pp. 17–18. Quoted by permission of the Controller of Her Britannic Majesty's Stationery Office.

the outcome of which, after long examination, was the famous Balfour Declaration which became the charter of the Zionist movement.[18]

Comments of Chaim Weizmann

Mr. George, in his *War Memoirs*, dates his acquaintance with me, and his interest in our movement, from the time (1917) when I came to work for the Ministry of Munitions, and centers the relationship on the subject of my chemical work for the Government during the second half of the war. His narrative makes it appear that the Balfour Declaration was a reward given me by the Government when Mr. Lloyd George became Prime Minister, for my services to England. I almost wish that it had been as simple as that, and that I had never known the heartbreaks, the drudgery and the uncertainties which preceded the Declaration. But history does not deal in Aladdin's lamps. Actually, Mr. Lloyd George's advocacy of the Jewish homeland long predated his accession to the Premiership, and we had several meetings in the intervening years. . . .[19]

Comments of Viscount Samuel in Reference to Lloyd George's *Memoirs*

It is dramatic, but incorrect and unfortunate, to represent so great an event as the Balfour Declaration . . . as though it were partly a douceur given, instead of a knighthood or a decoration, to a Jewish inventor for a timely discovery in the production of explosives; partly an induce-ment to Jews in the United States and other neutral countries to favour the Allies. In this account nothing is said of the causes that had in fact chiefly influenced the British Cabinet during its long-sustained deliberations—a genuine sympathy with the aspirations of Jews for a restoration in Palestine, as a factor of spiritual and moral value to them, and indirectly in some degree to the world; a belief that to bring to Palestine that new economic and cultural element would be the best means of promoting the regeneration of a land, of deep historic interest to mankind, that was now almost derelict; and, further, a proper measure of precaution against possible future dangers to legitimate and long-established interests of the British Commonwealth. Nor indeed does it do justice to Mr. Lloyd George's own part in the matter. Long before he had to cope with a shortage of acetone he had taken a close interest in the Palestine question and had shown a full understanding of its significance. From the beginning he had been unwavering in his support of the policy that was ultimately embodied in the Balfour Declaration. As Prime Minister his approval ensured its adoption. Afterwards, at the Peace Conference in Paris and subsequently, his tenacity was to carry it through many difficulties and over many obstacles. And it was Weizmann the enthusiast, Weizmann the diplomat, who is entitled to high credit whenever the story is told; Weizmann the chemist only in a very minor degree. Without derogation to his service in the manufacture of cordite, if acetone had never been heard of, I believe that the Balfour Declaration would have taken precisely the shape that it did, and been promulgated just when it was.[20]

---

[18]David Lloyd George, *War Memoirs* (New Haven, Conn.: Yale University Press, 1933), Vol. II, p. 50.

[19]Weizmann, *op. cit.*, pp. 149–50.

[20]Samuel, *op. cit.*, p. 147.

Great Britain received, after the war, the obligation of administering Palestine, and even before the Mandate became officially effective, Viscount Samuel was appointed High Commissioner. The determination of policy was transferrred from the Foreign Office to the Colonial Office, whose new minister, Winston Churchill, organized a Middle East Department to cope with the complex problems which the government inherited. Colonel Richard Meinertzhagen, whose diary is quoted, was Military Adviser in the Department. A strong sympathizer for the Zionist cause, he had previously been General Allenby's Political Officer in Cairo.

Churchill's pronouncement in 1922 was the official British interpretation of the Balfour Declaration. It pleased neither Arab nor Jew.

Conversation of Weizmann, Balfour, Lloyd George, and Churchill, July 22, 1921, as Recorded by Colonel Meinertzhagen

On the 20th instant I addressed a letter to General Smuts on the subject of Zionism. I feel that the time has come when something must be done unless the whole fabric is to crumble and disintegrate. . . .

I wrote to him in the hopes that he might use his influence with the Prime Minister and Winston before they met Weizmann at lunch, which they did at A. J. Balfour's house on July 22nd. A short résumé of the conversation which ensued is interesting and is given below.

It interested me to see that both Lloyd George and Balfour realized that, when they subscribed to the Balfour Declaration, they had in mind a Jewish State as the ultimate aim of Zionism. Balfour's real motive was to remedy the unsatisfactory state of the Jews in the world. That he told me in Paris in 1919. Lloyd George was influenced entirely by sentiment and by his belief in the Old Testament. But Smuts tells me he was influenced, when he agreed to the declaration, by a desire to have the Jews on his side during the war. He appreciated their force in world politics, and thought that by making such a declaration he would enlist their help.

Notes on conversation held at Mr. Balfour's house on July 22nd, 1921. Present: Mr. Lloyd George, Mr. A. J. Balfour, Mr. Winston Churchill, Sir Maurice Hankey, Mr. Edward Russell, Dr. Weizmann.

Dr. W. reported on his visit to America, explained the situation there—Zionist, Jewish and general—and delivered message to British Government entrusted to him by Sir A. Geddes—L. G. very interested.

Dr. W. further explained the fight with the Anglo-Zionist Organization at the results of which L. G. expressed great satisfaction and said "it is very creditable to you."

A. J. B. "You ought to tell the P.M. the position of Zionism at present."

Dr. W. replied that while he was away in America "building up", the whole position became vitiated by the developments of the situation in Palestine, e.g. Samuel's speech which was a negation of the Balfour Declaration.

W. C. (interrupting) "Why?"

Dr. W. produced speech and read it, showing difference between it and the Declaration. The Declaration meant an ultimate Jewish majority—and this speech would never permit such a majority to eventuate.

W. C. demurred at this interpretation of the speech.

L. G. and A. J. B. both said that by the Declaration they always meant an eventual Jewish State.

Dr. W. continuing on position of Zionism, stoppage of emigration, non-granting of necessary concessions for development, lack of security for Jewish population, apropos of which he said "We were gunrunning and I can't allow it."

W. C. (interrupting) "We won't mind it, but don't speak of it."

Dr. W. "I would like it sanctioned. Is it agreed?"

They all agreed to this.

W. C. took official view of the Administration showing the difficult situation that had arisen owing to the B. Declaration which was opposed by the Arabs, nine-tenths of the British officials on the spot, and some of the Jews in Palestine. He said it was a poor country in which destitute emigrants could not be dumped.

Dr. W. refuted this and spoke of "representative Government Project."

W. C. quoted Mesopotamia and Transjordania, to which

Dr. W. replied "You will not convince me that self-government has been given to these two lands because you think it right, it has only been done because you must," to which L. G., A. J. B. and W. C. all agreed.

Dr. W. "If you do the same thing with Palestine it means giving up Palestine—and that is what I want to know."

L. G. to W. C. "You mustn't give representative Government to Palestine."

W. C. "I might have to bring it before the Cabinet." Of course questions affecting the Jewish National Home would be eliminated from the purview of the representative Government.

Dr. W. said this was impossible, and after a general refutation of arguments used, the talk became general for a while.

Then W. C. spoke of the Arab delegation and felt sure that a modus operandi could be worked out with them for the next three years.

Dr. W. doubted this, he regarded the Arabs as political blackmailers and could only talk with them when he knew the position of the British Government.

L. G. "Frankly speaking, you want to know whether we are going to keep our pledges?"

Dr. W. "Yes." A. J. B. nodded.[21]

British Policy on Palestine as Formulated by Winston Churchill, British Colonial Secretary, June 3, 1922

So far as the Jewish population of Palestine are concerned, it appears that some

among them are apprehensive that His Majesty's Government may depart from the policy embodied in the Declaration of 1917. It is necessary, therefore, once more to affirm that these fears are unfounded, and that that Declaration, reaffirmed by the Conference of the Principal Allied Powers at San Remo and again in the Treaty of Sèvres, is not susceptible of change.

When it is asked what is meant by the development of the Jewish National Home in Palestine, it may be answered that it is not the imposition of a Jewish nationality upon the inhabitants of Palestine as a whole, but the further development of the existing Jewish community, with the assistance of Jews in other parts of the world, in order that it may become a centre in which the Jewish people as a whole may take, on grounds of religion and race, an interest and a pride. But in order that this community should have the best prospect of free development and provide a full opportunity for the Jewish people to display its capacities, it is essential that it should know that it is in Palestine as of right and not on sufferance. That is the reason why it is necessary that the existence of a Jewish National Home in Palestine should be internationally guaranteed, and that it should be formally recognised to rest upon ancient historic connection.

This, then, is the interpretation which His Majesty's Government place upon the Declaration of 1917, and, so understood, the Secretary of State is of opinion that it does not contain or imply anything which need cause either alarm to the Arab population of Palestine or disappointment to the Jews.

For the fulfilment of this policy it is necessary that the Jewish community in Palestine should be able to increase its numbers by immigration. This immigration cannot be so great in volume as to exceed whatever may be the economic capacity of the country at the time to ab-

---

[21]Col. Richard Meinertzhagen, *Middle East Diary, 1917–1956* (New York: Thomas Yoseleff, 1960), pp. 103–05.

sorb new arrivals. It is essential to ensure that the immigrants should not be a burden upon the people of Palestine as a whole, and that they should not deprive any section of the present population of their employment. . . .[22]

Mandate for Palestine, July 24, 1922

. . . . .

Article 1. The Mandatory shall have full powers of legislation and administration, save as they may be limited by the terms of this Mandate.

Article 2. The Mandatory shall be responsible for placing the country under such political, administrative, and economic conditions as will secure the establishment of the Jewish national home, as laid down in the preamble, and the development of self-governing institutions, and also for safeguarding the civil and religious rights of all the inhabitants of Palestine, irrespective of race and religion.

Article 3. The Mandatory shall, so far as circumstances permit, encourage local autonomy.

Article 4. An appropriate Jewish agency shall be recognized as a public body for the purpose of advising and cooperating with the Administration of Palestine in such economic, social, and other matters as may affect the establishment of the Jewish national home and the interests of the Jewish population in Palestine, and, subject always to the control of the Administration, to assist and take part in the development of the country.

The Zionist Organisation, so long as its organisation and constitution are in the opinion of the Mandatory appropriate, shall be recognised as such agency. . . .

. . . . .

Article 6. The Administration of Palestine, while ensuring that the rights and position of other sections of the population are not prejudiced, shall facilitate Jewish immigration under suitable conditions and shall encourage, in cooperation with the Jewish Agency referred to in Article 4, close settlement by Jews on the land, including State lands and waste lands not required for public purposes.

. . . . .

Article 25. In the territories lying between the Jordan and the eastern boundary of Palestine as ultimately determined, the Mandatory shall be entitled, with the consent of the Council of the League of Nations, to postpone or withhold application of such provisions of this Mandate as he may consider inapplicable to the existing local conditions, and to make such provision for the administration of the territories as he may consider suitable to those conditions. . . . [23]

---

[22]*British White Paper,* Cmd. 1700 (London: His Majesty's Stationery Office, 1922), pp. 18–19. Quoted by permission of The Controller of Her Britannic Majesty's Stationery Office.

[23]*Mandate for Palestine,* Cmd. 1785 (London: His Majesty's Stationery Office, 1922), pp. 2–11. Quoted by permission of The Controller of Her Britannic Majesty's Stationery Office.

BIBLIOGRAPHY

Sources Used in This Problem

1. *Collections and Official Documents*

Adamow, E. (ed.). *Die Aufteilung der asiatischen Türkei.* Dresden: Ministeriums für Auswärtige Angelegenheiten, 1932.

British White Paper, Cmd. 1700. London: His Majesty's Stationery Office, 1922.

British White Paper, Cmd. 5957. London: His Majesty's Stationery Office, 1939.

Documents on British Foreign Policy 1919–1939. First Series, Vol. IV. London: Her Majesty's Stationery Office, 1952.

The Times, London.

The Manchester Guardian.

Mandate for Palestine, Cmd. 1785. London: His Majesty's Stationery Office, 1922.

Parliamentary Debates. London: His Majesty's Stationery Office, 1922.

Report of the Executive of the Zionist Organization to the XIIth Zionist Congress. London: National Labour Press, 1921.

Report of the Palestine Royal Commission (Peel Report). London: His Majesty's Stationery Office, 1937 (reprinted 1946).

2. *Others*

LLOYD GEORGE, DAVID. *War Memoirs.* 2 vols. New Haven, Conn.: Yale University Press, 1933.

MEINERTZHAGEN, RICHARD. *Middle East Diary, 1917–1956.* New York: Thomas Yoseleff, 1960.

SAMUEL, VISCOUNT. *Grooves of Change: A Book of Memoirs.* London: Cresset, 1945.

SOKOLOW, NAHUM. *History of Zionism.* 2 vols. London: Longmans, Green and Company, 1919.

WEIZMANN, CHAIM. *Trial and Error.* New York: Harper, 1949.

SELECT LIST OF BOOKS RECOMMENDED FOR FURTHER READING

ANTONIUS, GEORGE. *The Arab Awakening.* Philadelphia: J. B. Lippincott, 1939.

BARBOUR, NEVILL. *Nisi Dominus: A Survey of the Palestine Controversy.* London: Harrap, 1946.

COCKS, F. SEYMOUR. *The Secret Treaties and Understandings.* London: Union of Democratic Control, 1918.

COOKE, HADLEY V. *Challenge and Response in the Middle East: The Quest for Prosperity, 1919–1951.* New York: Harper, 1952.

DUGDALE, BLANCHE E. *Arthur James Balfour.* 2 vols. New York: G. P. Putnam's Sons, 1937.

FRANK, GEROLD. *The Deed.* New York: Simon and Schuster, 1963.

GLUBB, SIR JOHN. *Britain and the Arabs.* London: Hadder & Stoughton, 1957.

HANNA, PAUL L. *British Policy in Palestine.* Washington, D.C.: American Council on Public Affairs, 1942.

HERTZBERG, ARTHUR (ed.). *The Zionist Idea: A Historical Analysis and Reader.* Garden City, N.Y.: Doubleday & Co. and Herzl Press, 1959.

LESLIE, SHANE. *Mark Sykes: His Life and Letters.* New York: Scribner's, 1923.

MARLOWE, JOHN. *The Seat of Pilate.* London: Cresset, 1959.

MONROE, ELIZABETH. *Britain's Moment in the Middle East 1914–1956.* London: Chatto and Windus, 1963.

RABINOWICZ, OSKAR K. *Fifty Years of Zionism.* London: Robert Auscombe, 1950.

STARK, FREYA. *Dust in the Lion's Paw.* London: John Murray, 1961.

STEIN, LEONARD. *The Balfour Declaration.* New York: Simon and Schuster, 1961.

STORRS, SIR RONALD. *Memoirs.* New York: G. P. Putnam's Sons, 1937.

SYKES, CHRISTOPHER. *Cross Roads to Israel.* London: Collins, 1965.

ZEINE, N. *The Struggle for Arab Independence.* Beirut: Khayat's, 1960.

SECTION II

The Uneasy Peace

THE LOCARNO TREATIES

Germany's effort under Stresemann to reestablish its place in Europe, 1925-26

The second half of the decade 1920–30 emerges in retrospect as a period in which men believed too optimistically that they had solved their problem of security and could live in peace. In those years Geneva, seat of the League of Nations, meeting place of prime ministers and statesmen, super- seded Paris, London, and Berlin in the headlines of the world's press. Ushered in by the withdrawal of French troops from the Ruhr, this period has variously been designated the Briand Era, or the Stresemann Era, from

GERMANY AFTER WORLD WAR I

the efforts of these two statesmen to resolve the differences between France and Germany. But it ended in the early thirties with the depression, with the failure of the disarmament conferences, with the Japanese conquest of Manchuria, with the rise of militant fascism, and with the world's subsequent disillusion in regard to the League as an instrument capable of dealing with aggression.

No understanding of this period can be achieved without a study of the Locarno Treaties, which endeavored to provide a security arrangement to quell Germany's dissatisfaction with Versailles and to quiet French suspicions of a German military revival. As a French writer has put it: "Locarno is the post-war focal point. Everything becomes clear if you consider the series of preceding events as converging on Locarno, just as all subsequent events must be viewed as developing from it."[1] The following set of documents attempts to present Locarno as such a focal point.

In 1924, the year preceding the Locarno negotiations, an effort was made within the framework of the League of Nations to establish a pact whereby through arbitration and conciliation war could be avoided. The effort failed; but it has significance insofar as it can be considered a precursor to the Locarno Treaties. This attempt is here described by Joseph Paul-Boncour, a member of the French delegation to Geneva, from his reminiscences published in 1945.

FOR CONSIDERATION   It was Austen Chamberlain, Foreign Minister of the Conservative government which succeeded MacDonald's Labour Ministry, who had to announce to the League, in March, 1925, that Great Britain would not support the Protocol. Notice that at the same time Chamberlain had under consideration the German offer for a security arrangement.

Comments of Paul-Boncour

The French delegation was presided over by Herriot. MacDonald, Labour Prime Minister, presided over the English delegation. It was the first time that the two heads of government of the two great democracies of Europe had come in person to Geneva; it was to force the League of Nations to face the essential problem for which it had been established. . . .

I do not recall which of the two first opened fire. But I see MacDonald, straightforward, with clear eyes, with his familiar gesture of striking one hand against the other to emphasize his argu-

[1]Bertrand de Jouvenel, *De Versailles à Locarno* (Paris: Calmann-Lévy, 1940), p. 379.

ment; Herriot leaning against the rostrum, like a schoolteacher, genial and convincing; and I hear the applause they received.

They were not however saying the same thing; but their faith was equal; their aims were similar; and the Assembly was very anxious to reach a compromise between the two positions.

.   .   .   .   .

The Assembly met on September 1, 1924. After the opening ceremonies, the Herriot-MacDonald meeting immediately took place. After September 6, the principal members of the two delegations met in a small room adjoining the chamber where the leaders had just met. We agreed on the trilogy: *Arbitration, Security, Dis-*

armament, those problems which were to provide work and discussion at Geneva over the years.

Unanimously adopted by the Assembly in the form of a Franco-British resolution, this provided the canvas on which the Committees worked. There then began the rapid and conscientious labor which would, five weeks later, finish with the famous *Protocol for the Pacific Settlement of International Disputes,* called simply *Protocol* for short; and anyone who has considered even for a moment the problem of war and peace knows what hopes went with it to its grave. At Geneva we used to speak of the "Year of the Protocol" as one speaks of great vintage years.

. . . . .

At the end of September we were able to come before the Assembly with a draft. There would be little point in seeking an analysis in the archives where it sleeps, awaiting the inevitable resurrection if Europe would live and live in freedom. . . .

Doubtless there was nothing in the Protocol which was not, in principle, already in the Covenant of the League of Nations. . . . But the Protocol pushed the ideas which inspired the Covenant to their logical conclusions. It introduced a new element into public law. It opened up a new future to people decimated by the war. Leaving to each sovereign state a latitude in using this or that method of conciliation, mediation, or arbitration, whichever seemed best to safeguard its interests and susceptibilities, it extended to relations between states certain rules which in all civilized countries govern the relations among private individuals, in the knowledge that no one has the right to take justice into his own hands. The obligation to accept such a solution, comparable to a court decision, became unavoidable. And the Protocol anticipated and worked out, against those who would not submit to it, a system of sanctions which was the most complete, the most redoubtable, ever set up against anyone who would assume the responsibility of unleashing a war.

. . . . .

After Herriot left, as soon as the Franco-British resolution was adopted on September 6, Briand, who replaced him, knowing the part I had played in the work of the Third Committee, turned over to me the responsibility of speaking for France at the session which ended this long and important Assembly, and of bringing to this Protocol, which was largely our work, complete adherence.

I ran into it again, on returning to the Chamber of Deputies in Paris, where I was charged with the report by the Foreign Affairs Committee. Herriot had wished France to be the first great Power to ratify it.

Alas! she was the only one.

In England, a Conservative Government had succeeded the Labour Government; it did not think it should accede to what the Labour delegates had done at Geneva. . . .

And Briand could only throw flowers on the grave.[2]

---

[2]Joseph Paul-Boncour, *Entre deux guerres* (Paris: Librairie Plon, 1945), Vol. II, pp. 148–52. Quoted by permission of the publishers, Librairie Plon, Paris; all rights reserved.

The first postwar French governments, haunted with the fear of a revived Germany, attempted to build up alliances and to safeguard Germany's western frontier. Thus France allied itself with Poland (February 19, 1921), with Czechoslovakia (January 25, 1924), and occupied the Ruhr in January, 1923. Opposed to this realistic and traditional policy, an important group, represented most capably by Aristide Briand, sought to achieve some form of collective security through conciliation and arbitration. To this group the German Foreign Minister Gustav Stresemann made his appeal, reasoning that an aggressive French policy would not subside while France remained uneasy about German aims. To this end, in September, 1924, Stresemann had approached the League of Nations with a view toward joining the League, but the move was rebuffed. In October the German government fell, to be replaced by a rightist coalition with Luther as Chancellor but with Stresemann still at the Foreign Office. Shortly after the new Ministry had been formed, Stresemann informally approached Great Britain on the question of a security agreement. This was followed by a formal note to France.

Excerpt from the Diary of British Ambassador to Germany, D'Abernon, January 21, 1925

The new Government has so far been a disappointment to its friends, and still more a disappointment to its opponents. . . . Everyone—friend and enemy alike—is surprised at the moderate and progressive tone adopted by Luther and Stresemann. Surprise would be even greater did the public know the contents of the memorandum Pact of Mutual Security which I forwarded to London last night. In readiness to meet Allied demands in the matter of Security, and in general conciliatoriness of tone, this document goes far beyond anything which the public in Germany expect. . . .

This German initiative is of the utmost importance. I have long thought the question of mutual security between France and Germany infinitely more important than the minor discussions on which we have been engaged and less difficult of solution than the smaller issues.

It remains to be seen what reception the German initiative will meet with in London and Paris. At first, surprise will be so great that no one will grasp the real importance of the negotiation, or believe in the *bona fide*. Some will suspect a German device for creating difficulties between France and England.[3]

[3]Lord D'Abernon, *The Diary of an Ambassador* (Garden City, N.Y.: Doubleday & Company,

German Memorandum to France, February 9, 1925

In considering the various forms which a pact of security might at present take, one could proceed from an idea similar to the source of the proposal made in December, 1922. . . . Germany could, for example, declare her acceptance of a pact by virtue of which the Powers interested in the Rhine—above all, England, France, Italy, and Germany—entered into a solemn obligation for a lengthy period (to be eventually defined more specifically) *vis à vis* the Government of the United States of America as trustee not to wage war against a contracting state. A comprehensive arbitration treaty, such as has been concluded in recent years between different European countries, could be amalgamated with such a pact. Germany is also prepared to conclude analogous arbitration treaties providing for the peaceful settlement of juridical and political conflicts with all other states as well.

Furthermore, a pact expressly guaranteeing the present territorial status on the Rhine would also be acceptable to Germany. The purport of such a pact could be, for instance, that the interested states bound themselves reciprocally to observe the inviolability of the present territorial status on the Rhine; that they further-

Inc., 1930), Vol. III, pp. 123–26. Reprinted by permission of the Trustees of the Estate of Lord D'Abernon.

more, both jointly and individually, guaranteed the fulfilment of this obligation; and finally, that they would regard any action running counter to the said obligation as affecting them jointly and individually. In the same sense, the treaty states could guarantee in this pact the fulfilment of the obligation to demilitarize the Rhineland which Germany has undertaken in Articles 42 and 43 of the Treaty of Versailles. Again, arbitration agreements of the kind defined above between Germany and all those states which were ready on their side to accept such agreements could be combined with such a pact.

To the examples set out above still other possibilities of solution could be linked. Furthermore, the ideas on which these examples are based could be combined in different ways. Again, it would be worth considering whether it would not be advisable so to draft the security pact that it would prepare the way for a world convention to include all states along the lines of the Protocol for the Pacific Settlement of International Disputes drawn up by the League of Nations, and that, in case such a world convention were achieved, it could be absorbed by it or worked into it.[4]

Comments of Herbert von Dirksen, then Deputy Director, Eastern Department, German Foreign Office

After the Dawes Conference in London a feeling prevailed in the Foreign Office that something should be done to bring Germany back into the comity of nations. The dictate of Versailles ought to be replaced or supplemented by a genuine understanding. It is almost impossible to decide whose head first conceived this idea; probably Gaus and Schubert, inspired by Lord d'Abernon, invented it. The rôle of Stresemann was more that of a nurse taking care of an infant than that of a parent. Quick to grasp a political idea, he immediately realized the importance of normalizing the relations of Germany with the outer world. Farsighted and courageous, he was prepared to run the risk of tactical disadvantages, such as internal political fights, in order to reach the strategic aim of re-establishing Germany as a great power.

From these roots sprang a note which he addressed in the beginning of February, 1925, to Great Britain and France, proposing a guarantee of Germany's western frontiers by a common treaty between the adjacent countries. The leading principle of his proposal was a renunciation of Alsace-Lorraine by Germany, whereas the problem of the eastern frontiers was left open. But, even with this limitation, Stresemann's offer meant a huge concession made in advance, whereas the compensation, the evacuation of Western Germany by Allied occupation armies, remained undecided. Only by being aware of the intensity of feeling in Germany about the dictated Treaty of Versailles and about the cession of territories considered to be Germany, is it possible to gauge the audacity of Stresemann's offer.[5]

---

[4]*British White Paper,* Cmd. 2435 (London: His Majesty's Stationery Office, 1925), p. 4. Quoted by permission of the Controller of Her Britannic Majesty's Stationery Office.

[5]Herbert von Dirksen, *Moscow, Tokyo, London: Twenty Years of German Foreign Policy* (Norman, Okla.: University of Oklahoma Press, 1952), pp. 53–54. Copyright 1952 by the University of Oklahoma Press.

The following excerpts give some indication of the character and personalities of the diplomats who negotiated the Locarno Treaties.

Comments of Harold Nicolson, British Diplomat and Historian

The four artificers of Locarno, although temporarily blended for a common purpose, were of contrasting type. Lord D'Abernon possessed all the impulse, virtuosity, glamour and impatience of a Renaissance patrician. Mr. Chamberlain combined the starched appearance of a city magnate with boyish emotionalism and adult force. M. Briand, with his heavy Breton face stuck neckless and awry upon heavy Breton shoulders, would suddenly allow his imagination to lash his shrewdness into an idealistic escapade. Dr. Stresemann's physical appearance reflected the composite nature of his character and mind. The thick neck reminded the observers that he was the son of a Berlin publican; the bald bullet head suggested Prussian obstinacy and rage; the pallid face and delicate white hands denoted sensitiveness and refinement; the small, watchful, restless, pink-lidded eyes flashed suspicion; the way his tongue would at moments dart between red lips indicated almost reptilian quickness and resource; his ears were huge. A Berliner, it would be supposed, with all the wit and pugnacity of a Berliner; a patriot who suffered horribly from his country's collapse; a man of power forced by bitter circumstances to become excessively adroit. Between these four different men Dr. Benes (who had not at that date adopted the slow movements of an elder statesman) scuttled rapidly: proposing, soothing, stimulating, mediating, with infinite good intention, persistence and ingenuity.[6]

Comments of American Journalist Louis Lochner

Stresemann was the commanding German figure during the 1920's. Cabinet af-

[6]Harold Nicolson, *King George the Fifth* (Garden City, N.Y.: Doubleday & Company, Inc., 1953), p. 408.

Geneva Is So Embracing

Referring to a successful session of the League Council (1927). Represented above are Chamberlain, Stresemann, and Briand.

ter cabinet fell, but the "fulfilment minister" was always reappointed to guide the foreign policies of the Weimar Republic.

At first sight he seemed unprepossessing. He was short, stocky, bald-headed, thick-necked, with rather small, watery-blue eyes, generous ears and mouth, and a strident voice that could not compare with the resonant baritone of his great competitor for international top rating as a public speaker, his friend Aristide Briand.

One's initial impression changed almost immediately after meeting him or listening to him for a while. Dr. Stresemann had an imperturbable sense of humor, a booming, wholehearted laugh, a warm, human approach, an enviable interest in music, the drama, history, the biographies of great men, especially Napoleon and

Goethe, and in oratory as an art. As a parliamentarian he was an excellent tactician, as foreign minister an able, alert negotiator. His oratorical ability was unmatched by the German statesmen of his time. Again and again he mounted the rostrum of the Reichstag with the odds against him. But by the time he had fin-

ished, after beginning somewhat haltingly, then becoming more and more fluent, and finally inspiringly passionate in defense of his policies, the house cheered him vociferously and a safe majority approved.[7]

---

[7]Louis P. Lochner, *Always the Unexpected* (New York: The Macmillan Company, 1956), p. 129.

At first the German offer evoked little enthusiasm in either London or Paris. British Foreign Minister Austen Chamberlain, however, felt the German note was worthy of serious consideration and reacted as indicated in the following documents.

FOR CONSIDERATION   Why was Chamberlain so concerned that the Eastern as well as the Western frontiers be guaranteed? What were the advantages to Great Britain that D'Abernon should be so anxious for a successful conclusion of the negotiations?

Excerpts from the Diary of British Ambassador to Germany, D'Abernon

March 19, 1925. It is now two months since the German Draft Proposal was sent from Berlin to London. The French Press continue to call it the "Stresemann-D'Abernon Memorandum." . . . As for my own share in the genesis of the Pact, I have steadily advocated something of the kind for the last three years. Since October I have frequently talked matters over with Schubert, more particularly after the set-back concerning the evacuation of Cologne. These conversations probably resulted in the German move of January 20, but whatever was done previous to that date was of minor importance compared with the obstacles overcome or avoided during the last six weeks. How "Das Kind" survived passes comprehension. A chilly, suspicious public; a putative parent more than half inclined to repudiate the obligations of paternity; no frank support from any side—all this to surmount in the first few weeks of existence.

Augustus John has been staying at the

Embassy for the last fortnight, and has begun several portraits. The principal one is that of Stresemann. . . . The sittings to John have been a unique opportunity to discuss with Stresemann the Pact of Reciprocal Guarantee. When these sittings began he was still affected by the chilly reception of his first initiative, and was apparently on the verge of dropping the whole negotiation. In conversation during the sittings I did my utmost to encourage him to persist, and have, I believe, succeeded in instilling new life into "Das Kind." A symbolic group might be designed, "Diplomacy assisted by Art."[8]

Excerpt from a Speech by British Foreign Minister Austen Chamberlain in the House of Commons, March 24, 1925

If I understand them rightly, they [the German proposals] amount to this: that Germany is prepared to guarantee volun-

---

[8]D'Abernon, *op. cit.*, Vol. III, pp. 151–53.

tarily what hitherto she has accepted under the compulsion of the Treaty, that is, the *status quo* in the West; that she is prepared to eliminate, not merely from the West but from the East, war as an engine by which any alteration in the Treaty position is to be obtained. Thus not only in the West, but in the East, she is prepared absolutely to abandon any idea of recourse to war for the purpose of changing the Treaty boundaries of Europe.[9]

Remarks of British Foreign Minister Chamberlain on the Locarno Negotiations, Made in Commons, November 10, 1932

I had only a short time resumed my seat on that bench [March 24, 1925] when I received a message from the German Ambassador urgently desiring to see me. . . . He told me that in what I had said I had gone beyond what was au-

thorized by the German Government. . . . I tried to ascertain exactly what he meant. . . . I put to him specifically this question: "Do you mean that the German Government reserve to themselves the right to use war as a means of changing the Eastern frontier?" . . .

I could not get any precise statement from him as to what the claim was. Accordingly . . . we telegraphed the passage from my speech . . . to Lord D'Abernon, asking him to explain the circumstances . . . and that we might be informed whether, in what I had said . . . we had gone beyond the intentions of the German Government. We got back a confirmation from the German Government of the view which we took of their position. That was, that they voluntarily abandoned any idea of revising the frontiers of Western Europe, and that, while they could not abandon hope of securing revision of the Eastern frontier, they excluded war as an instrument for securing it.[10]

[9]*Parliamentary Debates, Commons, 1924-25* (London: His Majesty's Stationery Office, 1926), Vol. 182, Col. 318. Quoted by permission of the Controller of Her Britannic Majesty's Stationery Office.

[10]*Parliamentary Debates, Commons, 1931-32* (London: His Majesty's Stationery Office, 1933), Vol. 270, Cols. 562-63. Quoted by permission of the Controller of Her Britannic Majesty's Stationery Office.

Coincidentally with negotiations for an agreement, the Allied Military Control Commission was expressing strong dissatisfaction regarding Germany's failure to abide by the disarmament provisions of the Versailles Treaty. On June 5, 1925, the Conference of Allied Ambassadors sent a sharp note regarding these shortcomings, some of which are summarized here.

General Hans von Seeckt, in command of the *Reichswehr*, had no intention of abandoning his policy of clandestine preparations for war. These activities, suspected at the time, have been abundantly documented in the Nuremberg Trials, testimony from which is here cited.

Summaries of Violations and Measures to be Taken from Note of Conference of Ambassadors, June 4, 1925

(1) The police must remain a state and municipal organization. Its effectives must be reduced to 150,000, and there

must be no reinforcement from auxiliary police or volunteers. The military character of the *Schutzpolizei* must entirely disappear.

(2) A detailed list of factories, &c., was given where rectifications were needed, the Control Commission being left to in-

dicate the precise measures of destruction, dispersal, or transformation to be adopted. The list was divided into (*a*) private factories other than authorized factories; (*b*) former state factories; (*c*) authorized factories; (*d*) military establishments; (*e*) military workshops with units; (*f*) police workshops.

(3) All existing war material in excess of the scales laid down by the Control Commission must be surrendered. With regard to police armament, machine guns were only authorized for armored cars and river police launches. All mountings enabling them to be used in any emplacement must be surrendered. With regard to gas masks, a concession was made: a stock of masks to be fixed by the Control Commission was allowed for the Reichswehr.

(4) The treaty laid down that the German army should be devoted exclusively to the maintenance of order within the territory and the control of the frontiers; consequently: (*a*) The decree of the 11th August, 1920, which had the effect of conferring the powers of a Commander-in-Chief on the head of the Army Directorate and of grouping the administrative services in a special organization under a Secretary of State directly responsible to the Reichswehr Minister (equivalent to a Commander-in-Chief and a Great General Staff), must be repealed.

[(*b*) (*c*) (*d*) (*e*) (*f*) omitted]

(5) Short term enlistment, the preparation of reserve cadres and the military activities of associations must be suppressed by decree.

(6) The German Government and the Control Commission were stated to be already in negotiation with regard to the settlement of the question of import and export of war material.

(7) Legislation regarding possession of, traffic in and illicit manufacture of war material must be brought into harmony with the treaty and put into force.

(8) Legislation must be promulgated and put into force for the suppression of all forbidden zones.

(9) Legislation regarding war requisitions must be brought into harmony with the treaty and put into force.

(10) All guns in the fortress of Königsberg must be placed on fixed mountings, and their excess spare parts delivered or destroyed.

(11) The guns in fortifications and coast defenses must be placed on fixed mountings. In regard to fortifications, in exceptional cases certain uncompleted work would be allowed to stand.

(12) and (13) Documents to enable accurate statistics respecting fortifications to be prepared, and documents relative to existing stocks of war material and production of German factories during the war and after the armistice must be delivered as required.[11]

Excerpt from Memorandum concerning Trips of the Chief of German Army Command (General von Seeckt) to the Ruhr, December 6, 1925

Discussion with Office Chiefs on 3 and 5 December 1925 (as far as the journey of His Excellency is concerned). Present were: Major General Wurtzbacher, General Hasse, v. Haack, Baron von Bolzhain, Wetzell.

Fixing for spring of the model of a "German tank." The designing period of 9 months considered necessary by the ordnance office must be shortened.

The industry is obliging towards the army administration. Krupp von Bohlen's change of opinion. Willingness of the leading personalities, structure of the administration Krupp: Aufsichtsrat, Directorate, general meeting.

Utilization of the still existing designers and offices of Krupp for new construction and alteration.

───────────
[11]Royal Institute of International Affairs, *Survey of International Affairs 1925* (Oxford University Press, 1928), p. 187.

Timely information to the industry regarding armament intentions, new introductions and scope. Moving of the armament industry to central Germany (Grusonwerk Magdeburg Backau). Industry willing to move. No production of guns etc., here, which need not be kept secret anyhow, but preparation of raw materials (small blocks) and equipment for same. Connection between Krupp and Bofors Sweden. Here manufacture of tank models, sale to foreign countries for the purpose of trying them out.

Possible utilization of Krupp installations near Munich. Short description of the visit in Dortmund and Bochum. Dr. Voeglein and Borbet.[12]

**Comments of Professor
J. W. Wheeler-Bennett**

Perhaps the greatest *coup* achieved by Krupp during the period of secret rearmament was the penetrating of the Bofors Arms factory in Sweden, to whom Krupp

proceeded to sell the most valuable of his assets in patents and secret armament processes in return for a substantial block of the company's shares. To these holdings he added by purchases on the stock exchange, the transaction being financed by a substantial grant from the Reich Government, ostensibly given for the rehabilitation of the Rheinmetall Company. By December 1925—that is to say, the month in which the Locarno Agreements were signed in London—Krupps had acquired a controlling interest in Bofors, holding six million out of nineteen million shares, and were again busily engaged in the manufacture and development of the latest patterns of heavy guns, anti-aircraft guns and tanks.

Such then is an example—and one example only—of the process of secret rearmament carried out by the heavy industry of Germany in co-operation with and under the stimulus of the *Reichswehr*. The process followed the lines sketched by von Seeckt and elaborated by the *Rüstamt;* it was enthusiastically executed by those whom it would chiefly benefit.[13]

---

[12]*Trials of the War Criminals before the Nuremberg Tribunals* (Washington, D.C.: U.S. Government Printing Office, 1951), Vol. X, p. 425.

[13]John W. Wheeler-Bennett, *The Nemesis of Power: The Germany Army in Politics 1918–1945* (New York: St. Martin's Press, Inc., 1954), pp. 146–47.

T o what extent did Stresemann know what General von Seeckt and the *Reichswehr* were doing? Hans Gatzke refers to a cabinet meeting in 1923 in which the *Reichswehr* Minister reported on illegal increases in army ranks.[14] Other evidence from the year 1928 is reproduced here.

FOR CONSIDERATION   Granted that Stresemann knew of certain violations of the Versailles Treaty, does it necessarily follow that his policy toward France and England was cynical or dishonest? Only since 1953 have scholars had access to Stresemann's personal papers, and even more recently to German Foreign Office files.[15] A revised assessment of Strese-

---

[14]Hans W. Gatzke, *Stresemann and the Rearmament of Germany* (Baltimore: The Johns Hopkins Press, 1945), pp. 18–19.

[15]See Hans Gatzke, "Gustav Stresemann: A Bibliographical Article," *Journal of Modern History*, Vol. XXXVI (March, 1964), pp. 1–13.

mann's policy, based on these materials, will be in process for some years to come.

Testimony of Former German Minister of the Interior, Karl Severing, at Nuremberg Trials

DR. SIEMERS: On 18 October 1928 the cabinet meeting which we have already mentioned took place. May I ask you to describe briefly that cabinet meeting. . . .

SEVERING: At this session, members of the cabinet were familiarized with the details of what might be considered a concealment of the budget or violations of the Versailles Treaty. Both gentlemen, the Commander-in-Chief of the Army and the Commander-in-Chief of the Navy, spoke, if I remember rightly.

DR. SIEMERS: Did the entire cabinet attend?

SEVERING: Yes, perhaps with the exception of one or two members who were ill, but it was a session which in general might be called a plenary session.

DR. SIEMERS: The principal members were present?

SEVERING: Yes.

DR. SIEMERS: Were Müller, Stresemann present?

SEVERING: I cannot tell you whether Stresemann was present. He was still ill in September and whether he had recovered by 18 October, I cannot say. But I might add, that if Herr Stresemann was not present, certainly someone else was present as an authorized deputy from the Foreign Office.

DR. SIEMERS: Did Admiral Raeder and General Heye at this meeting expressly give the assurance to the cabinet—as I remember, in form of an affidavit—that only those violations had occurred which were mentioned by them?

SEVERING: Whether that was proclaimed in a solemn manner by affidavit or by word of honor, I cannot say; but, in any event, at the request of the Reich Chancellor and especially at my own request, they said that no further violations would take place.[16]

---

[16]*Trial of the Major War Criminals before the International Military Tribunal* (Nuremberg: 1948), Vol. XIV, p. 255.

Since the Treaty of Rapallo (April 16, 1922), Germany had recognized the Soviet Union and had developed commercial relations with it. Part of the secret arrangements involved manufacture of German armaments in Russia. An aspect of this development is here described by Gustav Hilger, who at the time was on the staff of the German Ambassador, Count Brockdorff-Rantzau. Information about the Russian program was revealed by stories in *The Manchester Guardian,* December 3 and 6, 1926. During the spring and summer of 1925, however, the program was a well-guarded secret. Note, however, that the French Ambassador to Russia refers to rumors of a Russo-German *rapprochement,* even if he did not believe the stories.

Herbert von Dirksen was a German career diplomat. At this time he served in the Eastern division of the Foreign Office, and later became Ambassador to Russia. When World War II broke out he was Ambassador to London. In 1924–25 Leon Trotsky, Soviet Commissar for the Red army, was heavily involved in the disputes with Stalin that would lead to his exile. The Soviet Commissar for Foreign Affairs was Georgi Chicherin.

Memorandum of a Conversation with Trotsky by German Ambassador to Russia Brockdorff-Rantzau, June 9, 1924

It was also a shock that, as I heard from a reliable source, at the arms factories in Tula, which operate under German management, a foreign, either an English or an American, commission was received about two weeks ago. Trotsky said he will enquire about this immediately; the report was undoubtedly false.

I then asked abruptly if one were still negotiating with Colonel Bauer here. Trotsky replied that there is the intention of resuming the negotiations regarding the chemical factories in the near future; there was, after all, also German capital behind Bauer. I retorted that this seemed to be the case; nevertheless I wanted to inform the Peoples' Commissar that in Berlin there was not any intention of working together with Bauer. General von Seeckt has given me a categorical assurance to this effect. It is known that Bauer is in touch with General Ludendorff; cooperation between him and the Reichswehrministerium is out of the question. Trotsky said that this information was invaluable; he naturally did not want to jeopardize the working relationship with the Reichswehrministerium under any circumstances.

.   .   .   .   .

In the further course of the discussion I reminded Trotsky of his statement to me in December last year with regard to relations with France. At that time he had said that France was the common enemy of Russia and Germany. I suggested that this conception may have changed since Poincaré's fall from power. Trotsky replied with great emphasis that this was not the case at all; neither relations with France nor those with Britain could disrupt the German-Russian friendship. He was firmly convinced that this friendship would continue for years—he corrected himself—for decades to come. . . .

When I took my leave after about an hour I thanked Trotsky for his trust and candour and asked him to use his great authority to see to it that this incident is finally completely settled. I asked him directly if he thought that, in spite of this lamentable conflict, the old friendly relations between Germany and Russia might be restored. He answered affirmatively without any hesitation; whereupon I said my job here should be made easier for me and one should not forget that I want to work with the *Soviet Government*.[17]

Comments of Herbert von Dirksen

The Russians were kept informed from that time onwards [early 1925] and reacted with mounting vigor. Their ever-present distrust rose to a pitch. They had no confidence in Stresemann, whom they suspected of being a Westerner. But quite apart from the personal issue, their inborn suspicion was bound to be aroused by negotiations between Germany with the Western Powers, the more so when they sprang from German initiative and not from Allied pressure. The motive of this initiative could be nothing but the intention of the German Government to abandon the Rapallo-policy and to turn to the West.

More to the point, and better founded, was their anxiety regarding another problem: they foresaw that the German-Allied negotiations would somehow end with Germany becoming a member of the League of Nations. And that raised a problem of immense importance to them:

[17]Gerald Freund, *Unholy Alliance: Russian-German Relations from the Treaty of Brest-Litovsk to the Treaty of Berlin* (London: Chatto & Windus Ltd.; New York: Harcourt, Brace & World, Inc., 1957), pp. 256–57.

the problem of Article 16 of the Covenant of the League, which imposed upon members the obligation to join the sanctions which might be decided upon against a recalcitrant member or an aggressive non-member—or, at least, the members had to tolerate the march of the sanction contingents through their territory.

The initial conversations with the Russians led us to the conviction that some political equivalent would have to be offered to the Soviet Union in order to re-establish the equilibrium between East and West. This idea developed into a project ending in a political treaty in which the unaltered friendly attitude of both powers should be restated and some sort of guarantee be given to the Kremlin against potential dangers rising from Article 16. In a word—the Rapallo Treaty was to be rejuvenated. This was the trend of thought that led to the so-called Treaty of Berlin.

It was a long and arduous way to this goal. The distrust of the Kremlin was not to be allayed easily. Things were complicated by the fact that Count Rantzau shared Russian anxieties and was bitterly opposed to Stresemann's initiative. He felt esteem and some sympathy for the Foreign Minister, but did not trust the strength of his character if tempted by the Western Powers. He frankly disliked Schubert, who reciprocated this feeling. The Ambassador argued more as a spokesman of the Russians than as one who explained the German point of view to the Russian Government.

During one of Count Rantzau's prolonged stays in Berlin the combined efforts of Stresemann, Schubert, Gaus, and myself convinced him that at least an attempt should be made to induce the Soviet Government to accept our point of view and also the draft of the treaty which was under discussion. Gaus had invented a new formula which, he said, had a magic effect on the Russian mind. I was initiated

into the deepest secrets of every word, for the Ambassador's mind, being averse to the principle as such, did not react to such subtleties. At last the plans crystallized. I was to accompany Count Rantzau to Moscow and explain everything to Tchitcherin. Rantzau willingly agreed and postponed his threat of resignation.[18]

Comments of Gustav Hilger

Military missions came to Soviet Russia either without the knowledge of the ambassador, or, if they did report to the embassy, they paid no heed to the rules laid down by Rantzau for their negotiations. German officers in Russia made wholly irresponsible statements and proposed fantastic deals which the Russians seem to have taken for bare coin only for a while; later these proposals were nothing but a source of embarrassment for the political representative of the Reich.

The ambassador's chief complaint was focused on his suspicion that Soviet Russia continually got the better part of the deal in military agreements. I remember a conversation with Rozengolts, in the summer of 1923, in which Rantzau bluntly asserted that German orders for war material should really be regarded as an outright subvention of the Soviet armament industry, particularly in view of the exhorbitant prices Germany had to pay. Rantzau would have insisted on concrete political advantages to be derived from the military agreements. While von Seeckt either was satisfied with the military benefits of obtaining weapons, ammunition, and maintaining the instruction of his personnel, or believed that political advantages would be a natural and automatic consequence of close military co-operation, the ambassador continually demanded that the negotiators request of the Soviet government

---

[18]Dirksen, *op. cit.*, pp. 54–55.

at least an explicit guarantee against Poland.

The ambassador continuously bombarded his superiors in Berlin with all of these complaints. Although the causes for them were never removed to his complete satisfaction, he succeeded at least in compelling the cabinet to assume a certain amount of control over the matter of military collaboration.

When, therefore, in July, 1923, Chicherin told us that his government would send Arkady Rosengolts to Berlin for direct negotiations with the cabinet, Rantzau had won a tactical victory, which was made into a triumph when in one of the first conferences in Berlin it was decided that the embassy in Moscow should henceforth be in control of military agreements.

By the end of 1926, when the *Manchester Guardian* came out with its "revelations," the purely military co-operation in the aircraft and tank schools was in full swing. German financial participation and technical advice in the enlargement and improvement of Soviet ammunition plants had ceased, although the German Army

was still receiving shipments of ammunition from these factories.[19]

French Ambassador to Russia
Jean Herbette to Foreign Minister
Briand, March 26, 1925

. . . It is said that the Russo-German alliance has been signed, or rather that it is inevitable. That it may be signed, I have no reason to believe; in fact I have been assured the contrary in circumstances such that I do not see why anyone would want to deceive me; and furthermore, I do not see what advantage Russia would find in allying herself in advance. That a Russo-German alliance is inevitable, I believe even less. . . .[20]

[19]Gustav Hilger and Alfred G. Meyer, *The Incompatible Allies: A Memoir-History of German-Soviet Relations 1918–1941* (New York: The Macmillan Company, 1953), pp. 200–201. Reprinted with permission of The Macmillan Company. Copyright 1953 by The Macmillan Company.

[20]Georges Suarez, *Briand* (Paris: Librairie Plon, 1951), Vol. VI (1923-32), p. 88; all rights reserved.

Four months elapsed before France replied to the German Memorandum of February 9, 1925. In April the Herriot government, which had been suspicious of the proposal, fell from power. Briand, who had not been a member of the Herriot Ministry, returned to the Foreign Office.

French Note to Germany,
June 16, 1925

I. . . . An agreement could not be reached unless Germany, on her part, assumes the obligations and enjoys the rights established by the Covenant of the League of Nations. Thus an agreement cannot be realized unless Germany joins the League. . . .

II. The search for security guarantees

which the world desires must be carried on without introducing innovations into the Peace Treaties. The agreements to be concluded must imply neither a revision of these Treaties nor look toward a modification in practice of specific conditions for implementing certain of their clauses. . . .

III. . . . The French Government does not fail to appreciate how significant for the cause of peace would be, alongside of a reaffirmation of the principles set forth in the Treaty, a solemn repudiation of all warlike ideas (with no time limit) among the Contracting States.

Among the latter Belgium must obviously be included, although she is not specifically mentioned in the German note. . . . It must equally be understood . . . that the Treaty to be drawn up on this basis could not affect the clauses of the Versailles Treaty relative to the occupation of the Rhineland. . . .

IV. . . . France considers that an arbitration treaty like those proposed by Germany would form a natural complement to an agreement on the Rhineland. But it must be clearly understood that, between France and Germany, such a treaty would have to cover all disputes and not leave room for coercive action except where such action is undertaken under the Treaties in effect among the parties or under the Rhineland Pact, or by virtue of the guarantees given by the parties, or by any one of them, under an arbitration treaty. A similar arbitration treaty between Belgium and Germany would be no less necessary. . . .

V. The German Government added in its memorandum that it was ready to conclude arbitration treaties with all States so disposed. The Allied Governments note this assurance with satisfaction. . . .

VI. Nothing in the anticipated treaties must affect the rights and obligations pertaining to the members of the League of Nations by virtue of the League Covenant.

VII. . . . Finally, it is self-evident that if the United States should see fit to associate herself with the anticipated agreements, France would be most happy to see the great American nation participate in this work of security and general peace. . . .[21]

---

[21]*Livre jaune français* (French Yellow Book): *Pacte de Sécurité* (Paris: Ministère des Affaires Étrangères, 1925), Vol. I, pp. 27–29.

Throughout the summer of 1925 the preliminary negotiations continued. The following documents present evidence of British, German, and French attitudes at this time.

FOR CONSIDERATION   The Briand policy of treating Germany with justice and as an equal bore fruit in the withdrawal of French troops from the Ruhr on July 31, 1925. Can it be argued that the Briand policy contained the seeds of Hitler's reoccupation of the Rhineland? Was it thus ill-advised? Because Churchill's *Gathering Storm* was published in 1948, is it likely to be suspect in dealing with events of 1925? Stresemann's letter to the former Crown Prince is considered by many as one of the best statements of his policy.

Comments of Winston Churchill

The British attitude was debated in the House of Commons on June 24. Mr. Chamberlain explained that British commitments under the Pact would be limited to the West. France would probably define her special relationships with Poland and Czechoslovakia; but Great Britain would not assume any obligations other than those specified in the Covenant of the League. The British Dominions were not enthusiastic about a Western Pact. General Smuts was anxious to avoid regional arrangements. The Canadians were lukewarm, and only New Zealand was unconditionally prepared to accept the view of the British Government. Nevertheless, we persevered. To me the aim of ending the thousand-year strife between France and Germany seemed a supreme object. If we could only weave Gaul and Teuton so closely together economically, socially, and morally as to prevent the occasion of new quarrels, and make old antagonisms die in the realisation of mutual prosperity and interdependence, Europe would rise again. It seemed to me that the supreme interest of the British people in Europe lay in the assuagement of the Franco-German feud, and that they had no other interests comparable or contrary to that. This is still my view today.

Mr. Austen Chamberlain, as Foreign Secretary, had an outlook which was respected by all parties, and the whole Cabinet was united in his support.[22]

Excerpt from the Journal of German Foreign Minister Stresemann, July 19, 1925

The last two weeks have been completely occupied by the final struggle over the production of the German answer to the Briand Note. The differences that manifested themselves in the course of this struggle were more political and personal than material. . . . The attitude of the German Nationals was, for the rest, very dubious. There were continual attempts to avoid anything that might suggest that the Memorandum of February 9th was valid for Germany. . . . It is possible that matters may proceed as they did over the Dawes Plan, over which the Industrials and the Reichslandsbund won the victory over the politicians in the end.

In any event, if I am to carry on my office I must keep very much on the alert. . . .[23]

German Note Handed to French Foreign Minister Briand, July 20, 1925

.   .   .   .   .

1. . . . The conclusion of a pact of security as outlined in the German suggestions, does not represent a modification of existing treaties. . . . The German Government consider as self-evident that it is not meant to exclude for all future time the possibility of adapting existing treaties at the proper time to changed circumstances by way of peaceful agreement. They may point out that even the Covenant of the League of Nations allows for such necessities. If the Allied Governments emphasize for instance that the pact of security must not affect the treaty provisions in force concerning the military occupation of German territory, it is correct that the German Memorandum has not made the conclusion of the pact dependent on a modification of those provisions. But should the Allied Governments intend to set those provisions up as sacrosanct for the future, the German Government would, in answer to this, like to point out that the conclusion of a security pact would represent an innovation of such importance, that it could not but react on the conditions in the occupied territories and the questions of occupation in general.

2. . . . The German Government, judging by the terms of the note of the 16th June . . . cannot but assume that in those cases [arbitration treaties] in the opinion of the Allied Governments, coercive action can take place without any regular pro-

[22]Winston Churchill, *The Gathering Storm* (Boston: Houghton Mifflin Co., 1948), p. 27. Quoted by permission of the publishers, Houghton Mifflin Company.

[23]Gustav Stresemann, *His Diaries, Letters and Papers.* Ed. and tr. by Eric Sutton. (London: The Macmillan Company, Ltd., 1937), Vol. II, pp. 139–40. Copyright 1938 by The Macmillan Company. Reprinted with permission of the Macmillan Company.

cedure laid down in advance, either by arbitral or some other international procedure. . . . If this is correct . . . the German Government would by treaty have to concede to the Allied Governments the right to take military measures against Germany without any preceding regular procedure, whenever they are of the opinion that Germany had infringed the provisions regarding the demilitarization of the Rhineland. . . . The German Government, therefore, hope that their misgivings concerning these points can be removed by the Allied Governments. . . .

3. . . . The Allied Governments . . . are of the opinion that the security pact as suggested in the German Memorandum is only conceivable if Germany enters the League of Nations. . . . Even after the explanations by the Council of the League of Nations [of March 13] the danger remains that Germany, as a disarmed country, surrounded by strongly-armed neighbors, in a central position, having been in history repeatedly the theatre of great wars, would, after entering the League of Nations, be exposed without limitation to the danger of being involved in the armed conflicts of third states. . . . Therefore if the immediate entrance of Germany into the League is to be rendered possible, a solution has to be found to tide over the time until general disarmament has become a reality. This solution would have to pay due regard to the special military and economic as well as the special geographic situation of Germany.[24]

British Foreign Minister Chamberlain to British Ambassador to Germany, D'Abernon, August 11, 1925

I snatch ten minutes to answer your letter of the 7th, and give you news of

[24]*British White Paper*, Cmd. 2468 (London: His Majesty's Stationery Office, 1925), pp. 6–9. Quoted by permission of the Controller of Her Britannic Majesty's Stationery Office.

the result of my first conversation with Briand. . . . As to this meeting, Briand was the first to insist upon a point which I had intended to make, namely: That we must prepare for a real discussion with the Germans so as to arrive at a mutual agreement, and not another treaty imposed by the Allies upon Germany. . . .

In sketching the terms of a pact my object had been to secure that there shall be arbitration (judicial or by a tribunal of conciliation) in every case, and that the decision of the arbitrators should be of binding force. The only case justifying resort to force without first exhausting the procedure of conciliation would be where one of the parties had been guilty not of some minor infraction, but of such a flagrant act as constituted an immediate danger to others. . . .[25]

Excerpt from the Diary of British Ambassador to Germany, D'Abernon

August 11, 1925. During the last two months there has been a vast improvement in the situation here. This is mainly due to the French having evacuated the Ruhr, and to their intended evacuation of the three "Sanction" towns—Dusseldorf, Duisburg and Ruhrort. . . . This action on the part of the French has had two effects here—that of strengthening the position of the Luther-Stresemann Government, and that of increasing the number of adherents to a policy of reconciliation. . . . If the present negotiations for a Pact can be carried through rapidly on the strength of the good impression made by the Ruhr evacuation, a new era of mutual confidence between France and Germany may commence. . . .

No countries, except France and Germany, will gain more by this Agreement than Czechoslovakia and Poland, where

[25]Sir Charles Petrie, *Life and Letters of Sir Austen Chamberlain* (London: Cassell & Co. Ltd., 1940), Vol. II, pp. 281–83.

frontiers are hardly yet solidified and where stability would be greatly endangered by any outbreak of hostilities. The advantage of the Pact of Mutual Security will be most direct to the principal contractors—to Germany in the immediate present, since she is disarmed; to France in the further future, when she may have only 40 million inhabitants against Germany's 80 millions. Were I a statesman of either of these two countries, I should not rest until the Pact had been signed, sealed and ratified. The direct advantage to England is less obvious, but the indirect advantage of becoming arbiter between France and Germany gives us a position of enormous potentiality. It makes us a dominating factor in European politics.

A secondary effect of the Pact will be to relieve Germany of the danger of being driven into the arms of Russia. I have never been an alarmist on this subject, believing the difference of political temper between Germany and Russia to be such that a close alliance between Soviet Russia and a fundamentally aristocratic Germany is hardly conceivable. . . .[26]

Foreign Minister Stresemann to the Former Crown Prince, September 7, 1925

In my opinion there are three great tasks that confront German foreign policy in the more immediate future—

In the first place the solution of the Reparations question in a sense tolerable for Germany, and the assurance of peace, which is an essential promise for the recovery of our strength.

Secondly, the protection of Germans abroad, those 10 to 12 millions of our kindred who now live under a foreign yoke in foreign lands.

The third great task is the readjustment of our Eastern Frontiers; the recovery of Danzig, the Polish corridor, and the frontier in Upper Silesia.

[26]D'Abernon, *op. cit.*, Vol. III, pp. 182–84.

In the background stands the union with German Austria, although I am quite clear that this not merely brings no advantages to Germany, but seriously complicates the problem of the German Reich.

If we want to secure these aims, we must concentrate on these tasks. Hence the Security Pact, which guarantees us peace, and constitutes England, as well as Italy, if Mussolini consents to collaborate, as guarantors of our Western frontiers. The pact also rules out the possibility of any military conflict with France for the recovery of Alsace-Lorraine; this is a renunciation on the part of Germany, but, in so far, it possesses only a theoretic character, as there is no possibility of a war against France. The burden of Reparations laid upon us by the Dawes Plan will probably be unendurable by 1927. We shall then have to call for a new conference for a fresh estimate of German capacity to pay, a right that is in any case secured to us by the Treaty of Versailles. A comparison of the 2½ milliards, which is the maximum sum that we have to pay, with the average of more than 4 milliards which our opponents have to pay as interest on their War debt, may serve to remind us that the enemy is, from the point of view of taxation, not less heavily burdened than we ourselves.

Our anxiety on behalf of Germans abroad is an argument in favour of our joining the League. Even the Saar, and the politicians belonging to the extremest Right, are in favour of this. In Geneva we shall speak on behalf of German civilization as a whole, because the whole of the Germanic world sees in us its refuge and protector. The objection that we shall be outvoted on the League proceeds from the false assumption that, on the Council of the League, which has the power of decision, any outvoting is possible. The decisions of the League Council must be taken unanimously. Germany is assured of a permanent seat on the Council. If we had been on the Council at the present time, Poland would not have got her way over the question of postal arrangements at Danzig, since the objection of the German representative would have sufficed to dismiss the claim. Poland, Czecho-Slovakia, Jugo-Slavia, and Rumania, who are all bound by international treaties to take care of their minority population, *i.e.* more especially the German minorities, would not so disgracefully ignore their obligations if they knew that Germany could bring all these derelictions before the League. Moreover all the questions that lie so close to German hearts, as for instance, War Guilt, General Disarmament, Danzig, the Saar, etc., are matters for the League of Nations, and a skilful speaker at a plenary session of the League may make them very disagreeable for the Entente. France, indeed, is not very enthusiastic at the idea of Germany's entering the League, while England is anxious for it, in order to counteract France's hitherto predominant influence on that body.

The question of a choice between East and West does not arise as the result of our joining the League. Such a choice can only be made when backed by military force. That, alas, we do not possess. We can neither become a Continental spearhead for England, as some believe, nor can we involve ourselves in an alliance with Russia. I would utter a warning

against any Utopian ideas of coquetting with Bolshevism. When the Russians are in Berlin, the red flag will at once be flown from the Castle, and in Russia, where they hope for a world revolution, there will be much joy at the Bolshevization of Europe as far as the Elbe; the rest of Germany will be thrown to the French to devour. That we are perfectly ready to come to an understanding with the Russian State, in whose evolutionary development I believe, on another basis, and my contention that we are not selling ourselves to the West by joining the League, is a matter on which I would gladly enlarge to Your Royal Highness in a personal talk. The great movement now stirring all the primitive peoples against the colonial domination of the great nations, will in no way be influenced to the disadvantage of these peoples by our joining the League. The most important thing for the first task of German policy mentioned above is, the liberation of German soil from any occupying force. We must get the stranglehold off our neck. On that account, Germany policy, as Metternich said of Austria, no doubt after 1809, will be one of finesse and the avoidance of great decisions.[27]

----

[27]*Stresemann: Diaries, Letters and Papers,* Vol. II, pp. 503–4.

Further diplomatic exchanges between France and Germany took place during August, and preliminary technical problems were reviewed by French, German, and English legal advisers in London. In September, France extended Germany a formal invitation to a conference.

Note Given to German Foreign Minister Stresemann by French Ambassador to Germany de Margerie, September 15, 1925

. . . After the conversations which the legal experts have just completed at London, it appears to the French Government

and her allies that the nations concerned have a common interest in not prolonging the negotiations and should now fix a date for the planned meeting. In this connection, the end of September, or at the latest the first few days of October, would provide a suitable time. The Conference would take place on neutral territory, preferably in Switzerland, in a place to be agreed on by the Governments. The French Government and her allies strongly hope that the proposals will coincide with the wishes of the German Government and that the latter will be in a position shortly to forward her acceptance.[28]

Excerpt from the Diary of German Foreign Minister Stresemann, September 23, 1925

Within the Cabinet there is agreement that at the negotiations at the forthcoming conference of Ministers the following points are to be put forward as presenting the German standpoint:

(1) There must be definite assurance that the existing system of occupation shall be fundamentally altered, and more especially that the delegate system and the consequent limitation of German sovereignty shall be abolished. . . .

(2) There is a statement at the beginning of the preamble to the London draft relating to the consolidation of the *status quo*. Efforts are to be made to get the preamble wholly set aside if possible. If this cannot be managed, in drawing up the formula the aim should be to get the statement about the consolidation of the *status quo* entirely dropped, and to discover a formula expressing the fact that

the States contracting the treaty will refrain from any resort to war or force. . . .

(3) . . . An agreement from the countries affected that they will strongly urge that the question of general disarmament shall be immediately brought up for discussion at the League.

(4) The provisions of the League regarding the so-called right of investigation went beyond the Versailles Treaty. . . . These provisions were not recognized by us as justly founded, and the contracting Powers must be induced to adopt the German standpoint and undertake to urge on the League a similar modification of the resolutions.

(5) In connection with the Security Pact, it should be possible to consider a reduction of the period of occupation of the Second and Third Zones and also a reduction of the numbers of troops. . . .

(6) The arbitration treaties with Poland and Czechoslovakia are to be included on the basis of the agreements in the London draft. A guarantee for the Eastern boundaries will be refused by Germany, as also any possible arbitration treaty which includes these frontiers.

(7) In regard to Article 16, an interpretation accepted by all parties must secure Germany's right to decide for herself whether, in the case of an application of Article 16, she is prepared to take any part in the deliberations of the League.[29]

---

[28]*Livre jaune français*, Vol. II, p. 10.

[29]*Stresemann: Diaries, Letters and Papers*, Vol. II, pp. 165–67.

Meanwhile, in September, 1925, talks with the Russians for a commercial treaty were continuing.

Comments of Herbert von Dirksen

As soon as the most dangerous stumbling-blocks between Germany and the Western Powers had been overcome and an agreement had been reached to fix a date and a place for a conference—the first

days of October in Locarno—the Soviet Government started for an all-out offensive against the Wilhelmstrasse. A last desperate effort was made to keep Germany back from a road which was bound—according to the view of the Kremlin—to lead to disaster and to a break with the

Rapallo partner. Tchitcherin started on a voyage to Berlin which he linked with the extortionist gesture of staying a few days in Warsaw on the way, and of proclaiming his intention to visit Paris after his stay in the German capital. Thus we were meant to be intimidated by the prospect that the Soviet Union had political alternatives.

Especially in nightly talks with Stresemann, immediately before the departure of the German delegation, Tchitcherin exercised the highest pressure imaginable. He frightened Stresemann by allegedly secret pledges agreed upon by former German governments—a contention which was proved to be utterly unfounded when files and statements by the officials concerned were scrutinized. He had to be satisfied with the promise of the Chancellor, Luther, and of Stresemann that the German Government did not contemplate a change of its policy towards the Soviet Union; that the pact which was to be negotiated at Locarno would in no way contradict the words and the spirit of the Treaty of Rapallo; and that German statesmen would insist on safeguarding the common interest with regard to Article 16 of the Covenant of the League, in case Germany were to join the League.

On the day of his departure for Locarno Luther invited Tchitcherin, the Soviet Embassy, and numerous leading German Ministers and deputies to a formal lunch in Bismarck's Chancellery. Even my humble person was put in the scale in order to improve the equilibrium between East and West in Locarno. On the last day it was decided that I should join the delegation to allay Rantzau's and the Soviet's suspicion that Locarno was bound to be an entirely Western enterprise.

. . . . .

Another political reputation was impaired, almost annihilated, though not in so dramatic and tragic a manner as Stresemann's: that of Count Rantzau. It is true Stresemann had secured a satisfactory formula to allay the concern of Moscow. Count Rantzau could even boast of a little counter-Locarno. The negotiations concerning the commercial treaty had come to a successful end, as the Russians were at last abandoning their go-slow tactics for political reasons. The treaty had been signed with much pomp in Moscow on October 12 while the Locarno confusion was in progress. It is true that a revivifying injection was administered to the organism of Russo-German friendship and matters went on more smoothly. But the atmosphere between Moscow and Berlin had, nevertheless, changed fundamentally.

The romanticism of Rapallo had evaporated. The common destiny of the two great, humiliated, vanquished nations had been replaced on the part of Germany by a two-sided, well-balanced policy. This was utterly strange and repugnant to Count Rantzau. Locarno had brought about a fission in his policy. He had foreseen it, but he had acquiesced. He had been persuaded to stay in office. Now he regretted it. He continued his work in Moscow, but a cord of the instrument was broken. His friends agreed that it would have been more consistent with his career to retire. But fate was lenient to him. He did not have to live long in an utterly changed atmosphere. He died a few years later. His tragedy was not as striking as that of Stresemann, but a tragedy all the same.[30]

[30]Dirksen, *op. cit.*, pp. 58–59, 64–65.

Germany accepted the French invitation on September 26, 1925.

FOR CONSIDERATION   Compare the German Cabinet's "points to be put forward" with the terms of the final treaty. Notice, for example, that the expression status quo is retained. Notice also that the German acceptance was accompanied by certain informal reservations and recalled a memorandum of September, 1924. This memorandum had specified that before Germany could enter the League it must obtain a permanent seat, must participate in the Mandate system, must obtain a modification on the war guilt clauses, and must have clarified its obligations under Article 16 of the Covenant which involved implementation of League decisions. (As Germany was disarmed under the Versailles Treaty it could not employ the sanctions available to armed nations.) France accepted the German Note, pointing out that the reservations "should not in any way interfere with the negotiations at Locarno, for they have no connection with the discussion of the Security Pact." Were the German reservations in fact unrelated to the Locarno negotiations?

Verbal Declaration Annexed to German Note of September 26, 1925

. . . The German Government feels it necessary in all frankness to let the French Government know its opinion on two questions closely related to the aim of the discussions. In the notes already exchanged, the allied Governments subordinated the conclusion of a security pact to German membership in the League of Nations. The German Government has not objected to the joining of the two problems, but from this very fact feels that it must recall . . . its memorandum of September, 1924, to the Governments represented on the Council of the League of Nations. In this memorandum it reaffirmed a statement to the effect that the eventual entry of Germany into the League of Nations must not be understood as though the German Government recognized as established certain statements advanced to justify the international obligations of Germany, statements which imply a moral change for the German people. . . .

The ideal of understanding and reconciliation would moreover be hindered if, before Germany joined the League and before the conclusion of a security pact, a dispute which still separates Germany and the allied countries were not settled. This concerns the evacuation of the southern zone of the Rhineland [Cologne] and the definite settlement of disarmament. . . .[31]

---

[31]*Livre jaune français*, Vol. II, p. 11.

A t Locarno, Switzerland, from October 4th to 16th, the British, French, German, Belgian, Italian, Polish, and Czechoslovak delegations discussed the problem of security and worked out the series of agreements known as the Treaties of Locarno. The following documents provide information about the treaty and certain reactions to it.

FOR CONSIDERATION   Only the essential portions of the principal security pact have been reproduced here; the complete texts of all the Locarno Treaties run to 30 pages.

The Conference at Locarno, as Described by Herbert von Dirksen

The world in general yearned for the restoration of real peace. Well-meaning people everywhere hailed the German initiative and eagerly awaited a real reconciliation at Locarno. The searchlights of press and propaganda were turned on the statesmen there. Every step of theirs was watched and commented on as when Briand and Stresemann had a talk, or when they and Chamberlain had a motor-launch trip on the lake. It was no easy resolve to break off the Conference and to reject an unsatisfactory compromise. It was hard to be the villain of the piece once more, to return home empty-handed, met by the sneers of one's colleagues and the inevitable invective of all those who dare not shoulder a responsibility. And as the third and greatest threat, the shadow of the Russian giant loomed over the sunny beaches of the Lago Maggiore.

Thus the fortnight of the negotiations was bound to be loaded with excitement, drama, and tension. The stage fitted well into the scene: the conference-room of the town hall with its round table; the delegates with their experts; no crowd of spectators, not the unrest of the sessions in Geneva. The main actors of Locarno had a setting which displayed their character and personality with the utmost lucidity. From the beginning Briand and Stresemann dominated the scene. Sir Austen Chamberlain, by his nature and by the rôle assigned to Great Britain, limited himself to the part of the conciliating *père noble*, to the *Attinghausen* in Schiller's drama *Wilhelm Tell* and his exhortation, "*Seid einig, einig, einig!*" (Be united!) Mussolini, who made an appearance, remained silent and had to be satisfied with the publicity. To have witnessed the oratorical duel of these two great orators, Stresemann and Briand, was unforgettable. Never did I hear Stresemann defending and pleading for his ideas and the interests of his country with more courage, oratorical skill, and brilliance than during the Locarno debates. The very essence of his speeches was to demonstrate the necessity for Germany to obtain a guarantee against the potential consequences of Article 16, of the sanctions which might involve the Reich in a war or, at least, in becoming the battleground in an East-West conflict.

The rôle of Briand, who had to profess the peaceful intentions of his country and to persuade his opponent to join the comity of peaceful nations, was less thankless and difficult. The beautifully formed phrases also responded to the eminent oratorical qualities of his character and to the persuasiveness of the French language. Stresemann had to overcome the disadvantage of his somewhat husky, almost hoarse voice, and of an outward appearance which did not win sympathy at first sight. But when he warmed up, and the genuine pathos of a great and idealistic mind came to the surface, he was equal to Briand and carried as much weight and persuasiveness as the French statesman. I personally was bound to follow the debates with the closest attention, as it fell to my lot to draw up the minutes.

After many dramatic debates and private conversations, the most important of which was held during an excursion on the motor-launch *Orange Blossom*, an agreement was reached which satisfied our demands and represented a compromise between the maintenance, in principle, of Article 16, while giving us sufficient loopholes to evade consequences which might endanger our relations with the Soviet Union.[32]

Comments of British Foreign Minister Sir Austen Chamberlain

I first met Dr. Stresemann at the Conference of Locarno in October, 1925. . . .

----
[32]Dirksen, *op. cit.*, pp. 60–62.

The circumstances of the Locarno Conference were peculiar and his position one of extraordinary difficulty. He had made his first tentative proposal for a pact of mutual guarantee in the previous January. . . . The new proposal at first raised some suspicion in Great Britain, and even more across the Channel. It was thought in some quarters to be merely a skillful diplomatic move intended to drive a wedge between our two countries. But the British Government felt at once that it demanded their most serious consideration, and represented to the French Government that it was on these lines, and on these only, that the guarantee of French territory originally offered in the non-ratified Anglo-American treaty could be renewed by this country after all that had occurred in the interval. The long months of negotiation— not too long for the important work which had to be done—had convinced us of Dr. Stresemann's sincerity, and had evolved from his first sketch a practical scheme (already communicated through their legal adviser to the German Government) which was probably more definite and more far-reaching than Dr. Stresemann had contemplated.[33]

The Locarno Treaty, October 16, 1925

Final Protocol

The representatives of the German, Belgian, British, French, Italian, Polish and Czechoslovak Governments, who have met at Locarno from the 5th to 16th October, 1925, in order to seek by common agreement means for preserving their respective nations from the scourge of war and for providing for the peaceful settlement of disputes of every nature which might eventually arise between them.

Have given their approval to the draft treaties and conventions which respective-

---

[33]Sir Austen Chamberlain, *Down the Years* (London: Cassell & Co. Ltd., 1935), pp. 173–77.

ly affect them and which, framed in the course of the present conference, are mutually interdependent:

Treaty between Germany, Belgium, France, Great Britain and Italy.
Arbitration Convention between Germany and Belgium.
Arbitration Convention between Germany and France.
Arbitration Treaty between Germany and Poland.
Arbitration Treaty between Germany and Czechoslovakia.

.   .   .   .   .

Treaty of Mutual Guarantee between Germany, Belgium, France, Great Britain and Italy.

.   .   .   .   .

Article 1

The high contracting parties collectively and severally guarantee, in the manner provided in the following articles, the maintenance of the territorial *status quo* resulting from the frontiers between Germany and Belgium and between Germany and France and the inviolability of the said frontiers as fixed by or in pursuance of the Treaty of Peace signed at Versailles on the 28th June, 1919, and also the observance of the stipulations of articles 42 and 43 of the said treaty concerning the demilitarised zone.

Article 2

Germany and Belgium, and also Germany and France, mutually undertake that they will in no case attack or invade each other or resort to war against each other.

This stipulation shall not, however, apply in the case of—

1. The exercise of the right of legitimate defense. . . .

2. Action in pursuance of article 16 of the Covenant of the League of Nations.

3. Action as the result of a decision taken by the Assembly or by the Council of the League of Nations or in pursuance

of article 15, paragraph 7, of the Covenant of the League of Nations, provided that in this last event the action is directed against a State which was the first to attack.

Article 3

In view of the undertakings entered into in article 2 of the present treaty, Germany and Belgium and Germany and France undertake to settle by peaceful means and in the manner laid down herein all questions of every kind which may arise between them and which it may not be possible to settle by the normal methods of diplomacy....

Article 4

1. If one of the high contracting parties alleges that a violation of article 2 of the present treaty or a breach of articles 42 or 43 of the Treaty of Versailles has been or is being committed, it shall bring the question at once before the Council of the League of Nations.

2. As soon as the Council of the League of Nations is satisfied that such violation or breach has been committed, it will notify its finding without delay to the Powers signatory of the present treaty, who severally agree that in such case they will each of them come immediately to the assistance of the Power against whom the act complained of is directed.

3. In case of a flagrant violation of article 2 of the present treaty or of a flagrant breach of articles 42 or 43 of the Treaty of Versailles by one of the high contracting parties, each of the other contracting parties hereby undertakes immediately to come to the help of the party against whom such a violation or breach has been directed as soon as the said Power has been able to satisfy itself that this violation constitutes an unprovoked act of aggression and that by reason either of the crossing of the frontier or of the outbreak of hostilities

or of the assembly of armed forces in the demilitarised zone immediate action is necessary. Nevertheless, the Council of the League of Nations, which will be seized of the question in accordance with the first paragraph of this article, will issue its findings, and the high contracting parties undertake to act in accordance with the recommendations of the Council provided that they are concurred in by all the members other than the representatives of the parties which have engaged in hostilities.[34]

·   ·   ·   ·   ·

Comments of Winston Churchill

There were great rejoicings about the treaty which emerged at the end of 1925 from the Conference at Locarno. Mr. Baldwin was the first to sign it at the Foreign Office. The Foreign Secretary, having no official residence, asked me to lend my diningroom at Number 11 Downing Street for his intimate friendly luncheon with Herr Stresemann. We all met together in great amity, and thought what a wonderful future would await Europe if its greatest nations became truly united and felt themselves secure. After this memorable instrument had received the cordial assent of Parliament, Sir Austen Chamberlain received the Garter and the Nobel Peace Prize. His achievement was the high-water mark of Europe's restoration, and it inaugurated three years of peace and recovery. Although old antagonisms were but sleeping, and the drumbeat of new levies was already heard, we were justified in hoping that the ground thus solidly gained would open the road to a further forward march.

At the end of the second Baldwin Ad-

---

[34]*British White Paper*, Cmd. 2525 (London: His Majesty's Stationery Office, 1925), pp. 5–11. Quoted by permission of the Controller of Her Britannic Majesty's Stationery Office.

ministration, the state of Europe was tranquil, as it had not been for twenty years, and was not to be for at least another twenty. A friendly feeling existed towards Germany following upon our Treaty of Locarno, and the evacuation of the Rhineland by the French Army and Allied contingents at a much earlier date than had been prescribed at Versailles. The new Germany took her place in the truncated League of Nations.[35]

Comments of Harold Nicolson

The almost hysterical jubilation that greeted the Locarno treaties, the reaction that set in thereafter, have obscured the fact that they constituted a remarkable diplomatic achievement. Germany of her own free will had accepted some of the most vital provisions imposed upon her by the Treaty of Versailles. Had it not been for the economic crisis of 1930 to 1931 and the advent of Hitler, Locarno might well have justified the hopes that were formed at the time:

"The principal part," wrote Lord D'Abernon to the King, "of the honour which attaches

to the Locarno achievement should accrue to England and to Your Majesty's Government. As far back as January 1921 it was constantly urged by me that German ministers should consider the necessity of affording proof of their pacific orientation, and throughout subsequent years I have contended that there was no satisfactory solution to the problem of the pacification of Europe except on the basis of mutual security. Unless France were reassured as to the safety of her frontiers, there would always be anxiety and unrest. Unless, on the other hand, security was reciprocal and Germany was guaranteed against the recurrence of episodes such as the Ruhr invasion, it would be impossible for the German people to settle down and pursue the policy of conciliation. . . ."

On October 16, 1925, which happened to be Mr. Chamberlain's birthday, the treaties were initialled at Locarno amid scenes of almost orgiac gush. "I felt myself," wrote Mr. Chamberlain to Sir William Tyrrell, "a little child again in spirit." On December 1, the final signature took place in London in circumstances of greater dignity. "This morning," the King recorded in his diary, "the Locarno Pact was signed at the Foreign Office. I pray this may mean peace for many years. Why not for ever?"[36]

[35]Churchill, *op. cit.*, p. 31.

[36]Nicolson, *op. cit.*, p. 409.

It is not possible to view Germany only in its relations to the West. The commercial treaty with Russia had proven to be of value, and negotiations were pressed to develop closer ties between Germany and the Soviet Union. The following documents refer to these negotiations and the reactions to them.

Comments of Herbert von Dirksen

During the whole winter of 1925–26 the negotiations dragged on till at last the clauses of the treaty and the accompanying exchange of notes about the guarantee against the menace of sanctions were agreed upon. The non-cooperative attitude of Count Rantzau

made the task of the Foreign Office still harder. An insurmountable aversion to the Locarno-policy, stemming almost more from sentiment than from intellect, and the conviction that the blow inflicted on the Rapallo-spirit was irreparable, prevented the Ambassador from a wholehearted co-operation, though he tried to force himself to be helpful. He even declined the proposal which I made to him that the pact should be signed in Moscow. He did not want to link his name with this transaction. This time he lacked foresight as to the effects of the treaty. It was to be signed in Berlin, and the date was fixed for April 26. The Soviet Government managed to give quite an effective setting by proclaiming this fact on the very afternoon of the signature at a session of the so-called parliament in Moscow, thus securing the resounding applause of the obedient deputies

To invest the signing of the Pact with all the paraphernalia of ardent love and mutual friendship did not correspond with the intentions of Stresemann and Schubert. They regarded the whole matter rather as a ransom extorted to hush up an unsavory family affair. Thus the act of signing was reduced to the minimum of decent *mise-en-scène*. A perfunctory lunch, with some phrases of congratulation muttered by Stresemann, followed.[37]

Excerpt from a Memorandum of Conversation of British Ambassador D'Abernon with "a Leading German Authority," April 4, 1926

The main cause of Germany's decision finally to yield to the advances of Russia and sign a new agreement with her is to be attributed to fear of Poland—to alarm lest some alliance might be established between Russia and Poland or between Russia and France.

It was always clear that Germany would not allow close relations between Russia and either France or Poland without intervening. Whenever negotiations between Russia and either of the above-mentioned countries advanced to the stage of probable agreement, Germany was certain to cut in and not allow her-

self to be deprived of the Russian connection.

The conversion of German Ministers from a negative attitude towards Russia to one of acceptance of Russian proposals has been greatly facilitated by the reduction of the original Russian claim. Throughout 1925 Germany could have had an alliance with Russia for the asking. It was only necessary to make the alliance sufficiently close. This Germany refused. The Luther-Stresemann Government, while determined to maintain a certain connection with Russia, placed greater importance on joining the League of Nations. They refused to be intimidated by Russian menaces although such menaces were repeated in various forms both from Moscow and by Chicherin during his two stays in Berlin. Stresemann assured him that Germany had the most friendly disposition towards Russia but that it was quite impossible for Germany to refuse the advantages offered by the Pact of Locarno and a permanent seat on the Council.

When Russia saw that it was hopeless to deter the German Ministers from this purpose they [*sic*] came forward with more moderate proposals.

After the London meeting of December 1925 they no longer proposed an alliance but stated that they would be satisfied with a declaration from Germany that she would not join in any military or economic combination against Russia. Until quite recently however they have urged that a convention in this sense might advantageously be accompanied by a secret Treaty giving further guarantees of assistance on the part of Germany if Russia was attacked or unduly pressed. The German Government appear to have declined even to discuss the possibility of a secret treaty. They have, however, maintained their readiness to enter into a formal engagement with Russia not to join in any hostile combination, as well as to give Russia official cognisance of the interpretation

---

[37]Dirksen, *op. cit.*, pp. 66–67.

placed on Article 16 by the Locarno Powers.[38]

Treaty of Berlin between Germany and the Soviet Union, April 24, 1926

Art. 1. The basis of the relations between Germany and the Union of Socialist Soviet Republics remains the Treaty of Rapallo.

The German Government and the Government of the Union of Socialist Soviet Republics will remain in friendly touch with one another in order to bring about an understanding with regard to all questions of a political and economic character jointly affecting their two countries.

2. Should one of the contracting parties, despite its peaceful attitude, be attacked by one or more third Powers, the other contracting party will observe neutrality for the entire duration of the conflict.

3. If, on the occasion of a conflict of the nature mentioned in article 2, or at a time when neither of the contracting parties is involved in warlike complications, a coalition is formed between third Powers for the purpose of imposing upon one of the contracting parties an economic or financial boycott, the other contracting party undertakes not to adhere to such coalition.[39]

Report of Maxim Litvinoff to the Soviet Central Executive Committee, April 24, 1926

It is not superfluous to remark here that everything that has been signed in Berlin today will be published in full, and that no secret treaties, no secret protocols or annexes to the agreement have been signed.

The treaty is an appendix to, or rather an amplification of, the Rapallo treaty, and is in complete accordance with those friendly relations which were established between our Union and Germany, and which both parties wish to preserve in future. The Rapallo treaty was dictated both by the desire of the two countries to establish friendship, by their community of interests, and by the dangerous international position in which both States found themselves at that time, surrounded by a sea of enmity. Since then, of course, a great deal has changed on the international scene. I do not know whether Germany can at the present time count many friends among the European States, whether since Locarno and Geneva it regards its relations with other European States as adequately pacified and consolidated, whether it regards itself as free from any danger. That is Germany's affair. As to our Union, then, although relations with a whole series of States have improved, and they have recognized us *de jure,* it must just the same regard its position as somewhat threatened, and the enmity towards it on the part of the western non-Soviet world as continuing to exist. In such circumstances we cannot exclude the possibility of a general or collective attack on the Union. The object of Soviet diplomacy is therefore to lessen the danger of the formation of anti-Soviet blocs and combined attacks; the lessening of such dangers naturally increases the chances of general peace.

European diplomacy and its press have in the last few days been racking their brains over the question whether the Soviet-German treaty contradicts the so-called spirit of Locarno. The question and the reproach are not, of course, addressed

[38]*Documents on British Foreign Policy 1919–1939,* Series 1a (London: Her Majesty's Stationery Office, 1966), Vol. I, pp. 584–85. Quoted by permission of the Controller of Her Britannic Majesty's Stationery Office.

[39]*British and Foreign State Papers, 1926, Part III,* Vol. CXXV (London: His Majesty's Stationery Office, 1932), p. 738. Quoted by permission of the Controller of Her Britannic Majesty's Stationery Office.

to us, for we have retained full freedom of action and are bound by no agreements, neither by the Locarno agreements nor any other. But, objectively speaking, the answer to that question depends on the objects set by Locarno. If Locarno, as its authors try to convince us, really aimed at the pacification of Europe, at a real improvement and consolidation of the relations between European States, then its advocates should clearly give a warm welcome to the Soviet-German treaty as a further step in strengthening friendship between two great nations. But if, as we have always suspected, one of the aims of Locarno is the formation of a united anti-Soviet front and the isolation of our Union, then in that case we must admit that the treaty signed today really does contradict the spirit of Locarno, and we can only rejoice that we have succeeded to some extent in depriving Locarno of its anti-Soviet sting. I say "to some extent" because, judging by the fury and spite of the attacks on Germany for concluding this treaty, and the references to Locarno, it must be said that Locarno continues to represent a threat to our Union.[40]

Foreign Secretary Austen Chamberlain to British Ambassador to Russia, Hodgson, April 26, 1926

It is useless to argue with Soviet authorities upon supposed anti-Soviet object of Locarno treaties. They have been told in every capital in Europe that these treaties had no such object and that His Majesty's Government have never sought to form any kind of anti-Soviet bloc. They are really suffering from swollen head. They are of less consequence to us than they suppose and they grossly flatter themselves when they suppose that British policy is dictated by thought of them.[41]

[40]Royal Institute of International Affairs, *Soviet Documents on Foreign Policy*, Vol. II (1925–32) (London: Oxford University Press, 1952), pp. 107–08.
[41]*Documents on British Foreign Policy*, Series 1a, Vol. I, p. 671.

Locarno launched a halcyon period in Franco-German relations. French troops evacuated the First (Cologne) Rhineland Zone on January 31, 1926, and on September 8 of the same year Germany entered the League. With Stresemann and Briand at Geneva, there was talk of resolving all outstanding differences between Germany and France. The following excerpts from Stresemann's diary record a celebrated meeting of the two foreign ministers. The Thoiry meeting did not produce the results hoped for, as practical considerations and political opposition hindered the successful resolution of the negotiations; it is nevertheless symptomatic of the attitude prevailing at the time.

Memorandum of German Foreign Minister Stresemann on Conversation with French Foreign Minister Briand at Thoiry, September 17, 1926

Herr Briand let me know through Professor Hesnard that he was going to propose to me that the occupation of the Rhineland should be wholly terminated, that the Saar should be given back to Germany, and Military Control abolished. He would begin the conversation by quite openly laying his cards on the table and explaining his views. Professor Hesnard asked me to reply with equal candour to the question that Briand would put to me

—namely whether we would in that case be ready to meet the economic needs of France in the matter of the issue of bonds. The political interview started according to plan.

Herr Briand began the interview with the expression of his conviction that partial solutions were useless, as always involving the possibility of danger in the future. His purpose was to discuss a comprehensive solution of all the questions at issue between Germany and France, and he asked me to say openly whether we could come to terms with France in the economic sphere, if this question should be solved. In this connection he was not merely thinking of the return of the Saar, but the termination of the entire Rhineland occupation.

. . . . . .

STRESEMANN: If we are in agreement about the withdrawal of the troops from the Rhineland, the return of the Saar territory, and the abolition of Military Control, it is important that we should come to an understanding over Eupen and Malmedy.

I then gave Briand a detailed statement of the negotiations with Belgium . . . and asked what was the French Government's attitude to this matter.

BRIAND: . . . If the whole problem is solved, the question of Eupen and Malmedy will be solved with it. We have had various disputes over the occupied areas. I attach importance to establishing once and for all what

we have done in this connection. You produced a document at Locarno in which you detailed your wishes regarding the occupied areas. Let me tell you that almost all of these had alraedy been met by us before Germany entered the League. . . .

The strength of the occupying forces had, he said, also been sensibly diminished. I withdrew a division from the Rhineland and sent it to Morocco. . . . I also had the wives of officers and non-commissioned officers, who remained behind, sent back to France. I was told in the Ministry of War that there was then no accommodation for these families in France; to which I replied that it must be provided. The transport of these families cost us a great deal of money and in individual cases we have had to pay high compensation. But I did it by way of opposing the General Staff, which would hear of no reduction in the strength of the Army of Occupation.

STRESEMANN: I am greatly obliged to you and I can only regret that your good intentions of relieving the burden on the Rhineland met with so little support from the other side. You yourself said that the 6000 men now to be sent away were not enough. But I need not discuss any further reduction, since we are now considering the removal of all troops from the Rhineland. Will these 6000 men be sent in any event before the end of September?

BRIAND: Not a doubt of it, the orders have been issued.[42]

_____

[42]*Stresemann: Diaries, Letters and Papers,* Vol. III, pp. 17–18, 22–23.

After the rise of Hitler and the carnage of World War II, one must take a second look at the Locarno settlement. Here are two views, one French and one German, written after 1945.

Comments of Former French Premier Paul Reynaud

The three aims of German policy, after the Ruhr operation of 1923, were:

(1) to prevent France from again using

force to restrain Germany from violations of the treaty;

(2) to obtain the anticipated evacuation of the Rhineland, security for the treaty's implementation;

(3) to end the military disproportion between France and Germany by a recognition

of equal rights. Stresemann was the man of this policy and his success was complete. . . .

It was at Locarno, in 1925, at the suggestion of an England extremely hostile to our military interventions in Germany, that Stresemann achieved victory on the first point. "We have spoken European," said Briand to the Chamber on his return. French opinion heartily accepted this accord which, recognizing as definite the western frontiers of Germany, seemed like a renunciation on her part of a *guerre de revanche*. At that time however, the renunciation was small, for to take Alsace-Lorraine away from France it would have been necessary to make war and for that Germany was not prepared. . . . No commitment was made by Germany at Locarno in regard to Czechoslovakia or Poland, those two powder-kegs to the east. But everyone knew that Germany did not accept the Polish Corridor. It pleased the French to shut their eyes to this claim, but it remained there nonetheless and it was the real menace to the peace of Europe. The Locarno policy was thus an ostrich policy. In Locarno you can already see the mood of Munich, and that is a serious matter. So, an immediate advantage for Germany, a problematical and limited advantage for France; we have since seen what it was worth.[43]

Comments of Herbert von Dirksen

Has the Locarno policy paid in the long run? I pondered over this question for years, especially so far as Russo-German relations were concerned. From a convinced supporter of Locarno, I developed into a skeptic. Discussing with Russian

officials, also with Russophile Americans, the merits of Stresemann's policy, I used to stress the fact that Germany simply could not remain out in the cold, but that she was bound to find a *modus vivendi* with the Western Powers and to reassert her position as a Central European Power. I was refuted by the retort that Locarno was not necessary to achieve this end; that the settlement of the reparation problem at the Dawes Conference in London, 1924, or rather the re-entry of the United States into the arena of European politics, would have had just the same result as Locarno: to re-establish Germany's position in Europe. If we had been more patient, we might have saved the political expenses of Locarno and Geneva.

In a retrospective view I am inclined to agree with this opinion. The failure of Locarno—for a failure it was in the long run—evoked the most sinister consequences. It meant that Western European statesmanship had failed to reconcile Germany, to win her wholehearted collaboration in European reconstruction. She felt disappointed, almost cheated, as she had not received her reward for the goods delivered by her. It must be kept in mind that the German statesmen of this Weimar period cannot be blamed as Junkers, Fascists, reactionaries, crooks, or idiots. They were honest, capable, intelligent men, inspired by the one desire to restore their country, in collaboration with the other European nations, to an honorable position on the European continent. Their supreme effort to achieve this goal, initiated by the most capable of them, was Locarno. Together with Versailles, the non-fulfilment of President Wilson's Fourteen Points, and the breakdown of disarmament, the failure of Locarno was one of the roots from which National Socialism sprang.[44]

[43]Paul Reynaud, *La France a sauvé l'Europe* (Paris: Librairie Ernest Flammarion, 1947), pp. 47–48. Quoted by permission of the publishers, Librairie Ernest Flammarion, Paris.

[44]Dirksen, *op. cit.*, p. 65.

BIBLIOGRAPHY

Sources Used in This Problem

1. Collections and Official Documents

British and Foreign State Papers, 1926. Part III. London: His Majesty's Stationery Office, 1932.

British White Paper, Cmd. 2435. London: His Majesty's Stationery Office, 1925.

British White Paper, Cmd. 2468. London: His Majesty's Stationery Office, 1925.

British White Paper, Cmd. 2525. London: His Majesty's Stationery Office, 1925.

Documents on British Foreign Policy 1919–1939. Series 1a, Vol. 1. London: Her Majesty's Stationery Office, 1966.

Livre jaune français (French Yellow Book): *Pacte de Sécurité* Vols. I, II. Paris: Ministère des Affaires Étrangères, 1925.

Parliamentary Debates. London: His Majesty's Stationery Office.

Soviet Documents on Foreign Policy. Royal Institute of International Affairs. Vol. II (1925–32). London: Oxford University Press, 1952.

Trial of the Major War Criminals before the International Military Tribunal. Vol. XIV. Nuremberg, 1948.

Trials of the War Criminals before the Nuremberg Tribunals. Vol. X. Washington, D.C.: U.S. Government Printing Office, 1951.

Survey of International Affairs 1925. Royal Institute of International Affairs. London: Oxford University Press, 1928.

2. Others

Chamberlain, Sir Austen. *Down the Years.* London: Cassell, 1935.

Churchill, Winston. *The Gathering Storm.* Boston: Houghton Mifflin, 1948.

D'Abernon, Lord. *The Diary of an Ambassador.* 4 vols. Garden City, N.Y.: Doubleday, 1930.

Dirksen, Herbert von. *Moscow, Tokyo, London: Twenty Years of German Foreign Policy.* Norman, Okla.: University of Oklahoma Press, 1952.

Freund, Gerald. *Unholy Alliance: Russian-German Relations from the Treaty of Brest-Litovsk to the Treaty of Berlin.* London: Chatto & Windus Ltd.; New York: Harcourt, Brace, 1957.

Hilger, Gustav and Meyer, Alfred G. *The Incompatible Allies—A Memoir-History of German-Soviet Relations 1918–1941.* New York: Macmillan, 1953.

Lochner, Louis P. *Always the Unexpected.* New York: Macmillan, 1956.

Nicolson, Harold. *King George the Fifth.* Garden City, N.Y.: Doubleday, 1953.

Paul-Boncour, Joseph. *Entre deux guerres.* 3 vols. Paris: Librairie Plon, 1945.

Petrie, Sir Charles. *Life and Letters of Sir Austen Chamberlain.* 2 vols. London: Cassell, 1940.

Reynaud, Paul. *La France a sauvé l'Europe.* 2 vols. Paris: Flammarion, 1947.

Suarez, Georges. *Briand.* Vol. VI. Paris: Librairie Plon, 1952.

Sutton, Eric (ed. and trans.). *Gustave Stresemann: His Diaries, Letters and Papers.* 3 vols. London: Macmillan, 1937.

Wheeler-Bennett, John W. *The Nemesis of Power: The German Army in Politics, 1918–1945.* New York: St. Martin's Press, 1954.

SELECT LIST OF BOOKS RECOMMENDED FOR FURTHER READING

BRETTON, HENRY L. *Stresemann and the Revision of Versailles.* Stanford, Calif.: Stanford University Press, 1953.

CARR, EDWARD HALLET. *German-Soviet Relations between the Two World Wars.* Baltimore: The Johns Hopkins Press, 1951.

CRAIG, G., and GILBERT, F. (eds.). *The Diplomats.* Princeton, N.J.: Princeton University Press, 1953.

CRIPPS, CHARLES ALFRED (LORD PARMOOR). *A Retrospect.* London: Heinemann, 1936.

EYCK, ERICH. *A History of the Weimar Republic.* 2 vols. Cambridge: Harvard University Press, 1963 and 1964.

GATZKE, HANS W. *Stresemann and the Rearmament of Germany.* Baltimore: The Johns Hopkins Press, 1954.

GORDON, HAROLD J. *The Reichswehr and the German Republic 1919–1926.* Princeton, N.J.: Princeton University Press, 1957.

HALPERIN, S. WILLIAM. *Germany Tried Democracy: A Political History of the Reich from 1918 to 1933.* New York: Crowell, 1946.

JORDAN, W. M. *Great Britain, France, and the German Problem, 1918–1939.* New York: Oxford University Press, 1944.

LAQUEUR, WALTER. *Russia and Germany: A Century of Conflict.* Boston: Little Brown, 1965.

LITVINOV, MAXINE. *Notes for a Journal.* New York: William Morrow, 1955.

MORGAN, J. H. *Assize of Arms: The Disarmament of Germany and Her Rearmament, 1919–1939.* London: Oxford University Press, 1945.

PINSON, KOPPEL L. *Modern Germany.* New York: Macmillan, 1954.

REYNOLDS, PHILIP ALAN. *British Foreign Policy in the Inter-War Years.* London: Longmans, Green, 1954.

ROSENBAUM, KURT. *Community of Fate: German-Soviet Diplomatic Relations 1922–1928.* Syracuse, N.Y.: Syracuse University Press, 1965.

TURNER, H. A., JR. *Stresemann & the Politics of the Weimar Republic.* Princeton, N.J.: Princeton University Press, 1963.

VALLENTIN, ANTONIA. *Stresemann.* London: Constable, 1931.

WANDYCZ, PIOTR. *France and Her Eastern Allies, 1919–1925.* Minneapolis, Minn.: University of Minnesota Press, 1962.

WHEELER-BENNETT, J. W. *The Treaty of Brest-Litovsk and Germany's Eastern Policy.* New York: Farrar & Rinehart, 1939.

WOLFERS, ARNOLD. *Britain and France between Two Wars: Conflicting Strategies of Peace since Versailles.* New York: Harcourt, Brace, 1940.

THE LEAGUE OF NATIONS AND THE MANCHURIAN CRISIS

Collective Security and the Stimson Doctrine, 1931-33

With the conquest of Manchuria in 1931, Japan perpetrated the first major violation of treaty commitments since World War I. Both the Nine Power Pact and the Paris Peace Pact were patently disregarded as Japanese troops carried out the invasion. In one sense this act constitutes a symbol: it terminates the period of optimism that reigned in the 1920's and it marks the return to power politics that would lead ultimately to the Second World War.

The Manchurian Crisis also demonstrates very clearly the inadequacy of the League in dealing with aggression. The League reacted slowly and, recognizing the fact that no policy in the Far East could function without American support, spent long months in negotiations with a view toward United States–League cooperation. Hopes that the Japanese liberal element would prevail over the war party turned out to be unfounded, and in the end, as no forceful policy supported by Great Britain, the United States, and the League was forthcoming, Japan completed its occupation, opposed only by inadequate Chinese forces and by diplomatic notes of protest from the West.

As background one should appreciate the attitudes of Japanese militarists, who advocated a "strong" policy regarding expansionism. The logical area for expansion was Manchuria, lying north of Korea, but ostensibly part of the Nationalist China of Chiang Kai-shek. Both China and Japan hoped to control railroads which would be essential in the economic exploitation of this vast region.

In 1927 and 1928, when Tanaka Giichi was Prime Minister, the "strong" attitude predominated and led to the promulgation of the celebrated Tanaka Memorial.

Excerpts from the Tanaka Memorial, Presented to the Japanese Emperor July 25, 1927, by Premier Tanaka

. . . in order that we may lay plans for the colonization of the Far East and the development of our new continental empire, a special conference was held from June 27th to July 7th lasting in all eleven days. It was attended by all the civil and military officers connected with Manchuria and Mongolia, whose discussions resulted in the following resolutions. . . .

.   .   .   .   .

Manchuria and Mongolia are the Belgium of the Far East. In the Great War, Belgium was the battlefield. In our wars with Russia and the United States, we must also make Manchuria and Mongolia suffer the ravages. As it is evident that we have to violate the neutrality of these territories, we cannot help building the Kirin-Hueining and Changchun-Talai Railways in order that we may be militarily pre-pared. In time of war we can easily increase our forces and in time of peace we can migrate thousands upon thousands of people into this region and work on the rice fields. This line offers the key to economic development as well as to military conquests.

.   .   .   .   .

. . . the Manchuria Railway should be radically reorganized. . . . Chinese, Europeans, and Americans should be invited to invest money in the South Manchuria Railway on the condition that we have a plurality of its stocks. . . . by inviting international participation in the South Manchuria Railway, we can blind the eyes of the world. Having achieved that, we can push our advance in Manchuria and Mongolia at our will, free ourselves from the restraints of the Nine Power Treaty and strengthen our activities in that country with foreign capital.[1]

---

[1] *The China Critic*, Vol. IV, No. 39 (September 24, 1931), pp. 923–34.

After 1928, Japan's foreign policy was tempered somewhat by Foreign Minister Shidehara, advocate of a program which, while expansionist, sought to minimize military aggression. But while the General Staff did not receive unlimited support from the government, it made its own plans, as revealed in the following document.

"General Principles Concerning the Settlement of Manchuria-Mongolia Problems," Adopted by the Japanese General Staff and Ministry of War, June, 1931

1) The alleviation of anti-Japanese activities of the Chang regime shall continue to be undertaken primarily through negotiation by the Foreign Office, and the army shall maintain close contact with the Kwantung Army in order to make them act with discretion.

2) In spite of the above-mentioned efforts, should anti-Japanese activities be intensified, military action might become necessary.

3) Internal as well as international understanding are absolutely necessary for the settlement of Manchurian problems. The Minister of War through the Cabinet, and the Military Affairs Department [of the Ministry of War] and the Second Department of the General Staff, with close contact with the Foreign Office, shall make careful

preparations, such as publicizing the realities of anti-Japanese activities in Manchuria to the people of our country and of the powers, so that in the event of military action, public opinion will support the measure and the powers will not take opposing or suppressive steps.

4) The General Staff shall make plans concerning necessary forces and the guidance of their movement in the event of military action.

5) Measures with regard to cultivation of internal and international understanding shall be undertaken with a view to achieving results in approximately one year, that is, by the spring of 1932.[2]

[2]Quoted in Sadako N. Ogata, *Defiance in Manchuria* (Berkeley, Calif.: University of California Press, 1964), pp. 53–54.

In connection with its control of the South Manchuria Railway, Japan exercised the right to patrol the roadbed. Thus Japan had, in its Kwantung army, stationed in Manchuria, an instrument which could act without direct surveillance from Tokyo. On the night of September 18, 1931, an explosion on the railroad track, the "Mukden Incident," unleashed a Japanese advance which culminated in the absorption of Manchuria.

FOR CONSIDERATION   Was the explosion engineered by Chinese or by Japanese? Did it actually occur? Was it planned in advance? To what extent was the Cabinet informed? The Ministry of War? These questions were asked by the Lytton Commission, which studied the Manchurian question on the spot during five months in 1932. Since World War II, additional Japanese documents have become available.

The Mukden Incident, September 18, 1931 (Chinese Version)

On the night of September 18th, all the soldiers of the 7th Brigade, numbering about 10,000, were in the North Barracks. As instructions had been received from Marshal Chang Hsueh-liang on September 6th that special care was to be taken to avoid any clash with the Japanese troops in the tense state of feeling existing at the time, the sentries at the walls of the Barracks were only armed with dummy rifles. For the same reason, the west gate in the mud wall surrounding the camp which gave access to the railway had been closed. The Japanese had been carrying out night manoeuvres around the barracks on the nights of September 14th, 15th, 16th and 17th. At 7 P.M. on the evening of the 18th, they were manoeuvring at a village called Wenkuantun. At 9 P.M., Officer Liu reported that a train composed of three or four coaches, but without the usual type of locomotive, had stopped there. At 10 P.M. the sound of a loud explosion was heard, immediately followed by rifle fire. This was reported over the telephone by the Chief of Staff to the Commanding Officer, General Wang I-Cheh, who was at his private house situated near the railway, about six or seven miles from the barracks, to the south. While the Chief of Staff was still at the telephone, news was brought to him that the Japanese were attacking the barracks and that two sentries had been wounded.[3]

The Mukden Incident, September 18, 1931 (Japanese Version)

Lieutenant Kawamoto, with six men under his command, was on patrol duty on the night of September 18th, practising defence exercises along the track of the South Manchuria Railway to the north of Mukden. . . . When they reached a point at which a small road crosses the line, they heard the noise of a loud explosion a little way behind them. They turned and ran back, and after going about 200 yards they discovered that a portion of one of the rails on the down track had been blown out. . . . On arrival at the site of the explosion, the patrol was fired upon from the fields on the east side of the line. Lieutenant Kawamoto immediately ordered his men to deploy and return the fire. The attacking body, estimated at about five or six, then stopped firing and retreated northwards. The Japanese patrol at once started in pursuit and, having gone about 200 yards, they were again fired upon by a larger body, estimated at between three and four hundred. . . . Lieutenant Kawamoto then ordered one of his men to report to the Commander of No. 3 Company, who was also engaged in night manoeuvres some 1,500 yards to the north; at the same time, he ordered another of his men to telephone (by means of a box telephone near the spot) to Battalion Headquarters at Mukden for reinforcements. . . .

Lieutenant Kawamoto's patrol, reinforced by Captain Kawashima's Company,

was still sustaining the fire of the Chinese troops concealed in the tall kaoliang grass, when the two Companies arrived from Mukden. Although his force was then only 500, and he believed the Chinese army in the North Barracks numbered 10,000, Lieutenant-Colonel Shimamoto at once ordered an attack on the Barracks, believing, as he told us, that "offence is the best defence." . . . The attack was vigorously contested by the Chinese troops within, and there was fierce fighting for some hours. . . .[4]

Reaction of Members of the Lytton Commission to the Mukden Incident, as Described by George Blakeslee, an Assistant to the Commission

These conclusions were ample to condemn Japan for its actions upon that eventful night. But the Commissioners, after all their study of that event, after all the evidence they had read and the witnesses they had heard, including the leading Chinese and Japanese participants, still remained uncertain as to just what did happen on and near the railway tracks. They exchanged views at one meeting, and found that their several surmises were widely divergent. They all agreed that there was an explosion—the Chinese stated that there was one but they regarded it merely as a signal for the Japanese attack—but the majority of the Commission at least, as I remember it, did not believe that there was any explosion between ten and eleven o'clock which injured the railway track. At any rate, they were all convinced that the Japanese account, in its entirety, was untrue.[5]

[4]*Ibid.*, pp. 67–68.

[5]Letter of Blakeslee to Stanley K. Hornbeck, September 14, 1932, quoted in Armin Rappaport, *Henry L. Stimson and Japan, 1931–33* (Chicago: University of Chicago Press, 1963), pp. 218–19. Reprinted by permission of The University of Chicago Press.

[3]*Report of the Commission of Enquiry* [*Lytton Report*], League of Nations Publication C. 663. M. 320. 1932. VII (Geneva, 1932), p. 69. (Hereafter cited as *Lytton Report*.)

Official Opinion of the Lytton Commission on the Mukden Incident

The Chinese, in accordance with . . . instructions . . . had no plan of attacking the Japanese troops, or of endangering the lives or property of Japanese nationals at this particular time or place. They made no concerted or authorised attack on the Japanese forces and were surprised by the Japanese attack and subsequent operations. An explosion undoubtedly occurred on or near the railroad between 10 and 10:30 P.M. on September 18th, but the damage, if any, to the railroad did not in fact prevent the punctual arrival of the south-bound train from Changchun, and was not in itself sufficient to justify military action. The military operations of the Japanese troops during this night, which have been described above, cannot be regarded as measures of legitimate self-defence.[6]

Typical Statements of Col. Itagaki and Lt. Col Ishiwara, according to Diary of Harada Kumao

The Manchurian Incident was planned well in advance. Field pieces were arranged in positions around Mukden as early as July 25. Since we succeeded in Manchuria, our next move is to engineer a coup d'état after we return to Japan and crush the party government and set up a government based on national socialism with the Emperor at the center. Capitalists, such as Mitsui and Mitsubishi, will be liquidated and there will be equitable distribution of wealth. You can rest assured that we will do this.[7]

---

[6]*Lytton Report*, p. 71.
[7]Harada Diary, Vol. II, p. 77, as quoted in Takehiko Yoshihashi, *Conspiracy at Mukden* (New Haven, Conn.: Yale University Press, 1963), p. 135.

Comments of Japanese Premier Wakatsuki Addressed to Minister of War Minami, September 19, 1931, according to Diary of Harada Kumao

Did the incident break out because the Chinese troops destroyed the rail and opened fire on the Japanese guards? Was it truthfully an act of legitimate self-defence? If, on the contrary, it turns out to be an act of conspiracy by the Japanese army, what do you propose to do about our nation's standing in the world? . . . Whatever may have caused the incident, I will immediately instruct the commanding officer of the Kwantung Army not to enlarge the theater of conflict nor to bombard and occupy government buildings and fortifications.[8]

Excerpts from Report of British Military Attaché Regarding Visit to Manchuria, September 30 to October 2, 1931

In Japanese military circles attention was centred on convincing myself and my colleagues from Peking that Chinese were responsible for present state of affairs in that they attacked a railway protected by troops whose first axiom of war has always been "the best defence is attack." This remark I took as intended to convey the idea that, appearances to the contrary, Japanese had been and were still on the defensive.

I have not since heard nor can I find anything calculated to alter at all the impressions conveyed to you in my previous telegrams that Japanese were responsible for outbreak on the night of the 18th/19th. Japanese attack was a set piece, break in railway served as a pretext and was conveniently arranged at a point which put the Japanese railway guard in a favour-

---

[8]Harada Diary, Vol. II, p. 62; *ibid.*, p. 7.

able position for dealing with the only Chinese troops worth mentioning in the vicinity of Mukden. No other conclusions can be drawn from a detailed analysis of events on the night in question; moreover a careful sifting of facts and fancies goes far to show that Japanese military fearing a settlement of Nakamura case which would leave the issues as far as they were concerned in much the same position as before, decided to bring to an end what was to them intolerable arrogance of inferior soldiery who contrary to treaty occasionally dared to march in formed bodies across their railway or shoot individual sentries performing their normal duty.

Should necessity arise it is evident that Japanese Cabinet will exploit to the full the current idea that military alone were responsible for this *coup.* The Cabinet doubtless counselled patience and putting a brake on those enthusiasts who favoured positive action in Manchuria; but before military arguments to the effect that the army was every day losing men and prestige in Manchuria these men were powerless.[9]

---

[9]*Documents on British Foreign Policy 1919–1939,* 2d Series (London: Her Majesty's Stationery Office, 1960), Vol. VIII, pp. 709–10. Quoted by permission of the Controller of Her Britannic Majesty's Stationery Office.

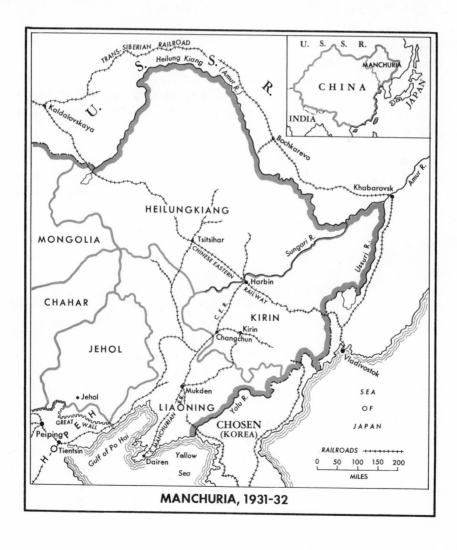

MANCHURIA, 1931-32

Aware of the situation in Manchuria, and cognizant of the debate going on in the League of Nations, Secretary of State Henry Stimson considered the policy which the United States should pursue. The three following documents include the official note sent to Japan on September 22, Stimson's comments from his book, *The Far Eastern Crisis*, published in 1936, and an analysis by the journalists Drew Pearson and Constantine Brown, published in 1935.

FOR CONSIDERATION   As Stimson's name will always be associated with the Manchurian problem in terms of the Stimson Doctrine, it is important to estimate the firmness of Stimson's stand at this time. How firm *is* the note of September 22? Although the note was not immediately made public, the Japanese press considered the United States as generally sympathetic toward Japanese interests. Would a stronger U.S. position have strengthened Shidehara?

How seriously should the allegations of Pearson and Brown be taken? Does the reputation of these journalists for "inside stories" and "predictions" invalidate their testimony? How could it be corroborated? A historian of this episode has stated: "Inquiries by this author support the story [of differences in the State Department] but the sources of information unfortunately cannot be quoted."[10]

**Memorandum of Secretary of State
Stimson to Japanese Ambassador
Debuchi, September 22, 1931**

Without going into the background, either as to the immediate provocation or remote causes or motivation, it appears that there has developed within the past four days a situation in Manchuria which I find surprising and view with concern. . . .

This situation is of concern, morally, legally and politically to a considerable number of nations. It is not exclusively a matter of concern to Japan and China. It brings into question at once the meaning

[10]Sara R. Smith, *The Manchurian Crisis, 1931–1932* (New York: Columbia University Press, 1948), p. 31 n. Compare Armin Rappaport, *Henry L. Stimson and Japan, 1931–1933* (Chicago: University of Chicago Press, 1963), pp. 37–38.

of certain provisions of agreements, such as the Nine-Powers Treaty of February 6, 1922, and the Kellogg-Briand Pact.

It is the hope of the American Government that the orders which it understands have been given both by the Japanese and the Chinese Governments to their military forces to refrain from hostilities and further movements will be respected and that there will be no further application of force. It is also the hope of the American Government that the Japanese and the Chinese Governments will find it possible speedily to demonstrate to the world that neither has any intention to take advantage, in furtherance of its own peculiar interests, of the situation which has been brought about in connection with and in consequence of this use of force.

What has occurred has already shaken the confidence of the public with regard to the stability of conditions in Manchuria, and it is believed that the crystallizing of a situation suggesting the necessity for an indefinite continuance of military occupation would further undermine that confidence.[11]

Comments of Secretary of State Stimson

I do not recall that there was any difference of opinion whatever in our group in the State Department as to the policy we should follow in the face of this diagnosis of the situation in Manchuria. The evidence in our hands pointed to the wisdom of giving Shidehara and the Foreign Office an opportunity, free from anything approaching a threat or even public criticism, to get control of the situation. We were well aware of the incomplete development of parliamentary government in Japan and that the Japanese constitution, instead of placing the army under the direction of the Cabinet, gave it direct and independent access to the Emperor as chief of state. We of course knew of the imperious economic problem Japan faced in the necessity of providing a livelihood for a constantly increasing population and we were well aware that in grappling with this problem during the period of the great war she had sought to use the tactics of conquest and colonization over China for its solution. But for nearly ten years under the guidance of Shidehara and his fellow liberals she had been "studiously and persistently sailing on the opposite tack to the militant course" which she had previously followed. . . .[12]

[11]*Papers Relating to the Foreign Relations of the United States, Japan: 1931–1941* (Washington, D.C.: U.S. Government Printing Office, 1943), Vol. I, pp. 5–7.

[12]Henry L. Stimson, *Far-Eastern Crisis* (New York: Harper & Row, 1936), p. 34. Copyright 1936, 1964 by Henry L. Stimson. Reprinted by permission of Harper & Row, Publishers.

Comments of the American Journalists, Drew Pearson and Constantine Brown

Mr. Stimson had other reasons for relying upon the good faith of the Japanese Government. He had inherited from his predecessors, Mr. Hughes and Mr. Kellogg, a secret understanding with Japan, which, although never reduced to writing and never called by any name, deserved the title of "Japanese-American Alliance." Supplanting the Anglo-Japanese Alliance, which died at the Washington Arms Conference, there had developed a tacit understanding based on the fact that the United States bought one-third of all Japan's exports, and Japan in turn bought the same proportion from the United States. It was an understanding between merchant princes. In Japan, Baron Shidehara, Minister of Foreign Affairs, spoke for the great House of Mitsubishi, whose daughter he had married, for the equally powerful Mitsuis, and for all the rest of Japan's ruling merchant class; while in the United States the Harding, Coolidge, and Hoover administrations spoke for General Electric, United States Steel, Standard Oil, General Motors, and for all the others which found Japanese markets profitable. Especially they spoke for J. P. Morgan, who even sought to loan $30,000,000 of American investors' money for Japanese exploitation of Manchuria.

At Mr. Stimson's right hand during these crucial days sat an Under Secretary of State who had been suckled on the same diplomatic dogma.

William R. Castle, Jr., sprang from a family of Hawaiian missionaries which had amassed great wealth from cheap Japanese labor. He, himself, had served as American ambassador to Japan, and despite the fact that Admiral Kato publicly refused to attend a dinner at the American Embassy because the ambassador had induced Japan to accept the London Naval Treaty, Castle had built up a healthy admiration for the Japanese. Certainly, he informed his chief, Japanese rule in Manchuria was vastly preferable to that of the mercurial son of that old brigand, Chang Tso-lin.

Unquestionably this view carried weight with Mr. Stimson.

At Mr. Stimson's left hand, however, sat another adviser whose views were diametrically different. Stanley K. Hornbeck, chief of the Far Eastern Division, had taught American political economy in Chi-

nese Government colleges, Chinese political economy at Wisconsin and Harvard, and in one way or another had devoted almost a lifetime to the study of China.

And Dr. Hornbeck knew what Stimson and Castle only vaguely knew, that for Japan the situation in Manchuria had become one where it had to fish or cut bait.[13]

---

[13]Drew Pearson and Constantine Brown, *The American Diplomatic Game* (Garden City, N.Y.: Doubleday & Company, Inc., 1935), pp. 300–01. Copyright 1935 by Doubleday & Company, Inc. Reprinted by permission of the publisher.

F aced with the first major crisis of its career, the League of Nations passed the resolution here quoted. Significant in this resolution is the recognition that U.S. support will be all-important.

FOR CONSIDERATION   To what extent could the League operate in the Far East without U.S. cooperation? Could the League have sent a Commission of Inquiry to Manchuria without U.S. approval? Are Stimson's arguments, written several years later, sufficient to explain his motivation in following the policy he chose?

**Resolution Adopted by the Council
of the League of Nations,
September 22, 1931**

(1) To make an urgent appeal to the Chinese and Japanese Governments to refrain from any action which might aggravate the situation or prejudice the peaceful settlement of the problem;

(2) To endeavor, in consultation with the Chinese and Japanese representatives, to find adequate means of enabling the two countries to withdraw their troops immediately without the lives of their nationals and the safety of their property being endangered;

(3) To forward the minutes of all the Council meetings and the documents relating to the subject to the Government of the United States for its information;

(4) To ask the two parties concerned to meet immediately after the meeting of the

Council together with certain other members of the Council.[14]

**Secretary of State Stimson to the
President of the League Council,
September 23, 1931**

. . . . I assure you that the Government of the United States is in wholehearted sympathy with the attitude of the League of Nations as expressed in the Council's resolution and will dispatch to Japan and China notes along similar lines.

I have already urged cessation of hostilities and a withdrawal from the present situation of danger and will continue earnestly to work for the restoration of peace.[15]

---

[14]League of Nations, *Official Journal*, December, 1931, p. 2454.

[15]Royal Institute of International Affairs, *Survey of International Affairs, 1932* (London: Oxford University Press, 1934), p. 247.

The Council of the League of Nations met on September 25, 1931, and for several days discussed the Manchurian situation. China argued for an immediate inquiry, while Japan, promising the troops would soon be withdrawn, insisted on direct negotiation with China. Finally, on September 30, the Council agreed to postpone further action in the hope that both parties would "do all in their power to hasten the restoration of normal relations." The Council would again consider the situation on October 14.

In Japan, Foreign Minister Shidehara continued to try to bring military activities under the control of the goverment. Public opinion was split, but the Kwantung army was largely a law unto itself.

Official Statement of the Kwantung Army Headquarters, October 4, 1931

Recently movements have been growing everywhere to establish a regime, and though the people all praise the dignity of the Japanese Army, they do not in the least attempt to uphold their former leader. This is none other than the result of indignation felt against many years of oppression by war lords. The [Kwantung] Army stands aloof from politics and diplomacy and concentrates on maintaining public peace by keeping its forces prepared and by holding quiet vigilance. . . . However, it sincerely wishes to realize rapidly the paradise of coexistence and co-prosperity for the thirty million residing in Manchuria and Mongolia, and believes that from a moral point of view to promote the unification [of various independent movements] is the urgently needed means of relief that proves the neighborly friendship of our country.[16]

Japanese Actions against Chinchow, October 8, 1931

The first of these operations was the bombing, on October 8th, of Chinchow, to which place the Provincial Government of Liaoning Province had been transferred by Marshal Chang Hsueh-liang at the end of September. According to the Japanese account, the bombing was chiefly directed against the military barracks and the Communications University, where the offices of the Civil Government had been established. The bombing of a civil administration by military forces cannot be justified, and there is some doubt whether the area bombed was in fact as restricted as the Japanese allege.[17]

[16]Quoted in Ogata, op. cit., p. 81.
[17]Lytton Report, p. 72.

In spite of strong protests against Japanese actions, the Japanese government took no steps to interfere with military operations in Manchuria. The Chinese delegation at Geneva insisted that developments required an immediate convocation of the League Council.

In Washington, President Herbert Hoover was not as strongly convinced as his Secretary of State that the United States should proceed without assurances from Great Britain and France.

Comments of President Herbert Hoover

At this time, early in October, Secretary Stimson laid before me two alternative courses of action, stated in his own words:

(1) Some form of collective economic sanctions against Japan, or in default of that,

(2) The exercise of diplomatic pressure and the power of world public opinion. . . .

I was fully in favor of the second proposal but was greatly disturbed over the first and told Mr. Stimson so. I was soon to realize that my able Secretary was at times more of a warrior than a diplomat. To him the phrase "economic sanctions" (boycott) was the magic wand of force by which all peace could be summoned from the vasty deep. On that point we developed a difference. Ever since Versailles I had held that "economic sanctions" meant war when applied to any large nation. I urged upon him that no nation of spirit would submit to having her whole economy totally demoralized and her people thrown out of employment and into starvation. It meant all the penalties of war except shooting. Sanctions or the threat of them also meant rising emotions, the development of incurable hatreds, and an insensate opposition to any remedial action. . . .

In order to get all the factors in hand and to avoid any public communications and any hurt feelings, I asked Secretary Mills to telephone a friend in London and ask him to find out personally and confidentially the real attitude of the British Ministry. Would the British join the United States in sanctions? If so, and if such action involved military danger, would their fleet join with ours? If this resulted in war, would they go along? The reply came quickly: "The answer to the first question will be certainly and emphatically 'No,' and therefore no replies to the other questions are necessary." I did not feel out the French, but later it was confirmed that they held the same view.[18]

Comments of Viscount Cecil

Meanwhile, on October 6th, Parliament had been dissolved. The General Election resulted in the virtual destruction of the Opposition, which only secured 56 seats as against 558 for the Ministerialists. . . .

Mr. MacDonald thereupon reconstituted and enlarged his Government—the most important change from the League point of view being the substitution of Sir John Simon as Foreign Secretary instead of Lord Reading. However, we did not then know its importance.

The Council met again at Paris on November 14th. I represented the United Kingdom, though Sir John Simon paid one or two visits to Paris during its sessions. It quickly became clear that he was not prepared to take any step to compel Japan to leave China—not even to urge that a diplomatic protest should be made by withdrawing the envoys of the League Powers from Tokyo. When I pointed out that, if we were to do nothing to make the time limit, which expired on November 16th, a reality, it would have been better not to have committed ourselves to it, he agreed but adhered to his attitude. It was clear that in these circumstances Japan would not comply with League admonitions.[19]

Report of a Conversation on the French Position with Sir Eric Drummond by American Consul in Geneva, Gilbert, November 6, 1931

In France as well as in the French press there are pro-Japanese elements, and

[18]Herbert Hoover, *The Memoirs of Herbert Hoover* (New York: The Macmillan Company, 1951), Vol. II, pp. 366–67. Copyright 1951, 1952 by Herbert Hoover and used with the permission of The Macmillan Company, publishers.

[19]Viscount Cecil, *A Great Experiment* (London: Jonathan Cape, 1941), pp. 226–27.

these are related in part to the sales by French munition manufacturers to Japan. This also is reflected somewhat in the French Foreign Office, with Briand far ahead of the latter in respect of the manner in which France and the League conduct the Sino-Japanese question. Briand's policy is supported entirely by Massigli, while Leger, who supports Briand personally, is inclined toward Japan as a phase of French foreign policy. As I have previously reported, Berthelot is more or less frankly pro-Japanese. Therefore, a great deal depends upon support for Briand's

leadership. Drummond learned in a telephone talk with Massigli that communications through the French Ambassador at Washington to Paris were very unsatisfactory. Drummond was told by Massigli that Briand was not at all clear in regard to the American memorandum to the Japanese Foreign Office . . . and was quite confused by what Claudel had reported on the whole American position.[20]

[20]*Papers Relating to the Foreign Relations of the United States, 1931*, Vol. III (Washington, D.C.: U.S. Government Printing Office, 1946), p. 388.

On October 16, 1931, the United States, having been invited to participate in the Council's deliberations, appointed its consul at Geneva, Prentiss Gilbert, as its representative. Gilbert's comments on this occasion follow.

FOR CONSIDERATION   Why did the United States designate a minor diplomatic agent rather than an outstanding statesman to represent it? Why was he instructed simply to observe, not to participate? It so happened that Gilbert's instructions brought only a physical change in his position in the council room, for Gilbert regularly attended the meetings as an observer.

Excerpt from Speech of United States Representative Gilbert, before the Council of the League of Nations, October 16, 1931

At this moment of deep international concern, I thank you for your invitation to sit in your deliberations and participate in your discussions in so far as the Pact of Paris, to which my country is a party, is concerned.

The Government of the United States of America has been following with the closest attention the proceedings before the Council for the settlement of the dispute at present unhappily existing between China and Japan. My government does not seek to intrude with respect to such measures as you may propose under the Covenant of the League of Nations; and is not in a position to participate with

the members of the Council in the formulation of any action envisaged under that instrument for the composing of differences existing between two of its members. . . .

In your deliberations as to the application of the machinery of the Covenant of the League of Nations, I repeat, we can take no part. But the Pact of Paris, bearing as it does, the signature of the President of this meeting, together with that of our former Secretary of State, as joint proponents, represents to us in America an effective means of marshaling the public opinion of the world behind the use of pacific means only in the solution of controversies between nations.[21]

[21]*Conditions in Manchuria*, U.S. Senate Doc. 55, 72nd Cong., 1st sess. (Washington, D.C.: U.S. Government Printing Office, 1932), pp. 18–19.

For a week the League Council debated the Manchurian crisis. During this period France, Great Britain, Spain, and the United States dispatched notes to Japan under the Paris Pact, but it was not until October 24 that the Council adopted another resolution calling for direct Sino-Japanese conciliation before November 16. Japan reacted with a statement two days later.

Statement by the Japanese Government, October 26, 1931

The Japanese Government . . . have already expressed . . . their readiness to enter into negotiations with the Chinese Government on certain basic principles that should regulate the normal interrelationship between the two countries. . . . The basic principles which they have had in mind relate to:

(1) Mutual repudiation of aggressive policy and conduct.

(2) Respect for China's territorial integrity.

(3) Complete suppression of all organized movements interfering with freedom of trade and stirring up international hatred.

(4) Effective protection throughout Manchuria of all peaceful pursuits undertaken by Japanese subjects.

(5) Respect for the treaty rights of Japan in Manchuria.

The Japanese Government believe that all these points, being in entire accord with the aims and aspirations of the League of Nations and embodying the natural basis upon which peace in the Far East must depend, will commend themselves to the approval of the public opinion of the world. . . . Their willingness remains unaltered and unabated to open negotiations with the Chinese Government on the subject of the basic principles above formulated relating to normal relations between Japan and China, and on the subject of the withdrawal of Japanese troops to the South Manchuria Railway Zone.[22]

[22]League of Nations, *Official Journal*, December, 1931, p. 2514.

A new phase of the Manchurian crisis developed in connection with a Chinese civil conflict. The Chinese General Chang Hai-peng, ambitious to become governor of Heilungkiang Province and probably backed by the Japanese, started an advance early in October against the forces of General Ma Chan-shan. To obstruct this advance, General Ma destroyed bridges over the Nonni River serving the Japanese-controlled Taonan-Angangchi Line.

Action at the Nonni Bridge and Tsitsihar, October 20–November 19, 1931

. . . The Japanese Consul General at Tsitsihar, on instructions from his Government, requested General Ma Chan-shan, who had arrived at Tsitsihar on October 20th, to have the bridges repaired as soon as possible, but no time-limit accompanied this request. . . . On October 28th, Major Hayashi, the representative of General Honjo at Tsitsihar, demanded the completion of the repairs by noon of November 3rd, stating that, if they were not carried out by that date, engineers of the South Manchuria Railway, under the protection of Japanese troops, would take over the work. The Chinese authorities asked for an extension of the time-limit, but no answer was returned to this request and Japanese troops were despatched from Ssupingkai for the purpose of protecting the execution of the repair work. . . . The engineers, under the command of Captain Hanai, started work on the morning of November 4th, and one infantry company, with two Japanese flags, began its advance to Tahsing Station by noon of that day.

Hostilities actually began during . . . the afternoon of the 4th. . . . As soon as firing began, Colonel Hamamoto realised that his men were in a very difficult position and went immediately to their support with whatever troops he had available. . . .

The Kwantung Army Headquarters, on receiving a report of the position, imme-

diately despatched strong reinforcements, and another battalion of infantry arrived during the night, enabling the Colonel to re-open his attack at dawn of November 5th. . . . A renewed attack on the morning of the 6th rolled up the entire Chinese front, and brought Tahsing Station into the hands of the Japanese troops by noon. . . . In order to relieve this tense situation, General Honjo demanded, on November 12th, that all Heilungkiang troops should retire to the north of Tsitsihar and that his troops should be allowed to proceed northward for the protection of the Taonan-Angangchi Railway. The advance did not begin before November 17th, when the Chinese sent cavalry troops around the right flank of the Japanese and attacked them. General Tamon informed the Commission that, in spite of his small strength of 3,000 infantrymen and 24 field-guns, he ventured to attack the Chinese forces, and completely defeated them on November 18th, with the result that Tsitsihar was occupied on the morning of the 19th.[23]

23*Lytton Report*, pp. 74–75.

As the Kwantung army moved on to victory, younger officers pushed forward the movement to establish an "independent" state of Manchuria. To head this state they needed a puppet, and their choice fell on the former Chinese Emperor, Hsuan Tung, who was living in retirement as Henry Pu Yi. They brought him to Manchuria and began propaganda activities for independence. The positions of the Ministry of War, and of the "emperor" himself, are reflected in the following.

Japanese Minister of War Minami to Commander in Chief, Kwantung Army, November 15, 1931

You are well aware of the fact that the powers are strictly following the course of action of Pu Yi [Hsuan Tung] as well as the movement of the new regime in Manchuria. . . . Should Pu Yi

suddenly enter into the midst of the establishment of the new regime today, even if the act is formally committed in the name of popular will, it would make the world suspicious of the intentions of the Imperial Army, . . . and might rapidly bring about a situation extremely disadvantageous to our national policy with regard to the powers. . . . Thus you are to give

directions to keep Pu Yi completely unin-
volved in the question of the political regime whether actively or passively for
some time.[24]

Testimony of Henry Pu Yi at the Tokyo War Crimes Trial

. . . the Manchurian people, officials
and myself lost freedom completely.

---

[24]Quoted in Ogata, op. cit., p. 121.

When Lord Lytton came to Manchukuo,
we were all under the supervision of the
Japanese military officers; and wherever
Lord Lytton went, he was under the supervision of Japanese gendarmes. When
I interviewed Lord Lytton, many of the
Kwantung military officers were beside
me supervising. If I had told him the
truth, I would have been murdered right
after the mission left Manchuria.[25]

---

[25]"International Military Tribunal for the Far
East" (Tokyo, 1946–49), pp. 605–06. (Mimeographed.)

The occupation of Tsitsihar introduced a new crisis. If Japan insisted on
continuing its aggression, it was possible that the League, with U.S.
cooperation, might undertake the implementation of its resolves by
imposing sanctions. Charles G. Dawes, U.S. Ambassador at London, was
sent to Paris, where on November 14 he conferred with French Foreign
Minister Briand. Five days later Stimson discussed the problems with
President Hoover. Various points of view on these developments are
brought out in the following documents.

FOR CONSIDERATION   Is the position of the United States in regard to sanctions
quite clear? To what extent at this point was the United States prepared
to take a strong stand against Japan?

Telephone Conversation between Secretary of State Stimson and Ambassador to Great Britain Dawes, November 10, 1931

SECRETARY: This is Secretary Stimson.
Is this General Dawes?

DAWES: Yes, Mr. Secretary.

SECRETARY: I have an important message for you. The President and I have
an important job for you to do,—a really
he-man's job—and that is to go over
to Paris next week or the end of this
week and to be there during the special
conference of the Council of the League
of Nations on the subject of Manchuria.
The situation, as you must know from
the press, is extremely critical, and yet

from the messages I get I am hopeful
—very hopeful—that it will be possible
with some of the astute good sense I
know you to have, to have a settlement
finally worked out that would vindicate
the peace treaties and save peace in Manchuria. I am sending you by cable today
a résumé of the situation to help you.
You see at present the Paris Embassy is
stripped. Edge is over here. Norman
Armour is on leave, and Marriner is here.
So I am sending Howland Shaw from
Turkey. He is one of the best men in
Europe.

DAWES: I do not get that name.

SECRETARY: Howland Shaw. He is to
be Attaché and he is stopping (this is
confidential) at Geneva on the way up

to confer with Gilbert. I can if necessary have Gilbert go up too but that might make a little excitement in the press here. The point is that we want to be represented by you because we require the necessary personality to give effect to our views in conferences which will be held with people like Briand. We do not want anybody to sit on the Council. We do not want you or anybody else to actually sit in the meetings of the Council but we want them to come to you.

DAWES: Yes.[26]

Comments of Secretary of State Stimson

November 19th, when the news came of the Japanese defeat of General Ma, was a day of excitement in Paris. Dr. Sze was reported as being anxious on behalf of China to invoke Article XV of the Covenant with a view to leading ultimately up to the imposition of sanctions. Members of the League were reported to have enquired from Mr. Dawes what our attitude would be in case they should proceed along that line. They were anxious to obtain commitments from us before they even discussed such action themselves. On our part we manifestly could give no such commitment. Our Congress was not in session and there was no statutory authority under which the Executive could impose economic sanctions. Furthermore it was quite unlikely that such authority would be granted. . . .

On the other hand if the League of Nations desired to proceed under Articles XV and XVI of the Covenant and themselves impose such sanctions we were anxious not to discourage them or put any obstacles or dangers in their path. With the authority of the President, after a conference with him on that day,

November 19th, I informed Mr. Dawes to that effect and authorized him in his discretion to make known our whole position to M. Briand.[27]

Comments of American Ambassador Charles G. Dawes

Briand then brought up the question of my personal attendance at the sessions of the Council of the League, which question had confronted me at every meeting I had had with the press, and indeed with nearly everybody else. Briand maintained that if I did not attend the sessions it would be considered generally as an indication of an attitude on the part of our Government of less cooperation than heretofore in the purposes of the League in this situation, and therefore be a decided injury to its prestige and influence.

In answer, I told him that in my present judgment, if I did attend the Council meetings, it would lessen the helpfulness of the United States in the situation, and that a parallel cooperation of the United States, reserving its independence of action and decision, would be more effective in securing peace than if, by attendance at the meetings, to the curiosity of the world press and the justified apprehension of my Government, I became involved in the discussions of methods to be adopted by a body of which the United States was not even a member. I told him, however, that I was holding in abeyance any final decision in this matter of attendance until contact with the situation in Paris for a time would better enable me to settle the question wisely.

I said further that if in the future I came to believe that the greatest influence of the United States for the common

[26]*Papers Relating to the Foreign Relations of the United States*, 1931, Vol. III, p. 407.

[27]Stimson, *op. cit.*, pp. 76–77.

objective of peace could be exercised by my attendance at the meetings of the Council, I would not hesitate to attend them.[28]

Comments of the American Journalists, Drew Pearson and Constantine Brown

Charlie had been picked for the job chiefly because of the protest of career diplomats against the continued functioning of Prentiss Gilbert. Like the career men, Charlie felt that Gilbert had bungled. And so strongly did he feel, that he even refused to let Gilbert come from Geneva to Paris, where the Council now convened, in order to give him the history of the case.

"I already know all about it," Dawes exploded.

Since Gilbert had worn out the headlines by sitting at the Council table, Dawes' instincts for good showmanship told him to do just the opposite. And since his chief in the White House had become a bit jittery over the new alliance with Geneva, he decided to boycott the Council, remain a shadowy figure in the background. For the first few days it worked. Dawes, and the vacant chair which stood awaiting him at the Council table, became the talk of Paris. . . .

What the League of Nations needed, in the opinion of the American observer, was more punch. And he groomed himself to be the savior who at the appropriate time would deliver that punch. Until then he busied himself with secret conversations in his suite at the Ritz. He called in his old friend and London colleague, Tsuneo Matsudaira, with whom he was sure he could talk business. An-

other caller was Dr. Alfred Sze, the Chinese Minister.

"Sit down, Dr. Sze," bellowed Dawes. "I know absolutely nothing about this business, or about diplomacy, either. So sit down and tell me all about it."

"Really?" replied Sze. "When a man tells me he knows nothing about a card game, then I am always on the alert."

Though he did not realize it himself, Dawes told Dr. Sze the truth, as Sir John Simon discovered when he tried to give the American observer a brief background of what had happened since the League took over the Manchurian dispute. Explaining a complicated diplomatic problem to Dawes was like teaching discipline to a pup. Nothing fazed him except the opinion of his own importance.

"I'll have a dead secretary if anything leaks out," he shrilled at newspaper men.

"But suppose, Mr. Ambassador, that news of what you are doing leaks out from other diplomats with whom you talk?"

"They are not telling anything about what I have been doing," he bellowed back, "because nobody knows that except myself."

Which, unfortunately, was all too true. No one, not even the State Department, knew what Dawes was doing. And there is grave doubt whether he did, himself.[29]

Statement of William E. Borah, Chairman of the Senate Foreign Relations Committee, November 21, 1931

The proposal made from Paris to intervene—in other words to employ force, for that is what it means, in the settlement of the Manchurian affair—seems incredible. In saying this I do not mean to ap-

---

[28]Charles G. Dawes, *Journal as Ambassador to Great Britain* (New York: The Macmillan Company, 1939), pp. 416–17.

[29]Pearson and Brown, *op. cit.*, pp. 321–22.

Cartoon by David Low and by arrangement with the London Evening Standard.

She Drew a Horse in the Manchurian Sweep

prove what Japan is doing; far from it. But this talk of the use of force or intervention, implied from the very beginning, has had the effect of the very reverse of bringing about peace.

When the United States employs its good offices in every reasonable way to bring about peace, it has done all it can or should do. No treaty and no duty devolving upon peace-loving nations requires or permits the United States to go further.[30]

---

[30]*The New York Times,* November 22, 1931.

The League of Nations had reached an impasse. The November 16 deadline for withdrawal had been ignored by the Japanese, and the Chinese absolutely refused to accept the idea of a League Commission of Inquiry. No one was prepared to use force, much less sanctions, and the only way to save face seemed to be the Commission, which would put the whole affair "on ice" for several months. A heroic effort on the part of the Japanese liberal element temporarily restrained the military, and Ambassador Dawes was influential in persuading the Chinese. As a result, the Japanese themselves introduced the resolution for an inquiry, and after some debate the motion was passed on December 10.

Order of the Chief of the General Staff to the Commander in Chief, Kwantung Army, November 24, 1931

(1) In accordance with established policy, the Division Headquarters and the main forces are to evacuate quickly to the prescribed area without considering the resulting situation, leaving a force of about one infantry regiment in the vicinity of Tsitsihar. The action is to be undertaken immediately. (2) It is necessary to evacuate the remaining corps within approximately two weeks.[31]

Comments of Elizabeth Green, Editor of *Pacific Affairs*, from Tokyo, December 3, 1931

On first stepping ashore in Japan depression greets one. It is like entering a country already definitely at war. The military scarlet cap-band and sleeve-stripe is everywhere—officers shouldering the mere civilian out of the way, loaded lorries on the streets, soldiers entraining. One is used to such manifestations in China, but not in Japan. Nor is one here used to the widespread use of the flamboyant poster. But today war maps and vivid pictures attract crowds to the show windows where they are displayed; at night electric ideographs flash across the faces of the great newspaper offices telling the day's happenings in Manchuria to the populace of Osaka and Tokyo. Young middle-school students, emphasizing their importance with pennants and arm bands, patrol the downtown streets, haranguing the crowds for funds to help the "heroes" up in the bitter northern territory. Girls make appeals for nursing volunteers. Newspaper headlines clamor about "the enemy," the "latest engagement," the "shifting front," "our troops' progress westward." It is difficult to reconcile all this activity, all this deliberate stirring of patriotism, with the solemn official pronouncements of "no war in Manchuria."[32]

Viscount Cecil (in Paris) to British Foreign Minister Sir John Simon, December 8, 1931

The settlement—if it is to be called such—which we hope to arrive at tomorrow might have been reached, as far as I can see, quite easily a fortnight ago. . . . Most of the intervening time has been wasted in fatuous interchanges of impossible proposals between the Japanese and Chinese, particularly the Japanese. What is much more disquieting is the threat of the Japanese soldiers to march on Chinchow. I believe it is pure militarism of the worst type and merely a desire to show their strength, for the reasons given for it are very unconvincing and it is quite evident that the Japanese Delegation here profoundly disapproves and, so far as I can make out, so does the civil Government in Tokyo. If they do attack Chinchow, it is at least on the cards that Chinese public feeling, or student feeling, will become unmanageable and insist on a declaration of war, making a formal appeal under Article 16 for assistance from all the Members of the League. If they do, it would be very awkward, in view of the existing domestic situation. For it would seem quite clear that, in the circumstances supposed, Japan will have resorted to war in breach of its covenant under Article 12.[33]

Resolution Adopted by the Council of the League of Nations, December 10, 1931

The Council,
(1) Reaffirms the resolution passed unan-

---

[31]Quoted in Ogata, *op. cit.*, p. 112.

[32]Elizabeth Green, "The Manchurian Disease," *Pacific Affairs*, Vol. V, No. 1 (January, 1932), pp. 52–53.

[33]*Documents on British Foreign Policy 1919–1939*, 2d Series, Vol. VIII, p. 1000.

imously by it on September 30th, 1931, by which the two parties declare that they are solemnly bound; it therefore calls upon the Chinese and Japanese Governments to take all necessary steps to assure its execution, so that the withdrawal of the Japanese troops within the railway zone may be effected as soon as possible under the conditions set forth in the said resolution.

(2) Considering that events have assumed an even more serious aspect since the Council meeting of October 24th,

Notes that the two parties undertake to adopt all measures necessary to avoid any further aggravation of the situation and to refrain from any initiative which may lead to further fighting and loss of life.

(3) Invites the two parties to continue to keep the Council informed as to the developments of the situation.

(4) Invites the other members of the Council to furnish the Council with any information received from their representatives on the spot.

(5) Without prejudice to the carrying out of the above-mentioned measures,

Desiring, in view of the special circumstances of the case, to contribute towards a final and fundamental solution by the two Governments of the questions at issue between them;

Decides to appoint a Commission of five members to study on the spot and to report to the Council on any circumstance which, affecting international relations, threatens to disturb peace between China and Japan, or the good understanding between them upon which peace depends.

The Governments of China and Japan will each have the right to nominate one assessor to assist the Commission.

The two Governments will afford the Commission all facilities to obtain on

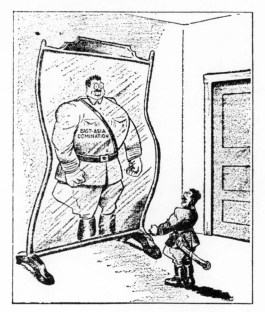

Elderman *in* The Washington Post
"The magic mirror."

the spot whatever information it may require.

It is understood that, should the two parties initiate any negotiations, these would not fall within the scope of the terms of reference of the Commission, nor would it be within the competence of the Commission to interfere with the military arrangements of either party.

The appointment and deliberations of the Commission shall not prejudice in any way the undertaking given by the Japanese Government in the resolution of September 30th as regards the withdrawal of the Japanese troops within the railway zone.

(6) Between now and its next ordinary session, which will be held on January 25th, 1932, the Council which remains seized of the matter invites its President to follow the question and to summon it afresh if necessary.[34]

---

[34]League of Nations, *Official Journal*, December, 1931, pp. 2375–76.

In Japan, the government found more and more difficulty in restraining the Kwantung army. On November 28, news reached the West that in violation of recent orders the army was proceeding against Chinchow. If Chinchow fell, all Manchuria would be in Japanese hands. Secretary Stimson was understandably upset that assurances given him had been spurious, and he determined to take a stronger line.

In Tokyo the Wakatsuki government also came under attack, partly from those moderates who believed Japan's treaty commitments should be met, and partly from the more militant Seiyukai party. Efforts to form a coalition cabinet failed and on December 11, 1931, Wakatsuki fell, to be replaced as Prime Minister by the Seiyukai leader, Tsuyoshi Inukai. The replacement of War Minister Minami by Araki Sadao, an outspoken militarist, boded ill for a policy of restraint. And continued army activity in Manchuria confirmed Western fears.

Actions in Manchuria, December 10, 1931, to January 3, 1932

It has usually been asserted [by Japanese officers] that the resoluton of December 10th "gave Japan the right to maintain her troops" in Manchuria, or made the Japanese Army responsible for the suppression of banditry there. In describing the subsequent operations, they assert that, while executing this right against the bandit forces near the Liao River, they incidentally came in conflict with the remaining Chinese forces near Chinchow, which were in consequence withdrawn within the Great Wall. The fact remains that, having made their reservation at Geneva, the Japanese continued to deal with the situation in Manchuria according to their plans.

The 2nd Division, with the exception of its garrison at Tsitsihar, was concentrated west of Mukden. Reinforcements soon began to arrive; the 4th Brigade of the 8th Division between December 10th and 15th. On December 27th, Imperial sanction was obtained for the despatch of the Staff of the 20th Division and another brigade from Korea. Changchun and Kirin were for the time being only protected by Independent Railway Guards.

As a Japanese advance on Chinchow was imminent, the Chinese Minister for Foreign Affairs made an attempt to prevent further fighting by offering to withdraw the Chinese troops to within the Great Wall, provided that three or four foreign Powers were willing to guarantee the maintenance of a neutral zone north and south of Chinchow. Nothing came of the proposal. . . .

The concentrated attack of the Japanese forces began on December 23rd, when the 19th Chinese Brigade was forced to give up its position. From that day, the advance continued with perfect regularity and hardly met with any resistance at all, the Chinese Commander having given out a general order to retreat. Chinchow was occupied on the morning of January 3rd and the Japanese forces continued their advance right up to the Great Wall at Schanhaikwan, where they established a permanent contact with the Japanese garrison in that place.[35]

[35]*Lytton Report*, pp. 77–78.

The policy of nonrecognition of territory acquired by aggression, the now-famous "Stimson Doctrine," evolved gradually in November and December, 1931. Stimson's diary reveals that the idea was brought up by the President in a Cabinet meeting on November 9. Hoover may have been a little piqued, as his memoirs show, that Stimson received more credit for the idea than he did. In actual fact nonrecognition was debated thoroughly in the State Department, and Walter Lippmann contributed some thoughts on the matter. It was the Japanese advance on Chinchow, after December 14, which decided the Secretary to go ahead with the statement. Stimson wrote a draft in longhand on January 3 and after some revisions the note was sent to Japan on January 7.

FOR CONSIDERATION   Notice that a new principle, nonrecognition, has been invoked and that it appears without previous discussion in the League. Notice also that there was no prior discussion with France or England. As this note came *after* the conquest of Manchuria and faced a *fait accompli,* is it correct to say that Secretary Stimson consistently maintained a firm attitude against Japanese aggression?

Comments of President Herbert Hoover

. . . After taking over the Presidency in 1929 I had discussed with Secretary of State Kellogg the possibility of proposing that the world put some moral teeth in the Kellogg Pact. . . . Secretary Kellogg and I considered several ideas for incorporation in it, including the nonrecognition of spoils or territory seized, advanced originally by Secretary of State William Jennings Bryan. . . .

Recollecting these ideas, I suggested to Secretary Stimson early in December, 1931, in Cabinet meeting, that we consider proposing to the League that the members refuse to recognize any territory obtained by the Japanese in violation of the Kellogg Pact and emphasize the refusal by withdrawing all legations from the offending nation.

In the latter part of December we took up the elaboration of this idea of non-

recognition. In the interest of accuracy of historic fact, I may mention here that an attempt was made to stamp this as the "Stimson Doctrine" with the implication that I had no part in it, nor Secretary Bryan, either. In consequence of such statements to the press before I left Washington in 1933, Secretaries Hurley and Wilbur wrote me letters of protest, both having been present at Cabinet meetings when I first proposed this idea (originally Bryan's).[36]

United States Note to Japanese Government, January 7, 1932

With the recent military operations about Chinchow, the last remaining administrative authority of the Government of the Chinese Republic in South Manchuria, as it existed prior to September 18th, 1931, has been destroyed. The Amer-

[36]Hoover, *op. cit.,* Vol. II, pp. 372–73.

ican Government continues confident that the work of the neutral commission recently authorized by the Council of the League of Nations will facilitate an ultimate solution of the difficulties now existing between China and Japan. But in view of the present situation and of its own rights and obligations therein, the American Government deems it to be its duty to notify both the Imperial Japanese Government and the Government of the Chinese Republic that it cannot admit the legality of any situation *de facto* nor does it intend to recognize any treaty or agreement entered into between those Governments, or agents thereof, which may impair the treaty rights of the United States or its citizens in China, including those which relate to the sovereignty, the independence, or the territorial and administrative integrity of the Republic of China, or to the international policy relative to China, commonly known as the open door policy; and that it does not intend to recognize any situation, treaty or agreement which may be brought about by means contrary to the covenants and obligations of the Pact of Paris of August 27, 1928, to which Treaty both China and Japan, as well as the United States, are parties.[37]

[37]*Papers Relating to the Foreign Relations of the United States, Japan: 1931–1941*, Vol. I, p. 76.

Secretary of State Stimson attempted to follow up his note to Japan with two steps: (1) an approval by the League of his nonrecognition policy and (2) an invocation of the Nine Power Pact against Japan. As the following documents show, he succeeded in the first but not in the second. He decided, then, to express his point of view in an open letter to the Chairman of the Senate Foreign Relations Committee, Senator Borah.

Comments of Secretary of State Stimson

On February 8th I broached the matter of the invocation of the Nine Power Treaty to the President. . . . On February 11th the President suggested that I call up the British Foreign Minister, Sir John Simon, directly on the telephone in order to hasten the matter and to have the best possible opportunity for fully discussing the proposition and ascertaining whether the British Government would cooperate. I did so the same day. . . .

I talked with the Foreign Minister again on the same subject at London on February 13th and February 15th and, while no explicit refusal to my suggestion was ever made, I finally became convinced that for reasons satisfactory to it, and which I certainly had no desire to inquire into or criticize, the British Government felt reluctant to join in such a *démarche*. I therefore pressed it no further.[38]

Comments of Hugh Wilson, American Minister to Switzerland

I was, of course, in the closest touch with Sir John Simon, British Secretary of State for Foreign Affairs. Messages were constantly coming and going between Mr. Stimson in Washington and Sir John in Geneva. . . . One day Sir John recounted to me a talk over the telephone which he had had with the Secretary of State in

[38]Stimson, *op. cit.*, pp. 161–64.

Washington. Sir John was perturbed. Mr. Stimson had suggested taking such vigorous action that Sir John felt that it might lead to the use of the American and British fleets to enforce it. He added that the British public was in no state of mind to support a war in such a remote region and for purposes which they would consider remote. From his reports received from Washington as to the state of mind of the American people he questioned whether the American public would not also be reluctant to assume such a risk.[39]

Excerpt from Secretary of State Stimson's Letter to Senator Borah, February 23, 1932

[In 1928] the policy of self-denial against aggression by a stronger against a weaker power, upon which the Nine Power Treaty had been based, received a powerful reinforcement by the execution by substantially all the nations of the world of the Pact of Paris, the so-called Kellogg-Briand Pact. . . .

That is the view of this Government. We see no reason for abandoning the enlightened principles which are embodied in these treaties. We believe that this situation would have been avoided had these covenants been faithfully observed, and no evidence has come to us to indicate that a due compliance with them would have interfered with the adequate protection of the legitimate rights in China of the signatories of those treaties and their nationals. . . .

In the past our Government, as one of the leading powers on the Pacific Ocean, has rested its policy upon an abiding faith in the future of the people of China and upon the ultimate success in dealing with

them of the principles of fair play, patience, and mutual goodwill. We appreciate the immensity of the task which lies before her statesmen in the development of her country and its government. The delays in her progress, the instability of her attempts to secure a responsible government, were foreseen by Messrs. Hay and Hughes and their contemporaries and were the very obstacles which the policy of the Open Door was designed to meet. We concur with those statesmen, representing all the nations in the Washington Conference who decided that China was entitled to the time necessary to accomplish her development. We are prepared to make that our policy for the future.[40]

British Ambassador Lindsay to Sir John Simon, March 3, 1932

Several times I have warned the State Department that they must not be too sanguine in their expectations of identic action by us. Only the other day I asked Stimson how he could expect a vigorous foreign policy from a country which was off the gold standard, and he admitted the difficulty. . . . I think there can surely be no real danger of our choosing the Japanese rather than the American part if we have to make a choice. I can see that there are advantages, particularly to ourselves as well as general, in staying neutral as long as possible. Let's hope it may be possible to do so for a long time, though it will be a task of the utmost difficulty and delicacy. I know that the Americans are dreadful people to deal with—they cannot make firm promises, but they jolly you along with fair prospects and when you are committed they let you down.[41]

[39]Hugh R. Wilson, *Diplomat between Wars* (New York: Longmans, Green & Co., Inc., 1941), pp. 276–77. Used by permission of David McKay Company, Inc.

[40]*Papers Relating to the Foreign Relations of the United States, Japan: 1931–1941*, Vol. I, pp. 83–87.

[41]*Documents on British Foreign Policy 1919–1939*, 2d series, Vol. IX, pp. 710–11.

Resolution Adopted by the Special
Assembly of the League,
March 11, 1932

The Assembly,

. . . Considering that the principles governing international relations and the peaceful settlement of disputes between Members of the League are in full harmony with the Pact of Paris, which is one of the corner-stones of the peace organization of the world . . .;

Pending the steps which it may ultimately take for the settlement of the dispute which has been referred to it;

Proclaims the binding nature of the principles and provisions referred to above and declares that it is incumbent upon the Members of the League of Nations not to recognize any situation, treaty or agreement, which may be brought about by means contrary to the Covenant of the League of Nations or to the Pact of Paris.[42]

[42]League of Nations, *Official Journal*, Special Supplement No. 101, p. 87.

With the fall of Tsitsihar, Chinchow, and Harbin, the Japanese had obtained control of all Manchuria. Not wishing to alienate the Western powers by outright annexation, the Inukai government now supported the "independence" movement which had been backed by junior officers. The following materials all pertain to the establishment of the new state.

Japanese Premier Inukai to Marshal
Uehara Yusaku, February 15, 1932

The end of the Manchurian Affair is approaching, but should an independent state be established [in Manchuria], head-on collision with the Nine Power Treaty would be inevitable. I have therefore been working hard at keeping the form of a separate regime and at attaining our objectives in substance. My aim is to terminate the present crisis as soon as possible, and my ideal is to take the occasion to improve relations with China. . . . As I have many old friends among the leaders of the various factions in both south and north China, I am in a much more advantageous position than the ordinary government officials to undertake negotiations.

.   .   .   .   .

What is most worrisome is the fact that the will of the senior officers is not thoroughly observed by their subordinates. For example, the action in Manchuria seems to have been brought about by the united power of the field-grade officers, who made their superiors acquiesce automatically. . . . It is feared that it might become customary to act single-mindedly upon the belief that should those who hold direct command over regiments unite and cause a disturbance, the superiors would finally give ex post facto approval to all matters, and that [such a trend] might create a major change in military control and discipline. . . . Therefore I wish the elders of the army to take remedial measures now, when the malady has not yet spread widely. The so-called coup d'état incident under the last cabinet was caused by the above mentioned tendency and is its outward expression.[43]

Excerpt from the "Proclamation on the
Establishment of Manchukuo,"
March 1, 1932

After thorough deliberations for several months past at numerous meetings, the

[43]Quoted in Ogata, *op. cit.*, pp. 139, 150.

leaders of Fengtien, Kirin, Heilungkiang and Jehol Provinces, Harbin Special District, and those under various banners of Mongolia, have come to a unanimous conclusion to adopt a practical application of good rule rather than a display of words in the administration of State affairs. Under whatever form of government, the primary duty of the State is to assure the inhabitants peace and security.

Manchuria and Mongolia constituted in the past a separate State detached from China Proper. The present situation places us in a position to strive for our own national independence. Accordingly, by the will of the thirty million people, we hereby declare on this day that we sever our relations with the Republic of China and establish the State of Manchuria, and we hereby make a public proclamation of the fundamental principles on which this new State is founded.

1. We believe that statecraft should be founded upon the principle of Tao or the Way, and Tao founded upon Tien or Heaven. . . .

2. There shall be no discrimination with respect to race and caste. . . .

3. In internal affairs the new State will reject the policies adopted in the dark days of the past. It will revise laws and enforce local autonomy, draft able men into the service of the government and elevate the officials deserving promotion, encourage industry, unify the currency system, open up the natural resources of the country, endeavour to maintain a good standard of living for the people, adjust and regulate the administration of the police, eliminate banditry, and promote and popularize education, respect Li-chiao, the teachings of Confucianism, and apply the principle of Wangtao, the Way of Benevolent Ruler, and practice its teachings.[44]

The Establishment of "Manchukuo," as Described in the Lytton Report

The North-Eastern Administrative Council met at once in urgent session and elected six delegates to proceed to Port Arthur, to convey their invitation to the former Emperor at Port Arthur, where he had been residing since he left Tientsin in the previous November. Mr. Pu-yi at first declined it, but on March 4th a second delegation comprising twenty-nine delegates obtained his consent to accept the post for one year only. Then the Administrative Council elected its chairman, Lieutenant-General Chang Chinghui, and nine others, to be the Reception Committee. On March 5th, the Committee went to Port Arthur and was received in audience. In response to its request, the former Emperor, on March 6th, left Port Arthur for Tangkangtze, and after two days began, on the 8th, to receive homage as the Regent of "Manchukuo."

The inauguration ceremonies were held at the new capital, Changchun, on March 9th. Mr. Pu-yi, as Regent, made a declaration in which he promised to found the policy of the new State upon the basis of "morality, benevolence and love." On the 10th, the principal members of the Government were appointed. . . . A notice regarding the establishment of "Manchukuo" was issued by telegram on March 12th to the foreign Powers.[45]

Report on Japanese Infiltration of Manchurian Government by American Consul General Myers at Mukden, October 1, 1932

It will be noted from the recapitulation that there are 509 natives (Chinese, Manchus and Mongols) and 312 Japanese holding official positions with the central Government at Changchun—these figures include subordinates as well as principal

[44]Quoted in Mo Shen (ed.), *Japan in Manchuria* (Manila: Grace Trading Co., 1960), p. 403.

[45]*Lytton Report*, p. 95.

officials. It is possible, as is obvious in the case of the Department of Defence, that the published list of office-holders is not complete. It is understood that the personnel of this Department is almost entirely Japanese. Too, some of the posts have apparently not yet been filled.

It is noteworthy that the most important branches of the Government have the largest proportion of Japanese. First in this category is the Council of State Affairs or Cabinet which comprises the Prime Minister and the heads of the various departments. This Council is dominated, or possibly more correctly speaking directed, by the General Affairs Board whose principal officers are all Japanese. . . .[46]

---

[46]*Papers Relating to the Foreign Relations of the United States, 1932*, Vol. IV (Washington, D.C.: U.S. Government Printing Office, 1948), pp. 283–85.

I ronically, the independence of Manchukuo was proclaimed simultaneously with the arrival in Japan of the League of Nation's Commission of Enquiry. Authorized by the declaration of December 10, 1931, the Commission had elected Lord Lytton its chairman on January 21, 1932. For four and a half months, from March to July, the Commission examined evidence in Japan, China, and Manchuria.

During the inquiry, Japan became more determined in its decision to hold Manchuria. On May 15, 1932, Premier Inukai was assassinated and Admiral Saito Makoto became Prime Minister. In July, Uchida Yasuya, formerly president of the South Manchuria Railway, was installed as Foreign Minister. The new cabinet marked the inauguration of a more militaristic, aggressive, anti-American policy which would continue until World War II. At about the same time, a new American ambassador, Joseph Grew, arrived in Tokyo.

The following excerpt comes from a long letter written by George H. Blakeslee to Stanley Hornbeck on his way home from the Far East, after the Lytton Commission had finished its work. Blakeslee was a State Department officer who had been assistant to General McCoy, the American representative.

Comments of George Blakeslee

The Earl of Lytton, as Chairman, sat at the head of the conference table. Distinguished in lineage and in public service, tall and dignified, he appeared an impressive figure, especially on those formal occasions when he stood wearing the insignia of his various orders and his many decorations. In the literary field, as well as in Governmental posts, he had won a high reputation, and he possessed a charm of literary style which came naturally to a son and a grandson of two of the leading authors of England. . . .

He worked intensely and continuously, read all the essential documents and papers, listened to the many witnesses who appeared before the Commission, and came to the conviction that the Japanese were completely unjustified in their actions in Manchuria. As Chairman, it was his wish to write a report for the Commission which should express these conclusions with the literary clarity and force of which he was an acknowledged master.

But, at the other end of the table from

Lord Lytton and separated from him in every other respect by more than the table length, sat General Claudel. As characteristically French as the Earl of Lytton was characteristically British, he was genial, even effusive at times, with a lovable strain in his character, highly emotional, expressing himself in conversation or at the conference table simultaneously with voice, face and hands.... While intellectually forced to condemn the Japanese, he was sympathethic with them and wished to drape the naked truth regarding their actions with the flowing phraseology of a a pleasing and somewhat illusive literary style. He was opposed to any expression which appeared to be an indictment of them. The whole problem he seemed to view sympathetically from the Japanese point of view. He spoke and understood only French, which Lord Lytton also spoke, though not with ease. As the days passed these two men misunderstood each other more completely and the gulf between them continually widened.

. . . . .

Dr. Schnee was typically German, combining much of the "Deutsche Gemutlichkeit" with a Prussian precision of mind. There were no effervescent emotions in either his manner or his character. He was quiet, thorough, dependable and genuine.

. . . . .

Count Aldrovandi, a former Ambassador at Berlin, could be unusually charming in the courtly, gracious Italian manner; but usually he appeared the cold diplomat with clear head and keen mind.

. . . . .

General McCoy possessed a rare combination of qualities desirable in a member of an international commission: keen insight, inflexible purpose, good judgment, and abiding patience and tact....

To General McCoy, all factors considered, probably more than to any other man, the Commission owes its unanimous report.

. . . . .

When it seemed probable that General Claudel would write a dissenting reservation, and Mr. Haas, the General Secretary, was preparing for this development by saying in small committee meetings that it would make no difference in Geneva should General Claudel make a reservation, General McCoy took him somewhat vigorously to task, "Whatever may be the effect in Geneva, it will make a tremendous difference in America whether the Report is unanimous or not".

And when the critical session arrived and General Claudel delivered to the Commission what appeared to be his ultimatum, it was General McCoy who saved the day by the wise recommendation that Count Aldrovandi should meet with General Claudel and attempt to draw up a statement which the Commission could accept....

And so a unanimous Report was achieved. Everyone knew that the rest of the Commission's work, some three days of it, related to mere detail. I do not know how General Claudel felt on that August 30th afternoon, but those of us on "our" side, felt almost hilariously happy.[47]

---

[47]Blakeslee to Hornbeck, September 14, 1932, quoted in Rappaport, *op. cit.*, pp. 211–23.

With general knowledge that the Lytton Commission had completed its work, the least that diplomats in Geneva could hope for was a delay on Japan's part until after the report had been discussed. In actual fact, Foreign Minister Uchida had told Lord Lytton in July that his government would soon recognize the new state. Secretary Stimson made one last attempt to support the League of Nations, affirming in a speech on August 8, 1932, that if the League pronounced an aggressor, the United States would not be neutral. This had no effect on Japan, however, and the Japanese government recognized Manchukuo on August 27, before the Lytton Report had been made public.

Ambassador Grew's reaction to the situation is given here.

Excerpts from the Diary of Ambassador Joseph Grew

September 1, 1932

When the Commission of Inquiry of the League of Nations visited Tokyo in July, 1932, the Japanese press published concerted and inspired articles affirming Japan's determination to pursue its "fixed policy." This was partly for the benefit of the Commission, but also partly to inspire the people to defy the League if necessary. The Foreign Office spokesman, Mr. T. Shiratori, as already stated in the diary, released to the Japanese press on August 9 an entirely uncalled-for, inaccurate, and provocative interpretation of the speech of the Secretary of State before the Council for Foreign Relations. This was obviously released for the purpose of arousing nationalistic and anti-American feeling.

The people throughout Japan (even school children) are being urged to subscribe to funds for purchasing and presenting to the Army "patriotism" airplanes, tanks, passenger motorcars, armored motorcars, and antiaircraft equipment. This is partly for the purpose of conserving Army funds and partly to encourage war fever.

September 3, 1932

. . . I don't want to be sensational, but I do want to go on record—continually—that the Japanese Government intends to proceed with its program in Manchuria unless prevented by superior physical force. . . .

Liberal statesmen carry little or no weight; the military preparations are going forward steadily. They expect an unfavorable report from the League of Nations but regard America as their greatest stumbling block; little is being said of friction with Soviet Russia just now.

I said that it was difficult to believe that the Japanese, as intelligent people, could really give credence to the obviously false premise of self-determination for Manchuria, but they regard their whole course of action as one of supreme and vital national interest, if not one of self-defense, and on that basis they are prepared to fight if necessary. All of these opinions have been confirmed with increasing intensity, especially during the past few weeks. After a careful study of the situation I can find no approach by which the present Japanese intransigence might be overcome or modified. . . .[48]

[48]Joseph C. Grew, *Ten Years in Japan* (New York: Simon and Schuster, Inc., 1944), pp. 38–39.

On October 1, 1932, the Lytton Commission reported to the League Council which, unwilling to make a decision, turned the Report over to the Assembly. In December, the Report was debated in the Assembly, where the small powers urged denunciation of Japan. The Japanese delegate, Matsuoka, threatened to withdraw. Not wishing to be responsible for the first weakening of the League, the Assembly referred the matter to a

Committee of Nineteen. On February 14, 1933, the Committee recommended approval, which the League supported ten days later. On March 27, Japan gave notice of its withdrawal from the League.

FOR CONSIDERATION   Could the absorption of Manchuria have been prevented, short of war? Did Stimson's moral indignation do more good than harm? Where did the League of Nation's failure lie? Compare League action in 1931 with UN action in Korea in 1950, with UN action in the Middle East in 1956 and 1967.

Excerpt from Conclusions of Lytton Commission, October 1, 1932

The evidence received from all sources has satisfied the Commission that, while there were a number of factors which contributed to the creation of "Manchukuo," the two which, in combination, were most effective, and without which, in our judgment, the new State could not have been formed, were the presence of Japanese troops and the activities of Japanese officials, both civil and military.

For this reason, the present regime cannot be considered to have been called into existence by a genuine and spontaneous independence movement.[49]

Japanese Foreign Minister Uchida to the Secretary-General of the League of Nations, March 27, 1933

The Japanese Government believe that the national policy of Japan, which has for its aim to ensure the peace of the Orient and thereby contribute to the peace throughout the world, is identical in spirit with the mission of the League of Nations, which is to achieve international peace and security....

They have repeatedly emphasized and insisted upon the absolute necessity of taking into consideration the fact that

China is not an organized State—that its internal conditions and external relations are characterized by extreme confusion and complexity, and by many abnormal and exceptional features—and that, accordingly, the general principles and usages of international law which govern the ordinary relations between nations are found to be considerably modified in their operation so far as China is concerned, resulting in the quite abnormal and unique international practices which actually prevail in that country.

However, the majority of the Members of the League evinced in the course of its deliberations during the past seventeen months a failure either to grasp these realities or else to face them and take them into proper account.... As a result, the Report adopted by the Assembly at the Special Session of February 24 last, entirely misapprehending the spirit of Japan, pervaded as it is by no other desire than the maintenance of peace in the Orient, contains gross errors both in the ascertainment of facts and in the conclusions deduced....

The conclusion must be that, in seeking a solution to the question, the majority of the League have attached greater importance to upholding inapplicable formulae than to the real task of assuring peace, and higher value to the vindication of academic theses than to the eradication of the sources of future conflict.

The Japanese Government, believing

---

[49]*Lytton Report,* p. 97.

that in these circumstances there remains no room for further cooperation, hereby give notice, in accordance with the provisions of Article 1, Paragraph 3, of the Covenant, of the intention of Japan to withdraw from the League of Nations.[50]

[50]League of Nations, *Official Journal,* May, 1933, p. 657.

BIBLIOGRAPHY

Sources Used in This Problem

1. *Collections and Official Documents*

The China Critic.

Conditions in Manchuria. U.S. Senate, Document 55, 72nd Congress, 1st Session. Washington, D.C.: U.S. Government Printing Office, 1932.

Documents on British Foreign Policy, 2d Series. Vols. VIII, IX. London: Her Majesty's Stationery Office, 1960, 1965.

"International Military Tribunal for the Far East." Tokyo (mimeographed), 1946–49.

Lytton Report. See *Report of the Commission of Enquiry.*

The New York Times.

Official Journal. League of Nations.

Pacific Affairs.

Papers Relating to the Foreign Relations of the United States. Japan: 1931–1941. Vol. I. Washington, D.C.: U.S. Government Printing Office, 1943.

Papers Relating to the Foreign Relations of the United States, 1931. 1932. Washington, D.C.: U.S. Government Printing Office, 1946, 1948.

Report of the Commission of Enquiry [into the Appeal of the Chinese Government] [*Lytton Report*]. League of Nations publication C. 663. M. 320. 1932. VII. Geneva, 1932.

Survey of International Affairs, 1932. Royal Institute of International Affairs. London: Oxford University Press, 1934.

2. *Others*

Cecil, Viscount. *A Great Experiment.* London: Jonathan Cape, 1941.

Dawes, Charles G. *Journal as Ambassador to Great Britain.* New York: Macmillan, 1939.

Grew, Joseph. *Ten Years in Japan.* New York: Simon and Schuster, 1944.

Hoover, Herbert. *The Memoirs of Herbert Hoover.* 2 vols. New York: Macmillan, 1952.

Ogata, Sadako N. *Defiance in Manchuria.* Berkeley, Calif.: University of California Press, 1964.

Pearson, Drew and Brown, Constantine. *The American Diplomatic Game.* Garden City, N.Y.: Doubleday, 1935.

Rappaport, Armin. *Henry L. Stimson and Japan, 1931–33.* Chicago: University of Chicago Press, 1963.

Shen, Mo (ed.). *Japan in Manchuria.* Manila: Grace Trading Co., 1960.

Smith, Sara R. *The Manchurian Crisis, 1931–1932.* New York: Columbia University Press, 1948.

Stimson, Henry L. *Far-Eastern Crisis.* New York: Harper's, 1936.

Wilson, Hugh. *Diplomat between Wars.* New York: Longmans, Green, 1941.

YOSHIHASHI, TAKEHIKO. *Conspiracy at Mukden.* New Haven, Conn.: Yale University Press, 1963.

SELECT LIST OF BOOKS RECOMMENDED FOR FURTHER READING

BASSETT, REGINALD. *Democracy and Foreign Policy: A Case History, the Sino-Japanese Dispute, 1931–1933.* London: Longmans, Green, 1952.

CURRENT, RICHARD N. *Secretary Stimson: A Study in Statecraft.* New Brunswick, N.J.: Rutgers University Press, 1954.

FERRELL, ROBERT H. *American Diplomacy in the Great Depression.* New Haven, Conn.: Yale University Press, 1957.

GREW, JOSEPH. *Turbulent Era.* Boston: Houghton Mifflin, 1952.

MAXON, Y. C. *Control of Japanese Foreign Policy: A Study in Civil-Military Rivalry 1930–1945.* Berkeley, Calif.: University of California Press, 1957.

MORISON, ELTING. *Turmoil and Tradition: A Study of the Life and Times of Henry L. Stimson.* Boston: Houghton Mifflin, 1960.

SCALAPINO, ROBERT A. *Democracy and the Party Movement in Pre-War Japan.* Berkeley, Calif.: University of California Press, 1953.

STROMBERG, ROLAND N. *Collective Security and American Foreign Policy: From the League of Nations to NATO.* New York: Praeger, 1963.

TAKEUCHI, TATSIYI. *War and Diplomacy in the Japanese Empire.* New York: Doubleday Doran, 1935.

WILBUR, R. L. and HYDE, A. M. *The Hoover Policies.* New York: Scribner's, 1937.

WILLOUGHBY, W. W. *The Sino-Japanese Controversy and the League of Nations.* Baltimore: The Johns Hopkins Press, 1935.

YANAGA, CHITOSHI. *Japan since Perry.* New York: McGraw-Hill, 1949.

SECTION III

Between the Wars: Democracy

ENGLAND—THE RISE OF LABOUR

British Socialism, in and out of

Parliament, 1918-37

When the Labour Party came to power in 1945, with Clement Attlee as Prime Minister, it brought with it political experience achieved painfully through half a century. The post-World War II ministry was the third in which Labour had formed the government, but during the first two, in 1924, and in 1929–31, the party had been unable to carry out an effective legislative program of social reform.

The following documents provide insights into British Socialism, into trade unionism, and into the Labour Party as the political organ of the socialist movement between the two World Wars.

Among the leftist influences in England were the Fabian Society (so called because it advocated a gradual evolution to socialism), and its intellectual guides, the social historians Beatrice and Sidney Webb. The comments below deal with British socialism directly after World War I. Sidney Webb had drafted most of *Labour and the New Social Order*. Both George Bernard Shaw (an enthusiastic Fabian) and Clement Attlee wrote brief summaries of the rise of Labour—Shaw in 1927 and Attlee in 1937.

The Fabian Society as Described by George Bernard Shaw, 1927

The Fabian Society . . . presented Socialism in the form of a series of parliamentary measures, thus making it possible for an ordinary respectable religious citizen to profess Socialism and belong to a Socialist Society without any suspicion of lawlessness, exactly as he might profess himself a Conservative and belong to an ordinary constitutional club. A leader of the society, Mr Sidney Webb, married Miss Beatrice Potter, who had made a study at first hand of working-class life and organization, and had published a book on Co-operation. They wrote the first really scientific history of Trade

Unionism, and thereby not only made the wage-workers conscious of the dignity of their own political history (a very important step in the Marxian class-consciousness) but shewed the middle-class Socialists what the public work of the wage-working world was really like, and convinced them of the absurdity of supposing that Socialists could loftily ignore the organization the people had already accomplished spontaneously in their own way. Only by grafting Socialism on this existing organization could it be made a really powerful proletarian movement.

The Liberals, still believing themselves to be the party of progress, assumed that all progressive movements would be grafted on the Liberal Party as a matter of course, to be patronized and adopted by the Liberal leaders in Parliament as far as they approved. They were disagreeably surprised when the first effect of the adoption of constitutional parliamentarism by the Fabian Society was an attack on the Liberal Government of that day.[1]

Comments of Clement Attlee

Labour and the New Social Order, which was the call of Labour to the men and women who had just come through a great war, was a remarkable document. It was very lengthy and diffuse, dealing with a great variety of subjects, including such matters as Home Rule for Ireland, married women's income tax, and temperance reform. Within it all Labour adherents could find their own particular reforms. It did not represent at all the attitude of mind of people who expected shortly to be called upon to administer the

affairs of the country. It was a declaration of faith and aspirations rather than a political programme. It was, however, an uncompromisingly Socialist document. It stated that its proposals proceeded from definitely held principles, and went on to declare that Labour stood for a deliberately planned co-operation in production and distribution for the benefit of all who participate by hand or by brain. The manifesto was drawn up while the war was still in progress, and it is, therefore, natural that it should have been much concerned with the question as to how the nation was to return to a peace-time basis. It did not consider for a moment the re-establishment of pre-war Capitalist industry. The war, it stated, saw "the culmination and collapse of a distinctive industrial civilisation, which the workers will not seek to reconstruct." The war had seen a rapid extension of Government control over industry. Labour was anxious to retain the power of the community over those industries which were essential to the welfare of the nation.

Allowing, however, for the difference in the country's position in 1918 and to-day, the programme shows that as far as general principles are concerned Labour stood then where it stands to-day. For nine years *Labour and the New Social Order* remained the Party's official programme.[2]

Excerpts from "Labour and the New Social Order," Labour Party Conference, June, 1918

. . . . .

What we now promulgate as our policy, whether for opposition or for office,

---

[1]George Bernard Shaw, *The Intelligent Woman's Guide to Socialism and Capitalism* (New York: Brentano's, 1928), p. 220. Used by permission of The Public Trustee and The Society of Authors.

[2]C. R. Attlee, *The Labour Party in Perspective—and Twelve Years Later,* foreword by Francis Williams (2d ed.; London: Victor Gollancz, Ltd., 1949), pp. 50–51.

is not merely this or that specific reform, but a deliberately thought out, systematic, and comprehensive plan for that immediate social rebuilding which any Ministry, whether or not it desires to grapple with the problem, will be driven to undertake. The Four Pillars of the House that we propose to erect, resting upon the common foundation of the Democratic control of society in all its activities, may be termed, respectively:

(a) The Universal Enforcement of the National Minimum;
(b) The Democratic Control of Industry;
(c) The Revolution in National Finance; and
(d) The Surplus Wealth for the Common Good.

(a) A National Minimum

The Labour Party to-day stands for the universal application of the Policy of the National Minimum, to which (as embodied in the successive elaborations of the Factory, Mines, Railways, Shops, Merchant Shipping, Trade Boards, and Truck Acts, the Public Health, Housing, and Education Acts, and the Minimum Wage Acts) the spokesmen of Labour have already gained the support of the enlightened statesmen and economists of the world. . . .

It is . . . the duty of the Government to adopt a policy of deliberately and systematically preventing the occurrence of unemployment, instead of (as heretofore) letting unemployment occur, and then seeking, vainly and expensively, to relieve the unemployed. . . .

In so far as the Government fails to prevent Unemployment—whenever it finds it impossible to discover for any willing worker, man or woman, a suitable situation at the Standard Rate—the Labour Party holds that the Government must, in the interest of the community as a whole, provide him or her with adequate maintenance. . . .

(b) Democratic Control of Industry . . .

The Labour Party stands not merely for the principle of the Common Ownership of the nation's land, to be applied as suitable opportunities occur, but also, specifically, for the immediate Nationalisation of Railways, Mines and the production of Electrical Power. . . .

But the sphere of immediate Nationalisation is not restricted to these great industries. We shall never succeed in putting the gigantic system of Health Insurance on a proper footing, or secure a clear field for the beneficent work of the Friendly Societies, or gain a free hand for the necessary development of the urgently called for Ministry of Health and the Local Public Health Service, until the nation appropriates the profit-making Industrial Insurance Companies, which now so tyrannously exploit the people with their wasteful house-to-house Industrial Life Assurance. . . .

.   .   .   .   .

The Labour Party . . . asks for a systematic reorganization of the whole educational system, from the nursery school to the University, on the basis of (a) social equality; (b) the provision for each age, for child, youth, and adult, of the best and most varied education of which it is capable, with whatever provision by way of maintenance is needed to enable the students to obtain full advantage of the instruction provided; . . .

(c) The Revolution in National Finance

The Labour Party stands for such a system of taxation as will yield all the necessary revenue to the Government without encroaching on the prescribed National Minimum Standard of Life of any family whatsoever; without hampering production or discouraging any useful personal effort, and with the nearest possible approximation to equality of sacrifice. We

definitely repudiate all proposals for a Pro-
tective Tariff, in whatever specious guise
they may be cloaked, as a device for bur-
dening the consumer with unnecessarily
enhanced prices, to the profit of the capitalist employer or landed proprietor, who
avowedly expects his profit or rent to be
increased thereby. We shall strenuously
oppose any taxation, of whatever kind,
which would increase the price of food or
of any other necessary of life. We hold
that indirect taxation on commodities,
whether by Customs or Excise, should be
strictly limited to luxuries; and concentrated principally on those of which it is
socially desirable that the consumption
should be actually discouraged. . . .

.   .   .   .

(d) Surplus for the Common Good

In the disposal of the surplus above the
Standard of Life society has hitherto gone
as far wrong as in its neglect to secure the
necessary basis of any genuine industrial
efficiency or decent social order. We have
allowed the riches of our mines, the rental

value of the lands superior to the margin
of cultivation, the extra profits of the
fortunate capitalists, even the material
outcome of scientific discoveries—which
ought by now to have made this Britain
of ours immune from class poverty or from
any widespread destitution—to be absorbed by individual proprietors; and then
devoted very largely to the senseless luxury of an idle rich class. Against this mis-
appropriation of the wealth of the community, the Labour Party—speaking in the
interests not of the wage-earners alone,
but of every grade and section of pro-
ducers by hand or by brain, not to mention also those of the generations that are
to succeed us, and of the permanent welfare of the community—emphatically protests. One main Pillar of the House that
the Labour Party intends to build is the
future appropriation of the Surplus, not
to the enlargement of any individual for-
tune, but to the Common Good. . . .[3]

---

[3]"Labour and the New Social Order," Labour
Party Conference, June, 1918.

The acceptance of socialist theory and the rise of the Labour Party must be
related to the grave economic difficulties which plagued Great Britain
between the two wars. Industrial production could not compete successfully on the world market, and the statistics of declining output found a
counterpart in statistics of unemployment and poverty. Over the two
decades of the 1920's and the 1930's hung the constant specter of millions
of men without work, of boys growing to manhood who could not find
jobs. The great depression of the 1930's found nearly 3,000,000 people
out of work, a total of 22.1 percent (as the following table shows) of the
working population.

The following documents are included to establish a very important
background against which the rise of Labour must be viewed. They suggest something of the human problems of morale as well as the purely
economic aspects. Lord Woolton was a Conservative, later Minister of Food.
George Orwell, celebrated as the author of 1984, was commissioned in 1937
by the Left Book Club to make a study of the distressed areas. Griffin Taylor is a British writer now living in the United States.

Statistics on Unemployment in Great Britain, 1921–38

Year	Percentage Unemployed	
	Great Britain	Great Britain and Northern Ireland
1921............	16.6	17.0
1922............	14.1	14.3
1923............	11.6	11.7
1924............	10.2	10.3
1925............	11.0	11.3
1926............	12.3	12.5
1927............	9.6	9.7
1928............	10.7	10.8
1929............	10.3	10.4
1930............	15.8	16.1
1931............	21.1	21.3
1932............	21.9	22.1
1933............	19.8	19.9
1934............	16.6	16.7
1935............	15.3	15.5
1936............	12.9	13.1
1937............	10.6	10.8
1938............	12.6	12.9

SOURCE: William H. Beveridge, *Full Employment in a Free Society* (London: George Allen & Unwin, Ltd., 1945)

Comments of the Earl of Woolton (Unemployment in 1926)

Unemployment in Liverpool had once again become acute and alarming in the year 1926. Large numbers of those who were unemployed were the children of men and women who had suffered so grievously from the same problem in the period from 1908 to 1910, which I have already described. Memories and stories of those earlier days were a vivid part of their inheritance, memories of the misery, the mental and physical degradation, and the hopelessness of those times. Some rebelled, but some accepted the conditions with a depressing fatalism. If the ships didn't come into the port, if there were no cargoes to load or unload and no ships to repair, what could they, or indeed any government, do about it? There were few alternative occupations independent of the trade of the port to which they could turn their hands.

The Labour and the Socialist Party of the present day owes much of its strength to the failure to solve this problem of the powerful Liberal government that came into office in 1906 and of the Conservative governments after the war.

It was no wonder that the unemployed asked whether all the powers of government and of finance couldn't provide something better than the current relief work. The question arose in the minds of some of us as to whether this great world seaport of Liverpool, which had so much to offer in its labour, in its easy access for the import of raw materials and for the export of goods, couldn't attract to itself manufacturing industry that could use those faculties. Meanwhile, the prospect was depressing. One saw men unaccustomed to the work slowly-wheeling barrow-loads of soil to make a new park, knowing full well that the people responsible for the work wanted it to last as long as possible. This relief work was demoralizing both in its nature and in the inefficiency of its organization. It was making no contribution to getting men back to the trades for which they had been trained. The tragedy was brought home to me most graphically when I was walking along one of the Liverpool streets near to the University Settlement, where I used to live; I met a David Lewis club member, whom I had known as a good steady worker as a boiler-maker. He was obviously unemployed, but I stopped and asked him how he was going on; in complete hopelessness he replied that he saw no chance of working again. With artificial cheerfulness I said, "Cheer up, you'll get work soon"—and then he opened out his hands to me, palms upwards, and said, "Look at those hands, sir: they've gone soft and I shall never be able to get a job again: I would break down with those hands within a week." That was an aspect of unemployment that had never occurred to me. I had thought of people being on short rations and still shorter pleasures, but it had never occurred to me that after two or three months of unemployment they would become technically incapable of doing a job.[4]

Comments of British Writer, F. H. Griffin Taylor (Conditions in 1934)

One dark, chilly, rainy morning in 1934 I turned mechanically out of the roaring traffic of Hammersmith Broadway into the street that took me to my school in North Kensington and was brought up short, completely surprised. It was a couple of miles to the heart of London and here was my accustomed street with, standing on one side of it for as far as I could see, an immense throng of men six or eight abreast. They were halted and keeping rough ranks like an army in defeat. They wore the crude uniform of the worker—drab grey and rusty black caps, chokers, thin overcoats, rumpled raincoats. Some carried rucksacks, some brown paper parcels, some World War One khaki haversacks. They were shockingly silent.

The police were keeping all traffic out of the area, but they let me through. The rain had eased off. I could hear only the swish of my bicycle tires and the lazy clipclop of the handful of mounted police who moved slowly up and down with nothing to do. I rode reluctantly, afire with a pity I dared not show, an emotion I was to recognize again years later when as duty officer in Norway I inspected the first group of German prisoners-of-war I

ever encountered. The men I now passed were young and old, but most seemed to be my father's age. Two white-faced younger men looked across the road at me, and, as I caught their ironic gaze, I felt a curious sense of guilt mingled with a sort of complicity, for at that moment I was the only witness of their shame. The rest of the men, clad in an uneasy dignity as ill-fitting as their awful clothes, gazed down at their feet or straight ahead, saying nothing.

These were the Hunger Marchers. They had come from all parts of the land on foot to show London the face of Unemployment. They came begging that something be done, yet these men were no beggers. As I turned towards school through a gap held open by a sleek-rumped police horse, I heard from some distant point ahead in that river of men the heartbreaking strains of singing, obviously Welsh.

I was perhaps sixteen then. There was very little about it in the newspapers the next day when I looked, nor in the days that followed. After a while, I sometimes wondered if the ghostly scene had ever taken place.[5]

Comments of George Orwell (Conditions in 1937)

I found great variation in the houses I visited. Some were as decent as one could possibly expect in the circumstances, some were so appalling that I have no hope of describing them adequately. To begin with, the smell, the dominant and essential thing, is indescribable. But the squalor and the confusion! A tub full of filthy water here, a basin full of unwashed crocks there, more crocks piled in

[4]Lord Woolton, *Memoirs of the Earl of Woolton* (London: Cassell & Co., Ltd., 1959), pp. 109–10. Reprinted by permission of A. D. Peters & Co.

[5]"The Hunger Marchers," extract from unpublished manuscript communicated by F. H. Griffin Taylor to the editor.

any odd corner, torn newspaper littered everywhere, and in the middle always the same dreadful table covered with sticky oilcloth and crowded with cooking pots and irons and half-darned stockings and pieces of stale bread and bits of cheese wrapped round with greasy newspaper! And the congestion in a tiny room where getting from one side to the other is a complicated voyage between pieces of furniture, with a line of damp washing getting you in the face every time you move and the children as thick underfoot as toadstools! There are scenes that stand out vividly in my memory. The almost bare living-room of a cottage in a little mining village, where the whole family was out of work and everyone seemed to be underfed; and the big family of grown-up sons and daughters sprawling aimlessly about, all strangely alike with red hair, splendid bones and pinched faces ruined by malnutrition and idleness; and one tall son sitting by the fireplace, too listless even to notice the entry of a stranger, and slowly peeling a sticky sock from a bare foot.

.   .   .   .   .

To sum up: There is no chance of righting the conditions I described in the earlier chapters of this book, or of saving England from Fascism, unless we can bring an effective Socialist party into existence. It will have to be a party with genuinely revolutionary intentions, and it will have to be numerically strong enough to act. We can only get it if we offer an objective which fairly ordinary people will recognise as desirable. . . .

All that is needed is to hammer two facts home into the public consciousness. One, that the interests of all exploited people are the same; the other, that Socialism is compatible with common decency.[6]

[6]George Orwell, *The Road to Wigan Pier*, with a foreword by Victor Gollancz. (2d ed.; New York: Harcourt, Brace & World, Inc., 1958), pp. 51–58, 262–63. Reprinted by permission of Harcourt, Brace & World, Inc.

After the war, under Lloyd George, Bonar Law, and Stanley Baldwin, the Conservatives retained a considerable margin of seats in parliament (in 1923, 347 as against 142 for Labour and 117 for the Liberal Party). But new elections were held on December 6, 1923, with the following results: Conservative: 257; Labour: 192; Liberal: 158. For the first time, Labour had its parliamentary opportunity, as described below.

Sidney Webb became a member of the government as president of the Board of Trade. His recollections, found among his papers, were published posthumously in 1961.

Hugh Dalton did not hold office at this time, but became Undersecretary for Foreign Affairs in the second MacDonald government in 1929. He describes a luncheon with writers of the *New Leader*, the Independent Labour Party organ, in 1924.

FOR CONSIDERATION   Some difference of opinion can be noted, in certain instances suggesting strong personality conflicts. A complete assessment of Labour politics would have to analyze these and to discount prejudiced testimony accordingly.

Comments of George Bernard Shaw

The Fabian Society followed up its attack by a proposal for the establishment of a Labor Party in Parliament to oppose both Conservatives and Liberals impartially. A working-class leader, Keir Hardie, formerly a miner, founded a Society called the Independent Labor Party to put this proposal into practice. Among the members of the Fabian Society who became a leader in this new Society was Mr Ramsay MacDonald, who, by his education and knowledge of the world outside the wage-working class, was better qualified than Keir Hardie for successful leadership in Parliament. From the Independent Labor Party sprang The Labor Party, a political federation, much more powerful, of Trade Unions and of Socialist Societies, whose delegates sat on its executive committee. . . . At the election of 1906 enough Labor members were elected to form an independent party in Parliament. By 1923 they had encroached so much that neither the Liberals nor the Conservatives had a majority in the House; and Mr Ramsay MacDonald was challenged to form a Government and shew whether Labor could govern or not. He accepted the challenge, and became British Prime Minister with a Cabinet of Socialists and Trade Unionists. It was a more competent government than the Conservative Government that preceded it, partly because its members, having risen from poverty or obscurity to eminence by their personal ability, were unhampered by nonentities, and partly because it knew what the world is like today, and was not dreaming, as even the cleverest of the Conservative leaders still were, of the Victorian mixture of growing cotton lordship and decaying feudal lordship in the capitalist class, with starved helpless ignorance and submissive servitude in the proletariat, which had not even lasted out Queen Victoria's lifetime.[7]

---

[7]Shaw, op. cit., p. 220.

Comments of Sidney Webb

I propose to write down, whilst fresh in memory, various comments on the Labour Government of 1924, just in the order in which they occur to me.

It may be desirable to place on record that the possibility of the Labour Party being called upon to take office, as the result of the election of 1923, never occurred to any of us before the day after the poll. Though the main numerical results of the election had been foreseen, with rather unusual accuracy, it does not seem to have been realised by anyone that such results would lead to J. R. MacDonald being sent for. For a new party forming only 31 per cent. of the House of Commons to be charged with office was quite without precedent (since 1868 at any rate). The decision of the electorate was, as we had foreseen, clearly against both socialism and Fiscal Protection, with the Unionists forming by far the largest party and constituting 41 per cent. of the House. This seemed to indicate a continuance of the Unionist Government, supported by the Liberals conditionally on its abandoning its newly adopted Tariff proposals. When this abandonment was definitely announced, the fateful decision rested with the Liberal Party. Asquith decided to support the Labour Party's projected amendment to the Address, and thus cause the decisive defeat of the Government. Lloyd George formally acquiesced in this decision, which the Liberal Party unanimously accepted. . . .[8]

Comments of Hugh Dalton

On February 4th MacDonald turned up at the lunch. We had had no notice to

---

[8]Sidney Webb, "The First Labour Government," *Political Quarterly*, Vol. XXXII (January–March, 1961), p. 6.

expect the Prime Minister and Foreign Secretary. . . .

J. R. M. deplores all strikes. Strikes by the dockers and the miners are threatened. This sort of thing will "knock us out" if it goes on. What is wanted is to "preach Socialism" in the country and the importance of political action. "Some reductions" of wages may be justifiable. Strikes may prevent trade revival. The military may have to be used to run lorries. "The complexities of the situation" may even become such as to compel us to have "a national Government", "nearly a Coalition but not quite". We may have "to bring in some people from the other parties and to bring some of ours out". Men never want to strike, unless they are instigated by their leaders. The dockers can't get an advance at the present time. He could not ask for a dissolution in any case for the next few months. Within a year he might be able to bring about a revolutionary change in the European situation.

I had a very nasty taste in my mouth at the end of all this. I intervened once or twice, but Allen, Angell and others sat round like a kindergarten. Some of the liveliest lunchers were absent. As for the "national government", we had been warned—seven years warning![9]

Comments of Beatrice Webb

June 23, 1924

... There is to be no Cabinet this week. Anyway, in a Cabinet of twenty members, all of whom attend a gathering absorbed in all the routine and more pressing work, it is obvious there can be no consultation about foreign affairs. Meanwhile each Minister is absorbed by his own department and thinks and talks of little else. There are, of course, advantages in this one-man-government—it works with little or no friction (if there is no consultation there cannot be divided counsels). And there is always the attack of the enemy to herd them together, when necessary for self-preservation. But democratic control *there is not:* not even the control by an inner circle—leave alone an Executive Committee depending on the support of a representative assembly. . . . What puzzles me—Is MacDonald an able statesman as well as a clever parliamentarian and attractive popular preacher? My mind is literally a blank on this subject: I have not the remotest idea whether the P.M. is a genius, a mere spinner of words, or a sufficiently able man to make a good job of the country's business, on more or less Labour lines? This year, I assume, will show his calibre. He has certainly had good luck, up to now; and persistent good luck usually means a strain of unusual talent, if not genius.[10]

Comments of Viscount Snowden on the First Labour Government

I had the satisfaction of introducing a measure modifying the hardship of the means limit in old age pensions. It had long been felt that taking a person's income derived from savings into account was unjust, and was in fact a discouragement of thrift. My Bill provided for the payment of larger pensions to certain people, and for the payment of pensions to others who had been disqualified from receiving them under the then existing Act, under which the whole of a person's income from whatever source was taken into consideration, and if it amounted to more than 10s. a week he was disqualified from getting the full pension. My Bill provided that an income from any form of

[9]Hugh Dalton, *Memoirs*, Vol. I, *Call Back Yesterday, 1887–1931* (London: Frederick Muller Ltd., 1953), p. 148.

[10]Beatrice Webb, *Beatrice Webb's Diaries 1924–1932*, ed. Margaret Cole (London: Longmans Green & Co., 1956), pp. 31–32.

savings should be disregarded unless it exceeded £39 a year in the case of a single person, or £78 a year in the case of a married couple.

I had to face the usual Party criticism from the Liberal and Tory Opposition that this was not a full redemption of Party pledges. But their criticism was nullified by the fact that both Parties had been in office over a period of years and had made no attempt to remove the obvious injustice of the thrift disqualification. The Bill was carried. It gave pensions to 225,-000 who had hitherto been deprived of them owing to the limitation which our Act removed.

The most important of the measures passed by the Labour Government was Mr. Wheatley's Housing Bill. . . . His Bill, which after a long debate in the House became law, was the greatest contribution which had been made towards the solution of the Housing problem. The shortcomings of previous Housing Acts had been that they catered only for a class of people who could afford to buy their houses. But the real need was to produce houses to let.[11]

_____

[11]Viscount Philip Snowden, *An Autobiography* (London: Ivor Nicholson & Watson, 1934), Vol. II, pp. 700–01. Reprinted by permission of the copyright owner.

In September, 1924, when both Conservatives and Liberals censured the government for allegedly using its influence to withdraw prosecution against J. R. Campbell, a leftist writer, MacDonald decided to use the case for a vote of confidence. The government lost, on October 8, and new elections were called.

The subsequent election campaign involved a letter, purportedly sent by the Communist International president, Zinoviev, to the British Communist Party. When this was published on October 25, it became an issue, although the letter's authenticity was then questioned and has never been established.

Herbert Morrison was not a member of the 1924 Cabinet, but he became Minister of Transport in 1929, in the second Labour government. In 1923 he achieved a signal victory in gaining control of the London County Council.

The Fall of the First Labour Government Described by Sidney Webb

When MacDonald came from the Palace to the Cabinet, we discussed the date of the election. It had already been elaborately considered by Henderson in consultation with the entire staff of Labour Party organisers; and a couple of days previously at a dinner party of about forty at 10 Downing Street, when past and potential donors to the Election Fund had been invited. At that dinner it was quite confidently declared by Henderson that, in order to fulfill all formalities and yet avoid both the English and the Scottish municipal election days, the formal Dissolution must be timed as to make the Polling Day November 8, thus involving a postponement for ten days. But the Cabinet, when MacDonald brought the King's consent, was strongly in favour of an immediate dissolution. . . .

At 6 p.m. . . . the House was summoned to the House of Lords to hear the Royal Assent given. . . .

Thus the Labour Government of 1924, with only 31 per cent. of the House of Commons behind it, lasted for eight and a half months, though defeated a dozen times in the House; and when it went to the electors increased its aggregate vote by 1,200,000 or 26 per cent.—though its 192 members were, by electoral ill-luck and the "pact" which partially united Liberals and Unionists against them, reduced to 151. We had always foreseen from the start that the Labour Government's episode could not last long—I don't think we expected as long a run as nine months—and that, when the election came, it must result in our being succeeded by a Unionist Government. But we certainly did not expect anything like so numerous a Unionist Party as 412; and on the other hand, we never dreamed, in our wildest moments, of a Liberal Party reduced to forty—a virtual obliteration of the Liberal Party that, together with our splendid increase of 1,200,000 votes, consoled us for the loss of forty seats.[12]

**Excerpt from the "Zinoviev Letter,"
Dated September 15, 1924, Published
October 25, 1924**

. . . . . .

Keep close observation over the leaders of the Labour Party, because these may easily be found in the leading strings of the *bourgeoisie*. The foreign policy of the Labour Party as it is already represents an inferior copy of the policy of the Curzon Government. Organize a campaign of disclosure of the foreign policy of MacDonald.

The Ikki [Executive Committee, Third (Communist) International] will willingly place at your disposal the wide material in its possession regarding the activities of British Imperialism in the Middle and Far East. In the meanwhile, however,

strain every nerve in the struggle for the ratification of the Treaty, in favour of a continuation of negotiations regarding the regulation of relations between the S.S.S.R. and England. A settlement of relations between the two countries will assist in the revolutionizing of the international and British proletariat not less than a successful rising in any of the working districts of England, as the establishment of close contact between the British and Russian proletariat, the exchange of delegations and workers, &c., will make it possible for us to extend and develop the propaganda of ideas of Leninism in England and the Colonies. Armed warfare must be preceded by a struggle against the inclinations to compromise which are embedded among the majority of British workmen, against the ideas of evolution and peaceful extermination of capitalism. Only then will it be possible to count upon complete success of an armed insurrection. . . .[13]

Comments of Herbert Morrison

The letter presumably existed a month before the press reproduced its text on the Saturday before polling day, which was a Wednesday. Ramsay MacDonald, who was Foreign Minister as well as Prime Minister, must have been aware of the letter at least ten days prior to the press revelations. He had said nothing at his election meetings nor to his colleagues in the cabinet.

With reason Jimmy Thomas commented to Philip Snowden after they had read the scare headlines: "We're sunk!" MacDonald may have thought so too, but he effectively disguised the feeling. On that Saturday afternoon he was due to address a mass meeting at Swansea. The public packed the hall to hear what he had to say about the letter, and the press

---

[12]Sidney Webb, *loc. cit.*, pp. 33–34.

[13]*The Times* (London), October 25, 1924.

were there in droves. We candidates anxiously awaited the evening papers so that we could study what we expected would be a clear lead on what to say at our meetings that Saturday evening.

There was not a single word in the MacDonald speech about it. Not until he spoke at Cardiff on Monday did he refer to it, and then he merely recited the known facts. He did not take a clear line.

Forty-eight hours later the nation went to the polls. The Tories achieved a big victory with 419 seats. Labour members dropped from 191 to 151, and I was among the defeated. . . .

My own election experience was much the same as that of other Labour candi-

dates. I took the line that it was not certain whether the Zinoviev letter was genuine or a forgery, but that in any case MacDonald's sharp note to the Soviet Government proved that the Labour Party was not toeing the bolshevik line and that we would defend our country against outside interference. It was probably the best line, but looking back I do not think it much mattered what line Labour candidates took. The swing to the Tories in marginal seats like mine was so definite that no argument could shift it.[14]

_____

[14]Lord Morrison of Lambeth, *Herbert Morrison: An Autobiography* (London: Odhams Press Ltd., 1960), pp. 108–09.

The collapse of Labour brought the Conservatives back into power, with Stanley Baldwin as Prime Minister. The new government inherited grave economic problems: decline in production and exports; rising costs; and a shaky currency. The return to the gold standard in 1925 necessitated a termination of the coal miners' subsidy. At the same time, the coal operators decided to abandon the supplementary wage scale of 1921. The miners' union, supported by the Trades Union Congress (T.U.C.), strongly protested, and Baldwin formed a royal commission to investigate.

Sir Herbert Samuel, leading member of the Liberal Party, whose comments are quoted below, was named chairman of the new commission.

Out of the miners' problems came the General Strike of May 4–12, 1926, a unique and controversial episode in British history. The following comments set forth varying points of view. Macmillan and Duff Cooper, both Conservative M.P.s at the time, later became, respectively, Prime Minister and Ambassador to France.

FOR CONSIDERATION   Note that there is little unanimity as to the effectiveness of the General Strike. Was it ever attempted again? Is Beatrice Webb correct in seeing it as the "death gasp" of Trade Union political control?

Comments of Sir Herbert Samuel

The Commission sat in a large room adjoining Westminster Hall; at the open sessions it was usually crowded with newspaper reporters and members of the public. When evidence was being taken

we invited representatives of the two parties to attend, and to put such questions as they wished. We heard nearly eighty witnesses; received a great mass of written evidence; and visited twenty-five mines in various parts of Great Britain, inspecting the underground workings of several. . . .

I think it was generally agreed that the inquiry was thorough and was fair.

· · · · ·

The Royal Commission's recommendations were generally approved—in Parliament, in the Press, and by public opinion. On March 24th the Government made a statement. They said that some of the proposals did not accord with their own views, and to some of them, taken singly, they were opposed. "Nevertheless, in face of the unanimous Report of the Commission and for the sake of a general settlement," they would undertake to carry out such of the recommendations as involved action by the State; . . . The employers, after some hesitation, declared that while they could not agree with the Commission on a number of points, it was their sincere desire "to do their utmost to give effect to the objects aimed at in the recommendations if a settlement by agreement can therefore be effected." But unhappily the Miners' Federation took a course which was bound to prove fatal.

The Report, taken as a whole, was very favourable to the miners. It endorsed their view that the organization of the industry was far from satisfactory; it found that the methods for utilizing coal were crude and unscientific; research inadequate; distribution and selling arrangements costly and often inefficient; the working conditions and terms of employment calling for many improvements. Our recommendations included: State ownership of the mineral; amalgamation of many hundreds of small mines to form strong and efficient units of production; the scientific use of coal and its derivatives; more economical methods of transport and sale; a National Wages Board, representing employers and employed with a neutral element, to determine rates of pay; and many reforms to promote the safety, health, comfort, and general welfare of the workers. But, on the immediate question of wage-rates, we felt bound to report that a temporary reduction was inevitable. . . .

The Miners' Federation, however, had declared beforehand that in no circumstances would they agree to any reduction, temporary or permanent, in the existing rates of pay, nor to any increase in working-hours. "Not a minute on the day, not a penny off the pay," was their slogan.

When the Report was published negotiations took place. The miners rejected uncompromisingly this crucial part of the Commission's proposals, and thereby put an end to our plan. On April 15th the mine-owners gave notice that the existing wage-contracts would be terminated on April 30th, the day when the subsidy came to an end; and that a new schedule of wage-rates would be applied on the following day. These were much lower than anything the Royal Commission had contemplated. The miners appealed to the Government to intervene. The Trade Union Congress came to their support. Last-minute proposals were made, but proved abortive. The Government undoubtedly committed some tactical errors in the final stages; but these made no difference, for a conflict was then inevitable. The hour struck. On Saturday, May 1st, the owners enforced their terms; on the Monday the miners refused to go to work, and the Trade Union Congress declared a General Strike from midnight of that day.[15]

Excerpts from the Journal of Hamilton Fyfe, Editor of the *Daily Herald* (Official Organ of the T.U.C. and the Labour Party)

First Day (May 4)

· · · · ·

Midnight. Well, it's settled. To-morrow we shall produce a newspaper, the *British Worker*, an evening paper, about the size

[15]Viscount Samuel, *Grooves of Change: A Book of Memoirs* (London: The Cresset Press, 1945), pp. 184–87.

of the London *Star,* eight pages, one penny. . . .

Trade unionism is a means to an end. It has been of immense benefit, but to make it an end in itself, to regard its machinery and regulations as if they were sacred, is to misapprehend and misuse it. I stress this because it is important that there should be understanding of the point and a lesson learned for the future.

When the strike began this morning all who saw the matter in its true perspective regarded themselves as being subject in all things to the orders of the General Council. I myself am ready to do anything which the General Council want done; to refrain from doing anything, no matter how good and useful it might seem to me, if they say it is to be left undone. There are many who do not share this view.

After long and, as it seemed to me, needless discussion, Mellor and I went back to our committee shortly before eleven to ask for a peremptory order from the General Council—in virtue of the complete powers given to it—that every one required for the production of the *British Worker* as an official strike news sheet should be authorised—if not instructed— to get to work.

Now at length we seem to have the way clear before us; I can go to bed with an easier mind than I had two hours ago.

. . . . .

FOURTH DAY (MAY 7)

You ask me what the House of Commons has been doing all this time? The answer is, Nothing.

What can it do? The General Council watches Labour politicians closely. It knows many of them consider the Strike a blunder. All who have theorised about general strikes take this view. They say it is a weapon which should only be used for a revolutionary purpose, and that it is out of place in an industrial dispute. . . .

General Strikes have been talked about and written about a great deal. The idea

has become familiar. It has now been put into execution because the need for some fresh weapon arose and there was this one ready to hand. A man who is attacked, and compelled suddenly to defend himself, doesn't stop to argue whether a poker was made to stir the fire with or to bring down on an assailant's head. He picks it up instinctively and uses it for the latter purpose.

. . . . .

AFTERWORD. There has never been anything like those Nine Days in any country. Not many thought it possible that so splendid a demonstration of comradeship, so marvellous a response by all sections to the cry of distress from one section, could ever occur here.

It did occur. It was a greater success than any one had dared to hope, this quiet, dignified withdrawal of labour by three million workers who felt that the miners' homes were in danger, and that next the attack would fall upon their own.

Three million out and the rest ready to join in as soon as they got the word. All orderly, all resolved to have no disturbances, to give no excuse for the violence which was there ready to be used. It was the most wonderful, the most inspiring illustration of Labour's new-found solidarity. After it nothing can ever be the same again.[16]

A Socialist View of the Strike. Comments of Beatrice Webb

May 4th. When all is said and done we personally are against the use of the General Strike in order to compel the employers of a particular industry to yield to the men's demands, however well justified these claims may be. Such methods cannot be tolerated by any Government—

[16]Hamilton Fyfe, *Behind the Scenes of the Great Strike* (London: Labour Publishing Co., Ltd., 1926), pp. 26-27, 48, 89.

even a Labour Government would have to take up the challenge. A General Strike aims at coercing the whole community and is only successful *if it does so* and in so far as it does so. Further, if it succeeded in coercing the community it would mean that a militant minority were starving the majority into submission to their will, and would be the end of democracy, industrial as well as political. . . .

To us it was as clear as noonday that with the T.U. Movement in its present state of mind this weapon of a final strike *would be used*. When it has been tried and failed, as fail it will, the workers will be in a better frame of mind for steady and sensible political action. Moreover, the governing class will have had a nasty shock and being English, they will learn from it and compel the coal-owners to reorganise or clear out.

For the British Trade Union Movement I see a day of terrible disillusionment. The failure of the General Strike of 1926 will be one of the most significant landmarks in the history of the British working class. Future historians will, I think, regard it as the death gasp of that pernicious doctrine of "workers' control" of public affairs through the Trade Unions, and by the method of direct action.

. . . . .

May 18th. Churchill's announcement in the House to-day that the General Strike will have cost the Government no more than three-quarters of a million—a sum which the death of a couple of millionaires will pay—puts the cap of ridicule on the heroics of the General Strike. The three million strikers will have spent some three million pounds of Trade Union money and lost another four or five in wages. . . .

The Government has gained immense prestige in the world and the British Labour Movement has made itself ridiculous. A strike which opens with a football match between the police and the strik-

ers and ends in unconditional surrender after nine days with densely-packed reconciliation services at all the chapels and churches of Great Britain attended by the strikers and their families, will make the continental Socialists blaspheme. . . .

Let me add that the failure of the General Strike shows what a *sane* people the British are. If only our revolutionaries would realise the hopelessness of their attempt to turn the British workman into a Russian Red and the British business man and country gentleman into an Italian Fascist! The British are hopelessly good-natured and common-sensical—to which the British workman adds pigheadedness, jealousy and stupidity. What oppresses me is the fear that these elements of crass stupidity and pigheaded obstinacy may prevent the revival of British trade and that Trade Unionism may diminish and not increase efficiency. . . .[17]

A Conservative View of the General Strike. Comments of Duff Cooper

Old men forget, and a few pages penned at the time have a higher value for the historian and, I hope, a livelier interest for the general reader than the most careful reconstruction of damaged hieroglyphs carelessly scattered in the recording vaults of the mind. I will therefore print what I wrote as it was written without altering a word.

. . . . .

Wednesday, May 5th. A wet morning and so dark that at midday it was impossible to see to read without electric light. The electric light was faint and yellow. I went to White's, where there were a lot of people discussing absurd rumours—one was that Winston had been assassinated. . . .

Thursday, May 6th. The weather still very cold. . . .

The streets are much emptier today owing to the taxis having come out. We lunched

17Beatrice Webb, *op. cit.*, pp. 91–92, 97–98.

at home. . . . We went down to the House afterwards. . . . It was a dull and trying afternoon. The more violent of the Labour Members spoke and made such ridiculous and tiresome speeches that it made me feel physically ill to listen to them. . . . At eleven o'clock Simon made a most important and impressive speech, in which he condemned the strike uncompromisingly and laid especial stress upon its illegality. The Labour Party left the Chamber before he began, but all the Liberal Party were there with the exception of Lloyd George, and they were solidly behind him. That speech may prove the way to his supplanting Lloyd George as their leader.

.   .   .   .   .

Friday, May 14th. I went to the House of Commons at eleven, when we discussed the financial resolution to the Electricity Bill. At four o'clock the Prime Minister made a statement to the effect that the railways had just arrived at an agreement, that negotiations with the dockers were going on satisfactorily, and that he had prepared proposals for settling the mines dispute which he was going to submit to both parties. Ramsay MacDonald and Lloyd George had nothing to say except to express the hope that Baldwin himself would take part in the negotiations between the mine-owners and the miners. It was the final culminating scene in the greatest personal and public triumph that any Prime Minister has ever had.

When I came to write my weekly article I insisted that the dispute in the coal industry was no more the real issue during the General Strike than was the levy of ship-money the real issue during the Civil War. On each occasion the issue had been whether the country was to be governed by Parliament or not. I believed that many members of the Labour Party had understood this, and while I strongly condemned their conduct in leaving the House in a body rather than listen to the important speech of Sir John Simon, I was able to praise the rest of their behaviour.[18]

---

[18]Duff Cooper, *Old Men Forget: The Autobiography of Duff Cooper (Viscount Norwich)*

A Conservative View. Comments of Harold Macmillan

The general tone and temper of the House of Commons was responsible and impressive. Except for the extreme Left wing of the Labour Party, speakers tried hard to be fair and moderate. Whatever might be the view of some of the trade unionists engaged in the conflict, it was clear that the leaders were deeply disturbed and as anxious for a settlement as everyone else. Now, years later, I have read much of the material which has been published, but still no very clear picture emerges. There was, no doubt, a difference, if not of opinion, at least of mood inside the Cabinet, just as there was inside the trade union movement. . . .

Looking back upon it all, it is clear that this tragic conflict was one of those into which both sides had drifted helplessly to disaster through the intransigence of their so-called "allies". Like so many wars between nations throughout history, this civil war could have been avoided. If the owners had unequivocally accepted and if the Government had undertaken to give immediate effect to the recommendations of the Samuel Commission as to the reorganisation of the industry—still better, had they gone even further than the actual Report along the lines of compulsory unification—the moral position of the Miners' Federation would have been much weakened, and the hands of the T.U.C. leaders strengthened. But Conservative opinion was not yet prepared for so drastic an interference of the State with industry. Similarly, the other trade union leaders should have recognised the plain fact that during the period which any reorganisation must have taken—a period of at least six months, perhaps even one or two years—some concession had to be

---

(New York: E. P. Dutton & Co., Inc., 1954) pp. 148-54. Copyright 1954, by E. P. Dutton & Co., Inc. Reprinted by permission of E. P. Dutton & Co., Inc.

made in the wage structure to allow the industry to continue. As it was, although we hardly realised it at the time, the bitterness felt by trade unionists throughout the country became more and more intense. Only the sound instincts and traditions of the people as a whole allowed the inevitable incidents to pass off without serious damage, and, indeed, without the loss of a single life.[19]

Comments of Sir Herbert Samuel

The General Strike was over, to the relief of the whole nation, but the coal

[19]Harold Macmillan, *Winds of Change, 1914–1939*, pp. 216–17. Copyright © 1966 by Thomas Newspapers Limited. By permission of Harper & Row, Publishers.

stoppage went on. It lasted for six months. The Union's funds were gradually exhausted; the miners' savings as well. Debts piled up in the mining villages; privation and suffering stalked through the idle coalfields. As was inevitable, the long patient endurance of the miners—nearly a million of them—their staunchness, their wonderful loyalty to their leaders and to one another, proved in vain. After one of the most bitter industrial conflicts the country has ever known, they were obliged to go back in the end; and on terms far, far worse than they could have had in the beginning. The nation suffered a loss from the stoppage estimated at from three to four hundred million pounds.[20]

[20]Viscount Samuel, *op. cit.*, p. 192.

Except for a militant minority, such as those in the Independent Labour Party, trade unionists in Great Britain concluded that there were more effective measures for social action than strikes. Between 1926 and 1939, the number of strikes declined to less than 10 percent of the previous averages. In 1926, Walter Citrine became general secretary of the Trades Union Congress, and he influenced the T.U.C. toward cooperation with management rather than toward violence. And the Labour Party undertook a reappraisal of its policies in an effort to recover from its recent setbacks. In 1928, it promulgated a new policy, "Labour and the Nation," largely drafted by Professor R. H. Tawney.

By 1929, many voters had been won over, and Labour had its second chance.

Comments of Clement Attlee

In 1928 a new programme was drawn up to replace *Labour and the New Social Order*. The new document, *Labour and the Nation*, differed considerably from its predecessor in its line of approach. It reflected in the first place the changed position of the Party. It was a bid for power by a Party which expected in the normal course to attain it. It was for this reason more constructive. It was, however, a

very long document, and, though not so all-embracing as its predecessor, comprised a bewildering number of subjects. A four-page summary set out no less than seventy-two proposals that a Labour Government, if elected, intended to carry out. It was obvious that nothing short of a miracle could have enabled the Party, even with an overwhelming majority, to get all these measures passed into law within the life of one Parliament, yet there was no suggestion as to which of them was to be given priority. It was, indeed, designed to rally to the Party a great variety of supporters. It gave the Prime Minister an opportunity to select which items suited him. It gave every malcontent unlimited opportunities of charging the Party with breaches of faith for not implementing all these promises.[21]

Summary of Proposals in "Labour and the Nation," 1928

I. INDUSTRIAL LEGISLATION

1. The Repeal of the Trade Unions Act and the Restoration of Trade Union Rights.
2. The establishment of a 48-hour week.
3. The improvement and extension of Factory Acts, Mines Regulation Acts, Workmen's Compensation Acts, Merchant Shipping Acts, Minimum Wage Acts, and other industrial legislation.
4. The establishment and enforcement of international labour standards.

II. UNEMPLOYMENT

1. The establishment of adequate provision for unemployed workers, under the control of a National Authority.
2. The amendment of the Unemployment Insurance Acts, the establishment of the scale of benefits recommended by the Labour Party in its evidence before the Blanesburgh Committee, and the extension of the principle of Unemployment Insurance to classes of workers at present outside its scope.
3. The withdrawal from the Labour market of children under 15, with the necessary provision of maintenance allowances.
4. The improvement of the provision made for widows and orphans and for the veterans of industry.
5. The repeal of the Eight Hours Act in the coal industry.

6. The transference and migration of unemployed miners.
7. The establishment of a superannuation scheme for aged miners.

III. THE DEVELOPMENT OF INDUSTRY AND TRADE

1. The establishment of a National Economic Committee to advise the Government as to economic policy, and of a National Development and Employment Board to prepare schemes for the development of national resources.
2. The control of the Bank of England by a public Corporation, including representatives of the Treasury, the Board of Trade, Industry, Labour and the Co-operative Movement; the encouragement of Co-operative and Municipal banking; the promotion of an International Conference, as proposed at Genoa in 1922, with a view to the regulation of the value of gold by international agreement; and the introduction of such further changes in the banking and financial system as will secure that the available supply of credit and savings is used to the greatest national advantage.
3. The transference to public ownership of the coal, transport, power, and life insurance industries.
4. The appointment of a Commission to prepare a scheme for the reconstruction of the cotton industry.
5. The relief of industry by the readjustment of the relations between national and local finance and by the taxation of land values.
6. The protection of the consumer against exploitation and the extension of the powers of the Food Council.
7. The establishment of the fullest possible publicity with regard to costs and profits.
8. The promotion of scientific research, with a view to the improvement of industrial technique.

[21]Attlee, *op. cit.*, p. 53.

9. The extension of the powers of the Economic Section of the League of Nations.

IV. Agriculture and Rural Life

1. The transference of land to public ownership. . . .

.   .   .   .   .

V. The Development of the Social Services

.   .   .   .   .

VI. Education and the Care of Childhood

.   .   .   .   .

VII. Financial Policy

.   .   .   .   .

VIII. International Peace and Cooperation

.   .   .   .   .

IX. The British Commonwealth of Nations

.   .   .   .   .

X. Political Democracy

.   .   .   .   [22]

Comments of Clement Attlee

The General Election of 1929 found Labour for the first time the largest Party in the House of Commons, with 288 members. Against it was ranged the Conservative Party, with 267, while holding the balance was the Liberal Party, with

[22]Labour and the Nation," The Labour Party, 1928.

59 members, temporarily united under the leadership of Mr. Lloyd George. The Liberal Party had gone to the country on a programme of advanced social reform. It had polled over five million votes, which, together with Labour's eight and a half million, made some fourteen millions against a total of less than nine million votes cast for a Conservative policy. There was, therefore, a clear mandate from the country for a programme which would be generally to the Left.

On the other hand, the Liberal Party was a collection of persons of very different views, united, it has been said, by a common distrust of their leader.

There were, it seems to me, three possible courses open to the Labour Party: to refuse office, to accept office and invite defeat by putting forward a Socialist programme and placing the onus of rejecting it on to the Liberal Party, or to come to some agreement with the Liberals on a programme which would secure joint action in the House. . . .

No one of these courses was followed. Mr. MacDonald was quite right in thinking that in the sphere of foreign affairs a great lead for peace and disarmament could be given, but he had no clear idea as to what course to follow in domestic affairs. He seemed to think that by a course of studious moderation he could conciliate opposition, while doing enough to retain the support of his own followers.[23]

[23]Attlee, op. cit., pp. 54-55.

The second Labour government lasted until August, 1931, when MacDonald, in what has been called "The Great Betrayal," repudiated some of his Labour colleagues and formed a "National" government. The following documents throw some light on MacDonald and on the vicissitudes of the Labour movement.

R. H. Tawney had been, in 1930, a member of MacDonald's Economic Advisory Council.

FOR CONSIDERATION   A complete judgment of the first and second Labour governments' accomplishments should include an assessment of foreign policy, to which MacDonald devoted a good deal of personal attention. What were the issues at this time?

Ramsey MacDonald in 1931, as Described by Hugh Dalton

And so gradually, and as these social circles widened—as they always will for rising politicians who desire to enter them—he contrasted to himself more and more sharply the drab, rude, coarse-grained, cocksure, uninstructed members of the Labour Party with those brighter spirits, the more elegant, refined, wealthy, thoughtful members of the aristocracy, with their wider interests and their more comfortable and hospitable homes. So he went to "the aristocratic embrace", as Webb, I think, first called it. And after that embrace, once or twice repeated, to the new political liaison, the "National" Government.

But though he wanted this badly, he wished to seem to have it forced upon him, by forces stronger than himself, outside himself, even against some faint gestures of resistance. Yet—and here, perhaps, is his greatest tragedy—when at last he got what he wanted, the first satisfaction soon passed, and he resumed his old unhappiness, his martyr's crown, his grievances against most of the world at home and abroad—including, of course, his old "followers" in the Labour Party. He never wanted to revive *that* dead relationship. But he had had his great new political love affair too late in life. When it came, at last, he was long past his best.[24]

Comments of Beatrice Webb

August 23rd. S.W. reported that at the Cabinet yesterday morning the Prime

Minister stated that the Conservative and Liberal leaders refused to accept the Labour Cabinet proposals and demanded 75% cuts mainly in the dole and 25% taxes. The Cabinet refused to compromise to that extent and the King was informed by telephone and decided to return to London from Balmoral. J.R.M. raised the question of a Coalition Government: some of the Labour Cabinet Ministers remaining in office. This, he intimated, was what the King desired and might propose. This proposal Henderson and other members hotly rejected. The impression left on S.W.'s mind was that J.R.M., Snowden and Jimmy *might consider it.* "A good riddance for the Labour Party," I said. . . .[25]

Comments of Viscount Snowden, Chancellor of the Exchequer

Mr. MacDonald at the Palace meeting on the Monday morning agreed to the formation of a National Government, with himself as Prime Minister, without a word of previous consultation with any of his Labour colleagues. . . .

It was a very strange thing that Mr. MacDonald should have taken this grave step without informing some at least of his Labour colleagues of his intention. He did tell his Cabinet, as I have mentioned, that he intended to advise the King to call the Opposition leaders into consultation, but this was not understood either by them or the Labour Cabinet as the prelude to a National Government.

When the Labour Cabinet as a whole declined to agree to a reduction of Unemployment pay, Mr. MacDonald assumed

---

[24]Dalton, *op. cit.,* p. 286.

[25]Beatrice Webb, *op. cit.,* p. 282.

too hurriedly that this involved the resignation of his Government. He neither shewed nor expressed any grief at this regrettable development. On the contrary, he set about the formation of the National Government with an enthusiasm which shewed that the adventure was highly agreeable to him.

Mr. Baldwin and Sir Herbert Samuel at once called their supporters together to endorse their action, which they promptly did. Mr. MacDonald, on the other hand, never sought to meet the Labour Party. Two days after the formation of the National Government he sent a private letter to each Labour member of Parliament in which he stated the reasons for the resignation of the Labour Government and the formation of the National Government. This letter was not intended to be published, but some Labour member who received it must at once have handed it to the Press, for it appeared in the evening newspapers the same day.

A meeting of the Parliamentary Labour Party was held on 28th August. Mr. MacDonald did not attend it, nor did he send any message or appeal. This was naturally taken as an indication that he had finally separated himself from the Party and did not want its support. I do not know if Mr. MacDonald had an invitation to attend this meeting. I was not aware of it until after it had been held. Labour members have since complained that Mr. MacDonald and myself did not attend this meeting.[26]

Comments of R. H. Tawney

. . . The events of the late summer of 1931 were the occasion, rather than the cause, of the débâcle of the Labour Party. In spite of the dramatic episodes which heralded its collapse, the Government did not fall with a crash, in a tornado from the blue. It crawled slowly to its doom,

---

[26]Snowden, *op. cit.,* Vol. II, pp. 952–53.

deflated by inches, partly by its opponents, partly by circumstances beyond its control, but partly also by itself. The gunpowder was running out of it from the moment it assumed office, and was discovered, on inspection, to be surprisingly like sawdust. Due allowance must be made, no doubt, for the cruel chance which condemned it to face the worst collapse in prices of modern history; and due credit must be given for the measures which it introduced, but failed, through no fault of its own, to pass into law. But, granted the inexorable limits, can it seriously be argued that it was audacious in working up to them? . . .

Industrial and social reconstruction, the favourite theme of Labour orators, owed little to the existence of a Labour Cabinet. It doubtless felt itself precluded, till the Macmillan Committee had reported, from making up its mind on the questions of currency and credit which were to prove its undoing. Even in matters, however, where delay was not imposed by circumstances, its actions did not err on the side of trenchancy. It found coal, cotton and steel with one foot in the nineteenth century; it left them there. What passed in its inner councils is, of course, unknown; but it gave few outward symptoms of realising that, if the modernisation of the major industries is to be handled at all, it must be planned as a whole, or of grasping the necessity of creating a permanent organ to press it steadily forward, or of appreciating the importance of devoting attention to the long-range aspects of unemployment, as distinct from monthly fluctuations in the number of unemployed. It had even to be stimulated by the protests of its followers in the House into proceeding—too late—with its little Education Bill. . . .

If the laments of some ex-ministers at the "conspiracy," which "stabbed them in the back"—as though a Titan, all energy and ardour, had been felled at his forge by the hand of assassins—were merely undignified, they would properly be ignored. Unfortunately, they are worse. What Labour most needs is not self-commiseration, but a little cold realism. . . .

It is the author, the unintending and pitiable author, of its own misfortunes. It made a government in its own image; and the collapse of that government was the result neither of accident—though that played its part—nor of unfavourable circumstances—though luck was against it—nor, least of all, it must be reported, of merely personal failings. It was in the logic of history; for 1929-31 repeated 1924. It sprang from within, not without; for it had begun within six months of the Gov-

ernment's return, and the flight from principles was both earlier and more precipitate than the flight from the pound. It was the consequence, not of individual defects, but of a general habit of mind and outlook on affairs which ministers had acquired long before they could anticipate that power would be their lot. What was tried, and found wanting, in short, in 1929-31, was, not merely two years of a Labour Cabinet, but a decade of Labour politics.[27]

_____

[27]R. H. Tawney, "The Choice before the Labour Party," *The Political Quarterly* (July-September, 1932), pp. 323–26.

With MacDonald, Snowden, and several others breaking ranks with Labour, it was necessary for the party and the Trades Union Congress to reorganize. On August 28, Arthur Henderson was chosen to lead the Parliamentary Labour Party. Two months later the Party Conference, here described by Beatrice Webb, took place at Scarborough.

FOR CONSIDERATION   What happened to the Independent Labour Party? How strong was it? Was Communism a serious threat in Great Britain?

Comments of Beatrice Webb

Scarborough Labour Conference

October 10th. Dull, drab, disillusioned but *not* disunited, is the impression I got of the Labour Party Conference of 1931. There are few women among 800 delegates; there is a marked absence of wives; there are numbers of pale and listless men in the Conference—there is an uncanny absence of laughter and mutual chaff— there is no anger and very little sympathy with rebels—the I.L.P. [Independent Labour Party] were steam-rollered by 2 million to 200,000 out of the Party. The Communists and their absurd little paper, the *Daily Worker*, are ignored. Henderson got a great reception; there was singularly little attempt to call the late Ministers on the platform to account. . . .

At Headquarters (Prince of Wales Hotel). The scene has completely changed from the last Conferences I attended, Margate, 1927, and Brighton, 1929. The smart set that surrounded MacDonald, and gave the tone to Headquarters—Thomson, Mosleys, De la Warrs, Jowitts, Usher, etc.— have disappeared. Henderson's bodyguard of intellectuals—Dalton, Noel Baker, Laski, Colin Clark—together with the younger Labour Ministers—Morrison, Johnston and Susan Lawrence—are very much in evidence. The most notable newcomer—one who is already acclaimed as *the future leader*—is Stafford Cripps. He moved among the younger men with ease and modesty—he is able and virtuous without personal vanity or airs of superiority—uncontaminated by "Society", a homely person—a distinguished intellectual and first-rate advocate, but not yet an artist like J. R. M. or Mosley. He is not to me, though he is my nephew, *personally* attractive. He has neither wit nor humour; neither subtlety nor artistry. But *if* he has sufficient physical vigour, he will go far, because he has character as well as intellect; he is pious in the best sense. . . .

We have got rid of the rotten stuff from the movement, but we have not yet sufficient will-power and knowledge to take control of the big formless business of capitalist production, distribution and exchange which is now disintegrating before our eyes in Great Britain and apparently in U.S.A. and Germany and other countries. What seems now to be the prevailing spirit among the new governing group of the P.L.P. is a dour determination never again to undertake the government of the country as the *caretaker of the existing order of society.* They intend to lay down, on the first day of office, a positive policy of immediate legislation and executive control of the nation's income and investment of savings—with no damned nonsense about H. of Lords obstruction or Court objection! I do not yet see the men for such a job! But there is the *Will* present—in this little group at Headquarters—at any rate the Will to elaborate a plan whilst in *opposition.*[28]

Program Advocated by Sir Stafford Cripps, 1933

The Labour Party is not now concerned so much with some particular political orientation of capitalist society as with the change from capitalism to Socialism. Continuity of policy—even in fundamentals—can find no place in a Socialist programme. It is this complete severance with all traditional theories of government, this determination to seize power from the ruling class and transfer it to the

---

[28]Beatrice Webb, *op. cit.*, pp. 291–92.

people as a whole, that differentiates the present political struggle from all those that have gone before. . . .

The first requisite in bringing about a peaceful revolution is to obtain a Parliamentary majority of adequate size to carry all necessary measures through the House of Commons. This majority must be definitely and irrevocably pledged to Socialism and must not depend in any way upon the assistance of merely radical or humanitarian elements. Given such a majority, success or failure will be proved in the first full Parliamentary term. Unless during the first five years so great a degree of change has been accomplished as to deprive capitalism of its power, it is unlikely that a Socialist Party will be able to maintain its position of control without adopting some exceptional means such as the prolongation of the life of Parliament for a further term without an election. Whether such action would be possible would depend entirely upon the temper of the country, and this in turn would be dependent upon the actual results which the Government could show.

The most critical period, however, for a Socialist Government will be the first few months of power. . . .

The Government's first step will be to call Parliament together at the earliest moment and place before it an Emergency Powers Bill to be passed through all its stages on the first day. This Bill will be wide enough in its terms to allow all that will be immediately necessary to be done by ministerial order. These orders must be incapable of challenge in the Courts or in any way except in the House of Commons.

This Bill must be ready in draft beforehand, together with the main orders that will be made immediately upon its becoming law. . . .

It is most probable that the House of Lords—the stronghold of capitalism—will either reject or more likely delay the passage of such a bill. The Commons will be in a strong position as the election will have so recently taken place, and it may be that guarantees as to the passage of such a Bill may have been obtained as a condition of the taking of office.

If this is not so, then immediate application will have to be made to the Crown to resolve the conflict by the creation of Peers, and although this will necessitate some delay, it is better to risk this delay, which need not be excessive, than to adopt any unconstitutional alternative. . . .[29]

Comments of Herbert Morrison

Very soon the quixotic remarks and actions, so improbable in a man with a trained legal mind, indicated that Cripps was not quite the unassailable asset to the Party I had thought he would be. He was prone to say things which I frankly do not believe that at times he really meant. An example was the comment he made in January, 1934, which aroused a furore in the press.

[29]Sir Stafford Cripps, "Can Socialism Come by Constitutional Methods?", in *Problems of a Socialist Government* (London: Victor Gollancz, Ltd., 1933), pp. 36–44.

It happened at a comparatively insignificant political meeting in Nottingham. He was reviewing problems which would arise for a future Labour government, and he said that opposition from the Palace and other places would have to be overcome. Not unexpectedly the reporters saw a big news story in the remark, and it was headline news the next morning, sending apprehensive shivers of bloody revolution down the spines of timid old ladies of both sexes as they read these remarks of Cripps over their breakfast tables. . . .

It may be that the unfortunate Nottingham reference to the Palace was made because Cripps for some reason believed that his audience would like to hear it. He could quite often be led astray like this, possibly because his legal training enabled him to put up cogent arguments to his brief, or because of experience in addressing a jury.

In private discussions he was invincible. There was many an occasion when in our personal talks I took the opposite view to his. We would argue until he got me to a point where my case could no longer be argued, yet I knew in my bones that he was wrong and I was right—which subsequent events usually proved to be so.[30]

[30]Lord Morrison, *op. cit.*, pp. 158–59.

The Labour Party gradually gained more support from the electorate, and in the elections of November, 1935, increased their seats from 59 to 154. (The Prime Minister, Stanley Baldwin, still had the support of 428 Conservative and Liberal votes.) New Labour leadership was emerging with men like Herbert Morrison, Hugh Dalton, Arthur Greenwood, and Clement Attlee playing the most prominent roles. But the movement was split over domestic and foreign policies. Cripps advocated a "Popular Front" of Communists and Socialists (such as gained power in France in 1936), and was ultimately expelled. When George Lansbury, leader of the Labour Party in parliament, resigned over the question of sanctions against Italy, he was succeeded by Clement Attlee.

Labour now undertook to organize a program which would be practical and effective. These policies are here described by Dalton and Attlee. It was essentially this planning which underlay the legislation of 1945-50 directly after World War II, when Labour's "Great Ministry" took office.

Comments of Hugh Dalton on
Labour's Immediate Programme,
1937

I spent some time also, in the early months of my Chairmanship, in carrying out our pledge, given at Edinburgh, to produce "a Short Programme of primary measures of Socialism and Social Amelioration to which legislative effect will be given by the next Labour Government". Previous programmes, it was widely felt, were too complicated, too miscellaneous and too long. What was wanted now was something short and simple, on which our propaganda could concentrate.

Labour's Immediate Programme was published in March. . . . Re-reading this programme eighteen years later and recalling the conditions of that time, I like it pretty well. It ran to only nine pages, including a page of summary. Labour's Aims, we said, were Socialism, Peace and Democracy. On the third of these we spoke words of determinism and reassurance. "A Labour Government will prove that, while preserving freedom and respecting the rights of minorities, the democratic system can work swiftly and effectively. Labour will not allow its measures to be defeated by obstruction from vested interests or unrepresentative bodies." This was our only reference, oblique but clear, to the House of Lords. "It will carry out its plans without inflicting injustice on individuals. A fair price will be paid for all private property transferred to public ownership." But "the community", we claimed, "must command the main levers which control the economic machine. These are Finance, Land, Transport, Coal and Power".

The Bank of England, like the Central Bank in most other countries, will become a Public Institution. It will be administered by practical and experienced men under the general direction of the Government. Through the Bank of England credit will be controlled in the interests of trade and employment. ("Through the Bank of England" other credit agencies, including the Joint Stock Banks, could be controlled.)

New investment would be controlled through a National Investment Board, "whose duty will be to mobilise our financial resources, to guide them into the right channels, and to advise the Government on a financial plan for the full employment of our people". Large schemes of Public Development would be carried out. "Taxation will be used to secure a better distribution of wealth and purchasing power, and to provide funds for the extension of the Social Services."

"The land," we said, "should belong to the people, and national planning requires that the use of land shall be controlled in the public interest." "A short Bill will be passed enabling the Government and other public authorities to acquire such land as they need for any purpose without delay and at a reasonable price." But "the small householder and owner-occupier will be left in undisputed possession of his home".

"A National Transport Board", we undertook, "will be set up to co-ordinate transport by road, rail, air and coastwise shipping, and to own and operate the railways and such other transport services as are suitable for transfer to public ownership."

"The coal industry, including coal treatment and marketing, will be unified under public ownership. The first charge on the industry will be a living wage and safety for the miner. The electricity and gas supply industries will likewise be brought completely under public ownership."

We pledged ourselves "to make available to all a plentiful supply of good food", through increasing home production, controlling imports, reorganising food distribution and assuring, through social services, "sufficient and suitable food for children and for expectant and nursing mothers".

A Labour Government would "co-operate with the Trade Unions to improve wage standards", and would "seek to promote through the International Labour Office the adoption of Conventions to raise labour standards throughout the world".

"A universal statutory period of holiday with pay each year will be enacted." Evan Durbin was very keen on this; we haven't done it yet.

"Vigorous measures", we promised, "will be adopted to increase employment, and to concentrate the available work on those best fitted to perform it." All children would be kept at school till 15 and, as soon as the necessary arrangements could be made, to 16, with maintenance allowances. There would be improved pensions on condition that pensioners retired from work. For those who were still unemployed, "proper maintenance will be provided and the Means Test will be abolished".

We had an emphatic section on the Distressed Areas. "Immediate remedies," we declared, "must be found for the terrible conditions" there. "The State must accept responsibility for the location of industry. Labour will bring new industries into these areas, will encourage existing industries, develop local resources and improve communications, assist Local Authorities and relieve the crushing burden of local rates. Drastic and immediate

action will be taken to raise the shockingly low standards of life, which, for large numbers of people in these areas, amount to slow starvation."

On Foreign Policy and Defence we added a little to previous pronouncements. A Labour Government, we said, would try its hardest "to remove the economic causes of international rivalry, and to enable all peaceful nations to share in the abundant wealth of the world. It will take the lead in seeking to strengthen and re-invigorate the League of Nations as an instrument of international co-operation and collective security. It will play its full part in every effort to check the present ruinous arms race, and to promote disarmament by international agreement."[31]

Comments of Clement Attlee, 1937

I believe that a Socialist Government must have always very clearly before it its ultimate aims and ideals. It must work throughout with the object of attaining them. It must not rest content with minor successes. It must, even when dealing with immediate problems, keep in mind always the goal to which it is tending. It is here that the Labour Party is so different from those parties which believe fundamentally in the retention of a class system of society and in a Capitalist system as the economic foundation of society. . . .

The new order of society will enable millions, who up to now have had to toil in factory and workshop all their lives without any prospect of ever experiencing the good things of life, to get their first opportunity of enjoying some of those luxuries that are now confined exclusively to the well-to-do. Let us consider for a moment the sort of life that we hope will be led by a working man and his family under Socialism.

[31]Hugh Dalton, *Memoirs*, Vol. II, *The Fateful Years, 1931–1945* (London: Frederick Muller Ltd., 1957), pp. 124–27.

A great part of the week, under Socialism as under any other system, will inevitably be spent in work. Whether that work is in factory or office, the worker will be able to feel that he is working in his own concern, which belongs to him as a British citizen. He will know that the work he is doing will be of benefit to himself and to every other person in the country. There will be no question of the goods he is producing being destined for destruction as "surplus" because the economic system cannot absorb them. Everything that is made will add to the sum of the country's wealth. He will know, too, that if he continues to work satisfactorily there is no chance of his losing his job.

. . . . .

I believe that the Labour Party is the instrument whereby this change will be affected. Typically British, the Labour Party has shown its power of adaptation to new conditions and new purposes. At its inception it was a party representing almost entirely organised Labour. Its programme was sectional, not national. It has since then developed into a national party, open to all, and has a policy which embraces every phase of national life. In its earlier days it would have been a fair criticism to have said that it could not aspire to power because its appeal was too narrow. It is not true to-day. Increasingly it draws its strength from men and women of all classes of society. Its achievement of power does not depend on an alteration in the quality of its adherents, but in their quantity. It has to convert to its faith many millions of workers who still cling to Capitalism. It has to persuade many members of the classes which depend in the main on their own work for their livelihood that true community of interest is based on fellowship in service, not on participation in profits.[32]

[32]Attlee, *op. cit.*, pp. 120–21, 192–93.

BIBLIOGRAPHY

Sources Used in This Problem

1. *Collections and Official Documents*

"Labour and the New Social Order," Labour Party Conference, June, 1918.
"Labour and the Nation," Labour Party, 1928.
The Political Quarterly.

2. *Others*

Attlee, Clement. *As It Happened.* New York: The Viking Press, Inc., 1954.

———. *The Labour Party in Perspective—and Twelve Years Later.* 2d ed., with Foreword by Francis Williams. London: Gollancz, 1949.

Beveridge, William H. *Full Employment in a Free Society.* London: George Allen & Unwin, Ltd., 1945.

Cooper, Duff. *Old Men Forget: The Autobiography of Duff Cooper (Viscount Norwich).* New York: E. P. Dutton & Co., 1954.

Dalton, Hugh. *Memoirs.* Vol. I, *Call Back Yesterday, 1887–1931;* Vol. II, *The Fateful Years, 1931–1945.* London: Frederick Muller, 1953, 1957.

Fyfe, Hamilton. *Behind the Scenes of the Great Strike.* London: Labour Publishing Co., 1926.

Macmillan, Harold. *Winds of Change, 1914–1939.* London: Macmillan, 1966.

MORRISON, LORD, OF LAMBETH. *Herbert Morrison: An Autobiography.* London: Odhams Press, 1960.

ORWELL, GEORGE. *The Road to Wigan Pier.* 2d ed. New York: Harcourt, Brace & World, 1958.

Problems of a Socialist Government. London: Gollancz, 1933.

SAMUEL, VISCOUNT. *Grooves of Change: A Book of Memoirs.* London: Cresset, 1945.

SHAW, GEORGE BERNARD. *The Intelligent Woman's Guide to Socialism and Capitalism.* New York: Brentano's, 1928.

SNOWDEN, PHILIP (VISCOUNT). *An Autobiography.* 2 vols. London: Nicholson & Watson, 1934.

TAYLOR, F. H. GRIFFIN. "*The Hunger Marchers.*" (manuscript).

WEBB, BEATRICE. *Beatrice Webb's Diaries.* Ed. MARGARET COLE. Vols. I, II. London: Longmans, Green, 1952, 1956.

WOOLTON, LORD. *Memoirs of the Earl of Woolton.* London: Cassell, 1959.

SELECT LIST OF BOOKS RECOMMENDED FOR FURTHER READING

BASSETT, R. S. *Nineteen Thirty-One: Poiltical Crisis.* London: Macmillan, 1958.

BEVAN, ANEURIN. *In Place of Fear.* New York: Simon & Schuster, 1952.

BRAND, CARL F. *The British Labour Party.* Stanford, Calif.: Stanford University Press, 1964.

BULLOCK, ALAN. *The Life and Times of Ernest Bevin.* London: Heinemann, 1963.

COLE, GEORGE D. *History of the Labour Party from 1914.* London: Routledge and Kegan Paul, 1948.

LYMAN, RICHARD W. *The First Labour Government, 1924.* London: Chapman and Hall, 1957.

McHENRY, D. E. *The Labour Party in Transition.* London: Routledge, 1938.

McKENSIE, R. T. *British Political Parties: The Distribution of Power within the Conservative and Labour Parties.* London: Heinemann, 1955.

Men without Work: A Report Made to the Pilgrim Trust. London: Cambridge University Press, 1938.

MILIBAND, RALPH. *Parliamentary Socialism: A Study in the Politics of Labour.* London: Allen & Unwin, 1961.

MOWAT, CHARLES. *Britain between the Wars 1918–1940.* London: Methuen, 1955.

PELLING, HENRY. *A Short History of the Labour Party.* New York: St. Martin's Press, 1965.

POLLARD, SIDNEY. *The Development of the British Economy 1914–1950.* London: Arnold, 1962.

REYNOLDS, E. E., and BRASHER, N. H. *Britain in the Twentieth Century.* London: Cambridge University Press, 1966.

SCANLON, JOHN. *Decline and Fall of the Labour Party.* London: Peter Davies, 1932.

SHINWELL, EMANUEL. *Conflict without Malice.* London: Odhams Press, 1955.

SYMONS, JULIAN. *The General Strike.* London: Cresset, 1957.

THOMAS, J. H. *My Story.* London: Hutchinson, 1937.

WATKINS, ERNEST. *The Cautious Revolution.* New York: Farrar, Straus, 1950.

WILLIAMS, FRANCIS. *A Prime Minister Remembers.* London: Heinemann, 1961.

————. *Fifty Years March: Rise of the Labour Party.* London: Odhams Press, n.d.

PROBLEM 6

FRANCE—THE POPULAR FRONT

From the February riots to the

fall of Leon Blum, 1934-37

While Great Britain managed to absorb a socialist onslaught within the framework of democratic government, France underwent a series of crises in the 1930's which sorely tried its republican institutions. The difficulties in France were basically economic, related to reparation payments, the world depression, decline of production, and low wages; but unrest expressed itself politically through large-scale demonstrations of Rightist semimilitary orders, patterned on blackshirt and brownshirt lines, and of Communists and Socialists on the Left. Whether the parliamentary regime, weakened by the continual instability of ministries based on *blocs*, could survive the onslaughts from Right and Left, was the dominating question in the decade preceding World War II. The following series of documents relates to these Rightist and Leftist movements, to the ministerial crises, and to the rise of the Popular Front during the years of agitation, 1934 to 1936.

Two factors constantly influenced the course of French history in the 1930's: economic conditions and the apportionment of seats in the Chamber of Deputies. Pierre-Etienne Flandin, a Left Republican, Prime Minister in 1935, had been Minister of Finance in 1932 and well understood France's financial difficulties. His remarks on economic conditions in France in the 1930's are worth considering. He later participated in Pétain's Vichy government, but was acquitted of collaboration after the war.

FOR CONSIDERATION   Compare French wages in industry with those in the United States, bearing in mind that the cost of living demonstrated no such great differences. Notice the apportionment of seats in the Chamber, that neither Right, Center, nor Left could control a majority, and that a coalition of several groups was necessary to establish a ministry. Would a *bloc* consisting of the Center plus the Socialists be the most logical method of gaining control of the government?

Comments of Former Premier Pierre-Etienne Flandin

The bankruptcy of Germany in 1931, the Hoover moratorium in June, and the depreciation of the pound sterling in September, 1931, brought Europe to a serious economic crisis. After 1931, the index of wholesale prices computed in gold fell, in England, to 98 and, after the devaluation of the pound in 1932, to 73. Later, the United States was forced to devaluate the dollar and in 1933 American wholesale prices went to 75. After a year of fluctuations, British and American wholesale indices levelled off, at the end of 1934, at 63 and 65 respectively. The price-index in gold had thus fallen to less than 50% of its 1928 value. Such a shock was truly catastrophic for the world economy and obviously brought about serious repercussions on the French economy.

If one would understand the political development of our country, he must keep these figures constantly in mind. They are the key to what would otherwise be an undecipherable enigma.

No one can deny that our fiscal system makes the State an associate in all economic activity. By indirect taxes, more than by direct taxes, the Treasury obtains about ⅓ of the profits and gains of all Frenchmen. The fall of wholesale prices, which approximately represent production costs, corresponds thus to a loss in budgetary receipts.

Our maximum governmental income was reached during the fiscal year 1929 . . . with receipts at 53 billion francs. . . . From 1929 to 1934, French wholesale prices fell about 40%. In the same period revenues fell from 53 to 41 billions, a reduction of about 22%. Thus an un-

balanced budget, which became more unbalanced as time went on, developed while the burden of the financial situation became heavier and risked paralyzing business initiative, hampering production, and resulting in dangerous underconsumption.[1]

Statistics Relative to Economic Matters in France

Hourly Earnings of Skilled Labor in Manufacturing[2] (Equivalents in U.S. currency according to exchange rate prevalent at the time)

	Paris		Other Towns	
	francs		francs	
1932	6.34	(25¢)	3.99	(16¢)
1934	6.34	(25¢)	3.89	(15¢)
1936	7.06	(42¢)	4.42	(27¢)
1938	10.67	(31¢)	6.17	(18¢)

Cost of Living Indices in Towns of more than 10,000 (1937 = 100)

1932	94
1934	83
1936	92
1938	100

National Income at Market Prices (in 1000 million francs)

1930	243
1932	206
1934	184
1936	189-200
1938	348 (excluding net income from abroad)

Wholesale Price Indices (1937 = 100)

1928	111
1930	95
1932	74
1934	65
1936	71
1938	112

[1]Pierre-Etienne Flandin, *Discours* (Paris: Editions Gallimard, 1937), pp. 22–24. Quoted by permission of Editions Gallimard, Paris. All rights reserved.

[2]United Nations, *Statistical Yearbook, 1948.*

Results of the Elections of May, 1932

Left	Number of Seats in Chamber of Deputies	Right	Number of Seats in Chamber of Deputies
Communists	12	Popular Democrats	16
Dissident Communists	11	Independent Republicans	28
Socialists	130	Conservatives	5
Dissident Socialists	36	Republicans (Republican-Democratic Union)	76
	189		125
Center			
Radical Socialists	157	Total: 605	
Radicals (*Non-Valoisiens*)	62	Needed for Majority: 303	
Left Republicans	72		
	291		

Throughout 1932 and 1933 ministry followed ministry, and none was able to introduce much-needed economic reforms. At the end of 1932 Camille Chautemps, a Radical Socialist later tried for his association with Pétain in 1940, headed a government made up primarily of Radical Socialists and Socialists. In December the Stavisky Scandal broke. Who was Stavisky? The French Chamber was asking the same question; a Socialist deputy provided an answer.

FOR CONSIDERATION   Lagrange implies that the French Police, and in particular the Chief of Police Jean Chiappe, had been guilty of gross incompetence. Chiappe, an extreme Rightist, was a favorite target of the Socialist and Communist Press, which accused him of fascist leanings. Can the comments of a Socialist about an official on the far Right be accepted by the historian without reservations?

Excerpt from Speech in Chamber of Deputies of M. Lagrange, January 11, 1934

Who was Stavisky? A crook and adventurer whom scandal brought to light for the first time? No! He has been known for a long while. In July, 1915, he went to prison for six months. . . . In July of 1926, on the complaint of M. Labbé, an agent of the National Bank of Credit, he was arrested at Marly-le-Roi under curious circumstances. After a time in prison he appeared for trial in July, 1928. But since December 29, 1927, he had been out on bail. Today, the case has still not been tried. . . . In January, 1928, he found the *Etablissements Alex*; on April 18, 1929, he established the *Compagnie Foncière d'Entreprises Générales de Travaux Publics*: pompous title, important company, brilliant Board of Directors, including a former Prefect of Police, a general, a former high official and a little later, an ambassador from an ill-defined country. (*Very good! Very good! from the Extreme Left.*) . . .

But, gentlemen, alongside of these activities, there was another Stavisky: the man of society, the gambler. He gambled at Cannes..., he owned race horses.... But, while carrying on these pursuits, and meanwhile acquiring a theater, he became interested in pawnshops and municipal treasuries. In 1930— note the date, gentlemen—he was at Orleans: he pawned emeralds, real or imitation, obtaining an advance of several millions. A complaint was followed by an inquiry, and Stavisky paid back the money. He then went to Bayonne where he was going to set up the *Crédit Municipal* fraud.... To float his bonds, Stavisky had to be established in society. He had his own press, his newspapers, his theater. He became Serge Alexandre, a king of Paris. . . . If he could float the Bayonne municipal pawnshop bonds—500 million francs—he could make good the bonds and get away with it. . . . But the whole thing collapsed. His colleague at Bayonne was arrested. Stavisky fled from Paris. A Deputy was arrested. The Police finally found Stavisky at Chamonix. He was dead. And then came the scandal....

How was it possible that a well-known crook, living in "provisional freedom" since 1927, that a gambler with a police record, who was barred from all casinos; how

was it possible that this notorious crook who, we are told, was closely watched by the police and the Sûreté Générale, could have gone on dazzling Paris during six years, and steal millions and millions of francs? It is simply because he found in our principal social organisms—in the police, in the judiciary, in public and private offices, in the Press and in Parliament, a sufficient number of greedy people and a sufficient amount of carelessness and corruption....

And yet we now learn from a press interview that a high official of the police now in retirement, M. Pachot, had been watching Stavisky all the time and that he had drawn up several reports. I ask you what has happened to M. Pachot's reports? Such are the questions, M. le Président, which require an answer. M. Chiappe, returning from Florence, stated that he had been watching Stavisky for ten years, drawing up report after report. If this should be true, what were the pressures which kept the authorities from acting?[3]

---

[3]*Journal Officiel, Débats, Chambre des Députés* (Paris, 1934), Vol. I, pp. 21–22.

Because those government figures who were implicated in the Stavisky Affair came from the Center and the Left, the scandal afforded considerable ammunition to the Right. Rightists, such as Charles Maurras, the articulate leader of the Action Française, saw the government, the parliament, the law courts and the police honeycombed with corrupt and intriguing henchmen of the Premier. Typical of the Rightist position was that of André Tardieu, the veteran politician who had been Clemenceau's right-hand man at Versailles.

FOR CONSIDERATION   Ultimately some 20 persons were arrested and tried in connection with the Stavisky case; 11, including Mme. Stavisky, were acquitted in 1936; of the 9 who received sentences only 2, Bonnaure and Garat, were parliamentarians mentioned by Tardieu. No charges could be sustained against any Cabinet member or against any major political figure. In view of these facts, what sort of interpretation should be given the charges of men like Tardieu?

Comments of Andre Tardieu

Suppose a band of criminals, using public institutions in their work, had confided their interests for ten years to three lawyers of a family prominent in Parliamentary and judicial circles. Suppose that the head of this family had become prime minister, his brothers and cousins were attorneys attached to his office and working under his patronage, and his brother-in-law director of the *Parquet* of the Seine. Suppose, along with them, operating in a similar fashion, were Parliamentary lawyers, in many instances former cabinet ministers or *Gardes des Sceaux*: you would assume that in such a hypothesis reposed a danger for the public interest. Now all this is not a hypothesis. It is the history of the Stavisky Affair. In the service of the principal accused person, in the service of his wife, of his accomplices, of his business, are . . . two young lawyers, MM. Pierre and Robert Chautemps, supported by older men, nearly all of them former ministers and all of them deputies who counsel and argue cases: MM. André Hesse, René Renoult, Bonnaure, Garat, Odin, Proust, Puis, Curral, Julien Durrand, Georges Bonnet; to receive their petitions, the public prosecutor of the Seine, Pressard, always ready to cover up and to prescribe "an extreme prudence"; in the middle, wielding the conductor's baton, the head of the family, the head of the government, M. Camille Chautemps, brother-in-law of the prosecutor, brother and cousin of the two lawyers who carry his name and plead before the bar, M. Camille Chautemps, Premier, Minister of the Interior, Chairman of the Radical Socialist Party.[4]

[4]André Tardieu, *La Révolution à refaire*, Vol. II, *La profession parlementaire* (Paris: Librairie Ernest Flammarion, 1937), pp. 317–31. Quoted by permission of the publishers, Librairie Ernest Flammarion, Paris.

The following newsaper account provides some idea of the agitated emotions evoked by the Stavisky Affair. A verbatim record of this incident can be found in the *Journal Officiel* of the Chamber of Deputies, but it fails to suggest the violence of the occasion. After the session, M. de Monzie fainted in the antechamber. The accusations of Henriot, a Rightist firebrand who delighted in making exaggerated charges, were typical of his political tactics. Paul-Boncour confirmed the fact that he had been Mlle. Simon's lawyer, but maintained that he did not know she had later married Stavisky; no charges were ever made that he had collaborated with Stavisky.

Session of the Chamber of Deputies, January 18, 1934, as Described in the Paris *Herald*

A row of classic proportions . . . broke out in the French Chamber last night, when the Stavisky scandal came up again. . . .

The trouble began when M. Henriot intervened in the discussion of the budget estimates for the judiciary with a vigorous attack upon the government for "attempting to hush up the Stavisky scandal." The speaker followed his general onslaught with a running fire of personal attacks on Georges Bonnet, minister of finance; Eugene Raynaldy, minister of justice; M. de Monzie, minister of education, and M. Paul-Boncour, the foreign minister, for alleged implication in the Stavisky affair.

The sitting became so turbulent that it had to be suspended. When it was resumed, M. Henriot recalled the circumstances surrounding the arrest of Stavisky in 1926, when, after a two-month police hunt, he was found at a villa in Marly-le-Roi, giving a farewell dinner to his friends before fleeing the country.

Among the friends present at the banquet was Mlle. Arlette Simon, the present Mme. Stavisky, who was hurt in a fight with police at the villa and was removed to a clinic after arrest. "Two men only were allowed to see the woman Simon then," the Bordeaux deputy shouted amid a tumultuous hubbub, "and those two are now sitting on the government bench." "Names, names!" the Chamber roared.

"I am ready to give the names to a magistrate," M. Henriot replied. "No doubt they went to see her as lawyers." "Names, names," the deputies again shouted in chorus. "I dare say," the deputy continued, "that M. Pachot (a police official) could name them, and would designate M. de Monzie and M. Paul-Boncour. That is a serious matter, even if the two ministers went to see her as lawyers."

Here pandemonium was let loose.... Amid the turmoil only the stentorian voice of Renaud Jean, the Communist deputy, was heard, "You are all in the same boat," he shouted. "You are all rotten to the core. Long live the Soviets! To the garbage can with all of you!"[5]

------

[5]*New York Herald* (Paris edition), January 19, 1934. Reprinted by permission of the *New York Herald Tribune*.

T he attacks against Prime Minister Chautemps provoked his resignation on January 27, 1934. His was the first Cabinet to resign under pressure of public opinion, without first receiving an adverse vote in the Chamber.

Comments of Foreign Minister Paul-Boncour

M. Chautemps had succeeded M. Sarraut, who had succeeded M. Daladier, who had succeeded me. In spite of his skill, which was considerable, his oratorical talent, which was no less, a mastery of corridor politics, and even though votes of confidence had concluded the repeated questionings he had undergone during an affair which should have remained a strictly legal question, M. Chautemps felt that the danger was increasing. Perhaps greater firmness in the street and more brutality at the rostrum would have been better. In any event his majority

continued to hold; it remained constant up to the last debate. I don't know, or rather I know only too well, why, from the very heart of his cabinet, M. Chautemps was persuaded to refuse a Commission of Inquiry, under pretext of governmental prestige, and to resign, under pretext of appeasement. This was the opposite of what he should have done: accept the one and refuse the other; bring everything out into the open, which could only disturb a few supernumeraries, leaving intact the republican heads they were out for, and not give in to portfolio seekers who wanted to chalk up another fall of government. We were too few to maintain this point of view when we discussed it at our last meeting. Feeling that he received little encouragement from his own colleagues, injured by a personal campaign which tried to smear his entire family and which raged against a magistrate, later dead from these attacks, he tendered the resignation of his government to the President of the Republic.[6]

[6]Joseph Paul-Boncour, *Entre deux guerres* (Paris: Librairie Plon, 1945), Vol. II, pp. 298–99. Quoted by permission of the publishers, Librairie Plon, Paris; all rights reserved.

Another Radical Socialist, Edouard Daladier, succeeded Chautemps on February 3. His ministry lasted four days. He concluded that the Stavisky matter necessitated a thorough housecleaning and decided to remove the Chief of Police, Chiappe, from office. According to Daladier, Chiappe threatened to start a riot in the street (*dans la rue*); according to Chiappe, he merely said that he would be in the street out of a job (*à la rue*). In any event, Rightist organizations like the Action Française, the Croix de Feu, the Camelots du Roi, sympathetic with Chiappe, called for street demonstrations against the government; the result was the famous Riot of February 6. After the riots, the Chamber of Deputies established a Commission of Inquiry into the events of February 6, which investigated the affair.

FOR CONSIDERATION   Historians have questioned whether this demonstration was truly a fascist uprising with a coordinated plan for overthrowing the government. Although there is some evidence for this view, most writers would probably share the opinion of Eugen Weber that "there was no plan of united action among the different leagues, and there was no single group that could seriously have hoped to take power by itself."[7]

Testimony of M. Chiappe

The Prime Minister (Daladier) . . . said: "Chiappe, I am going to appeal to you as the good citizen and good Frenchman you are. I am asking you to carry on the heritage of Marshal Lyautey in Morocco." Then I answered: "The very thought of succeeding Marshal Lyautey in Morocco fills me with pride, embarrassment and deep emotion. But under the present circumstances I cannot leave Paris, I cannot leave my post." . . . But M. Daladier continued: "You must accept." I replied: "There is no use continuing like this. No matter what post you offer me, no matter what reason you give for offering it to me, I cannot leave Paris. I know —I feel it—you will probably run me out of the Prefecture de Police, the prefecture to which I and my wife have devoted seven years of our lives. Well, never mind! I entered the Prefecture a rich man and I leave it poor; I shall be in the street (*à la rue*), perhaps unhappy, but honest." . . .[8]

[7]*Action Française* (Stanford, Calif.: Stanford University Press, 1962), pp. 332–33.

[8]*Rapport général fait au nom de la Commission d'Enquête chargée de rechercher les causes et les origines des Evénements du 6 Février 1934, Annexes* (Paris: Imprimerie de la Chambre des Deputés, 1934), Vol. I, pp. 170–71. (Hereafter cited as *Evénements du 6 Février.*)

Testimony of M. Daladier

I then asked to be put in touch by telephone with M. Chiappe as I wished to ask him to come and see me. It was more than a quarter of an hour before Chiappe deigned to come to the phone. M. Bressot said that Chiappe was not able to answer the phone because he was tired and suffering from sciatica. At any rate it was over a quarter of an hour before I could get in touch with Chiappe. I entreated him to come by car and see me immediately. Chiappe answered that he was sick in bed, and could not be disturbed. That being the case I had to discuss the matter by telephone.

The conversation went more rapidly than Chiappe's testimony would seem to indicate, and its tone—at least at one end of the wire—was very sharp, violent, and irritable. . . . I spoke to him about the Governorship of Morocco, and pointed out that it was an extremely important post. . . . No sooner had I approached the subject when I received the categorical and brutal reply: "No, never, I refuse, you are trying to dishonor me." . . . And when I appealed to Chiappe's civic duty, reminding him at the same time that the Government had a perfect right to transfer officials, he answered: "I refuse, you will find me in the street (*dans la rue*)."[9]

Appeal to the People of Paris by the *Action Française*, February 6, 1934

Called to power in the hope that they would restore justice and order, MM. Daladier and Frot commenced their work by running out the policemen, thus giving free rein to Socialist anarchy and saving the Masonic thieves. In trying to force this abject regime on us, in trying to smother the voice of public indignation,

MM. Daladier and Frot are hurling violent threats at decent people, which they must do because they are frightened and have a bad conscience. They hope to have things their own way. What do they take Frenchmen for?

The people of France will react to this ignominious challenge. In defiance of corrupt public authorities they will assert their own rights. After the factories and offices are closed they will meet before the Chamber tonight and crying "Down with the Thieves!" they will tell the Government and its parliamentary supporters that they have had enough of this abject regime.[10]

Chamber of Deputies Meeting of February 6, 1934, as Witnessed by Alexander Werth

When the President announced that the Premier would "make a communication to the Chamber," there was a wild uproar on the same benches. Never, in all the history of Parliament, had a Premier been howled down before he had even read the Ministerial Declaration. M. Daladier did not seem to have thought that things would be quite so bad. He mounted the tribune with a sour look and began:

"During the past month, the scandal which arose from the fault of certain individuals . . ."

This was already too much for the Opposition. They roared and laughed and M. Henriot shouted: "No, not only individuals!"

Daladier continued, in spite of the noise: "Sharp antagonism between the parties . . . Parliament demoralised . . . vigilance of the Republicans. . . ." There was another outburst of noise from the Right. ". . . We cannot escape from this stifling atmosphere unless we throw the fullest light on this affair, with unrelenting

---

[9]*Ibid.*, p. 271.

[10]*Action Francaise*, February 6, 1934.

energy and courage." (Ironical laughter on the Right.)—"The Government"—M. Daladier continued in the midst of the infernal din—"has already begun its work. It was formed a week ago, and wishes to be judged on the strength of its first acts."

"Don't worry, we have judged you already!" the Right roared.

"You will tell us whether we have done well. . . ."

"The Country has already told you!" the Opposition cried.

". . . to have restored the authority of the Republican State . . ." More roars.

"While the Committee of Inquiry . . ."

"*Vivent les Soviets!*" the Communists cried.

". . . While the Committee of Inquiry, composed of representatives of all parties makes sure that all the truth becomes known, Parliament should return to its normal duties."

The pandemonium became worse than ever. The Left rose to their feet and cheered, the Opposition shouted inarticulately; there were cries of "Resign!" the Communists began their rhythmical chant —*Les Soviets partout! les Soviets partout!*— "What a zoo, what a zoo!" an old journalist in the Press gallery remarked, shaking his head.

Daladier leaned against the back of the tribune, waiting for the storm to subside. But it went from bad to worse. The Communists then began to sing the "Internationale": a free fight was about to start round M. Frot at the foot of the tribune, and the President could do no more than suspend the sitting.

Never before had a sitting been suspended in the middle of a Ministerial Declaration. There was no doubt about it: the Opposition had made up their minds to obstruct and sabotage the sitting. It is true that when it was resumed five minutes later, they let Daladier read the rest of his Declaration in comparative quiet. "The Budget must be voted before March 31st . . . the peasant is wondering how he

will sell his crops . . . scandals come and go, but the great problems remain . . . France's will for peace and security . . . faithful to the League of Nations . . ."— God! it all sounded so flat, so unreal; what did the League of Nations matter at a moment when thousands of people were beginning to crowd into the Place de la Concorde?

"To carry out this work, we need a majority . . ."

"You've got one!" the Opposition cried, pointing to the Socialists.

In conclusion, Daladier said something about "our fathers who in more troubled times than these, had the energy to defend the democratic order . . . progress . . . freedom . . . democracy . . ."

"Mee-ow!" the Opposition replied.[11]

The Riot of February 6, 1934, Described by Joseph Kessel

I went down [toward the Place de la Concorde] cocking my ear anxiously at a low sound, which began to rumble at the foot of the avenue. Then flames flickered over a mass of confused forms. I quickened my pace. At the square there were men running. A youth, head bleeding, stumbled into a comrade's arms.

"Night sticks," cried the latter with hysterical emphasis. "But that's nothing. *They fired!*"

The more I pushed through this crowd aroused with indignation, tremendous stupefaction and unspeakable fury, and in which workers, amputees, employees, students were all mixed together, the more I understood the incomprehensible words: "They fired!"

Everyone was giving details, atrociously precise.

"I saw three of them fall."

[11]Alexander Werth, *France in Ferment* (New York: Harper & Bros., 1940), pp. 147–48. Reprinted by permission of Harper & Row, Publishers.

"He was carried off, shot in the head."

"It's the Guards."

"He collapsed holding his stomach with his hands."

"It's a massacre."

The sidewalks were littered with pieces of railings, bolts, twisted benches. The outlines of barricades stretched one after the other, lamp-posts torn up, kiosks knocked over, sections of pavement turned on end. . . .

.   .   .   .   .

Arriving at the Place de la Concorde, I slid through the barriers. There, I saw a scene which will never be erased from my memory.

A heavy column of smoke spiralled above the noblest and best-proportioned area that men have ever laid out in a city. Near the Obelisk an autobus had just burned. Already its carcass looked black, hideous. Blood was spattered on the ground. Broken street-lights, remnants of shelters for pedestrians, lay under the immobile regard of the great statues, their white outlines blurred in the darkness.

Policemen were massed in the middle of the square. All around the helmets of the *Garde Mobile* glistened. And, drawn up in strict order, the horses' heads were outlined, the riders' plumes floating in the air.

Against this human bulwark charged a howling mob. You could hear:

"Murderers!"

"Long live Chiappe!"

"We're not afraid of you!"

Then you could hear the noise of a charge, of a skirmish. New cries went up even though, on the magnificent facades, remained the glare of several untouched searchlights.

Near the bridge which led to the Chamber, goal of the whole riot, I met some newspapermen.

"I thought the defense was going to be swept away," one of them said to me. "Veterans, members of the Croix de Feu,

camelots du roi [Royalists] and even Communists, furious, broke the police barriers, threw the *Garde Mobile* into confusion, unhorsed the municipal policemen, hamstrung their mounts and forced the entrance to the bridge. Then the *Mobile* lost its head and fired. Finally reinforcements cleaned up the square."

I listened, stupefied, incredulous. I simply could not grasp the real, living picture of this deed which, however, a thousand tongues repeated: armed men had opened fire on their unarmed countrymen.[12]

Official Conclusions of the Commission of Inquiry into the Events of February 6

On Fascist Organizations

There does not exist in France at this time any political group having a military or semi-military character in the sense that it is actively preparing for military service or war. Groups do exist however which by their authoritarian organization, their discipline, their orientation, and by the virtually absolute power of their leaders, constitute powerful organs which through politically-oriented manifestations in the street, can endanger the public order.

On the Removal of Chiappe from Office

As M. Chiappe's leaving the Prefecture of Police had an important bearing on the demonstrations, the Commission has examined the conditions under which he left office and finds: A Government coming to power has the right, through legal procedures, to transfer high officials. . . . The Lescouve, Plytas and Mossé reports, to which M. Daladier had access on February 2, showed that following the Stavisky Affair detailed investigations of the Par-

---

[12]Joseph Kessel, *Stavisky, l'homme que j'ai connu* (Paris: Editions Gallimard, 1934), pp. 150–54. Quoted by permission of the publishers.

quet, the Sûreté Générale and the Prefecture of Police were required. M. Daladier indicated to his cabinet that . . . it was necessary to reorganize and renovate these services and that, in his opinion, this could be accomplished only under conditions which entailed the removal of the administrative chiefs. M. Daladier's decision, on February 3, to remove these three department heads was a consequence of these reports; the Commission hereby states that the decisions were unrelated to any deal with representatives of the Socialist Party.

On the Use of Firearms on February 6

(Questions and Opinions of the Commission)

Were machine guns, sub-machine guns, rifles or carbines fired at any time by the Police? (No; unanimous)

Did the government give the order to fire on the demonstrators? (No; unanimous of those voting; three abstentions)

Did the Police, *Gardes Mobiles,* and *Gardes Républicains* fire spontaneously on the demonstrators? (Yes; unanimous)

Did violence and assault provoke the Police before the firing from 7:30 to 8:00 p.m.? (Yes; unanimous)

Were cease and desist orders given before the firing? (Yes; unanimous)

Were these orders associated with the firing and given just before? (No; unanimous)

Did the demonstrators fire pistol shots before the first Police volley? (Fourteen members of the Commission approved the statement: "Rather numerous shots from small arms were fired at the Police by the crowd before any general firing by the Police.")

On the Extent of Casualties from Gunfire

Fourteen civilians died from bullet wounds.

One policeman died from a violent blow, possibly from a piece of metal.

82 civilians were wounded by bullets. . . .

Two *Gardes Mobiles* were wounded by bullets.

On the Casualties to Horses of the Gardes Mobiles:

Most of the casualties came from projectiles of various sorts (pieces of metal, glass, fence-posts, pavement, sheet iron, etc.). Certain wounds—to the number of nine—appeared to have been inflicted by razor blades attached to the ends of sticks. . . . There were no casualties from bullets.[13]

———

[13]*Evénements du 6 Février,* pp. 92–99, 106–07.

Faced with tremendous popular resentment, the Daladier Cabinet resigned on February 7. The venerable Radical Socialist Gaston Doumergue, who had been Premier before World War I, came out of retirement to form a "nationalist" government based on a coalition of Rightist groups. Several days later the Communists and Socialists protested by calling a one-day general strike.

Official Report on the General Strike of February 12, 1934

The General Strike of February 12 was decided upon and organized by the General Confederation of Labor (C.G.T.) to reaffirm the unions' will to defend their fundamental liberties and to oppose attempts at dictatorship.

The *Conféderation Générale du Travail Unitaire* also invited its members to participate.

The Socialist Party, the Communist Party, the *Parti d'Unité Proletarienne*, *L'Union Anarchiste* [and five other leftist groups] also invited their members to participate.

The strike order was completely carried out in industrial centers; partly carried out in rural centers.

Numerous civil employees took part in the movement.

The General Strike came off quietly in Paris and the provinces. However, incidents developed at Marseilles, in the North and in the Paris suburbs, where they assumed an unusual gravity.[14]

[14]*Evénements du 6 Février*, p. 112.

The February demonstrations intensified the antagonisms between Left and Right. This conflict was marked by the development of semimilitary organizations on the Right and by a tendency toward coalition, as indicated by the Socialist-Communist Pact of July, 1934, on the Left.

Not least among the weapons used on both sides was the political poster, a common sight on every street corner of Paris. Two typical posters from the collection of the Bibliothèque Nationale, Paris, are here reproduced. The Francists, a relatively small Rightist group founded by Marcel Bucart, attempted to wean workers away from the Communist Party, using a vulgar language which does not easily lend itself to translation. The League of the Rights of Man was a Leftist group which later joined the Popular Front. The Croix de Feu, led by Colonel de la Rocque, came closest of all the military groups to Hitler's brownshirts.

Political Poster of the Rightist Semi-military Organization, the Francists

AH! THE FILTHY SCUM!

Comrades in factory, office and field

They are playing you all for suckers

.   .   .   .   .

They try to persuade you that the people's paradise is Soviet Russia when the U.S.S.R. is the most imperialistic, the most militaristic, the most nationalistic country in the world.

THEY ARE USING YOU

to "springboard" or to put in the "gravy" a certain number of hail fellows who claim to be "revolutionaries" when they are quite

simply trustees of capitalistic interests or secret agents of the financial feudal system or exploiters of human misery.

WORKERS!

The Socialist and Communist Parties lie to you and deceive you odiously

THEY WERE INCAPABLE OF BRINGING ABOUT A SOCIAL REVOLUTION

.   .   .   .   .

They are the dirty pigs of International Capitalism

.   .   .   .   .

COME TO FRANCISM

—to throw "all that" in the garbage can or in the brig.

—to bring about total Revolution.

—to bring it about that, willing or not, the "big shots" and the "liberal bourgeoisie," forgetful of their social role, should hold themselves to the law of the general interest and should work for the Nation.

—to create in peace, justice and order, the TRUE FRENCH REPUBLIC.

THE FRANCIST WORKERS

Political Poster of a Leftist Organization, the League of the Rights of Man

For honesty and
        liberty in opposition to Fascism
AN APPEAL

of the League of the Rights of Man to the People of France

Blood has run, and it is terrible that so shortly after the war men should still be killing men.

Bands of the Action Française and Young Patriots, fanatically aroused by abominable agitators and supported by the Croix de Feu, are alone responsible, in all human conscience, for the slaughter of February 6.

The League of the Rights of Man sadly affirms that under the sign of Fascism a Government has been established which calls itself a Government of National Union.

But, along with the Royalists and Fascists who wanted to install a Hitlerian regime in France with gunfire, there are thousands of good people who wanted, and believed in, a demonstration for honesty in opposition to the thieves.

To these good people, the League of the Rights of Man cries: They deceived you!

.   .   .   .   .

This is why the League of the Rights of Man asks:

1st—that there be formed a Government of unquestionably honest men, a Government which would throw light on things and make quick justice, without any consideration of persons or parties;

2nd—that all the political parties, beginning with the parties of the Left, should carry out without pity or delay a moral housecleaning.

. . . . .

With all the Republicans, the League cries, against all scoundrels and all Fascists: *Honesty! Liberty!*

A Croix de Feu Meeting, June 29, 1934, as Described by Alexander Werth

The people were neither rowdy nor stupid like the Solidarité Française. They were earnest, well-disciplined and, on the whole, decent-looking people. The elder men, the real Croix de Feu, wore tricolor armlets decorated with a fiery cross with a skull in the centre. . . .

What class did these people belong to? Except for a few ostentatiously proletarian-looking old men—some of them with wooden legs—stationed in front of the platform, nearly all these people were middle class and, I should say, upper middle class. The young people were of the *fils de famille* or University student type—a well-dressed and a well-washed crowd.

. . . . . .

[The speakers] spoke about recruiting new members among the working classes; the Communist Party, they said, was a gang of criminals—*qui se ressemble, s'assemble;* there might be some good fellows among them, but they must be won over, and effective resistance against the Communists must be organized; the friends of Stavisky and the murderers of Prince were still living on the fat of the land; Freemasonry was a plague; when all culprits were punished, the Constitution must be revised; a pure wind had passed over France on February 6; the voice of France must be heard; a change had come over France since February 6, when the Croix de Feu saved the country. . . .

And then there was a sudden commotion in the audience, "La Rocque! La Rocque! La Rocque!" Pushing his way through the crowd La Rocque stepped briskly on to the platform. He greeted the audience with a charming smile and a wave of the hand. He was far less like Hitler than like a lieutenant of the *Ancien Régime*. Uncle Toby must have met many men in Flanders who looked like La Rocque. Such was the first impression of the *Chef* of the Croix de Feu.

He was not an orator: He began,

Mesdames, Mesdemoiselles, mes chers amis, I am glad to see that so many of you have come. . . . You are Frenchmen of the front line. You must know that you belong to an immense force, independent of any party. Before there is a new order of things, an end must be put to disorder, and the idea of authority must be restored. The men of the United Front who call us rioters, reason like Asiatics. We stand above little party combinations and electoral intrigues. We are patriots among patriots, *nous sommes des sociaux parmi les sociaux.* All that I want to tell you is this: be on your guard, always be ready to do your duty. Your duty is to serve France. Do it without any personal ambition, in the name of honour and security, for your own sake and for the sake of your children.[15]

United Action Pact between Socialists and Communists, July 27, 1934

The General Committee of the Communist Party and the Permanent Administrative Committee of the Socialist Party are determined to beat Fascism. . . . In view of the Fascist danger arising from the organized attacks by armed gangs upon the proletariat, the Socialist and Communist Parties recognize the necessity of a common plan of action. . . .

1. The Communist and Socialist Parties sign this pact of united action, and agree to organize a joint campaign with the following ends in view:

---

[15]Werth, *op. cit.,* pp. 275-77.

(*a*) To mobilize the entire working population against the Fascist organizations, which must be disarmed and disbanded.

(*b*) To defend democratic liberties. . . .

(*c*) To prevent the preparation for war.

(*d*) To abolish the decree-laws.

(*e*) To combat the Fascist terror in Germany and Austria . . .

2. This campaign will be conducted by means of joint meetings in the largest possible number of places. . . . If in the course of it the members of one of the parties comes to grips with Fascists, the members of the other will come to their assistance.

3. In the course of this joint campaign the two parties will refrain from attacking and criticizing those of each other's members and organizations. . . .[16]

[16]*Le Populaire*, July 28, 1934. Quoted by permission.

Doumergue and his Rightist adherents believed that the country's difficulties could be blamed on the French Constitution, which hampered the Prime Minister's freedom of action. He appealed to the country in a series of radio broadcasts but, failing to obtain popular support, his ministry fell in November, 1934, to be succeeded by a new government formed by Pierre-Etienne Flandin.

Excerpt from Radio Address of Premier Doumergue, September 24, 1934

The most urgent thing, in the present regime, and especially under the present circumstances, is to have an authoritative government. We do not have one. There may be some of you who will say that, in a parliamentary and democratic regime there cannot be a government with authority. I do not agree with this.

.   .   .   .   .   .

In France the head of the government, who is called the *Président du Conseil,* is only a fiction. He has no special authority, and is not mentioned in the Constitution. Both legally and in fact he is similar to any other Minister, without adequate authority over Parliament. In our country governments do not last long: They have no homogeneous majority; for there are too many parties. They can be overthrown for the slightest reason; and nothing ever happens to those who participate in such assassinations. . . .

Let us give the government authority by putting several words into the Consti-

tution, which would provide the head of the government with the title and rights of a Prime Minister. Let us permit the Prime Minister, when the government disagrees with the majority of the Chamber, to appeal immediately to the country without having to go through the present formalities and procedures. A small modification of the Constitution will suffice; except in a few clearly indicated situations when the preliminary authority of the Senate, which has rendered such great services to the Republic, will be necessary. You can be assured that cabinet crises will become rare when the fear of immediate dissolution will put a brake on impatient and usually unjustifiable ambitions, which are more frequently at the bottom of such crises than a conflict of principles and ideas.[17]

Comments of Prime Minister Pierre-Etienne Flandin

The governmental coalition formed by M. Doumergue broke up over the ques-

[17]*Documents politiques* (1934), pp. 528–29.

tion of constitutional reform proposed by M. Doumergue. M. Herriot and the Radical-Socialist ministers withdrew from the Government. My task was to immediately regroup the coalition by postponing constitutional reform, but without losing the support of the conservative elements. I was unable to obtain that of M. Tardieu and his friends of the extreme right who were making a question of principle out of the immediate reform of the constitution. But I kept that of M. Marin and the moderate republicans. My ministry was formed between noon and midnight—which was a record under the Third Republic. Having thus been able to keep public order well in hand, the demonstrations which were anticipated in the same circles as those which had organized the activities of February 6, did not take place. The resignation of M. Doumergue provoked no disorders in the streets. All the same, I had to sustain subsequently the permanent hostility of M. Tardieu, of M. Franklin-Bouillon, reconciled, of Colonel de la Rocque and of the French Social Party, and of all elements outside of Parliament who, from this time, had begun to fight against the Third Republic and Parliamentarism.[18]

[18]Pierre-Etienne Flandin, *Politique française, 1919–1940* (Paris: Nouvelles Editions Latines 1947), p. 169, n. Quoted by permission of Nouvelles Editions Latines, publishers, Paris.

Throughout the history of the Third Republic ministries came and went with disconcerting rapidity. Although in many instances the fall of a cabinet affected neither the general policy nor the day-to-day workings of governmental administration, these frequent collapses nevertheless did nothing to enhance the prestige or the power of the French government. It has therefore seemed worthwhile to examine in some detail, as a test case, the circumstances leading to the fall of a cabinet. The collapse of the Flandin Ministry, exemplifying an interplay of political rivalries, the instability of the *bloc* system, and the pressure of financial influences, provides such an example. Behind Flandin's fall stood the opposition of the Bank of France, the conservative, privately controlled institution, established by Napoleon, which refused to support Flandin's financial policy. The comments on the Bank which follow appeared in *La Flèche,* a moderate Left journal representing the opinions of Gaston Bergery's "Common Front," a movement opposed to communism, fascism and the influence of financial cartels. (Bergery associated himself with Pétain during the war, was later imprisoned but acquitted in 1949.)

Excerpt from an Anti-capitalist Article, "Who Controls the Bank of France Controls the Trusts," by Francis Delaisi, February 1, 1936

The Regents of the Bank of France are at once judge and plaintiff. Six of them are themselves heads of private banks: the houses of Rothschild, Mallet, Mirabaud, Hottinguer, de Neuflize, Vernes (temporarily replaced by the *Banque Lazard*). Besides, they control, either by themselves or through their sons and brothers, 21 other banks, . . . through which they can rediscount their own notes and always ensure their solvency. They direct 17 transportation and shipping companies (including five railway lines), of which none shows a deficit. Let us add 43 industries, among which are the great steel corporations (*Creusot, Etablissements de Wendel*), chemical concerns (*Saint-Gobain, Kuhlmann*), and various utilities companies. Finally, there are eight insurance firms (*Phénix, Nation, Union, Providence*, etc.), most of which are embarrassed by depreciation of buildings constructed with their reserves, and now without tenants.

All these enterprises live only through orders and subsidies from the State; all, after four years of depression, need credit from the Bank of France. They would be very humble before these two powers except that by an extraordinary coincidence they themselves run the monetary institution on which their lives depend! Better yet. As the State also depends on the Bank to meet its deficits, by controlling the Bank they control the State and can dictate to it on their own terms. Every time that the Chamber overthrows a Ministry, the man designated by the President of the Republic to form a new cabinet must first of all, according to tradition, "consult with his friends," not least among which are the Regents, whom he must ask whether they are willing to advance the funds to cover his "first-of-the-month bills." If they refuse, he renounces the mission the Head of State has entrusted to him. Generally they agree quite readily, but on condition that he does not interfere with war contracts or naval appropriations indispensable to their steel and chemical concerns, nor with their shipping subsidies, nor with the high interest rate of the Treasury Bonds which ensures the banks' profits.[19]

Statement Released by the Bank of France, 1935

The Bank of France will rediscount public notes, but within such limits that

it will never find itself in the position of having effected an appreciation of the State's credit. It will maintain control of its own rediscounting. Its credit, that is to say of the franc, and on the other hand the credit of the State, that is, the quality of its bonds, belong to two distinct categories. M. Flandin's government has done some things which may be considered praiseworthy. The Budget was voted early enough. It has shown good sense in opposing the abolition of the economy decrees. Its economic measures—although somewhat less certain—deserve nevertheless a "satisfactory grade," when the difficulties of the situation are considered. M. Flandin has been rewarded for this grade in the form of credit facilities. These may not prove to be enough. He may ask for more. Our response will then depend on the extent to which we are satisfied with the government's actions during the first respite we have granted as a reward for its present determination to defend the currency.[20]

Pro-Doumergue Political Poster of the National Republicans

THE REPUBLIC IS DONE FOR IF . . .

The present parliamentary regime slides into anarchy.

.   .   .   .   .

IT IS NECESSARY TO REESTABLISH AUTHORITY IN THE STATE.

To restore authority in the State, it is necessary to reform the electoral law and the Constitution from top to bottom.

1st—By changing the abominable system of balloting twice by wards which lends itself to every sort of scandal and corruption. On a rotten electoral base, nothing fitting or proper can be achieved.

2nd—By granting to the Premier, in the Constitution, the right of dissolution. This

[19]*La Flèche*, February 1, 1936.

[20]*La Flèche*, February 1, 1936.

LA RÉPUBLIQUE EST FICHUE SI...

Le régime parlementaire actuel glisse dans l'anarchie. Les partis politiques sont débordés par les clans, les clubs, certains syndicats révolutionnaires. Les intérêts privés se coalisent contre l'intérêt national. Le parlement paralysé n'aboutit plus à rien, et surtout le gouvernement ne gouverne plus.

Les partis républicains nationaux sont unanimes à dire qu'une chose pareille ne peut pas durer.

IL FAUT RESTAURER L'AUTORITÉ DANS L'ÉTAT.

Les notabilités politiques les plus diverses l'ont reconnu. Le président Doumergue, M. Jeanneney, président du Sénat, M. Maurice Ordinaire, président de l'Union Républicaine du Sénat. M. Caillaux, M. Lamoureux, etc.... etc...

Pour restaurer l'autorité dans l'Etat, il faut réformer la loi électorale et la Constitution de fond en comble.

1° - En changeant l'abominable mode de scrutin d'arrondissement à deux tours qui prête à tous les scandales et à toutes les corruptions. — Sur une base électorale pourrie, on ne peut rien faire de solide et de propre.

2° - En accordant au Président du Conseil, dans la constitution, le droit de dissolution. C'est le système anglais qui a fait ses preuves depuis des siècles.

Depuis la révolution française aucun régime politique n'a duré soixante ans en France ! Il ne faut pas s'étonner que notre République soit vieille. Il faut la rénover, la transformer, changer dans le système politique ce qui est usé, brisé, inutilisable.

SINON, CE SERA BIENTOT
L'ODIEUSE DICTATURE OU LA RÉVOLUTION !

is the English system which has proved itself for centuries.

Since the French Revolution no political system has lasted sixty years in France. It should not astonish anyone that our Republic is decrepit. We must renovate her, transform her, change everything in the political system which is out-of-date, worn out, or unusable.

IF NOT, THERE WILL SOON BE A NASTY DICTATORSHIP OR A REVOLUTION!

Comments of Former Premier Pierre-Etienne Flandin

To lower interest rates M. Germain-Martin, Finance Minister, and M. Tannery, who was named Governor of the Bank of France to carry out this policy, had agreed that for several months the Treasury would refrain from seeking long term loans on the open market. . . . As the Treasury, whose revenues were at this time near the low-water mark, urgently needed funds, it had been agreed that the Bank of France . . . would help the Treasury borrow the necessary disposable funds on the financial market so that it could meet its obligations. I never deceived myself into thinking that this policy was devoid of certain risks, and I knew that it should be practiced with great prudence. But it was certainly less dangerous than a policy of direct advances from the Bank, which my successors employed. Loans on the open market, which I then planned, would not have amounted to 5 billions. Since then, direct loans from the Bank have added up to 20 billions.

If financial orthodoxy influenced the Bank of France's Regents, in January and February, 1935, to thwart the policy my Government wished to follow, I should think that, after the experience with the deflation policies of Laval and the "reflaiton" of Blum, they might regret having refused to lend me their assistance.

Even then, when this policy was first announced, it brought about some favorable economic consequences. . . . But, it soon appeared that the interest of the State did not square with certain private interests. I was probably wrong in proclaiming that fact in a speech. Thereafter opposition increased daily. Unable to obtain the Bank of France's indispensable cooperation, the Treasury had to turn indirectly to the market, through loans backed by the credit of the national railroads, colonial governments and the City of Paris. . . . On the Bank of France's final statement for March, 1935, it showed that gold reserves had risen to 82,634 millions, a figure only surpassed in 1932. . . . Early in May, when I was ready to request exceptional powers from Parliament, so that I could override a certain opposition in economic and financial circles, I was badly injured in an automobile accident. At the same time speculation started. The pretext was the result of the municipal elections which, while they provided a Communist landslide around Paris, were for the most part favorable to the republican groupings, more or less comparable to the bloc which formed the Government. But the opposition, allying themselves with the devaluation enthusiasts, whose zeal suddenly increased, helped promote a great drain of capital and speculation on the fall of the franc which, within several weeks, depleted the gold reserves of the Bank of France by about 10 billion francs.

Wishing to leave my successor free to choose his own monetary policy, I did my best to argue for the full powers which I knew would be refused me, but which could possibly be accorded to a new Government.[21]

Results of the Municipal Elections of May 5 and 12, 1935[22]

Major Parties (Controlling Majorities in More Than 57 of the Communes with More Than 5000 Inhabitants)	Total Number of Municipal Councils in Which a Majority Is Held	Change from Previous Situation	
		Gains	Losses
Communists	90	52	9
Socialists	168	32	39
Radical Socialists	221	57	61
Left Republicans	145	40	51
Democratic Republicans	99	20	35

Debate in the Chamber of Deputies, May 28, 1935

M. GERMAIN-MARTIN, *Minister of Finances* (Left Radical): . . . The situation, while serious, can be rectified. But to do that prompt decisions must be made. . . . If you refuse to understand both the ex-

tent of the danger and the urgency of the remedy, I wonder how, tomorrow, a Minister of Finances could resist an attack on the franc and on public credit. I have elaborated on the whole situation, simply and sincerely. I hope I have convinced you of the need of voting confidence, not just to certain men, but to the Government, which is charged with the country's interests. . . .

M. LÉON BLUM (Socialist): The Finance Minister invites the Parliament to defend the national currency. . . . But who is attacking the franc? Why is it attacked? Since when has it been attacked? What are the secret but basic reasons for this attack? And what determined the circumstances and the moment chosen for this attack? (Applause from Extreme Left and several Left benches.) . . . The budget deficit is no novelty. We knew that there would be a budget deficit the moment we voted it. The Treasury's embarrassment is chronic, but has been more serious in the last two weeks than before. And you knew it was inevitable when you failed to get the Bank of France to rediscount your Treasury bonds. (Applause from Extreme Left and from several Left and Center benches.) . . . You have told us, *Monsieur le Ministre des Finances*, with an emotion which we feel deeply . . . that the whole edifice would be threatened, perhaps ruined. Who, I ask you, put the stick of dynamite there?

M. PHILIPPE HENRIOT (Republican): The Common Front!

M. LÉON BLUM: We face a veritable speculative blaze. Who ignited it? I ask the question, but if I had to, I would find the answer and an admission in your speech. You said that the drain on gold began on May 13, after the municipal elections.

M. PHILIPPE HENRIOT: Because you destroyed confidence! (Exclamations from the Extreme Left.)

M. LÉON BLUM: The drain on gold began on May 13. I noted the figures. There

---

[21]Flandin, *Discours*, pp. 34–37.
[22]Released to the Press by the Ministry of the Interior, May 13, 1935.

are big jumps. May 11, 36,000,000 in gold withdrawals; the 13th, more than 200. Since then the rate has increased as you know. Was this a surprise? For a month we have been able to denounce this developing plot and warn public opinion and Parliament that, for the next session, you could look to a financial panic for reprisals against the election results. (Applause from Extreme Left and numerous Left benches.) . . . We are in the presence of a real conspiracy against . . . the Government, as well as against the Parliament and the sovereign will of the country. What is happening now is the same thing that happened in 1924 and 1925, M. Herriot, and what happened just before the general elections of 1932. . . .

M. PHILIPPE HENRIOT: Take over! Try to reform the Cartel.[23]

Debate in the Chamber of Deputies, May 30, 1935

M. ARTHUR RAMETTE (Communist): . . . Gentlemen, it is clear. The Full Powers that are requested are only a preface . . . to a violent political reaction and Fascism. The re-entrance of M. Tardieu, the activity of devaluation proponents like M. Paul Reynaud, his former lieutenant, the agitation undertaken by the Fascist leagues and their top leader, M. Chiappe, are indications of the direction French capitalistic policy is taking. . . . This policy of deflation has not been adopted simply to balance the budget. Labor's wages have been reduced considerably while the amount of production per worker has constantly risen. . . . The results of this policy have been the misery of the urban and rural proletariat, the ruin and bankruptcy of the small peasant and the small businessman. . . .

[23]*Journal Officiel, Débats, Chambre des Députés* (1935), Vol. II, pp. 1674–75.

The economists subsidized by Capital admit that the national income has decreased in considerable proportions. M. Dessirer, for example, estimates that the national income has decreased in the period 1930–1934 from 243 billions to 165 billions. Very well. But who has lost these 78 billions? I have done a little figuring. . . . For the whole of the exploited groups: wage-earners, pensioners and retired people, small and middle peasants, small businessmen, artisans, small property-owners, the reduction in income from 1930 to 1934, amounts to 38 or 39%. That is more than 67 billions per year which the depression has cost the poorest social groups. On the other hand, the capitalist class has undergone a reduction of their income which is less than 15%. . . . The *Observation économique*—which is not a Communist journal—states that in November, 1934, the profits of the main gas and electric companies increased from 180 millions in 1929 to 217 millions in 1933. The declared profits for banks, in the same period, remained about even, going from 433 millions to 393 millions. Those of the principal farm-products companies increased from 81 millions to 86 millions. Does this not prove that the deflation policy has had no other result than to make the exploited classes pay for the costs of the depression? They have paid and they continue to pay, through a 65 to 70 billion franc reduction in income, a hidden tax which is added to the 70 billions in open taxes they have to pay. What are the results for the budget? Contraction of taxable goods, constantly increasing deficit. All the measures taken by the different governments since 1932 have increased the misery of the masses and the only result obtained has been to open up a new deficit alongside the old one. (Applause from the Communist Extreme Left.)

.   .   .   .   .

M. EDOUARD HERRIOT (Radical Socialist), *Cabinet Minister:* The Government asks for a vote of confidence on the bill as a whole. . . .

The vote is taken.

THE CHAIRMAN: Here, after checking,

are the results: number voting, 555; simple majority, 278; for the bill, 202; against the bill, 353. The Chamber of Deputies has not adopted the bill.[24]

[24]*Ibid.*, pp. 1733–34.

As a result of his failure to obtain full powers from the Chamber of Deputies, Flandin fell and in June, 1935, was succeeded by Pierre Laval. The Laval Ministry, which lasted until January, 1936, is here described by the Socialist journalist and politician, Louis Frossard.

Comments of L. O. Frossard, Socialist Deputy

The fall of the Flandin cabinet brought Pierre Laval to power, with Marcel Régnier as Minister of Finances. . . . As soon as he could, he read the cloture decree and in the second half of July a tornado of decree-laws swept the country. Laval's "brain-trust," Gignoux, Dautry and Rueff, had prepared them along with Marcel Régnier. The deflation policy vigorously attacked the parties favored in the budget. The policy was not entirely stupid because it derived from the idea, simple but reasonable, that State finances ought to be managed like private finances, adjusting expenses to receipts, not receipts to expenses. But it lowered salaries and pensions 10%. In vain the "victims" of deflation were assured that these 10% reductions were to consolidate the 90% which remained; what they saw clearest was that at the end of the month they got 10% less. What an admirable platform,

eight months from the legislative elections, for the recently-formed Popular Front! These 10% reductions formed a batallion of a million impassioned propagandists. It promised to substitute "reflation" for "deflation," recovery to be obtained by raising the "purchasing power." Instead of reducing expenses as a small shopkeeper would, expenses would be increased and a flood of gold would spill over the country, filling up the Treasury. Between those who were taking money from the people and those who promised to provide it, what could you expect the country to do? The people chose quickly. And most of those who signed the deflationary decree laws paid with their posts for their inability to realize that, far from ruining itself, a country which spends too much is sure to get rich.[25]

[25]L. O. Frossard, *De Jaurès à Léon Blum* (Paris: Librairie Ernest Flammarion, 1934), pp. 183–84. Quoted by permission of the publishers, Librairie Ernest Flammarion, Paris.

It is impossible entirely to separate internal and foreign policies. The following documents, which refer to matters of French defense and armament, bear on an issue which is essentially domestic but which has a very significant connection with foreign policy.

FOR CONSIDERATION   French shortcomings in questions of national defense are especially brought out in terms of Hitler's rise to power. On January 26, 1934, Hitler signed a nonaggression pact with Poland. What effect did this have on France's alliance with Poland, dating from 1921? On March 16, 1935, Germany, breaking the Versailles Treaty, reintroduced compulsory military service; and a year later, on March 7, 1936, it reoccupied the Rhineland in violation of the Locarno Pact. To what extent was France's domestic policy responsible for its inability to take action at these times? Could France aid Russia, with whom a mutual aid pact had been signed (May 2, 1935) and ratified (February 27, 1936)?

Debate in the Chamber of Deputies, March 15, 1935

M. FLANDIN (Prime Minister): To the 480,000 men in camps and immediately available in Germany, to which can be added a number of semi-military groups . . . , we can oppose only about 278,000 in Europe. . . . After 1936, as everyone knows, Germany will have at her disposal at least 600,000 men, while we, on the basis of present estimates, will fall to 208,000. . . .

M. LÉON BLUM (Socialist): Gentlemen, I don't believe there is any more determined adversary to Hitler than we Socialists are. . . . But against this danger, I defy any of you to find any way of stopping him, any kind of guarantee, other than enrolling Germany in a system of disarmament and control which would be accepted voluntarily by her or would be imposed on her by the unanimous agreement of all the other powers.[26]

Excerpt from Official Report of Parliamentary Commission Investigating the Events of March 7, 1936 (German Reoccupation of the Rhineland)

Sunday evening (March 8), M. Albert Sarraut [the Premier] made a vehement

[26]*Journal Officiel, Débats, Chambre des Députés* (1935), Vol. II, pp. 1021–23.

speech over the radio: "We are not inclined to leave Strasbourg within range of German guns," he should have said. But after having declared that the French Government intended to uphold Locarno, "the essential guarantee of French and Belgian security," he limited himself to announcing an appeal to the Council of the League of Nations and "exchanges of views" among the Locarno signatories.[27]

Memorandum of War Minister Jean Fabry to Premier Laval, January 18, 1936

The armament plan now being carried out is no more than a beginning in the reorganization of the French Army. . . .

Tanks: Complete replacement, item by item, of 3000 outmoded FT tanks [1918 model], which can no longer be kept in service, is indispensable. An initial set of 1500 modern tanks must be placed in use to prepare for the most urgent needs. As 500 are now on order, it is urgent that *1000 new tanks* still be constructed, which will require, including spare parts and am-

[27]*Rapport fait au nom de la Commission chargeé d'enquêter sur les événements survenus en France de 1933 à 1945*, Part I, *Les événements du 7 mars 1936*, Assemblée Nationale, Annexe au procès-verbal de la 2ᵉ séance du 8 août 1947 (Paris: Imprimerie de l'Assemblée Nationale, 1951), p. 31.

munition, a total sum of *400 million francs* ($26,000,000) in 1936.[28]

Introduction to the *Instructions for the Tactics of Major Military Units,* August 12, 1936

The Commission for drawing up the preliminary *Instructions of 1921* proposed, in its report to the Minister of War, to set forth the considerations governing the tactics of major units. This was to be done while the lessons learned during the war were still fresh in everyone's memory.

Without underestimating the importance of subsequent progress in the realms of combat techniques and in transportation, the Commission for drawing up the present *Instructions* feels nevertheless that this progress of a technical nature has not sensibly modified the fundamental tactical doctrine established by its predecessor.

It has consequently admitted that the rules objectively established after the 1918 victory by the eminent military leaders who had only recently relinquished their high commands, should remain the basic tactical doctrine of our major units.[29]

Comments of Charles de Gaulle

At this period I was detailed to the Secrétariat Général de la Défense Nationale, a permanent body at the disposal of the Prime Minister for preparing the State and the nation for war. From 1932 to 1937, under fourteen Governments, I found myself involved, in a planning capacity, in the whole range of political, technical and administrative activity concerning the country's defence. I had, in particular, to be familiar with the plans for security and for limitation of armaments presented by André Tardieu and Paul-Boncour respectively at Geneva; to supply the Doumergue Cabinet with the elements for its decisions when it chose to adopt a different course after the arrival of the Führer; to weave the Penelope-web of the bill for the wartime organisation of the nation; and to go into the measures involved by the mobilisation of the civil departments, of industry and of public services. The work I had to do, the discussions at which I was present, the contacts I was obliged to make, showed me the extent of our resources, but also the feebleness of the State.

For the disjointedness of the authorities was rife all over this field. Not—certainly—that the men who figured there lacked intelligence or patriotism. On the contrary, I saw men of incontestable value and, sometimes, of great talent come to the head of the ministries. But the political game consumed them and paralysed them. As a reserved but passionate witness of public affairs, I watched the constant repetition of the same scenario. Hardly had the Premier taken office when he was at grips with innumerable demands, criticisms and bids for favour, which all his energy was absorbed in warding off without ever contriving to master them. Parliament, far from supporting him, offered him nothing but ambushes and desertions. His ministers were his rivals. Opinion, the Press and sectional interests regarded him as the proper target for all complaints. Everyone, indeed—and he first of all—knew that he was there for only a short time. In fact, after a few months, he had to give place to another. As regards national defence, such conditions prevented those responsible from achieving that organic whole of continuous plans, matured

[28]Jean Fabry, *De la Place de la Concorde au Cours de l'Intendance* (Paris: Les Editions de Paris, 1942), pp. 95–96. Quoted by permission of the publishers, Les Editions de Paris.

[29]Paul Reynaud, *La France a sauvé l'Europe* (Paris: Librairie Ernest Flammarion, 1947), Vol. I, p. 339. Quoted by permission of the publishers, Librairie Ernest Flammarion, Paris.

decisions and measures carried to their conclusion, which we call a policy.

For these reasons the military, who received from the State no more than spasmodic and contradictory impulses, fell back within their deference to doctrine. The Army became stuck in a set of ideas which had had their hey-day before the end of the previous war. It was all the more inclined that way because its leaders were growing old at their posts, wedded to errors that had once constituted their glory.

Hence, the concept of the fixed and continuous front dominated the strategy envisaged for a future action. Organisation, doctrine, training and armament derived from it directly. It was understood that, in case of war, France would mobilise the mass of her reserves and would build up the largest possible number of divisions, designed not for manoeuvring, attacking and exploiting, but for holding sectors. . . .

To my mind, such an orientation was as dangerous as could be. I considered that, from the strategic point of view, it handed the initiative over to the enemy, lock, stock and barrel. From the political point of view, I believed that by proclaiming our intention to keep our armies at the frontier, Germany was being egged on to act against the weak, who were from that moment isolated: the Sarre, the Rhineland, Austria, Czechoslovakia, the Baltic States, Poland, and so on; that Russia was being discouraged from forming any bond with us; and that Italy was being assured that, whatever she might do, we would not impose any limit to her malevolence. Lastly, from the moral point of view, it seemed to me deplorable to make the country believe that war, if it came, ought to consist, for her, in fighting as little as possible.[30]

-----
[30]Charles de Gaulle, *The Complete War Memoirs of Charles de Gaulle* (New York: Simon and Schuster, Inc., 1955), pp. 6-8.

Comments of Jean Fabry, Former War Minister

The Socialists cried: "More than 100 billion francs ($7,000,000,000) spent on national defense in fifteen years! And still no armaments! Where did the money go?" On billboards and in campaign speeches there could be no rebuttal. The good people, whose gullibility is infinite, as readily believed that their leaders stole it as they accepted the idea that they were betrayed [in 1940] by their generals.

This myth of "100 billions spent for non-existent armaments" was exploded by Pierre-Etienne Flandin. He clearly proved early in 1935 that of the 92 billions—not 100—received by the War Ministry to provide for "the maintenance of the army," "the liquidation of the war," "the occupation of the Rhineland," "the pacification of Morocco," "the Riff and Near East campaigns," "the construction of the Maginot Line," and finally for "the construction of new equipment," hardly 8,500 million francs had been spent for the last two items. By 1935 the War Ministry had already spent four and a half billions on the Maginot Line, so that hardly four billions ($260,000,000) had been expended for equipment. The conclusion is clear and brutal: the French Army, up to 1935, had been far from having the means indispensable for its modernization.

.   .   .   .   .

Here are facts which cannot be denied: at the end of 1936 armament construction was six to eight months behind schedule; in 1937 this delay was extended to twelve and fourteen months, and even more for certain material, some of which was extremely important.

In 1936, in Germany (where two and three shifts worked 24 hours a day) output had reached three times the normal in the automobile industry (277%) and one-and-a-half in the machine industry (177%). . . . In France the reduction of labor had diminished output 40 to 60%. Thus the same factory which in France would put out 40 cars per month would put out 277 in Germany. Where we counted man-hours in the 100,000's, Germany was counting in millions. Thus when the two armies met on the battlefield one had 1000 tanks, the other 10,000; one had 500 planes, the other 5000. This may appear to be an over-simplification, but it is a certain and perhaps the truest explanation of our defeat in 1940.

Several examples illustrate this point, which, however, is not accepted by any responsible member of the Popular Front. For example:

Light tanks: An initial order of 300 Renault light tanks, and an initial order of 200 Hotchkiss tanks should have been ready in August–September, 1936. At the end of July, 1936, we had: 300 Renault tanks ready (bodies only); the 200 Hotchkiss would be available early in December,

1937, (bodies only). Six months behind schedule. But deliveries on the turrets, as a result of production delays, had hardly started; so that by the middle of 1936 only *twenty turrets* had been mounted on the new light tanks. . . .

If the general situation did not improve, if order was not re-established in the factories, if the strikes did not end, the anticipated deliveries would get even farther behind schedule!

Let us add that all these light tanks *had no modern armament. The old 37 mm. guns that armed the 1918 model FT's would have to arm the new light tanks,* as we lacked the up-to-date 37 mm. still under study. Now the old 37 mm., with its weak initial velocity, had no effect on armor plate. Our modern light tanks, *in a fight against tanks*, would thus have been powerless.[31]

---

[31]Fabry, *op. cit.*, pp. 79–80, 117–19.

T he Rightist governments of Doumergue, Flandin, and Laval, and the agitations of militant groups like the Croix de Feu, resulted in the Socialists and Communists drawing closer together. Since the Pact of July 27, 1934, the union had developed into the Popular Front, and it celebrated its power in a monster rally and parade on Bastille Day, 1935. Following are the reactions to this event by the two leaders, respectively, of the Communist and Socialist Parties.

Comments of Communist Leader Maurice Thorez

The Amsterdam-Pleyel Movement [the "Congress against Fascism" of 1932] had launched the idea of a vast gathering of the People's Front for July 14th, 1935. . . . Ten thousand mandated delegates, people who bore responsibility for the great movement which only the working masses could bring to victory, first took the sol-

emn oath to bar the way to Fascism.

Of all the speeches, it was the speech made by Jacques Duclos, the great builder of the People's Front, which brought the spark that flared up in a moment of intense communion of feeling. All the delegates, rising to their feet in one single movement and raising their clenched fists, began to sing the "Marseillaise," and followed it with the "International." . . .

Then the oath was read out:

We solemnly pledge ourselves to remain united for the defense of democracy, for the disarmament and dissolution of the Fascist leagues, to put our liberties out of the reach of Fascism. We swear, on this day which brings to life again the first victory of the Republic, to defend the democratic liberties conquered by the people of France, to give bread to the workers, work to the young, and peace to humanity as a whole.

The ten thousand delegates replied in one single voice: "We swear it!" . . .

Forty-eight associations had affiliated to the Organizing Committee of the July 14th rally: among them, in the first line, the Communist Party, the Socialist Party, the Radical Socialist Party, the Inter-Group of Socialist Parties (*Socialistes de France, Socialistes Francais, Républicains Socialistes*), the central trade union bodies (*Confédération Générale du Travail, Confédération du Travail Unitaire*), the Amsterdam-Pleyel Movement, the *Ligue des Droits de l'Homme*, the *Anciens Combattants Républicains*, . . . etc.

At the other end of Paris, in the districts of idleness and luxury, the Fascists were massing their feeble deaths-head bands to climb to the Arc de Triomphe. . . .

And at the same time a mighty torrent, a tidal wave of half a million people, was sweeping for eight hours, under the burning sun, through the old suburb of St. Antoine, from which so many revolutionary fighters had set out in the past. All along the route the windows were decked with red flags, and there was tremendous cheering, tremendous happiness in the fusion of all the working masses who are the real Paris, and who that day felt once again the sense of their strength and of their historic mission.[32]

---

[32]Maurice Thorez, *France To-day and the People's Front* (New York: International Publishers Co., Inc., 1936), pp. 186–89. Quoted by permission of International Publishers Co., Inc., New York. Copyright © 1936.

Excerpt from an Editorial of Leon Blum, July 16, 1935

Fascism did not pass. Fascism shall not pass. Following the unforgettable procession on Sunday, I wondered whether the dictatorial movement, now overwhelmed, should not be considered as a happy circumstance for us. The sense of danger has made the people aware of their strength.

On the morning of the 7th of February, 1934, I heard men talking about the possible risks and chances of resistance: "The workers' party is not even capable of holding the street in Paris." Perhaps we should be on our guard against a certain feebleness, an inertia among the masses of the populace. We could even believe that the spring had been broken, that all this deception, wretchedness and rancor had finally worn out and debilitated the old heroic elasticity. I won't labor the point, but who today would dare formulate those dreadful sacrileges?

Since the 12th of February, Paris and all France has roused itself at our appeal. The people of France suddenly felt the revolutionary blood surging through their veins. There they stood, free and proud as in the great days of their history, sure of themselves, ready for the struggle, ready for the sacrifice. Sunday they celebrated their victory with a majesty so powerful and serene that you could feel the adversary, almost respectful, humble himself to the ground. Let us then render thanks to *Messieurs les Fascistes*: they forced the wholesome waters to gush forth from the sand; it is to their effronteries of the past year that the revolutionary and resurrected people owe this celebration, symbol of which is the 14th of July, the Day of the Bastille.[33]

---

[33]*Le Populaire*, July 16, 1935.

In 1936 the Popular Front concentrated its efforts on winning the May elections, where in fact it obtained a significant victory, bringing Léon Blum to the premiership for the first time.

Program of the Popular Front, January 11, 1936

A. Political

  I. *The Defense of Freedom*
1. A general amnesty.
2. Against the Fascist Leagues:
   a) The effective disarmament and dissolution of all semi-military formations, in accordance with the law.
   b) Putting into effect legal measures to provide for cases involving provocation to murder or attempts against the security of the State.
3. Purification of public life, especially in regard to Parliamentary qualifications.
4. The press:
   a) Abrogation of the infamous laws and decrees restraining freedom of opinion.
   b) Reform of the press by adoption of legislative measures
      1) which would permit the effective repression of calumny and blackmail.
      2) which would assure newspapers of a normal means of subsistence, which would require them to make public the origins of their resources, which would put an end to the scandal of financial publicity, and which would prevent the formation of press trusts.
   c) Organization of State broadcasting to ensure accuracy of information and equality of all

social and political organizations before the microphone.
5. Trade Union Liberties:
   a) Universal application and respect for trade union laws.
   b) Respect for the rights of working women.
6. The School and Freedom of Conscience:
   a) To assure the life of public schools, not only by the necessary funds, but by reforms to make education compulsory up to fourteen years. . . .
   b) To guarantee to all, students and teachers alike, liberty of conscience. . . .
7. Colonial Territories:
   Establishment of a Parliamentary Commission of Inquiry into the political, economic and moral conditions in French territories overseas, especially in French North Africa and Indochina.

  II. *Defense of the Peace*
[Program of Foreign Policy]

B. Economic

  I. *Restoration of Purchasing Power Destroyed or Reduced by the Depression.*
1. Against unemployment and industrial depression:
   Establishment of a national unemployment fund.
   Reduction of the working week without reduction of wages.
   Attracting youth to labor by establishing adequate retirement systems.
   Rapidly setting up a public works program.

2. Against commercial and agricultural depression.

Normalization of farm-produce prices, to counteract speculation and the high cost of living....

Creation of a national grain bureau....

Support of agricultural cooperatives, government control and sale of fertilizers, extension of credit to farmers....

Suspension of distraints and regulation of debt re-payments.

II. *Against the Plundering of Reserves. For a Better Organization of Credit.*

Regulation of banking...

New regulations on the powers of corporation directors...

To keep the national credit and savings from the control of the economic oligarchy, to make of the Bank of France, now a private bank, the Bank of the French Nation....

III. *Financial Reform*

Regulation of the armament trade in conjunction with the nationalization of war industries.

Reduction of waste in military and civilian administration....

Democratic reform of the tax system.... Introduction of a graduated income tax and reorganization of inheritance taxes.[34]

Results of the Elections of May 3 and 13, 1936*

Popular Front

Communists	72
Dissident Communists	10
Socialists	146
Dissident Socialists	37
Radical Socialists	116
	381

Center

Left Radicals	31
Democratic Alliance	84
(Left Republicans)	115

Right

Popular Democrats	23
Democratic Republicans	88
Conservatives	11
	122

Total: 618
Needed for Majority: 310

Excerpt from Ministerial Declaration of Premier Léon Blum, June 6, 1936

At the beginning of next week we shall lay before the House a number of bills that we shall ask both assemblies to vote before their vacations.

These bills will deal with political amnesty; a forty-hour week; collective contracts; paid holidays; a large public works program for improved economic, sanitary, scientific, sport and tourist equipment; nationalization of the manufacture of arms of war; creation of a wheat board, which will serve as an example for the revalorization of other agricultural products, like wine, meat, and milk; extension of the school age; reform of the statutes of the Bank of France guaranteeing a preponderance of national interests in its direction; partial revision of the decree laws in favor of the public servants and war veterans who are most severely affected.

As soon as these measures are voted we shall present in Parliament a second series of bills concerning national funds for unemployment, insurance against agricultural calamities, management of the agricultural debt system and pensions guaranteeing aged workers in the cities and country against misery.

Shortly afterward we shall lay before you a large system of fiscal simplification and relief, which will ease produc-

[34]*Archives contemporaines, 1934–1937* (Brussels: Système Keesing, 1938), p. 1902. Quoted by permission.

*Released to the press by the Ministry of the Interior, May 14, 1936.

tion and commerce and call for no new revenues except out of the accumulated fortunes of repression and fraud and, above all, out of a return of general activity.

While we shall be seeking in full collaboration with you to reanimate French economy, to absorb the unemployed, to increase the mass of incomes and to furnish the mass some happiness and security to all those who create the real wealth by their labor, we shall have to govern the country.

We shall govern as republicans. We shall assure republican order. We shall apply with quiet firmness the laws in defense of the Republic. We shall show that we intend to animate the whole administration and all public services with the republican spirit. If democratic institutions are attacked we shall assure them inviolable respect with a vigor equal to any threats or resistance.[35]

———

[35]*Journal Officiel, Débats, Chambre des Députés* (1936), Vol. II, p. 1316.

The Popular Front victory was complete, but a not insignificant opposition developed among the vanquished Rightists. While fascist and semimilitary groups were suppressed (June 30, 1936), they reorganized as political parties and continued their propaganda campaigns. The following document provides an interesting example of Rightist schemes, if only because it so closely anticipates the developments of 1940. Gustave Hervé was editor of the extremely nationalist journal *La Victoire*.

Rightist Reaction to the Popular Front: a Proposal by M. Gustave Hervé, 1936

The only barrier, the only dam known that can protect a country plunged into anarchy by the normal interplay of political factions, is an authoritative regime, in which a single man, personifying the vital interests of the State, unites political factions by suppressing them all and in which he imposes his supreme arbitration on all individual or collective egotisms. . . . When the First Republic fell into difficulties under the Directory it was with real relief, and even enthusiasm, that the French people accepted the *coup d'état* which brought Napoleon to power. . . .

The Fascist regime which has just saved Italy from Bolshevism is an Italian form of Bonapartism. The Hitlerian regime is a German form of Bonapartism. . . .

But without aping Mussolini or Hitler,

or reviving Napoleon, the least we can do is to substitute for the parliamentary Republic an authoritarian Republic on a corporate base. There would be no room for political factions. An authoritarian Republic? This means that the Head of the State would concentrate in his own hands all legislative and executive power, and that he would govern by decrees, with a Vice-President of his own choosing, and with ministers responsible to him alone. . . .

A corporate base? This means that in place of the present sovereign Parliament, elected by political parties, there would be a Council of State, representing the corporate interests of agriculture, industry, commerce, and the major utilities. This Council of State would have only an advisory capacity, its principal function would be to aid the Head of the State in drawing up his decrees. . . .

But it is necessary to have a Chief in order to rally public opinion to such a program. . . . It is necessary to have a name to bring out the voters, a name which appeals to their hearts and minds, a popular name, one to conjure with, an illustrious name which can dispense with long introductions and long speeches.

We have this name, illustrious and magic and popular; we have the man— the man of destiny which France always finds in her hour of extreme danger.

Who?

Pétain, the grand soldier of Verdun, the most illustrious survivor of the World War, now that Clemenceau, Joffre, and Foch have left us.

.   .   .   .   .

You say: "And suppose Pétain refuses to take office, after a victory in his name at the polls?"

Pétain will not refuse. He cannot refuse. He is used to serving. When the country calls, can you imagine this great soldier betraying her? When the nation needs him to save her, can you see Pétain refusing to march?

.   .   .   .   .

Note well that the May elections of 1936 brought victory not to a single party, but to a coalition of four Left and Extreme Left parties, those of Blum, Thorez, Paul-Boncour, and Herriot-Daladier.

Among the Nationalists, there is already a Marin party (*Fédération Républicaine*), a Flandin party (*Alliance Démocratique*), a Popular-Democratic party, a La Rocque party, a Doriot party, a Taittinger party, without speaking of the *Action Française* and the Bonapartist groups. . . . It is up to the disinterested fighters of each one of these groups to force their leaders, if they are not disinterested enough to decide for themselves, to join a great national coalition behind Pétain, and behind the program of an authoritarian Republic on a corporate base.[36]

----

[36]Gustave Hervé, *C'est Pétain qu'il nous faut!* (Paris: Editions La Victoire, 1936), pp. 23–25, 34–39, 51.

The Popular Front put some reforms into effect—such as the 40-hour week— but it turned out to have no greater permanence than other governments, and it fell on June 23, 1937. After Pétain came to power after the fall of France in 1940, Blum was imprisoned and brought to trial at Riom in 1942. The remarks of Paul-Boncour, a dissident Socialist who did not hold a portfolio in the Blum Cabinet, and Blum's own defense before his Vichyite accusers, provide a fitting conclusion for this series of documents.

Comments of Paul-Boncour

In regard to his [Blum's] legislation, some was purely humanitarian, like paid vacations; it was a shame to have delayed them. . . .

Other parts, like compulsory arbitration, passed by the next government but introduced by his, simply came too late and were still inadequate. It was necessary to go much farther in substituting a new order for the anarchy of economic

liberalism. But they were timely and needed; all parties had more or less hailed them; you cannot fasten on them the slogan which tries to blame the Popular Front for our defeat and all our faults.

I know: it was the forty-hour week! Of all our disasters, that takes the prize. I do not think the legislation was timely, at least in the way it was conceived and administered, considering the effort which was required of the country. Several May firsts ago the C.G.T. (General Federation of Labor) had replaced their demand for an eight-hour day, which had passed into law and custom, with this one. The C.G.T. demanded a forty-hour week; all to the good. But for what purpose? *To reduce unemployment.* That presumed a succession of shifts, thus increasing production. A double selfishness, of management and labor, made out of it a simple reduction of working hours to the profit of those already taken care of, labor pleased to receive the benefits and management not caring to see the mass of wages raised.

But the Government?

Ah yes, the Government! Which should have imposed on both groups the measure of public interest: a forty-hour week to reduce unemployment; a succession of shifts to increase production. But what Government, Right or Left, would have had the strength? My forty days in power were there to show how costly it was, on a single budget item, to have wanted to impose equal sacrifices on every one, without favoring either one or the other of the private interests which opposed the State. To act in this way a feeble government— and at a time when a strong republican tradition had not corrected our Constitution's inadequacies, all governments were more or less feeble—consolidated against it both the one and the other.

One year and three weeks after having come to power and excited so much hope among the masses, Blum fell before the Senate's hostility. As after 1924, so after 1932, by a gradual process, the legislature was about to end up with a majority and with a policy different from those designated by universal suffrage. In November, 1938, after Munich, Daladier undertook the struggle against those Communists with whom he had squared off on July 14, 1935, broke the strike, and declared that it was necessary to revise the social legislation passed two years before by a Government of which he and his Radical friends were a part. . . .

One must admit that these blows and contradictions were not elements to raise the prestige of a regime which was going to have to undergo the terrible assault of the Dictatorships, and to safeguard the existence and faith of a menaced Republic.[37]

Excerpt from the Testimony of Léon Blum at the Riom Trial, March 12, 1942

I see—you will excuse me—the good I have been able to do, I see how I smoothed out great social conflicts, I see that for the first time I secured unanimous support for war credits; I see that I prepared the minds of the people for this conception of French unity which was surely as splendid as in the early months of the war of 1914, for it was a spectacle which those who saw it will never forget. I see what I have done. I see the good I have been able to do, that I have been fortunate enough to do. What is the wrong which even involuntarily, even in spite of my good-will and good intentions which nobody I think can doubt, what is the wrong I have done? Is it my crime, as poisoner and traitor, that I have, as is asserted, ruined the authority of the employers and destroyed the pillars of discipline? I do not think so, for, if it were so, my Collective Agreements Act would have been impeached. It was this Collective Agreements Act which introduced democracy into the factories, it is this Act which balks the employer of the right, perhaps essential, linked up as it is to a certain extent with his right of property, of discussing conditions of labour with each of his employees or workers individually. It is this act which makes Collective Agreements the subject of discussion upon a basis of equality or parity, between workers and employers, between the workers as a group and the employers as a group.

If ever there was a law which modified

---

[37]Paul-Boncour, *op. cit.,* Vol. II, pp. 332–34.

the employers' authority, it is this law. However, it is not in the charge. I am not one of those who have tried to ruin the authority of the industrial chiefs. Too often, alas, the employers have themselves been responsible for doing that. I believe that, in a Labour democracy, as in a political democracy, authority is necessary, and the leader gains this authority by an example of competence, industry, justice and goodness But, on the other hand, one form of employers' authority has, I believe, disappeared and will not be seen again; the form of authority of which during that difficult period some employers seemed to retain a rather painful memory. The divine right of employers is dead.

.   .   .   .   .

Gentlemen, I retract nothing of what I have said. I do not think there is one single argument which I have not supplied. I have told you why repression, regret for the non-employment of which seems to be expressed in some of the evidence, appeared impossible to me, for had it been possible it would have been the worst of mistakes, the worst of crimes, against our country.

But, suppose I did what they appeared to ask me, what certain witnesses at least seemed to want me to do, what they seem to regret that I did not do. Let us suppose I had made a blood-bath for the workers, that I had been the cause of more days like those of June, for that is where historically, the most probable analogy may be found. I agree that I would

have established order, material order. Do you think I would have established it for long? Don't you know that in this country there exists an underlying generosity of feeling to which the use and abuse of force is repugnant? Don't you know that after a certain time in any movement of this kind, however blameworthy it may appear, in the end public sympathy always goes to the victims? I played a rôle for which I would almost venture to say I was destined, the rôle of conciliator. Had I done otherwise, had I been the arm that strikes, the arm that avenges so many fears, and had I used force, the order which I should have restored would have been but a fragile and precarious thing, for I should have wounded the deepest, most sensitive, and most generous feelings in the heart of this country. In the Chamber, Briand, in an inspired moment, once said: "Look at my hands; not a drop of blood." He responded to this deep popular sentiment. Yesterday evening in my cell I was reading Michelet's *French Revolution,* and, as if by chance, just as so often happens in opening the Bible to look up a text, I lit upon this sentence: "My heart bleeds to see French blood flowing." The sentence was in inverted commas. Who said it? Joan of Arc.[38]

---

[38]*Léon Blum before His Judges,* at the Supreme Court of Riom, March 11, 12, 1942. Foreword by The Right Hon. Clement R. Attlee, M.P. and introduction by Felix Gouin (London: Routledge & Kegan Paul, Ltd., 1943), pp. 154–55.

BIBLIOGRAPHY

SOURCES USED IN THIS PROBLEM

1. *Collections and Official Documents*

Action Française (newspaper).
Archives contemporaines 1934–1937. Brussels: Système Keesing.
Documents politiques. Paris, 1934.
Journal Officiel, Dèbats, Chambre des Députés. Paris.

La Flèche (newspaper).

Le Populaire (newspaper).

New York Herald. Paris edition (newspaper).

Rapport fait au nom de la Commission chargée d'enquêter sur les événements survenus en France de 1933 à 1945. Paris: Imprimerie de l'Assemblée Nationale, 1951.

Rapport général fait au nom de la Commission d'Enquête chargée de rechercher les causes et le origines des Evénements du 6 Février 1934. Paris: Imprimerie de la Chambre des Députés, 1934.

United Nations *Statistical Yearbook.*

2. Others

DE GAULLE, CHARLES. *The Complete War Memoirs of Charles de Gaulle.* New York: Simon and Schuster, 1955.

FABRY, JEAN. *De la Place de la Concorde au Cours de l'Intendance.* Paris: Les Editions de Paris, 1942.

FLANDIN, PIERRE-ETIENNE. *Discours.* Paris: Gallimard, 1937.

FLANDIN, PIERRE-ETIENNE. *Politique française, 1919–1940.* Paris: Nouvelles Editions Latines, 1947.

FROSSARD, L. O. *De Jaurès à Léon Blum.* Paris: Flammarion, 1934.

HERVÉ, GUSTAVE. *C'est Pétain qu'il nous faut!* Paris: Editions La Victoire, 1936.

KESSEL, JOSEPH. *Stavisky, l'homme que j'ai connu.* Paris: Gallimard, 1934.

Lèon Blum before His Judges. At the Supreme Court of Riom, March 11, 12, 1942. London: Routledge, 1943.

PAUL-BONCOUR, JOSEPH. *Entre deux guerres.* 3 vols. Paris: Librairie Plon, 1945.

REYNAUD, PAUL. *La France a sauvé l'Europe.* 2 vols. Paris: Flammarion, 1947.

TARDIEU, ANDRÉ. *La révolution à refaire.* Vol. II, *La profession parlementaire.* Paris: Flammarion, 1937.

THOREZ, MAURICE. *France To-day and the People's Front.* New York: International Publishers, 1936.

WERTH, ALEXANDER. *France in Ferment.* New York: Harper & Row, 1940.

SELECT LIST OF BOOKS RECOMMENDED FOR FURTHER READING

BINION, R. *Defeated Leaders (Caillaux, Jouvenel, Tardieu).* New York: Columbia University Press, 1960.

BOSWORTH, WILLIAM. *Catholicism and Crisis in Modern France.* Princeton, N.J.: Princeton University Press, 1962.

BROGAN, D. W. *France under the Republic.* New York: Harper & Row, 1940.

COLTON, JOEL. *Leon Blum: Humanist in Politics.* New York: Knopf, 1966.

CURTIS, MICHAEL. *Three against the Third Republic: Sorel, Barrès, Maurras.* Princeton, N.J.: Princeton University Press, 1959.

DERFLER, LESLIE. *The Third French Republic, 1870–1940.* New York: Van Nostrand (Anvil), 1966.

EARLE, EDWARD MEAD (ed.). *Modern France.* Princeton, N.J.: Princeton University Press, 1950.

EHRMANN, HENRY W. *French Labor from Popular Front to Liberation.* Ithaca, N.Y.: Cornell University Press, 1947.

GOGUEL, FRANÇOIS. *La politique des partis sous la IIIe République.* 2 vols. Paris: Editions du Seuil, 1946.

JOLL, JAMES (ed.). *The Decline of the Third Republic.* St. Antony's Papers, No. 5. New York: Praeger, 1959.

LARMOUR, PETER J. *The French Radical Party in the 1930's.* Stanford, Calif.: Stanford University Press, 1964.

LA ROCQUE, FRANÇOIS DE. *The Fiery Cross: The Call to Public Service in France.* London: Dickson, 1936.

MARCUS, JOHN T. *French Socialism in the Crisis Years, 1933–1936.* New York: Praeger, 1958.

NOLTE, ERNST. *Three Faces of Fascism: Action Française, Italian Fascism, National Socialism.* New York: Holt, Rhinehart & Winston, 1966.

OSGOOD, SAMUEL M. *French Royalism under the Third and Fourth Republics.* The Hague: Martinus Nijhoff, 1960.

PICKLES, DOROTHY. *The French Political Scene.* London: Nelson, 1938.

TANNENBAUM, EDWARD R. *The Action Française: Die-hard Reactionaries in 20th-Century France.* New York: Wiley, 1962.

THOMSON, DAVID. *Democracy in France since 1870.* 4th ed. London: Oxford University Press, 1964.

WEBER, EUGEN. *Action Française: Royalism & Reaction in 20th-Century France.* Stanford, Calif.: Stanford University Press, 1962.

WERTH, ALEXANDER. *The Twilight of France 1933–1940.* New York: Harper & Row, 1942.

SECTION IV

Between the Wars: Totalitarianism

RUSSIA—THE CONSOLIDATION OF COMMUNISM

Stalin's rise to power and the Moscow Trials, 1924-38

The fact that Joseph Stalin had become undisputed master of the Soviet Union by the beginning of World War II has left its mark on history. In an age of dictators, he outlasted his contemporaries Mussolini, Chiang Kai-shek, and Hitler, whose regimes collapsed at a time when his gave every appearance of constantly increasing solidity. Stalin's struggle against the Opposition, first typified by Trotsky and later by Zinoviev, Kamenev, Bukharin, and a score of others, represented a conflict between him and elements of both Right and Left which disagreed with his program for the Soviet Union. In the end, after a series of purges which culminated in the dramatic Moscow Trials between 1936 and 1938, Stalin had removed from his path all opposition, had destroyed his major rivals, and had relegated thousands of lesser personalities to prison and forced-labor battalions. There was no group left to resist him.

Interpretation of Stalin's rise to power raises many problems: was he governed by a personal lust for power, or did he work primarily in the interests, as he understood them, of the Revolution? Was his struggle personal or ideological? Did the Opposition plan in reality to overthrow Stalin or did it seek merely a reversal of his policies? Was the Opposition a potential fifth column? Why did Opposition members confess so readily to appalling plots against the government? Those who have read Arthur Koestler's novel *Darkness at Noon* will wonder to what extent his theories about the Opposition can be corroborated.[1]

The following documents simplify the story greatly, limiting it to the

---

[1]For critical assessment of these issues, the student may find a variety of interpretations in Robert V. Daniels (ed.), *The Stalin Revolution: Fulfillment or Betrayal of Communism?*, "Problems in European Civilization" (Boston: D. C. Heath & Company, 1965).

struggle between Stalin and Trotsky and a few others, and commenting particularly on the agricultural issue, although that was but one of many under discussion at the time.

Although during his lifetime Lenin dominated the activities of the Bolsheviks, the other major leaders, such as Trotsky, Kamenev, Zinoviev, and Stalin, were by no means in accord as to the direction the revolution should take. Stalin, who had gained influence as head of the Rabkrin (Workers' and Peasants' Inspectorate) and as Commissar of Nationalities, became Secretary General of the Communist Party's Central Committee, a position which enabled him to line up various blocs in such a way that he came to dominate the Party Congresses. The danger of a split between Stalin and Trotsky was foreseen by Lenin, who commented on it in his famous "testament."

Lenin died on January 21, 1924, and the conflict between Stalin and Trotsky began almost immediately. Trotsky's and Stalin's own comments on the beginning of this struggle present an interesting comparison.

FOR CONSIDERATION   Why does Stalin appear to oppose a complete purge of Trotsky? Did he reverse himself later? Why did he preach moderation in 1924 and 1925? Is there any consistency in Stalin's policy? To what extent are Trotsky's memoirs, published after his expulsion from the party, likely to be suspect?

Excerpts from the "Testament of Lenin," December 25, 1922, January 4, 1923

Our party rests upon two classes, and for that reason its instability is possible, and if there cannot exist an agreement between those classes its fall is inevitable. . . . I think that the fundamental factor in the matter of stability . . . is such members of the Central Committee as Stalin and Trotsky. . . .

Comrade Stalin, having become General Secretary, has concentrated an enormous power in his hands; and I am not sure that he always knows how to use that power with sufficient caution. On the other hand Comrade Trotsky, as was proved by his struggle against the Central Committee in connection with the question of the People's Commissariat of Ways

of Communication, is distinguished not only by his exceptional abilities—personally he is, to be sure, the most able man in the present Central Committee; but also by his too far-reaching self-confidence and a disposition to be too much attracted by the purely administrative side of affairs.

These two qualities of the two most able leaders of the present Central Committee might, quite innocently, lead to a split; if our party does not take measures to prevent it, a split might arise unexpectedly. . . .

December 25, 1922.

Postscript. Stalin is too rude, and this fault, entirely supportable in relations among us Communists, becomes insupportable in the office of General Secretary. Therefore, I propose to the comrades to

find a way to remove Stalin from that position and appoint to it another man who in all respects differs from Stalin only in superiority—namely, more patient, more loyal, more polite, and more attentive to comrades, less capricious, etc. This circumstance may seem an insignificant trifle, but I think that from the point of view of preventing a split and from the point of view of the relation between Stalin and Trotsky which I discussed above, it is not a trifle, or it is such a trifle as may acquire a decisive significance.[2]
January 4, 1943

Comments of Trotsky

After Lenin's death . . . Stalin not only has remained the general secretary, contrary to Lenin's wish, but has been given unheard-of powers by the apparatus. . . . A "regrouping" has been effected in the entire directing personnel of the party and in all the parties of the International, without exception. The epoch of the epigones is separated from that of Lenin not only by a gulf of ideas, but also by a sweeping overturn in the organization of the party.

Stalin has been the chief instrument in carrying out this overturn. He is gifted with practicality, a strong will, and persistence in carrying out his aims. His political horizon is restricted, his theoretical equipment primitive. . . . His mind is stubbornly empirical, and devoid of creative imagination. To the leading group of the party (in the wide circles he was not known at all) he always seemed a man destined to play second and third fiddle.

[2]Leon Trotsky, *The Real Situation in Russia*, trans. Max Eastman (New York: Harcourt, Brace & World, Inc., 1928), pp. 320–23. Copyright 1928, by Harcourt, Brace & World, Inc.; renewed, 1956, by Max Eastman. Reprinted by permission of the publishers.

And the fact that today he is playing first is not so much a summing up of the man as it is of this transitional period of political backsliding in the country. Helvetius said it long ago: "Every period has its great men, and if these are lacking, it invents them." Stalinism is above all else the automatic work of the impersonal apparatus on the decline of the revolution.

.   .   .   .   .

In the autumn of 1924 . . . another discussion had blazed up. . . . In Leningrad, in Moscow, and in the provinces, hundreds and thousands of preliminary secret conferences had been held to prepare the so-called "discussion," to prepare, that is, a systematic and well-organized baiting, now directed not at the opposition but at me personally. When the secret preparations were over, at a signal from the *Pravda* a campaign against Trotskyism burst forth simultaneously on all platforms, in all pages and columns, in every crack and corner. It was a majestic spectacle of its kind. The slander was like a volcanic eruption. It was a great shock to the large mass of the party. I lay in bed with a temperature, and remained silent. Press and orators did nothing but expose Trotskyism, although no one knew exactly what it meant. Day after day they served up incidents from the past, polemical excerpts from Lenin's articles of twenty years' standing, confusing, falsifying and mutilating them, and in general presenting them as if everything had happened just the day before. No one could understand anything of all this. If it had really been true, then Lenin must have been aware of it. But was there not the October revolution after all that? Was there not the civil war after the revolution? Had not Trotsky worked together with Lenin in creating the Communist International? Were not Trotsky's portraits hanging everywhere next to those of Lenin? But slander poured forth in a cold lava stream. It pressed down automatically on the consciousness, and was even more devastating to the will.[3]

Comments of Stalin in Report to the Fourteenth Congress of the Communist Party of the Soviet Union, December 23, 1925

Permit me now to pass to the history of our internal struggle within the majority on the Central Committee. What did our disagreement start from? It started from the question: "What is to be done with Trotsky?" That was at the end of 1924. The Leningrad group at first proposed that Trotsky be expelled from the Party. Here I have in mind the period of the discussion in 1924. The Leningrad Gubernia Party Committee passed a resolution that Trotsky be expelled from the Party. We, i. e., the majority on the Central Committee, did not agree with this

(*voices:* "Quite right!"), we had some struggle with the Leningrad group and persuaded them to delete the point about expulsion from their resolution. Shortly after this, when the Plenum of the Central Committee met and the Leningrad group, together with Kamenev, demanded Trotsky's immediate expulsion from the Political Bureau, we also disagreed with this proposal of the Opposition, we obtained a majority on the Central Committee and restricted ourselves to removing Trotsky from the post of People's Commissar for War. We disagreed with Zinoviev and Kamenev, because we knew that the lopping policy was fraught with grave danger for the Party, that the lopping method, the blood-letting method—and they demanded blood—was dangerous, contagious: today you lop off one, tomorrow another, the day after tomorrow a third—what will we have left in the Party? (*Applause.*)[4]

---

[3]Leon Trotsky, *My Life* (New York: Charles Scribner's Sons, 1930), pp. 506, 513–14. Copyright 1930, by Charles Scribner's Sons. Quoted by permission of the publishers, Charles Scribner's Sons.

[4]*Strategy and Tactics of World Communism: The Communist Conspiracy,* U.S. House of Representatives, 84th Cong., 2d sess., House Report No. 2241, Part I, Sec. B, May 29, 1956 (Washington, D.C.: U.S. Government Printing Office, 1956), p. 114.

The Fourteenth Congress, in 1925, voted against Trotsky, but also saw the Kamenev and Zinoviev groups turn from Stalin to a *rapprochement* with Trotsky. In 1926, Trotsky, Zinoviev, and Radek were expelled from the party. What the Oppositionist policies consisted of is suggested in the following documents.

FOR CONSIDERATION   Can any judgment be formed as to the true attitude of the Opposition on overthrowing the government by force? Were Stalin's actions based on personal ambition for power or on his concern to further the revolutionary program? As it would be impossible, in the limited space of this volume, to characterize all aspects of Oppositionist policy, emphasis has been placed on the controversy over industrialization and the *kolkhozes* (or collective farms). Note Serge's comment that "Party democracy" and the collapse of Chinese communism were equally important issues. Another great question—whether the Revolution should be pursued on a worldwide basis, especially in capitalist countries, or consolidated in the Soviet Union—split the party leadership. Stalin supported the latter view, of socialism in one country, and successfully maintained this position in the Communist International.

It would be profitable to study the complete text of the Oppositionist Platform, which runs to 172 pages in the edition edited by Max Eastman (*The Real Situation in Russia*).

Excerpts from the Oppositionist Platform, September, 1927

The saying of Lenin, "Whoever believes things on a mere say-so is a hopeless idiot," has been replaced by a new formula: "Who does not believe the official say-so, is an Oppositionist." Workers in the industries who incline toward the Opposition are compelled to pay for their opinions with unemployment. The rank-and-file member of the party cannot speak his opinion aloud. Old party workers are deprived of the right to express themselves either in the press or at meetings.

Bolsheviks defending the ideas of Lenin are slanderously accused of desiring to create "two parties." This accusation was deliberately invented in order to array against the Opposition the workers, who naturally defend with passion the unity of their party. Every word of criticism against the crude Menshevik mistakes of Stalin . . . is described as a "struggle against the party." This, although Stalin has never asked the party any preliminary question, either about the policy in China or about any other important problem. This accusation that the Opposition desires to create "two parties" is repeated every day by those whose own purpose is to crowd out of the party the Bolshevik-Leninist members, so that they may have a free hand in carrying out their opportunist policy. . . .

The political course of the Central Committee (which was laid down at the Fourteenth Congress upon the principle of the solidarity with Stalin) is erroneous. Although wavering, the present nucleus of the Central Committee moves continually to the right. The abolition of inner-party democracy is an inevitable result of the fact that the political course is radically wrong. In so far as it reflects the pressure of petty-bourgeois elements, the influence of the non-proletarian layers which envelop our party, it must inevitably be carried through by force from above.

.   .   .   .   .

The Opposition is for the unity of the party. Stalin propagates his own program —to "cut off" the Opposition—under the false flag of a pretense that the Opposition wants to create a "second" party. The Opposition answers with its slogan: "Unity of the Leninist Russian Communist Party at all costs." The platform of the Opposition is expounded in the present document. The working-class sections of the party and all genuine Leninist Bolsheviks will be for it.

.   .   .   .   .

Nothing testifies so surely to the erroneous political course of the Stalin group as their unceasing determination to quarrel not with our real opinions, but with imaginary opinions which we do not and never did hold. . . . After shutting the lid down tight on the party, and cutting off the Opposition from the party press, the Stalin group carries on against us an uninterrupted argument, attributing to us from day to day a continually increasing series of stupidities and crimes. The party member becomes every day less inclined to believe these accusations.

When we state that the present stabilization of capitalism is not a stabilization for decades, and that our epoch remains an epoch of imperialist wars and social revolutions (Lenin), the Stalin group attributes to us a denial of all the elements of stabilization of capitalism.

When we say, in the words of Lenin, that for the construction of a socialist society in our country, a victory of the proletarian revolution is necessary in one or more of the advanced capitalist countries, that the final victory of socialism in one country, and above all a backward country, is impossible . . . , the Stalin group makes the wholly false assertion that we "do not believe" in socialism and in the building of socialism in the Soviet Union.

When, following Lenin, we point out the growing bureaucratic distortions of our proletarian state, the Stalin group attributes to us the opinion that our Soviet state in general is not proletarian. . . .

When we point out that Thermidorian elements with a sufficiently serious social basis are growing in the country; when we demand that the party leadership offer a more systematic, firm, and planful resistance to these phenomena and their influence upon certain links in our party, the Stalin group attributes to us the announcement that the party is Thermidorian, and that the proletarian revolution has degenerated. . . .

When we point to the enormous growth of the Kulak; when we, following Lenin, continue to assert that "the Kulak cannot peacefully grow into socialism," that he is the most dangerous enemy of the proletarian revolution—the Stalin group accuses us of wishing to "rob the peasants."

When we draw the attention of our party to the fact of the strengthening position of private capital, of the immoderate growth of its accumulations and its influence in the country, the Stalin group accuses us of attacking the NEP and demanding a restoration of military Communism. . . .[5]

---

[5]Trotsky, *The Real Situation in Russia*, pp. 118–21, 124–25, 174–77.

Comment of Victor Serge, Former Member of the Executive Committee of the Communist International and Member of the Trotskyite Opposition

The battle of ideas was joined on three issues, on which the maximum possible silence was maintained: agricultural system, Party democracy, Chinese Revolution. Chiang Kai-shek, with Blücher (Galen) and my comrade Olgin (lately one of the victors at Bokhara) as his counsellors, was beginning his triumphal march from Canton to Shanghai and winning startling victories on the way; the Chinese Revolution was in its ascendancy. From the very beginning the discussion in the whole party was falsified, on orders from the bureaucracy. The cell committee, in obedience to the district committee, called an aggregate meeting every fortnight. Attendance was compulsory and all names were checked off at the door. A hack orator took two hours to prove the possibility of constructing Socialism in a single country and denounce the Opposition's "lack of faith." All he did was to spin out the statements published by the Central Committee's Agitation Department. . . .

The Chinese Revolution galvanized us all. I have the impression of a positive wave of enthusiasm heaving up the whole Soviet world—or at least the thinking part of it. The country felt, however confusedly, that a Red China could be the salvation of the U.S.S.R. Then came the Shanghai fiasco. . . .

When he arrived before Shanghai [April, 1927], Chiang Kai-shek had found the town in the hands of the trade unions, whose rebellion had been superlatively organized with the assistance of the Russian agents. Day by day we followed the preparation of the military *coup,* whose only possible outcome was the massacre of the Shanghai proletariat. Zinoviev, Trotsky, and Radek demanded an immediate change of line from the Central Committee. It would have been enough to send the Shanghai Committee a telegram: "Defend yourselves if you have to!" and the Chinese Revolution would not have been beheaded. One divisional commander put his troops at the disposal of the Communist Party to resist the disarmament of the workers. But the Politbureau insisted on the subordination of the Communist Party to the Kuomintang. The Chinese Party, led by an honest man, Ch'en Tu-Hsiu, had disavowed the peasant uprisings in Hopei and left the insurgent farmers of Chan-Sha to be slaughtered in their thousands.

On the very day before the Shanghai incident Stalin came to the Bolshoi Theatre to explain his policy to the assembled activists of Moscow. The whole Party noted one of his winged remarks: "We are told that Chiang Kai-shek is making ready to turn against us again. I know that he is playing a cunning game with us, but it is he that will be crushed. We shall squeeze him like a lemon and then be rid of him."

This speech was in the press at *Pravda* when we heard the terrible news. Troops were wiping out the working-class quarters of Shanghai with sabre and machine-gun. (Malraux was later to describe this tragedy in *Man's Estate*.)

Despair was in us all when we met. The arguments within the Central Committee were repeated with equal violence in every Party cell where there were Oppositionists. When I began to speak in my own branch, just after Chadayev, I felt that a paroxysm of hatred was building up and that we would be lynched on the way out. I ended my five minutes by flinging out a sentence that brought an icy silence: "The prestige of the General Secretary is infinitely more precious to him than the blood of the Chinese proletariat!" The hysterical section of the audience exploded: "Enemies of the Party!"[6]

[6]Victor Serge, *Memoirs of a Revolutionary* (London: Oxford University Press, 1963), pp. 215–17.

Testimony of Leon Trotsky before the Preliminary Commission of Inquiry on the Charges Made at the Moscow Trials

TROTSKY: During the period from 1922 until 1929 I fought for the necessity of an accelerated industrialization. I wrote in the beginning of 1925 a book in which I tried to prove that by planning and direction of industry it was possible to have a yearly coefficient of industrialization up to twenty. I was denounced at that time as a fantastic man, a super-industrializer. It was the official name for the Trotskyites at that time: super-industrializers. . . .

GOLDMAN: And Stalin at that time called you a super-industrialist?

TROTSKY: Yes.

GOLDMAN: He was opposed to the rapid industrialization of the country?

TROTSKY: Permit me to say that in 1927, when I was chairman of the commission at Dnieprostroy for a hydro-electric station, a power station, I insisted in a session of the Central Committee on the necessity of building up this station. Stalin answered, and it is published. "For us to build up the Dnieprostroy station is the same as for a peasant to buy a gramophone instead of a cow. . . ."[7]

Comments of Trotsky

The next landmark was the Moscow demonstration [1927] in honor of the tenth anniversary of the October revolution. . . .

The oppositionists decided to take part in the general procession, carrying their own placards, with their slogans. These were in no sense directed against the party; they read, for example: "Let us turn our fight to the right—against the kulak, the nepman and the bureaucrat."

[7]*Not Guilty*, Report of the Committee of Inquiry into Charges Made against Trotsky (Dewey edition) (New York: Harper & Bros., 1938), p. 260.

. . . "Let us carry out Lenin's will." . . . "Against opportunism, against a split, and for the unity of Lenin's party."

It is difficult even to imagine anything more disgraceful than the preparations for the fifteenth congress. Zinoviev and his group had no difficulty in perceiving that the congress would put the political capsheaf on the physical rout that had begun in the streets of Moscow and Leningrad on the tenth anniversary of the October revolution. The only concern of Zinoviev and his friends was to capitulate while there was yet time. They could not fail to understand that the Stalin bureaucrats saw their real enemy not in them, the oppositionists of the second draft, but in the main group of the opposition, linked to me. They hoped to buy forgiveness, if not to win favor, by a demonstrative break with me at the time of the fifteenth congress. They did not foresee that by a double betrayal they would achieve their own political elimination. Although they weakened our group temporarily by stabbing it in the back, they condemned themselves to political death.

The fifteenth congress resolved to expel the opposition *en bloc*. The expelled were placed at the disposal of the G.P.U.[8]

Excerpt from Program of the Communist International, Adopted September 1, 1928

As the land of the dictatorship of the proletariat and of socialist construction,

---

[8]Trotsky, *My Life,* pp. 533–34, 538.

the land of great working class achievements, of the union of the workers with the peasants and of a new culture marching under the banner of Marxism, the U. S. S. R. inevitably becomes the base of the world movement of all oppressed classes, the center of international revolution, the greatest factor in world history. In the U. S. S. R., the world proletariat for the first time has acquired a country that is really its own, and for the colonial movements the U. S. S. R. becomes a powerful center of attraction.

Thus, the U. S. S. R. is an extremely important factor in the general crisis of capitalism, not only because it has dropped out of the world capitalist system and has created a basis for a new socialist system of production, but also because it plays an exceptionally great revolutionary role generally; it is the international driving force of proletarian revolution that impels the proletariat of all countries to seize power; it is the living example proving that the working class is not only capable of destroying capitalism, but of building up socialism as well; it is the prototype of the fraternity of nationalities in all lands united in the world union of socialist republics and of the economic unity of the toilers of all countries in a single world socialist economic system that the world proletariat must establish when it has captured political power.[9]

---

[9]*Strategy and Tactics of World Communism: The Communist Conspiracy,* U.S. House of Representatives, 84th Cong., 2d sess., House Report No. 2242, Part I, Sec. C, May 29, 1956 (Washington, D.C.: U.S. Government Printing Office, 1956), pp. 214–15.

The Fifteenth Party Congress, in 1927, succeeded in solidifying Stalin's position. Zinoviev, Kamenev, and Radek were unsuccessful in regaining lost ground and Trotsky was banished in January, 1928. The time had come for Stalin to strengthen his hand still more by overriding all opposition. To this end the Soviet interior police, the famous G.P.U., was the important instrument for carrying out the government's political purges.

The following documents throw some light on the G.P.U., from the Stalinist and the Oppositionist point of view.

FOR CONSIDERATION   It is obviously difficult for an internee to approach the question of concentration camps without bias. How can the historian allow for this bias? The arguments for the G.P.U., like those for the Terror during the French Revolution, derive from an acceptance of the principle that ends justify means. Does Stalin make a convincing case?

Interview of Stalin with Foreign Workers' Delegation, November 5, 1927

QUESTION: Judicial powers of the G.P.U., trial without witnesses, without counsel, secret arrests. Considering that these measures are not approved of by French public opinion, it would be interesting to hear their justification. Is it intended to substitute or abolish them?

ANSWER: The G.P.U., or the Cheka, is a punitive organ of the Soviet Government. It is more or less similar to the Committee of Public Safety which existed during the great French Revolution. It punishes primarily spies, plotters, terrorists, bandits, speculators, and forgers. It is something in the nature of a military political tribunal set up for the purpose of protecting the interests of the Revolution from attacks on the part of the counter-revolutionary bourgeoisie and their agents.

. . . . . .

It is not surprising . . . that the bourgeoisie of all countries hate the G.P.U. All sorts of legends have been invented about the G.P.U. The slander which has been circulated about the G.P.U knows no bounds. And what does that mean? It means that the G.P.U. is properly defending the interests of the Revolution. The sworn enemies of the Revolution curse the G.P.U. Hence it follows that the G.P.U. is doing the right thing.

But this is not how the workers regard the G.P.U. You go to the workers' districts and ask the workers what they think of it. You will find that they regard it with great respect. Why? Because they see in it a loyal defender of the Revolution. . . .

I do not mean to say by this that the internal situation of the country is such that it is necessary to have a punitive organ of the Revolution. From the point of view of the internal situation, the Revolution is so firm and unshakable that we could do without the G.P.U. But the trouble is that the enemies at home are not isolated individuals. They are connected in a thousand ways with the capitalists of all countries who support them by every means and in every way. . . .

The G.P.U. is necessary for the Revolution and it will continue to live and strike terror into the heart of the enemies of the proletariat. (Loud applause.)

ONE OF THE DELEGATES: Allow me, Comrade Stalin, to thank you on behalf of the delegates present for your explanations and refutations of the falsehoods circulated about the U.S.S.R. abroad. You can rest assured that we will be able to tell our workers at home the truth about the U.S.S.R.

STALIN: You are welcome, comrades. I consider it my duty to answer your questions and to report to you. . . .[10]

Anti-Communist Report from Russia, 1929

The two Moscow prisons in charge of the G.P.U.—the Lubianka and the Bu-

[10]Stalin, *op. cit.*, Vol. I, pp. 419–21.

tirsky—are overcrowded with politicals. They are compelled to sleep in fearfully congested quarters, the mattresses and bedding being veritable nests of vermin. The food is bad; the bread half-baked, mixed with indigestible ingredients. Occasionally there is soup or stew consisting of frozen potatoes and decayed vegetables, with now and then some meat offal. New political arrivals are placed together with ordinary criminals, and it requires several weeks of energetic protest before they are transferred to the political wing of the prison.

There are numerous workers and peasants among the politicals, as well as scores of Communists of the Opposition, foreign and Russian. The most prominent of them are kept in strict isolation, while the others —those of the rank and file—are permitted certain work, such as cleaning the cells, assisting in the kitchen, distributing the rations, and so forth. It is interesting to mention that the attitude of the prisoners to the new political element—the Communist Opposition—in no way differs from their treatment of other new arrivals. They are neither shunned nor discriminated against. And, as a matter of fact, the Communist prisoners are generally even more bitter and antagonistic to the authorities than the other politicals.

Twice every month prisoners are transferred from Moscow to the Solovietzki Islands and to Kem, in the far North. Their number is usually so great that there are never enough railroad cars on hand to hold them all. Then one witnesses a sight that has become common: with the butts of their guns the G.P.U. agents force the prisoners into the cars. The Kem concentration camp now has over 18,000 prisoners, while 27,000 are in the Solovietzki. Conditions in Solovietzki are so fearful that it has been popularly christened the "red Sakhalin," after the dreaded Sakhalin colony of Tzarist times.

Members of various political parties and movements are represented among the politicals: there are Socialists, Communists, Anarchists. . . . There are men convicted in the Shaktin (Don Basin) Trial, with a goodly sprinkling of Trotsky followers and foreign Communists. . . .

Among the group of the Shaktin prisoners the most tragic case is that of one of the chief witnesses named Bashkin. Long imprisonment and the nerve-wrecking trial have unbalanced his mind. His comrades in the case tell of the continuous nightly "pumping" that Bashkin and the others underwent at the hands of the G.P.U. in its attempts to force confessions out of them. Few, even the strongest men, could mentally survive the agonizing night hearings, and particularly the experience of having the death mask placed over their heads, preparatory to being taken out and shot. These were the Bolshevik third degree methods: leading men out at night to execution, going through all the harrowing formalities and then, at the last moment, returning them to their cells—only to have the performance repeated a few days later.[11]

Statement of a Prisoner Charged with Sabotage, 1930

They kept me five months in isolation, without papers, without anything to read, without mail, without contact with the outside world, without visits from my family; I was hungry, I suffered from solitude; they demanded of me that I confess having committed an act of sabotage that never took place; I refused to take upon myself crimes that had never been committed, but they told me that if I was really for the Soviet power, as I said I was, I ought to confess in this affair, for the Soviet power needed my confession;

[11] Bulletin of the Relief Fund for Anarchists (May, 1929). Reprinted by permission of the Alexander Berkman Aid Fund.

that I need have no fear of the consequences; the Soviet regime would take into consideration my open-hearted confession, and would give me the opportunity to work and to make good my mistakes through work. At the same time I would have visits from my family, letters, walks, newspapers. But if I persisted in maintaining silence I would be subjected to pitiless repression, and not myself alone, but my wife and children also. For months I resisted; but my situation became so intolerable that nothing, it seemed to me, could be worse; in any case I had become indifferent to everything. And I signed everything the examining judge demanded of me.[12]

Comments of Victor Serge, Former Member of the Executive Committee of the Communist International and Member of the Trotskyite Opposition

Most of the oppositionists were expelled from the party in 1928 and immediately imprisoned: they still were in 1936. The G.P.U. disdained to seek any legal pretexts to motivate the three years of imprisonment that it inflicted upon them by administrative measure—to begin with. . . . These first three years terminated, their penalties were prolonged two years when they rejected apostasy. . . . The prisoners of 1928 finished their five years in 1933–1934, were deported, *arrested again* without any special reason after the Kirov affair, and *once more imprisoned for five years.*

.   .   .   .   .

May I be permitted to dwell here for a moment on my own experience? . . . I was arrested and deported in 1933. Deported for three years, at the same time with me, were two valiant communists of

Moscow, guilty of knowing me: Sheva Ghenkina, secretary of the Red International of Miners, whose husband was already in Central Asia, and Nadyezhda Moisseyevna Almaz, fighter in the Urals in 1918, secretary to Losovsky, sent to Astrakhan where she was doomed to unemployment. My sister-in-law, Anita Russakova, who worked as my typist, did three months in the secret prison and was then released. Imprisoned again at the beginning of 1936. . . . Nothing is clearer in my mind than the reasons behind this all-too-common affair. Right after my arrival in the West, I wrote on this point to my friend, Magdeleine Paz:

They finished at the magistrate's examination by presenting me with a forgery—a flagrant, unmistakable forgery, signed, apparently, by my sister-in-law. . . . When I grew angry, it was withdrawn and the young woman was given back her freedom. But last December, when my departure abroad and consequently my passage through Moscow became imminent, she was arrested; after three months of secret examination, she has just been deported to Viatka for five years. She is a minor employee, entirely apolitical, of a skittish and timid nature. The game is odiously clear; it had to be made impossible for me, meeting her in Moscow, to have any light thrown on the dirty trick that had failed against me. Inquisitors who, in spite of everything, may be called upon to answer for their conduct—above all when they fail! defend their careers.

I name the principal one among them: Rutkovsky. He attempted, by making use of this forgery, to dictate to me, I repeat it, *entirely false* confessions. . . . I declare that no definite charge was brought to my attention.

.   .   .   .   .

Thousands of names would be needed here, totalling tens of thousands of years of proscription for the Opposition, and nobody knows how many hidden dramas. Here are some data on the arrests: At the beginning of 1928, from 3,000 to

---

[12]Reported by Anton Ciliga in *Not Guilty*, p. 364.

4,000; October 1929, about 1,000 in the large centres; January 1930, 300 in Moscow; May 1930, on the occasion of the Sixteenth Congress of the party, from 400 to 500 in Moscow; August 1930, several hundreds. In 1931–1932 there were no more oppositionists at large. At the end of 1932, hundreds of former oppositionists, readmitted into the party, were again arrested.[13]

---

[13]Victor Serge, *Russia Twenty Years After* (New York: Hillman-Curl, Inc., 1937), pp. 106, 111–12, 114. Copyright 1937 by Hillman-Curl, Inc.

Zinoviev and Kamenev, in 1928, having recanted, were accepted back into the party. They were far, however, from agreement with Stalin. The following document, according to its editor, Victor Serge, was published clandestinely in Moscow in 1928. Zinoviev was still in exile, but Kamenev had returned to Moscow where he held discussions with Nikolai Bukharin, economist and journalist and leader of the Right Opposition. The document purports to consist of notes on the conversations which Kamenev made and sent to Zinoviev.

Kamenev to Zinoviev (July, 1928), Presumed Report on Conversation with Bukharin

BUKHARIN: . . . We estimate that Stalin's line of conduct places the entire revolution in danger. We can perish with it. The differences in views existing between him and us are infinitely deeper than those we have had in the past with you. . . . For several weeks I have not spoken to Stalin. He is an unprincipled intriguer who subordinates everything to the possession of power. He alters his theories to eliminate one person or another. In the septumvirat (Politburo of seven members) we treated each other like liars and bluffers. He gave in the better to strangle us. . . . I read there a statement without letting it get out of my hands. (The least paper can't be trusted to him.) His present task is to get Moscow and Leningrad, and *Pravda* away from us, and to replace Uglanov, who is completely with us, by Kaganovitch. In regard to his policy, it is the following:

1) Capitalism has developed either at the expense of colonies, or by loans, or by exploitation of the workers. We have no colonies, no one makes us loans, our base is thus: a levy on the peasantry. . . .

2) The more socialism develops, the more resistance will increase. This is idiotic and totally ignorant.

3) If it is necessary to make a levy on the peasants, and if resistance increases, firm management will be necessary. Self-criticism must not touch the policy-makers, but the administrative officials.

As a matter of fact, self-criticism is directed against Tomski and Uglanov. Result: a police régime. It is no longer a matter of finding a scapegoat, it is really the fate of the revolution which is being decided. Everything can perish with such a theory.

If we intervene, they will strangle us by accusing us of schism. If we don't intervene, they will strangle us with shabby manoeuvers and hold us responsible for the wheat shortage in October.

KAMENEV: . . . And on what do they count to have wheat?

BUKHARIN: . . . Right there is the difficulty: on the repetition of emergency measures in the presence of the renewal of difficulties. (On requisitions.) Now, this is war communism, slaughter.

KAMENEV: . . . And you?

BUKHARIN: . . . Perhaps what would be needed is a manoeuver of vast compass to conciliate the middle-class peasant. You can run down the Kulak as much as you wish, but it is necessary to reconciliate the middle-class peasant. But under Stalin and this lout Molotov who wants to outdo me in Marxism and whom we call "Slow poke," there's nothing to do. . . .[14]

_____

[14]Victor Serge, "De Lénine à Staline," *Crapouillot*, January, 1937, p. 56.

W ith Trotsky's direct opposition safely curbed (Trotsky had been expelled from Russia in January, 1929), Stalin could proceed without interference from the Left. He found, however, that opposition "to the Right" had developed.

Comments of Stalin on "Right Deviationism" in a Speech of November 19, 1928

Are there representatives of the Right deviation among our Party members? Certainly there are. Comrade Rykov referred to the case of Comrade Shatunovsky. . . . Nevertheless, I believe that Comrade Shatunovsky is not typical. . . . I think that in this respect the palm must go to Comrade Frumkin. I refer to his first letter (June, 1928) . . . which has been distributed here. . . . Let us examine the "fundamental postulates" of the first letter.

1. *"The countryside, with the exception of a small section of the poor peasants, is opposed to us."* Is that true? Obviously not. If it were true there would not be even a trace left of the *smychka* (bond) between the working class and the peasantry. . . . Why does Comrade Frumkin write such absurdities? In order to scare the Party and thereby have it adopt a more conceding attitude towards the Right deviation.

2. *"The policy pursued lately has brought the main mass of the peasantry into a state of gloom and despair."* Is that true? Absolutely untrue. It is obvious that if the main mass of the middle peasants had been in a state of economic despair this spring they would not have extended the spring crop area in all the main grain-bearing regions as they did. . . . Comrade Frumkin is talking patent nonsense. . . .

3. *"We must turn back to the Fourteenth and Fifteenth Congresses."* . . . Comrade Frumkin, in advocating the return to the Fourteenth Congress, rejects that forward step made by the Party between the Fourteenth and Fifteenth Congresses, and by so doing is trying to pull the Party back. The July Plenum of the Central Committee had this matter under discussion, and in its resolution plainly stated that those who tried to "evade the decision of the Fifteenth Congress," namely, "to extend the drive against the kulaks," were "expressing the bourgeois tendencies within our country." . . .

4. *"The utmost assistance to the poor peasants joining the collective farms."* . . . When he speaks of giving the utmost assistance to the poor peasant who joins the collective farms, Comrade Frumkin is, in fact, evading the task of the Party to develop the collective farm movement to the utmost, which was laid down by the Fifteenth Congress. . . .

5. *"Not to carry on the development of the Soviet farms in shock or super-shock order."* Comrade Frumkin ought to know that *we have only just begun* to work

seriously on the development of the old Soviet farms and the creation of new ones. Comrade Frumkin must know that we are assigning much less resources for this work than we should if we had any reserves for the purpose. . . .

Assemble all Comrade Frumkin's postulates and you obtain a bouquet which is characteristic of the Right deviation.

.   .   .   .   .

And we say that wherever there is a Right deviation there must be a "Left" deviation. The "Left" deviation is the shadow of the Right deviation. . . . Those who incline toward Trotskyism are, in fact, Rights turned inside-out, they are Rights concealing themselves behind "Left" phrases. . . .

Then what is the difference between them?

The difference consists in the fact that their platforms are different, their demands are different, and their approach and methods are different. If, for instance, the Rights say, "It is a mistake to build Dnieprostroy," while the "Lefts" on the contrary say, "What is the good of one Dnieprostroy? Give us a Dnieprostroy every year" (laughter), it must be admitted that there is some difference between them. If the Rights say, "Do not interfere with the kulak, give him freedom to develop," while the "Lefts," on the contrary, say, "Strike not only at the kulak, but also at the middle peasant, since he is just as much a private-property owner as the kulak," it must be admitted that there is some difference between them. If the Rights say, "The difficulties have set in, is it not time to quit?" while the "Lefts," on the contrary, say, "What are difficulties to us: a fig for difficulties, let us dash ahead" (laughter), it must be admitted that apparently there is some difference between them.[15]

---

[15]Joseph Stalin, *Leninism* (New York: International Publishers Co., Inc., 1933), Vol. II, pp. 88–90, 94–95. Reprinted by permission of International Publishers Co., Inc. Copyright © 1933.

W ith the launching of the First Five-Year Plan, on October 1, 1928, the Soviet government undertook a program the general nature of which is indicated in the following.

FOR CONSIDERATION   What resemblance does this program bear to the Oppositionist program of 1926 and 1927? Were Stalin's objections to the Opposition related simply to matters of timing? If Stalin was finally carrying out the plan long advocated by Trotsky, could Trotsky have any reason to continue the opposition? Notice that Stalin admitted, in his article "Dizzy with Success" and in his report to the Sixteenth Congress, that the new policy had encountered a resistance which imperiled the entire Soviet economy. To what extent did Stalin admit he was wrong and to what extent did he reverse his policy?

Stalin's Statement of the Party Line, from a Speech of April, 1929

The Party's Plan

1. We are re-equipping (reconstructing) industry.

2. We are beginning seriously to re-equip agriculture (reconstruction).

3. For this we must expand the development of collective farms and state farms, employ on a mass scale the contract system and machine and tractor

stations as means of establishing a *bond* between industry and agriculture along the line of *production*.

4. As for the present grain-purchasing difficulties, we must admit the necessity for temporary emergency measures, reinforced by the public support of the middle and poor peasant masses, as one of the means of breaking the resistance of the kulaks and of obtaining from them the maximum grain surplus necessary in order to be able to dispense with importing grain and to save foreign currency for the development of industry.

5. Individual poor and middle-peasant farming plays, and will continue to play, a predominant part in supplying the country with food and raw materials. But

alone it is no longer adequate; the development of individual poor and middle-peasant farming must therefore be *supplemented* by the development of collective farms and state farms, by the contract system applied on a mass scale, by accelerating the development of machine and tractor stations, in order to facilitate the squeezing out of the capitalist elements from agriculture and the gradual transfer of the individual peasant farms to the lines of large-scale collective farming, to the lines of collective labor.

6. But in order to achieve all this, it is necessary first of all to accelerate the development of industry, of metals, chemicals, machinery construction, of tractor works, agricultural machinery works, etc. Without this, it will be impossible to solve the grain problem and to reconstruct agriculture.

Conclusion: The key to the reconstruction of agriculture is the speedy rate of development of our industry.[16]

Hutton—Philadelphia Inquirer

Bedtime Stories
Said the anaconda . . .

Comments of Andrei Vyshinsky

The socialist reorganization of the village—grand in range and in results—was realized in the years of the first and second five-year plans, making the USSR a land of socialist agricultural production, the greatest in the world, mechanized and with modern technical equipment. Millions of individual peasant homesteads joined the kolkhozes. In 1937 only seven percent of the peasant households were outside the kolkhoz associations. The land occupied by the kolkhozes was secured in their behalf for their free and unlimited use—that is to say, in perpetuity. This was given final, formal shape, in accordance with the directive of the Council of Peo-

[16]Joseph Stalin, *Leninism: Selected Writings* (New York: International Publishers Co., Inc., 1942), p. 111. Reprinted by permission of International Publishers Co., Inc. Copyright © 1942.

ple's Commissars of the USSR (July 7, 1935), by transferring special state documents to the kolkhozes.

In 1936 there were as many as 4,137 sovkhozes. There were 4,993 machine tractor stations with 289,000 tractors and approximately 30,000 combines. In 1937 there were already 5,617 machine tractor stations with 356,800 tractors and 96,300 combines. . . .

The process of collectivizing agriculture was combined with that of complete liquidation of capitalist (kulak) economy in the village. The directive of the Central Executive Committee and the Council of People's Commissars of the USSR of February 1, 1930, transferred to local organs of government (the regional and territorial executive commissars and the governments of autonomous republics) the right to put complete collectivization into operation in their districts. They were to take "all necessary measures in the struggle with the kulaks—even including the complete confiscation of their property and settling them outside the limits of separate districts and territories." The same directive suspended—in districts of complete collectivization—the operation of the law allowing the lease of land and the use of hired labor in the individual peasant homesteads. Capitalism was liquidated in agriculture as it had been in industry. . . .

Such were the results of the steps taken to construct socialist economy (1924-1936)—results attained in the most savage struggle with capitalism (and its political agents) and with enemies of the people—the Trotskyists, the Bukharinists, the Zinovyevists, and the bourgeois nationalists. Under the guidance of the party of Lenin and Stalin, the toilers of the USSR achieved the complete victory of socialism in all branches of national economy.[17]

---

[17]Andrei Y. Vyshinsky (ed.), *The Law of the Soviet State*, trans. H. W. Babb (New York: The

Comments of American Journalist, Eugene Lyons

. . . Obliteration of the allegedly kulak elements was not only an end in itself, but a means for stampeding the rest of the population into submission to collectivization. Whatever hocus-pocus of village meetings of the poor might be invoked to select the quota of victims, the palpable objective was to scare the poor and middling peasants themselves into merging their land, livestock, and implements. Indeed, the only sure way to prove that they were not kulaks was to apply and be accepted as collective members. . . .

Hell broke loose in seventy thousand Russian villages. The pent-up jealousies of a generation, the sadistic instincts of self-important little officials, the inflamed zeal of local communists, were unleashed and whipped into fury. The haphazard persecutions of the preceding months were systematized and legalized and invested with a high crusading fervor. . . .

A population as large as all of Switzerland's or Denmark's was stripped clean of all their belongings—not alone their land and homes and cattle and tools, but often their last clothes and food and household utensils—and driven out of their villages. They were herded with bayonets at railroad stations, packed indiscriminately into cattle cars and freight cars, and dumped weeks later in the lumber regions of the frozen North, the deserts of Central Asia, wherever labor was needed, there to live or die. Some of this human wreckage was merely flung beyond the limits of their former villages, without shelter or food in those winter months, to start life anew if they could, on land too barren to have been cultivated in the past.

I saw batches of the victims at provincial railroad points, under G.P.U. guards, like bewildered animals, staring vacantly into space. These meek, bedraggled, work-worn creatures were scarcely the kulaks of the propaganda posters. The spectacle of peasants being led by soldiers with drawn revolvers through the streets even of Moscow was too commonplace to win more than a casual glance from the crowds on the sidewalks. I talked to refugees who came to our doors to beg a few crumbs of bread, to officials who had taken part in the liquidation in Ukrainian villages, to Soviet reporters assigned to describe the great Stalinist "successes." No man can see with his own eyes a social upheaval of such scope. But from isolated tales of terror, from the scenes I happened to witness, from the hints and tell-tale circumlocutions in the press, I came to know and to feel some part at least of the unfolding nightmare.[18]

Comments of Victor Kravchenko Regarding the Liquidation of Kulaks

Evening was falling when I drove into the village, with several companions. Immediately we realized that something was happening. Agitated groups stood around. Women were weeping. I hurried to the Soviet building.

"What's happening?" I asked the constable.

"Another round-up of kulaks," he replied. "Seems the dirty business will never end. The G.P.U. and District Committee people came this morning."

A large crowd was gathered outside the building. Policemen tried to scatter them, but they came back. Some were cursing. A number of women and children were weeping hysterically and calling

the names of their husbands and fathers. It was all like the scene in a nightmare. . . .

In the back yard, guarded by the G.P.U. soldiers with drawn revolvers, stood about twenty peasants, young and old, with bundles on their backs. A few of them were weeping. The others stood there sullen, resigned, helpless.

So this was "liquidation of the kulaks as a class"! A lot of simple peasants being torn from their native soil, stripped of all their worldly goods, and shipped to some distant lumber camps or irrigation works. For some reason, on this occasion, most of the families were being left behind. Their outcries filled the air. As I came out of the Soviet house again, I saw two militiamen leading a middle-aged peasant. It was obvious that he had been manhandled—his face was black and blue and his gait was painful; his clothes were ripped in a way indicating a struggle.

As I stood there, distressed, ashamed, helpless, I heard a woman shouting in an unearthly voice. Everyone looked in the direction of her cry and a couple of G.P.U. men started running towards her. The woman, her hair streaming, held a flaming sheaf of grain in her hands. Before anyone could reach her, she had tossed the burning sheaf onto the thatched roof of the house, which burst into flame instantaneously.

"Infidels! murderers!" the distraught woman was shrieking. "We worked all our lives for our house. You won't have it. The flames will have it!" Her cries turned suddenly into crazy laughter.

Peasants rushed into the burning house and began to drag out furniture. There was something macabre, unreal, about the whole scene—the fire, the wailing, demented woman, the peasants being dragged through the mud and herded together for deportation.[19]

[18]Eugene Lyons, *Assignment in Utopia* (New York: Harcourt, Brace & World, Inc., 1937), pp. 279–81. Copyright 1937, by Harcourt, Brace & World, Inc.

[19]Victor Kravchenko, *I Chose Freedom* (New York: Charles Scribner's Sons, 1946), p. 104. Quoted by permission of Victor Kravchenko.

Excerpt from Stalin's Article
"Dizzy with Success," March 2, 1930

The artel is the *main link of the collective farm movement* because it is the most expedient form for solving the grain problem. And the grain problem is the *main link in the whole system of agriculture* because, unless that problem is solved, it is impossible to solve either the problem of livestock raising (large and small livestock), or the problem of industrial and special crops which provide the basic raw materials for industry. That is why the agricultural artel is at the present moment the main link in the system of the collective farm movement.

It is from this that the "Model Rules" for collective farms—the final text of which is being published today—proceeds.

It is from this, too, that our party and Soviet functionaries should proceed; it is their duty to make a thorough study of these rules and carry them out to the full.

This is the party's line at the present moment.

Can it be said that the line of the party is being carried out without infractions and distortions? No, unfortunately, that cannot be said. We know that in a number of districts in the U.S.S.R., where the struggle for the existence of the collective farms is far from being at an end, and where the artels are not yet consolidated, attempts are being made to skip the artel form and to organize agricultural communes from the outset. The artel is not yet consolidated, but they are already "socializing" dwellings, small livestock and poultry; and this sort of "socialization" degenerates into bureaucratic paper decrees, for the conditions which would make such socialization necessary do not yet exist. One might think that the grain problem has already been solved in the collective farms, that it is already a superseded stage, that the main task at the present moment is not to solve the grain problem, but to solve the problem of livestock and poultry farming. The question arises: Who benefits by this blockhead "work" of lumping together the various forms of the collective farm movement? Who benefits by this stupid and harmful precipitancy? Irritating the peasant collective farmer by "socializing" dwellings, all the dairy cattle, all the small livestock and the poultry when the grain problem is still *unsolved,* when the artel form of collective farming is *not yet consolidated*—is it not obvious that such a "policy" can please and benefit only our sworn enemies? One such overzealous "socializer" even went so far as to issue an order to an artel calling for "the registration within three days of every head of poultry in every household," for the appointment of special "commanders" to register and supervise, "to take over the key position in the artel," "to be in command of the battle for socialism, without quitting their posts," and—of course—to hold the artel in a tight grip. What is this—a policy of leading the collective farm, or a policy of *disintegrating and discrediting it*? And what about those "revolutionaries"—save the mark—who *begin* the work of organizing an artel by removing the church bells. Remove the church bells—how r-r-revolutionary indeed![20]

Trotsky's Open Letter to the
Ruling Party of the Soviet Union,
April, 1930

Dear Comrades: The present letter is impelled by a feeling of greatest alarm over the future of the Soviet Union, and the destiny of the proletarian dictatorship. The policy of the present leadership, that is, the narrow group of Stalin, is driving the country at full speed towards the most dangerous crises and convulsions.

The immediate tactical task is: *To retreat from the positions of adventurism.*

[20]Stalin, *Leninism* (1942 edition), pp. 172-73.

A retreat is in any case inevitable. It is therefore necessary to carry it out as soon as possible, and in the most orderly manner possible.

To call a halt to "wholesale" collectivization, and to replace it with a careful selection based on genuine voluntary desire.

To put an end to record-breaking jumps in industrialization. To reconsider the question of tempos in the light of experience, from the standpoint of the necessity of raising the living standard of the working-class masses.

To abandon the "ideals" of a self-contained economy. To work out a new variant of the plan, calculated on the widest possible interaction with the world market.

To carry out the necessary retreat and then a strategic rearming, without too much damage and, above all, without losing its sense of perspective—this can be done only by a Party clearly cognizant of its aims and strength. . . . The fraud and the falsehoods of "self-criticism" must be replaced by honest Party democracy. . . .

It is impossible to find a way out from the present contradictions without crises and struggle. A favorable change in the relation of forces on a world scale, i.e., important successes of the international revolution, would, of course, introduce a very significant and even decisive factor into Soviet internal affairs. But it is impermissible to build a policy on expectations of some saving miracle "in the shortest possible period of time."[21]

Excerpt from Stalin's Report to the Sixteenth Congress of the Communist Party, June 27, 1930

If we take the number of head of cattle of all kinds in 1916 as equivalent to 100,

[21]*Bulletin of the Opposition* (April, 1930), quoted in *Not Guilty*, pp. 301–02.

we get the following picture year by year. In 1927 the number of horses was 88.9 per cent, large-horned cattle 114.3 per cent, sheep and goats 119.3 per cent, pigs 111.3 per cent. In 1928 the figure for horses was 94.6 per cent, large-horned cattle 118.5 per cent, sheep and goats 126 per cent, pigs 126.1 per cent. In 1929 the figure for horses was 90.9 per cent, large-horned cattle 115.6 per cent, sheep and goats 127.8 per cent, pigs 103 per cent. In 1930 the figure for horses was 88.6 per cent, large-horned cattle 89.1 per cent, sheep and goats 87.1 per cent, pigs 60.1 per cent of the 1916 level.

Thus you see that, taking into account the data of last year, we have patent signs of the beginning of decline in our stock breeding.

Even less consoling is the picture we get in respect of the *marketing* of animal products, particularly as regards meat and fat. If we take the gross output of meat and fat each year as 100, the part marketed represented in 1926, 33.4 per cent; in 1927, 32.9 per cent; in 1928, 31.4 per cent; in 1929, 29.2 per cent.

.   .   .   .   .

The distinctive feature of our difficulties consists in this, that *they themselves provide us with a basis for overcoming them.*

What follows from all this?

From this it follows, in the first place, that our difficulties are not difficulties of petty and accidental "mismanagement" but difficulties of class struggle.

It follows, secondly, that behind our difficulties are concealed our class enemies, that those difficulties are complicated by the desperate resistance of the dying classes in our country, the support these classes receive from outside, the presence of bureaucratic elements in our own institutions, the uncertainty and conservatism which exist in certain sections of our Party.

It follows, thirdly, that in order to overcome the difficulties it is necessary first of all to beat off the attacks of the capitalist elements, crush their resistance, and in this way clear the road for a rapid move forward. . . .

Therefore the *organisation of the offensive of Socialism along the whole front*—this is the task which has now arisen before us in developing our work of reconstructing the *whole* of national economy. . . .

But is an offensive, particularly an offensive along the whole front, permissible at all in the conditions of N.E.P. (the New Economic Policy)? . . .

In passing to the offensive along the whole front we are not abolishing the N.E.P., for private trade and capitalist elements still remain, commodity circulation and money economy still remain; but we are certainly abolishing the initial stage of N.E.P. and developing its further stage, the present stage of N.E.P., which is its last stage. . . .

But now comes the question, Has the time already arrived to pass to the offensive, is the moment mature for the offensive? . . .

To this question the Party has already given a clear and definite reply.

Yes, such a moment has already arrived.[22]

[22]Stalin, *Leninism* (1933 edition), Vol. II, pp. 275, 295–98.

From 1931 to 1933 the Stalinist government further tightened its grip on the country. The Five-Year Plan, barely under way, was accelerated so that it might achieve in four years, that is by January, 1933, what had originally been planned for five. The intensive collectivization movement, causing widespread destruction of crops and livestock, was followed by a severe famine in the Ukraine. But no matter how great the discontent, the inflexible Stalin never relaxed his control, and ever-increasing repression stifled whatever voice was left among the Opposition. Zinoviev and Kamenev, once more expelled from the Party in October, 1932, were exiled to Siberia. During the Seventeenth Party Congress, the "Congress of Victors," at which Zinoviev, Kamenev, and others publicly recanted their anti-Stalinist tendencies, Stalin made the following observations.

Excerpt from Stalin's Report to the Seventeenth Congress of the Communist Party, January 26, 1934

The anti-Leninist Trotskyite group has been defeated and scattered. Its organizers are now to be found in the backyards of the bourgeois parties abroad.

The anti-Leninist group of the Right deviationists has been defeated and scattered. Its organizers have long since renounced their views and are now trying in various ways to expiate the sins they committed against the party.

The national deviationist groups have been defeated and scattered. Their organizers have either completely merged with the interventionist emigrés, or else recanted.

The majority of the adherents of these anti-revolutionary groups have been compelled to admit that the line of the party was correct and have capitulated before the party.

At the Fifteenth Party Congress it was still necessary to prove that the party line was correct and to wage a struggle against certain anti-Leninist groups; and at the Sixteenth Party Congress we had to deal the final blow to the last adherents of these groups. At this Congress, however, there is nothing more to prove and, it seems, no one to fight. Everyone now sees that the line of the party has triumphed. . . .

Does this mean, however, that the fight is ended, and that the offensive of socialism is to be discontinued as unnecessary?

No, it does not mean that.

Does this mean that all is well in our party; that there will be no more deviations, and that, therefore, we may now rest on our laurels?

No, it does not mean that.

We have defeated the enemies of the party, the opportunists of all shades, the national deviationists of all types. But remnants of their ideologies still live in the minds of individual members of the party, and not infrequently they find expression. The party must not be regarded as something isolated from the people who surround it. It lives and works in its environment. It is not surprising that at times unhealthy moods penetrate into the party from outside. And the soil for such moods undoubtedly still exists in our country, if only for the reason that there still exist in town and country certain intermediary strata of the population who represent the medium that breeds such moods.

.   .   .   .   .

We have always said that the "Lefts" are also Rights, only they mask their Right-ness behind Left phrases. Now the "Lefts" themselves confirm the correctness of our statement. Take last year's issues of the Trotskyite *Bulletin*. What do Messieurs the Trotskyites demand; what do they write about; how does their "Left" program express itself? They demand: *the dissolution of the state farms* because they do not pay; *the dissolution of the majority of the collective farms* because they are fictitious, *the abandonment of the policy of eliminating the kulaks; reversion to the policy of concessions, and the leasing of a number of our industrial enterprises to concessionaires because they do not pay.*

There you have the program of these contemptible cowards and capitulators— their counter-revolutionary program of restoring capitalism in the U.S.S.R.!

What difference is there between this program and that of the extreme Rights? Clearly, there is none.[23]

-----

[23]Stalin, *Leninism* (1942 edition), pp. 339–40, 349.

The "Congress of Victors" in 1934 turned out to be but the entr'acte to the last phase of Stalin's consolidation of power and destruction of the Opposition. On December 1, 1934, Kirov, a member of the Politburo, was assassinated. The murder touched off a round of arrests, followed by trials, of most of the old Bolsheviks and Oppositionists. Zinoviev and Kamenev were put on trial in January, 1935, and sentenced to prison. Over a year later, from August 19 to 25, 1936, the same two, with fourteen others, were tried at the First Moscow Trial. They were accused of establishing a Terrorist Center, allied to the banished Trotsky, in 1932, shortly before their exile to Siberia. Found guilty, they were shot.

Five months later, from January 23 to 30, 1937, the Stalinist government staged a Second Trial, in which Radek, Pyatakov (vice-chairman of the People's Commissariat of Heavy Industry) and others were accused of establishing a center parallel to the original Terrorist Center.

Definition of the Charge, Second Moscow Trial, January, 1937

That, on the instructions of L. D. Trotsky, there was organized in 1933 a parallel center consisting of the following accused in the present case: Y. L. Pyatakov, K. B. Radek, G. Y. Sokolnikov, and L. P. Serebryakov, the object of which was to direct criminal, anti-Soviet, espionage, diversive and terrorist activities for the purpose of undermining the military power of the U.S.S.R., accelerating an armed attack on the U.S.S.R., assisting foreign aggressors to seize territory of the U.S.S.R. and to dismember it and overthrowing the Soviet Power and restoring capitalism and the rule of the bourgeoisie in the Soviet Union.

That, on the instructions of the aforesaid L. D. Trotsky, this center, through the accused Sokolnikov and Radek, entered into communication with representatives of certain foreign states for the purpose of organizing a joint struggle against the Soviet Union. . . .[24]

[24]*Report of Proceedings in the Case of the Anti-Soviet Trotskyite Centre . . . January 23–30, 1937* (Moscow: People's Commissariat of Justice of U.S.S.R., 1937), p. 18.

The verbatim record of the trial, amounting to over 500 pages, has been made available by the Soviet government. The procedure differed markedly from that of Western courts. Witnesses and evidence were largely lacking, and the bulk of the trial consisted of "confessional" statements amplified by interrogations of the state prosecutor, Andrei Vyshinsky, who first came to public attention at this time. The sum total of the testimony seemed to incriminate the defendants in large-scale conspiracy and treason, inspired by Trotsky from outside Russia. Shortly after the trial the complete testimony was analyzed at length by the "Trotsky Commission of Inquiry," headed by the distinguished philosopher John Dewey. Thus, even before World War II, the weakness of the government's case was revealed. These findings were confirmed by W. G. Krivitsky[25] in 1939, and after World War II, notably by Alexander Orlov, a former NKVD director who broke with Stalin in 1938. If any further evidence was needed, it was provided by Nikita Krushchev in 1956 and 1961 in his famous denunciations of Stalin.

The student will find further readings on the trials in A. E. Senn, *Readings in Russian Political and Diplomatic History* (Homewood, Ill.: The Dorsey Press, 1966), Vol. II, pp. 157–82. The great scholar of the Soviet Union, David J. Dallin, devoted part of his last book to the Second Trial.[26]

[25]W. G. Krivitsky, *In Stalin's Secret Service* (New York: Harper Bros., 1939).
[26]David J. Dallin, *From Purge to Coexistence* (Chicago: Henry Regnery Co., 1964), pp. 3–116.

**Testimony of Y. L. Pyatakov
at the Second Moscow Trial,
January 23, 1937**

PYATAKOV: I have already testified that during my conversations with Radek at the end of 1935 the question arose that it was necessary to meet Trotsky by one way or another. As I had that year to go to Berlin on official business for a few days, I agreed that I should attempt to see Trotsky. . . .

VYSHINSKY: When was this approximately?

PYATAKOV: It was on December 10, in the first half of December. That same day, or the next, I met Bukhartsev. . . . The next day Trotsky sent a messenger, with whom Bukhartsev brought me together in the Tiergarten. . . . He asked me if I was prepared to travel by airplane. I said I was prepared, although I realized how risky such an operation was. . . .

VYSHINSKY: Did your conversation with him end there?

PYATAKOV: He arranged to met me next morning at the Tempelhof Airport. . . .

VYSHINSKY: What happened next day?

PYATAKOV: Early next morning I went straight to the entrance of the airdrome. He was waiting at the entrance and led the way. . . . We got into an airplane and set off. We did not stop anywhere, and at approximately 3 p.m. we landed at the airdrome in Oslo. There an automobile awaited us. We got in and drove off. We drove for about 30 minutes and came to a country suburb. We got out, entered a small house that was not badly furnished, and there I saw Trotsky, whom I had not seen since 1928. It was here that my conversation with Trotsky took place. . . .

VYSHINSKY: How long did your conversation last?

PYATAKOV: About two hours.

VYSHINSKY: Tell us what you talked about.

PYATAKOV: The conversation began,

first of all, by my giving some information. I told him what the Trotskyite-Zinovievite centre had already done. . . . When we came to the subject of wrecking activity, he delivered himself of a veritable philippic. . . . At the same time he formulated very sharply, I would say perhaps for the first time, so clearly and precisely, his position with regard to wrecking activities. That is why he made those scathing statements. He said that socialism could not be built in one country alone, and that the collapse of the Stalin state was absolutely inevitable. . . . Wrecking and diversionist cadres were to be trained, not in any general way, but in order to draw a line of demarcation between the Stalin state and the Trotskyite organization, so that we might say, if anything happened, that we are not the Soviet state. That was one task. The other task was a more practical one: to train cadres for the event of war, that is to say, to train diversionists and those who would engage in destruction, helpers for the fascist attack on the Soviet Union. . . .

As to the international situation, he said that the proletarian revolutionary movement was being destroyed and that fascism was triumphant. If we intended to come to power, the real forces in the international situation were in the first place the fascists, and with these forces we must establish contact . . . and ensure that the attitude towards us should be favourable if we came to power. . . .

In connection with the international question Trotsky very emphatically insisted on the necessity of preparing diversionist cadres. He rebuked us for not engaging energetically enough in diversive, wrecking and terrorist activities.

He told me that he had come to an absolutely definite agreement with the fascist German government and with the Japanese government that they would adopt a favourable attitude in the event of the Trotskyite-Zinovievite *bloc* coming to power. But, he added, it went without saying that such a favourable attitude was not due to any particular love these governments cherished for the Trotskyite-Zinovievite *bloc*. It simply proceeded from the real interests of the fascist governments and from what we had promised to do for them if we came to power.

VYSHINSKY: What did you promise?

PYATAKOV: . . . A general favourable attitude towards German interests and towards the German government on all questions of international policy; certain territorial concessions would have to be made. . . .

The next point of the agreement dealt with the form in which German capital would be enabled to exploit in the Soviet Union the raw material resources it needs. It concerned the exploitation of gold mines, oil, manganese, forests, apatites, etc.

In short, it was agreed in principle between Trotsky and Hess that German capital would be allowed to come in and obtain a necessary economic complement but the definite forms which this was to assume would evidently be worked out later.[27]

Summary of Trotsky's Testimony before the Dewey Commission of Inquiry

Leon Trotsky testified that . . . the last time he saw Pyatakov was in 1927. He denied that he had seen Pyatakov in or near Oslo in December, 1935, or at any other place, or that he had seen him since 1927 or had any communication with him, either directly or through some intermediary. He denied that he had ever heard the name of Bukhartsev before the trial.[28]

Summary of an Affidavit Signed by Konrad Knudsen, His Wife, Hilda Knudsen and Their Daughter, Hjordis Knudsen, in the Possession of the Dewey Commission of Inquiry

[The affidavit states that] Trotsky and his wife were guests in the Knudsen home from June 18, 1935, to August 27, 1936, and that during this whole period, with the exception of a couple of brief interruptions for treatment at a hospital in Oslo, Trotsky resided with them . . .; that no visitor could enter the house without the knowledge of members of the household, and that Trotsky introduced them to all his visitors; . . . that the few times Trotsky was away from the house he left in Knudsen's car and in Knudsen's company; . . . that his visitors were Czechoslovaks, German emigrants, Englishmen, Frenchmen and Americans, and that there were no Russians among them; that Trotsky received no visitors during the month of December, 1935; that he spent two days of that month at their hut in the woods, and that this hut was not generally known and no one would have been able to find him there.[29]

Statement of Erwin Wolf, Trotsky's Secretary and Bodyguard

. . . Trotsky received no visit from a foreigner in the month of December, 1935, and a secret visit to Trotsky was out of the question, since not only I myself but also the members of the Knudsen family knew every step of Trotsky's. . . . I am above all in a position to state and to swear that Pyatakov's alleged visit to Trotsky is a pure invention, for the latter was in fact under my constant guardianship in December, 1935.[30]

[27]*Report of Proceedings in the Case of the Anti-Soviet Trotskyite Centre . . . January 23–30, 1937*, pp. 58–65.

[28]*Not Guilty*, p. 117.

[29]*Ibid.*, p. 182.

[30]*Ibid.*, p. 183.

**Excerpt from a Letter to Trotsky's
Lawyer from Director Gullichsen,
in Charge of the Kjeller (Oslo)
Airport, February 14, 1937**

In reply to your letter of the 10th inst.
I beg to state that my statement published
in *Arbeiderbladet* is correct, as no foreign
aeroplane landed here in December,
1935.[31]

Comments of Alexander Orlov

Pyatakov . . . signed a false deposition
which stated that, having taken advantage
of his trip to Berlin in December of 1935,
he wrote from there a letter to Trotsky
who was then in Norway, asking his directives on issues connected with the conspiracy. . . .

When at a conference at the Kremlin
Stalin listened to the report about Pyatakov's "testimony," he asked whether it
wouldn't be better to say in the deposition
of Pyatakov that he had received the directives from Trotsky not by mail, but
during a personal meeting with him. Thus
was born the notorious legend that Pyatakov had made a trip to Norway to see
Trotsky.

In order not to get into a scrape with
the new version, Stalin ordered Slutsky,
chief of the Foreign Department of the
NKVD, to work out a legend about Pyatakov's trip to Trotsky, taking into account
railroad schedules between Berlin and
Oslo. . . .

I learned in detail what occurred at the
next conference in the Kremlin from Slutsky himself, when he visited me in Paris
at the sanatorium of Professor Bergeré, in
February 1937.

At that conference Slutsky reported to
Stalin that the data which he had gathered made it expedient to adopt the story

of Pyatakov's trip to Norway. He explained that because of the existing railroad schedules Pyatakov's trip . . . would
require at least two days. . . .

Stalin was dissatisfied with Slutsky's report and didn't let him cite all his reasons
against the legend of Pyatakov's trip to
Oslo. "The things you said about the train
schedules might be true," said Stalin, "but
why couldn't Pyatakov fly to Oslo in an
airplane? Such a flight there and back
could most likely be made in one night."

In answer to that Slutsky remarked that
airplanes carry very few passengers and
that the name of every passenger is entered into the register of the air-line company. But Stalin had already made his
decision: "It must be said that Pyatakov
flew in a special plane," ordered Stalin.
"For such a job the German authorities
would glady give an airplane."

Slutsky, who loved to boast of every
talk he had with Stalin, told me about
that conference in strict confidence. . . .

It seemed that the legend invented by
Stalin about Pyatakov's flight to Oslo was
fully guaranteed from exposure: Pyatakov
could make the flight to Oslo and back in
one night, and even the shrewdest critic
wouldn't be able to prove that a lone
plane did not fly to Norway under the
cover of the night.

But a terrible shock awaited Stalin.

On the 25th of January, 1937, only two
days after Pyatakov had told at the trial
how he flew to Oslo in the middle of December of 1935, the Norwegian newspaper
Aftenposten made the following announcement:

PYATAKOV'S CONFERENCE
WITH TROTSKY
AT OSLO QUITE IMPROBABLE
. . . He is supposed to have arrived in a
monoplane at the Kjeller Airfield. Information
obtained at that field, however, states that no
civil airplane landed there during December
1935.

The sudden announcement that not a
single plane had landed at the Kjeller

_____
[31]*Ibid.*, p. 185.

Airdrome caught Stalin and his falsifiers unawares.

. . . . .

Pyatakov had faithfully carried out his part of the deal. Painful as it was to disgrace himself in public and blacken his immaculate and heroic past, he hoped that at the price of his humiliations he was saving the lives of his wife and child.

Pyatakov, like all other defendants, made a "last plea" speech before the court at the end of the trial. Of that short speech the following words struck me by their dramatic power:

"Any punishment which you may adjudge," said Pyatakov, "will be lighter than the very fact of confession . . .

"In a few hours you will pass your sentence; and here I stand before you in filth . . . a man who has lost his party, who has no friends, who has lost his family, who has lost his very self."

On January 30, 1937, the military court condemned thirteen out of the seventeen defendants to death before a firing squad. All the thirteen men, and among them Pyatakov, Serebriakov and other intimate friends of Lenin, were murdered in the cellar of the NKVD.[32]

Excerpts from Khrushchev's Secret Speech of February 25, 1956

Having at its disposal numerous data showing brutal willfulness toward Party cadres, the Central Committee has created a Party Commission under the control of the Central Committee Presidium; it was charged with investigating what made possible the mass repressions against the majority of the Central Committee members and candidates elected at the XVIIth Congress of the All-Union Communist Party (Bolsheviks).

The Commission has become acquainted with a large quantity of materials in the NKVD archives and with other documents and has established many facts pertaining to the fabrication of cases against Communists, to false accusations, to glaring abuses of socialist legality—which resulted in the death of innocent people. It became apparent that many Party, Soviet and economic activists who were branded in 1937–1938 as "enemies" were actually never enemies, spies, wreckers, etc., but were always honest Communists; they were only so stigmatized, and often, no longer able to bear barbaric tortures, they charged themselves (at the order of the investigative judges-falsifiers) with all kinds of grave and unlikely crimes. The Commission has presented to the Central Committee Presidium lengthy and documented materials pertaining to mass repressions against the delegates to the XVIIth Party Congress and against members of the Central Committee elected at that Congress. These materials have been studied by the Presidium of the Central Committee.

It was determined that of the 139 members and candidates of the Party's Central Committee who were elected at the XVIIth Congress, 98 persons, i.e., 70 percent, were arrested and shot (mostly in 1937–1938). (*Indignation in the hall.*)

. . . . .

The same fate met not only the Central Committee members but also the majority of the delegates to the XVIIth Party Congress. Of 1966 delegates with either voting or advisory rights, 1,108 persons were arrested on charges of anti-revolutionary crimes, i.e., decidedly more than a majority. This very fact shows how absurd, wild and contrary to common sense were the charges of counter-revolutionary crimes made out, as we now see, against a majority of participants at the XVIIth Party Congress. (*Indignation in the hall.*)

. . . . .

[32]Alexander Orlov, *The Secret History of Stalin's Crimes* (New York: Random House, Inc., 1953), pp. 182–87.

Now when the cases of some of these so-called "spies" and "saboteurs" were examined it was found that all their cases were fabricated. Confessions of guilt of many arrested and charged with enemy activity were gained with the help of cruel and inhuman tortures.

At the same time Stalin, as we have been informed by members of the Political Bureau of that time, did not show them the statements of many accused political activists when they retracted their confessions before the military tribunal and asked for an objective examination of their cases. There were many such declarations, and Stalin doubtlessly knew of them.

The Central Committee considers it absolutely necessary to inform the Congress of many such fabricated "cases" against the members of the Party's Central Committee elected at the XVIIth Party Congress.

.   .   .   .   .

Many thousands of honest and innocent Communists have died as a result of this monstrous falsification of such "cases," as a result of the fact that all kinds of slanderous "confessions" were accepted, and as a result of the practice of forcing accusations against oneself and others. In the same manner were fabricated the "cases" against eminent Party and state workers—Kossior, Chubar, Postyshev, Kosarev, and others.

In those years repressions on a mass scale were applied which were based on nothing tangible and which resulted in heavy cadre losses to the Party.

The vicious practice was condoned of having the NKVD prepare lists of persons whose cases were under the jurisdiction of the Military Collegium and whose sentences were prepared in advance. Yezhov would send these lists to Stalin personally for his approval of the proposed punishment. In 1937–1938, 383 such lists containing the names of many thousands of

Party, Soviet Komsomol, Army and economic workers were sent to Stalin. He approved these lists.

A large part of these cases are being reviewed now and a great part of them are being voided because they were baseless and falsified. Suffice it to say that from 1954 to the present time the Military Collegium of the Supreme Court has rehabilitated 7,679 persons, many of whom were rehabilitated posthumously.

Mass arrests of Party, Soviet, economic and military workers caused tremendous harm to our country and to the cause of socialist advancement. . . .

Only because our Party has at its disposal such great moral-political strength was it possible for it to survive the difficult events in 1937–1938 and to educate new cadres. There is, however, no doubt that our march forward toward socialism and toward the preparation of the country's defense would have been much more successful were it not for the tremendous loss in the cadres suffered as a result of the baseless and false mass repressions in 1937–1938.

We are justly accusing Yezhov for the degenerate practices of 1937. But we have to answer these questions: Could Yezhov have arrested Kossior, for instance, without the knowledge of Stalin? Was there an exchange of opinions or a Political Bureau decision concerning this? No, there was not, as there was none regarding other cases of this type. Could Yezhov have decided such important matters as the fate of such eminent Party figures? No, it would be a display of naivete to consider this the work of Yezhov alone. It is clear that these matters were decided by Stalin, and that without his orders and his sanction Yezhov could not have done this.[33]

---

[33]*The Anti-Stalin Campaign and International Communism*, ed. Russian Institute of Columbia University (New York: Columbia University Press, 1956), pp. 22–39.

Few victims of Russian trials have testified concerning the methods by which confessions were obtained. In 1945, a Polish resistance leader, Zbigniew Stypulkowski, was subjected to a trial in the Soviet Union. He later wrote a book about his experiences,[34] and also testified before an American Congressional inquiry. His comments provide one of the most vivid accounts of what presumably happened during the trials of the 1930's.

Testimony of Polish Underground Leader Zbigniew Stypulkowski

MR. STYPULKOWSKI: . . . The method applied by the Russian judge—he is not a judge, he is in fact a NKVD man, in my case a major of the NKVD called Senior Judge for special cases. He applied a sci-entifically worked-out method of interro-gation, which can be applied only by very few able men. Therefore all the best trained judges are concentrated in Mos-cow and are in the Security Ministry, which is attached to the Lubianka prison; it forms one block of buildings. In my opinion this method is based on the co-ordination of physical pressure in time with psychological pressure. The physical pressure applied on the body of the vic-tim consists, in my case, and in all cases when they are to be brought to public trial, of such means as light, cold, hunger, atmosphere of terror, and especially sleep-lessness, lack of sleep. I was lying in a bed in the cell facing a very large bulb fixed at the door in this fashion: the beams were beaming directly on my face; it was about 300 watts. This light was in my cell day and night. During the night, if I tried to hide my eyes from this beaming light, and I turned over on my back, or hid my eyes with my hands, the warder would immediately come in and say in a whis-per, "It is not allowed to sleep like that.

[34]*Invitation to Moscow* (London: Thames & Hudson, 1951).

I must see your eyes." And he turned my body so that I had to face all the time the light. This was repeated every time I turned for a moment on my back. This was one tool of physical pressure.

Another was hunger. We were getting in the morning two slices of bread and a huge amount of water. For lunch we were getting some water with cabbage leaves in it, sometimes some fish bones were added to it. At 5 o'clock we were getting two spoonfuls of barley, and that was all. Of course, I could stand this diet in the first days very easily, my reserves allowed me. But after a few weeks, thinking that the time had come when the warder would bring these two slices of bread, I would spring like a tiger to grasp them. As a result, after a few weeks my legs were swollen, I was trembling all the time. During the hearings I left on the desk the wet from my fingers amounting to a good glass for brandy.

Then sleeplessness. I was allowed to sleep, according to the rules on the walls of the prison, between 2 and 4 in the af-ternoon, and then from 10 to 6 at night. Excellent. I think all the delegates who are still visiting Russia representing the Labor Federation, and so on, are shown these rules on the wall. But what they do not know is that I was being called to the judge always all the nights except 1 dur-ing 70 days, and many afternoons just at the time when I was allowed to sleep ac-cording to the rules. If I tried to have a sleep even in a sitting position during the daytime I was immediately warned by the warder that "It is not allowed," and my nap was interrupted. After some weeks I lived in a semiconscious state due to this torture.

Then cold. It was very cold, not freezingly so, but enough for the weakened body of the man hungry and not sleeping to tremble all the time. So that when I have seen my colleagues during the confrontations I had the impression that I have met somebody completely changed from what I used to know, only the name remained the same. This man was completely representative of some creature like a man, but was not as a real man. I looked much the same.

I told you that also the general atmosphere of terror is helping the Russian aims. I have in mind the fact that I was being physically examined during the 70 days more than once, 200 or 300 times. The Russians even examined all the days my soles, to see whether something is not sticking to them. . . .

That was the physical side of pressure, the exercise of pressure on the body of the victims. This would give no result in a few days, so that the judge waits very patiently until the evident signs of the weakening of the body appear. In the meantime he held interminable discussions with me in his study. I had 41 examinations. The shortest one lasted about 3 hours, but not infrequently I was being examined for 15 hours without respite. Sometimes I was called at 10 o'clock in the evening, sometimes at 1 in the morning, sometimes 3 times during 1 night, and so on. During the examinations I had to sit at that position, with outstretched arms.

(Let the record show the witness is sitting up with his hands in front of him on the table.) I looked straight-forwardly to the judge, who, for security reasons, was sitting at the end of the study.

.   .   .   .   .

But as to what happened to my col-leagues, 1 of them was very old, about 70 years, and he had left in the country his 3 sisters who were even older than he. He was deceived by this friendly atmosphere of the first conversation, and he gave the addresses of his sisters. After 3 days, on the desk of the judge were dispersed small things of sentimental value taken out of the house of those sisters, some books, some photographs. The judge would not ask any questions about these things to the arrested man, but if he noticed that he did not observe it, then he took it and said, "Is this yours?" Nothing more, and then the inner struggle starts, and the conscience of the arrested man left alone in the cell. He begins to consider, "What have I done? I have given my sisters into Communist hands. Their fate is precluded unless I will act according to their will. I must do my best to save them."

.   .   .   .   .

Here is the basic difference between the methods which the Germans applied toward their arrested people and the Russians. The Germans, when they arrested—I know it from my own experience—they dealt with the person very quickly. They tried to achieve by force, brutal force, the confession, the details about the underground movement and anti-German activity; they beat the victim, sometimes to the extent that he sometimes died from it. But if the Germans did not achieve the confession of the material which they sought to have, they sent the victim after a short time to some concentration camp, sentenced him to death or left him in this concentration camp to die. The matter was settled.

The Russians acted quite contrary to this strategy. They have always plenty of time to deal with the victim. They are never impatient, they are seeking to get the result by very slow and psychological action to achieve this main aim, which is to transform the psychological attitude of the victim. . . .

I told you at the beginning that the psychological pressure must be well coordinated in time with the physical pressure because the man who is still sound, who is still strong, has his critical sense, but under these circumstances he loses his critical sense. He is left with an imagination. He makes as fact some rumors he has heard. His division of opinion grows to the extent of being of essential importance. He learns by heart the ideas which were put in his mind through these weeks and weeks by the judges, and then he accepts them as his own, to the extent that after our trial I was sitting with some of my companions who pleaded guilty. The trial was over, and some of them discussed with me the procedure of investigation, and they were still convinced that many of the judges' arguments were right and that they were their own.

·   ·   ·   ·   ·

MR. McTIGUE: Did any rules of evidence apply in the Soviet trials, as they apply, for example, in the courts of the United States?

MR. STYPULKOWSKI: They considered to be fully proved material that the judges extracted from us during the period of interrogation. But they had witnesses. They called about 15, I think. These witnesses without exception were brought from prison. The majority of them were already under sentence of death. So that their appearance in the court was the last chance for them to save their heads, and therefore we observed a very tragic situation. The witnesses knew their lessons by heart and sometimes exaggerated their evidence even beyond what the prosecutor wanted from them, so that the prosecutor sometimes tried to break their evidence. But they would continue by saying "But I have not yet told this or that." This was really an extremely tragic moment during the hearings. Their depositions were very funny, but also very important from the point of view of Soviet Russian policy.[35]

[35]Testimony before the House of Representatives Committee, 1954, in *Communist Aggression Investigation:* Fourth Interim Report of Hearings before the Select Committee on Communist Aggression, House of Representatives, 83rd Cong., 2d sess., Part 2 (Washington, D.C.: U.S. Government Printing Office, 1954), pp. 1079–90.

A noteworthy element of the Moscow Trials was the lack of documentary evidence produced in court. Although several Trotsky letters were referred to, none apparently was still in existence; in any event no very incriminating document was exhibited or became, so far as the verbatim text is concerned, a part of the record. However, one of the few references to a specific document was included in the summing-up of the prosecutor, here reproduced in part.

FOR CONSIDERATION   The Trotsky statement referred to by Vyshinsky has been printed, in another translation, in this collection (See Trotsky's Open Letter of April, 1930). Does the complete text uphold Vyshinsky's allegations of treason, conspiracy, and terrorism? If the program set forth in Trotsky's Open Letter "in essence, is the same thing" as the program summarized in the prosecutor's charge, how much reliability can be placed on Vyshinsky's accusations?

**Excerpt from the Speech for the
Prosecution by the Soviet Procurator,
A. Y. Vyshinsky, at the Second
Moscow Trial, January 28, 1937**

The united Zinovievite-Trotskyite centre and its active members persistently tried to prove that they did not advance any political program demands—that they were merely imbued with a "bare thirst for power." This is untrue.... It turned out that they did have a program, just as the Trotskyite terrorist centre had a program. This program was an open assertion of the need for capitalist restoration in the U.S.S.R....Sokolnikov said:

... We were of the opinion that fascism is the most organized form of capitalism, it is conquering, seizing Europe, strangling us. Therefore, it would be better to arrive at some compromise in the sense of retreating from socialism to capitalism. ...

Radek said that it was clear that:
"The master of the situation would be fascism—German fascism on the one hand, and the military fascism of a Far-Eastern country, on the other."

And, of course, Trotsky, their teacher, understood this no less than they did. The whole Trotskyite centre understood it. They accepted it with open eyes. This was the second point of their "remarkable" program.

The third point was the question of war and the defeat of the U.S.S.R.

The fourth was the question of the consequences of the defeat: not only leasing as concessions the industrial enterprises which the imperialist states regarded as important, but selling outright to private owners important economic units which they had already earmarked for this purpose....

The fifth point was what they called the agrarian problem.... This was the manner in which they proposed to solve the agrarian problem: burn all the gains of the proletarian revolution—dissolve the collective farms, liquidate the state farms, hand over the tractors and other complex agricultural machinery to individual farmers....

The sixth question was the question of democracy. Radek has related what Trotsky had written him on this subject. ... "In this letter Trotsky said" (I am quoting Radek's testimony):

There can be no talk whatever about democracy. The working class has experienced 18 years of revolution and its appetite is enormous. ... In order to hold on, a strong government will be needed, irrespective of the forms in which it will be clothed. ...

Finally, the seventh question was the program of foreign policy, of partitioning the country: "Give the Ukraine to Germany; the Maritime Province and the Amur region to Japan."...

The existence of this program was admitted here by Pyatakov, Radek, and Sokolnikov; they themselves told us about it in this Court.

But perhaps it is all an invention? Perhaps they said this simply because they wanted to play the comedy of repentant sinners? Since they have repented they must talk about something or other, they must expose something or other. Perhaps Trotsky never gave them such a line?

But, Comrade Judges, you know, everybody knows, that abroad, Trotsky publishes the so-called *Bulletin of the Opposition*, and if you take No. 10 of this *Bulletin*, for April, 1930, you will find that it contains what, in essence, is the same thing: [Omissions in the quotation are Vyshinsky's.]

... All the same, retreat is inevitable. It must be carried out as soon as possible. ...
... Put a stop to "mass" collectivization. ...
... Put a stop to the hurdle race of industrialization. Revise the question of tempo in the light of experience. ...

. . . Abandon the "ideals" of self-contained economy. Draw up a new variant of a plan providing for the widest possible intercourse with the world market. . . .

. . . Carry out the necessary retreat, and then strategical rearmament. . . .

. . . It will be impossible to emerge from the present contradictions without crises and struggle. . . .[36]

[36]*Report of Proceedings in the Case of the Anti-Soviet Trotskyite Centre . . . January 23–30, 1937*, pp. 489–94.

How many people were involved in the purges? What did people think about them? The following documents give some insight into these questions. Alexander Weissberg had been imprisoned in Russia at the time. Ilya Ehrenburg was one of the Soviet Union's best-kown journalists. Joseph E. Davies and Robert Coulondre were, respectively, the American and French Ambassadors to Russia.

Comments of Ilya Ehrenburg

I realized that people were being accused of crimes which they had not and could not have committed, and I asked myself and others: why, what for? No one could give me an answer. We were completely at sea.

I was present at the opening session of the Supreme Soviet—the newspaper gave me a press card. The oldest deputy, the eighty-year-old academician A. N. Bach, who had been a member of the *Narodnaya Volya* (The People's Will) in the remote past, read his speech from a paper and, naturally, ended it with the name of Stalin. A thunder of applause greeted it. I had the impression that the old scholar reeled as from the blast of an explosion. I was sitting up above, there were ordinary Muscovites—factory and office workers—all around me, and they were in a frenzy.

. . . In the minds of millions of people Stalin had become a sort of mythical demi-god; everyone uttered his name with awe and believed that he alone could save the Soviet State from invasion and disruption.

We thought (perhaps we wanted to think) that Stalin knew nothing about the senseless violence committed against the Communists, against the Soviet intelligentsia.

Meyerhold said: "They conceal it from Stalin."

One night, when I was taking Chuka for a run, I met Boris Pasternak in Lavrushensky lane; he waved his arms about as he stood between the snowdrifts: "If only someone would tell Stalin about it".

Yes, not only I, but many other people thought that the evil came from the small man whom they called the "Stalin People's Commissar". People who had never belonged to any opposition, who were loyal followers of Stalin or honest non-party specialists were arrested. Those years came to be known as *"Yezhovshchina"* (The Yezhov time).

In my opinion Babel was more intelligent than I, and cleverer than most. He had known Yezhov's wife before her marriage. He sometimes went to see her, aware that this was unwise, but wanting, as he told me, "to find a key to the puzzle". One day he said, shaking his head: "It's not a matter of Yezhov. Of course Yezhov plays his part, but he's not at the bottom of it". Yezhov shared the fate of Yagoda. His place was taken by Beria in whose time Babel, Meyerhold, Koltsov and many other innocent people perished.

I remember a terrible day at Meyer-hold's. We were sitting peacefully look-ing through an illustrated monograph on Renoir, when a friend of Meyerhold, the Corps Commander I. P. Belov, arrived. He was very worked up and, without paying any attention to our presence, began to describe the trial of Tukhachev-sky and other high ranking officers. Belov was a member of the Military Collegium of the Supreme Court. "They were sitting like that—facing us. Uborevich looked me in the eyes ..." I remember another phrase of Belov's: "And tomorrow I'll be put in the same place." Then he suddenly turned to me: "Do you know Uspensky? Not Gleb, Nikolay. There's a man who wrote the truth." And he gave us rather incoherently the gist of a story by Uspen-sky, I do not recall which, but a very cruel one. Belov left soon after. I glanced at Meyerhold; he sat with his eyes shut looking like a wounded bird. (Belov was arrested soon after.)[37]

Comments of Alexander Weissberg

Throughout 1937 I made a systematic note of the happenings and drew up statistics. I reckoned which groups of the population, according to age, nationality and class, were most represented among the arrested, and I never lost an oppor-tunity of discussing the various hypothet-ical explanations put forward by my fel-low prisoners. It was not until the autumn of 1938 that a theory gradually began to take shape to fit the facts as we knew them.

As early as the spring of 1937 we be-gan to calculate our numbers. There was one quite simple method of doing it. Every new prisoner who came in had

some money with him and various objects which he was not allowed to have with him in the cells, for instance, his braces, a pocket knife, a metal comb and such things. When he was formally entered into the prison books, these things were taken away from him and he was given two receipts, one for the money and the other for the things. These receipts were all numbered so that when two prisoners came into our cell within a month of each other all we had to do was to compare the numbers on their receipts and we could tell approximately how many people had been arrested in that time. Now, the Kholodnaya Gora was the central prison for Kharkov and its sur-roundings, and this meant that all pris-oners passed through it before they were sent off to the camps even if their inter-rogations had taken place in some other prison. It was in our prison that the camp transports were made up. In this way we were able to obtain the approximate number of prisoners and then we related it to the total population. By the time I left on February 20, 1939, we had ar-rived at the conclusion that within the past two years 5.5 per cent of the total population of Kharkov and its surround-ings had been arrested.

This is a fairly large territory and we were therefore in a position to draw ap-proximate conclusions from the numbers arrested there as to the numbers arrested throughout the country as a whole. How-ever, we were not entirely satisfied with that. From the prisoners who came to us from other towns or were brought back from the camps for further interrogation, or perhaps confrontation, we learned that our methods of counting were in opera-tion in all central prisons everywhere, and that our results were approximately the same as those obtained elsewhere. The results varied between 5.5 and 6 per cent of the total population. If we take the lower figure it gives us a grand total of about nine million arrests.

---

[37]Ilya Ehrenburg, *Men, Years—Life,* Vol. IV, *Eve of War, 1933–1941,* trans. Tatania Shebu-niana in collaboration with Yvonne Kapp (Lon-don: MacGibbon and Kee, 1963), pp. 196–97.

From this total we must deduct about two millions for men charged with criminal offenses and whose arrest had nothing to do with the purge.[38]

Comments of Joseph E. Davies

With an interpreter at my side, I followed the testimony carefully. Naturally I must confess that I was predisposed against the credibility of the testimony of these defendants. The unanimity of their confessions, the fact of their long imprisonment (*incommunicado*) with the possibility of duress and coercion extending to themselves or their families, all gave me grave doubts as to the reliability that could attach to their statements. Viewed objectively, however, and based upon my experience in the trial of cases and the application of the tests of credibility which past experience had afforded me, I arrived at the reluctant conclusion that the state had established its case, at least to the extent of proving the existence of a widespread conspiracy and plot among the political leaders against the Soviet government, and which under their statutes established the crimes set forth in the indictment.

.   .   .   .   .

On the face of the record in this case it would be difficult for me to conceive of any court, in any jurisdiction, doing other than adjudging the defendants guilty of violations of the law as set forth in the indictment and as defined by the statutes.

I have talked to many, if not all, of the members of the Diplomatic Corps here and, with possibly one exception, they are all of the opinion that the proceedings established clearly the existence of a political plot and conspiracy to overthrow the government.

.   .   .   .   .

It is the prevailing opinion here of the Diplomatic Corps, as well as that of American journalists, that the Stalin government is thoroughly entrenched in power and, in the absence of foreign war, will continue to be so for a long time.[39]

Comments of French Ambassador to Russia, Robert Coulondre

I personally attended the Second and Third Moscow Trials, those of 1937 and 1938, from the reading of the charge to the final sentence. . . .

After the chairman declared the session open, the defendants entered and silently took their places. . . . They were mute, acting somewhat like automatons. . . . They made their statements in a monotone; there was something impersonal about most of them which must have struck everyone who was there. Free defendants, I mean mentally free, have a natural lively attitude of defense which you find in all our courts, unless the accused persons are prostrated. But the Moscow defendants were not prostrated. The word would be inappropriate, for they expressed themselves lucidly and with facility. They were entirely detached, as if outside of themselves; they were truly impersonal. . . .

I went from astonishment to astonishment, listening to the confessions of these defendants at the Second Trial. At first the impressions I have just recorded were not strong enough to make me suspicious and I told myself that the police had really got hold of a nest of vipers. Only gradually, as their confessions stressed their rascality, as the acts of

[38]Alexander Weissberg, *The Accused*, trans. Edward Fitzgerald (New York: Simon and Schuster, Inc., 1951), pp. 318–19.

[39]Joseph E. Davies, *Mission to Moscow* (New York: Simon and Schuster, Inc., 1941), pp. 42–46. Reprinted by permission of Simon and Schuster, publishers. Copyright 1941, by Joseph E. Davies.

contrition emphasized their repentance, did I gather the impression that there had been "intervention," and I wondered how it would come out.

When Pyatakov got up and spoke, the cup was full.

Pyatakov was well known abroad, where he had often come as head of the Soviet oil monopoly; he was the typical loyal businessman, clear and precise in speech and with a cool head on his shoulders. Nothing I knew about him would lead me to believe that he was a fanatic or a sadist. Yet I heard Pyatakov, with a faraway voice and an absent manner, declare that he had intrigued abroad with Trotsky to support the latter's treasons; that he had raised the price of Soviet goods to finance this treason; that he had blown up factories in Russia and had had trains derailed; that he had even tried to poison all the workers of one factory. I felt like getting up, as Krestinsky was to do at the Third Trial, and shouting at Pyatakov: "It's not true, you lie, you are even deceiving yourself." ...

Only one of the defendants, Radek, seemed to me to be himself in the course of the Second Trial. He was, if I am not mistaken, a Jew of Polish extraction, highly intelligent and a brilliant speaker. He provided his part of the trial with an appearance of reality. He spoke to the point; unfortunately, he wanted to prove too much. Radek's attitude contrasted with that of the other defendants and revealed the false front of the whole trial. It is not impossible that this great publicity man was also a great actor and that the G.P.U. had obtained his cooperation in this second capacity, with promises to save his life.

.   .   .   .   .

Was there some truth in the "confessions" of the defendants? Probably. The worst lies are those based on truth. What seems reasonable is that those who were guilty were not guilty of all the crimes enumerated in the charge. But that they

had shown themselves hostile to the Stalin regime, that they had more or less plotted "à la russe," is possible and even probable. I think there is a born conspirator in every Slav.

.   .   .   .   .

The lesson recited by the defendants must have been imposed, otherwise it is incredible that they would have recited it. How? Not being an expert on torture, I am in no position to say.... It is possible that some of the defendants, having failed to put across their brand of communism, and realizing that they had lost out, acquiesced in dying for Stalin so that, in all events, communism might live. All that one can say for this theory is that it is better adapted to the Russian than to the Western mentality.

It is entirely probable that most of the guilty persons had been subjected to other forms of pressure, and, primarily, torture—not physical, for those who were to be publicly exhibited must obviously not show traces of violence, but some psychological kind. Don't you think that if a person was kept awake over long periods, if every night he was prepared for execution, if his nervous system was so upset he couldn't see a member of the G.P.U. without fainting, he would sign any confession? Some would give in to save their families, others in the hope of saving their own lives....

I think that neither conception nor execution of these spectacle-trials was Stalin's work. The conception and execution was too elementary, too sophomoric; the authorship must have been left to the Soviet police. However, Stalin necessarily not only knew about them, but he approved and controlled these base works. He was thus responsible for them. Were they really necessary for the success of his policy?[40]

---

[40]Robert Coulondre, *De Staline à Hitler* (Paris: Librairie Hachette, 1950), pp. 87–92. Quoted by permission of Librairie Hachette, Paris, publishers.

BIBLIOGRAPHY

Sources Used in This Problem

1. *Collections and Official Documents*

The Anti-Stalin Campaign and International Communism. Edited by the Russian Institute of Columbia University. New York: Columbia University Press, 1956.

Bulletin of the Relief Fund for Anarchists (periodical).

Communist Aggression Investigation: Fourth Interim Report of Hearings before the Select Committee on Communist Aggression. House of Representatives (83rd Cong., 2d Sess.). Washington, D.C.: U.S. Government Printing Office, 1954.

Crapouillot (periodical) .

Report of Proceedings in the Case of the Anti-Soviet Trotskyite Centre. . . . January 23–30, 1937. Moscow: People's Commissariat of Justice of U.S.S.R., 1937.

Strategy and Tactics of World Communism: The Communist Conspiracy. House of Representatives, 84th Cong., 2d sess. Washington, D.C.: U.S. Government Printing Office, 1956.

2. *Others*

Coulondre, Robert. *De Staline à Hitler.* Paris: Hachette, 1950.

Dallin, David J. *From Purge to Coexistence.* Chicago: H. Regnery, 1964.

Davies, Joseph E. *Mission to Moscow.* New York: Simon and Schuster, 1941.

Ehrenburg, Ilya. *Men, Years—Life,* Vol. IV, *Eve of War, 1933–1941.* Tr. by Tatania Shebuniana with Yvonne Kapp. London: MacGibbon & Kee, 1963.

Kravchenko, Victor. *I Chose Freedom.* New York: Scribner's, 1946.

Lyons, Eugene. *Assignment in Utopia.* New York: Harcourt, Brace, 1937.

Not Guilty. Report of the Committee of Inquiry into Charges Made against Trotsky (John Dewey, Chairman). New York: Harpers, 1938.

Orlov, Alexander. *The Secret History of Stalin's Crimes.* New York: Random House, 1953.

Serge, Victor. *Memoirs of a Revolutionary.* London: Oxford University Press, 1963.

Serge, Victor. *Russia Twenty Years After.* New York: Hillman, 1937.

Stalin, Joseph. *Leninism.* New York: International Publishers, 1933. 2 Vols.

Stalin, Joseph. *Leninism: Selected Writings.* New York: International Publishers, 1942.

Trotsky, Leon. *My Life.* New York: Scribner's, 1930.

Trotsky, Leon. *The Real Situation in Russia.* Tr. by Max Eastman. New York: Harcourt, Brace, 1928.

Vyshinsky, Andrei (ed.). *The Law of the Soviet State.* Tr. by H. W. Babb. New York: Macmillan, 1948.

Weissberg, Alexander. *The Accused.* Tr. by Edward Fitzgerald. New York: Simon and Schuster, 1951.

Select List of Books Recommended for Further Reading

Alliluyeva, Svetlana. *Twenty Letters to a Friend.* New York: Harper and Row, 1967.

ASPATURIAN, VERNON V. *The Soviet Union in the World Communist System.* Stanford, Calif.: Stanford University Press, 1966.

AVTORKHANOV, A. *Stalin and the Soviet Communist Party.* New York: Praeger, 1959.

BARMINE, ALEXANDER. *One Who Survived.* New York: G. P. Putnam's, 1945.

BECK, F. and GORDON, W. *Russian Purge and the Extraction of Confession.* New York: Viking, 1951.

BRZEZINSKI, ZBIGNIEW. *The Permanent Purge.* Cambridge, Mass.: Harvard University Press, 1956.

BUKHARINE, NIKOLAI I. *Letter of an Old Bolshevik.* London: Allen & Unwin, 1938.

CARR, EDWARD H. *History of Soviet Russia.* London: Macmillan, 1950.

CHAMBERLIN, WILLIAM M. *The Russian Enigma.* New York: Scribner's, 1943.

DALLIN, DAVID J. *The Real Soviet Russia.* New Haven, Conn.: Yale University Press, 1947.

DANIELS, ROBERT V. *The Conscience of the Revolution: Communist Opposition in Soviet Russia.* Cambridge, Mass.: Harvard University Press, 1960.

DANIELS, ROBERT V. (ed.) *The Stalin Revolution: Fulfillment or Betrayal of Communism.* Problems of European Civilization. Boston: D. C. Heath, 1965.

DEUTSCHER, ISAAC. *The Prophet Outcast: Trotsky.* New York: Oxford University Press, 1963.

DEUTSCHER, ISAAC. *Stalin: A Political Biography.* New York: Oxford University Press, 1949.

DEWAR, HUGO. *The Modern Inquisition.* London: Wingate, 1953.

DJILAS, MILOYAN. *Conversations with Stalin.* New York: Harcourt, Brace, World, 1962.

ERLICH, ALEXANDER. *The Soviet Industrialization Debate, 1924–1928.* Cambridge, Mass.: Harvard University Press, 1950.

FAINSOD, MERLE. *How Russia Is Ruled.* Cambridge, Mass.: Harvard University Press, 1953.

FAINSOD, MERLE. *Smolensk under Soviet Rule.* Cambridge, Mass.: Harvard University Press, 1958.

GINSBURG, EUGENIA SEMYONOVNA. *Journey into the Whirlwind.* New York: Harcourt, Brace, 1967.

KRIVITSKY, W. G. *In Stalin's Secret Service.* New York: Harper, 1939.

KULSKI, W. W. *The Soviet Regime.* Syracuse: Syracuse University Press, 1959.

LEITES, N. and BERNAUT, E. *Ritual of Liquidation.* New York: Free Press, 1954.

LIPPER, ELINOR. *Eleven Years in Soviet Prison Camps.* Chicago: H. Regnery, 1951.

LYONS, EUGENE. *Workers' Paradise Lost: Fifty Years of Soviet Communism.* New York: Funk & Wagnalls, 1967.

MACLEAN, FITZROY. *Escape to Adventure.* Boston: Little Brown, 1950.

PAYNE, ROBERT. *The Rise and Fall of Stalin.* New York: Simon and Schuster, 1965.

PONOMARYOV, BORIS N. *History of the Communist Party of the Soviet Union.* Moscow: Foreign Languages Publishing House, 1960.

RANDALL, F. B. *Stalin's Russia.* New York: Free Press, 1965.

SCHAPIRO, LEONARD. *The Communist Party of the Soviet Union.* New York: Random House, 1960.

SENN, A. E. *Readings in Russian Political and Diplomatic History.* Homewood, Ill.: The Dorsey Press, 1966, Vol. II.

STALIN, JOSEPH. *Works.* 13 vols. Moscow: Foreign Languages Publishing House, 1954–.

STEINBERG, J. (ed.) *Verdict of Three Decades*. New York: Duell, Sloan & Pearce, 1950.

STYPULKOWSKI, ZBIGNIEW. *Invitation to Moscow*. London: Thames & Hudson, 1951.

TROTSKY, LEON. *The Revolution Betrayed*. New York: Pioneer Publishers, 1937.

TUCKER, R. C., and COHEN, S. F. (eds.). *The Great Purge Trial*. New York: Grosset & Dunlap, 1965.

VON LAUE, THEODORE H. *Why Lenin? Why Stalin? A Reappraisal of the Russian Revolution, 1900–1930*. Philadelphia: J. B. Lippincott, 1964.

WOLFE, BERTRAM D. *Khrushchev and Stalin's Ghost*. New York: 1956.

GERMANY—THE THREAT OF NAZI POWER

From Munich to the outbreak of World War II, 1937-39

Of the many elements which comprise the complex syndrome known as fascism, foreign policy stands out as one of the most significant and characteristic. Adolf Hitler was determined to bring Germany once more to a position of power, and to accomplish this he had first to rebuild the *Wehrmacht* and expand Germany's territorial limits. By 1937 he had already obtained the Saar, had remilitarized the Rhineland, had negotiated a naval agreement with Great Britain, and was ready to consider the direction and aims of future policy.

The degree to which Hitler possessed fanatical aggressive intentions, and consequently was personally to blame for World War II, has been variously estimated by historians. Hitler's rabble-rousing speeches, his autobiographical *Mein Kampf*, and his so-called "Secret Book" (written in 1928 but not published until 1961), all testify to his concern for German living space and the need for rearmament. At the Nuremberg Trials no serious questions were raised concerning German war guilt, and documents such as the Hossbach Memorandum (part of which is here reproduced) seemed to confirm the generally accepted opinion regarding Hitler's responsibility for the war.

In 1961, the British historian A. J. P. Taylor set forth a provocative thesis maintaining that Hitler's war plans were after all nothing more than the hypothetical operation plans developed by any efficient general staff, that the Führer was no more "aggressive" than previous German leaders, and that he simply took skillful but unpremeditated advantage of diplomatic blunders. Taylor's thesis has been strongly attacked, especially by Professor H. R. Trevor-Roper.[1] In any case, Taylor is merely one of many

---

[1] A. J. P. Taylor, *The Origins of the Second World War* (New York: Fawcett Publications, 1961). H. R. Trevor-Roper, "A. J. P. Taylor, Hitler, and the War," *Encounter*, Vol. XVII (July, 1961), pp. 88–96.

historians who have tried to reassess the war guilt problem not only in terms of German involvement, but of the responsibility of Britain, Russia, France, Italy, Poland, and, as American documents have now appeared, of the United States. An excellent and useful study of these modern interpretations can be found in the volume of critical excerpts edited by John L. Snell, *The Outbreak of the Second World War: Design or Blunder?* (Boston: D. C. Heath & Co., 1962).

This set of materials devoted to the Munich settlement and the origins of the war starts with the controversial Hossbach Memorandum. Taylor affirms that the memorandum was no "blueprint," but was simply a matter of Hitler's daydreaming, written up not even in the form of official minutes but rather as a personal recollection. One should of course read the entire document and study it in the context of other materials in order to evaluate it properly. The student who is interested in the Taylor thesis should be sure to read Taylor's reply to critics in the "Second Thoughts" section of his revised edition.

Comments of Hitler to His Commanders in Chief, November 5, 1937, from the Hossbach Memorandum

The German question can be solved only by way of force, and this is never without risk. . . . If we place the decision to apply force with risk at the head of the following expositions, then we are left to reply to the questions "when" and "how". . . .

For the improvement of our military-political position, it must be our first aim in every case of entanglement by war to conquer Czechoslovakia and Austria simultaneously in order to remove any threat from the flanks in case of a possible advance westwards.

.   .   .   .   .

The annexation of the two States to Germany militarily and politically would constitute a considerable relief, owing to shorter and better frontiers, the freeing of fighting personnel for other purposes, and the possibility of reconstituting new armies up to a strength of about twelve divisions. . . .

Generaloberst von Fritsch mentioned that it was the purpose of a study which he had laid out for this winter to investigate the possibilities of carrying out operations against Czechoslovakia . . . ; the Generaloberst also stated that owing to the prevailing conditions he would have to relinquish his leave abroad, which was to begin on 10 November. This intention was countermanded by the Fuehrer, who gave as a reason that the possibility of the conflict was not to be regarded as being so imminent. . . . The Fuehrer stated that the date which appeared to him to be a possibility was summer, 1938.[2]

---

[2] *Nazi Conspiracy and Aggression: A Collection of Documentary Evidence and Guide Materials Prepared by the American and British Prosecuting Staffs for Presentation before the International Military Tribunal at Nürnberg, Germany* (Washington, D.C.: U.S. Government Printing Office, 1946), Vol. III, pp. 298–305. Also in *Documents on German Foreign Policy*, Series D, Vol. I (Washington, D.C.: U.S. Government Printing Office, 1949), pp. 29–39.

Major collections of documents on the origins of the war have been appearing since the end of hostilities. Documents for use in the Nuremberg Trials were published in 10 volumes as *Nazi Conspiracy and Aggression* (Washington, D.C.: U.S. Government Printing Office, 1946–48), and the many volumes of the trials themselves (*The Trial of German Major War Criminals*) contain a large quantity of material. Obviously Russian material is not included in the foregoing, and under the influence of the cold war, the United States published *Nazi-Soviet Relations, 1939–1941*, in 1948. Russia countered with *Documents*

Affidavit of Friedrich Hossbach,
Presented to the Nuremberg Tribunal[3]
June 18, 1946

At the session of November 5, 1937,

and Materials Relating to the Eve of the Second
World War (Moscow: Ministry of Foreign Affairs of the Soviet Union), in the same year. Both
collections contained material captured from Germany at the end of the war. Most of these documents also appear in the series Documents on
German Foreign Policy, Series D (Washington,
D.C.: U.S. Government Printing Office, 1949–
56), edited by a team of English and American
scholars between 1949 and 1956. To facilitate
checking complete documents, references have
been made in some instances to more than one
source. Occasionally the translations differ
slightly.

[3]International Military Tribunal (Nuremberg,
1949), Vol. XLII, p. 228.

I did not take any minutes. Several days
later I drew up from memory a handwritten text which I believe was faithful
to what Hitler had said. I did not make,
nor did I have made, a copy of this handwritten draft.

Twice I brought this draft to Hitler's
attention but he said that he had no time
to read it. . . . I left the draft with General
Blomberg and I believe he initialed it
"Bl" on the first sheet and also read it.
The draft was placed in Blomberg's files.
The contents of the draft were never au-
thenticated by any signatures. I have no
knowledge as to how several typed copies
may have been made, I have knowledge
only of my handwritten draft.

On March 12, 1938, Hitler carried out the *Anschluss* with Austria, and German troops entered Austria without resistance. This move obviously concerned Germany's neighbors, especially Czechoslovakia, which saw itself
as the next victim. Russia, fearing an eventual German push to the East,
made it known to Great Britain, on March 17, that it was "prepared
immediately to take up in the League of Nations or outside of it the
discussion with other powers of the practical measures which the circumstances demand." British Prime Minister Neville Chamberlain's reaction
is well demonstrated in the following letter, and the British government
rejected Russia's offer in a note of March 24.

FOR CONSIDERATION   What evidence, down until Munich, is there that Chamberlain modified his position?

Prime Minister Chamberlain to
His Sister, March 20, 1938

You have only to look at the map to
see that nothing that France or we could
do could possibly save Czechoslovakia
from being overrun by the Germans, if
they wanted to do it. The Austrian frontier
is practically open; the great Skoda munition works are within easy bombing distance of the German aerodromes, the railways all pass through German territory,
Russia is 100 miles away. Therefore we
could not help Czechoslovakia—she would

simply be a pretext for going to war with
Germany. That we could not think of unless we had a reasonable prospect of being
able to beat her to her knees in a reasonable time, and of that I see no sign. I
have therefore abandoned any idea of
giving guarantees to Czechoslovakia, or
the French in connection with her obligations to that country.[4]

---

[4]Keith Feiling, The Life of Neville Chamberlain (London: Macmillan & Co., Ltd., 1946),
pp. 347–48. Quoted by permission of Macmillan
& Co., Ltd., London.

If Chamberlain could disclaim the existence of any vital connections between England and central Europe, the same disinterested attitude could
not be maintained by France. Since 1920 her basic policy had been to
build up a series of alliances with the small countries east of Germany.
France had signed a mutual assistance pact with Poland in 1921, and in
1924 had agreed with Czechoslovakia to provide mutual aid in case of
unprovoked attack by a third power. These pacts had been reinforced at
Locarno in 1926 and further strengthened through agreements with
Rumania and Yugoslavia.

It could be argued that once Germany reoccupied the Rhineland in
1936, France lost her capability of bringing meaningful assistance to her
eastern allies. As a consequence the French foreign office was extremely
anxious to make sure of British support in case it became necessary to
uphold treaty commitments with Czechoslovakia. In April French Premier
Daladier and Foreign Minister Georges Bonnet held conversations in
London with their British counterparts, Chamberlain and Halifax.

**Excerpt from British Official Record
of Anglo-French Conversations,
April 29, 1938**

M. Bonnet said that there was one
question he wished to ask. If we accepted
as a hypothesis that such a *démarche*
were made in Prague and that the Czechoslovak Government agreed to further concessions, at that moment and under those
particular circumstances would the British
Government then be prepared to affirm its
solidarity with the French Government
with a view toward the maintenance of a
settlement on the lines agreed upon with
Dr. Benés? He felt it was essential that
when such a point had been reached we
should no longer remain in the present
state of uncertainty.

Lord Halifax said that, if he had rightly

understood M. Bonnet, the latter had
asked whether, after Dr. Benés had informed His Majesty's Government of the
concessions which he was prepared to
make, and the latter had found them reasonable, His Majesty's Government would
then be prepared, in the event of the rejection of these concessions by Germany
and of a German attack on Czechoslovakia
to accept an obligation to defend Czechoslovakia against the results of such German aggression. If this was M. Bonnet's
question, he could only answer that, for
the reasons already given, it would be
impossible to accept such a commitment.[5]

[5]*Documents on British Foreign Policy*, 3d
Series, Vol. I (London: Her Majesty's Stationery Office, 1948), p. 229. Quoted by permission
of the controller of Her Britannic Majesty's Stationery Office.

Hitler began military preparations. At least as early as April 21, 1938, it is
known that he held preliminary discussions with General Keitel on
Operation "Green," the attack on Czechoslovakia. Keitel submitted to

Hitler a draft plan on May 20, and the final directive, part of which is here quoted, was signed ten days later. The other document here reproduced throws some light on the basic directive.

Directive for Operation "Green" (Political Sections), from Hitler, May 30, 1938

It is my unalterable decision to smash Czechoslovakia by military action in the near future. It is the business of the political leadership to await or bring about the suitable moment from a political and military point of view.

An unavoidable development of events within Czechoslovakia, or other political events in Europe providing a suddenly favorable opportunity which may never recur, may cause me to take early action.

The proper choice and determined exploitation of a favorable moment is the surest guarantee of success. To this end preparations are to be made immediately.

.   .   .   .   .

Most favorable from a military as well as a political point of view would be lightning action as the result of an incident which would subject Germany to unbearable provocation, and which, in the eyes of at least a part of world opinion, affords the moral justification for military measures.

Moreover, any period of diplomatic tension prior to war must be terminated by sudden action on our part, unexpected in both timing and extent, before the enemy is so far advanced in his state of military readiness that he cannot be overtaken.[6]

Excerpt from Report of British Military Attaché at Berlin Mason-MacFarlane, August 7, 1938

Rittmeister a. D. Viktor von Koerber, late of the 2nd Leibhusaren, called on me yesterday. . . . He is entirely convinced that war in September has already been decided upon by Herr Hitler and his intimate advisers. He says that Goring, Himmler and Ribbentrop are determined on war this autumn, and that General Keitel is 100 per cent on their side.[7]

---

[6]*Documents on German Foreign Policy*, Series D, Vol. II, *Germany and Czechoslovakia* (Washington, D.C.: U.S. Government Printing Office, 1949), pp. 358–59. (Cited hereafter as *Germany and Czechoslovakia*.)

[7]*Documents on British Foreign Policy*, 3d Series, Vol. II, pp. 65-66.

On May 21 a crisis developed when Czechoslovakia partially mobilized because of rumors that German troops were approaching. The Sudetens (German-speaking inhabitants of western and northern Czechoslovakia) claimed that the government simply wished to intimidate them during the elections. Throughout June and July the agitations continued, and there appeared no possibility of agreement between the Sudeten Party and the Czech government.

France attempted, during early September, to obtain a specific commitment from Great Britain. The French Ambassador saw Halifax on September 7 and again on September 9. Daladier, the French Premier, had seen the British Ambassador, Sir Eric Phipps, telling him that France would abide by commitments to Czechoslovakia. On September 10, Bonnet had a conversation with British Ambassador Phipps and asked him: "Tomorrow Germany may attack Czechoslovakia. In this case France will mobilize at once. She will turn to you saying: 'We march. Do you march with us?' What will Great Britain's answer be?" Phipps transmitted this point-blank inquiry to Halifax who replied with the following letter, which was sent to Bonnet.

Lord Halifax, British Foreign Minister, to Sir Eric Phipps, British Ambassador to France, September 12, 1938

I got your private and confidential letter of September 10th last night, in which you transmitted to me the question that Bonnet had put to you, not as Ambassador, but as a friend. I naturally recognize of what importance it would be to the French Government to have a plain answer to such a question. But, as you pointed out to Bonnet—and I think, if I may say so, that your language was admirable—the question itself, though plain in form, cannot be dissociated from the circumstances in which it might be posed, which are necessarily at this stage completely hypothetical.

Moreover in this matter it is impossible for His Majesty's Government to have regard only to their own position, inasmuch as in any decision they may reach or action they may take they would, in fact, be committing the Dominions. Their Governments would quite certainly be unwilling to have their position in any way decided for them in advance of the actual circumstances of which they would desire themselves to judge.

So far, therefore, as I am in a position to give any answer at this stage to M. Bonnet's question, it would have to be that while His Majesty's Government would never allow the security of France to be threatened, they are unable to make precise statements of the character of their future action, or the time at which it would be taken, in circumstances that they cannot at present foresee.[8]

_____

[8]*Ibid.*, p. 303.

The tension of the first week in September, intensified by a speech of Hitler's on the 12th, had become so acute that on September 13 Chamberlain wrote to Hitler proposing that he "come over at once to see you with a view to trying to find a peaceful solution." Hitler accepted the proposal and held talks with the British Prime Minister at Berchtesgaden on the 15th.

Description of the Berchtesgaden Conference in Letter of Prime Minister Chamberlain to His Sister, September 19, 1938

For the most part H. spoke quietly and in low tones. I did not see any trace of insanity, but occasionally he became very excited and poured out his indignation against the Czechs in a torrent of words, so that several times I had to stop him and ask that I might have a chance to hear what he was talking about. I soon saw that the situation was much more critical than I had anticipated. I knew that his troops and tanks and guns and planes were ready to pounce, and only awaiting his word, and it was clear that rapid decisions must be taken if the situation was to be saved. At one point he seemed to be saying that he was going in at once, so I became indignant saying that I did not see why he had allowed me to come all this way, and that I was wasting my time. He quieted down then, said if I could assure him that the British Government accepted the principle of self-determination (which he had not invented), he was prepared to discuss ways and means. I said I could give no assurance without consultation. My personal opinion was that on principle I didn't care two hoots whether the Sudetens were in the Reich, or out of it, according to their own wishes, but I saw immense practical difficulties in a plebiscite. I could, however, break off our talk now, go back and hold my consultations, and meet him again. That is a possible procedure, he said, but I am very sorry that you should have to make two journeys. However, next time I shall come to meet you somewhere near Cologne. Then I asked him how the situation was to be held in the meantime, and he promised not to give the order to march unless some outrageous incident forced his hand.

. . . I had established a certain confidence, which was my aim, and on my side, in spite of the hardness and ruthlessness I thought I saw in his face, I got the impression that here was a man who could be relied upon when he had given his word.[9]

---

[9]Feiling, op. cit., p. 367.

As a result of the Berchtesgaden meeting, and after further consultation between the British and French governments, the two powers determined to intervene and use their combined weight to bring Czechoslovakia to an agreement with Germany. The following four documents include the Anglo-French proposals, Czechoslovakia's initial reaction, Britain's further pressure, and Czechoslovakia's final acquiescence.

Anglo-French Proposals to the Czechoslovak Government, September 19, 1938

. . . both Governments have been compelled to the conclusion that the maintenance of peace and the safety of Czechoslovakia's vital interests cannot effectively be assured unless these areas are now transferred to the Reich.

This could be done either by direct transfer or as the result of a plebiscite. . . .

The area for transfer would probably have to include areas with over 50 per cent German inhabitants, but we should hope to arrange by negotiation provisions for adjustments of frontiers, where circumstances render it necessary, by some international body including a Czech representative. . . .[10]

Excerpt from Reply of the Czechoslovak Government to the Anglo-French Proposals, September 20, 1938

The Czechoslovak Government cannot for constitutional reasons take a decision which would affect their frontiers. Such a

---

[10]Documents on British Foreign Policy, 3d Series, Vol. II, p. 405.

decision would not be possible without violating the democratic régime and juridical order of the Czechoslovak state. In any case it would be necessary to consult Parliament.[11]

Excerpt from British Note to the Czechoslovak Government, September 21, 1938

In the opinion of His Majesty's Government, the reply of the Czechoslovak Government does not meet the critical situation which the Anglo-French proposals were designed to remove and, if it should be adhered to, would lead, after publication, in the opinion of His Majesty's Government, to an immediate German invasion. His Majesty's Government therefore appeals to the Czechoslovak Government

[11]Hubert Ripka, *Munich: Before and After* (London: Victor Gollancz, Ltd., 1939), p. 75. Quoted by permission of the publisher, Victor Gollancz, Ltd., London, and the author.

to retract their answer and to consider speedily an alternative which would take account of realities.[12]

Note Communicated by Czechoslovak Government to French and British Ministers in Prague, September 21, 1938

1. Under severe duress and extreme pressure of the French and British Governments, the Government of the Czechoslovak Republic accepts with bitterness the Anglo-French proposals, on the presumption that the two Governments will do everything to ensure that in the carrying out of the said proposals the vital interests of the Czechoslovak Republic are safeguarded. . . .[13]

[12]*Ibid.*, pp. 78–79.
[13]*Documents and Materials Relating to the Eve of the Second World War* (Moscow: Ministry of Foreign Affairs of the Soviet Union, 1948), Vol. I, pp. 203–04.

Russia had not been a party to the Anglo-French negotiations. Litvinov expressed the Soviet position in a speech before the League of Nations, part of which is here reproduced.

Excerpt from Speech of Soviet Foreign Minister Maxim Litvinov before Assembly of the League of Nations, September 21, 1938

When, a few days before I left for Geneva, the French Government for the first time inquired of my Government as to its attitude in the event of an attack on Czechoslovakia, I gave the French representative in Moscow, in the name of my Government, the following perfectly clear and unambiguous reply:

We intend to fulfil our obligations under

the pact, together with France, to afford assistance to Czechoslovakia by the way open to us; our War Department is ready immediately to participate in a conference with representatives of the French and Czechoslovak War Departments in order to discuss measures appropriate to the moment. In an event like this, we shall consider desirable that the question be raised in the League of Nations, if only as yet under Article XI, with the object, first, of mobilizing public opinion, and secondly, ascertaining the position of certain other States whose passive aid might be extremely valuable.[14]

[14]*The New York Times*, September 22, 1938.

As the Czech government finally acceded to the Anglo-French Proposals, Chamberlain returned to Germany and met Hitler at Godesberg on September 23. The documents which follow are associated with this meeting.

British Notes on the Conversation between Chamberlain and Hitler at Godesberg, September 22, 1938

.   .   .   .   .

Herr Hitler said he would like to thank the Prime Minister for his great efforts to reach a peaceful solution. He was not clear, however, whether the proposals, of which the Prime Minister had just given him an outline, were those submitted to the Czechoslovak Government.

The Prime Minister replied: Yes.

Herr Hitler said that he was sorry, since these proposals could not be maintained.

.   .   .   .   .

The Prime Minister said that he was both disappointed and puzzled at the Fuehrer's statement. The Fuehrer had said during their previous conversation that if he, the Prime Minister, could arrange for a settlement on the basis of self-determination he would be prepared then to discuss procedure . . . He [Mr. Chamberlain] had induced his colleagues, the French and the Czechs, to agree to the principle of self-determination, in fact he had got exactly what the Fuehrer wanted and without the expenditure of a drop of German blood. In doing so he had been obliged to take his political life in his hands. As an illustration of the difficulties which he had to face, he mentioned that when he undertook his first flight to Germany he was applauded by public opinion. Today he was accused of selling the Czechs, yielding to dictators, capitulating, and so on. He had actually been booed on his departure today. . . .

.   .   .   .   .

After further agreement Herr Hitler said that he would give instructions to General Keitel that no military action was to be taken. But Mr. Chamberlain must understand that the Czechs must be spoken to sharply and firmly, or an admonition would have no effect. He never believed himself that a peaceful solution could be reached, and he admitted that he never thought that the Prime Minister could have achieved what he had. That was why he had made his military preparations and Germany was ready today to move at a moment's notice.[15]

Excerpt from Diary of William Shirer, American Correspondent, September 23–24, 1938

It seems that Hitler has given Chamberlain the double-cross. And the old owl is hurt. All day long he sulked in his rooms at the Petershof up on the Petersberg on the other side of the Rhine, refusing to come over and talk with the dictator. At five p.m. he sent Sir Horace Wilson, his "confidential" adviser, and Sir Nevile Henderson, the British Ambassador in Berlin (both of whom, we feel, would sell out Czecho for five cents), over the river to see Ribbentrop. Result: Chamberlain and Hitler met at ten thirty p.m. This meeting, which is the last, broke up at one thirty a.m. without agreement and now it looks like war, though from my "studio" in the porter's lodge twenty-five feet away I could not

[15]*Documents on British Foreign Policy,* 3d Series, Vol. II, pp. 465–73.

discern any strain or particular displeasure in Chamberlain's birdy face as he said his farewell to Hitler, who also was smiling and gracious. Still the Germans are plunged in deep gloom tonight, as if they really are afraid of war now that it's facing them. They are gloomy and yet feverishly excited.[16]

---

[16]William L. Shirer, *Berlin Diary* (New York: Alfred A. Knopf, Inc., 1940), pp. 138–39. Reprinted by permission of Alfred A. Knopf, Inc. Copyright 1940, 1941 by William L. Shirer.

During September 26 and 27, impressive efforts were made to conserve the peace. Chamberlain wrote moving personal appeals to Hitler, and sent his close personal adviser, Sir Horace Wilson, to intercede. President Roosevelt addressed two personal letters to Hitler, begging him to refrain from aggression. Hitler replied to these letters in terms which conceded nothing but which implied that the door was open for further pressure on Prague. Chamberlain also asked Mussolini to intervene on behalf of peace. (These letters have not been reproduced here because they introduced no new element into the crisis.) The following documents throw light on the developments preceding the meeting of the four heads of government at Munich.

British Ambassador to France Phipps to British Foreign Minister Halifax, September 26, 1938

. . . The Minister for Foreign Affairs summoned me to the Quai d'Orsay, and asked me to put to you the following questions on behalf of the French Government:

Supposing that, as a result of German aggression on Czechoslovakia, France mobilised and proceeded to an act of war against Germany, will Great Britain:

1) Mobilise immediately and at the same time as France?
2) Introduce conscription?
3) Pool the economic and financial resources of the two countries?[17]

French Foreign Minister Bonnet to French Ambassador to Germany, Francois-Poncet, September 28, 1938

According to the British Ambassador it is not only mobilisation but the opening

---

[17]*Documents on British Foreign Policy*, 3d Series, Vol. II, p. 558.

of hostilities which could be planned for tomorrow at 2 P.M.

Sir Eric Phipps has just communicated to me a proposition which his Government is submitting to Berlin and which deals with the immediate entry of German troops into Egerland.

Please ask your British colleague to let you know without delay if this proposition is accepted.

In the negative, and in order to make a final effort to avoid the irreparable, you are to submit as urgent, in the name of the Government, to M. Hitler himself, a proposition which, retaining the means of application of this latest British suggestion, would deal with an immediate occupation of a more important area.

.   .   .   .   .

If the German Government indicates to you that it would be ready to accept this proposition, the French Government will employ all its power to bring the Czechoslovak Government into line with it before October 1. But this would obviously be impossible if military operations were to begin tomorrow.

This sketch-map is approximate and the details would have to be worked out, it being understood that the fortifications would rest in the hands of the Czechs. ....[18]

Comments of Andre Francois-Poncet, French Ambassador to Germany

At 11 o'clock [September 28] Hitler requests me to come immediately to the Chancellery. I find his entourage greatly excited. The S.S. men, the *Wehrmacht* officers, come and go, busy, obviously preoccupied. In the ante-room of the large salon where Hitler receives me are several tables set with tablecloths, napkins, spoons and forks. I make inquiries. I am told that a lunch will be served here, at 1 o'clock, to the commanders of the invasion army units. Mobilization is set for 3 o'clock.

The *Führer*, next to whom stands Ribbentrop, has an animated face. He is nervous, strained. I get in touch with him directly. I place my map [of Czechoslovakia] before his eyes. I recall to his attention that once already, by a frank analysis at a critical moment in the Spanish war, we safeguarded the peace. He is mistaken if he thinks it possible, today, to localize the conflict. If he attacks Czechoslovakia, a fire will ignite all Europe. Will he perpetrate such a disgraceful act when his claims are three-quarters satisfied? Hitler seems dubious. Ribbentrop intervenes to mitigate the effect of my words. I rebuke him sharply. I am not talking to him but to Hitler. I continue to argue in urgent terms.

At this moment, an S.S. man enters the room and announces that the Italian Ambassador, Attolico, has just arrived, carrying an urgent message for the Chancellor. Hitler leaves the room and remains absent

for about a quarter of an hour. When he returns, he says: "Now it's Mussolini himself, who asks me to delay!" I resume my previous exposition to which, I remark, the Duce has just brought unanticipated support.

The *Führer* listens to me with less attention. His mind is somewhere else. A look of hesitancy appears on his face. Finally, he gets up. I ask him if I must advise my Government that he remains adamant. He tells me he will send his reply early in the afternoon. I take away the impression that he is wavering. At his door, I meet Goering and Neurath, who make signs of encouragement to me. I pass the generals of the *Wehrmacht*, who begin to arrive for the lunch to which they have been invited. I return to my Embassy.

At 2:30, Goering telephones me, on behalf of the Chancellor, that Hitler proposes the calling of a conference for the next day, the 29th, at Munich, and asks me to invite the French Prime Minister to attend. I transmit the invitation without commentary. An hour later, it is accepted. I inform Goering about it on the spot. He cries: "*Gott sei Dank!* (God be thanked!) *Bravo!*"[19]

Comments of Ivone Kirkpatrick, then an Official in the British Embassy in Berlin, later British High Commissioner for Germany

We also received instructions for a second interview with Hitler. By this time it was clear to me that Hitler was bent on having his little war. I felt that the interview could have little result and Hitler's behaviour was so offensive that I wanted never to see him again. He seemed to be

---

[18]Georges Bonnet, *De Washington au Quai d'Orsay* (Geneva: Les Editions du Cheval Ailé, 1947), pp. 283–84. Quoted by permission of the publisher, Les Editions du Cheval Ailé, Geneva.

[19]André François-Poncet, *Souvenirs d'une Ambassade à Berlin* (Paris: Librairie Ernest Flammarion, 1947), pp. 327–28. Quoted by permission of the publisher, Librairie Ernest Flammarion, Paris.

enveloped in an aura of such ruthless wickedness that it was oppressive and almost nightmarish to sit in the same room. . . . The time for the interview was fixed for 12:15. The ante-room was full of high officials, all manifestly depressed by the turn of events. . . . We went in. Hitler looked as black as thunder. He told us several times, grinding his heel into the carpet, that he had had enough of the Czechs. "I will smash the Czechs", he shouted. One could sense that he was itching to drop a bomb on Prague, to see Benés in flight. . . .

Sir Horace Wilson, speaking very slowly and quietly, then said that he had a message to give from the Prime Minister. He would try to give it in the Prime Minister's words and manner. If, he continued, the Germans attacked Czechoslovakia and the French in pursuance of their treaty obligation became engaged in a conflict with Germany, then Britain would feel obliged to support France. Hitler replied angrily that he could only take note of this statement. If France felt obliged to attack Germany, then Britain also felt obliged to commit an act of aggression against Germany. Sir Horace Wilson retorted that Hitler had clearly misunderstood the purport of the message. He must therefore in the interest of history repeat it. Still speaking very slowly, Wilson then repeated the formula to a Hitler who was showing signs of rising exasperation, wriggling in his seat, slapping his knee, drumming on the floor with his heel. But quite unperturbed, Wilson slowly recited his piece to the end. Before the translation was complete Hitler bellowed furiously: "It's just what I said. If France attacks Germany, then England must attack Germany too." He added, "If France strikes and England strikes, I don't care a bit. I am prepared for every eventuality"; and Ribbentrop sagely nodded his agreement. Sir Horace Wilson, looking very pained, said that it was evident that the Chancellor still misunderstood the message and he must ask

leave to repeat it. But this time Hitler was on his feet shouting that he understood the purport of the message only too well. It meant that in six days' time we should all be at war with one another. . . .

The same evening the Prime Minister informed Dr. Benes that it seemed likely that German troops would cross the frontier almost at once unless the Czechoslovak Government accepted the German terms forthwith. In this situation the British Government felt unable to tender advice as to what Dr. Benes should do. Later a further effort was made to induce Hitler to come to terms, and at 11 P.M. a note was handed to the German State Secretary embodying a proposed time-table for the evacuation of the Sudeten territory. He replied that the plan was out of date and he did not believe that it could possibly be accepted. While all this was going on our work in the Chancery was disturbed by the rattle of an enormous motorised and armoured column which passed down the Wilhelmstrasse in an easterly direction. The column took over three hours to pass and represented the flower of the German Army. I went out for a moment or two to have a look at it and returned to my desk both impressed and depressed. The people of Berlin who were standing glumly on the pavement stared at the passing troops but showed no emotion whatever. My friends in the Reich Chancellery told me that Hitler, who was watching from a window, was disgusted with the crowd for their apathy.

On September 28th the British fleet was mobilised. Meanwhile there was much coming and going in Berlin. Mussolini, appalled at the prospect of a general war for which he was not ready, had urged Hitler to compromise. Similar advice was being tendered by Goering and the German generals. In consequence Hitler decided to draw in his horns. A mass meeting at which Goebbels was to have announced mobilisation was cancelled at the last moment and Hitler informed the

Ambassador in the morning that at Mussolini's request he had consented to postpone mobilisation until 2 P.M. on September 29th. After more telephoning around Europe the project of a four-power meeting at Munich, to be held the following day, was put forward and accepted. That evening Henderson and I set forth for Munich.[20]

[20]Ivone A. Kirkpatrick, *The Inner Circle: Memoirs* (New York: St. Martin's Press, Inc., 1959), pp. 124–27.

Hitler's invitation for a conference was accepted promptly by Daladier. At the moment that Chamberlain received his invitation, he was addressing the House of Commons. He paused, then told the House, "I need not say what my answer will be." The following documents all throw some light on the Conference itself.

FOR CONSIDERATION   To what extent is it possible that Mussolini's leadership at the Conference led to concessions more drastic than Daladier or Chamberlain wished to make? Is it possible to argue that France and Britain did not care how great their concessions were, so long as war was avoided? Could Chamberlain and Daladier, acting in concert, have obtained better terms? Why did Daladier appear more distraught—and ashamed—than Chamberlain? (The mob which received him at Paris on his return was far from hostile, probably as enthusiastic as the British crowd which hailed Chamberlain.) When Chamberlain returned to London he said: "This is the second time there has come back from Germany peace with honour. I believe it is peace in our time."

Comments of German Foreign Office Official Erich Kordt

He [Weizsäcker] got hold of Neurath and Göring and elaborated with them a short paper with possible conditions of a compromise, for a plebiscite to be taken in the regions, for evacuation dates in the case that the plebiscite should be favorable to Germany. Then Göring submitted this draft to Hitler, who took a quick look at this paper and said, "Well, it might perhaps be acceptable" to him. Now this paper has a special significance because the moment afterward I was asked to have Schmidt translate it into French. The State Secretary passed it on to Ambassador Attolico. Attolico rushed to meet Mussolini on his way to Munich. And when the meeting opened in Munich, to the great surprise of Ribbentrop and others present, Mussolini presented this suggestion as his own, and therefore the whole proceedings of the Munich Conference were conducted on the basis of this paper.[21]

Memorandum on the Munich Conversation at 4:30, September 29, 1938, by Erich Kordt of the German Foreign Office

At the Duce's suggestion it was first decided to discuss point by point the Italian proposal submitted to the delegations in the morning.

Point 1) (beginning of evacuation on

[21]*Germany and Czechoslovakia*, p. 1005 n.

October 1) was at once agreed to unanimously.

On point 2) the Führer stated that, if agreement could be reached on this point too, the question of procedure would no longer present any great difficulties. His proposal was first to define on the map certain stages of the German occupation, the procedure of which could then be established by a commission, on which there would also be a Czech representative.

Prime Minister Chamberlain expressed his agreement with the date fixed in point 2) for the completion of the evacuation of the German area, October 10. However, he expressed doubts on the possibility of giving a guarantee to Germany as long as he did not know Czechoslovakia's attitude to the question of evacuation.

On the question whether Czechoslovakia's previous agreement had to be obtained for the granting of the guarantee provided for in the Italian proposal, as Mr. Chamberlain seemed to suggest, Daladier stated that such agreement did not seem necessary to him.[22]

**Excerpt from the Diary
of William Shirer,
September 30, 1938**

Dr. Mastný, the intelligent and honest Czech Minister in Berlin, and a Dr. Masaryk of the Prague Foreign Office, were told at one thirty a.m. that Czechoslovakia would *have* to accept, told not by Hitler, but by Chamberlain and Daladier! Their protests, we hear, were practically laughed off by the elder statesman. Chamberlain, looking more like some bird—like the black vultures I've seen over the Parsi dead in Bombay—looked particularly pleased with himself when he returned to the Regina Palace Hotel after the signing early this morning, though he was a bit sleepy, *pleasantly* sleepy.

Daladier, on the other hand, looked a completely beaten and broken man. He came over to the Regina to say good-bye to Chamberlain. A bunch of us were waiting as he came down the stairs. Someone asked, or started to ask: *"Monsieur le Président,* are you satisfied with the agreement?..."* He turned as if to say something, but he was too tired and defeated and the words did not come out and he stumbled out the door in silence. The French say he fears to return to Paris, thinks a hostile mob will get him. Can only hope they're right. For France has sacrificed her whole Continental position and lost her main prop in eastern Europe. For France this day has been disastrous.

How different Hitler at two this morning! After being blocked from the Führerhaus all evening, I finally broke in just as he was leaving. Followed by Göring, Ribbentrop, Goebels, Hess, and Keitel, he brushed past me like the conqueror he is this morning. I noticed his swagger. The tic was gone! As for Mussolini, he pulled out early, cocky as a rooster.[23]

**Comments of Dr. Hubert Masaryk on
the Czechoslovak Delegation at
Munich September 30, 1938**

At 1:30 a.m. we were taken into the hall where the Conference had been held. There were present Mr. Neville Chamberlain, M. Daladier, Sir Horace Wilson, M. Léger, Mr. Ashton-Gwatkin, Dr. Mastný and myself. The atmosphere was oppressive; sentence was about to be passed. The French, obviously embar-

[22]*Ibid.,* pp. 1011–14.

[23]Shirer, *op. cit.,* pp. 144–45.

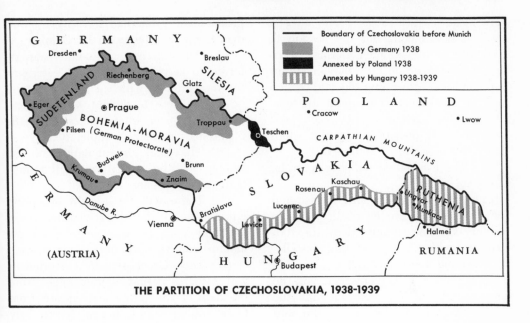

THE PARTITION OF CZECHOSLOVAKIA, 1938-1939

rassed, appeared to be aware of the consequences for French prestige. Mr. Chamberlain, in a short introduction, referred to the agreement which had just been concluded and gave the text to Dr. Mastný to read out. During the reading of the text, we asked the precise meaning of certain passages. Thus, for example, I asked MM. Léger and Wilson to be so kind as to explain the words "preponderantly German character" in Article 4. M. Léger, without mentioning a percentage, merely remarked that it was a question of majorities calculated according to the proposals we had already accepted. Mr. Chamberlain also confirmed that there was no question except of applying a plan which we had already accepted. . . .

While M. Mastný was speaking with Mr. Chamberlain about matters of perhaps secondary importance (Mr. Chamberlain yawned without ceasing and with no show of embarrassment), I asked MM. Daladier and Léger whether they expected a declaration or answer to the agreement from our Government. M. Daladier, obviously embarrassed, did not reply. M. Léger replied that the four

statesmen had not much time. He added positively that they no longer expected an answer from us; they regarded the plan as accepted and that our Government had that very day, at latest by 5 p.m. to send its representative to Berlin to the meeting of the International Commission and finally that the Czechoslovak official whom we sent would have to be in Berlin on Saturday, in order to fix the details of the evacuation of the first zone. The atmosphere was becoming oppressive for everyone present.

It had been explained to us in a sufficiently brutal manner, and that by a Frenchman, that this was a sentence without right of appeal and without possibility of modification. . . .[24]

Essential Portion of the Munich Agreement, September 29, 1938

Germany, the United Kingdom, France and Italy, taking into consideration the

[24]From Hubert Ripka, *op. cit.,* pp. 225-27.

agreement, which has been already reached in principle, for the cession to Germany of the Sudeten German territory, have agreed on the following terms and conditions governing the said cession and the measures consequent thereon, and by this agreement they each hold themselves responsible for the steps necessary to secure its fulfilment:

(1) The evacuation will begin on 1st October.

(2) The United Kingdom, France and Italy agree that the evacuation of the territory shall be completed by the 10th October, without any existing installations having been destroyed, and that the Czechoslovak Government will be held responsible for carrying out the evacuation without damage to the said installations.

(3) The conditions governing the evacuation will be laid down in detail by an international commission composed of representatives of Germany, the United Kingdom, France, Italy and Czechoslovakia.

(4) The occupation by stages of the predominantly German territory by German troops will begin on 1st October....

(5) The international commission referred to in paragraph 3 will determine the territories in which a plebiscite is to be held. These territories will be occupied by international bodies until the plebiscite has been completed....

(6) The final determination of the frontiers will be carried out by the international commission....

(7) There will be a right of option into and out of the transferred territories, the option to be exercised within six months from the date of this agreement.

(8) The Czechoslovak Government will within a period of four weeks from the date of this agreement release from their military and police forces any Sudeten Germans who may wish to be released, and the Czechosolvak Government will within the same period release Sudeten German prisoners who are serving terms of imprisonment for political offences.[25]

_____

[25]*Germany and Czechoslovakia*, pp. 1014–15.

Between the settlement at Munich and the outbreak of World War II came a year of tension during which statesmen wondered if Hitler's appetite for power and territory would be satiated with the portions of Czechoslovakia he had obtained. They could see clearly enough that the question of the Polish Corridor continued to be unresolved from the German point of view; but less certain were the odds on whether France and Great Britain would once more "appease" the Führer in new demands.

Although not known at the time, Hitler very shortly gave orders to the army to prepare for the liquidation of Czechoslovakia.

FOR CONSIDERATION   A. J. P. Taylor has argued that such orders constitute no more than the plans which all general staffs prepare for all possible eventualities, and that therefore Hitler was no more "aggressive" than any other chief of state. (See his *The Origins of the Second World War* [2d ed.; Greenwich, Conn.: Fawcett Publications, 1965], p. 187.)

Hitler Directive to Armed Forces, October 21, 1938

. . . The Armed Forces must be prepared at all times for the following eventualities:

1. The securing of the frontier of Germany and the protection against surprise air attacks.

. . . . .

2. Liquidation of the remainder of Czechoslovakia.

It must be possible to smash at any time the remainder of Czechoslovakia if her policy should become hostile toward Germany. . . . The organization, order of battle and state of readiness of the units earmarked for that purpose are in peacetime to be so arranged for a surprise assault that Czechoslovakia herself will be deprived of all possibility of organized resistance. The object is the swift occupation of Bohemia and Moravia and the cutting off of Slovakia.

3. Annexation of the Memel District.[26]

. . . . .

Appendix by General Keitel to Hitler Directive, November 24, 1938

The Fuehrer has ordered:—

1. Apart from the three contingencies mentioned in the instructions of the 21 October 1938, preparation are also to be made to enable the Free State of Danzig to be occupied by German troops by surprise. . . .

Condition is a *quasi-revolutionary* occupation of Danzig, exploiting a politically favorable situation, *not a war against Poland*. . . .[27]

---

[26]*Nazi Conspiracy and Aggression*, Vol. VI, pp. 947–48. Also in *Documents on German Foreign Policy*, Series D, Vol. IV, pp. 99–100.

[27]*Nazi Conspiracy and Aggression*, Vol. VI, p. 949.

T he possibility of a German push toward the East brought the Soviet Union to a sharp realization of her defenselessness. Russia needed alliances, either with the West or, notwithstanding the ideological opposition of Communism to Fascism, with Germany. In the following address, Stalin put forth feelers.

Excerpts from an Address by Stalin, March 10, 1939

Formally speaking, the policy of non-intervention might be defined as follows: "Let each country defend itself from the aggressors as it likes and as best it can. That is not our affair. We shall trade with both the aggressors and their victims." . . . The policy of non-intervention reveals an eagerness, a desire, not to hinder the aggressors in their nefarious work: . . . not to hinder Germany, say, from enmeshing

herself in European affairs, from embroiling herself in a war with the Soviet Union. . . .

Cheap and easy!

. . . take Germany, for instance. They let her have Austria, despite the undertaking to defend her independence; they let her have the Sudeten region; they abandoned Czechoslovakia to her fate, thereby violating all their obligations; and then they began to lie vociferously in the press about the "weakness of the Russian army," "the demoralization of the Russian air force," and "riots" in the Soviet Union, egging the Germans on to march farther east, promising them easy pickings, and prompting them: "Just start war on the Bolsheviks, and everything will be all right." It must be admitted that this too looks very much like egging on and encouraging the aggressor.

. . . Certain European and American politicians and pressmen . . . are saying quite openly, putting it down in black and white, that the Germans have cruelly "disappointed" them, for instead of marching farther east, against the Soviet Union, they have turned, you see, to the west and are demanding colonies. One might think that the districts of Czechoslovakia were yielded to Germany as the price of an undertaking to launch war on the Soviet Union, but that now the Germans are refusing to meet their bills and are sending them to Hades.

.   .   .   .   .

The foreign policy of the Soviet Union is clear and explicit.

1. We stand for peace and the strengthening of business relations with all countries. That is our position; and we shall adhere to this position as long as these countries maintain like relations with the Soviet Union, and as long as they make no attempt to trespass on the interests of our country.

2. We stand for peaceful, close and friendly relations with all the neighboring countries which have common frontiers with the U.S.S.R.

3. We stand for the support of nations which are the victims of aggression and are fighting for the independence of their country.

4. We are not afraid of the threats of aggressors, and are ready to deal two blows for every blow delivered by instigators of war who attempt to violate the Soviet borders.

Such is the foreign policy of the Soviet Union. (*Loud and prolonged applause.*)[28]

[28]*Land of Socialism Today and Tomorrow* (Moscow: Foreign Languages Publishing House, 1939), pp. 14–18.

C onfronted with a German military threat, Czechoslovakia was powerless. President Hacha hurried to Berlin on March 14 in an effort to save his country, but was handed an ultimatum. Hacha surrendered, and on March 16 Bohemia and Moravia were incorporated as protectorates into the German Reich.

Chamberlain was dismayed and felt greatly let down, but no one in Britain or France was prepared to counter force with force. The threat to Poland and to Rumania could not be overlooked, however, and on March 21 Chamberlain initiated a proposal whereby France, Britain, Poland and the Soviet Union should consult on the question of aggressive threats. France agreed, but Russia made its consent dependent on Poland's. Poland's foreign relations, dominated by Colonel Jozef Beck, a diplomat who was considered cynical and untrustworthy by many, were indeed tortuous.[29] Beck expressed an unwillingness to go along with the quadrapartite arrangement, but suggested a secret Anglo-Polish pact. At the same time, as indicated in the following, he made gestures toward Germany, which were formally rejected.

[29]See, for example, the study on Beck in G. A. Craig and F. Gilbert (eds.), *The Diplomats 1919–1939* (Princeton, N.J.: Princeton University Press, 1953).

FOR CONSIDERATION   Certain revisionist interpretations of the origins of World War II, especially those of A. J. P. Taylor, place a heavy responsibility for the outbreak on Beck's deviousness and intransigence. Why was Poland so unwilling to negotiate with Russia?

Polish Ambassador to Germany
Lipski to Polish Minister for Foreign
Affairs Beck, March 26, 1939

I was received today by the Minister for Foreign Affairs, M. von Ribbentrop. The conversation lasted from 12:30 till 2. M. von Ribbentrop gave me a distinctly cold reception. . . .

M. von Ribbentrop stated, with some excitement, that news had been received of our "mobilisation measures." Certain movements of troops had also been observed in Pomorze. This had made a very bad impression. He pointed out that whereas on March 21 he had made a certain offer of a wide agreement, we had subsequently taken military measures. It reminded him of similar risky steps taken by another State (obviously he was thinking of Czechoslovakia). He added that all

aggression on our part against Danzig would be an aggression against the Reich. . . .

M. von Ribbentrop said that our answer would be communicated to the Chancellor, who at present is in Bavaria, but that he himself would be bound to adopt a critical attitude toward it. He was afraid the Chancellor might come to the conclusion that it is impossible to reach an understanding with Poland, which he would like to avoid. As from what I said it resulted that a meeting between you and the Chancellor could take place only if the bounds of discussion were clearly established, he said that he did not see any possibility of this at present.[30]

---

[30]*Polish White Book, Official Documents concerning Polish-German and Polish-Soviet Relations, 1933–39* (London: Polish Ministry of Foreign Affairs, 1940), pp. 67–68.

W ith the collapse of its proposal for a four-power agreement, Great Britain on March 27 decided to propose an agreement with Poland. Having accepted this on March 30, Polish Foreign Minister Beck came to London where the general terms of the guarantee were worked out. Russia had not been consulted.

FOR CONSIDERATION   It has been claimed that the German policy toward Poland was caused by the Anglo-Polish *rapprochement*. Does the documentary evidence support this contention? What aid could Great Britain bring Poland in case of an attack by Germany? Does this agreement have any bearing on German-Soviet relations? Why did Great Britain prefer an agreement with Poland to a possible alliance with the Soviet Union? In this regard notice that British Prime Minister Neville Chamberlain wrote in his diary, under date of March 26, 1939: "I must confess to the most profound distrust of Russia. I have no belief whatever in her ability to maintain an effective offensive, even if she wanted to." (Feiling, *The Life* *of Neville Chamberlain,* page 403.) When was the permanent agreement between England and Poland finally signed? Inasmuch as France also was allied to Poland, why did not an Anglo-Polish pact eventuate?

**Summary of Conclusions,
Anglo-Polish Conversations,
April 6, 1939**

.   .   .   .   .

2. The Polish Government and His Majesty's Government in the United Kingdom have decided to place their collaboration on a permanent basis by the exchange of reciprocal assurances of assistance. They are accordingly prepared to enter into a formal agreement on the following basis:

(a) If Germany attacks Poland His Majesty's Government in the United Kingdom will at once come to the help of Poland.

(b) If Germany attempts to undermine the independence of Poland by processes of economic penetration or in any other way, His Majesty's Government in the United Kingdom will support Poland in resistance to such attempts. If Germany then attacks Poland, the provisions of paragraph (a) above will apply. In the event of other action by Germany which clearly threatened Polish independence, and was of such a nature that the Polish Government considered it vital to resist it with their national forces, His Majesty's Government would at once come to the help of Poland.

(c) Reciprocally, Poland gives corresponding assurances to the United Kingdom. . . .

5. The following points remain to be settled before the formal agreement can be concluded:

(a) His Majesty's Government desire that the formal agreement should provide that if the United Kingdom and France went to war with Germany to resist German aggression in Western Europe (the Netherlands, Belgium, Switzerland, Denmark), Poland would come to their help. (M. Beck appreciated the vital importance of this question for the United Kingdom, and undertook that the Polish Government would take it into serious consideration.)

(b) The obligations which His Majesty's Government have accepted towards Poland during the period necessary for the conclusion of the formal Agreement have also been accepted by France. It is understood that the obligations to be accepted by His Majesty's Government in the formal Agreement itself should also be accepted by France; the method of arranging this would be a matter for discussion with the French Government.

6. His Majesty's Government wished it to be part of the formal Agreement that Poland should come to the help of Roumania if the latter were the State threatened. The Polish Government, while respecting to the full the obligations of mutual assistance which exist between Poland and Roumania, thought it premature to express a definite opinion as to the desirability of including the case of Roumania in the formal Agreement.[31]

---

[31]*Documents on British Foreign Relations,* 3d Series, Vol. V, pp. 47–48.

The following three documents are printed to present an idea of Hitler's strategic thinking. "Fall Weiss," or "Operation White," was the military plan for an invasion of Poland.

Revised German Chief-of-Staff Directive, April 3, 1939

The Fuehrer has added the following directives to Fall Weiss: (1) Preparations must be made in such a way that the operation can be carried out at any time from the 1st September 1939 onwards. (2) The High Command of the Armed Forces has been directed to draw up a precise timetable for Fall Weiss and to arrange by conferences the synchronized timings between the three branches of the Armed Forces.[32]

Annex II to German Directive to Armed Forces, Signed by Hitler, April 11, 1939

German relations with Poland continue to be based on the principle of avoiding any quarrels. Should Poland, however, change her policy toward Germany, based up to now on the same principles as our own, and adopt a threatening attitude towards Germany, a final settlement might become necessary, notwithstanding the pact in effect with Poland.

The aim then will be to destroy Polish military strength, and create in the East a situation which satisfies the requirements of national defense. The Free State of Danzig will be proclaimed a part of the Reich-territory at the outbreak of the conflict, at the latest.

The political leadership considers it its task in this case to isolate Poland if possible, that is to say, to limit the war to Poland only.[33]

---

[32]*Nazi Conspiracy and Aggression,* Vol. VI, p. 916.
[33]*Ibid.,* pp. 918–19. Also in *Documents on German Foreign Policy,* Series D, Vol. VI, pp. 224–25.

Hitler to Chiefs of Staff, Secret Meeting of May 23, 1939

Danzig is not the subject of the dispute at all. It is a question of expanding our living space in the East and of securing our food supplies, of the settlement of the Baltic problems. . . . If fate brings us into conflict with the West, possession of extensive areas in the East will be advantageous. . . . The Polish problem is inseparable from conflict with the West. There is therefore no question of sparing Poland, and we are left with the decision: *to attack Poland at the first suitable opportunity.* We cannot expect a repetition of the Czech affair. There will be war. Our task is to isolate Poland. The success of the isolation will be decisive. Therefore, the Fuehrer must reserve the right to give the final order to attack. There must be no simultaneous conflict with the Western Powers (France and England).

If it is not certain that a German-Polish conflict will not lead to war in the West then the fight must be primarily against England and France. . . . Economic relations with Russia are possible only if political relations have improved. A cautious trend is apparent in Press comment. It is not impossible that Russia will show herself to be disinterested in the destruction of Poland. Should Russia take steps to oppose us, our relations with Japan may become closer. If there were an alliance of France, England, and Russia against Germany, Italy, and Japan, I should be constrained to attack England and France with a few annihilating blows. We must prepare ourselves for the conflict.[34]

---

[34]*Nazi Conspiracy and Aggression,* Vol. VII, pp. 849–50. Also in *Documents on German Foreign Policy,* Series D, Vol. VI, pp. 575–80.

To French Foreign Minister Georges Bonnet it appeared that a closer understanding with Russia in connection with aid to Poland and Rumania was imperative. On April 9, the French Committee of National Defense agreed that military discussions should be initiated with the Soviet Union.

Five days later British Foreign Minister Halifax in London, and Bonnet in Paris, sounded out the respective Russian Ambassadors on a possible three-power accord. The following is the text of the French proposal.

FOR CONSIDERATION   Is this French proposal a suggestion that France and Russia should develop a military alliance? Bonnet, in his memoirs, implies that it is.[35] Is he correct? If not, does this put into question Bonnet's reliability in other matters?

French Foreign Minister Bonnet to the Soviet Ambassador to France, April 14, 1939

In case France and Great Britain should find themselves in a state of war with Germany as a result of action taken in bringing aid and assistance to Rumania or Poland, victims of unprovoked aggression, the U.S.S.R. will bring them immediate aid and assistance.

[Second paragraph identical except that France and Great Britain pledge themselves to aid Russia under similar circumstances.]

The three Governments will get together without delay on the means of providing this assistance in both envisaged cases, and they will make every effort to ensure that it will be entirely efficacious.[36]

[35]Georges Bonnet, *Fin d'une Europe: De Munich à la Guerre* (Geneva: Les Editions du Cheval Ailé, 1948), p. 178–80.

[36]*Ibid.*, p. 180.

The danger to Europe's peace was everywhere apparent. President Roosevelt on April 14 addressed identical letters to Hitler and Mussolini asking them for assurances that they would not attack other countries. No such assurances were forthcoming. The German Foreign Office was more interested in exploring the possibilities suggested in Stalin's speech of March 10. On April 17, a conversation took place between Ernst von Weizsäcker, German career diplomat and Secretary of State, and Russian Ambassador Merekalov. The conversation is here described by Weizsäcker.

FOR CONSIDERATION   These discussions apparently started without Hitler's knowledge or approval. Remember that Hitler had consistently fulminated against Communism in general and the Soviet Union in particular. Notice also that in this summer of 1939 the Russians were negotiating with both Britain and Germany.

Memorandum of Secretary of State in German Foreign Office, Weizsacker, April 17, 1939

.   .   .   .   .

It had appeared to me that the Russian press lately was not fully participating in the anti-German tone of the American and some of the English papers. As to the German press, Herr Merekalov could form his own opinion, since he surely followed it very closely.

The Ambassador thereupon stated approximately as follows:

Russian policy had always moved in a straight line. Ideological differences of opinion had hardly influenced the Russian-Italian relationship, and they did not have to prove a stumbling block with regard to Germany either. Soviet Russia had not exploited the present friction between Germany and the Western democracies against us, nor did she desire to do so. There exists for Russia no reason why she should not live with us on a normal footing. And from normal, the relations might become better and better.

With this remark, to which the Russian had led the conversation, Herr Merekalov ended the interview. He intends to go to Moscow in the next few days for a visit.[37]

[37]*Nazi-Soviet Relations*, pp. 1–2. Also in *Documents on German Foreign Policy*, Series D, Vol. VI, pp. 266–67.

Each day of delay in effecting an Anglo-French-Soviet understanding brought Russia and Germany closer together. That this danger was not unknown to the Western Powers is suggested by the following comments of the French Ambassador to Germany.

Comments of Robert Coulondre, French Ambassador to Germany

It was at this time [early May] that I received, on Hitler's intentions, some hints of primary importance. The Officer associated with our Attaché for Air, Captain Stellin, handsome as well as intelligent and brave, was quite close to one of Marshal Goering's aides de camp, General Bodenschatz, who seemed to have for him a sort of sentimental regard, and he had already received from him some confidential statements which had proved correct. I asked him to see the General and the latter, on May 6, made some declarations of which I only summarize the essential points.

(1) M. Beck's speech will change nothing in the situation. The Führer is resolved to bring about the return of Danzig to Germany and the juncture of eastern Prussia with the Reich.

(2) The Führer, patient and thoughtful, will not attack the question directly, for he knows that from now on France and England would not give in and that the coalition he would run into would be too strong. He will manoeuver right up to the end.

(3) With a view to this, the Führer will come to terms with Russia. A day will come when he will thus attain his objectives without the Allies having had any reason, or even any intention of intervening. Perhaps one will see the fourth partition of Poland. In any case "one will soon see that something is going on in the East, *dass etwas im Osten in Gange ist.*"[38]

[38]Robert Coulondre, *De Staline à Hitler* (Paris: Librairie Hachette, 1950), pp. 270–71. Quoted by permission of the publisher, Librairie Hachette, Paris.

The Soviet government also made a proposal to the British and French governments for a military pact on April 17. This proposal suggested: that England, France, and the U.S.S.R. pledge reciprocal assistance in case of aggression against any one of them; that the Baltic countries be included in the pact; that military implementation be studied in common; that no separate peace be signed; that England limit its assistance to Poland in case of German aggression; that Poland and Rumania agree to cancel their longstanding alliance.[39] The British government could not reach any compromise with France whereby they both could accept this proposal. Meanwhile, on April 28, Hitler denounced the Anglo-German Naval Treaty and the German-Polish Nonaggression Pact. A week later, on May 4, Litvinov was replaced, as Soviet Foreign Minister, by V. M. Molotov. A British refusal of the Soviet proposal was finally sent on May 9. The following documents throw some light on these negotiations.

FOR CONSIDERATION   As Litvinov's policy had long been oriented toward the West, his fall very likely indicates the turning point in Soviet foreign policy. At the time, however, it was felt, and Molotov himself insisted, that no modification was planned. Were Western diplomats shortsighted in not reading the signs more clearly? What aspects of the Soviet proposals were objectionable to Britain? Why could not Russia accept the French proposals?

Communiqué of the Soviet Government, May 9, 1939

.   .   .   .   .

The proposals [of the British Government] state that the Soviet Government must give immediate help to Britain and France in case the latter are involved in military operations in execution of their obligations toward Poland and Rumania. However, the counter-proposals of the British Government include no pledge of help to be given by the British and French Governments to the Soviet Union on a reciprocal basis, should the Soviet Union become engaged in military operations in execution of the obligation it would undertake concerning any Eastern European State.[40]

Statement of British Prime Minister Chamberlain, May 10, 1939

His Majesty's Government . . . made it plain that it is in no part their intention

that the Soviet Government should commit themselves to intervene, irrespective of whether Britain and France are already intervening in the discharge of their own obligations. His Majesty's Government added that if the Soviet Government wished to make their own intervention contingent on that of Britain and France, His Majesty's Government for their part would offer no objection. . . .[41]

Polish Attitude toward Russia in May, 1939, as Stated by Polish Ambassador to Russia Grzybowski in his *Final Report*, dated November 6, 1939

Some days later (more or less at the time of M. Potemkin's stay in Warsaw [May 10, 1939]) I gave to M. Molotov a résumé of our attitude.

We could not accept a one-sided Soviet guarantee. Nor could we accept a mutual guarantee because, in the event of a conflict with Germany our forces would be

[39]Bonnet, *op. cit.*, p. 182; L. B. Namier, *Diplomatic Prelude* (London: Macmillan Company, Ltd., 1948), p. 155.

[40]Keesing's *Contemporary Archives, 1937–1940* (Keynsham, Bristol: Keesing's Publications, Ltd.), p. 3570 B. Quoted by permission.

[41]*Parliamentary Debates, Commons, 1938–39* (London: His Majesty's Stationery Office, 1940), Vol. 347, Col. 454. Quoted by permission of the Controller of Her Britannic Majesty's Stationery Office.

completely engaged, and so we would not be in any position to give help to the Soviets. Also we could not accept collective negotiations, and made our adoption of a definite attitude conditional on the result of the Anglo-Franco-Soviet negotiations. We rejected all discussion of matters affecting us other than by the bilateral method. Our alliance with Rumania, being purely defensive, could not in any way be regarded as directed against the U.S.S.R.[42]

---

[42]*Polish White Book,* p. 208.

France as well as England took steps to guarantee Poland's integrity. On April 13, 1939, Premier Daladier issued such a guarantee during a speech to the Chamber of Deputies, and thereafter negotiations ensued between France and Poland to determine a definitive text for the guarantee. But certain difficulties, as suggested in Bonnet's letter to the Polish ambassador, prevented these negotiations from reaching a conclusion. In the end, no agreement was signed until after the Germans had invaded Poland.

French Foreign Minister Bonnet to Polish Ambassador to France Lukasiewicz, May 26, 1939

. . . I have kept you fully informed about the condition in which I found the preparatory work at the [British] Foreign Office, about the exchange of views I had with Lord Halifax . . . and about the joint study at Geneva. . . .

This study has demonstrated the impossibility of the English to accept the final draft of the Franco-Polish protocol, as proposed by you, since it would depart too far from the basic elements already agreed on by M. Beck and Lord Halifax. . . . I have, however, been able to work out a new formula . . . which departs in the smallest degree possible from your proposal. . . .

This new proposal is at the moment under consideration by the British Government, which will furthermore let me know about other terms in the Anglo-Polish draft agreement.

But without waiting for London's decisions . . . I believe I should . . . personally communicate to you the formula which was provisionally drawn up at Geneva in agreement with the British legal expert:

The French and Polish Governments simultaneously declare that henceforward they understand their agreements to indicate a commitment for France and Poland to lend each other all aid and asistance in their power immediately, if either one is the object of an action clearly threatening its independence, directly or indirectly, and if this country, to defend its vital interests, resists this action with arms.

.   .   .   .   .

While awaiting the signature of the Franco-Polish interpretive protocol, which will simply confirm explicitly the broad reassurances already made publicly in regard to the reciprocal aid commitments existing between France and Poland, I can only call to your attention the *de jure* and *de facto* situation which should already cover all possible concerns of the Polish Government; a guarantee of immediate and direct intervention by France has been, and continues to be, ensured by the solemn declaration of the head of the French Government, on April 13th last.[43]

---

[43]L. B. Namier, *Europe in Decay, a Study in Disintegration* (London: The Macmillan Company, Ltd., 1950), pp. 308–10. Quoted by permission of The Macmillan Company.

Meanwhile, between May 14 and 21, 1939, a Polish military mission conferred with French Commander in Chief Gamelin on the military aid which France should furnish Poland. On May 19 the following agreement was signed.

FOR CONSIDERATION   This convention has given rise to considerable controversy. According to Bonnet this secret military convention was signed without prior notification having been given the French Foreign Ministry, which, however, put it into effect by signing on September 4, 1939, a Franco-Polish Mutual Assistance Pact calling for military implementation in accordance with plans already worked out by the military authorities.[44] Gamelin maintains, however, that he not only had Daladier's authorization for signing, but had inserted into the convention a reservation to the effect that the French and Polish High Commands acted "within the framework of decisions taken by the two Governments . . .". Another aspect of the document also has interest. What has been translated as "a body of her forces" is in the original "les gros de ses forces." While this might appear to mean the *major part* of her forces, in French military terminology, according to General Gamelin, it means *a third*. In any event, because the political agreement was not signed, Gamelin considered the military convention null and void.[45] Is it not possible that Poland took the convention into account in its diplomatic actions toward Germany?

Excerpts of the Franco-Polish Military Convention, Signed May 19, 1939

France will undertake immediately action in the air according to a plan fixed beforehand. . . .

When a part of the French forces are ready (about the third day after the initial day of general French mobilization), France will launch offensive actions progressively against limited objectives.

Should the major German effort be concentrated on Poland, France would launch an offensive action against Germany with a body of her forces (after the fifteenth day following the initial day of general French mobilization).[46]

---

[44]Bonnet, *op. cit.*, pp. 229–33.
[45]General Gamelin, *Servir* (Paris: Librairie Plon, 1946), Vol. II, p. 421, and *passim*. For a discussion of this problem, see Namier, *Diplomatic Prelude*, pp. 454–66.

[46]Bonnet, *op. cit.*, p. 229.

In May, German-Soviet negotiations began to make headway. While these were ostensibly discussions for a trade agreement, both parties, as the following documents show, were not unwilling to discuss a political arrangement. Toward the end of June, Hitler almost broke off the negotiations, but permitted them to be resumed in July. Meanwhile he continued military preparations.

FOR CONSIDERATION   The Axis Pact, between Germany and Italy, was signed on May 22. What bearing would this have on the strategic positions of France, Poland, and Russia?

Memorandum by German Ambassador to Russia Schulenburg, on a Conversation with Soviet Foreign Minister Molotov, May 20, 1939

. . . . .

I opened the conversation by saying to Herr Molotov that the last proposals of Herr Mikoyan in our economic negotiations had presented several difficulties which could not be immediately removed. . . .

Herr Molotov replied that the course of our last economic negotiations had given the Soviet Government the impression that we had not been in earnest in the matter and we had only played at negotiating for political reasons. . . . The Soviet Government could only agree to a resumption of the negotiations if the necessary "political bases" for them had been constructed [wenn hierfür die notwendige "politische Grundlage" geschaffen sein werde].

I told Herr Molotov that we had never regarded the economic discussions as a game, but we had always conducted them entirely in earnest. We always had and still have the sincerest intention to come to an agreement, and Berlin was of the opinion, if I understood it correctly, that a successful conclusion of the economic discussions would also help the political atmosphere.[47]

German Third Army Group Directive, June 14, 1939

The commander-in-chief of the army has ordered the working out of a *plan of deployment against Poland* which takes in account the demands of the political leadership for the opening of war by surprise and for quick success. . . .

The order for deployment "Fall Weiss" will be put into operation on August 20, 1939; all preparations have to be concluded by this date.

. . . . .

Enclosure 1. The operation, in order to forestall an orderly Polish mobilization and concentration, is to be opened by surprise with forces which are for the most part armored and motorized, placed on alert in the neighborhood of the border. . . .[48]

German Ambassador to Russia Schulenburg, to German Foreign Office, July 3, 1939

I opened the discussion [with Molotov] with the statement that on the basis of the talks in Berlin, particularly with the Reich Foreign Minister, I had the impression that we would welcome a normalization of relations with the Soviet Union. . . .

Molotov listened attentively and stated that he received this communication with satisfaction. I continued that since the conversation of the State Secretary with Astakhov, we had waited for a Soviet statement as to what Molotov had meant in his conversation with me on May 20 by the words "creation of a political basis for the resumption of economic negotiations"; . . .

In his answer Molotov did not go into the question as to the meaning of the con-

[47]*Nazi-Soviet Relations*, p. 6. Also in *Documents on German Foreign Policy*, Series D, Vol. VI, pp. 559–60.

[48]*Nazi Conspiracy and Aggression*, Vol. IV, pp. 1035–37.

cept "political basis," but he declared that the Soviet Government in accordance with the enunciations of its leaders desired good relations with all countries and therefore—provided there was reciproci-

ty—would also welcome a normalization of relations with Germany. . . .[49]

[49]*Nazi-Soviet Relations*, pp. 28–29. Also in *Documents on German Foreign Policy*, Series D, Vol. VI, pp. 834–35.

In spite of the uncertainties of arrangements with Britain and Russia, and the failure of France to sign the guarantee promised Poland, France indicated on July 1 that it would support Poland.

French Foreign Minister Bonnet to German Ambassador to France Welczek, July 1, 1939

. . . At a moment when measures of all kinds are being taken in Danzig, whose scope and object it is difficult to appreciate, it is particularly essential to avoid any risk of misunderstanding about the extent of the obligations and about the attitude of the French Government: a misunderstanding whose consequences might be incalculable. I therefore regard it as

my duty to state definitely that any action, whatever its form, which would tend to modify the *status quo* in Danzig, and so provoke armed resistance by Poland, would bring the Franco-Polish agreement into play and oblige France to give immediate assistance to Poland.[50]

[50]*The French Yellow Book: Diplomatic Documents, 1938–1939* (Eng. ed.; New York: Harcourt, Brace & World, Inc., 1940), p. 197. Quoted by permission of Harcourt, Brace & World, Inc.

British-French-Soviet negotiations went on at Moscow during the spring and summer of 1939. Early in June, Great Britain sent William Strang, a competent career diplomat heading the Foreign Office's Central European Department (but not an outstanding figure in the government) to assist in the conversations. As his participation was later criticized, Lord Strang's own comments are pertinent. In the course of the discussions many problems developed, particularly in connection with guarantees to the Netherlands and the Baltic states. Neither group could agree on a definition of "indirect aggression." As one may note from the following, negotiations almost broke down in July, but were patched up sufficiently to permit a draft treaty to be drawn up on July 23. Although the treaty was never signed, Molotov agreed that military discussions could start and Strang left Moscow on August 7, to be replaced by the Anglo-French military missions.

Comments of Sir William Strang

On June 6 in Warsaw, I received a telegram from the Foreign Office warning me

that I might have to return to London at very short notice in order to join Sir William Seeds, the Ambassador at Moscow, who was due to return to his post with fresh instructions to resume negotiations with the Soviet Government for a treaty of mutual assistance. The next day a second telegram said that the Ambassador was ill and had been unable to travel to London, and that it had been decided to send me to Moscow. I was to return to London by the quickest way in order to receive instructions. I was back in London on the following day, June 8, and arrived in Moscow via Warsaw on June 14.

This so-called mission of mine to Moscow has been the subject of such widespread misapprehension that the facts should be stated. I did not go to Moscow to open negotiations with the Soviet Government: these had already been going on for several months. I did not go to Moscow to carry on the negotiations: I went to help the British Ambassador, who had been conducting them from the beginning, and had been more recently joined in them by his French colleague, M. Naggiar.

·   ·   ·   ·   ·

It is still sometimes stated that the negotiations broke down on the question of the Baltic States. This, as a matter of history, is not so. The break occurred in the military conversations, not in the political conversations; and it came on the question of Poland. The political conversations had not been abandoned; they had been left in suspense when the military conversations started. They were, in fact, very largely successful. There was one main point left outstanding; but its eventual solution need not have proved any more difficult than that of other stubborn differences that were surmounted during the negotiations. Indeed, after I had left Moscow, and while the political conversations were in suspense and the military conversations were proceeding, instructions were sent to Sir William Seeds, upon which he was never able to act, permitting him to agree to a definition of indirect aggression

which would have substantially weakened the criterion of "threat of force", and would thus have gone far to meet the Soviet view.[51]

Instructions of British Foreign Office (Lord Halifax) to British Ambassador to Russia, Seeds, July 12, 1939

I see grave objections to the provision which is made in M. Molotov's formula with reference to aggression against the State in question in addition to aggression against one of the contracting parties. This no doubt is intended to cover the case of a civil war or *coup d'état* in which foreign forces were participating, but I do not think that this eventuality can be safely covered by any form of words and it ought not to be attempted.

I will now turn to the new difficulty which M. Molotov has raised in insisting that the political agreement must wait upon a military agreement, which will only be signed simultaneously. We most strongly object to this completely abnormal procedure. The fact that M. Molotov should make this demand reveals a suspicion of our sincerity and *bona fides* which is most offensive and quite unjustifiable, more especially as we are prepared immediately on signature to start military conversations.

I appreciate the fact that I am setting you an arduous task in instructing you to reject the two chief proposals which M. Molotov made to you at your last interview. But we are nearing the point where we clearly cannot continue the process of conceding each fresh demand put forward by the Soviet Government. In order to meet M. Molotov we have made the following concessions:—(1) we have met the Soviet Government's demand that the

[51]Lord (William) Strang, *Home and Abroad* (London: A. Deutsch, 1956), pp. 157, 190.

treaty should cover the case of the Baltic States; (2) we have abandoned our demand that the Netherlands, Switzerland and Luxemburg should be included among the countries to be covered by the agreement; (3) we have agreed to provide for the case of indirect aggression; (4) we have against our better judgement undertaken to define it; (5) we are prepared to insert this definition in the agreement itself; (6) we have accepted M. Molotov's proposal that the agreement should contain a provision prohibiting the signatories from concluding a separate armistice or peace.

If in return for all these concessions the Soviet Government are unwilling to meet us on the two points now at issue, His Majesty's Government may have to reconsider their whole position. I do not suggest that you should actually say this to M. Molotov at the present stage, but it would be useful if you could find means of giving him to understand that our patience is well-nigh exhausted and that he will do well not to presume any further on our readiness to yield to the Soviet Government each time they put forward a new demand.[52]

Sir William Strang to British Foreign Office, July 20, 1939

Molotov does not become any easier to deal with as the weeks pass. He has, it is true, now made himself familiar with the details of our problem; and you will have noticed that the drafts he produces, whether they are his own or prepared by his experts, are ingeniously constructed, though they are, I am told, couched in inelegant Russian. But it is difficult to get to grips with him. He seems to be bored

with detailed discussion; and the admirable argumentative material with which you supply us makes little impression on him. It took us, for example, an inordinate time trying to make clear to him the difference between initialling an agreement, signing an agreement, and bringing an agreement into force, and even now we are not sure that he has grasped it. Indeed we have sometimes felt that the differences which have arisen between us might perhaps be based on some colossal misunderstanding. And yet we have usually come to the conclusion in the end that this is not so, and that Molotov has seen clearly the extent of the difference between the respective positions of the two sides.

On the whole the negotiations have been a humiliating experience. Time after time we have taken up a position and a week later we have abandoned it; and we have had the feeling that Molotov was convinced from the beginning that we should be forced to abandon it.[53]

Draft Anglo-Franco-Soviet Agreement, July 23, 1939 (Sections in Italics Still under Discussion)

Article 1

The United Kingdom, France and the U.S.S.R. undertake to give to each other immediately all effective assistance if one of these three countries becomes involved in hostilities with a European Power as a result either

(1) of aggression aimed by that Power against one of these three countries, or

(2) of aggression, direct or indirect, aimed by that Power against any European State whose independence or

[52]*Documents on British Foreign Policy*, 3d Series, Vol. VI, pp. 334–36.

[53]*Ibid.*, p. 422.

neutrality the contracting country concerned feels obliged to defend against such aggression.

It is agreed between the three contracting Governments that the words "indirect aggression" in paragraph 2 above are to be understood as covering action accepted by the State in question under threat of force by another Power and involving the abandonment by it of its independence or neutrality.

The assistance provided for in the present article will be given in conformity with the principles of the League of Nations, but without its being necessary to follow the procedure of, or to await action by, the League.

Article 2

The three contracting Governments will concert together as soon as possible as to the methods, forms and extent of the assistance to be rendered by them in conformity with Article 1, with the object of making such assistance as effective as possible.

Article 3

The three contracting Governments will exchange information periodically about the international situation and will lay down the lines of mutual diplomatic support in the interests of peace....

Article 4

The three contracting Governments will communicate to one another the terms of any undertakings of assistance which they have already given to other European States....

[*Articles 5, 6, 7*]

PROTOCOL

The three contracting Governments have agreed as follows:

1. Paragraph 2 of Article 1 of the agreement signed by them today will apply to the following European States:

Turkey, Greece, Roumania, Poland, Belgium, Estonia, Latvia, Finland.

2. The foregoing list of States is subject to revision by agreement between the three contracting Governments.

3. *In the event of aggression or threat of aggression by a European Power against a European State not named in the foregoing list, the three contracting Governments will, without prejudice to the immediate action which any of them may feel obliged to take, immediately consult together at the request of any one of them with a view to such action as may be mutually agreed upon.*

4. The present supplementary agreement will not be made public.[54]

Comments of Winston Churchill on Anglo-Soviet Negotiations of 1939

At the Kremlin in August, 1942, Stalin, in the early hours of the morning, gave me one aspect of the Soviet position. "We formed the impression," said Stalin, "that the British and French Governments were not resolved to go to war if Poland were attacked, but that they hoped the diplomatic line-up of Britain, France, and Russia would deter Hitler. We were sure it would not." "How many divisions," Stalin had asked, "will France send against Germany on mobilisation?" The answer was: "About a hundred." He than asked: "How many will England send?" The answer was: "Two and two more later." "Ah, two and two more later," Stalin had repeated. "Do you know," he asked, "how many divisions we shall have to put on the Russian front if we go to war with Germany?" There was a pause. "More than three

---
[54]*Ibid.*, pp. 539–42.

"SO YOU CAN'T DEFINE 'INDIRECT AGGRESSION', EH?
WELL, SUPPOSE WE GIVE YOU ANOTHER DEMONSTRATION!"

Cartoon by David Low and by arrangement with the London Evening Standard.

If It's Expert Assistance That's Needed—

hundred." I was not told with whom this conversation took place or its date. It must be recognised that this was solid ground, but not favourable for Mr. Strang of the Foreign Office.[55]

Excerpt from Speech of Soviet Foreign Minister Molotov, August 31, 1939

They [the negotiations] encountered the difficulty that Poland, which was to be jointly guaranteed by Great Britain, France and the U.S.S.R., rejected military assistance on the part of the Soviet Union. Attempts to overcome the objec-

[55]Winston Churchill, *The Gathering Storm* (Boston: Houghton Mifflin Company, 1948), p. 391. Quoted by permission of Houghton Mifflin Company.

tions of Poland met with no success. More, the negotiations showed that Great Britain was not anxious to overcome these objections of Poland, but on the contrary encouraged them. It is clear that, such being the attitude of the Polish Government and its principal ally towards military assistance on the part of the Soviet Union in the event of aggression, the Anglo-French-Soviet negotiations could not bear fruit. After this it became clear to us that the Anglo-French-Soviet negotiations were doomed to failure.

What have the negotiations with Great Britain and France shown? The Anglo-French-Soviet negotiations have shown that the position of Great Britain and France is marked by howling contradictions throughout. Judge for yourselves. On the one hand, Great Britain and France demanded that the U.S.S.R.

should give military assistance to Poland in case of aggression. The U.S.S.R., as you know, was willing to meet this demand, provided that the U.S.S.R. itself received like assistance from Great Britain and France. On the other hand, precisely Great Britain and France brought Poland on the scene, who resolutely declined military assistance on the part of the U.S.S.R. Just try under such circumstances to reach an agreement regarding mutual assistance, when assistance on the part of the U.S.S.R. is declared beforehand to be unnecessary and intrusive.[56]

[56]*Strategy and Tactics of World Communism*, Supplement I (Washington, D.C.: U.S. Government Printing Office, 1948), pp. 158–59.

At the same time that the Anglo-Soviet conversations were proceeding in Moscow, informal discussions on a trade agreement between Germany and Great Britain took place in England. These were carried on in July and August by Helmuth Wohlthat, a German economic adviser; Herbert von Dirksen, the German Ambassador; and Robert Hudson, British Secretary of Overseas Trade. Occasionally Sir Horace Wilson, close adviser of Prime Minister Chamberlain, participated in the discussions.

Although neither the British nor German governments placed very much importance on the negotiations, they nevertheless had an effect on Russia. Russia knew they were going on.

FOR CONSIDERATION   Reports of the Dirksen conversations were among the documents published by the Soviet Union (*Documents and Materials Relating to the Eve of the Second World War*, 1948) as an instrument of cold war propaganda. The interested student will find British reports in *Documents on British Foreign Policy*, Series 3, Vol. VI, pp. 407–10, 579–82.

Excerpt from the Memoirs of Herbert von Dirksen, German Ambassador to Great Britain

The program developed by Sir Horace Wilson embraced in its entirety the mutual relations of both countries. It was not only confined to the economic sphere, but extended also to political and military matters. It dealt with the Colonial problem and included proposals for the purchase of raw materials for Germany. It provided financial arrangements for the two countries, it referred to a settlement of international debts, and took Hudson's ideas into account. The further working out of the program was left to the German side. The decisive question was: would Hitler authorize the appointment of a suitable person to take charge of the negotiations? . . .

Ribbentrop reacted at once when my own and Wohlthat's reports reached Berlin. In two telegrams he demanded an immediate report on the political questions which Wohlthat had raised with my permission. Wohlthat had apparently omitted to ask Wilson whether the proposals were to be considered as an abandonment of the negotiations (especially with Moscow) for an encirclement of Germany. . . .

That the importance of the British proposals was recognized by persons less warlike than Ribbentrop was shown by Göring's reaction to Wohlthat's report. As has only recently become known, through his adjutant-in-chief, Göring visited Hitler three times in August, earnestly urging him to avoid getting entangled in a war, seeing that a complete compromise with Britain on the basis of Wohlthat's reported offers would bring to Germany the fulfillment of her claims. Hitler, of course, repulsed him. But this episode is significant, showing that in August Göring did not believe in the inevitability of war, on the assumption that Hitler, in his incalculable manner, took irrevocable decisions only at the last moment. This frees those working unceasingly for peace from charges of quixotic behavior.

.   .   .   .   .

I sent a detailed report on the conversations to Berlin on the same day. The action of the British Government, which reached its zenith by this proposal,

made me ask myself: were these overtures really serious? . . . I came to the conclusion that I could express my full confidence in Chamberlain and in the initiative of his cabinet. In view of the ever-increasing threat of war, Chamberlain, as a responsible statesman, felt obliged to make one last and desperate attempt for the preservation of peace. . . . During my term of office in London Hitler did not once trouble to respond to Britain's offers, not even for form's sake. He never even replied to them. The historical significance of Chamberlain's last peace efforts consists in this: they placed the onus on Hitler's shoulders. . . .

And so a proposal which should have been examined with the utmost care, even if not considered trustworthy, was simply thrown into the waste-paper basket by Hitler and Ribbentrop.[57]

[57]Herbert von Dirksen, Moscow, Tokyo, London: Twenty Years of German Foreign Policy (Norman, Okla.: University of Oklahoma Press, 1952), pp. 225–28. Copyright 1952 by the University of Oklahoma.

In August, Germany accelerated its military and diplomatic preparations. An attack on Poland would have to start before weather conditions deteriorated in the winter. Ribbentrop himself took over the direction of German-Soviet negotiations. Having broken off negotiations with Poland in March, Germany now at the beginning of August came to the defense of Danzig and intensified its diplomatic and press campaign. Hitler conferred with Carl Burckhardt, League of Nations Commissioner for Danzig. One of his revelations to Burckhardt is astonishingly portentous.

Comments of William Shirer, American Correspondent, August 10, 1939

How completely isolated a world the German people live in. A glance at the newspapers yesterday and today reminds you of it. Whereas all the rest of the world

considers that the peace is about to be broken by Germany, that it is Germany that is threatening to attack Poland over Danzig, here in Germany, in the world the local newspapers create, the very reverse is being maintained. (Not that it surprises me, but when you are away for a while, you forget.) What the Nazi papers are proclaiming is this: that it is Poland which is disturbing the peace of Europe; Poland which is threatening Germany with armed invasion, and so forth. This is the Germany of last September when the steam was turned on Czechoslovakia.

"POLAND? LOOK OUT!" warns the B.Z. headline, adding: "ANSWER TO PO-LAND, THE RUNNERAMOK (AMOK-LÄUFER) AGAINST PEACE AND RIGHT IN EUROPE!"

Or the headline in *Der Führer*, daily paper of Karlsruhe, which I bought on the train: "WARSAW THREATENS BOM-BARDMENT OF DANZIG—UNBE-LIEVABLE AGITATION OF THE POLISH ARCHMADNESS (POLNI-SCHEN GRÖSSENWAHNS)!"

For perverse perversion of the truth,

this is good. You ask: But the German people can't possibly believe these lies? Then you talk to them. So many do.[58]

Comments of Carl J. Burckhardt

On August 11 Hitler had told me:

Everything I undertake is directed against Russia: if the West is too stupid and blind to realize this, then I will be obliged to align myself with the Russians, to attack the West, and then after their defeat to gather up all my forces for an onslaught against the Soviet Union. I need the Ukraine so that we will not be starved out as we were in the last war.[59]

[58]Shirer, *op. cit.*, pp. 172–73.

[59]Carl Jacob Burckhardt, *Meine Danziger Mission, 1937–39* (Munich: Verlag Georg D. W. Callwey, 1960), p. 348.

Whether or not Hitler could count on Italy is made fairly clear by the following extract from the papers of Italian Foreign Minister Galleazzo Ciano.

Ciano's Notes on a Conversation with Hitler at Berchtesgaden, August 13, 1939

Hitler asks if I have anything to say. I thank him and reply that I am waiting to learn his decisions. Hitler then begins to speak. . . .

Germany will take action against Po-land as soon as possible. That action will be rapid, decisive, implacable. The West-ern Powers will not intervene. . . . I take note of the Fuehrer's assertions and ask, should he be able and willing to tell me, when the operation will begin. Hitler says that that is not yet fixed. However, every-thing is ready and, should the operation have to begin as the result of a serious incident, it could take place at any minute. If, on the other hand, the operation is to

have a different origin, one can put it a little later. *The last date for the beginning of the operation is the end of August.* As a last resort for justifying the attack, and in case no other opportunity offers, he will consider as serious one of the many local incidents which occur daily in Danzig and in the Corridor. No delay would be pos-sible in view of the fact that the German General Staff consider four to six weeks necessary to liquidate the Polish question militarily, and in view of the fact that, after the 15th of October, mist and mud make the roads and aerodromes on the Polish front unusable. . . .[60]

---

[60]Malcolm Muggeridge (ed.), *Ciano's Diplo-matic Papers* (London: Odhams Books, Ltd., 1948), p. 302–03. Quoted by permission of the publisher, Odhams Books Ltd., London.

The Franco-British military mission, which on August 11 had replaced William Strang in Moscow, made little progress. Ribbentrop, to whom time was tremendously important, was convinced that direct negotiations with Stalin and Molotov were called for. His proposal to Russia, and the Russian reaction, are indicated in the following.

FOR CONSIDERATION   Why did the Russians give indications of being less in a hurry to conclude an agreement than the Germans?

German Foreign Minister von Ribbentrop to German Ambassador to Russia Schulenburg, August 14, 1939

As we have been informed, the Soviet Government also has the desire for a clarification of German-Russian relations. Since, however, according to previous experience this clarification can be achieved only slowly through the usual diplomatic channels, Reich Foreign Minister von Ribbentrop is prepared to make a short visit to Moscow in order, in the name of the Führer, to set forth the Führer's views to Herr Stalin. Only through such a direct discussion, in view of Herr von Ribbentrop, can a change be brought about, and it should not be impossible thereby to lay the foundations for a definite improvement in German-Russian relations.[61]

[61]*Nazi-Soviet Relations*, pp. 51–52. Also in *Documents on German Foreign Policy*, Series D, Vol. VII, p. 64.

Report of Conversation with Molotov from German Ambassador to Russia Schulenburg, to German Foreign Office, August 18, 1939

. . . . .

With regard to the proposed trip of the Reich Foreign Minister to Moscow, he declared that the Soviet Government was very gratified by this proposal, since the dispatch of such a distinguished public figure and statesman emphasized the earnestness of the intentions of the German Government. This stood in noteworthy contrast to England, who, in the person of Strang, had sent only an official of the second class to Moscow. A journey by the Reich Foreign Minister, however, required thorough preparation. The Soviet Government did not like the publicity that such a journey would cause. They preferred that practical work be accomplished without so much ceremony.[62]

[62]*Nazi-Soviet Relations*, p. 60. Also in *Documents on German Foreign Policy*, Series D, Vol. VII, p. 116.

On August 15 the Anglo-French military discussions in Moscow had reached an impasse over Russian insistence that Poland and Rumania agree to let Soviet troops pass through their countries. On August 17 the discussions were adjourned until the 21st. Immediate pressure was put on Poland, which transmitted the following official response to France.

FOR CONSIDERATION   Was this Polish refusal the major factor which prevented an Anglo-French-Soviet agreement? Or had Russia long before decided on a *rapprochement* with Germany?

Polish Prime Minister Beck to the French Government, August 19, 1939

I do not admit that in any way whatsoever the use of a part of our territory by foreign troops can be discussed. For us this is a question of principle. We have no military agreement with the U.S.S.R., we do not want to have one.[63]

---

[63]Bonnet, *Fin d'une Europe*, p. 282.

The negotiations for a German-Soviet trade agreement were successfully concluded on August 19, 1939. Hitler's comments on the *rapprochement* with Russia are here set forth. (Marshal von Manstein does not concur that the last line, about mediation, was in fact delivered.) Ribbentrop wished immediately to conclude a political arrangement in the nature of a nonaggression pact and strong German pressure was placed on the cautious Russians. On August 23 the pact was signed. Meanwhile the failure of England and France to modify the Polish position, and the refusal of Russia to accept a French assurance on Poland's behalf, had meant the complete breakdown of the Anglo-French-Russian military discussions.

Hitler to Commanders in Chief, August 22, 1939

It was clear to me that a conflict with Poland was bound to come sooner or later. I had already made this decision in the spring, but I thought I would first turn against the West in a few years, and only afterwards against the East. But the sequence cannot be fixed. One cannot close one's eyes even before a threatening situation. I wanted to establish an acceptable relationship with Poland in order to fight first against the West. But this plan, which was agreeable to me, could not be executed, since essential points have changed. It became clear to me that Poland would attack us in case of a conflict with the West. . . . My propositions to Poland (Danzig corridor) were disturbed by England's intervention. Poland changed her tone toward us. The initiative cannot be allowed to pass to the others. This moment is more favorable than in two to three years.

. . . . .

We will hold our position in the West until we have conquered Poland. We must be conscious of our great production. It is much bigger than in 1914–1918.

The enemy had another hope, that Russia would become our enemy after the conquest of Poland. The enemy did not count on my great power of resolution. Our enemies are little worms. I saw them at Munich.

I was convinced that Stalin would never accept the English offer. Russia has no interest in maintaining Poland and Stalin knows that it is the end of her regime no matter whether his soldiers come out of a war victoriously or beaten. Litvinov's replacement was decisive. I brought about the change toward Russia gradually. . . . The day after tomorrow von Ribbentrop will conclude the treaty. Now Poland is in the position in which I wanted her.

We need not be afraid of a blockade. The East will supply us with grain, cattle, coal, lead and zinc. It is a big arm, which demands great efforts. I am only afraid that at the last minute some *Schweinhund* will make a proposal for mediation.[64]

[64]*Nazi Conspiracy and Aggression*, Vol. III, pp. 581–85. Also in *Documents on German Foreign Policy*, Series D, Vol. III, pp. 200–04.

Comments of Marshal von Manstein on Hitler's Conference of August 22, 1939

The conference—or rather Hitler's address, as he was not going to let the occasion turn into an open discussion after his experience at a conference with the Chiefs-of-Staff the previous year, before the Czech crisis—took place in the big reception-chamber of the Berghof that looked out towards Salzburg. . . .

Hitler's speech on this occasion was the subject of various prosecution "documents" at the Nuremberg trial. One of these asserted that he had indulged in the vilest of language and that Göring, delighted at the prospect of war, had jumped on the table and yelled "*Sieg Heil!*" All this is quite untrue. It is equally untrue that Hitler said anything about "his only fear being a last-minute offer of mediation from some pig-dog or other." While the tone of his speech was certainly that of a man whose mind was firmly made up, he was far too good a psychologist to think he could impress a gathering of this kind with tirades or bad language. . . .

The impression left on those of us generals who did not belong to the top circle of military leaders was approximately this:

Hitler was absolutely determined to bring the German-Polish question to a head this time, even at the price of war. If, however, the Poles were to give in to German pressure, now approaching its climax in the deployment—albeit still camouflaged—of the German armies, a peaceful solution still did not seem excluded, and Hitler was convinced that when it came to the point the Western Powers would once again not resort to arms. He was at special pains to develop the latter thesis, his main arguments being: the backwardness of British and French armaments, particularly with regard to air strength and anti-aircraft defence; the virtual inability of the Western Powers to render Poland any effective help except by an assault on the Siegfried Line—a step

which neither power was likely to risk in view of the great sacrifice of blood it would entail; the international situation, particularly the tension in the Mediterranean, which considerably reduced Britain's freedom of movement; the internal situation in France; and last but not least the personalities of the responsible statesmen. Neither Chamberlain nor Daladier, Hitler contended, would take upon themselves the decision to go to war.[65]

Essential Sections of the Treaty of Nonaggression between Germany and the Soviet Union, August 23, 1939

Article I

Both High Contracting Parties obligate themselves to desist from any act of violence, any aggressive action, and any attack on each other, either individually or jointly with other powers.

Article II

Should one of the High Contracting Parties become the object of belligerent action by a third power, the other High Contracting Party shall in no manner lend its support to this third power.

Article III

The Governments of the two High Contracting Parties shall in the future maintain continual contact with one another for the purpose of consultation in order to exchange information on problems affecting their common interests.

Article IV

Neither of the two High Contracting Parties shall participate in any grouping of powers whatsoever that is directly or indirectly aimed at the other party.

．　　．　　．　　．　　．

[65]Field Marshal Erich von Manstein, *Lost Victories* (Chicago: Henry Regnery Co., 1958), pp. 28–29.

Secret Additional Protocol

On the occasion of the signature of the Nonaggression Pact between the German Reich and the Union of Socialist Soviet Republics the undersigned plenipotentiaries of each of the two parties discussed in strictly confidential conversations the question of the boundary of their respective spheres of influence in Eastern Europe. These conversations led to the following conclusions:

1. In the event of a territorial and political rearrangement in the areas belonging to the Baltic States (Finland, Estonia, Latvia, Lithuania), the northern boundary of Lithuania shall represent the boundary of the spheres of influence of Germany and the U.S.S.R. In this connection the interest of Lithuania in the Vilna area is recognized by each party.

2. In the event of a territorial and political rearrangement of the areas belonging to the Polish state the spheres of influence of Germany and the U.S.S.R. shall be bounded approximately by the line of the rivers Narew, Vistula, and San.

The question of whether the interests of both parties make desirable the maintenance of an independent Polish state and how such a state should be bounded can only be definitely determined in the course of further political developments.

In any event, both Governments will resolve this question by means of a friendly agreement.

3. With regard to Southeastern Europe, attention is called by the Soviet side to its interests in Bessarabia. The German side declares its complete political disinterestedness in these areas.[66]

---

[66]*Nazi-Soviet Relations*, pp. 76–78

Polish-German relations were on the verge of breaking. On August 25, the Anglo-Polish Mutual Assistance Pact was signed, but in some quarters there was still hope that war could be avoided. A Swedish Civil Engineer, Birger Dahlerus, played an interesting role in the negotiations preceding the attack on Poland. He had helped to arrange unofficial conferences between British businessmen and German officials. This group was hopeful of negotiations between British and German representatives.

FOR CONSIDERATION   Does Goering appear less enthusiastic for war than Hitler? Are there possibilities that the Anglo-Polish accord intensified rather than lessened the conflict?

Excerpts from Testimony of Birger Dahlerus at the Nuremberg Trial

DAHLERUS: I received a confirmation from Göring personally that Hitler agreed to such a conference. The matter was then discussed in London, and on 19 August, a request came to me to go to Paris, evidently to receive a reply from the British side. . . . On 23 August I was requested by Göring . . . to come to Berlin. . . . I arrived in Berlin on the 24th and saw Göring at 2 o'clock in the afternoon. . . . Göring stated that Germany wanted to come to an understanding with England.

DR. STAHMER: Then when did you leave for London?

DAHLERUS: The following morning. . . . I met Lord Halifax on Saturday, the 26th at 11 o'clock. . . . I suggested to Lord Halifax that he should write a letter to Göring. . . .

DR. STAHMER: Was your suggestion taken?

DAHLERUS: Yes, Lord Halifax conferred with Chamberlain, and afterwards wrote an excellent letter in which he indicated in very clear and distinct words the desire of His Majesty's Government to bring about a peaceful settlement.

DR. STAHMER: Did you then fly back to Berlin with this letter?

DAHLERUS: Yes. . . . I met Göring in his train. . . . I handed him the letter. . . . He declared that in his opinion Hitler must be informed immediately of the contents of this letter. . . .

DR. STAHMER: Did you then have a further conversation with Hitler?

DAHLERUS: I was visited by two officers at a quarter past twelve, midnight [August 27], who requested me to go with them immediately to Hitler. . . . He gave me a long report on his discussions on Friday with Henderson, and finally he asked me to go to London at once and explain his viewpoint. . . .

DR. STAHMER: What proposals were you specifically to make?

DAHLERUS: In condensed form, they were as follows:

(1) Germany wanted an agreement or an alliance with England.

(2) England was to help Germany in the annexation of Danzig and the Corridor.

(3) Germany gave the assurance that it would guarantee Poland's boundaries.

(4) An agreement should be reached on Germany's colonies.

(5) Adequate guarantees should be given for the treatment of German minorities.

(6) Germany gave its word to defend the British Empire with the German Wehrmacht wherever it should be attacked. . . .

I left in a special plane the next morning, after I had got in touch with London. I met Mr. Chamberlain, Lord Halifax, Sir Horace Wilson, and Sir Alexander Cadogan. . . .

DR. STAHMER: Did you also have a conference that day with Sir Alexander Cadogan? . . . Did you receive certain proposals from him?

DAHLERUS: Yes. . . . I must say that the English made the greatest effort to deal in a fair and peaceful way with the various points. Naturally, Point 6 . . . was rejected. Similarly, they did not want to have any discussion on the colonies as long as Germany was not mobilized. With regard to the Polish boundaries, they wanted these boundaries to be guaranteed by the five great powers; Russia, Germany, England, France and Italy. Concerning the Corridor, they proposed that negotiations with Poland be undertaken immediately. With reference to the first point, England was willing in principle to come to an agreement with Germany.

DR. STAHMER: Did you then return to Germany with these proposals?

DAHLERUS: Yes. . . . I met with Göring . . . on Sunday evening [August 27] and told him the results. . . . He did not consider the reply very favorable. . . . Finally he said that it would probably be better if he talked with Hitler alone. . . . At about one o'clock on Monday morning, the 28th, I received a telephone call and heard that Hitler would accept the English standpoint provided that the reply expected from Henderson on the next day was, in general, what I had said. . . . On Tuesday morning, or at 1:15, that is, shortly after midnight, on the 29th, I received a telephone call from the Reich Chancellery, made at Göring's request by Lieutenant Colonel Konrad. He told me that Henderson had submitted his reply in writing, that it was highly satisfactory, and there was every hope that the threat of war was past.[67]

---

[67] *Trial of the Major War Criminals before the International Military Tribunal* (Nuremberg, 1947), Vol. IX, pp. 461–67. For further documentation of the Dahlerus negotiations, see *Documents on British Foreign Policy*, 3d Series, Vol. VI, pp. 751–61, and Vol. VII, pp. 281–86, 395–98; also Birger Dahlerus' memoirs, *The Last Attempt* (London: Hutchinson & Co., 1947).

France as well as England attempted to thwart German aggression, as indicated by the following French note and comment of the French Ambassador.

FOR CONSIDERATION   Does Daladier's note show anything of the tone of Munich? Compare Coulondre's comments with those of François-Poncet in September 1938.

Daladier to Hitler, August 26, 1939

.   .   .   .   .

I can vouch not only for the good will of France, but also for that of all her allies. I can personally guarantee the readiness which Poland has always shown to have recourse to methods of free conciliation, such as may be envisaged between the Governments of two sovereign nations. In all sincerity I can assure you that there is not one of the grievances invoked by Germany against Poland in connection with the Danzig question which might not be submitted to decision by such methods with a view to a friendly and equitable settlement.

I can also pledge my honour that there is nothing in the clear and sincere solidarity of France with Poland and her allies which could modify in any manner whatsoever the peaceful inclinations of my country. This solidarity has never prevented us, and does not prevent us to-day, from helping to maintain Poland in her pacific inclinations.[68]

Comments of Robert Coulondre, French Ambassador to Germany

On the same day [August 26] at 7:00 P.M., I place this letter in the Chancellor's

hands. While he is reading it, I note his clouded face, his frozen expression, and I understand that the struggle in which he is engaged is desperate. . . .

Hitler has read the message, he has his eyes on me. In a few words he renders homage to the sentiments expressed by M. Daladier. His voice is hard and dry. "Since Poland has the British guarantee, it is vain," he says, "to want to carry away a sane comprehension of the situation. After all, things have now gone too far." As at this point I was going to speak, he makes a gesture with his hand which seems to imply that it is entirely useless. But nothing in the world could stop the words which mount from my heart to my lips. "Things have not gone so far," I say to him, "that war cannot be avoided so long as nothing irremediable develops. . . . You who have built an empire without spilling blood, don't spill that of soldiers and also that of women and children without finding out whether it could have been avoided. . . ."

Several seconds roll by in silence. I hear Hitler murmur: "*Ach! die Frauen und die Kinder, daran habe ich oft gedacht.*" (Oh! the woman and children, I have often thought about them.) He raises his eyes to Ribbentrop, who is standing by his side and who has maintained from the beginning of the discussion a face of stone. Then he stands up, takes Ribbentrop by the arm and leads him to a corner of the room. I have a minute of foolish hope. Foolish is certainly the word. Hitler comes

---

[68]*French Yellow Book*, No. 253, pp. 311–12. Quoted by permission of the publisher, Harcourt, Brace and World, Inc.

back. His face, which had held an instant before a more human expression, has become hard, savage. Has this all been only a comedy and have I succeeded in moving no one but myself? I will never know. "It is useless," he tells me, "Poland will not cede Danzig and I want Danzig returned to the Reich. . . ."[69]

---

[69]Coulondre, *op. cit.*, pp. 290–91.

The extent to which Hitler could count on help from his Axis partner Mussolini is indicated in the following passage.

Comments of Dr. Paul Schmidt, German Foreign Office Interpreter, Describing Events of August 25

The next caller was already waiting outside. It was Attolico, who now brought Mussolini's urgently awaited answer to Hitler's intimation that he was about to intervene actively in Poland. "In one of the most painful moments of my life," wrote Mussolini, "I have to inform you that Italy is not ready for war."

The letter was a bombshell. Hitler seemed to have forgotten Ciano's clear indication a few days before at Berchtesgaden that Italy was militarily unprepared. He was bitterly disappointed at this sudden, and to him completely unexpected defection of his ally. . . .

When I left Hitler's room with Attolico and bade him goodbye, I saw Keitel passing me swiftly on his way in to see Hitler. While I was still wondering which of the various groups standing in the hall I should join, Keitel came rushing out again from Hitler's room. I heard him speaking excitedly to his adjutant, and caught the words: "The order to advance must be delayed again." . . .

That same evening, August 25th, Hitler replied to Mussolini's letter briefly and coolly. He asked for particulars of the raw materials and weapons that Italy needed in order to make war. The following day we translated Mussolini's answer, brought by Attolico. The demands were so exorbitant that Germany could not possibly have met them. It was quite clear that Mussolini was taking evasive action. Italy again came in for abuse—but not Mussolini.

We had to translate yet another letter from Hitler to Mussolini. He asked his ally to keep his decision to remain neutral a strict secret, and to give every appearance of preparing for war, in order to intimidate the Western Powers. A few hours later Attolico reappeared—Mussolini agreed to do both.[70]

---

[70]Paul Schmidt, *Hitler's Interpreter*, ed. R. H. C. Steed (New York: International Press Alliance Corp., 1951), pp. 145–47. Quoted by permission of International Press Alliance Corporation.

The last negotiations before German troops moved into Poland were complicated and frustrating. As the British Ambassador played a significant role in receiving, under peculiar circumstances, the Sixteen Points which the Polish government was supposed to accept, the events are best related in his own words. The version of the German interpreter is included for comparison. These excerpts are followed by the Sixteen Points and the report of the Polish Ambassador.

FOR CONSIDERATION   What was behind the maneuver of the German government? Was there any desire to reach an agreement with Poland? Is Henderson's description of the events suspect on any point? Would the proposals, if taken seriously, have produced disunion between Poland and the Western Powers?

Comments of Nevile Henderson, British Ambassador to Germany

Such information, indeed, as reached me during the course of the following day [August 29] tended to represent the atmosphere as well disposed and to foreshadow readiness on Hitler's part to open direct negotiations with the Poles. I was consequently all the less prepared for the reception which I got on being summoned to the Reichschancery again at 7:15 on the evening of August 29th. Perhaps I should have been, as the German midday press had reported the alleged murder of six German nationals in Poland; and this story, which was probably fabricated by the extremists in fear lest Hitler was weakening, together with the news of the Polish general mobilization, was just the kind of thing which was most calculated to upset him. I immediately sensed in any case a distinctly more uncompromising attitude than the previous evening on Hitler's part when he handed me the answer which he had promised me.

Therein Germany's demands were declared to be the revision of the Versailles Treaty by means of the return of Danzig and the Corridor to Germany and the security for the lives of German national minorities in the rest of Poland. In reply to the British proposals for direct German-Polish negotiations and for an international guarantee of any settlement, it was stated, firstly, that the German Government, in spite of skepticism as to the prospect of their success, accepted direct negotiations with Poland, solely out of a desire to insure lasting friendship with Britain; but, secondly, that, in the event

of any modifications of territory, the German Government could neither undertake nor participate in any guarantee without first consulting the U.S.S.R.[71]

Comments of Nevile Henderson on His Interview with Ribbentrop, Night of August 30–31, 1939

.   .   .   .   .

Be that as it may, it is probable that Hitler's mood in the hour when he had to decide between peace or war was not an amiable one. It was reflected in Ribbentrop, whose reception of me that evening was from the outset one of intense hostility, which increased in violence as I made each communication in turn. He kept jumping to his feet in a state of great excitement, folding his arms across his chest and asking if I had anything more to say. I kept replying that I had; and, if my own attitude was no less unfriendly than his own, I cannot but say in all sincerity that I had every justification for it. When I told him that I would not fail to report his comments and remarks to my Government, he calmed down a little and said that they were his own and that it was for Herr Hitler to decide. As for inviting the Polish Ambassador to come to see him, such a course would, he indignantly said, be utterly unthinkable and intolerable.

After I had finished making my various communications to him, he produced a

---

[71]Sir Nevile Henderson, *Failure of a Mission* (New York: G. P. Putnam's Sons, 1940), pp. 277–79. Copyright 1940, by Sir Nevile Henderson. Courtesy of G. P. Putnam's Sons.

lengthy document which he read out to me in German or rather gabbled through to me as fast as he could, in a tone of the utmost scorn and annoyance. Of the sixteen articles in it I was able to gather the gist of six or seven, but it would have been quite impossible to guarantee even the comparative accuracy of these without a careful study of the text itself. When he had finished, I accordingly asked him to let me read it for myself. Herr von Ribbentrop, who always mistook rudeness for strength, refused categorically; threw the document with a contemptuous gesture on the table; and said that it was now out of date (*"überholt"*), since no Polish emissary had arrived at Berlin by midnight. I observed that in that case the sentence in the German note of August 29th to which I had drawn his and his Führer's attention on the preceding evening had, in fact, constituted an ultimatum in spite of their categorical denials. Ribbentrop's answer to that was that the idea of an ultimatum was a figment of my own imagination and creation.[72]

Comments of Dr. Paul Schmidt, German Foreign Office Interpreter

For a while the conversation proceeded in relative calm. Then Ribbentrop drew a paper out of his pocket: it contained Hitler's "League of Nations" proposals for the settlement of the Polish dispute. He read them out to Henderson in German, without, however, particularly hurrying over them as he was afterwards said to have done. On the contrary, he elaborated on some of the points. Then occurred the surprise.

Henderson asked whether he could be given the text of these proposals for transmission to his Government. According to normal diplomatic usage, that would follow as a matter of course, and I was rather surprised that Henderson should bother to ask at all. Expecting that Ribbentrop would hand him the paper with no more ado, I could scarcely believe my ears when I heard his answer. "No," he said with a rather misplaced smile, "I cannot hand you these proposals."

Henderson must have thought he had misheard, and repeated his request. Again Ribbentrop declined. He threw the document on the table, saying: "It is out of date, anyhow, as the Polish envoy has not appeared."[73]

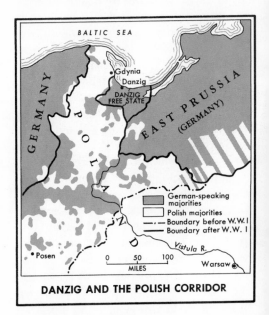

DANZIG AND THE POLISH CORRIDOR

German Proposal for a Settlement of the Polish Question (The Sixteen Points)

(1) . . . the Free City of Danzig shall return to the German Reich.

(2) The territory of the so-called Polish Corridor . . . shall itself decide as to whether it shall belong to Germany or Poland.

(3) For this purpose, a plebiscite shall take place in this territory. . . .

(4) The Polish port of Gdynia . . .

---

[72]*Ibid.*, pp. 283–87.

[73]Schmidt, *op. cit.*, pp. 152–54.

shall be excluded from the above territory. . . .

(5) . . . this plebiscite shall not take place before the expiry of twelve months.

(6) In order to guarantee unrestricted communication between Germany and East Prussia and between Poland and the sea during this period, roads and railways shall be established to render free transit traffic possible.

(7) The question as to the party to which the area belongs is to be decided by simple majority of the votes recorded.

(8) . . . Germany shall, in the event of the plebiscite area going to Poland, receive an extra-territorial traffic zone . . . in which to lay down an autobahn and a four-track railway line. . . . Should the plebiscite be favorable to Germany, Poland is to obtain free rights . . . for the purpose of free and unrestricted communication with her port of Gdynia.

(9) In the event of the Corridor returning to the German Reich, the latter declares its right to proceed to an exchange of population with Poland. . . .

(10) Any special rights desired by Poland in the port of Danzig would be negotiated on a basis of territory against similar rights to be granted to Germany in the port of Gdynia. . . .

(11) . . . Danzig and Gdynia would have the character of exclusively mercantile towns, that is to say, without military installations and military fortifications.

(12) The peninsula of Hela, which as a result of the plebiscite might go to either Poland or Germany, would in either case have similarly to be demilitarized.

(13) . . . both parties declare their agreement to have these complaints about treatment of minorities laid before an International Committee of Inquiry. . . .

(14) . . . Germany and Poland agree to guarantee the rights of both minorities by means of the most comprehensive and binding agreement. . . .

(15) In the event of an agreement on the basis of these proposals, Germany and Poland declare themselves ready to decree and to carry out the immediate demobilization of their armed forces.

(16) The further measures necessary for the more rapid execution of the above arrangement shall be agreed upon by both Germany and Poland conjointly.[74]

Comments of Polish Ambassador to Germany Lipski in His *Final Report,* Dated October 10, 1939

Soon after 12 o'clock [Aug. 31] I received telegraphic instructions from Warsaw to hand the Minister for Foreign Affairs a declaration of the Polish Government's favorable attitude to any proposal for direct negotiations.

At 1 p.m. I asked for an interview with the Minister of Foreign Affairs for the purpose of presenting my Government's communication. At 3 p.m. the State Secretary, M. von Weizäcker, telephoned to inquire if I sought an interview with the Foreign Minister in the capacity of a fully empowered delegate or in some other capacity. I replied that I was asking for an interview as Ambassador, to present a declaration from my Government. . . .

I informed the French and British Ambassadors of the nature of my discussion with M. von Ribbentrop. I learned of the invitation extended by the State Secretary to both Ambassadors and the American Chargé d'Affaires to call at the Ministry of Foreign Affairs between nine and ten p.m. There they were informed that as a Polish plenipotentiary had not arrived it was considered that the German proposals contained in sixteen points had been rejected by Poland. I desire to state emphatically that the German demands, contained in sixteen points, have never been handed or communicated to me by the German Government.

[74]*Documents on British Foreign Policy,* 3d Series, Vol. VII, pp. 460–62.

The German wireless had broadcast a similar communiqué at nine o'clock publishing the German proposals as comprised in the Sixteen Points, while the Press issued special editions. Not until the German proposals were published in the Press did I learn of their exact nature. . . .

During the same night the German wireless stations broadcast false information of aggressive action taken by Polish military detachments on the German frontier. The same night, I had yet another conversation with the French and British Ambassadors. In the early hours of September 1, I learned from the wireless that German armed forces had invaded Poland, and that the German Air Force had bombed a number of Polish towns.[75]

----

[75]*Polish White Book,* pp. 149-51.

After German troops entered Poland on September 1, France and England, grasping at straws, endeavored to stop the conflict by threatening to declare war on Germany unless Hitler withdrew his troops within 24 hours. When Hitler refused, France and England declared war on Germany on September 3. The following document describes Hitler's reception of the British ultimatum.

Comments of Dr. Paul Schmidt, German Foreign Office Interpreter

I then took the ultimatum to the Chancellery, where everyone was anxiously awaiting me. . . .

When I entered the next room Hitler was sitting at his desk and Ribbentrop stood by the window. Both looked up expectantly as I came in. I stopped at some distance from Hitler's desk, and then slowly translated the British Government's ultimatum. When I finished, there was complete silence.

Hitler sat immobile, gazing before him. He was not at a loss, as was afterwards stated, nor did he rage as others allege. He sat completely silent and unmoving.

After an interval which seemed an age, he turned to Ribbentrop, who had remained standing by the window. "What now?" asked Hitler with a savage look, as though implying that his Foreign Minister had misled him about England's probable reaction.

Ribbentrop answered quietly: "I assume that the French will hand in a similar ultimatum within the hour."

As my duty was now performed, I withdrew. To those in the anteroom pressing round me I said: "The English have just handed us an ultimatum. In two hours a state of war will exist between England and Germany." In the anteroom, too, this news was followed by complete silence.

Göring turned to me and said: "If we lose this war, then God have mercy on us!"

Goebbels stood in a corner, downcast and self-absorbed. Everywhere in the room I saw looks of grave concern, even amongst the lesser Party people.

Coulondre handed Ribbentrop an identical ultimatum soon afterwards, which was to expire at 5 o'clock in the afternoon.[76]

Comments of Ernst von Weizsacker, State Secretary in the German Foreign Office

Those who have written the history of this last phase have so far understandably

----

[76]Schmidt, *op. cit.,* pp. 157-58.

confined themselves to the diplomatic course of events, to the official books of various colors, to the confiscated documents, memoirs, etc. But in doing so they have underestimated certain political realities—namely, how, as a result of Hitler's frivolous game, in the last ten days of August, 1939, so much unrest had been engendered in the German minority, so many frontier infringements had occurred, so many people had been carried away into Central Poland, and so many other incidents had been reported, that all these things weighed heavier in the scales than the reverberating dispute of the so-called statesmen about how the original problem was to be solved. One may well ask whether the chariot had not already been rolling inexorably towards the abyss in the spring of 1939; but in the last week of August it certainly was. Hitler was now the prisoner of his own methods. He could no longer pull the horses to one side without being thrown out of the chariot. And riding on the leading horse was the Devil.

·   ·   ·   ·   ·

Historians in pursuit of truth will for a long time to come be trying to establish the ultimate causes of the war. If they use sources from the Third Reich, then they must remember that no one could achieve anything in Germany at that time unless he made concessions to the prevailing style of expressing himself. Officials and officers who had remained reasonable made their proposals or couched their arguments in terms suited to the person they were addressing; and the historian must beware of using such documents unless he has a thorough knowledge of the people to whom they were addressed and of the persons indirectly concerned. No one who wanted to accomplish anything in politics in Germany at that time wrote in order to appear later as one who had uttered wise warnings; nor did he write to save his own soul. He wrote and spoke in competition with psychopaths and for psychopaths. Historians will realize this, and will not be misled by the catchwords of today [1944]. And they will not content thmselves with studying the final phase before the war, but will probe into the past, year by year, until they come to a point where our knowledge of history will clearly forbid us to measure the great and profound causes of events, and the connections between them, with our human measuring-rods.[77]

[77] Ernst von Weizsäcker, *Memoirs of Ernst von Weizsäcker*, trans. John Andrews (Chicago: Henry Regnery Co., 1951), pp. 205–06, 213.

BIBLIOGRAPHY

SOURCES USED IN THIS PROBLEM

1. *Collections and Official Documents*

British White Book, Cmd. 5848. London: His Majesty's Stationery Office, 1938.

Documents on British Foreign Policy, 1919–1939. Third Series, Vols. I–IX. London: Her Majesty's Stationery Office, 1949–55.

Documents on German Foreign Policy. Series D, Vols. I–VII. Washington, D.C.: U.S. Government Printing Office, 1949–56.

Documents and Materials Relating to the Eve of the Second World War. 2 vols. Moscow: Ministry of Foreign Affairs of the Soviet Union, 1948.

French Yellow Book: Diplomatic Documents, 1938–1939. English ed. New York: Harcourt, Brace, 1940.

KEESING's *Contemporary Archives, 1937–1940*. Keynsham, Bristol: Keesing's Publications.

Land of Socialism Today and Tomorrow. Moscow: Foreign Languages Publishing House, 1939.

MUGGERIDGE, MALCOLM (ed.). *Ciano's Diplomatic Papers.* London: Odham's Books, 1948.

Nazi Conspiracy and Aggression: A Collection of Documentary Evidence and Guide Materials Prepared by the American and British Prosecuting Staffs for Presentation before the International Military Tribunal at Nürnberg, Germany. 10 vols. Washington, D.C.: U.S. Government Printing Office, 1946–48.

Nazi-Soviet Relations, 1939–1941. Documents from the Archives of the German Foreign Office. Edited by R. J. Sontag and J. S. Beddie. Washington, D.C.: U.S. Government Printing Office, 1948.

New York Times.

Parliamentary Debates. Commons. London: His Majesty's Stationery Office.

Polish White Book. Official Documents concerning Polish-German and Polish-Soviet Relations, 1933–39 (London: Polish Ministry of Foreign Affairs, 1940).

Trial of the Major War Criminals before the International Military Tribunal. Vol. IX. Nuremberg, 1947.

Strategy and Tactics of World Communism. Supplement I. Washington, D.C.: U.S. Government Printing Office, 1948.

2. Others

BONNET, GEORGES.   *De Washington au Quai d'Orsay.* Geneva: Les Editions du Cheval Ailé, 1947.

BONNET, GEORGES.   *Fin d'une Europe: de Munich à la Guerre.* Geneva: Les Editions du Cheval Ailé, 1948.

BURCKHARDT, CARL JACOB.   *Meine Danziger Mission, 1937–39.* Munich: GDW Callwey, 1960.

CHURCHILL, WINSTON.   *The Gathering Storm.* Boston: Houghton Mifflin, 1948.

COULONDRE, ROBERT.   *De Staline à Hitler.* Paris: Hachette, 1950.

DAHLERUS, BIRGER.   *The Last Attempt.* London: Hutchinson, 1947.

DIRKSEN, HERBERT VON.   *Moscow, Tokyo, London: Twenty Years of German Foreign Policy.* Norman, Okla.: University of Oklahoma Press, 1952.

FEILING, KEITH.   *The Life of Neville Chamberlain.* London: Macmillan, 1946.

FRANÇOIS-PONCET, ANDRÉ.   *Souvenirs d'une Ambassade à Berlin.* Paris: Flammarion, 1947.

GAMELIN, GENERAL.   *Servir.* 2 vols. Paris: Plon, 1946.

HENDERSON, SIR NEVILE.   *Failure of a Mission.* New York: Putnam's, 1940.

KIRKPATRICK, IVONE A.   *The Inner Circle: Memoirs.* New York: Macmillan, 1959.

MANSTEIN, ERICH VON.   *Lost Victories.* Chicago: Regnery, 1958.

NAMIER, L. B.   *Diplomatic Prelude.* London: Macmillan, 1948.

NAMIER, L. B.   *Europe in Decay, a Study in Disintegration.* London: Macmillan, 1950.

RIPKA, HUBERT.   *Munich: Before and After.* London: Gollancz, 1939.

SCHMIDT, PAUL.   *Hitler's Interpreter.* Ed. by R. H. C. STEED. London: Heinemann, 1951.

SHIRER, WILLIAM L.   *Berlin Diary.* New York: Knopf, 1940.

STRANG, LORD (WILLIAM).   *Home and Abroad.* London: A. Deutsch, 1956.

WEIZSÄCKER, ERNST VON. *Memoirs of Ernst von Weizsäcker.* Tr. by JOHN ANDREWS. Chicago: Regnery, 1951.

SELECT LIST OF BOOKS RECOMMENDED FOR FURTHER READING

BIRKENHEAD, F. W. F. S. *Halifax.* Boston: Houghton Mifflin, 1966.

BLUM, J. M. *From the Morgenthau Diaries.* Boston: Houghton Mifflin, 1959.

BULLOCK, ALAN. *Hitler: A Study in Tyranny.* New York: Harper & Row, 1962.

CHAMBERLAIN, NEVILLE. *In Search of Peace.* New York: Putnam's, 1939.

CRAIG, G. A. and GILBERT, F. (eds.). *The Diplomats 1919-1939.* Princeton, N.J.: Princeton University Press, 1953.

DALTON, HUGH. *The Fateful Years.* London: Muller, 1957.

EUBANK, KEITH. *Munich.* Norman: University of Oklahoma Press, 1963.

GEORGE, MARGARET. *The Warped Vision: British Foreign Policy, 1933-1939.* Pittsburgh: University of Pittsburgh Press, 1965.

GILBERT, MARTIN and GOTT, RICHARD. *The Appeasers.* Boston: Houghton Mifflin, 1963.

HASSELL, V. VON. *The von Hassell Diaries.* London: Hamish Hamilton, 1948.

HOLBORN, HAJO. *The Political Collapse of Europe.* New York: Knopf, 1951.

LOEWENHEIM, FRANCIS L. (ed.). *Peace or Appeasement? Hitler, Chamberlain, and the Munich Crisis.* Boston: Houghton Mifflin, 1965.

MACLEOD, R. and KELLY, D. (eds.). *The Ironside Diaries.* London: Constable, 1962.

MAISKY, I. *Who Helped Hitler?* London: Hutchinson, 1964.

MILWARD, A. S. *The German Economy at War.* London: Athlone Press, 1965.

MINNEY, R. J. *The Private Papers of Hore-Belisha.* London: Collins, 1960.

NICOLSON, HAROLD. *Diaries & Letters 1930-1939.* Ed. by NIGEL NICOLSON. New York: Atheneum, 1967.

ROBERTSON, E. M. *Hitler's Pre-War Policy.* London: Longmans, 1963.

ROCK, WILLIAM R. *Appeasement on Trial: British Foreign Policy & Its Critics 1938-39.* New York: Archon, 1966.

ROWSE, A. L. *Appeasement: A Study in Political Decline.* New York: W. W. Norton, 1961.

SALVEMINI, GAETANO. *Prelude to World War II.* London: Gollancz, 1953.

SCOTT, WILLIAM E. *Alliance against Hitler: The Origins of the Franco-Soviet Pact (1935).* Durham, N.C.: Duke University Press, 1962.

SETON-WATSON, R. W. *From Munich to Danzig.* London: Saunders, 1939.

SHIRER, WILLIAM L. *The Rise and Fall of the Third Reich.* New York: Simon and Schuster, 1960.

SNELL, JOHN L. (ed.). *The Outbreak of the Second World War: Design or Blunder?* Problems in European Civilization. Boston: D. C. Heath, 1962.

TAYLOR, A. J. P. *The Origins of the Second World War.* 2d ed. New York: Fawcett (Premier), 1961.

TAYLOR, TELFORD (ed.). *Hitler's Secret Book.* Tr. by SALVATOR ATTANASIO. New York: Grove Press, 1962.

TEMPLEWOOD, LORD (SIR SAMUEL HOARE). *Nine Troubled Years.* London: Collins, 1954.

THORNE, CHRISTOPHER. *The Approach to War. 1938-39.* New York: St. Martin's Press, 1967.

Toynbee, A. J. and V. M. *The Eve of War, 1939.* Royal Institute of International Affairs. Survey of International Affairs. London: Oxford University Press, 1958.

Waite, Robert G. L. (ed.). *Hitler and Nazi Germany.* European Problem Studies. New York: Holt, Rinehart and Winston, 1965.

Wheeler-Bennett, J. W. *Munich: Prologue to Tragedy.* New York: Duell, Sloan and Pearce, 1948.

Wheeler-Bennett, J. W. *The Nemesis of Power: The German Army in Politics 1918–45.* New York: St. Martin's Press, 1954.

SECTION V

Consequences of the

Second World War

POLAND AT YALTA,

POTSDAM, AND AFTER

A representative problem at the

Big Three Conferences, 1944-47

A significant aspect of World War II was the manner in which major political decisions were reached on a high level at conferences, such as those at
Casablanca, Quebec, Moscow, Teheran, Yalta, and Potsdam, which were
attended by the leaders of the great powers. The major conferences, at
which scores of diplomatic and military experts exchanged views, were
so complex that it is difficult to comprehend the issues without an extensive
study of backgrounds. Because the documentary evidence for all the major
issues discussed at any one conference would fill volumes, it has seemed
desirable to choose only a single issue which, running through all the
meetings, would provide an example of how a problem was handled and
to what extent the arrangements proved successful. The problem of Poland
presents such an issue: it was discussed at all the three-power conferences
and consumed more time at Yalta than any other problem. The Polish issue
has additional significance in that it constituted one of the major differences between the Soviet Union and the West after the war and played
a considerable part in contributing to the inception of the cold war.

After Poland was overrun in September, 1939, by the armies of Germany
and Russia, the Polish government established itself in London. Later,
when Germany turned against the Soviet Union, this Polish government
faced the unpleasant necessity of coming to terms with its Russian conqueror, now fighting on the Allied side. This was done on July 30, 1941,
but many decisions, such as arrangements on frontiers, and many grievances, such as the fate of some 8,000 Polish officers presumably captured
by Russia in 1939, remained unresolved. Although negotiations proceeded

all through 1942, no permanent Soviet-Polish understanding was attained, largely due to Polish refusal to surrender to Russia any of the territory in eastern Poland obtained after World War I. After 1943, when Russia saw more and more clearly that it would be able to occupy Poland, it became less willing to negotiate with the Polish government-in-exile. Then, on April 13, 1943, the German radio announced that there had been discovered, in the Katyn Forest, the graves of thousands of Polish officers apparently murdered by Russians in 1939. When the government-in-exile attempted to obtain particulars, Russia seized the opportunity to sever relations with the London group.

Thus, just at the time when Russia was assuming the offensive, Poland had no official contacts with the Soviet Union. Such was the situation when Churchill and Roosevelt met Stalin at the Teheran Conference, November 28 to December 1, 1943. Here the three powers tentatively agreed that the Curzon Line would provide a reasonable base for negotiation, although Poland would obtain recompense in the West at Germany's expense.

The position of the Polish underground, and of their representatives in London, the Polish government-in-exile, is given here, as well as comments representing the British and Soviet views.

FOR CONSIDERATION   Churchill was in a difficult position. He had agreed that the Curzon Line would be an equitable frontier, but he did not wish to repudiate the Polish government-in-exile, which would provide Britain with influence in central Europe if it returned to Poland. Stalin was understandably concerned that Churchill might not stand by his Teheran pledge.

From the Council of National Unity (Polish Underground Organ) to Prime Minister Mikolajczyk, February 15, 1944

1. We agree to the proposed Western boundaries and welcome the pledge of removing the Germans.

2. We do not agree to the tying up of our Eastern frontier with the question of our Western boundaries. The Western territories cannot be an equivalent as their reincorporation to Poland constitutes in fact the return of territories seized from her in the past.

3. We favor entering into conversations, with the participation of the Allies,
with a view to the resumption of diplomatic relations with the Soviets, on condition of full respect of our sovereignty and of non-interference in our internal affairs.

4. We object firmly to any discussions with the Soviets with regard to the revision of the Eastern boundaries. We stand by the inviolability of the frontiers as settled by the Treaty of Riga which was signed also by the representatives of the Ukraine, for the reason that the Soviets do not want frontier readjustments, just as the Danzig Corridor was not the real aim of the Germans, but an aim at the sovereignty and integrity of Poland.

5. No one in Poland would understand

why Poland is to pay the Soviets the costs of war with her territories and her independence. And no one would understand why Poland went to war against Germany and is waging it for the fifth year. Poland was first to oppose the German invaders, not only in defense of her independence, but also in defense of the freedom of Europe. She was called the inspiration of the world. Even now, in spite of enormous sacrifice, the Polish people are decided to fight against the new Soviet aggression in defense of their own independence and for the freedom of Europe. The Polish nation trust that the Allies and the peoples of the world will understand their attitude and will support it actively.[1]

Excerpt from Speech of Prime Minister Churchill in House of Commons, February 22, 1944

I may remind the House that we ourselves have never in the past guaranteed, on behalf of His Majesty's Government, any particular frontier line to Poland. We did not approve of the Polish occupation of Vilna in 1920. The British view in 1919 stands expressed in the so-called "Curzon Line," which attempted to deal, at any rate partially, with the problem. I have always held the opinion that all questions of territorial settlement and readjustment should stand over until the end of the war, and that the victorious Powers should then arrive at formal and final agreement governing the articulation of Europe as a whole. That is still the wish of His Majesty's Government.

However, the advance of the Russian armies into Polish regions in which the

Polish underground army is active makes it indispensable that some kind of friendly working agreement should be arrived at to govern the war-time conditions and enable all anti-Hitlerite forces to work together with the greatest advantage against the common foe. During the last few weeks the Foreign Secretary and I have labored with the Polish Government in London with the object of establishing a working arrangement upon which the fighting forces can act, and upon which, I trust, an increasing structure of good will and comradeship may be built between Russia and Poland.[2]

Stalin to Churchill, March 23, 1944

The Soviet Union's efforts to uphold and implement the Curzon Line are referred to in one of your messages as a policy of force. This implies that you are now trying to describe the Curzon Line as unlawful and the struggle for it as unjust. I totally disagree with you. I must point out that at Tehran you, the President and myself were agreed that the Curzon Line was lawful.

At that time you considered the Soviet Government's stand on the issue quite correct, and said it would be crazy for representatives of the Polish émigré Government to reject the Curzon Line. But now you maintain something to the contrary.

Does this mean that you no longer recognise what we agreed on in Tehran and are ready to violate the Tehran agreement? I have no doubt that had you persevered in your Tehran stand the con-

---

[1]Stanislaw Mikolajczyk, *The Rape of Poland* (New York: McGraw-Hill Book Co., 1948), pp. 284–85.

[2]*Parliamentary Debates, Commons* (London: His Majesty's Stationery Office, 1943–44), Vol. 397, Cols. 697–98. Quoted by permission of the Controller of Her Britannic Majesty's Stationery Office.

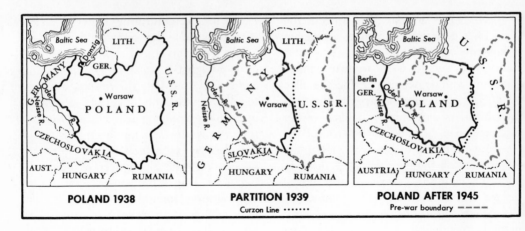

POLAND 1938   PARTITION 1939   POLAND AFTER 1945
Curzon Line ·······   Pre-war boundary − − − −

flict with the Polish emigré Government could have been settled. As for me and the Soviet Government, we still adhere to the Tehran standpoint, and we have no intention of going back on it, for we believe implementation of the Curzon Line to be evidence, not of a policy of force, but of a policy of re-establishing the Soviet Union's legitimate right to those territories, which even Curzon and the Supreme Council of the Allied Powers recognised as non-Polish in 1919. . . .

In your message of March 21 you tell me of your intention to make a statement in the House of Commons to the effect that all territorial questions must await the armistice or peace conferences of the victorious Powers and that in the mean-time you cannot recognise any *forcible* transferences of territory. As I see it you make the Soviet Union appear as being hostile to Poland, and virtually deny the liberation nature of the war waged by the Soviet Union against German aggression. That is tantamount to attributing to the Soviet Union something which is non-existent, and, thereby, discrediting it. I have no doubt that the peoples of the Soviet Union and world public opinion will evaluate your statement as a gratui-tous insult to the Soviet Union.[3]

[3]*Correspondence between the Chairman of the Council of Ministers, the Presidents of the U.S.A. and the Prime Ministers . . .* (Moscow: Foreign Languages Publishing House, 1957), Vol. II, pp. 133–34.

The Polish government-in-exile clearly saw that it needed strong support from the Western powers. Its Prime Minister, Stanislaw Mikolajczyk, leader of the Polish Peasant Party, came to the United States in June, 1944, to appeal personally to President Roosevelt. Roosevelt expressed interest and sympathy, promised his good offices as mediator, and strongly urged Mikolajczyk to see Stalin. After July such a direct approach at high level became urgent: Soviet troops had occupied all of eastern Poland, and a Polish Committee of National Liberation, headed by the Russian-trained Communist Boleslav Bierut, had been established at Lublin. Mikolajczyk hastened to Moscow where, in August, he held fruitless con-ferences with Stalin and members of the Lublin Committee.

Although Mikolajczyk did not know it at the time, the Lublin Committee had already made a deal with Stalin concerning the Polish borders. Mikolajczyk describes how he later learned of this deal.

Polish Discussions with Molotov, Moscow, August 15, 1945, as Described by Stanislaw Mikolajczyk

The second problem discussed at that time in Moscow was the question of the frontier, the Polish eastern frontiers.

I raised this question not only because it has been agreed in Yalta without the consultation of the Polish people and confirmed at Potsdam, but from the interest of the Polish people I wanted to open the discussion about the frontiers.

At this moment Mr. Molotov brought a map signed by Osobka-Morawski, on the 24th of July 1944 concerning the eastern frontiers of Poland. It means the day before the Lublin Committee was recognized as the administrative body for Poland by the Soviets, this agreement already was signed. It coincided with my flight to the first conference to Moscow in 1944. Then I was just on the way to Moscow as Prime Minister of London Government. Before we arrived, this agreement was signed for the price of recognition of the Lublin Committee. And in 1945 when I raised again the problem of the eastern Polish frontiers, Molotov said, "For us this thing has been agreed in Tehran, in Potsdam, in Yalta. For us this problem is settled and signed already in July 1944 and we can only discuss some changes not greater than a few kilometers. Certainly, Mr. Mikolajczyk, you don't intend to start a war over the problem of the frontiers and break the Soviet-Polish Alliance."[4]

---

[4]Mikolajczyk Testimony before House Committee on Communist Aggression, *Investigation of Communist Aggression,* Tenth Interim Report of Hearings before the Select Committee on Communist Aggression, House of Representatives, 83rd Cong., 2d sess., Poland, Rumania, Slovakia (Washington, D.C.: U.S. Government Printing Office, 1954), p. 24.

With the Lublin Committee recognized by Russia as the administrative authority in conquered Poland, Soviet forces began the attack on Warsaw. On August 1, 1944, General Bor-Komorowski, the Polish underground chief, ordered an attack on the retreating Germans. Nine miles from Warsaw, the Russian offensive halted. Before it was resumed, Bor had been forced to surrender on October 2, and the Polish forces had been virtually annihilated.

Under these tragic circumstances Mikolajczyk again went to Moscow, in October. He joined Churchill and British Foreign Minister Eden, who were anxious to negotiate with Stalin on questions pertaining to central Europe and the Balkans.

FOR CONSIDERATION   The meetings are well documented. The Mikolajczyk papers have been made available to historians (see for example Rozek, *Allied Wartime Diplomacy,* pp. 268–77), and a large quantity of Polish diplomatic papers were given the House of Representatives Committee investigating Communist Aggression, which has published them as "Polish Documents Report." See also the comments of Churchill[5] and U.S. Ambassador Harriman.[6]

Comments of Mikolajczyk on Moscow Conference of October, 1944

I arrived in Moscow on October 12, 1944, with Professor Grabski, General Tabor and Polish Foreign Minister Tadeusz Romer. . . .

We met on the thirteenth with Stalin, Churchill, and Eden. Harriman was the observor for the United States. Molotov, the chairman, seated us around an oval table and welcomed the Americans and the Britishers. At the end of his flowery speech he referred to my party as "our Polish guests" and then unexpectedly called on me to speak first.

I restated the postwar plan that Stalin had apparently ignored, emphasized its fairness to all parties and its consonance with all existing Big Three declarations, and concluded, "Our aim is to bring about an agreement between Poland and Russia, not between Russia and a handful of Poles—arbitrarily and unilaterally chosen by a foreign power."

.   .   .   .   .

"Your plan has two big defects," Stalin said. "It ignores the Lublin Poles, who have done such a good job in that part of Poland which the Soviet Army has liberated. And, secondly, if any Polish government wants relations with the Soviet Union, it must recognize the Curzon line as an actuality."

Stalin thought a moment and then added, "Perhaps the rest of your plan is

[5]Winston Churchill, *The Second World War,* Vol. VI, *Triumph and Tragedy* (Boston: Houghton Mifflin Company, 1953), pp. 235–43.

[6]*Foreign Relations of the United States: The Conferences at Malta and Yalta, 1945* (Washington, D.C.: U.S. Government Printing Office, 1955), pp. 202–4. (Hereafter cited as *The Conferences at Malta and Yalta.*)

acceptable. But these two flaws must be corrected."

Churchill now expressed a great and sudden happiness.

"I see now a new hope for agreement," he said with enthusiasm. "Regarding the new frontier along the Curzon line, I must announce in the name of the British government that, taking into account the huge losses suffered by the USSR in this war and how the Red Army has helped liberate Poland, the Curzon line must be your eastern frontier.

"Don't worry," he added, looking at me. "We will see to it that for the land you lose in the east there will be compensations in Germany, in East Prussia, and Silesia. You'll get a nice outlet to the sea, a good port at Danzig, and the priceless minerals of Silesia."

.   .   .   .   .

I said, "I cannot accept the Curzon line. I have no authority to forsake millions of my countrymen and leave them to their fate. If I agreed, everyone would have the right to say, 'It was for this that the Polish soldiers fought—a politician's sellout.' "

However, there was no way of evading the matter of the Curzon line and its acceptance, and when I continued to argue against it, Molotov suddenly stopped me roughly.

"But all this was settled at Teheran!" he barked. He looked from Churchill to Harriman, who were silent. I asked for details of Teheran. And then he added, still with his eyes on Churchill and the American Ambassador:

"If your memories fail you, let me recall the facts to you. We all agreed at Teheran that the Curzon line must divide Poland. You will recall that President

Roosevelt agreed to this solution and strongly endorsed the line. And then we agreed that it would be best not to issue any public declaration about our agreement."

Shocked, and remembering the earnest assurance I had personally had from Roosevelt at the White House, I looked at Churchill and Harriman, silently begging them to call this damnable deal a lie. Harriman looked down at the rug. Churchill looked straight back at me.

"I confirm this," he said quietly.

The admission made him angry, and he demanded that I agree then and there to the Russian demands. He reminded me of Britain's aid to Poland and of my duty now to accede to demands that Britain had come to support. I could answer only that while there were no words to express Poland's gratitude for Britain's war aid, I personally had no authority to agree to give up half of Poland.

"I didn't expect to be brought here to participate in a new partition of my country," I shouted.[7]

Polish Report of Conference between Churchill, Eden, and Mikolajczyk at Moscow, October 14, 1944

MR. MIKOLAJCZYK: Should I sign a death sentence against myself?

MR. EDEN: If the formula on the Curzon Line is agreed upon, then it will be possible to gain from Stalin full guarantees of the independence of Poland. . . .

MR. MIKOLAJCZYK, coming back to the frontiers question, states that Stalin de-

clared that the Curzon Line must be the boundary line between Poland and Russia.

MR. CHURCHILL (angrily): I wash my hands of it; as far as I am concerned we shall give the business up. Because of quarrels between Poles we are not going to wreck the peace of Europe. In your obstinacy you do not see what is at stake. It is not in friendship that we shall part. We shall tell the world how unreasonable you are. You will start another war in which 25 million lives will be lost. But you don't care.

MR. MIKOLAJCZYK: I know that our fate was sealed in Teheran.

MR. CHURCHILL: It was *saved* in Teheran.

MR. MIKOLAJCZYK: I am not a person completely washed out of patriotic feeling, to give away half of Poland.

MR. CHURCHILL: What do you mean by saying "you are not washed out of patriotic feeling"? Twenty-five years ago *we* have reconstituted Poland although in the last war more Poles fought against us than for us. Now again we are preserving you from disappearance, but you will not play. You are absolutely crazy.

MR. MIKOLAJCZYK: But this solution does not change anything.

MR. CHURCHILL: Unless you accept the frontier you are out of business forever. The Russians will sweep through your country and your people will be liquidated. You are on the verge of annihilation.[8]

[7]Mikolajczyk, *op. cit.*, pp. 93–98.

[8]"Polish Documents Report," Appendix to Committee Report on "Communist Takeover and Occupation of Poland," House Report No. 2684, Part 4, 83rd Cong., 2d sess., *House. Reports*, Vol. 13 (Washington, D.C.: U.S. Government Printing Office, 1955), pp. 126–27.

Mikolajczyk could not give in, and Churchill could not, even after they had both returned to London, persuade him—or at least, could not persuade the government-in-exile. Mikolajczyk again appealed to Roosevelt, who sent the reply printed here. A week later Mikolajczyk resigned as Prime Minister.

FOR CONSIDERATION   What were Mikolajczyk's alternatives?

Conversation between Mikolajczyk and Churchill in London, November 2, 1944, as Reported by Polish Minister T. Romer

MIKOLAJCZYK: . . . Why is Poland, alone among the United Nations, to bear territorial sacrifices, and so soon?

CHURCHILL (restraining his impatience): All right, then! Let the Lublin Poles continue to hold the leadership of Polish affairs in their hands, since you do not want to take it away from them. Dirty, filthy brutes, Quisling Poles will be at the head of your country! You may continue to sit here, but Russia will not want to talk with you any more. After all, it concerns the third world power! On my part, I did what I could, I explained to Stalin and convinced him of the need of an understanding with Poland. Today you could again be in Moscow close to success; instead, you sit here perplexed. I am very sorry.

MIKOLAJCZYK: The difficulty is that even despite our consent, the independence of Poland is not secured.

CHURCHILL: Surely you can say that you recognize the Curzon Line on condition that the independence of Poland shall be respected and guaranteed in the agreement. If this condition should not be possible of realization and the negotiations break down on that, you will not be bound in the matter of frontiers and us, as also, surely, the Americans, you will have behind you.[9]

Roosevelt to Prime Minister Mikolajczyk of the Polish Government-in-Exile, November 17, 1944

While I would have preferred to postpone the entire question of this Government's attitude until the general postwar

settlement in Europe, I fully realize your urgent desire to receive some indication of the position of the United States Government with the least possible delay. Therefore, I am giving below in broad outline the general position of this Government in the hope that it may be of some assistance to you in your difficult task.

1. The United States Government stands unequivocally for a strong, free and independent Polish state with the untrammeled right of the Polish people to order their internal existence as they see fit.

2. In regard to the future frontiers of Poland, if a mutual agreement on this subject including the proposed compensation for Poland from Germany is reached between the Polish, Soviet and British Governments, this Government would offer no objection. In so far as the United States guarantee of any specific frontiers is concerned I am sure you will understand that this Government, in accordance with its traditional policy, cannot give a guarantee for any specific frontiers. As you know, the United States Government is working for the establishment of a world security organization through which the Unit-

Seibel in The Richmond Times Dispatch

Jig-saw Puzzle.

[9]Ibid., pp. 150-51.

ed States together with the other member states will assume responsibility for general security which, of course, includes the inviolability of agreed frontiers.

3. If the Polish Government and people desire in connection with the new frontiers of the Polish state to bring about the transfer to and from the territory of Poland to national minorities, the United States Govern-

ment will raise no objection and as far as practicable will facilitate such transfer.

4. The United States Government is prepared, subject to legislative authority, to assist in so far as practicable in the post-war economic reconstruction of the Polish state.[10]

---

[10]*The Conferences at Malta and Yalta, 1945,* p. 210.

O n the question of official support to the Lublin Committee, Stalin sent Roosevelt the following note.

FOR CONSIDERATION   Russia recognized the Lublin Committee as the Provisional Government of Poland on January 5, 1945. What was the significance of this in terms of the Yalta Conference, only a month away? Is it possible that Roosevelt's policy toward Poland after the presidential election could be at variance with his pre-election position?

Stalin to Roosevelt, December 27, 1944

A number of things that have taken place since Mr Mikolajczyk's last visit to Moscow, in particular the wireless correspondence with the Mikolajczyk Government, which we found on terrorists arrested in Poland—underground agents of the émigré Government—demonstrate beyond all doubt that Mr Mikolajczyk's talks with the Polish National Committee served to cover up those elements who, behind Mr Mikolajczyk's back, had been engaged in terror against Soviet officers and soldiers in Poland. We cannot tolerate a situation in which terrorists, instigated by Polish émigrés, assassinate Red Army soldiers and officers in Poland, wage a criminal struggle against the Soviet forces engaged in liberating Poland and directly aid our enemies, with whom they are virtually in league. The substitution of Arciszewski for Mikolajczyk and the ministerial changes in the émigré Government in general have aggravated the situation and have resulted in a deep rift between Poland and the émigré Government. . . .

I must say frankly that in the event of

the Polish Committee of National Liberation becoming a Provisional Polish Government, the Soviet Government will, in view of the foregoing, have no serious reasons for postponing its recognition. It should be borne in mind that the Soviet Union, more than any other Power, has a stake in strengthening a pro-Ally and democratic Poland, not only because it is bearing the brunt of the struggle for Poland's liberation, but also because Poland borders on the Soviet Union and because the Polish problem is inseparable from that of the security of the Soviet Union. To this I should add that the Red Army's success in fighting the Germans in Poland largely depends on a tranquil and reliable rear in Poland, and the Polish National Committee is fully cognisant of this circumstance, whereas the émigré Government and its underground agents by their acts of terror threaten civil war in the rear of the Red Army and counter its successes.[11]

---

[11]*Correspondence between the Chairman of the Council of Ministers, the Presidents of the U.S.A., and the Prime Ministers . . .* Vol. II, pp. 180–81.

After the elections of November, 1944, President Roosevelt, through Harry Hopkins, began to negotiate with Stalin and Churchill for another Big Three Conference; finally preparations were concluded for a meeting at Yalta in the Crimea. President Roosevelt, who sailed to the Conference on the cruiser *Quincy*, included among his political advisers Secretary of State Stettinius, Admiral Leahy, Harry Hopkins, and James F. Byrnes. Prime Minister Churchill was accompanied by Foreign Minister Eden, Ambassador to Russia Kerr, Sir Alexander Cadogan; Marshal Stalin brought Foreign Minister Molotov, Andrei Vyshinski, and Andrei Gromyko. During the preconference discussions aboard the *Quincy* it was anticipated, according to Admiral Leahy, "that the Polish problem probably would be one of the most controversial."[12] After a meeting with the British group at Malta, the delegations flew to Yalta, where they arrived on February 3, 1945. Stalin and the Russian delegation arrived the next day.

The following documents provide an insight into the negotiations at Yalta.

FOR CONSIDERATION   A vital part of the controversy over Yalta is the question: which country made the greatest concessions? It is of course true that Poland was but one of many issues discussed, but the question is nevertheless applicable and pertinent. Did either the United States or Great Britain have such interests in Poland that concessions cost them much? Was there a moral obligation to Poland? The Polish government-in-exile had "immediate misgivings" at the possibility of an equitable settlement. Were they justified? Was it wise to settle one boundary but not the other?

Examination of the map showing the relative positions of the western and eastern offensives against Germany is important. Note that in early February, 1945, while the Russians were sweeping through Poland, the western Allies had not yet reached the Rhine.

Plenary Session of February 6, 1945:
Comments of James F. Byrnes

Closely related to the reparations issue was the problem of fixing Poland's boundaries. President Roosevelt said, at the outset of the discussion, that the United States felt that Poland's eastern boundary should generally follow the so-called Curzon Line. He still held, he said, the view he had expressed at Teheran that it would

[12]Admiral Leahy, *I Was There* (New York: McGraw-Hill & Co., 1950), p. 292.

be desirable to adjust the southern end of the line so that the city of Lwow and at least a portion of the oil fields should be inside Polish territory.

Prime Minister Churchill pointed out he had supported the Curzon Line in Parliament including the Soviet Union's retention of Lwow. The claim of the Soviet Union to this area, he said, "is one not founded on force but upon right." But if the Soviet Union made a "magnanimous gesture to a much weaker power" such as that suggested by the President, Mr.

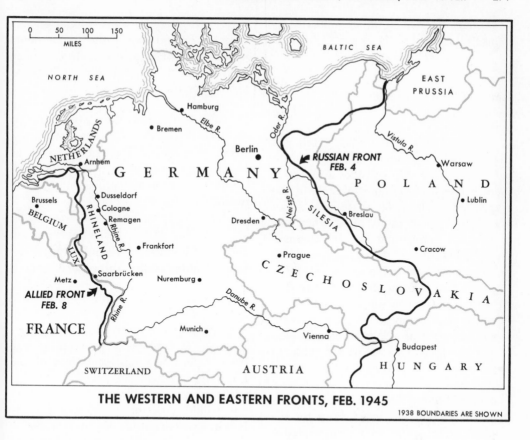

THE WESTERN AND EASTERN FRONTS, FEB. 1945

1938 BOUNDARIES ARE SHOWN

Churchill said, Britain "would admire and acclaim the Soviet position."

Marshal Stalin replied with an impassioned statement.

"The Curzon Line is the line of Curzon and Clemenceau and of those Americans who took part in 1918 and 1919 in the conference which then took place," Stalin declared. "The Russians were not invited and did not take part. . . . Lenin was not in agreement with the Curzon line. . . . Now some people want that we should be less Russian than Curzon was and Clemenceau was. You would drive us into shame. What will be said by the White Russians and the Ukrainians? They will say that Stalin and Molotov are far less reliable defenders of Russia than are Curzon and Clemenceau. I could not take such a position and return to Moscow with an open face."

At this point, Stalin stood at the con-ference table as he spoke. It was the only time during the entire conference that he exhibited his strong feelings in such a manner.

"I prefer the war should continue a little longer although it costs us blood and to give Poland compensation in the west at the expense of the Germans," he continued. "I will maintain and I will ask all friends to support me in this. . . . I am in favor of extending the Polish western frontier to the Neisse River."

Mr. Churchill doubted the wisdom of extending the western boundary of Poland to the Neisse River. He agreed that Poland's western boundary should be moved into what had been German territory but asserted "it would be a pity to stuff the Polish goose so full of German food that he would die of indigestion." He estimated that the taking of territory in East Prussia as far west as the Oder would necessitate the moving of six million Germans.[13]

Letter of Roosevelt to Stalin, February 6, 1945

You must believe me when I tell you that our people at home look with a critical eye on what they consider a disagreement between us at this vital state of the war. They, in effect, say that if we cannot get a meeting of minds now when our armies are converging on the common enemy, how can we get an understanding on even more vital things in the future?

I have had to make it clear to you that we cannot recognize the Lublin Government as now composed, and the world would regard it as a lamentable outcome of our work here if we parted with an open and obvious divergence between us on this issue.

You said today that you would be prepared to support any suggestions for the solution of this problem which offered a fair chance of success, and you also mentioned the possibility of bringing some members of the Lublin government here.

Realizing that we all have the same anxiety in getting this matter settled, I would like to develop your proposal a little and suggest that we invite here to Yalta at once Mr. Bierut and Mr. Osubka-Morawski from the Lublin government and also two or three from the following list of Poles, which according to our information would be desirable as representatives of the other elements of the Polish people in the development of a new temporary government which all three of us could recognize and support: Archbishop Sapieha of Cracow, Vincente Witos, Mr. Zurlowski, Professor Buyak, and Professor Kutzeba. If, as a result of the presence of these Polish leaders here, we could jointly agree with them on a provisional government in Poland which should no doubt include some Polish leaders from abroad such as Mr. Mikolajczyk, Mr. Grabski and Mr. Romer, the United States Government, and I feel sure the British Government as well, would then be prepared to examine with you conditions in which they would disassociate themselves from the London government and transfer their recognition to the new provisional government.[14]

Session of February 7, 1945: Excerpt from Minutes of the Yalta Conference

PRESIDENT: Shall we go on with the discussion of Poland?

STALIN: I have received the President's message. It contains a proposal to call from Poland two representatives of the Lublin government and two from the opposite camp, so that in our presence these four would settle the question of the new Polish government. If this is successful, the new provisional government should in the shortest possible time organize elections in Poland. This message of the President's also proposes that some more Poles from London—Mikolajczyk, Romer and Grabski, should also take part in the new government. I received this letter an hour and a half ago. I immediately gave instructions to find Bierut and [Osóbka-]Morawski so that I could talk with them on the phone. The result was that at the moment they are outside Warsaw at Lodz or Cracow but they will be found and I must ask them how to find the representatives on the other side and what they think of the possibility of their coming. I can then tell how soon they will arrive. If Vicente Witos or Sapieha could come here it would facilitate a solution but I do not know their addresses. I am afraid we have not sufficient time.[15]

[13]James F. Byrnes, *Speaking Frankly* (New York: Harper & Row, Publishers, 1947), pp. 29–30. Copyright 1947, by James F. Byrnes. Quoted by permission of Harper & Row, Publishers.

[14]*The Conferences at Malta and Yalta, 1945*, p. 728.
[15]*Ibid.*, p. 719.

Session of February 8, 1945: Excerpt from Minutes of the Yalta Conference

STALIN: . . . Molotov is right. We could not talk about a presidential committee without Poles. Perhaps they would agree. But as a result of their *amour propre* and feelings, the prestige of the provisional government is greatly increased. If we do not talk to them they would accuse us of being occupiers and not liberators.

PRESIDENT: How long before elections could be held?

STALIN: In about one month unless there is a catastrophe on the front and the Germans defeat us. (smiling) I do not think this will happen.

PRIME MINISTER: Free elections would of course settle the worries of the British government at least. That would supersede at a stroke all questions of legality. Of course, we must not ask anything that would impair military operations. But if it is possible to learn the opinion of the population in Poland in one or even two months no one could object.

PRESIDENT: That is why it is worth pursuing the subject. I move that we adjourn our talks until tomorrow. I suggest that meanwhile the matter be referred to the three foreign secretaries. They are very effective.

MOLOTOV: The other two will outvote me. (laughing)[16]

Stettinius' Description of Plenary Session at the Yalta Conference, February 10, 1945

At the plenary session that Saturday afternoon the President was wheeled into his usual place at the great circular table with his back to the brisk log fire crackling in the fireplace. Both Churchill and Stalin were late for this plenary session. When the Prime Minister arrived he went directly to the President to apologize and

---

[16]*Ibid.*, p. 790.

told him, "I believe that I have succeeded in retrieving the situation." When Stalin arrived five minutes after the Prime Minister, he too came to the President and apologized for his lateness.

Both Churchill and Stalin were late with good reason. After the close of the foreign ministers' meeting a sub-committee had worked out a wording on the questions of diplomatic recognition of the new Polish Government and observance of the elections which the Prime Minister persuaded Stalin to accept during his call at the Soviet headquarters.

As the plenary session opened the President asked Eden to report on the meeting of the foreign ministers. Eden read the following formula for Poland with one correction made by Molotov:

[First three paragraphs of "Report of Crimea Conference: Poland." See page 283.]

The Prime Minister observed that the document made no mention of the Polish boundaries. "We have all agreed on the eastern frontier," he said, and he expressed his belief that Poland should receive compensation in the west. He did not believe, however, that the British War Cabinet would accept the line of the western Neisse. Although there would be some criticism, he thought that the Polish statement should mention something about the territorial settlement.

While Churchill was speaking I scribbled a note to the President informing him that Eden had told me he had just received a "bad" cable from the War Cabinet telling the British delegation that they were going too far on Poland. At the same time, Harry Hopkins wrote the following note to Roosevelt:

Mr. President:—

I think you should make clear to Stalin that you support the eastern boundary but that only a general statement be put in communiqué saying we are considering essential boundary changes. Might be well to refer exact statement to foreign ministers.

Harry

The President then told the plenary session that the Polish Government should be consulted before any statement was made about the western frontier.

The Marshal said he agreed with the Prime Minister that some statement should be made on the eastern frontier. Molotov suggested that the statement on the eastern frontier be drafted by the foreign ministers. He added that it was not necessary to be as specific in regard to the western frontier as it was to the eastern frontier.

The Prime Minister remarked that he had already gone on record that Poland would receive a good slice of territory in the north and in the west, but that the opinion of the new Polish Government of National Unity should be ascertained. The President said that he had no objection in principle to such a statement, but that he thought the Prime Minister should draft it. Molotov suggested that it should form a last sentence to the Polish agreement.

.   .   .   .   .

The plenary session closed with another discussion of the Polish question. The President said that he now wished to propose some small amendments to the paragraph regarding frontiers in the Polish statement. While the Polish frontiers were being discussed earlier that afternoon, Harry Hopkins and I had jotted down some notes for the President. Hopkins, who sat just behind the President and me, frequently passed notes, written on ordinary lined paper, to the President. The one on the Polish question was most pertinent and helpful. He warned the President that it was doubtful that he had the constitutional power to commit the United States to a treaty establishing boundaries. The note read:

Mr. President:

You get into trouble about your legal powers & what senate will say.

Harry

During one adjournment that afternoon the President asked me to get a lawyer to consult with him over the wording of the Polish boundary statement. I called Alger Hiss and while the two of us were trying to work out a solution for the President, Roosevelt suddenly looked up at us and said, "I've got it."

The President told the Conference that the amendments he was proposing were necessary for American constitutional reasons. He suggested, therefore, that instead of the first words, "The three powers," he would like to substitute, "The three Heads of Government consider." In the second sentence he proposed eliminating the words "three powers," and in the last sentence, the word "feel" instead of "agree" should be used. These changes transformed the statement on boundaries from a governmental commitment to an expression of views in which Roosevelt concurred.

The amendments were accepted and the following text was approved:

[Fourth paragraph of Yalta Agreement on Poland. See page 283.]

Molotov thereupon suggested adding to the second sentence, "with the return to Poland of her ancient frontiers in East Prussia and on the Oder." The President asked how long ago these lands had been Polish, and Molotov replied: "Very long ago."

Such a statement then, the President observed, might lead the British to ask for the return of the United States to Great Britain. Stalin replied that the ocean would prevent this.

The Prime Minister declared that he agreed with the President that the western frontier not be designated at this time. He added that he was not opposed to the line of the Oder in principle if the Poles desired it. Stalin thereupon withdrew Molotov's amendment and left the draft as it was.[17]

---

[17]Edward R. Stettinius, *Roosevelt and the Russians* (Garden City, N.Y.: Doubleday & Company, Inc., 1949), pp. 258–71. Copyright 1949 Stettinius Fund, Inc. Reprinted by permission of Doubleday & Company, Inc.

**Report of Crimea Conference,
February 11, 1945**

POLAND

A new situation has been created in Poland as a result of her complete liberation by the Red Army. This calls for the establishment of a Polish provisional government which can be more broadly based than was possible before the recent liberation of Western Poland. The provisional government which is now functioning in Poland should therefore be reorganized on a broader democratic basis with the inclusion of democratic leaders from Poland itself and from Poles abroad. This new government should then be called the Polish Provisional Government of National Unity.

M. Molotov, Mr. Harriman and Sir A. Clark Kerr are authorized as a commission to consult in the first instance in Moscow with members of the present provisional government and with other Polish democratic leaders from within Poland and from abroad, with a view to the reorganization of the present government along the above lines. This Polish Provisional Government of National Unity shall be pledged to the holding of free and unfettered elections as soon as possible on the basis of universal suffrage and secret ballot. In these elections all democratic and anti-Nazi parties shall have the right to take part and to put forward candidates.

When a Polish Provisional Government of National Unity has been properly formed in conformity with the above, the government of the U.S.S.R., which now maintains diplomatic relations with the present provisional government of Poland, and the government of the United Kingdom and the government of the U.S.A. will establish diplomatic relations with the new Polish Provisional Government of National Unity, and will exchange ambassadors by whose reports the respective governments will be kept informed about the situation in Poland.

The three heads of government consider that the Eastern frontier of Poland should follow the Curzon line with digressions from it in some regions of five to eight kilometres in favour of Poland. The recognize that Poland must receive substantial accessions of territory in the North and West. They feel that the opinion of the new Polish Provisional Government of National Unity should be sought in due course on the extent of these accessions and that the final delimitation of the western frontier of Poland should thereafter await the peace conference.[18]

---

[18]*The Conferences at Malta and Yalta*, pp. 973–74.

Presumably in the interest of implementing the Yalta Agreement, Russia began to invite Polish underground leaders to enter into political discussions. Letters like the one here printed were sent to 15 Polish leaders, who, on March 27 and 28, met with General Ivanov near Warsaw.

**Invitation from Soviet Colonel
Pimenov to Polish Underground
Leader Jan Jankowski, March 6, 1945**

My good intentions and modest aims which I hope will meet with your full support and appreciation are limited to one thing only—namely, to help you to meet in the next few days the representative of the High Command of the First White Ruthenian Front, Col.-Gen. Ivanov. I am, of course, aware of the difficulties of this action. But realizing its absolute necessity and its immense importance—I cannot show this at length in this short letter—I am of the opinion that this meeting between you and Col.-Gen. Ivanov may and, of course, should, settle matters which it is altogether doubtful can be settled quickly in any other way. . . .

For my part, as an officer of the Red army who has been entrusted with such a greatly important mission, I guarantee to you, under my word as an officer, that from that moment your fate will be in my hands and that after your arrival at our quarters you will be absolutely safe.[19]

---

[19]"Communist Takeover and Occupation of Poland," Special Report No. 1 of the Select Committee on Communist Aggression, House Report No. 2684, Part 3, 83rd Cong., 2d sess., *House Reports*, Vol. 13 (Washington, D.C.: U.S. Government Printing Office, 1955), p. 24.

T he 15 Polish underground leaders who responded to the Russian invitation simply disappeared. President Roosevelt spent his last days attempting to obtain guarantees from Stalin that the Yalta agreement would be implemented and Harry Truman, when he succeeded to the presidency on April 13, 1945, inherited a badly deteriorated situation. He came to grips with it personally when on April 23 he met Molotov, traveling through Washington on his way to the San Francisco Conference. After deliberating with his advisers, the President bluntly informed the Soviet Foreign Minister that the United States could not agree to be a party to the formation of a Polish government which was not representative of all Polish democratic elements. He declared that friendship with Russia had to be based on mutual observation of agreements and "not on the basis of a one-way street." Molotov, taken aback, observed that he had never been talked to like that in his life.[20] Stalin received a report of this encounter immediately and reacted accordingly.

Stalin to Truman, April 24, 1945

Poland is to the security of the Soviet Union what Belgium and Greece are to the security of Great Britain.

You evidently do not agree that the Soviet Union is entitled to seek in Poland a Government that would be friendly to it, that the Soviet Government cannot agree to the existence in Poland of a Government hostile to it. This is rendered imperative, among other things, by the Soviet people's blood freely shed on the fields of Poland for the liberation of that country.

I cannot understand why in discussing Poland no attempt is made to consider the interests of the Soviet Union in terms of security as well.

One cannot but recognise as unusual a situation in which two Governments— those of the United States and Great Britain—reach agreement beforehand on Poland, a country in which the U.S.S.R. is interested first of all and most of all, and place its representatives in an intolerable position, trying to dictate to it.

I say that this situation cannot contribute to agreed settlement of the Polish problem.

---

[20]Harry S Truman, *Memoirs*, Vol. I, *Year of Decisions* (Garden City, N.Y.: Doubleday & Company, Inc., 1955), pp. 76–82.

I am ready to accede to your request and to do all in my power to reach an agreed settlement. But you are asking too much. To put it plainly, you want me to renounce the interests of the security of the Soviet Union; but I can-not proceed against the interests of my country.[21]

[21]*Correspondence between the Chairman of the Council of Ministers, the Presidents of the U.S.A. and the Prime Ministers . . .*, Vol. II, p. 220.

On May 4 delegates at the San Francisco Conference were shocked to learn from Molotov that the Polish underground leaders were being held in Moscow and would be placed on trial for anti-Soviet activities.

FOR CONSIDERATION   It must be borne in mind that these trials were being held at exactly the same time that negotiations for broadening the Lublin government proceeded. Ultimately 12 were convicted and given sentences ranging from 4 months to 10 years. One who received a short sentence was Zbigniew Stypulkowski, who later recounted his experiences before the House Committee.[22]

Testimony of Polish Underground Leader Zbigniew Stypulkowski before House Committee Investigating Communist Aggression, 1954

MR. STYPULKOWSKI: We in Poland realized very clearly that if we refused this invitation the Poles would be branded immediately as stubborn fellows who did not understand anything, who made difficulties in the peaceful and friendly relations between the big allies, and would be responsible, if they refused this invitation for the future fate of their country. So, knowing well that we would be in the course of time victims of the Soviet regime, we accepted this invitation.

MR. McTIGUE: How many of you accepted the invitation to Moscow?

MR. STYPULKOWSKI: We were 16—15 delegates and 1 gentleman who served as interpreter and secretary. . . .

MR. McTIGUE: So you went to Moscow?

[22]Those seeking further details should consult Zbigniew Stypulkowski's book, *Invitation to Moscow* (London: Thames and Hudson, 1951).

MR. STYPULKOWSKI: After several friendly negotiating meetings, we summarized results, and we asked the Russians to be allowed to go by plane over the frontline to London to consult our Polish authorities there and to consult the representatives of the Western Powers in London. The Russians agreed to that, but they put one condition on it, which was very understandable at that time. They said that we must attend the luncheon party arranged for us by Marshal Zukov to mark publicly the smoothing of the relations between the Poles and the Russian authorities, and in this way to help to create favorable conditions in the rear of the army when it started the last offensive against Germany. We had to accept this invitation because we knew that the Russians knew our whereabouts. . . .

MR. McTIGUE: So you were invited to attend this fabulous lunch with the Russian Marshal Zukov?

MR. STYPULKOWSKI: Yes. . . . we were gathered in the Russian headquarters, greeted ostentatiously by the Russian generals, and other officers of various ranks who stood at attention before us but reported that unfortunately Marshal Zukov was not there because the latest Russian offensive against the Germans had just started. . . .

But the next day we were informed by a Russian general that Marshal Zukov had ordered him to apologize for not having come yet but he thought that it would be very much better if we came to his field headquarters. And for this he sent us his personal plane. We accepted this proposal and quickly realized that we were heading not toward the west, where the front line was, but to the east. But the aide-de-camp who was with us explained immediately that it was all right because at the last moment Marshal Zukov was called to Moscow to report to the Russian Government, so that we would have a chance to make an arrangement straightforwardly with the representatives of the Russian Government. . . .

We were taken in luxurious cars through the streets of Moscow and then we stopped at a very imposing building. When we got there my colleague, Jasiukowicz, said "Stypulkowski, it looks to me like we have come to a very nice hotel", but from my experience as a lawyer I realized, when I noticed the wire netting on the windows, that it was a prison, and so I told him.

This was our last exchange of words. I was put by a Russian MVD colonel very quickly into a dark corridor where booths were dispersed like telephone booths. . . .

Then I was held alone in a small dark cell, and in a few days the process of interrogation started.

.   .   .   .   .

At my 63rd questioning, when I was suffering more than usual because I had a developing scurvy—and my judge knew about it from the report of the medical assistants—when I was trembling more

than usual, at 3 o'clock in the morning he called me again. . . .

So that the Sovet agent gave me some illusions about a bright future within the so-called Polish patriotism, and at the same time he gave me another chance to be put into concentration camp, disappear or die.

.   .   .   .   .

I had a chance to look at the minutes and on that basis I can say that the first of my colleagues pleaded guilty after 44 examinations. Some resisted to the extent of 67 or 80 examinations. Once the confessions are started there is no limit to them because then the judges do not let him stop. . . .

My colleagues pleaded guilty. The story given by the news agencies was that the leading Poles had confessed to sabotaging the Red army's endeavors in the war against Germany, although the Communists always tried appeasement. And people said: "We do not share their methods, we do not accept the methods which are applied by the Russians but nevertheless the Poles pleaded guilty, so there must have been something in it. Anyhow, Stalin was very magnanimous and gave very light sentences, so we can now expect smooth relations between west and east."

MR. MADDEN: I think the committee would be interested now if you would briefly outline the happenings after your conviction, telling us how you got out of Russia.

MR. STYPULKOWSKI: After my sentence was over I was freed and spent about 3 weeks in Moscow as a free man. I had many impressions, but I will not bother you with them. But later on I was allowed to return to Poland, and what was the situation there? I was left free.

. . . I did not realize the reason why I was temporarily left free, but I quickly understood it. At the time, the capital, Warsaw, was completely destroyed and there were only two or three restaurants left in which all the visitors had to lunch or dine. So many members of the foreign missions who tried to establish diplomatic relations, trade relations, etc., with Warsaw had to be present twice a day in those restaurants.

MR. MADDEN: What year was this?

MR. STYPULKOWSKI: It was September 1945. I was present in the restaurants and then the Soviet agents who accompanied those foreign missions told them "You see, that is Mr. Stypulkowski, one of the 16 men at the Moscow trial, and now you see he is smiling, he is keeping well, he is flirting with the girls. Well,

that is the best proof that your information in the West is very false about our dictatorial regime. He is walking about quietly. That is the best proof that we are a democratic state." And such things were said on the radio.

But I had a chance to leave the country at the last moment, because the next day the NKVD visited my home, but I successfully crossed the frontier.[23]

---

[23]*Communist Aggression Investigation:* Fourth Interim Report of Hearings before the Select Committee on Communist Aggression, House of Representatives, 83rd Cong., 2d sess., Part 2 (Washington, D.C.: U.S. Government Printing Office, 1954), pp. 1076–91.

By the middle of May, shortly after V-E Day, the United Nations Conference at San Francisco had reached an impasse over the problem of voting procedure in the Security Council. At this point President Truman asked Harry Hopkins, ill though he was, to go to Moscow. The following excerpt deals with the Hopkins-Stalin conversations on Poland.

FOR CONSIDERATION   On the basis of other evidence, how accurate are Stalin's statements? Does Stalin's proposal that 4 out of 18 portfolios should be held by non-Lublin Poles appear to fulfill the terms of the Yalta Agreement? What was behind Stalin's holding the Polish underground leaders for trial?

Comments of Stalin, from the Record of a Meeting Involving Stalin, Molotov, Pavlov, Hopkins, Harriman, and Bohlen, Held in the Kremlin on May 27, 1945

Marshal Stalin . . . said Poland's weakness and hostility had been a great source of weakness to the Soviet Union and had permitted the Germans to do what they wished in the East and also in the West since the two were mixed together. It is therefore in Russia's vital interest that Poland should be both strong and friendly. He said there was no intention on the part of the Soviet Union to interfere in Poland's internal affairs, that Poland would live under the parliamentary system which is like Czechoslovakia, Belgium and Holland and that any talk of an intention to Sovietize Poland was stupid. He said even the Polish leaders, some of whom were communists, were against the Soviet system since the Polish people did not desire collective farms or other aspects of the Soviet system. In this the Polish leaders were right since the Soviet system was not exportable—it must develop from within on the basis of a set of conditions which were not present in Poland. He said all the Soviet Union wanted was that Poland should not be in a position to open the gates to Germany and in order to prevent this Poland must be strong and democratic. ... Mr. Hopkins had spoken of Russian unilateral action in Poland and United States public opinion concerning it. It was true that Russia had taken such unilateral action but they had been compelled to. He said the Soviet Government had recognized the Warsaw Government and concluded a treaty with it at a time when their Allies did not recognize this government. These were admittedly unilateral acts which would have been much better left undone but the fact was they had not met with any understanding on the part of their Allies. The need for these actions had arisen out of the presence of Soviet troops in Poland; it would have been impossible to have waited until such time as the Allies had come to an agreement on Poland. The logic of the war against Germany demanded that the Soviet rear be assured and the Lublin Committee had been of great assistance to the Red Army at all times and it was for this reason that these actions had been taken by the Soviet Government. He said it was contrary to the Soviet policy to set up Soviet administration on foreign soil since this would look like occupation and be resented by the local inhabitants. It was for this reason that some Polish administration had to be established in Poland and this could be done only with those who had helped the Red Army. ... Stalin then turned to his suggestion for the solution of the Polish problem.

Marshal Stalin said that he felt that we should examine the composition of the future Government of National Unity. He said there were eighteen or twenty ministries in the present Polish Government and that four or five of these portfolios could be given representatives of other Polish groups taken from the list submitted by Great Britain and the United States (Molotov whispered to Stalin who then said he meant four and not five posts in the government). He said he thought the Warsaw Poles would not accept more than four ministers from other democratic groups. He added that if this appears a suitable basis we could then proceed to consider what persons should be selected for these posts. He said of course they would have to be friendly to the USSR and to the Allies.[24]

---

[24]*Foreign Relations of the United States: The Conference of Berlin (Potsdam), 1945* (Washington, D.C.: U.S. Government Printing Office, 1960), Vol. I, pp. 39–40. (Hereafter cited as *The Conference of Berlin.*)

Harry Hopkins obtained from Stalin a concession that permitted the San Francisco Conference to continue; he also broke the deadlock of the Molotov-Harriman-Kerr Commission. On the other hand, he had agreed that only four non-Lublin Poles should be added to the Polish government and had obtained no concessions on the trials of the underground leaders. Great Britain and the United States supported the Hopkins arrangement, and on June 16, 1945, Mikolajczyk and Jan Stanczyk, representing the London group, flew to Moscow for conferences on broadening the government. The following agreement was reached.

FOR CONSIDERATION   On June 18 the trial of the underground leaders started.

Agreement Governing the Polish Provisional Government of National Unity, June 23, 1945

ARTICLE I

All parties entering the Coalition have full freedom of organizational work, freedom of assembly, press and propaganda.

Important decisions are to be arrived at by means of an understanding, not by majority vote.

The basic foreign policy is friendship, cooperation and alliance with democratic states, especially with the Soviet Union, Great Britain, France and friendship with the U.S.A. . . .

Poland will participate in an international organization for peace and security.

The Western border of Poland will be fixed as soon as possible.

Elections to the *Sejm* [Parliament] on the basis of universal, equal, direct and secret ballot, will be made as soon as pos-

sible, possibly before the end of 1945. . . .

The Red Army, as well as all other civilian, party and security organs of foreign powers, will be evacuated.

ARTICLE II

The Peasant Party's participation in the Government should be at least one-third, its candidates to be designated by its competent authorities.

The National Council will be enlarged and the Peasant Party will participate in it in the ratio mentioned above.

Wincenty Witos will be First Vice President of the National Council and Prof. Stanislaw Grabski its Third Vice President.

Six members of the Peasant Party will hold Cabinet posts. The Peasant Party will provide a Vice Premier and Ministers of Public Administration, Agriculture and Agrarian Reform, Education, Post and Telegraphs, Culture and Arts, and Health. . . .[25]

---

[25]Mikolajczyk, *op. cit.*, p. 126.

On June 28, 1945, the membership of the new Polish government was announced: Bierut, Communist, President; Osubka-Morawski, Socialist, Prime Minister; Mikolajczyk, the outstanding Peasant Party leader, became Second Deputy Premier and Minister of Agriculture. Fourteen of the 21 cabinet posts, and these the most important ones, went to Lublin Poles.

American Ambassador to Russia Harriman here gives his reactions to the new government, which was recognized by the Western powers on July 5.

Harriman to Department of State, June 28, 1945

I feel that Mikolajczyk is better off not to be Prime Minister under the present difficult situation both economic and political and that he has as strong a position as he could hope for as Deputy Prime Minister and Minister of Agri-

culture which latter post will necessitate his traveling around the country. With four new members of the Peasant Party in important posts in the Govt he should be in a position to exercise substantial influence.

The matter which gives all concern is the retention of the independent Ministry of Internal Security under a Communist. This Ministry is developing a secret police on the Russian style. The manner in which this Ministry is administered is the crux of whether Poland will have her independence, whether reasonable personal freedoms will be permitted and whether reasonably free elections can be held....

During the course of the negotiations I spent a good many hours with the principal Warsaw leaders, Bierut, Morawski and Gomulka. ... Mikolajczyk recognizes the importance of the Communist Party and of these men particularly the two Communists in the all important relations with Russia and says that he is ready to work closely with them even though they represent only a very small fraction of the Polish people.[26]

[26]*The Conference of Berlin,* Vol. I, p. 728.

F rom July 16 to August 1, 1945, the Big Three powers discussed the future of Europe at the Conference of Berlin, held at nearby Potsdam. The following documents all pertain to the Polish issue as there discussed.

FOR CONSIDERATION   Was the settlement on Poland a victory for the Soviet Union or the West?

Excerpt from Minutes of Plenary Session, Potsdam, July 21, 1945

TRUMAN: I propose that the matters of the Polish frontier be considered at the peace conference after consultation with the Polish government of national unity. We decided that Germany with 1937 boundaries should be considered starting point. We decided on our zones. We moved our troops to the zones assigned to us. Now another occupying government has been assigned a zone without consultation with us. We can not arrive at reparations and other problems of Germany if Germany is divided up before the peace conference. I am very friendly to Poland and sympathetic with what Russia proposes regarding the western frontier, but I do not want to do it that way.

STALIN: The Crimea decision was that the eastern frontier of Poland should follow the Curzon line. As to the western frontier, it was decided that Poland was to receive territory in the west and north in compensation.

TRUMAN: That is right, but I am against assigning an occupation zone to Poland.

STALIN: The new Polish government has already expressed its views on boundaries. What is our proposal for the Polish western frontier?

TRUMAN: I understand that the Secretary of State has received a communication from the new Polish government but I have not seen it.

STALIN: Our view is that we should express our view in acordance with that of the Polish government, but final question should be left to the peace conference. As to our giving the Poles a zone of occupation without consulting the other powers, this is not accurate. We received several proposals from the American and British governments that we should not permit the Poles in the disputed western frontier area. We could not follow this because German population fled and Poles remained. Our armies needed local administrations. Our armies are not set up to fight and clear country of enemy agents at the same time. We so informed our British and American friends. The more ready we were to let the Polish administration function, the more we were sure the Poles would receive territory to the west. I do not see the harm of permitting the Poles to set up administrations in territories in which they are to remain.

TRUMAN: I wanted the administrations in the four zones to be as we have agreed. We can not agree on reparations if parts of Germany are given away.

STALIN: We are concerned about reparations but we will take this risk.

TRUMAN: We are not concerned about reparations for ourselves but we do not want to pay reparations as we did before.

STALIN: The western frontier of Poland then remains open and no discussions are binding on us.[27]

Excerpt from Minutes of Plenary Session, Potsdam, July 22, 1945

TRUMAN: May I re-state my view point. The eastern frontier should follow the Curzon line, with slight digression in favor of Poland. The Allies recognize that Poland must receive substantial compensation in the north and west. They believe the new Polish government should be heard, and the final settlement await the peace conference. That was the agreement of Mr. Roosevelt with the Big Three at Crimea. I am in complete accord with it; but Poland has in fact been assigned a zone of occupation contrary to our agreement. We can agree, if we wish to give the Poles an occupying zone, but I don't like the way the Poles have taken or been given their zone.

STALIN: I also proceed on the decision of the Crimea Conference cited by the President. After the Government of National Unity has been formed, we are bound to seek its opinion. The Polish government have communicated their views. We have two alternatives: one, to approve

the Polish proposal; or, two, to hear the Poles and settle the question.

I think it expedient to settle the question now. As we are not in agreement with the Polish government, the Poles should be summoned here. But the view was expressed by the President that the Poles cannot be heard here, so we must remit the question to the Foreign Ministers.

At Crimea, the President and Mr. Churchill suggested the line should be along the Oder until it joined the Neisse. I insisted on the western Neisse. Under Churchill's plan, Stettin and Breslau would remain German. The question to be settled is the frontier, and not a temporary line. We can either settle the question or ignore it.

CHURCHILL: Or decide it without the Poles.

STALIN: If we disagree with the Poles we cannot decide it without them. It has been said that a fifth country has been brought into occupied Germany, and in a manner contrary to our agreement. If anyone is to blame, circumstances as well as the Russians are to blame.

CHURCHILL: I withdraw my objection to the Poles coming here and trying to work out arrangements pending the peace conference.

TRUMAN: I have no objection to the Poles coming here, and for the Foreign Secretaries to hear them.

STALIN: The Chairman should invite them.[28]

Comments of Stanislaw Mikolajczyk

Bierut, Foreign Minister Rzymowski, and I were chosen to express the Provisional Government's views on a variety of problems confronting the Big Three at their Potsdam meeting. Professor Grabski was permitted to submit his views in writing.

---

[27]*Ibid.*, Vol. II, p. 217.

[28]*Ibid.*, Vol. II, pp. 263–64.

My position was extremely difficult. Acting directly on instructions from the Kremlin, Bierut and Rzymowski set out to alienate the paternal interest of President Truman, Churchill, and—after Churchill's defeat in the British general elections that came in the middle of the Big Three hearings—Prime Minister Attlee.

By word and deed, the two Polish Communists made demands for western territory, worded in a way calculated to stir the British and Americans to dissent. The double game was obvious: If the United States and Great Britain refused to grant Poland new western lands, the Bierut government would then be able to announce that the Yalta obligations were no longer valid. And Bierut's physical and spiritual leader, Stalin, could then say to the people of Poland, "Russia is your only friend. The United States and Britain agreed to take the eastern part of your country from you and now do not wish to abide by their promise to compensate you with land in the west."

The Communists had another thought in mind, too. The Red Army controlled that part of Germany which had been promised to Poland. If Poland's demands were rejected, the land would remain under the custody of Russia as long as the period of occupation lasted.[29]

Section Pertaining to Poland from Protocol of the Proceedings of the Berlin (Potsdam) Conference, August 1, 1945

VIII. POLAND

A. *Declaration*

We have taken note with pleasure of the agreement reached among representative Poles from Poland and abroad which has made possible the formation, in accordance with the decisions reached at the

[29]Mikolajczyk, *op. cit.*, pp. 137–38.

Crimea Conference, of a Polish Provisional Government of National Unity recognized by the Three Powers. The establishment by the British and United States Governments of diplomatic relations with the Polish Provisional Government of National Unity has resulted in the withdrawal of their recognition from the former Polish Government in London, which no longer exists. . . .

The Three Powers note that the Polish Provisional Government of National Unity, in accordance with the decisions of the Crimea Conference, has agreed to the holding of free and unfettered elections as soon as possible on the basis of universal suffrage and secret ballot in which all democratic and anti-Nazi parties shall have the right to take part and to put forward candidates, and that representatives of the Allied press shall enjoy full freedom to report to the world upon developments in Poland before and during the elections.

B. *Western Frontier of Poland*

In conformity with the agreement on Poland reached at the Crimea Conference the three Heads of Government have sought the opinion of the Polish Provisional Government of National Unity in regard to the accession of territory in the north and west which Poland should receive. The President of the National Council of Poland and members of the Polish Provisional Government of National Unity have been received at the Conference and have fully presented their views. The three Heads of Government reaffirm their opinion that the final delimitation of the western frontier of Poland should await the peace settlement.

The three Heads of Government agree that, pending the final determination of Poland's western frontier, the former German territories east of a line running from the Baltic Sea immediately west of Swinamunde, and thence along the Oder River to the confluence of the western Neisse

River and along the Western Neisse to the Czechoslovak frontier, including that portion of East Prussia not placed under the administration of the Union of Soviet Socialist Republics in accordance with the understanding reached at this conference and including the area of the former free city of Danzig, shall be under the administration of the Polish State and for such purposes should not be considered as part of the Soviet zone of occupation in Germany.[30]

[30]*The Conference of Berlin*, Vol. II, pp. 1490–92.

C onditions in Poland indicated that according to Western interpretations the spirit of the Yalta Agreement was in no manner being upheld. The elections were postponed until January, 1947, and reports came out of Poland of imprisonments, deportations, and threats. The following documents indicate the turn that United States–Soviet relations were taking over the Polish question.

Excerpt from Press Interview Given by Stalin, October 23, 1946

QUESTION: Does the Soviet Union consider the Western frontiers of Poland to be final ?

STALIN: Yes, it does.[31]

Note Delivered by American Ambassador to Russia Smith, to Deputy Foreign Minister Vyshinsky, January 5, 1947

. . . My Government is especially perturbed by the increasingly frequent reports of repressive measures which the Polish Provisional Government has seen fit to employ against those democratic elements in Poland which have not aligned themselves with the "bloc" parties.

According to information reaching my Government from various authoritative sources, these repressive activities on the part of the Provisional Government have now increased in intensity to the point where, if they do not cease immediately, there is little likelihood that elections can be held in accordance with the terms of the Potsdam Agreement which call for free and unfettered elections "on the basis of universal suffrage and secret ballot in which all democratic and anti-Nazi parties shall have the right to take part and put forward candidates."

On December 18, 1946, Vice-Premier Stanislaw Mikolajczyk addressed a communication to the American Ambassador in Warsaw in which he called attention to the reprehensible methods employed by the Provisional Government in denying freedom of political action to the Polish Peasant Party. . . . Authoritative reports from other quarters in Poland serve to substantiate the charges brought by Mr. Mikolajczyk in the communication cited.[32]

Note Delivered by Soviet Foreign Minister Molotov to Ambassador Smith, January 13, 1947

. . . The Government of the United States of America advancing in its note

[31]*Information on Poland* (Warsaw: Ministry of Foreign Affairs, Press and Information Department, n.d.), p. Dx 38.

[32]*A Decade of American Foreign Policy: Basic Documents, 1941–49.* Sen. Doc. No. 123, 81st Cong., 1st sess. (Washington, D.C.: U.S. Government Printing Office, 1950), pp. 1198–99.

of January 5 a series of accusations against the Polish Government, states that the basis therefor are reports coming to the American Government. . . .

In the note are repeated the accusations against the Polish Provisional Government contained in Mikolajczyk's statement of repressive measures directed against certain members of the party he represents. In this connection, however, there are completely ignored widely known facts concerning the participation of certain of the members of Mikolajczyk's party in the activities of underground organizations, who resort to every kind of threat, to violence, and to murder in order to interfere with the normal conduct of the electoral campaign for the Sejm. . . .

In this situation, the Polish Government cannot remain indifferent and not undertake decisive measures with respect to the criminal elements who are endeavoring to disrupt the free and unfettered elections for the Sejm, even though certain members of Mikolajczyk's party should be guilty in this.[33]

[33]*Department of State Bulletin*, January 26, 1947, p. 164.

The United States sent Arthur Bliss Lane as Ambassador to the newly recognized Poland. It was expected that in accordance with various agreements, elections would be held in 1945. But President Bierut announced in August that due to the snow it would be impossible to hold elections that winter. In the following note Ambassador Lane reports his reactions to the State Department.

American Ambassador to Poland Lane to Director of the Office of European Affairs in the State Department, Matthews, March 1, 1946

We have been giving considerable thought to the political situation which is developing here and what our attitude should be in the event that "free and unfettered elections" are not held as promised, or if Mikolajczyk and members of his party are forced out of the government. The pessimism which I expressed to you in my letter of September 6, 1945, has been increasing as the months have passed and as I have observed the repressive measures which the Government has taken through the Security Police against those who were connected with the Armja Krajowa during the German occupation. In addition, as you are well aware, the Government has taken a violent line in the press against the PSL, Mikolajczyk's party, and has subjected Mikolajczyk's paper, *Gazeta Ludowa,* to rigid censorship.

Regardless of such freedom as may exist on the day elections are held, "free and unfettered elections" will not have been held in Poland in the broader sense of the term. Not only will supporters of Mikolajczyk have been, through their imprisonment, deprived of the privilege of voting, but the example of their imprisonment will undoubtedly indicate to those who have been fortunate enough to escape the wrath of the Security Police the fate which awaits them in case they take an active political part against the government. . . .

From the foregoing you will appreciate that I consider Mikolajczyk's chances of winning the elections are virtually nil.[34]

[34]Arthur Bliss Lane, *I Saw Poland Betrayed* (Indianapolis, Ind.: Bobbs-Merrill Company, Inc., 1948), pp. 193–94. Copyright 1948, used by special permission of the publishers, The Bobbs-Merrill Company, Inc.

The elections of 1947 had great significance since they would indicate whether or not there was a chance of free government in Poland. The following excerpts reflect the views of Mikolajczyk, of Joseph Swiatlo, a Communist defector, and of Wladyslaw Gomulka who, after a period of imprisonment, emerged in 1956 as Poland's top leader.

Comments of Mikolajczyk, December, 1946 and January, 1947

In the few remaining weeks before the elections more than one hundred thousand members of the Polish Peasant Party were arrested. One hundred and thirty members were murdered. One hundred and forty-two of our candidates were kept in prison throughout the entire campaign period. One of these, Mr. Szygula, a Silesian farmer, was tortured to death in prison. So was Lewandowski, a farmer near Inowroclaw. When the arrests became so numerous that there was no more room in prisons, our people were herded into fields, stripped of outer clothing, and forced to stay in the cold for forty-eight hours up to two weeks. The health of thousands was broken.

. . . . .

A week before the elections, the names of our candidates in ten of the fifty-two electoral districts were stricken from the ballot. The excuse was that their sponsors, many of them still undergoing torture because of their refusal to recant, "were not valid." Then ten districts—Przemyśl, Myślenice, Chrzanów, Bielsko, Ostrowiec, Kielce, Radom, Kalisz, Przasnysz, and Lódź—had a population of 5,342,000, which comprised about a quarter of the people of Poland. From these areas, which constituted 12 percent of the land in Poland, came seventy-six Communist bloc M.P.'s who walked in unopposed, after our slate was abolished. These areas were traditionally Peasant Party-minded.

. . . . .

The government was obliged to publish the names of all candidates on January 7, 1947. The names were not published until the twelfth; then they were posted, in most instances, in the one place where the average Pole would not think of visiting —the Security Police stations.

Sunday, January 19, 1947, will forever remain a black day in Polish history. Yet there was glory and hope and stirring valor mixed with the galling story of our official downfall as a democracy.

The millions who were ordered to vote openly gathered at their factories, offices, and other appointed places, and with band music in the air were marched by armed guards to their polling places.

. . . . .

Even after all the intimidation the Polish Peasant Party gained officially recognized majorities of from 65 to 85 per cent in the thirty-six polling places where our representatives had been permitted to watch the count. In Gniezno, one of the three districts in which I personally ran for a seat in the parliament, the Polish Peasant Party gained 96 per cent of the votes cast. The over-all majority rung up by our party candidates throughout the country—a figure that included the extermination of our chances in ten districts— was 74 per cent. This the Communists were forced to tell Stalin. Terror, murders, and intimidation had failed to break the will of our people.

However, these were the figures for the fifty-two districts that the government released on January 22, 1947 (and which the *Gazeta Ludowa* was forced to print).

Total votes cast	11,413,618*
Government Bloc	327 seats
Polish Peasant Party	24 seats
Catholic Labor Party	10 seats
PSL-New Liberation Party	7 seats
Others	4 seats

*Of a total electorate of 12,701,056.

Six days later the government announced the result of voting for the so-called "state lists" and said that the final results would be 394 seats for the government bloc, 28 for the Polish Peasant Party, 12 for the Christian Labor Party, 7 for the Polish Peasant Party–New Liberation, and 3 seats for the Catholic Progressive party.[35]

Testimony of a Former Member of the Polish Ministry of Public Security, Joseph Swiatlo, before House Committee Investigating Communist Aggression, 1954

MR. SWIATLO: I will try to describe how elections in 1947 were falsified.

In the first place, although the members of electoral boards were supposed to come from their own districts, the party changed this. Communist Party organizers from other districts were appointed as members of electoral boards.

In principle, this is a breaking of the constitution. The second part of members of the electoral boards or committees were strict agents of the security police.

Even these two factors were not enough to secure the proper results of the elections. This is why every electoral committee had a so-called—as we called him—a party mathematician.

This so-called party mathematician usually would receive from the central committee of the party the results of elections as he was to secure them. I don't speak now about such factors as terror or forcing the people to vote openly.

I speak exclusively about the process of falsification of elections.

[35]Mikolajczyk, op. cit., pp. 189–200.

Now, after the elections of 1947, the Government would boast very much about popular support, about its popularity. Nevertheless, the regime realized that too many people knew about falsifications of elections, and too many people took part in the falsifications.

MR. MACHROWICZ: Just one moment, please. I presume you want now to explain the difference between the 1947 and the 1952 elections, but before you go into that, I would like to ask you one question with regard to the 1947 elections.

Besides the fact that each district had already in advance instructions as to what the results must be of that district, is it true that every candidate who ran for the office was compelled in advance to submit his written resignation from that office which could be used whenever the party so required it?

MR. SWIATLO: Yes; that is right. I didn't speak about this particular fact since it applied also to the elections of 1952.

The party has no absolute confidence in its own members. Even from the strict party members, such written commitments are taken.

In connection with the impressions the elections of 1947 made in the country, the party hierarchy came to the conclusion that the elections of 1952 had to be carried out and falsified in a completely different way. . . .

When elections were announced, the security police received orders to send agents all over the country to determine the opinion and the political feeling of the country. The censorship of the correspondence at that time was very much strengthened. . . .

Now came the next important step: On orders, a special unit was organized in the Ministry of Security, a unit which had a specific task: To falsify elections. . . .

MR. KERSTEN: Were you in this unit?

MR. SWIATLO: Yes, sir.

MR. KERSTEN: And this unit was for the very express purpose of falsifying the elections, is that correct, in the 1952 elections?

MR. SWIATLO: Yes, sir.

The director of that unit was the Vice Minister of Public Security, General Romkowski. One of the members of that unit was myself.[36]

Comments of Wladyslaw Gomulka, 1960

Poland owes her liberation and independence to the Soviet Union and the Soviet Army, which together with the forces of the United States, Great Britain and other allies in the anti-Nazi coalition routed Nazi Germany. Moreover, it was thanks to the Soviet Union and its stand at the Yalta and Potsdam Conferences that an independent Poland was able to emerge within new and just frontiers, encompassing in their entirety the historic Polish lands from the River Bug up to the Rivers Oder and Neisse, with an access over 300 miles wide to the Baltic Sea. . . .

She benefits now from having the Soviet Union as a neighbor. Having learned from experience, Poland has chosen the road of close friendship and alliance with the Soviet Union and other socialist countries. This guarantees peace and the security of our frontiers and is an unfailing safeguard against the revanchist aspirations of the German militarists.

Having socialized the means of production, Poland is making great economic efforts to rebuild the country from wartime destruction and to eliminate the backwardness inherited from former rulers, so as to ensure a higher standard of living and culture in the shortest possible time. . . .

Some dissatisfaction may be and is voiced by people because of difficulties or shortages they may have to cope with. To the rather amusing surprise of Western correspondents who visit Poland, our citizens express opinions on such matters quite freely. But there are no differences of opinion among the overwhelming majority of Poles as to the fundamental principles of our People's Republic. The best proofs of this were the results of the elections to the Sejm and the people's councils held during the last few years in an atmosphere of such freedom that even unsympathetic Western reporters could not but recognize it. Socialism in Poland is growing out of Polish soil and has struck deep roots in it.[37]

---

[36]*Investigation of Communist Takeover and Occupation of Poland, Lithuania, and Slovakia:* Sixth Interim Report of Hearings before the Subcommittee on Poland, Lithuania, and Slovakia of the Select Committee on Communist Aggression, House of Representatives, 83rd Cong., 2d sess. (Washington, D.C.: U.S. Government Printing Office, 1954), pp. 143–46.

[37]Wladyslaw Gomulka, "The Policy of the Polish People's Republic," *Foreign Affairs* (April, 1960), pp. 404–06.

BIBLIOGRAPHY

SOURCES USED IN THIS PROBLEM

1. *Collections and Official Documents*

Correspondence between the Chairman of the Council of Ministers [Stalin], *the Presidents of the U.S.A.* [Roosevelt, Truman] *and the Prime Ministers* [Churchill, Attlee] . . . 2 vols. Moscow: Foreign Languages Publishing House, 1957.

A Decade of American Foreign Policy: Basic Documents, 1941–49. Sen. Doc. 123, 81st Cong., 1st sess. Washington, D.C.: U.S. Government Printing Office, 1950.

Foreign Relations of the United States: The Conference of Berlin (Potsdam), 1945. Washington, D.C.: U.S. Government Printing Office, 1960.

Foreign Relations of the United States: The Conferences at Malta and Yalta, 1945. Washington, D.C.: U.S. Government Printing Office, 1955.

House of Representatives Select Committee Investigating Communist Aggression, 83rd Cong., 2d sess. Washington, D.C.: U.S. Government Printing Office, 1954, 1955.
Fourth Interim Report of Hearings.
Tenth Interim Report of Hearings.
"Communist Takeover and Occupation of Poland," Special Report No. 1. *House Reports,* Vol. 13.
"Polish Documents Report," Appendix to Committee Report, House Report No. 2684, Part 4. *House Reports,* Vol. 13.
Sixth Interim Report of the Subcommittee on Poland, Lithuania, and Slovakia.

Information on Poland. Warsaw: Ministry of Foreign Affairs, Press and Information Department, n.d.

Parliamentary Debates. Commons. London: His Majesty's Stationery Office.

2. Others

BYRNES, JAMES F. *Speaking Frankly.* New York: Harper's, 1947.

LANE, ARTHUR BLISS. *I Saw Poland Betrayed.* Indianapolis, Ind.: Bobbs-Merrill, 1948.

MIKOLAJCZYK, STANISLAW. *The Rape of Poland.* New York: McGraw-Hill, 1948.

STETTINIUS, EDWARD R. *Roosevelt and the Russians.* Garden City, N.Y.: Doubleday, 1949.

SELECT LIST OF BOOKS RECOMMENDED FOR FURTHER READING

ANDERS, GENERAL W. *An Army in Exile.* New York: Macmillan, 1949.

BOR-KOMOROWSKI, GENERAL. *Secret Army.* London: Gollancz, 1950.

BREGMAN, A. (ed.). *Faked Elections in Poland.* London: Polish Freedom Movement, 1947.

BUTLER, DAVID E. (ed.). *Elections Abroad.* London: Macmillan, 1959.

CHURCHILL, WINSTON. *The Second World War.* Vol. VI, *Triumph and Tragedy.* Boston: Houghton Mifflin, 1953.

CIECHANOWSKI, JAN. *Defeat in Victory.* Garden City, N.Y.: Doubleday, 1947.

DZIEWANOWSKI, M. K. *The Communist Party of Poland: An Outline of History.* Cambridge, Mass.: Harvard University Press, 1959.

FEIS, HERBERT. *Between War and Peace: the Potsdam Conference.* Princeton, N.J.: Princeton University Press, 1960.

GALLAGHER, MATTHEW. *The Soviet History of World War II.* New York: Praeger, 1963.

GIBNEY, FRANK. *The Frozen Revolution.* New York: Farrar, Straus & Cudahy, 1959.

GRAEBNER, NORMAN A. *Cold War Diplomacy: American Foreign Policy, 1945–1960.* Princeton, N.J.: Van Nostrand, 1962.

GRIFFIS, STANTON. *Lying in State.* Garden City, N.Y.: Doubleday, 1952.

HALECKI, OSCAR (ed.). *East-Central Europe under the Communists: Poland.* New York: Praeger, 1957.

HALLE, LOUIS J. *The Cold War as History.* New York: Harper & Row, 1967.

HERZ, MARTIN F. *Beginnings of the Cold War.* Bloomington, Ind.: Indiana University Press, 1967.

HISCOCKS, RICHARD. *Poland: Bridge for the Abyss?* London: Oxford University Press, 1963.

KARBONSKI, STEFAN. *Warsaw in Chains.* London: Allen & Unwin, 1959.

Karski, Jan. *The Story of a Secret State*. Boston: Houghton Mifflin, 1945.

Luard, David (ed.). *The Cold War—a Re-Appraisal*. New York: Praeger, 1964.

Lukacs, John A. *A History of the Cold War*. Garden City, N.Y.: Doubleday, 1961.

Mayewski, Pawel (ed.). *The Broken Mirror*. New York: Random House, 1958.

Murray, Joseph P. *From Yalta to Disarmament: Cold War Debate*. New York: Monthly Review Press, 1961.

Rozek, Edward J. *Allied Wartime Diplomacy: A Pattern in Poland*. New York: Wiley, 1958.

Smith, Walter Bedell. *My Three Years in Moscow*. Philadelphia: J. B. Lippincott, 1950.

Snell, John L. *Illusion and Necessity: The Diplomacy of Global War, 1939–1945*. Boston: Houghton Mifflin, 1963.

Snell, John L. (ed.). *The Meaning of Yalta*. (Especially Chap. III, "Russian Power in Central-Eastern Europe," by Charles F. Delzell.) Baton Rouge: Louisiana State University Press, 1956.

Staar, Richard F. *Poland, 1944–1962: The Sovietization of a Captive People*. Baton Rouge: Louisiana State University Press, 1962.

Stypulkowski, Zbigniew. *Invitation to Moscow*. London: Thames and Hudson, 1951.

Truman, Harry S. *Memoirs*. Vol. I, *Year of Decisions*. Garden City, N.Y.: Doubleday, 1955.

Woodward, E. L. *British Foreign Policy in the Second World War*. London: His Majesty's Stationery Office, 1962.

Zurawski, Joseph W. *Poland, the Captive Satellite*. Detroit: Endurance Press, 1962.

THE SETTLEMENT IN GERMANY

Partition, the Soviet blockade, and the Berlin airlift, 1945-49

From the year 1945, when Russian, American, British, and French soldiers embraced each other during the common campaign against Germany, to 1948, when Russia imposed its blockade on Berlin, the East-West relationship turned from cordial cooperation to the strained antagonisms of the cold war. Obviously, the cause for this change cannot be found in Germany alone. There was friction over Poland, the Balkans, the Peace Treaties, the Near and Far East. But the postwar arrangements in Germany, the principal Western enemy, became the focal point for the Western *rapprochements* that led ultimately to the Atlantic Pact, and the dramatic countermeasure to the blockade, the airlift, provides a symbol of Soviet miscalculations and of Allied resourcefulness. The following documents pertain to the widening breach between Russia and the Western powers in Germany, and to the place of the Berlin blockade in the larger picture of Soviet-Western relationships.

With the collapse of Germany in May, 1945, the responsibility of occupying and governing the country fell to the victorious Allied powers, who divided Germany into four Occupation Zones. A basic occupation agreement was signed on June 5, and later, when Russia, the United States, and the United Kingdom met at Potsdam, the general policies for the occupation were laid down. The significant elements of the control agreement are here quoted.

Statement on Control Machinery in Germany, June 5, 1945

1. In the period when Germany is carrying out the basic requirements of unconditional surrender, supreme authority in Germany will be exercised, on instructions from their Governments, by the Soviet, British, United States, and French Commanders-in-Chief, each in his own zone of occupation, and also jointly, in matters affecting Germany as a whole.

The four Commanders-in-Chief will to-gether constitute the Control Council. Each Commander-in-Chief will be assisted by a political adviser.

2. The Control Council, whose decisions shall be unanimous, will ensure appropriate uniformity of action by the Commanders-in-Chief in their respective zones of occupation and will reach agreed decisions on the chief questions affecting Germany as a whole.

.   .   .   .   .

7. The administration of the "Greater Berlin" area will be directed by an Inter-Allied Governing Authority, which will operate under the general direction of the Control Council, and will consist of four Commandants, each of whom will serve in rotation as Chief Commandant. They will be assisted by a technical staff which will supervise and control the activities of the local German organs.[1]

---

[1] *A Decade of American Foreign Policy: Basic Documents, 1941–49,* Sen. Doc. No. 123, 81st Cong., 1st sess. (Washington, D.C.: U.S. Government Printing Office, 1950), pp. 512–13.

After Potsdam a clear-cut split developed between the Soviet Union and the Western occupying powers. While extremely complex in its details, the split basically revolved around three problems: reparations, economic unity, and political centralization. To determine the amount of reparations, it was first necessary to establish the level of German production, so that sufficient supplies would remain to provide for the German population. The Soviet Union, however, wished to reduce the German standard of living and level of industry far below that deemed acceptable by the Western powers. The West, furthermore, claimed that Russia had provided insufficient information and cooperation in the matter of economic production in the Eastern Zone and of reparations already taken. And while Russia was vociferous in its advocacy of political centralization, the West insisted that economic unity be first achieved.

These differences had become quite apparent by the time a Four-Power Reparations and Level of Industry Agreement was drawn up in March, 1946, but the impeding tactics of the Soviet Union forced the Western powers to reconsider their entire policy in Germany. In a significant address at Stuttgart, in September, 1946, Secretary of State Byrnes indicated a stiffening U.S. policy.

Excerpts from Address of Secretary of State Byrnes, Stuttgart, Germany, September 6, 1946

The United States is firmly of the belief that Germany should be administered as an economic unit and that zonal barriers should be completely obliterated so far as the economic life and activity in Germany are concerned.

The conditions which now exist in Germany make it impossible for industrial production to reach the levels which the occupying powers agreed were essential for a minimum German peacetime economy. Obviously, if the agreed levels of industry are to be reached, we cannot continue to restrict the free exchange of commodities, persons, and ideas throughout Germany. The barriers between the

four zones of Germany are far more difficult to surmount than those between
normal independent states.

The time has come when the zonal
boundaries should be regarded as de-
fining only the areas to be occupied for
security purposes by the armed forces
of the occupying powers and not as self-
contained economic or political units.

We favor the economic unification of
Germany. If complete unification cannot
be secured, we shall do everything in our
power to secure the maximum possible
unification.

.   .   .   .   .

So far as many vital questions are concerned, the Control Council is neither governing Germany nor allowing Germany
to govern itself.

A common financial policy is essential
for the successful rehabilitation of Germany. Runaway inflation accompanied by
economic paralysis is almost certain to
develop unless there is a common financial policy directed to the control of
inflation. A program of drastic fiscal reform to reduce currency and monetary
claims, to revise the debt structure, and
to place Germany on a sound financial
basis is urgently required.

.   .   .   .   .

All that the Allied governments can
and should do is to lay down the rules
under which German democracy can govern itself. The Allied occupation forces
should be limited to the number sufficient to see that those rules are obeyed.

But of course the question for us will
be: What force is needed to make certain
that Germany does not rearm as it did
after the first World War? Our proposal
for a treaty with the major powers to
enforce for 25 or even 40 years the demilitarization plan finally agreed upon
in the peace settlement would have made
possible a smaller army of occupation.
For enforcement we could rely more
upon a force of trained inspectors and
less upon infantry.

For instance, if an automobile factory,
in violation of the treaty, converted its
machinery to the production of weapons
of war, inspectors would report it to the
Allied Control Council. They would call
upon the German Government to stop
the production and punish the offender.
If the German Government failed to
comply then the Allied nations would
take steps to enforce compliance by the
German Government. Unfortunately our
proposal for a treaty was not agreed to.

Security forces will probably have to
remain in Germany for a long period. I
want no misunderstanding. We will not
shirk our duty. We are not withdrawing.
We are staying here. As long as there is
an occupation army in Germany, American armed forces will be part of that
occupation army.

The United States favors the early
establishment of a provisional German
government for Germany. Progress has
been made in the American zone in developing local and state self-government
in Germany, and the American Government believes similar progress is possible
in all zones.

It is the view of the American Government that the provisional government
should not be hand-picked by other governments. It should be a German national
council composed of the democratically
responsible minister-presidents or other
chief officials of the several states or
provinces which have been established in
each part of the four zones.

Subject to the reserved authority of
the Allied Control Council, the German
National Council should be responsible
for the proper functioning of the central
administrative agencies. Those agencies
should have adequate power to assure
the administration of Germany as an economic unit, as was contemplated by the
Potsdam Agreement.[2]

---

[2]*Ibid.*, pp. 523–26.

Following Byrnes' address, the Western powers determined to establish their own policies without regard to Russia. On December 2, 1946, Britain and the United States effected an economic fusion of their zones. At the Council of Foreign Ministers meeting at Moscow, in March and April, 1947, Germany was the chief subject of discussion, but high-level agreement broke down over problems of unification and reparations. More and more it became apparent to the Western powers that if the occupation was not to remain a steady drain on their resources, it would be necessary to increase production in the Western Zones. In consequence, France, Britain, and the United States concluded a new Level of Industry Agreement for the Western Zones on August 29, 1947. In November and December, the Council of Foreign Ministers again met, in London. The following documents express the positions of the Western group and of the Soviet Union at that time.

OR CONSIDERATION   Both East and West appear to claim that they desire economic unity and governmental centralization in Germany. Is it clear exactly where the differences lie? What would be the advantage to the Soviet Union in having a political centralization take place before an economic fusion of the four zones was obtained?

Statement of Secretary of State Marshall at the London Meeting of the Council of Foreign Ministers, December 15, 1947

It was accepted by all at Moscow that full agreement on economic principles was essential to the establishment of political unification. We are unable to agree on what shall be the area of the German economy; we cannot agree how to make German resources available to Germany as a whole, a condition prerequisite to the revival of German economy; we are confronted with a demand for reparations in excess of the Potsdam agreement which would make a German government subservient to its reparations creditor. It is therefore clear that agreement can be reached only under conditions which would not only enslave the German people but would seriously retard the recovery of all Europe.

If real economic unity could have been established, the United States would have been ready for the German people to be immediately accorded, under agreed controls, self-government with the authority, responsibility, and initiative this entails. But free government cannot succeed under conditions of economic serfdom. True political and economic unity would require a free movement of goods, persons, and ideas throughout Germany and the establishment of a rule of law and political freedom which the occupying powers themselves would respect. . . .

The simple fact is, the present division of Germany has been caused by the policies and practices of the occupying powers themselves. Only the occupying powers can create German unity in the present circumstances. That is why the United States has consistently pressed for certain fundamental decisions by the occupying powers themselves as the absolutely essential first step for the achievement of a unified Germany.

Three delegations at this conference have registered their willingness to take these decisions here and now. The Soviet Union alone refuses to agree.

In view of these facts, it seems impossible at this time to make practical progress. Therefore, I reluctantly conclude that no useful purpose would be served by a debate on the other points on our agenda; and I suggest that the Council of Foreign Ministers might now consider adjournment of this session.[3]

Whitelaw in The London Daily Herald

"Come on, let's finish this German puzzle."

Statement of Soviet Foreign Minister Molotov, Published in Moscow, December 31, 1947

At present the American plan provides for billions of dollars of credit to Bizonia over a period of years. . . .

This plan to a great extent reflects the desire to convert the western part of Germany into a base for extending the influence of American imperialism in Europe. The American plan embraces a number of European states, whose rehabilitation is made dependent on definite economic and political terms dictated to them too by the U.S.A. Undivided sway of American imperialism in the western part of Germany is designed to facilitate the strengthening of its influence in other European countries as well. And the development in Bizonia of such industries as iron and steel and coal mining creates the prerequisites for exploiting Western Germany as a strategical base for the reckless and aggressive plans of American imperialism.

It should also be said that the American plan by no means envisages the ful-

filment by Germany of her reparation obligations towards the states which suffered German aggression and occupation. It does not reckon with their interests, and disregards the decision of the Potsdam conference on this subject. Allegations that the settlement of the problem of reparations for the U.S.S.R. is hindered by the absence of information from the Soviet zone are, of course, utterly unfounded. The Soviet Union has always expressed and still expresses its readiness to present full information on this subject, if the Western Powers are prepared to proceed to the settlement of the reparations problem in deeds and not in words. As to the other Allied states to which reparations from Germany's Western zones are due, it is an open secret that Anglo-American and French policy has reduced the provisions of the Potsdam agreement practically to naught as far as those countries are concerned.[4]

. . . . .

[3]*Ibid.,* pp. 572–73.

[4]V. M. Molotov, *Problems of Foreign Policy Speeches and Statements, April 1945–November 1948* (Moscow: Foreign Languages Publishing House, 1949), pp. 546–55.

**Statement of British Foreign Minister
Bevin in House of Commons,
January 22, 1948**

We have been in favour of a centralised German Government, but not
an over-centralised German Government
which, in our view, could be a danger to
peace. In this I believe the Americans,
the French and ourselves, despite slight
differences between us, can reconcile our
views. On the other hand, the Soviet
Government are pressing for an over-
centralised Government which we know
could be used in the same way to develop
a one-party dictatorship as has been done
in the Eastern European countries, and
we cannot agree to it.

It became clear a year ago that Germany was to be made, as a result of the
series of disagreements between the
Great Powers, a terrific financial liability
on the United States and ourselves. No
food was to come from the East into the
West, no exchange, and hence the burden would fall upon our exchequers. I
indicated that we had to make it pay by
hook or by crook. We really had to make
our Zone go, and take the liability off
the taxpayer here. Then the Americans
offered fusion of the two Zones in 1946,
and negotiations for the first fusion
agreement then took place in New York
. . . we have tried to make this fusion
work, and work better, by setting up an
Economic Council. We are still hopeful
in Germany, and I hope I shall not be
told I am too patient—because I am not
waiting. We are going on with the work.
By taking the right lines in our bi-zonal
organization in Germany, I believe that
in the end we shall achieve a proper
organisation of Central Europe. We have
first to get the organisation on our own
side efficient.[5]

[5]*British White Paper,* Cmd. 7534 (London:
Her Majesty's Stationery Office, 1948), p. 13.
Reprinted by permission of the Controller of Her
Britannic Majesty's Stationery Office.

The London meeting of Foreign Ministers broke down completely. It
seemed then, at the beginning of 1948, that the only possibility left was
to develop a German policy without Soviet cooperation. Discussions in
London, between February 23 and March 6, led to a tentative agreement
among the Western powers which could lead to a unification of the three
zones, the establishment of a federal government, and even to a bestowal of
Marshall Plan aid to Western Germany. On March 17, 1949, five Western
states, Great Britain, France, Belgium, the Netherlands and Luxembourg,
signed a pact at Brussels which provided for joint defense, economic
cooperation, and cultural exchanges. At approximately this time, Russian
noncooperation in Germany became more marked than usual, as indicated
by the comments of the American Military Governor, General Lucius D.
Clay.

FOR CONSIDERATION   Is it likely that the actions of the Soviet Military
Governor, Marshal Sokolovsky, were determined by the meetings of the
Western powers?

**Comments of General Lucius Clay,
American Military Governor**

The last meeting of the Control Council took place on March 20, 1948. Sokolovsky had introduced in the Control Council the declaration of the Prague conference of the foreign ministers of Czechoslovakia, Yugoslavia, and Poland a Soviet-inspired attack on the policies of the Western Powers in Germany. At the time the representatives of the three Western Powers advised Sokolovsky that this declaration had been addressed to the governments of the occupying powers and hence was not a proper subject for discussions in the Control Council. At this meeting I advised Sokolovsky that our government had stated publicly that it could see no useful purpose in considering resolutions which were based on misstatements and distortions of fact.

.   .   .   .   .

Suddenly Sokolovsky demanded to be advised of all agreements on western Germany reached by the three Western Powers in London in February and March. He was informed that this conference had been held between governments and its report had been submitted for the approval of these governments. We considered his request to be reasonable but we could not provide him with the information he desired until we had heard from our governments. I reminded him, too, of the exchange of notes in which the United States had rejected the Soviet protest against the conference. Sokolovsky expected our answer and barely waited for its translation by the interpreters before reading a long statement which repeated all of the old charges against the Western Powers in more aggravating language.

The British representative started to reply as the interpreter completed the translation of the Soviet charge. Rudely interrupting and without explanation, the Soviet delegation, following what must have been a prearranged plan, rose as one as Sokolovsky declared: "I see no sense in continuing this meeting, and I declare it adjourned." Without further word the Soviet delegation turned on its heels and walked out of the conference room.

No chairman had ever attempted to adjourn a meeting without the approval of his colleagues. No chairman had ever adjourned a meeting without arranging for the date of the next meeting. And, significantly, no chairman had hitherto left a meeting without inviting his colleagues to join him for coffee and light refreshments. We knew of course that this was no spur-of-the-moment action. It was a last attempt to strike doubt in Western minds as to the advisability of proceeding with the program for western Germany.

The three Western military governors remained in their seats to invalidate the adjournment, to select a chairman, to continue the meeting, and then to formally adjourn. The Allied Control Council was dead. An international undertaking which if successful, might have contributed to lasting peace, had failed. We knew that day as we left the conference room that quadripartite government had broken up and that the split in Germany which in view of Soviet intransigence had seemed inevitable for some months had taken place.[6]

----

[6]Lucius D. Clay, *Decision in Germany* (Garden City, N.Y.: Doubleday & Company, Inc. 1950), pp. 355–57. Copyright 1950 by Lucius D Clay, reprinted by permission of Doubleday & Company, Inc.

T he Russian walkout in the ACC was followed 10 days later, on March 30 1948, by a Soviet order slowing down shipments to Berlin: personnel freight, and baggage had to be properly cleared at Russian checkpoints. This was the first symptom of the blockade to come. The American commander in Berlin, Colonel (later General) Frank Howley, reported evidence of a possible break with the Russians, as did his senior, General Clay, when asked by Washington about the possibilities of staying in Berlin.

Comments of General Frank Howley

As early as April, Kotikov began a series of tirades in the Kommandatura, accusing us of preventing its smooth functioning and attempting to end quadripartite government of Berlin. Any action we took unfavorable to the Russians was interpreted in this light. To me, Kotikov's attacks seemed all part of the new campaign by the Russians to "kill" the Kommandatura, blame the West for its demise, and then try to drive us all out of the city.

I went to Major General Walsh, the United States Intelligence chief in Berlin, and told him frankly the Russians were getting ready for this *coup*. I supported my statement with references to the meetings I had attended, where it was patent to the least prejudiced that the Russians were building up a case, step by verbal step, to make their action plausible.

General Clay appeared to think that there was nothing unusual in the Russian attitude at that time. Other commanders had pooh-poohed the idea, but Walsh forwarded my report to Washington.

I was later summoned to James W. Riddleberger, assistant in Berlin to Ambassador Murphy. After seeing General Walsh, I had repeated to a State Department man, Perry Laukhuff, what I had told the General and he had prepared a report for Washington.

Laukhuff, with all the inconclusiveness and circumlocution of a government official, indicated that "it would appear a possible responsible assumption" and "subject to later observation and study"

the Russians were embarking upon a course for blaming the Western powers for what they were going to do, namely, kill the Kommandatura and take other steps to drive the Western powers out of Berlin.

Riddleberger asked me if the report by Laukhuff wasn't too extreme.

"Too extreme?" I gasped. "Why, if anything, it's too weak!" praying I wasn't overestimating Russian perfidy.[7]

General Clay to Secretary of Army Royall, Teleconference of April 10, 1948

We have lost Czechoslovakia. Norway is threatened. We retreat from Berlin. When Berlin falls, western Germany will be next. If we mean . . . to hold Europe against Communism, we must not budge. We can take humiliation and pressure short of war in Berlin without losing face. If we withdraw, our position in Europe is threatened. If America does not understand this now, does not know that the issue is cast, then it never will and communism will run rampant. I believe the future of democracy requires us to stay. . . . This is not a heroic pose because there will be nothing heroic in having to take humiliation without retaliation.[8]

---

[7]Frank Howley, *Berlin Command* (New York: G. P. Putnam's Sons, 1950), pp. 174–75. Copyright 1950, by Frank Howley. Courtesy of G. P. Putnam's Sons.

[8]Clay, *op. cit.*, p. 361.

The following document is included to present specific evidence of the sort of problem which confronted Western representatives when they negotiated with Soviet delegates. While the issue in this case was not of great significance, nevertheless the incident serves as a revealing example of the difficulties encountered during East-West conversations.

Excerpt from Minutes of Allied Kommandatura Meeting, May 26, 1948

BRITISH: Last time I said there was one question of major importance to which I wished an answer. [Herbert was referring to the parcel-post question.] You can divide it into two, if you like. The first part can be answered quite simply by "yes" or "no." Does the Soviet delegation adhere to the various treaties providing for quadripartite government of Berlin?

RUSSIAN: Would you please ask the second question? I will answer them at once.

BRITISH: I have had a smoke screen thrown out before by asking too many questions at once and I would like to have an answer to this one now, thank you. If you cannot answer "yes" or "no" to this simple question, it will be very significant.

RUSSIAN: I would like to ask General Herbert not to worry about that and to ask his second question.

BRITISH: I am asking for an answer to a simple question and I propose to go on asking it until I get it, or until you refuse to give it. If you refuse to give it, we will know what the answer is.

RUSSIAN: If General Herbert has not listened attentively to my first statement, that is not my fault. At the end of that statement there is a very direct reply to the question put by General Herbert.

BRITISH: General Kotikov is still declining to reply to me. He refers to some statement. Perhaps he will give it. If it is more than a plain "yes" or "no," I shall consider it to be an unsatisfactory answer.

RUSSIAN: I just wanted to repeat the end of my first statement, but because of the ultimatum I have received I cannot do that now. General Herbert probably knows that the Soviet delegation does not consider it possible to answer any ultimatums of this kind.

BRITISH: There is no question of any ultimatum. I merely said that if his answer was not given in a certain form it would be an unsatisfactory answer. I asked General Kotikov to repeat the portion of his statement to which he has referred.

RUSSIAN: That is quite another thing. That is a more or less form of request. I will willingly comply with it. At the end of my first statement I said, "As to the question of the quadripartite management of the City of Berlin, the position of the Soviet delegation on this question is well known."

BRITISH: It is exactly because the position of the Soviet delegation is *not* well known that I have asked my question. I am asking him what appears to me to be an extraordinarily easy question to answer, and if he was a witness in the witness box I would describe him as the most evasive witness I have ever heard.

RUSSIAN: I don't know anything about the traditions in a British court. . . . Let us discuss the question of parcels now.

BRITISH: I do not wish to be treated like a small boy and told that I may have my sweet in due course, when Father Kotikov is ready to give it to me. There is to my mind no object in discussing the matter of parcels when this major item is not settled, and I propose that the matter be withdrawn. I think we have heard quite enough from the Soviet for one day.[9]

---

[9]Howley, *op. cit.*, pp. 173–74.

Soviet interference with traffic to Berlin was intensified throughout April with restrictions on mail, alternate rail routes, and power stations. An explanation can be sought in terms of the Six-Power Conference (United States, Great Britain, France and the three Benelux countries) concurrently meeting at London, April 20 to June 1, 1948, to discuss German trade, the Ruhr, and the possibilities of a German central government. On June 7, a communiqué on the results of this meeting was issued.

FOR CONSIDERATION   While the Conference was in session, Russia clamped restrictions on barge traffic and on June 12 closed the Elbe River bridge for "repairs." Examine the various documents published here for evidence that the blockade was a countermeasure against efforts to unify Western Germany.

Communiqué Issued by the Representatives of the United States, the United Kingdom, France, and the Benelux Countries at the Conclusion of the London Discussions, June 7, 1948

.   .   .   .   .

III (A) Further consideration has been given by all delegates to the problem of the evolution of the political and economic organization of Germany. They recognize, taking into account the present situation, that it is necessary to give the German people the opportunity to achieve on the basis of a free and democratic form of government the eventual re-establishment of German unity at present disrupted. In these circumstances they have reached the conclusion that it would be desirable that the German people in the different states should now be free to establish for themselves the political organization and institutions which will enable them to assume those governmental responsibilities which are compatible with the minimum requirements of occupation and control and which ultimately will enable them to assume full governmental responsibility. The delegates consider that the people in the States will wish to establish a constitution with provisions which will allow all the German states to subscribe as soon as circumstances permit.

Therefore the delegates have agreed to recommend to their governments that the military governors should hold a joint meeting with the Ministers-President of the western zone in Germany. At that meeting the Ministers-President will be authorized to convene a Constituent Assembly in order to prepare a constitution for the approval of the participating states.

Delegates to this Constituent Assembly will be chosen in each of the states in accordance with procedure and regulations to be determined by the legislative bodies of the individual states.

The constitution should be such as to

enable the Germans to play their part in bringing to an end the present division of Germany not by the reconstitution of a centralized Reich but by means of a federal form of government which adequately protects the rights of the respective states, and which at the same time provides for adequate central authority and which guarantees the rights and freedoms of the individual.

If the constitution as prepared by the Constituent Assembly does not conflict with these general principles the military governors will authorize its submissions for ratification by the people in the respective states.

.   .   .   .   .

V (A) The United States, United Kingdom and French Delegates reiterated the firm views of their governments that there could not be any general withdrawal of their forces from Germany until the peace of Europe is secured and without prior consultation. During this period there should be no general withdrawal of the forces of occupation of the United States, France or the United Kingdom without prior consultation. It was further recommended that the governments concerned should consult if any of them should consider that there was a danger of resurgence of German military power or of the adoption by Germany of a policy of aggression.[10]

Declaration of the Foreign Ministers of the Soviet Union, Albania, Poland, Bulgaria, Czechoslovakia, Yugoslavia, Rumania, and Hungary, at the Warsaw Conference, June 24, 1948

.   .   .   .   .

1. The decisions of the London Conference are directed to *complete the splitting and dismemberment of Germany.* . . .

---

[10]*A Decade of American Foreign Policy*, pp. 577–78.

2. The carrying out of a policy of the splitting and dismemberment of Germany *disrupts the conclusion of a peace treaty with Germany.* . . .

3. The adoption by the London Conference of the decision on the creation of a state in the western zones of Germany is permeated *by an anti-democratic spirit.* . . .

4. The policy pursued by the occupying powers in the western zones of Germany encourages German revisionist elements. . . . In particular the campaign of the German revisionist elements is directed against the Polish German frontier on the Oder and Western Nyssa which is an unshakable frontier—the frontier of peace. . . .

5. The declaration of the London Conference of the three Powers *subordinates the economy of Western Germany to the purposes of the United States of America and Great Britain.* . . .

6. The London Conference adopted a special decision on the Ruhr [which] . . . ensures the maintenance of the dominating position of American and British financial and industrial monopolies in the Ruhr industries. . . .

From all that has been said it follows that the London discussions are a *flagrant violation of the Yalta and Potsdam Agreements.* . . . In view of the above we refuse to recognize the decisions of the London Conference as a legal force or any moral authority. In accordance with the Yalta and Potsdam Agreements . . . [we] consider the settlement of the following questions above all as urgent:

First: The execution, by agreement between Great Britain, the USSR, France and the USA, of measures which will ensure the completion of the demilitarization of Germany.

Second: The establishment for a definite peroid of the Four Power Control—Great Britain, the USSR, France and the USA, over the Ruhr heavy industries with a view to developing peaceful branches of the Ruhr industry and prevention of the war potential of Germany.

Third: The formation by agreement between the Governments of Great Britain, the USSR, France and the USA of a provisional democratic peace-loving all-German Government consisting of representatives of democratic parties and organizations in Germany for the purpose of creating a guarantee against the repetition of German aggression.

Fourth: The conclusion of a peace treaty with Germany in accordance with the Potsdam decisions so that the forces of occupation of all powers be withdrawn from Germany in a year's time after the conclusion of the peace treaty.

Fifth: The preparation of measures for the fulfillment by Germany of her reparation obligations to the States which suffered from German aggression.[11]

------

[11]*Information on Poland* (Warsaw: Ministry of Foreign Affairs), pp. Dx 150-55.

The Soviet walkout in the ACC (March 20, 1948) made possible a banking and currency reform that had been long overdue. Such a reform had been approved by the U.S. government since August, 1946, and new currency had been printed before the end of 1947, but it had been impossible to reach four-power agreement as to its introduction. One of the serious obstacles had been Soviet insistence on printing the money at Leipzig; but the Western powers, recalling the billions of Reichsmarks the Russians had put into circulation in 1945, were unwilling to entrust this privilege

Yefimov in New Times (Moscow)

A Russian View: "Eyes Right! Line Up on Wall Street."

to the U.S.S.R. After the ACC had broken down, however, the American and British authorities shortly agreed to introduce the new Deutschemark into Bizonia by June 1; later the French joined, and the date was advanced to June 20.

The reforms included the establishment of a bank of issue, the *Bank deutscher Lander*, and a devaluation of credit balances, 10 Reichsmarks for 1 Deutschemark, to be put into effect in the three Western Zones, but not in Berlin. Events in Berlin, however, complicated the situation. On June 16, the Soviet representative walked out of the Kommandatura, leaving Berlin with no central government of occupying powers. When, on June 18, the Soviet authorities were notified about the currency reform in Trizonia, they countered, on June 22, by announcing that a new East mark would be introduced into Berlin and the Russian Zone. After an effort to bring about four-power administration of the East mark in Berlin had failed, the Western powers decided to introduce the Deutsche-mark, stamped with a "B", into the western sectors of Berlin.

These conditions precipitated a crisis in Berlin, as shown by the following documents.

Excerpt from a Proclamation by Soviet Military Governor Marshal Sokolovsky, June 19, 1948

German banking and industrial monopolies have been preserved in the Western zones and many of them have actually become branches of Wall Street, i.e., branch offices of American banking and industrial monopolies.

In carrying out the policy of dismembering Germany, the American, British and French monopolies are relying for support, in the Western zones of occupation, on the big German capitalists and the Junkers who ensured the advent to power of fascism and prepared and unleashed the second World War. The separate currency reform strengthens the political and economic position of these reactionary circles in Western Germany to the detriment of the interests of the working people. . . .

Taking into account the situation that has arisen, the Soviet Military Administration in Germany declares:

1. Currency issued in the Western zones of occupation in Germany will not be permitted to circulate in the Soviet zone of occupation and in the area of Greater Berlin which comes within the Soviet zone of occupation and is economically part of the Soviet zone.

2. The Soviet Military Administration notifies the population of Germany that the new currency issued in the Western zones of occupation, as well as Reichsmarks, Rentmarks and the Marks of the Allied Military Command, may not be introduced into the Soviet zone of occupation or in Greater Berlin from the Western zones of occupation in Germany.

3. Introduction of the new currency issued in Western Germany, as well as of Reichsmarks, Rentmarks and Marks of the Allied Military Command of the Western zones, or the acceptance of the new currency of the Western zones as payment in the Soviet zone of occupation in Germany and in Greater Berlin will be regarded as actions designed to undermine the economy, and those guilty will be punished accordingly.[12]

---

[12]*The Soviet Union and the Berlin Question* (Moscow, 1948), quoted in W. Heidelmeyer and G. Hindrichs (eds.), *Documents on Berlin 1943–1963* (Munich: R. Oldenbourg Verlag, 1963), pp. 60–61.

British Military Governor General Robertson to Soviet Military Governor Marshal Sokolovsky, June 23, 1948

I have received your letter of 22nd June advising me of the measures which you propose to take for currency reform in the Soviet Zone and Berlin.

I have no wish to cause difficulties to you in your Zone nor to complicate economic life in the city of Berlin. I was, and am, prepared to consider any reasonable arrangements for the use of a single currency in Berlin under quadripartite control, not excluding the possibility of this being the same as that in use in your Zone. At the meetings between our respective staffs yesterday, my representatives made this clear. They stipulated however that the orders for introducing these measures in Berlin must be quadripartite orders, since Berlin is under quadripartite jurisdiction, and no one Power can make enactments valid for the city as a whole.

I am sorry that you have been unable to accept this stipulation, the justice of which cannot be questioned. I note with regret that your orders purport to apply to the entire city of Berlin. It is impossible for me to accept this position, and I am compelled to join with my American and French colleagues in the issue of separate instructions and currency in order to protect the interests of the German population of my sector.[13]

Comments of General Frank Howley

On the eve of the blockade, the City Assembly met at the City Hall, in the Russian sector, to discuss the predicament facing Berlin.

The city fathers had two pistols pointed at their heads. Sokolovsky had proclaimed that economically Berlin was part of the Soviet zone and ordered them to accept this decision and adopt the East mark. On the other hand, the three Western

---

[13]*British White Paper*, Cmd. 7534, p. 18.

powers had ordered the city government not to obey this unilateral Soviet order since it breached the city constitution, agreements at the Allied Kommandatura, and agreements signed at the highest authority, the Allied Control Council.

To make sure that the city fathers knew their own minds and would reach an appropriate decision, a crowd of five thousand jostled outside the building, hooting and trying to intimidate Assembly members. The majority of the demonstrators were professional Communists, wearing party badges, and had been brought to the scene in Russian military trucks—all "made in the U.S.A." and given to Russia under Lend-Lease. City officials were mobbed on the street, and even inside the building, while loudspeakers harangued the crowd outside. Russian-sector police stood by idly. They had their orders, I was told, to "keep hands off and let the mob have its way!" The office of Soviet Police Chief Markgraf was next door to the City Hall, but calls for police protection were ignored.

Denied police assistance, Assembly officers did manage to clear the floor of interlopers and to open discussion. The Communist minority of 18 per cent instantly demanded that the Russian order be implemented and obeyed, climaxing their speeches with wild attacks on the Western powers. Boldly, in view of the massed menace outside, the three democratic parties—Social Democrats, Liberal Democrats, and Christian Democrats—stood up for the rights of the city, embodied in the international agreements. They stoutly insisted that the Assembly must abide by the constitution that Russia and the other three powers had given Berlin.

After a debate lasting four hours, the meeting ended with the announcement that the Assembly could not accept the Russian order, thereby intimating their ultimate refusal to see Berlin incorporated into the Russian zone.

Strange things were happening outside

while the Assemblymen were making this decision. Despite the efforts of agitators to start a riot and incite the mob to break windows and attack democratic leaders as they left the building, when the meeting finally ended most of the crowd had vanished. Only a few hundred diehards remained, and from their ranks sneaked a typical Russian-paid goon squad. Under the noses of the inactive police, they started beating up Assemblymen, injuring five who had shown the courage to stand out against the Russian edict. Satisfied, the hired thugs then scurried down their ratholes.

So the Assembly meeting ended with a major defeat for the Russians, as well as for their riot organizers. Berlin's elected representatives refused to be bullied by Sokolovsky into breaking agreements with the Western powers, and organized efforts to generate public indignation had failed ignominiously, even among their own Communist sympathizers.

The Muscovite mind then swung over to the next phase, one that had been long contemplated and refined in concept. The Germans refused to be propagandized or intimidated into accepting the will of Russia. All right. We'll try starving them, the mind decided, and the blockade was on in full force the next day. The Russian reason was the only excuse available at the time—the Western currency reform.[14]

---

[14]Howley, op. cit., pp. 190–92.

O n June 24, 1948, at 6 A.M., Russia proclaimed a total restriction on communication with Berlin. This was immediately countered by the introduction of the airlift, as here described. Robert D. Murphy, whose remarks are quoted, was Political Adviser, with rank of Ambassador, to the Military Government.

FOR CONSIDERATION   What were the reasons behind the blockade of Berlin? Was it the currency reform? Remember that partial blockades started in March and April, whereas the reform was not announced until June 18. Certainly the Russians may have suspected what was happening, but currency reform was nevertheless kept a highly classified, secret operation. Was it the London Agreement to form a West-German government? This agreement had been ratified by the Western powers by June 18 and steps would soon be taken for implementation: the German Minister-Presidents were to begin meetings at Coblentz on July 8. Was it an effort to obtain control of Berlin? General Howley's remarks would suggest this, and the Russians announced that Berlin would be considered economically part of the Soviet Zone. Was it to distract the Western powers from Communist actions in other areas? What was happening, for example, in the Far East?

When the Berlin crisis broke, it was immediately discussed in Washington. President Truman did not delay in making a basic decision, as indicated in the following.

Excerpts from the Diary of Secretary of Defense James Forrestal

27 June 1948 [*Conference of Royall, For-*

restal, Lovett, Sullivan, Bradley, Norstad and a number of other State, Defense and military leaders]

Definite conclusions reached at the

meeting were the following:

1. That State and Civil Affairs Division should prepare a currency paper for transmittal to Clay which might be used by him as a basis for resuming discussions with Sokolovsky.

2. That Secretary Royall, Mr. Lovett, and I should meet with the President the next morning and present the major issues involved for his decision, and that in the meantime Departments of Army and State should prepare a short statement of the possible alternative courses of action and the arguments in favor and against each.

3. Clay's reaction should be obtained as to whether two additional B–29 squadrons should go to Germany.

4. A proposed dispatch to Ambassador Douglas, which was read by Mr. Lovett, was approved. . . .

5. Douglas should be informed that we saw no particular merit in CCS [Combined Chief of Staff] discussions.

6. Douglas should be asked to explore the possibility of basing two B–29 groups in England.

28 June 1948   *Meeting at White House—Berlin Situation*

Present: Lovett, Royall and myself

Lovett recited the details of the meeting at the Department of the Army, Sunday afternoon. When the specific question was discussed as to what our future policy in Germany was to be—namely, were we to stay in Berlin or not?—the President interrupted to say that there was no discussion on that point, we were going to stay period.[15]

Comments of Robert D. Murphy

After prolonged exchanges of cablegrams and teletype conversations between Berlin and Washington, Clay and I were summoned home to present our views in person. We discovered immediately that several extraneous factors were influencing the momentous decision. For one thing, Truman was up for election in November and all polls showed he was far behind Thomas Dewey. If the President were to approve action in Berlin which the voters considered reckless, his election chances would diminish still further. In spite of his personal predicament, Truman was more disposed than his military advisers to take chances. . . .

The Berlin blockade is the one occasion in my long career where I feel I should have resigned in public protest against Washington's policy. My resignation almost certainly would not have affected events, but if I had resigned I would feel better today about my own part in that episode. I suffered anguish over this decision of our government not to challenge the Russians when they blockaded Berlin, and I still deeply regret that I was associated with an action which caused Soviet leaders to downgrade United States determination and capability, and led, I believe, to the subsequent Communist provocation in Korea.

When Clay and I flew to Washington, we had hoped for permission to try to break the blockade of ground access to Berlin. But the National Security Council did not share our confidence that the Russians were bluffing. With all ground routes thus ruled out, Berlin could receive its supplies only by air. During the intermittent traffic stoppages prior to the all-out blockade, we had discovered that airplanes could bring in a surprising amount of essentials. The National Security Council therefore decided that we should enforce only our written agreements for use of specific corridors.[16]

[15]Walter Millis and E. S. Duffield (eds.), *The Forrestal Diaries* (New York: The Viking Press, Inc., 1951), pp. 453–54. Quoted by permission of Princeton University.

[16]Robert D. Murphy, *Diplomat among Warriors* (Garden City, N.Y.: Doubleday & Company, Inc., 1964), pp. 316–17. Copyright © 1964 by Robert Murphy. Reprinted by permission of Doubleday & Co., Inc.

Once President Truman's decision had been made, the stage was set for that remarkable phenomenon, the Berlin airlift.

Comments of Robert D. Murphy

. . . The Airlift was accepted as a challenge by the Air Force commander in Europe, General Curtis E. LeMay. Once the decision was made, the British Government threw itself wholeheartedly into the Airlift. But they had only a fraction of our air transport so Americans had to do most of the flying. The French decided to stay in Berlin as long as the others did, but they did not participate in the Airlift. Even the French garrison and community in Berlin were supplied almost entirely by American and British planes.

A few days after Clay and I returned to Berlin from Washington, Clay telephoned to LeMay in Frankfurt. Clay asked: "Have you any planes there that can carry coal?"

"Carry what?" asked LeMay.

"Coal," repeated Clay.

"We must have a bad connection," said LeMay. "It sounds as if you are asking if we have planes for carrying coal."

"Yes, that's what I said—coal."

Rallying quickly, LeMay said stoutly, "The Air Force can deliver anything!"[17]

Comments of General Lucius Clay

Berlin under blockade was like a besieged city with only one supply line linking it to the Western world, the airlift bringing food, clothing, coal, raw materials, and medicines to the 2,500,000 men, women, and children in its western sectors. Operation Vittles, as the pilots designated the airlift, grew steadily from the few outmoded planes we had in Germany to the fleet of giant flying transports which on the record day delivered almost 13,000 tons to our three airports.

At the start our C–47s had flown the clock around; pilots, plane and ground crews worked far beyond normal hours to achieve a maximum effort. This effort showed the high number of landings which could be made, thus demonstrating that with larger planes we could sustain the Berlin population. It was a welcome sight to see the pilots of the C–47s when the first C–54's began to arrive on June 30, 1948, from Alaska, Panama, and Hawaii. It was impressive to see these planes with their insignia indicating the parts of the world from which they had come to participate in the airlift.

In July when I visited Washington I had been promised more planes to give us a total of 160 C–54s, and as they came in squadron by squadron, our freight to Berlin increased consistently. We proved on Air Force Day our ability with planes on hand to bring in 6987.7 tons, and the replacement of C–47s still in operation would have given us the 8000 tons which was essential to a sustaining economy in Berlin. We believed that in good weather we had to be able to carry twice the minimum quota of 4000 tons, although this provided a substantial safety factor.

By December our daily average exceeded 4500 tons. In January and February it had climbed to 5500 tons. We were over the minimum quota of 4000 tons a day by a substantial margin. This minimum provided no fuel for either domestic heating or industrial production. It did supply coal to maintain the available electric generating facilities in the western sectors.

---

[17] *Ibid.*, p. 318.

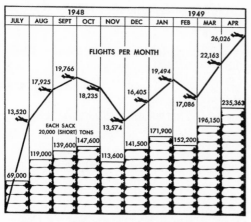

1948						1949			
JULY	AUG	SEPT	OCT	NOV	DEC	JAN	FEB	MAR	APR

FLIGHTS PER MONTH

26,026
22,163
19,766
19,494
17,925
18,235
16,405
13,520
17,086
235,363
13,574
196,150
171,900
EACH SACK
20,000 (SHORT) TONS
152,200
147,600
139,600
141,500
119,000
113,600
69,000

SOURCE: Adapted from *Berlin Airlift: An Account of the British Contribution*

How the Berlin Airlift Grew.

THE BERLIN AIR LIFT

Highways =====   Canal ------
Railroads ++++   Iron ------   Air Corridors
                    Curtain

The airlift was no makeshift operation. From the beginning it was a carefully planned split-second operation. It started with the determination of priority requirements in Berlin. The next steps were the requisition of supplies by the Bizonal Administration in Frankfurt, then the coordinated movement, of these supplies by ship, rail, and truck to the planes at the five airports in the western zones, the airlift delivery to the three Berlin airports, and the transfer of cargo from these airports to the German authorities.

Latest radar techniques made landings possible under almost unbelievable weather conditions and with a remarkable safety record. Two systems of radar were used, one to track the plane in the air corridor and as it left the corridor to enter the approach pattern to the airport, and the other to pick up the plane in the approach pattern and bring it safely to ground. The first system was operated from the tower, the second from the ground. The latter system, known as GCA or Ground Control Approach, had always been liked by our Air Forces but was not used very much in civil aviation as the pilots preferred another system in which they remained in control instead of having to take instructions from the ground. The

success of GCA in Germany did much to change the view and GCA is becoming more widely used in commercial flight.

To provide experience, pilots en route to Germany were given four-engine flight training in Montana, where a duplicate of the air corridor and approach paths was set up with navigation aids exactly like those in Germany. Moreover, pilots in the airlift flew the same pattern in good weather and bad.

·   ·   ·   ·   ·

When spring came in 1949, with our British colleagues we achieved a daily average of 8000 tons, which was as much as we had been able to bring into Berlin by rail and water prior to the blockade. Obviously, given the larger planes now coming off the production lines, this tonnage could be doubled, or, if maintained at the same figure, delivered in Berlin at from 25 to 35 per cent less cost. We were gaining invaluable experience in the use of air transport to support military operations and for civil use. The cost of the airlift could well be justified in its contribution to national defense.

Volumes can be written, and perhaps will be written, to cover in detail the work of the airlift, though I doubt if they will do it justice. Mechanically, it proved the efficiency of the Western Powers in the air in a way that the Soviet Government could understand. Morally and spiritually, it was the reply of Western civilization to the challenge of totalitarianism which was willing to destroy through starvation thousands of men, women, and children in the effort to control their souls and minds.[18]

18Clay, op. cit., pp. 381–82, 386.

Airlift Statistics, June 28, 1948 to May 11, 1949[19]

	U.S.A.F.	R.A.F.	Civil
Flights to Berlin and back	131,378	49,733	13,879
Miles flown ...	69,257,475	18,205,284	4,866,093
Tonnage flown in (short tons) ...	1,214,339	281,727	87,619

19Berlin Airlift: An account of the British Contribution. Prepared by the Air Ministry and Central Office of Information. Text by Dudley Barker. Used by permission of the Controller of Her Britannic Majesty's Stationery Office.

The institution of the Berlin blockade brought immediate protests from the West, but it was not until the end of July that Stalin expressed a willingness to negotiate. Early in the following month, conversations started in Moscow between the Russian leaders and the ambassadors of the Western powers.

Record of Meeting between Stalin and Molotov and the Representatives of the United States, the United Kingdom, and France, August 2, 1948

Ambassador Smith opened the conversation by presenting the following oral statement to Generalissimo Stalin:

.   .   .   .   .

Action taken by the Soviets in interfering with rights in connection with occupation, derived through the defeat and surrender of Germany and through international agreement and usage, by interrupting communications between Berlin and the Western zones, thus interfering with duties of Allied Military Forces of Occupation, is viewed with extreme seriousness by the Governments of the United States, the United Kingdom and France. . . . It was the feeling of our Governments that if these measures arose from technical difficulties, such difficulties can be easily remedied. The Three Governments renew their offer of assistance to this end. If in

any way related to the currency problem, such measures are obviously uncalled for, since this problem could have been, and can now be, adjusted by representatives of the four powers in Berlin. If, on the other hand, these measures are designed to bring about negotiations among the four occupying powers they are equally unnecessary, since the Governments of the United Kingdom, the United States and France have never at any time declined to meet representatives of the Soviet Union to discuss questions relating to Germany. However, if the purpose of these measures is to attempt to compel the three Governments to abandon their rights as occupying powers in Berlin, the Soviet Government will understand from what has been stated previously that such an attempt could not be allowed to succeed. . . .

The Soviet Government will, however, appreciate that the three Governments are unable to negotiate in the situation which the Soviet Government has taken the initiative in creating. Free negotiations can only take place in an atmosphere relieved of pressure.

This is the issue. Present restrictions upon communications between Berlin and the Western zones offend against this principle. When this issue is resolved, such difficulties as stand in the way of resumption of conversations on the lines set out above should be removed.

The remainder of the two hour meeting was taken up with a discussion which developed from the points brought out in Ambassador Smith's statement.

. . . . .

Stalin developed the argument that the communication restrictions in Berlin had been made necessary because of the decisions taken at London in regard to the establishment of a new German government at Frankfort and because of the introduction of a special Western currency in Berlin. The Western representatives explained that, contrary to the Generalissimo's apparent understanding, it had never been contemplated that the government at Frankfort would be a central German government. The agency now to be set up under the London decisions would in no way hamper eventual understanding on a central government for a united Germany. The Western representatives added that they were not authorized to discuss the London decisions. They would report Stalin's views; but in the meanwhile they felt strongly that agreement should be reached on the immediate issues in regard to Berlin.

At the end of the discussion Stalin asked whether the Western representatives wanted to settle the matter that night. If so, he could meet them and make the following proposal:

(1) There should be a simultaneous introduction in Berlin of the Soviet zone Deutsche mark in place of the Western mark B, together with the removal of all transport restrictions.

(2) He would no longer ask as a condition the deferment of the implementation of the London decisions although he wished this to be recorded as the insistent wish of the Soviet Government.[20]

---

[20]*The Berlin Crisis: A Report on the Moscow Discussions, 1948*, Department of State Publication No. 3298 (Washington, D.C.: U.S. Government Printing Office, 1948), pp. 17–19.

As there appeared to be a possibility of settling the Berlin crisis, it was agreed that the Western ambassadors should continue to work with Molotov on the details of the financial arrangements for Berlin. These are the instructions to the American Ambassador, W. Bedell Smith.

Instructions of the American Government to Ambassador to Russia Smith, August, 1948

We agree to the outline of the draft statement developed at your August 2 meeting with Stalin and Molotov.

Our acceptance of Soviet zone currency in Berlin *cannot* be unconditional and its use must be subject to some form of quadripartite control. This requirement is essential for the maintenance of our position in Berlin and is made doubly necessary because of Soviet action of the last few days in freezing the accounts of western sector enterprises in Berlin.

The substitution of the Soviet zone mark for the B mark in Berlin can now be accepted in principle but our agreement must be supplemented by a satisfactory agreement providing for quadripartite control of the availability and use of the Soviet currency in Berlin. . . .[21]

---

[21]*Ibid.*, p. 20.

The negotiations with Molotov, continuing throughout August, proved to be extremely difficult. A second meeting with Stalin took place on August 23, which resulted in new efforts to draft a compromise. An agreement was finally reached on August 27, 1948, and a few days later a directive was sent to the Military Governors, who were requested to reply by September 7. Following are Ambassador Smith's and General Clay's observations on the meetings.

FOR CONSIDERATION   While these negotiations proceeded, the airlift was succeeding. Are there possibilities that Russia wished to postpone a settlement until winter, when to supply Berlin would be much more difficult? Notwithstanding the blockade, efforts were continued to form a central government for Western Germany. On September 1, delegates went to the Parliamentary Council at Bonn to draw up a constitution or "basic law" for Germany.

Comments of American Ambassador to Russia Bedell Smith on Negotiations with Stalin, August, 1948

. . . Before we had time to become too elated, Stalin gave us a dash of cold water by insisting that something be said in the agreement about the plan to establish a Western German government. I reminded him that he had not made suspension of these plans a condition of the agreement. He persisted, however, that some mention of this question be made and suggested the following paragraph be included in a four-power communiqué:

The question of the London decision was also discussed, including the formation of a Western German government. The discussion took place in an atmosphere of mutual understanding.

Taken by themselves, these words would seem harmless enough to the average Western reader—indeed, they might seem desirable, as indicating a friendly understanding. But in this context, they were dynamite. The people of Germany and all Western Europeans knew very well that it would have been impossible for us to have discussed this question in an "atmosphere of mutual understanding" unless we had secretly accepted the Soviet condition and had agreed to abandon the Western German government idea in exchange for some blockade concessions—an action we could have taken only with a figurative pistol pointed at our heads. The effect on the people of Western Germany would have been enormous.

I had learned previously from reliable sources that Soviet diplomats in satellite countries had predicted confidentially the imminent announcement of a great political-diplomatic victory. This was to be it. The point of the hook was cleverly covered, but the barb was there none the less.

I said that I would inform my government of Stalin's desire, but that I did not anticipate that the United States could accede to any such wording unless the proposed paragraph also contained the definite statement that "no agreement was reached on the subject."

For all practical purposes, I believe

the conference really ended at this moment.

    •   •   •   •   •

At our last meeting with Stalin, we had agreed to meet again on the date fixed for the military governors to conclude their discussions. But before this day came I heard that Stalin had left Moscow on vacation, and I knew beyond question that the Politburo intended the session in Berlin to end in disagreement. But I still was astonished at the open hostility and indifference displayed by the Soviet commander, who not only disregarded the terms of the joint directive but even insisted on new traffic restrictions.

I was not, however, surprised at the final result. Molotov had tried to make a trade and failed. Stalin, confident of the effectiveness of the blockade, had given us a chance to delay our plans for a Western German government, without loss of prestige. When we refused, he lost interest in discussions that would produce nothing of benefit to the Soviet Union. From the Kremlin's point of view, it remained only to conclude the incident in such a way as to get the greatest amount of propaganda for itself and to place the maximum blame on the West.[22]

Comments of General Clay on Allied Military Governors' Meetings, August 31 to September 7, 1948

The discussions to implement the directive were technical. We offered to accept the East mark as the sole Berlin currency provided the city banking system was placed under quadripartite control. We insisted that we have access to reasonable amounts of East marks, which would be derived from the sale of food we brought into the city, and also the opportunity to export from the western sectors finished products to pay for the raw materials we would bring into the industrial plants. Sokolovsky rejected these proposals and brought up a point which had not previously been discussed in suggesting restrictions on the movement of commercial aircraft into Berlin. We made it very clear that we would not discuss any restrictions on the only transport facility which remained under our control. The seventh and last session of these meetings adjourned on September 7, the date on which our report had to be submitted to governments. We had spent many hours in discussions during which agreement had been reached only on technical details involved in the proposed currency change-over. The basic principles which appeared to have been solved in the Moscow directive remained unsolved and our efforts to obtain agreement had failed.

The three Western military governors submitted a joint report which said in part:

> We can sum up the over-all position by reporting that after some days of little progress, Marshal Sokolovsky has given ground on most of the subsidiary issues. . . . There remain three main points of disagreement. We see no sign of an intention on the part of Soviet representatives to yield on these three points and we see no chance of real progress here until action has been taken on a governmental level.

These three points of disagreement were: Soviet rejection of a four-power finance committee with supervisory power over the issue of East marks by the German Bank of Emission; their insistence on complete control of trade with Berlin; and their demand for restrictions in civil air traffic.[23]

[22]Walter Bedell Smith, *My Three Years in Moscow* (Philadelphia: J. B. Lippincott Co., 1949), pp. 240–44. Copyright 1949, by Walter Bedell Smith. Published by J. B. Lippincott Company.

[23]Clay, *op. cit.*, pp. 369–71.

With the breakdown of the Military Governors' Meeting, the only course remaining was to resume negotiations at a higher level. The Western governments protested in a note of September 14 to which Russia replied four days later, refusing to accept any point of the Western arguments. Finally, on September 26, 1948, the Western powers, "in view of the insistence of the Soviet Government upon maintaining the blockade and upon the institution of restrictions on air communications," felt compelled to refer the problem to the Security Council of the United Nations. There, early in October, arguments ensued as to whether the Security Council could deal with such an issue.[24]

FOR CONSIDERATION   In spite of Soviet opposition, the Security Council did decide to undertake the solution of the Berlin problem and established a Technical Committee on Currency and Trade of Berlin, which started work on November 30. Was the issue fundamentally a technical one? With Russia possessing a veto in the Security Council, was there any real chance of settling the problem by UN action? Did the Western powers turn the problem over to the UN in the hope of reaching a solution?

Excerpt from a Speech by Russian Delegate Andrei Vyshinsky to the Security Council, October 5, 1948

This legal procedure should be to refer the question to the Council of Foreign Ministers. We are told that the four Powers have been unable to agree on anything until now. Now I ask you . . . when and where did the Council of Foreign Ministers study the Berlin question? Will you who have raised the question of Berlin be good enough to show me a document, mention a date, or name those present and tell me the subject, and the decisions if any, taken by the Council at any discussion of the Berlin question. I maintain that no one has examined the question.

.   .   .   .   .

Now attempts are again being made to circumvent the Council of Foreign

Ministers and to include this question forthwith on the agenda of the Security Council. Such haste is very suspicious. The situation with which we are now faced is that a legal organ established by international agreements is being ignored. An attempt is being made to justify this on the grounds that the negotiations held so far have not led to any positive results and that consequently this question has been referred to the Security Council. But in fact no such negotiations have taken place. There have been no negotiations on the Berlin question in the Council of Foreign Ministers. There have only been preliminary discussions—an informal discussion—in Moscow. The Council of Foreign Ministers has not had its say. Are we then not justified in saying that the three Governments which have appealed to the Security Council are pursuing aims which have nothing in common with any real desire to settle the German question?[25]

[24]See *Germany 1947–1949: The Story in Documents,* Department of State Publication No. 3556 (Washington, D.C.: U.S. Government Printing Office, 1949), pp. 223–30.

[25]UN Security Council, *Official Records,* 3rd Year, No. 114 (1948), pp. 16–18.

Press Interview of Stalin with *Pravda* Correspondents, October 28, 1948

QUESTION: Is it true that in August of this year agreement had already once been reached between the four Powers on the Berlin question?

REPLY: Yes, it is true. . . . This agreement does not infringe upon anyone's prestige: it takes account of the interests of the parties to it and guarantees the possibility of further cooperation. But the Governments of the United States of America and Britain disavowed their representatives in Moscow and declared that this agreement was null and void, i.e., they violated it, deciding to place the question before the Security Council where the Anglo-Americans have an assured majority.

QUESTION: Is it true that recently in Paris, when the question was being discussed in the Security Council, in unofficial talks agreement was again reached on the question of the situation in Berlin already before it was voted on in the Security Council?

REPLY: Yes, it is true. . . . But the representatives of the U.S.A. and Britain again declared this agreement nonexistent.

QUESTION: What is the fact of the matter? Can it not be explained?

REPLY: The point is that the inspirers of the aggressive policy of the United States of America and Britain do not consider themselves interested in agreement and cooperation with the U.S.S.R. . . . The instigators of war, who are striving to unleash a new war, fear more than anything else agreement and cooperation with the U.S.S.R., since a policy of agreement with the U.S.S.R. undermines the positions of the warmongers and deprives the aggressive policy of these gentlemen of its objective. . . .[26]

[26]V. M. Molotov, *Stalin's Policy of Peace and Democracy*, Supplement to *Soviet News, London* (1948), pp. 23–24. Quoted by permission of *Soviet News*, London.

A lasting result of the Berlin crisis was a division in the Berlin city administration. On September 6, 1948, the City Assembly had been broken up and the democratic members fled to the British Zone where a Rump Assembly was established. As the constitution, approved by the four occupying powers in 1946, called for city-wide elections, there was some anxiety as to what would happen. The elections completed the split: thereafter the city had not only two currencies, but two governments. The events at the time of the breakup in December, 1948, are here described.

Comments of General Frank Howley

The final date set for the elections was December 5. As we anticipated, the Russians refused to approve the constitution, the election procedure, or the date. They didn't exactly say no, they merely attached conditions that the city government couldn't possibly meet.

Although the Russian obstruction machine had shifted into high gear against us, the democratic parties in the city government went ahead with preparations. They had to surmount high obstacles in the preliminary stages of organizing a city-wide ballot. To block election preparations, a Soviet tribunal was convened and found the leading democratic leaders guilty of being "Fascists and warmongers." Ignoring this ludicrous charge, the city government decided to proceed with the elections and, in all fairness, to permit delegations from the Russian zone to sit in on sessions of the *Magistrat* and the Assembly, if they desired.

Five days before the elections, the Russians completed the split in the Berlin administration. A puppet *Magistrat* was established in the Russian sector, after an *opéra bouffe* meeting in the Berlin Opera House.

.   .   .   .   .

Reports were circulated that Communist gangs would march into the Western sectors and attack voters. I let the Russians and their Red stooges know that, if anyone marched into our sector, he wouldn't run into a handful of frightened, unarmed Germans but into the United States Army. I put it very bluntly: Attempts to use force would be met by force. The democratic parties did what they should have done before: they organized their own strong-arm squads to take care of Communist rowdies at pre-election rallies.

Berliners in the three Western sectors replied to Russian threats and blandishments by going to the polls in greater numbers than anyone expected. No longer did the multiplicity of party programs obscure the decision. The issue was as clear as a newly washed windowpane.

My official report reads:

It was a choice between two fundamentally opposed political systems: Totalitarianism, supported by a police state devoid of any basic civil rights for the individual, and Western World Democracy, where the traditional constitutional safeguards of individual rights and political liberty prevail.

With no Communist candidates, the election campaign of the three democratic parties was not conducted along strictly party lines but as a joint demonstration against totalitarianism. Voting reached a total of 83.6 per cent of the electorate, far larger than in any American presidential election, in spite of bad weather and lack of public transport. The biggest turnout was in the American sector, followed by the British and the French.

The results were:

SPD (Social Democrats)
 64.5 per cent   76 seats
CDU (Christian Democrats)
 19.4 per cent   26 seats
LDP (Liberal Democrats)
 16.1 per cent   17 seats[27]

Excerpt from an Article, "Divisive Tactics of Anglo-American Authorities in Berlin," by E. Zhukov, Published in *Pravda*, December 6, 1948

On October 20, General Kotikov, the Soviet commandant of Berlin . . . declared himself in favor of holding elections, but with the provision that [certain] elementary and essential conditions be observed. These minimum conditions [freedom for activity of Soviet-sponsored political groups] necessary for holding unified democratic elections throughout the whole of Berlin, which provided, first of all, for the creation of a normal atmosphere for holding such elections in the Western sectors of the city, were rejected. . . . The Anglo-American authorities gave instructions for holding separate "elections" in the Western sectors of Berlin.

The terror employed against the democratic elements in these sectors was further intensified. The American garrison was brought into fighting readiness; armored cars and tanks began to parade through the streets of the Western sectors for the obvious purpose of intimidating the voters, or, as Colonel Howley expressed it, in order "to make the elections safe."

The separate elections that took place on December 5 in the Western sectors were the usual farce; their goal was the final division of Berlin.

.   .   .   .   .

The Anglo-American stage managers of

---

[27]Howley, *op. cit.*, pp. 225–28.

the separate "elections" cannot shirk the responsibility for systematically conducting a policy of separatism and for refusing to cooperate and to observe the quadripartite agreements relating to Germany and Berlin. No subterfuges, no false references to a non-existent "Soviet blockade" can obscure the fact that the American, English and French occupation authorities have consistently and with premeditation refused to exercise quadripartite control over Germany, and that they have proceeded from illegal, separatist tactics in relation to Western Germany to illegal, separatist tactics in Berlin.[28]

Comments of Willy Brandt

The stock of coal was supposed to last for thirty days, but it was impossible to replenish it to the same extent as the urgently needed food. Apartments and the greater part of offices—even the administration buildings—could no longer be heated. Every family got for the whole winter an allotment of twenty-five pounds of coal and three boxes of wood. Some fuel was smuggled in by black-marketeers. Most of the families were glad when they could keep one room of their apartment moderately warm for a few hours of the day. Fortunately, the winter was not particularly severe.

Cooking in Berlin was done ninety per cent by gas. During the first five months

of the blockade consumers were limited to half of their previous gas consumption. Electric current was only available for four hours daily, usually in two periods of two hours each. These periods came at different times of the day in different sections of the city, and people had to rise at odd hours in order to take advantage of the available current. The preparation of a cup of hot ersatz coffee or of a bowl of soup put the housewife before a nearly insoluble problem. . . .

In the meantime the Communists had changed their tactics: after threats and intimidations they all of a sudden made a tempting offer to the West Berliners. They asserted that the Soviet government had brought large quantities of foodstuffs into the East sector. All the West Berliners had to do if they wanted to get that food was to register with ration offices in the East sector. The answer was very impressive. The ration office in Treptow had sent out invitations to 285,000 persons. At first only twenty persons from the West sector registered. Sixteen persons registered in Prenzlauer Berg, and nineteen in Pankow. By the end of the year 85,000 of two million Berliners had accepted the Communist offer—four per cent of the population. And most of them were people who lived in the West sectors, but who worked in the East sector and continued to buy their rations there as they had always done.[29]

[28]*Soviet Press Translations*, January 1, 1949 (Seattle: Far Eastern and Russian Institute, University of Washington, 1949), pp. 3-4.

[29]Willy Brandt (as told to Leo Lania), *My Road to Berlin* (Garden City, N.Y.: Doubleday & Co., Inc., 1960), pp. 196-97. Copyright © 1960 by Leo Lania. Reprinted by permission of Doubleday & Co., Inc.

During the winter of 1948–49, while the UN unsuccessfully wrestled with the Berlin problem, and while the airlift continued to supply the city, other matters, more or less closely related to the crisis, were developing. At Bonn, representatives of Western Germany attempted to draw up a "basic law" that would satisfy the Western powers; the powers themselves were trying to draw up an occupation statute which would meet all the requirements of retaining certain basic controls. Meanwhile the signatories of the Brussels Pact began serious work to draw up a North Atlantic

Treaty of Defense, the basic plan of which was concluded on March 15. The Pact itself, expanded to include Norway, Canada, Denmark, Iceland, Italy, and Portugal, was signed on April 4, 1949.

The discussions on West German government proceeded with great difficulty. Russia, in fact, stole a march on the West by sponsoring a constitution for East Germany which was adopted by the People's Council on March 19, 1949. Finally, however, on April 8, during the meetings of the Western Foreign Ministers at Washington, an occupation statute, which is quoted in part, was drawn up.

FOR CONSIDERATION   To what extent was the North Atlantic Pact a result of the Berlin blockade? Was the earlier Brussels Pact a cause or a result of tension in Germany?

Occupation Statute Issued by the Governments of France, the United States, and the United Kingdom, April 8, 1949

1. During the period in which it is necessary that the occupation continue, the Governments of France, the United States and the United Kingdom desire and intend that the German people shall enjoy self-government to the maximum possible degree consistent with such occupation. The Federal State and the participating Laender shall have, subject only to the limitations in this Instrument, full legislative, executive and judicial powers in accordance with the Basic Law and with their respective constitutions.

2. In order to ensure the accomplishment of the basic purposes of the occupation, powers in the following fields are specifically reserved, including the right to request and verify information and statistics needed by the occupation authorities:

(*a*) disarmament and demilitarization, including related fields of scientific research, prohibitions and restrictions on industry and civil aviation;

(*b*) controls in regard to the Ruhr, restitution, reparations, decartelization, deconcentration, nondiscrimination in trade matters, foreign interests in Germany and claims against Germany;

(*c*) foreign affairs, including interna-

Kukrynisky in Literaturnaya Gazeta *(Moscow)—Sovfoto*

A Russian Comment on the 'Western Bloc'

tional agreements made by or on behalf of Germany;

(*d*) displaced persons and the admission of refugees;

(*e*) protection, prestige, and security of Allied forces, dependents, employees, and representatives, their immunities and satisfaction of occupation costs and their other requirements;

(*f*) respect for the Basic Law and the Land constitutions;

(*g*) control over foreign trade and exchange;

(*h*) control over internal action, only to the minimum extent necessary to ensure use of funds, food and other supplies in such manner as to reduce to a minimum the need for external assistance to Germany;

(*i*) control of the care and treatment in German prisons of persons charged before or sentenced by the courts or tribunals of the occupying powers or occupation authorities; over the carrying out of sentences imposed on them; and over questions of amnesty, pardon or release in relation to them.[30]

[30]*A Decade of American Foreign Policy*, pp. 586–87.

It appeared that nothing now could hinder the announcement that a government had been formed in West Germany. But while the occupation statute had been delivered to the Parliamentary Council (the West German constitutional convention), difficulties on the degree of centralization held up the final drafting of the "basic law." The three military governors met with German representatives on April 14 and agreed to hold further discussions on April 25. Robert D. Murphy, representing the State Department, came to Frankfurt to speed up the negotiations. At this point a story released by the Soviet news agency *Tass* provoked a State Department communiqué revealing that negotiations to end the Berlin blockade had been in progress for weeks. Quoted below are the Stalin interview referred to by *Tass*, the *Tass* release, the State Department communiqué and pertinent comments by Generals Clay and Howley, and by Robert Murphy.

FOR CONSIDERATION   Communists accused the State Department of prolonging the Berlin crisis in order to bring about an "aggressive military alliance." Is there validity to such an accusation? Why was Murphy anxious to conclude quickly the arrangements for a West German government? The recommendations of the UN Technical Committee,[31] which had completed its work in February, were rejected by the Western powers in March. Why were extra-UN negotiations more successful? What are possible theories as to why Russia decided to end the blockade?

Interview of Stalin Given to Kingsbury Smith, January 27, 1949

QUESTION: If the U.S.A., the United Kingdom, and France agreed to postpone the establishment of a separate Western German State, pending a meeting of the Council of Foreign Ministers to consider the German problem as a whole, would the U.S.S.R. be prepared to remove the restrictions which the Soviet authorities have imposed on communications between Berlin and the Western zones of Germany?

ANSWER: Provided the U.S.A., Great Britain and France observe the conditions set forth in the question, the Soviet Government sees no obstacles to lifting transport restrictions, on the understanding however that transport and trade restrictions introduced by the three Powers should be lifted simultaneously.[32]

Statement on Berlin Blockade Negotiations Released by *Tass*, April 26, 1949

.   .   .   .   .

On February 15 the United States representative in the UN, Dr. Jessup, requested the USSR representative, M. Malik . . .

[31]*Germany 1947–1949, op. cit.*, pp. 230–71.

[32]Released by *Tass*, January 30, 1949.

to explain the circumstances that, in Marshal Stalin's reply to correspondent Mr. Kingsbury Smith, . . . nothing is said with regard to a single currency for Berlin. M. Malik told Dr. Jessup in this connection that the absence . . . was not accidental, and that the question of currency for Berlin could be discussed at the Foreign Ministers' Council during examination of the question of Germany. Dr. Jessup then asked M. Malik to explain whether the . . . restrictions . . . could be lifted prior to the meeting of the Foreign Ministers' Council.

On March 21 M. Malik said . . . that, if agreement were reached as to the date when the Council of Foreign Ministers would meet, the . . . restrictions . . . could be lifted before the Council of Foreign Ministers started its work. . . .

According to the information at the disposal of *Tass*, M. Malik's last talk with Dr. Jessup on the questions touched upon took place on April 10.[33]

Statement on Berlin Blockade Negotiations Released by Department of State, April 26, 1949

.   .   .   .   .

On April 10 Mr. Malik again asked Mr. Jessup to call upon him at that time and again stated the position of the Soviet Government. From this statement it appeared that there were still certain points requiring clarification.

As a result of this meeting, further discussions took place between the three Governments, which have resulted in a more detailed formulation of their position, which will be conveyed by Mr. Jessup to Mr. Malik.

If the present position of the Soviet Government is as stated in the *Tass* Agency release as published in the American press, the way appears clear for a lifting of the blockade and a meeting of the Council of Foreign Ministers. No final conclusion upon this can be reached until further exchanges of view with Mr. Malik.[34]

Comments of General Clay

At this time informal conversations were taking place in New York between Dr. Jessup and Jacob Malik, Soviet representative to the Security Council. I knew nothing of these conversations and on the day preceding the press report of the discussions I had stated in a press conference in Berlin that I knew of no talks looking to the lifting of the blockade. Mr. Murphy, who had returned from Washington to Berlin to help me in the negotiations for the approval of the constitution of western Germany, had not felt free to tell me what he knew. I first learned of these discussions from the newspapers and subsequently from General Robertson after Dr. Jessup had included French and British representatives in the discussions. While I understood the necessity for keeping these conversations secret and the difficulties of maintaining secrecy when information passes through many hands, I was somewhat chagrined to hear the story this way.[35]

Comments of General Howley

With customary unconcern for the men on the spot, Washington neglected to inform us directly in Berlin of what was happening. I knew nothing about the negotiations, and I am sure that Clay was in the same unenviable position. We didn't even know that the American and Russian delegates at Lake Success were discussing the matter, although we did hear faint rumors that something in our department was developing. Robert Murphy visited Berlin during the discussions

---

[33]Released by *Tass*, April 26, 1949.

[34]*A Decade of American Foreign Policy*, pp. 936–37.

[35]Clay, *op. cit.*, p. 390.

and never dropped a hint. He must have had orders from Washington to keep it dark. It was a disconcerting position for Clay and me, responsible for American Military Government in Germany and Berlin.

I first learned that the blockade had been lifted from a State Department release to the newspapers.[36]

Comments of Robert Murphy

The end of my assignment to Germany came suddenly when I was recalled to Washington by the new Secretary of State, Dean Acheson, to serve there as Director of the Office of German and Austrian Affairs. It was a snowy night in February 1949 when my friends bade me farewell at Tempelhof, the airport in the American sector of Berlin. . . .

When I reached Washington, I learned that top-secret negotiations for ending the Berlin blockade had been going on for some time at the United Nations in New York between the Soviet delegate there, Jacob A. Malik, and Dr. Philip C. Jessup, who at this writing is a member of the International Court of Justice at The Hague. . . .

Jessup felt that he had achieved an exceptionally cordial relationship with the Soviet diplomat, and he depended heavily upon Malik's good will to reach an agreement on Berlin. I did not succeed in convincing Jessup . . . that Soviet negotiators cannot be influenced by personal friendships. At first Malik proposed outrageous conditions, making acceptance impossible.

But after weeks of talk Malik receded from this extreme position, thus giving the impression of substantial Soviet concessions. The Jessup-Malik talks were kept so secret that I was not permitted to tell even Clay about them when I made a quick trip to Germany that spring. Clay was put in the embarrassing position of first hearing about the negotiations from his British colleague in Berlin. . . .

The success of the Airlift provided a heady sense of triumph, but actually the Washington policymakers had limited themselves to an experiment which merely proved that it was possible to keep alive a great modern city by the use of air transport alone. Few observers seemed to realize that our decision to depend exclusively upon the Airlift was a surrender of our hard-won rights in Berlin, a surrender which has plagued us ever since. The crucial point of the Berlin settlement was that the United States Government failed to ensure its legitimate claims for surface-level access to that city. During the entire period of the blockade the Russians denied the Western powers the use of ground and water routes to Berlin, and access was made no more secure by the terms of the settlement than before the blockade.

Could the Western powers have obtained better terms from Stalin in the Berlin settlement? In my view, the answer is "Yes!" Stalin was getting nowhere in this skirmish and had intimated that he was disposed to cut his losses. Stalin must have been both surprised and pleased when the American negotiators permitted Moscow to retain virtually all the controls which had made trouble for us in Berlin.[37]

[36]Howley, op. cit., p. 262.

[37]Murphy, op. cit., pp. 320–21.

The Jessup-Malik discussions reached a successful conclusion on May 5, 1949, when it was announced that on May 12 the blockade would be lifted. All restrictions imposed since March 1, 1948, were to be removed, and 11 days thereafter the Council of Foreign Ministers was to meet at Paris. On the same day that the blockade was lifted, the Western military governors approved the Bonn constitution, and shortly thereafter a government in West Germany began to function.

From May 23 to June 21, 1949, the Sixth Meeting of the Council of Foreign Ministers attempted to arrange the following German problems: unity, including economic principles, political principles, and Allied control; Berlin and the currency problem; a peace treaty.

Excerpt from Statement by President Truman, June 21, 1949

The American delegation went to Paris with the serious intention of developing a constructive program which would meet the requirements for all of Germany and would safeguard the interests of all Four Powers in insuring that Germany would achieve its reconstruction along peaceful and democratic lines. At the same time, the Western powers were determined not to compromise the democratic principles and the conditions which must be established throughout Germany before an economically sound and workable solution can be found for German unity. They were equally determined not to jeopardize the basic freedoms as they now exist in Western Germany merely to obtain a nominal political unity. In these objectives they knew they had the support of the freely elected representatives of the majority of the German people.

The Soviet Union, on the other hand, sought a return to Potsdam and its system, which the Russians had rendered unworkable by their misuse of the unlimited veto. They refused to recognize the important progress which has been made in Western Germany since 1945.

In these circumstances, real progress for the unification of Germany and its people was impossible. The most that could be achieved was a working arrangement designed to mitigate the abnormal situation of a still divided Germany. This arrangement is no more nor less than what it professes to be—a means of dealing with what actually exists. It reaffirms the lifting of the Berlin blockade and contains the recognition of the occupation authorities of their obligation to insure the movement of persons and goods between the Eastern and Western zones and between Berlin and the zones.[38]

[38]*A Decade of American Foreign Policy*, pp. 113–14.

POSTSCRIPT   As President Truman stated in 1949, the raising of the blockade produced no permanent settlement, and the split into East and West became solidified with the establishment of the Western Federal Republic, of which Adenauer became Chancellor. In 1955, Russia granted sovereignty to East Germany. No easy resolution of differences presented itself, and Russia continued to be confronted by an embarrassing exodus to the West of some 230,000 East Germans per year. By 1961, the flow had increased to unacceptable proportions, and on August 13 the Wall gave physical evidence of Communist failure. Berlin had become a symbol of Western resistance and a manifestation to the entire world of what freedom meant. No one has expressed the spirit of West Berlin more cogently than President Kennedy, in a speech delivered five months before his death.

Excerpt from a Speech of President Kennedy in Berlin, June 26, 1963

I know of no town, no city that has been besieged for 18 years that still lives with the vitality and the force and the hope and the determination of the city of West Berlin.

While the wall is the most obvious and vivid demonstration of the failures of the Communist system, all the world can see we take no satisfaction in it, for it is, as your Mayor has said, an offense not only against history, but an offense against humanity, separating families, dividing husbands and wives and brothers and sisters and dividing a people who wish to be joined together.

What is true of this city is true of Germany. Real lasting peace in Europe can never be assured as long as one German out of four is denied the elementary right of free men, and that is to make a free choice.

In 18 years of peace and good faith this generation of Germans has earned the right to be free, including the right to unite their families and their nation in lasting peace with good-will to all people.

You live in a defended island of freedom, but your life is part of the main. So let me ask you as I close, to lift your eyes beyond the dangers of today to the hopes of tomorrow, beyond the freedom merely of this city of Berlin and all your country of Germany to the advance of freedom everywhere, beyond the wall to to the day of peace with justice, beyond yourselves and ourselves to all mankind.

Freedom is indivisible and when one man is enslaved who are free? When all are free, then we can look forward to that day when this city will be joined as one and this country and this great continent of Europe in a peaceful and hopeful globe.

When that day finally comes, as it will, the people of West Berlin can take sober satisfaction in the fact that they were in the front lines for almost two decades.

All free men, wherever they may live, are citizens of Berlin. And therefore, as a free man, I take pride in the words "ich bin ein Berliner."[39]

_____
[39]*New York Times,* June 27, 1963.

BIBLIOGRAPHY

SOURCES USED IN THIS PROBLEM

1. *Collections and Official Documents*

The Berlin Crisis: A Report on the Moscow Discussions, 1948. Department of State Publication No. 3298. Washington, D.C.: U.S. Government Printing Office, 1948.

British White Paper, Cmd. 7534. London: Her Majesty's Stationery Office, 1948.

A Decade of American Foreign Policy: Basic Documents, 1941–49. Sen. Doc. No. 123, 81st Cong., 1st sess. Washington, D.C.: U.S. Government Printing Office, 1950.

Germany 1947–1949: The Story in Documents. Department of State Publication No. 3556. Washington, D.C.: U.S. Government Printing Office, 1949.

HEIDELMEYER, W. and HINDRICHS, G. (eds.). *Documents on Berlin 1943–1963.* Munich: R. Oldenbourg Verlag, 1963.

Information on Poland. Warsaw: Ministry of Foreign Affairs.

MOLOTOV, V. M. *Problems of Foreign Policy: Speeches and Statements, April 1945– November 1948.* Moscow: Foreign Languages Publishing House, 1949.

MOLOTOV, V. M. *Stalin's Policy of Peace and Democracy.* Supplement to *Soviet News* (*London*), 1948.

The New York Times.

Official Records. UN Security Council.

Soviet Press Translations. Seattle: Far Eastern and Russian Institute, University of Washington, 1949.

Tass. Soviet News Agency.

2. Others

BRANDT, WILLY (as told to LEO LANIA). *My Road to Berlin.* Garden City, N.Y.: Doubleday, 1960.

CLAY, LUCIUS D. *Decision in Germany.* Garden City, N.Y.: Doubleday, 1950.

HOWLEY, FRANK. *Berlin Command.* New York: Putnam's, 1950.

MILLIS, WALTER and DUFFIELD, E. S. *The Forrestal Diaries.* New York: Viking, 1951.

MURPHY, ROBERT D. *Diplomat among Warriors.* Garden City, N.Y.: Doubleday, 1964.

SMITH, WALTER BEDELL. *My Three Years in Moscow.* Philadelphia: J. B. Lippincott, 1952.

SELECT LIST OF BOOKS RECOMMENDED FOR FURTHER READING

ALMOND, G. A. (ed.). *The Struggle for Democracy in Germany.* Chapel Hill, N.C.: University of North Carolina Press, 1949.

BRODERICK, A. H. *Danger Spot of Europe.* New York: Philosophical Library, 1952.

BRZEZINSKI, Z. *Alternative to Partition.* New York: McGraw-Hill, 1965.

DAVIDSON, EUGENE. *The Death and Life of Germany.* New York: Knopf, 1959.

DAVIDSON, W. PHILLIPS. *The Berlin Blockade: A Study in Cold War Politics.* Princeton, N.J.: Princeton University Press, 1958.

FREUND, GERALD. *Germany between Two Wars.* New York: Harcourt, Brace, 1961.

FRIEDERICH, CARL J. *The Soviet Zone of Germany.* New Haven, Conn.: Yale University Press, 1956.

GOLAY, JOHN F. *The Founders of the Federal Republic of Germany.* Chicago: University of Chicago Press, 1958.

HEIDENHEIMER, ARNOLD J. *Adenauer and the CDU.* The Hague: Martinus Nijhoff, 1960.

HILL, RUSSELL. *The Struggle for Germany.* New York: Harper, 1947.

HISCOCKS, RICHARD. *Democracy in Western Germany.* New York: Oxford University Press, 1957.

LaFEBER, WALTER. *America, Russia, and the Cold War, 1945–1966.* New York: Wiley, 1967.

MORGENTHAU, HANS J. (ed.). *Germany and the Future of Europe.* Chicago: University of Chicago Press, 1951.

NETTL, J. P. *Eastern Zone and Soviet Policy in Germany, 1945–1950.* New York: Oxford University Press, 1951.

PRITTIE, TERENCE. *Germany Divided.* Boston: Little Brown, 1960.

RATCHFORD, B. U. and ROSS, W. D. *Berlin Reparations Assignment.* Chapel Hill, N.C.: University of North Carolina Press, 1947.

STAHL, WALTER. *The Policies of Post-war Germany.* New York: Praeger, 1963.

WILLIS, FRANK ROY. *The French in Germany.* Stanford, Calif.: Stanford University Press, 1962.

WINDSOR, PHILIP. *City on Leave: Berlin, 1945–1962.* New York: Praeger, 1963.

ZINK, HAROLD. *The United States in Germany, 1944–1955.* Princeton, N.J.: Van Nostrand, 1957.

SECTION VI

The Twilight of Colonialism

THE FRENCH IN VIETNAM

Independence, Dien Bien Phu, and the Geneva Conference, 1945-54

The ending of colonialism has proved to be one of the most agonizing processes inherited by the world after 1945. In Africa, in the Middle East, and in Southeast Asia the transfer of power, effected sometimes peacefully and sometimes violently, has caused the greatest basic changes and up-heavals of the postwar era. Nowhere have there been such dislocations and violence as in Indochina which, caught between the West and the vast Communist land masses of China and Russia, has been fighting a struggle not merely for independence but for ideologies as well.

Shortly after the Japanese surrender, and before the French returned in force to Indochina, it appeared barely possible that a Vietnamese Republic, declared on September 2, 1945, might achieve recognition. Head of the short-lived Republic was Communist Ho Chi-minh, who was interviewed in November, 1945, by Harold Isaacs.

Comments of Harold Isaacs

When I saw his picture painted on a huge banner on one of the main streets, I was fairly certain. When he walked into the sitting room on the second floor of the Résidence Supérieure and held out his hand smiling, I knew he was indeed my Shanghai friend of long ago.

"You have changed," he said, looking me over with cocked head.—"So have you," I replied.—"You used to have black hair and you were thinner," he said; "and I? How have I changed?"

Ho Chi-minh had become an old man in these twelve years. His hair had turned gray. He wore now a scraggly little moustache and a beard of thin long strands. His cheeks were deep hollows, his skin like old paper. His brown eyes shone with a quizzical brightness. He wore a faded khaki jacket and trousers, a white shirt and old slippers.

"And now," he said, "I'm president of

the provisional government of the Republic of Viet Nam. They call me 'Excellency.' Funny, eh?"

He spoke much better English than I remembered him speaking. As he told me of what had passed with him in these years, I understood his painful thinness and the two teeth missing, fallen from the front of his mouth. He had gotten to Europe, then returned to Hong Kong. He made his way to the Indochinese frontier region, where for years he lived the life of a wanderer in the mountains, meeting friends, tortuously keeping contact with his fellows farther south, slipping into Indochina again and again and making good his escape. There was a long siege in Chinese prisons. "All the way up to Liuchow and Kweilin," he grinned. "It was at Kweilin that my teeth began to fall out. I looked at myself once and then tried never to look again. I was skin on

bones, and covered with rotten sores. I guess I was pretty sick." The Chinese held him as, of all things, a French spy!

Clear finally of his Chinese jailers, he returned to the border region, began organizing guerrillas in the mountains that rim southern Kwangsi and the Tonkin frontier. In March he crossed over and was the leader of the bands which made contact with the Americans, received arms and training and direction from American officers, and succeeded in three months in liberating large areas in the northern provinces. When the Viet Minh congress met at Coabang just as the Japanese surrendered, they named him president of the provisional government. He entered Hanoi and was riotously greeted in streets jammed with demonstrators.[1]

---

[1]Harold Isaacs, *No Peace for Asia* (New York: The Macmillan Company, 1947; Cambridge, Mass.: MIT Press, 1967), pp. 163–64.

Toward the end of 1945, the French had brought 50,000 troops into Indochina, and had appointed Admiral d'Argenlieu as Governor-General. The French were willing to negotiate with the new government, but not in terms of complete immediate independence. An agreement was reached in March, 1946.

Agreement between France and Vietnam, March 6, 1946

The French Government recognizes the Republic of Vietnam as a free state, having its own government, parliament, army and treasury, belonging to the Indo-Chinese Federation and to the French Union. . . .

The Government of Vietnam declares itself ready to accept amicably the French Army when, in conformance with international agreements, it relieves the Chinese forces. . . .

Annex

. . . The relief forces will be composed of

(*a*) 10,000 Vietnamese with their Vietnamese cadres, under the military control of Vietnam.

(*b*) 15,000 French, including the French forces now located in the territories of Vietnam north of the sixteenth parallel. These elements must be composed solely of French of metropolitan origin, except for soldiers guarding Japanese prisoners.

These forces, as a whole, will be placed

under supreme French command with the assistance of Vietnamese representatives.

The advance, stationing, and employment of these forces will be defined during a general staff conference between the representatives of the French and Vietnamese commands, which will be held upon the landing of the French units.

Mixed commissions will be created at all echelons to ensure liaison in a spirit of friendly cooperation between the French and Vietnamese forces. . . .[2]

[2]From *Notes Documentaires et Etudes*, No. 548, in Allan B. Cole (ed.), *Conflict in Indo-China and International Repercussions* (Ithaca, N.Y.: Cornell University Press, 1956), pp. 40–42. © 1956 by the Fletcher School of Law and Diplomacy. Used by permission of Cornell University Press.

The convention of March, 1946, was never adequately implemented. To the Vietminh (a contraction of "Viet Nam Doc Lap Dong Minh": League for the Independence of Vietnam) d'Argenlieu seemed to be using French power to reestablish the old colonial relationship. Fighting broke out in December, 1946, and by 1947, with the failure of French negotiations with Ho Chi-minh at Fontainbleau, full-scale war was in progress. D'Argenlieu was recalled and Paris arranged for the former emperor, Bao Dai, to become head of a pro-French regime. This development was confirmed by an agreement of June, 1948.

Agreement of Ha Long Bay Recognizing the Independence of Vietnam with Bao Dai as Head, June 5, 1948

(1) France solemnly recognizes the independence of Vietnam whose right it is to bring about freely its unity. Vietnam, on its part, proclaims its adhesion to the French Union as a state associated with France. The independence of Vietnam has no limits other than those emanating from its membership in the French Union.

(2) Vietnam undertakes to respect French national rights and interests, to assure in its Constitution respect for democratic principles, and to utilize preferably French counsellors and technicians for its needs in its internal and economic organization.

(3) After the constitution of a Provisional Government, the representatives of Vietnam will agree with the representatives of the French Republic on various special arrangements in the cultural, diplomatic, military, economic, financial, and technical spheres.[3]

[3]Cole, *op. cit.*, p. 72.

By March, 1949 (in the Elysée Agreements), Bao Dai's government had concurred in a formula that would unite an independent Vietnam "within the framework of the French Union." This state was recognized in February, 1950, by the United States, which began to send aid, both financial (some $500,000,000 annually) and military.

In 1950, the situation changed radically, because by this time Mao

Tse-tung had gained control of China and was able to bring significant assistance to the Vietminh. Under their capable general, Vo Nguyen Giap, the Vietminh had by their guerilla tactics infiltrated all of Northern Vietnam, had encircled Hanoi, and were in position to move onto the offensive. Against them France sent its distinguished general Jean de Lattre de Tassigny who, however, died of cancer in 1952 before any significant progress had been made.

At this time the French had established a fortified post (which they referred to as a *herisson*: hedgehog) at Na Sam. This was an "airhead," a foothold supplied by air from which sallies could be made. Na Sam was visited in 1953 by a British writer who here describes it.

Comments of Bernard Newman

The troops lived in dug-outs or shelters, but the nerve centres were completely underground. I waded through mud to see the staff rooms, radio installations, and the like. The centralised control ensured that the full weight of the fort's armaments could be directed against any point of attack. There was a strong force of artillery, but the mortars were perhaps more useful —they could toss their bombs *over* the mountains into the adjacent valleys.

The garrison numbered from 10,000 to 15,000 men, according to the situation. In addition there were 1,500 Viet Minh prisoners employed on labour duties. These were *not* fanatical Communists; they had few if any political interests. "We get 700 grammes of rice a day, which is about double what we had as civilians in the delta," said one. "There are plenty of vegetables, and fish, and occasionally meat. This is not a bad way of waiting for the war to end." He resumed his task of chopping wood: I noticed that the group of prisoners was working without a guard. True, they would find it very difficult to get out of Na Sam!

I met most of the senior officers, and argued long about Na Sam. One declared that the hedgehog cut an important line of communication. That would have been a sound argument in Europe, but not in a country where most supplies were carried along footpaths on coolie back. Na Sam had been effectively by-passed.

He also claimed that it was a good place for a counter-attack. This was absurd. The French would have to move across broken country, with a hundred opportunities for ambush, before they could reach the nearest Viet Minh forces fifty or sixty miles away.

Some officers still hoped for another attack from Viet Minh, but I thought this highly improbable. I was certain that Giap was content to contain Na Sam—with the minimum of effort and expenditure of forces.

One of the generals raised a more serious argument—that the French would suffer very heavy casualties from a withdrawal. The evacuation itself was bound to cost heavily in prestige, and if it also entailed serious losses there would be acid comment in Paris. I believed that no serious losses need be incurred, and gave as my reason our evacuation of Gallipoli in 1916—under the very noses of the Turks, and without losing a man. The Viet Minh were used to the daily procession of aircraft. This could continue as at present— but with the planes taking supplies and men out instead of bringing them in. When, some weeks later, the general sent for me to talk more about Gallipoli, it was obvious that something was afoot. My stock was high when, in July 1953 Na Sam *was* evacuated without loss, and 10,000 of France's best troops were released for more effective service. I have never been told officially why, soon after my return home, the French appointed me Chevalier

of the Legion of Honour, but I can make at least one guess.[4]

---

[4]Bernard Newman, *Background to Vietnam* (New York: Roy Publishers, Inc., 1965), pp. 76–77.

In May, 1953, General Henri Navarre was appointed commander in chief in Vietnam. He decided to withdraw from Na Sam as a part of overall strategy. In the course of the next few months he developed a concept of operations which is generally referred to as the "Navarre Plan." It is described here in his own words.

FOR CONSIDERATION   Because of the Dien Bien Phu debacle, there have been intensive arguments over the planning and implementation of Navarre's strategy. The differences between Navarre and his second in command, General René Cogny, even led to a lawsuit in 1955 and to angry debates in 1963.[5]

The "Navarre Plan," as Described by General Henri Navarre

Summed up, the overall plan presented by me to the Government—the first, to my knowledge, since the beginning of the war —was divided up into distinct plans: a plan of reinforcement from France of land, air, and naval forces; a plan of re-organizing troops; a plan of making the forces more mobile (itself supported by a plan of pacification); a plan of developing national armies in the Associated States [Laos, Cambodia, Vietnam]; these various plans all leading to a plan for building up a battle force.

Altogether these plans, which were spread over the years 1953, 1954, and 1955, formed an indivisible whole, for the realization of one depended closely on that of the others. The whole set of plans were based on political assumptions: defi-

nition of war aims, unified politico-military action, and getting the Associated States into the war. The operation plan was the cap-stone of this edifice.

.   .   .   .   .

The Operation Plan . . .

(1) During the 1953-1954 campaign, maintain a strategically defensive attitude north of the 18th parallel, and try to avoid a major battle. On the other hand, take the offensive in the south as soon as possible. . . .

(2) Once a superiority in mobile forces is obtained, that is, after the autumn of 1954, take the offensive north of Porte d'Annam, with the intention of creating a military situation which will permit a political solution to the conflict. . . .

.   .   .   .   .

As soon as studies for executing the plan were started, a serious question immediately arose: the defense of North Laos. . . .

From a military viewpoint, the abandonment of North Laos presented us with

---

[5]Details may be found in Bernard Fall's excellent study of Dien Bien Phu, *Hell in a Very Small Place* (Philadelphia: J. B. Lippincott Co., 1966).

THE FRENCH WAR IN VIETNAM

fend upper Laos was thus a military decision which, if not immediately too serious, bore the seeds of a general catastrophe several months off.

From the political point of view, the decision was even more serious. Of the three Associated States, Laos remained most loyal to France and was the only one which did not pose too many questions to joining the French Union. . . . To this strong political argument was added another. The United States aided us because we guarded an essential Southeast Asian sector: Thailand, Burma, Malaysia. To let the enemy reach the Mekong was to fail in this task. There was fear of a sharp American reaction.

The political and military arguments favored a decision to defend upper Laos. But defense against a large-scale attack posed difficult problems because of the terrain: high mountains, covered with thick forests traversed by only a few poor trails. . . . Defense was possible only by "hedgehogs," strong points established at landing strips and commanding the essential access routes. . . . It was dangerous, as it required building up garrisons which were isolated and difficult to supply. It required very heavy support by air. But it was the only defense suitable for facing an attack in force.[6]

considerable long-range risks. It was clear that the Vietminh, once they reached the Thailand frontier, even if they refrained from an armed invasion, would find themselves at a political advantage insofar as they might infilter and threaten all the South via the Mekong valley. Not to de-

T he Navarre Plan was discussed by the French government in July, 1953.

FOR CONSIDERATION   The government discussions were top secret, but they leaked out to the press and caused a considerable scandal in 1955. General Catroux, a former Governor of Indochina, a long-time Gaullist and former Ambassador to Russia, was appointed chairman of a commission to inquire into Dien Bien Phu. Although the official conclusions have not been made public, Catroux has written memoirs, which presumably reflect the commission's findings.

The defense of Laos became an important issue, as Dien Bien Phu was but a few miles from the border. Navarre did not learn the government's decision until December 4, after Dien Bien Phu had been taken by the French. Was the decision to defend Laos political or military?

Comments of General Catroux

The Committee of National Defense met on July 24, 1953, in the presence of General Navarre, to reach decisions regarding his plan which several days earlier had been examined by the Chiefs of Staff committee.

The advice of this committee was essentially the following: The overall conception and economy posed no objections; on the other hand, considering the troops available, the requests for reinforcement of the Expeditionary Force exceeded capabilities and could not be met. Consequently . . . it was recommended to limit General Navarre's responsibility *by not making him assume the defense of Laos,* in case this associated kingdom was attacked.

The position taken by the Chiefs of Staff had the merit of being coherent and concise. On the other hand, that adopted by the Committee of National Defense was less clearly expressed. In effect, of all the various problems, it made a firm decision only on reinforcements. The Commander in Chief was informed that he could count on only 9 battalions instead of 12—without the parachutist artillery group requested—one group of air transport, a few supplementary B-26's (but not a complete group), only one sixth of the air personnel requested, and less than the total sea transport estimated, as well as funds to improve airports. General Navarre was told that the Government was at the limit of its resources and could not go beyond them.

· · · · ·

. . . Was there an implication that General Navarre should revise his plan? It might have been desirable and even necessary that this be spelled out. This is especially true since General Navarre has consistently maintained that his plan was *an integral one* and only had value as such. . . . It does seem that the Committee, without *specifically* approving the plan, *tacitly* accepted the basic concept.

In any case this was the impression General Navarre took from the discussions. He believed he could assume that his overall strategy had been approved and he was inclined to expect that in the last analysis the means which had been refused at first, and declared indispensable by him, would ultimately be supplied.

This was the beginning of the misunderstanding between the Commander in Chief and the Government, a misunderstanding which might have been avoided if the organ responsible for the conduct of the war had taken the pains to formulate its decision in an unequivocal way as a *directive* or an *instruction* for General Navarre's guidance.[7]

[7]General Georges Catroux, *Deux actes du drame indochinois* (Paris: Librairie Plon, 1959), pp. 142-44; all rights reserved.

By 1953, the Vietminh armed forces consisted of much more than a few ragged guerrillas. Equipped with Russian and Chinese (as well as captured French) matériel, they constituted a formidable opponent. The following passage gives General Giap's estimate of the situation.

FOR CONSIDERATION   Bear in mind that the cease-fire in Korea took effect on July 27, 1953, releasing considerable Chinese men and equipment.

Comments of General Giap

The situation . . . in summer 1953 can be summarized as follows:

ON OUR SIDE

Through eight years of fighting and training, our *people's armed forces*, the core of the Resistance, had grown up from their infancy to full maturity. The People's Army then comprised many regular divisions and regiments besides a great number of local regiments and battalions. Militia and guerrilla forces also developed quickly.

The coming into being and speedy growth of these *three forces* was the result of our Party's correct policy of *mobilizing and arming the whole people and waging a people's war.*

It was also the result of the correct tactics for a protracted revolutionary war: *To wage guerrilla warfare, to advance from guerrilla to regular warfare, to closely combine these two forms of war, and to develop from guerrilla to mobile and siege warfare....*

All our regular divisions and regiments had been organizationally strengthened and re-equipped with new weapons partly taken from the enemy and partly manufactured by ourselves in spite of great difficulties and the scarcity of necessary means. The technical and tactical level and fighting capacity of our men had visibly risen through successive drives of training and through major campaigns. They were now quite familiar with mobile and siege warfare and concentrated operations involving sizeable forces and a vast scope of action, particularly in mountain regions, and could carry out annihilating attacks, make deep thrusts, withdraw quickly and fight with initiative, mobility and flexibility.

Our people's armed forces, especially our regular forces, owed their visible and rapid progress to the fact that our *Party* had paid due attention to strengthening its *leadership* as regards the army, promoting *political education and ideological* guidance, and had continuously heightened the revolutionary and class character of our armymen. As a result of political remoulding classes, our armymen had a clearer view of the goal of their fight, their hatred for the enemy and their fighting spirit had heightened. The ideological remoulding campaign in summer 1953 especially reserved for the army was carried on while our Party was implementing the policy of Thorough Reduction of Land Rent and Agrarian Reform. The class consciousness and revolutionary strength of our armymen was thus further enhanced. Internal unity, unity between the army and people, international unity to disintegrate the enemy, internal democracy combined with strict discipline, determination and courage in fighting, and dynamism and diligence in duty and production, had become good habits and good tradition in our army's life.

Our *people* were unswervingly united as one man around the Party, Government and President Ho Chi Minh. They were resolved to carry through the Resistance, and had an iron conviction in final victory.[8]

[8]General Vo Nguyen Giap, *Dien Bien Phu* (Hanoi: Foreign Languages Publishing House, 1964), pp. 26-28.

As preparations to implement the Navarre Plan gained momentum in the fall of 1953, both sides wondered whether negotiation was still possible. Ho Chi-minh answered questions posed by the Swedish newspaper *Expressen.*

Statement of French Prime Minister Laniel in the Chamber of Deputies, October 27, 1953

Surely, it is desirable to negotiate. No one has ever fought a war for the pleasure of fighting, especially for seven years. It would be inadmissible for someone in this Assembly to imagine that the French Government does not think, in this affair, of peace as its supreme objective.

But to make peace, at least two are necessary, and those who speak of peace and of negotiation have said nothing as long as it was not said with whom it was necessary to negotiate, with whom it was necessary to make peace. . . .

Numerous speakers have told us: it is necessary to negotiate with Ho Chi Minh!

I will simply reply to them thus: is it at the moment when Ho Chi Minh has just declared on September 2 that only his total victory could lead to peace, is it at the moment when he builds so many hopes on his autumn campaign, is it at this moment that France should ask of him his conditions for year? . . .[9]

Ho Chi-minh's Replies to Questions of the Stockholm *Expressen*, November 29, 1953

QUESTION 1. A recent debate in the French National Assembly has shown a desire among a large number of French politicians to arrive at a settlement of the conflict in Indo China through direct negotiations with your government. Can it be expected that this desire, which is now to an increasing degree shared by all French people, will find response among you and your government?

ANSWER: The war has been forced upon us by the French Government. The Vietnamese people who were forced to resort to arms during the past 7 to 8 years have fought heroically to defend their national independence and their right to live in peace. If the French Colonials continue their war of conquest the Vietnamese people are determined to carry out their patriotic war to a victorious end. But if the French Government has learned from these war years and wishes to bring about an armistice and solve the Vietnam problem through negotiations, the people and Government of the Democratic Republic of Vietnam will be prepared to discuss the French proposal.

QUESTION 2: Are there at present any prospects for an armistice or truce? On what terms?

ANSWER: The French Government must suspend hostilities. An armistice will then become a reality. The basis for such an armistice is that the French Government really respect the independence of Vietnam.[10]

---

[9]*Journal Officiel, Débats*, October 27, 1953, trans. and quoted in Cole, *op. cit.*, pp. 137–38.

[10]Translated and cited in Cole, *op. cit.*, pp. 148–49.

O n November 21, 1953, French forces occupied Dien Bien Phu and began to build up the defenses. On December 3 and December 12, General Navarre issued supplementary battle plans which envisaged breakouts from Dien Bien Phu and other points after three or four weeks.

In France there was little enthusiasm for the war, and the government of Joseph Laniel was interested in exploring the reactions of the major powers. The following passages reveal something of President Eisenhower's attitudes, together with Foreign Minister Bidault's reaction when, later, he read the President's memoirs.

General Ridgway was U.S. Army Chief of Staff at the time. The United States sent 200 technicians to Vietnam in February, 1954, and several B-25's. The American military observer in Vietnam, Lt. General John O'Daniel, visited Dien Bien Phu on February 2.

Comments of President Eisenhower

The Berlin Conference of Foreign Ministers convened on January 25, without agenda. Its purpose was to discuss such world problems as Austria, Germany, and the Far East.

Before departure for Berlin, Foster Dulles said that this meeting might represent the last major Soviet effort to disrupt the Western Alliance. If they were successful, we would have to reassess our views on at least two features of that alliance, EDC and NATO. If they failed, we could count it an achievement. There was a possibility of obtaining a peace treaty for Austria; none of us held a shred of hope on the reunification of Germany at this conference.

Unfortunately, Molotov was fully aware of the political pressures on French Foreign Minister Bidault to achieve a settlement in Indochina. Bidault, in fact, felt that if the Laniel government was to survive, he had to bring back at least a tentative pledge to discuss Indochina at a meeting scheduled later for Geneva.

The life of the Laniel government was important to United States policies. We were convinced that no succeeding government would take a stronger position than his on the defense of Indochina, or in support of the European Defense Community. We had to be sympathetic to the French desire. But there was danger in the attitude developing among the Western allies which, to us, seemed to put too much faith in the validity of negotiations with the Soviets and Chinese Communists. Secretary Dulles attempted to discourage Bidault from overanxiety to negotiate,

pointing out that this could lead to further deterioration of morale in Indochina and France itself.

Bidault persisted. On February 9 Foster notified me from Berlin that French pressure for a conference on Indochina at Geneva was mounting. He held little hope of being able to withstand it, and said that if the United States was held responsible for blocking such a conference, the moral obligation to carry on the war in Indochina might be shifted from French shoulders to ours. Finally, Foster himself found it necessary to propose a restricted four-power conference on the Far East.[11]

Comments of Georges Bidault

. . . I will limit myself to the following observations: (1) the appearance of facts and the reading of texts by someone who has several assistants and access to all the documents reveal, at least partly, a kind of presentation which is facilitated by knowledge of what happened later. (2) I don't remember Foster Dulles definitely emphasizing that a conference on Indochina would endanger morale in France and in Indochina. To the contrary, he repeated several times that one must negotiate from strength, like the United States in Korea. I observed that the Korean war had ended in an armistice and that the Indochinese war had already gone on for

[11]Dwight D. Eisenhower, *The White House Years*, Vol. I, *Mandate for Change 1953–1956* (Garden City, N.Y.: Doubleday & Co., Inc., 1963), pp. 342–43. Copyright © 1963 by Dwight D. Eisenhower. Reprinted by permission of Doubleday & Co., Inc.

twice as long. I replied also that the situation in Korea resulted in a position of force: the Americans were neither conquered nor conquerors. (3) In any case, if the United States had reasons for transforming an armistice into a lasting arrangement, France, whom the Korean armistice placed in greater danger, could not imagine that she would be left to fight with French soldiers and only American subsidies, without UN approval and without anticipated limitations.[12]

President Eisenhower to Secretary of State Dulles, February 10, 1954

. . . It is true that certain legislators have expressed uneasiness concerning any use of American maintenance personnel in Indochina. They fear that this may be opening the door to increased and unwise introduction of American troops into that area. Administration has given assurances to guard against such developments. . . .

There is no ground whatsoever for assuming we intend to reverse or ignore U. S. commitments made to French. Those commitments were based upon assumptions that French would act comprehensively and vigorously in prosecuting war; and their commitment in this regard is as binding as is ours in providing additional money and equipment. The so-called Navarre Plan visualized substantial victory by summer of 1955.

General O'Daniel's most recent report is more encouraging than given to you through French sources. I still believe that the two things most needed for success are French will to win and complete acceptance by Vietnamese of French promise of independence as soon as victory is achieved. To summarize, administration has no intention of evading its pledges in the area providing the French perfor-

mance measures up to the promises made by them as basis for requesting our increased help.[13]

Comments of General Matthew Ridgway

I was deeply concerned to hear individuals of great influence, both in and out of government, raising the cry that now was the time, and here, in Indo-China, was the place to "test the New Look," for us to intervene, to come to the aid of France with arms. At the same time that same old delusive idea was advanced—that we could do things the cheap and easy way, by going into Indo-China with air and naval forces alone. To me this had an ominous ring. For I felt sure that if we committed air and naval power to that area, we would have to follow them immediately with ground forces in support.

I also knew that none of those advocating such a step had any accurate idea what such an operation would cost us in blood and money and national effort. I felt that it was essential therefore that all who had any influence in making the decision on this grave matter should be fully aware of all the factors involved. To provide these facts, I sent out to Indo-China an Army team of experts in every field: engineers, signal and communications specialists, medical officers, and experienced combat leaders who knew how to evaluate terrain in terms of battle tactics. They went out to get the answers to a thousand questions that those who had so blithely recommended that we go to war there had never taken the trouble to ask. How deep was the water over the bar at Saigon? What were the harbor and dock facilities? Where could we store the tons of supplies we would need to support us there? How good was the road net—how could supplies be transported as the fighting forces moved inland, and in what tonnages?

---

[12]Georges Bidault, *D'une résistance à l'autre* (Paris: Les Presses du Siècle, 1965), p. 196.

[13]Eisenhower, *op. cit.*, pp. 343–44.

What of the climate? The rainfall? What tropical diseases would attack the combat soldier in that jungle land?

Their report was complete. The area, they found, was practically devoid of those facilities which modern forces such as ours find essential to the waging of war. Its telecommunications, highways, railways—all the things that make possible the operation of a modern combat force on land—were almost non-existent. Its port facilities and airfields were totally inadequate, and to provide the facilities we would need would require a tremendous engineering and logistical effort.

The land was a land of rice paddy and jungle—particularly adapted to the guerrilla-type warfare at which the Chinese soldier is a master. This meant that every little detachment, every individual, that tried to move about that country, would have to be protected by riflemen. Every telephone lineman, road repair party, every ambulance and every rear-area aid station would have to be under armed guard or they would be shot at around the clock.

If we did go into Indo-China, we would have to win. We would have to go in with a military force adequate in all its branches, and that meant a very strong ground force—an Army that could not only stand the normal attrition of battle, but could absorb heavy casualties from the jungle heat, and the rots and fevers which afflict the white man in the tropics. We could not again afford to accept anything short of decisive military victory.

We could have fought in Indo-China. We could have won, if we had been willing to pay the tremendous cost in men and money that such intervention would have required—a cost that in my opinion would have eventually been as great as, or greater than, that we paid in Korea. In Korea, we had learned that air and naval power alone cannot win a war and that inadequate ground forces cannot win one either. It was incredible to me that we had forgotten that bitter lesson so soon—that we were on the verge of making that same tragic error.

That error, thank God, was not repeated. As soon as the full report was in, I lost no time in having it passed on up the chain of command. It reached President Eisenhower. To a man of his military experience its implications were immediately clear. The idea of intervening was abandoned, and it is my belief that the analysis which the Army made and presented to higher authority played a considerable, perhaps a decisive, part in persuading our government not to embark on that tragic adventure.[14]

---

[14]Matthew Ridgway (as told to Harold W. Martin), *Soldier: The Memoirs of Matthew B. Ridgway* (New York: Harper & Row, Publishers, 1956), pp. 276–77. Reprinted by permission of Harper & Row, Publishers.

Great questions about Navarre's strategy were being raised at all levels. Between February 7 and 28, 1954, French Defense Minister René Pleven and Chief of the French Joint Staff General Paul Ely made an inspection tour of Vietnam, including an examination of the Dien Bien Phu defenses. The local commander, Colonel de Castries, and his able deputy, Colonel Langlais, were doing their best to fortify the camp, but the position, on a plain surrounded by hills, needed more men and matériel than were available. Bernard Fall has estimated that 30,000 men (not 10,000) should have been provided, and 34,000 tons of matériel were needed, not the 4,000 for which priorities had been given (*Hell in a Very Small Place*, pp. 40–42, 88–97). Understandably, General Ely, part of whose reaction is given here, was concerned.

Comments of General Paul Ely

Three ideas must be emphasized: we were not afraid of being put in really serious straits if China did not intervene directly, and as long as the Viet-Minh lacked planes; on the other hand, the most we could hope for was to establish military conditions most favorable to a political solution to the problem; finally, time so far seemed to have played against us, and could not turn in our favor unless Viet-nam truly and totally got into the war and adopted the same tactics as the Viet-Minh.

. . . . .

The contacts with reality [after the inspection tour] confirm the government's policy, and establish certain points. To grant total independence without any looking back must be the basic element of this policy. To bring the [Vietnamese] army, the most solid institution in the country, to maturity, by working out stages whereby the army, and especially the ground forces, will be "vietnamised"—this was the essential condition required for bringing the country to total war. . . .

The application [of this policy] necessitated an unambiguous convention with Viet-nam leading to the grant of independence. It also required that we be assured, through a specific understanding with the United States, of material and financial assistance while these plans were being executed, definite guarantees in case of Chinese intervention by air or other massive aid, and fully political guarantees to avoid American interference with French actions. A convention with Viet-nam, agreement with the United States, comprised a whole. If one of these elements were missing, a reappraisal of the entirety would be necessary. . . .

Such were the conclusions of the Pleven mission. . . .[15]

[15]Général d'Armée Paul Ely, *Mémoires,* Vol. I, *L'Indochine dans la tourmente* (Paris: Librairie Plon, 1964), pp. 52, 55–56; all rights reserved.

Part of the strategic error was the assumption that General Giap could not, or would not, bring a large concentration of his forces against the French outpost. Or even if he did, French firepower would exceed that of the Vietminh. But General Navarre was wrong. With bicycles, men on foot, and a few Soviet trucks, Giap brought in, along 500 miles of jungle trail, nearly 50,000 men and 200 guns larger than 57 mm., including 45 105-mm. howitzers captured in Korea. The attack opened on March 13, and two weeks later General Giap sent out the following appeal to his men.

General Giap to the Forces Besieging Dien Bien Phu, March 29, 1954

In brief, the coming attack is far greater than the previous ones. What is to be done to secure success?

Answer:

The only requirement is that all officers and men must be imbued with the determination of the High Command, behave resolutely and valiantly, strike rapidly, settle rapidly, attack fiercely and not let slip an opportunity to wipe out the enemy. Should one fall, another will take his place, officers and Party members must set good examples to the entire army, each man must set a good example when assaulting the enemy, everyone must show a strong mettle, not be afraid of difficulties or casualties, strike terror into the enemy's heart at the sight of our troops. All of you must have such a determination, and emulate to raise aloft President Ho Chi Minh's banner "Determined to fight and to win".

Comrades,

Once this attack won, we shall inflict most heavy losses upon the enemy, creating the required conditions to wipe out the whole enemy force at Dien Bien Phu.

Once this attack won, our army will make a step forward from destroying an enemy battalion in a siege battle to putting out of action several battalions in a battle.

This is a great trial for both officers and men.

Our entire army on all fronts, our compatriots throughout the country are longing for the news of this victory.

Our Party Central Committee and President Ho Chi Minh are waiting for the news of this victory.

All men, all units, all arms must enhance their determination, and fulfil at any cost this glorious coming task.

I wish you many shining deeds![16]

_____

[16]Giap, *op. cit.*, pp. 226–27.

W ith news of the all-out attack on Dien Bien Phu, the French government decided to send General Ely to Washington.

Comments of General Paul Ely

My stay in Washington from Monday to Friday (March 22–26) included talks with President Eisenhower, Mr. Foster Dulles, Secretary of Defense Wilson, and with Mr. Allen Dulles. I also attended a meeting of the Joint Chiefs of Staff, chaired by Admiral Radford, and also a meeting of the NATO military committee. . . .

The meeting with President Eisenhower took place in the presence of Admiral Radford. We did not go too much into detail, but I was aware of the fact that the President attached a great deal of importance to Dien Bien Phu. In my presence he instructed the admiral to give priority, without any apparent limitation, to all our requests in order to save the besieged stronghold. . . .

Mr. Foster Dulles commented on American attitudes toward the Indochinese conflict. According to him, no solution was possible without the support of local popular opinion and this would best be obtained if the people of the associated states were assured that the last vestige of colonialism would be removed. . . .

On leaving the State Department, I was a bit perturbed, in spite of everything, that possible American intervention, brought up at that time—and I insist on this point—was only contemplated, except perhaps in the minds of a few, in the event of a Chinese air attack on Indochina. Admiral Radford must have sensed my misgivings, and by a few things he said, gave me the impression, though only a personal impression, that President Eisenhower's position might be slightly different from that of his Secretary of State. . . .

⋅   ⋅   ⋅   ⋅   ⋅

[Before I left Washington] Admiral Radford stated with a certain insistence that if the French Government requested it, the United States would be ready to examine the possibility of intervening on behalf of Dien Bien Phu with their Pacific Strategic Air Force, and especially, with bombers based at Manila. . . .

Our discussions ended on this under-standing during a final meeting in which we exchanged signatures on a memorandum concerning an American guarantee in case of Chinese air intervention. . . .[17]

[17]Ely, *op. cit.,* pp. 64, 67, 76–77.

The big question in April, 1954, was: would the United States intervene in Vietnam? If so, would atomic weapons be used? Two years later, Secretary Dulles was quoted as saying: "If you are scared to go to the brink, you are lost. We've had to look it square in the face—on the question of enlarging the Korean war, on the question of getting into the Indochina war. . . ."[18] The following documents pertain to the Indochinese "brink" during that frenetic month.

FOR CONSIDERATION   Who let whom down? Both Washington and Paris seem to place the blame on London.

Comments of French Prime Minister Laniel

I immediately improvised a War Council attended by Paul Reynaud and Georges Bidault, as well as Marshal Juin. It was decided to request the intervention of our allies' heavy bombers. . . . This was the government's reaction within twelve hours of General Ely's return. . . .[19]

Meeting Held by Dulles, April 3, 1954, as Described by Chalmers Roberts, Chief of the National News Bureau of the *Washington Post & Times-Herald.*

. . . That Saturday morning eight members of Congress, five Senators and three Representatives, got the scare of their lives. They had been called to a secret conference with John Foster Dulles. They entered one of the State Department's fifth-floor conference rooms to find not only Dulles but Admiral Arthur W. Rad-ford, chairman of the Joint Chiefs of Staff, Under Secretary of Defense Roger Kyes, Navy Secretary Robert B. Anderson, and Thruston B. Morton, Dulles's assistant for Congressional Relations. A large map of the world hung behind Dulles's seat, and Radford stood by with several others. "The President has asked me to call this meeting," Dulles began.

The atmosphere became serious at once. What was wanted, Dulles said, was a joint resolution by Congress to permit the President to use air and naval power in Indochina. Dulles hinted that perhaps the mere passage of such a resolution would in itself make its use unnecessary. But the President had asked for its consideration, and, Dulles added, Mr. Eisenhower felt that it was indispensable at this juncture that the leaders of Congress feel as the Administration did on the Indochina crisis.

Then Radford took over. He said the Administration was deeply concerned over the rapidly deteriorating situation. He used a map of the Pacific to point out the importance of Indochina. He spoke

[18]*Life,* January 16, 1956, p. 78.
[19]Joseph Laniel, *Le drame indochinois* (Paris: Librairie Plon, 1957), p. 85; all rights reserved.

about the French Union forces then already under siege for three weeks in the fortress of Dienbienphu.

The admiral explained the urgency of American action by declaring that he was not even sure, because of poor communications, whether, in fact, Dienbienphu was still holding out. (The fortress held out for five weeks more.)

Dulles backed up Radford. If Indochina fell and if its fall led to the loss of all of Southeast Asia, he declared, then the United States might eventually be forced back to Hawaii, as it was before the Second World War. And Dulles was not complimentary about the French. He said he feared they might use some disguised means of getting out of Indochina if they did not receive help soon.

The eight legislators were silent: Senate Majority Leader Knowland and his G.O.P. colleague Eugene Millikin, Senate Minority Leader Lyndon B. Johnson and his Democratic colleagues Richard B. Russell and Earle C. Clements, House G.O.P. Speaker Joseph Martin and two Democratic House leaders, John W. McCormack and J. Percy Priest.

What to do? Radford offered the plan he had in mind once Congress passed the joint resolution.

Some two hundred planes from the thirty-one-thousand-ton U.S. Navy carriers *Essex* and *Boxer*, then in the South China Sea ostensibly for "training," plus land-based U.S. Air Force planes from bases a thousand miles away in the Philippines, would be used for a single strike to save Dienbienphu.

The legislators stirred, and the questions began.

Radford was asked whether such action would be war. He replied that we would be in the war. . . .

Clements asked Radford the first of the two key questions: "Does this plan have the approval of the other members of the Joint Chiefs of Staff?"

"No," replied Radford.

"How many of the three agree with you?"

"None."

"How do you account for that?"

"I have spent more time in the Far East than any of them and I understand the situation better."

Lyndon Johnson put the other key question in the form of a little speech. He said that Knowland had been saying publicly that in Korea up to ninety per cent of the men and money came from the United States. The United States had become sold on the idea that that was bad. Hence in any operation in Indochina we ought to know first who would put up the men. And so he asked Dulles whether he had consulted nations who might be our allies in intervention.

Dulles said he had not.

The Secretary was asked why he didn't go to the United Nations as in the Korean case. He replied that it would take too long, that this was an immediate problem.

There were other questions. Would Red China and the Soviet Union come into the war if the United States took military action? The China question appears to have been sidestepped, though Dulles said he felt the Soviets could handle the Chinese and the United States did not think that Moscow wanted a general war now. Further, he added, if the Communists feel that we mean business, they won't go "any further down there," pointing to the map of Southeast Asia. . . .

In the end, all eight members of Congress, Republicans and Democrats alike, were agreed that Dulles had better first go shopping for allies.[20]

President Eisenhower to Prime Minister Churchill, April 4, 1954

I am sure . . . you are following with

[20]Chalmers M. Roberts, "The Day We Didn't Go to War," *The Reporter*, Vol. XI (September 14, 1954), pp. 31–32.

the deepest interest and anxiety the daily reports of the gallant fight being put up by the French at Dien Bien Phu. Today, the situation there does not seem hopeless.

But regardless of the outcome of this particular battle, I fear that the French cannot alone see the thing through, this despite the very substantial assistance in money and matériel that we are giving them. It is no solution simply to urge the French to intensify their efforts. And if they do not see it through and Indochina passes into the hands of the Communists the ultimate effect on our and your global strategic position with the consequent shift in the power ratios throughout Asia and the Pacific could be disastrous and, I know, unacceptable to you and me. . . . This has led us to the hard conclusion that the situation in Southeast Asia requires us urgently to take serious and far-reaching decisions.

I believe that the best way to put teeth in this concept and to bring greater moral and material resources to the support of the French effort is through the establishment of a new, ad hoc grouping or coalition composed of nations which have a vital concern in the checking of Communist expansion in the area. I have in mind in addition to our two countries, France, the Associated States, Australia, New Zealand, Thailand and the Philippines. The United States government would expect to play its full part in such a coalition. . . .[21]

----

[21]Eisenhower, *op. cit.*, pp. 346–47.

T he British reply to Eisenhower's proposal was lukewarm. Dulles stopped in London on his way to Paris for a session of NATO.

Comments of British Foreign Minister Anthony Eden

Mr. Dulles arrived in London on April 11 for talks which took place informally that evening and formally on the two succeeding days. . . .

At my invitation, Mr. Dulles gave us a long explanation of the background to his Government's proposals on Indo-China. The United States Government, he said, had come to the conclusion that the French could no longer deal with the situation, either politically or militarily, on their own resources alone. If the French position in Indo-China collapsed, the consequences would be extremely grave. Not only Thailand, but also Malaya, Burma and Indonesia would be exposed to eventual absorption by communism. The battle at Dien Bien Phu had reached a crucial phase and American military authorities did not rate the French chances of victory highly. For these reasons, Mr. Dulles went on, the United States Chiefs of Staff had suggested three weeks ago that American naval and air forces should intervene in the Indo-China war. He told us that some aircraft-carriers had already been moved from Manila towards the Indo-China coast. On reflection, Mr. Dulles had considered that the United States should not act alone in this matter and that before a decision to intervene were taken, two conditions should be met. First, there must be some assurance that the French Government were willing to grant the Associated States real independence within the French Union, so as to provide the necessary political basis for effective resistance. Second, the United States Government must ascertain whether their allies, especially the United Kingdom, Australia and New Zealand, took an equally grave view of the situation. For these reasons, although he no longer had in mind a warning declaration specifically directed against China, Mr. Dulles wanted to see the formation of an *ad hoc* coalition which might develop into a South-East Asia defence organization. He thought that this in itself would deter China from further interference in Indo-China, and would strengthen our position at Geneva by giving evidence of our solidarity....

I told Mr. Dulles that we welcomed the idea of an organization for collective defence in South-East Asia, but that it would require the most careful thought and study, particularly on the question of membership. I emphasized that on no account should India and the other Asian Commonwealth countries be deliberately excluded. The other question was that of Indo-China itself, where fighting was in progress and where we were committed to a discussion with the Soviet and Chinese Governments at Geneva. If there was to be any question of allied intervention, military or otherwise, or of any warning announcement before Geneva, that would require extremely careful consideration. It was doubtful whether the situation in Indo-China could be solved by purely military means and we must at least see what proposals, if any, the Communists had to make at Geneva.[22]

Secretary of State Dulles to President Eisenhower, April 23, 1954

Please inform President and Radford urgently that Bidault received in the middle of afternoon council session copy of message from Navarre to Laniel which he gave me to read. He will talk to me further on subject at dinner tonight but, in brief, situation at Dien Bien Phu is desperate. Attempt to regain Huguette has

claimed last reserves. Only alternatives Navarre sees are (1) operation Vautour which would be massive B-29 bombing (which I understand would be U. S. operation from U. S. bases outside Indochina) or (2) request for cease fire (which I assume would be at Dien Bien Phu and not throughout all Indochina).

I told Bidault B-29 intervention as proposed seemed to me out of question under existing circumstances but that I would report all this urgently to the President and that I would discuss it with Admiral Radford immediately upon latter's arrival in Paris tomorrow evening.

Bidault gives the impression of a man close to the breaking point. His mental condition at this morning's session was greatly improved over yesterday, but it has been painful to watch him presiding over the council at this afternoon's long session. He is obviously exhausted and is confused and rambling in his talk.[23]

Comments of Georges Bidault

My conversations with Foster Dulles were without ambiguity just as my appeals were pressing. I pointed out that the powerful American Pacific fleet was in the Gulf of Tonkin, and that while he proclaimed, to me and everyone, in private and in public, that the United States could not tolerate a new Communist aggression in Southeast Asia, there was a means whereby theory could be made practical: namely, to relieve the garrison at Dien Bien Phu by intensive bombing, which would save the besieged forces and the morale of others. Aware, no doubt, of the difficulties he would face in the President and in Congress, Foster Dulles only scowled and did not even promise to support my request in Washington.

---

[22] Anthony Eden, *Full Circle* (Boston: Houghton Mifflin Company, 1960), pp. 106-07.

[23] Eisenhower, *op. cit.*, p. 350.

On the other hand, taking me aside, he said: "Suppose we gave you two atomic bombs?" I suspect, from what followed, that he had posed this hypothesis more or less clearly to others, for he was accustomed to seek approval without bothering himself too much about whether this procedure was pleasant or only correct. In any case, I answered him, and my reply did not require much reflection: "If these bombs are dropped in the Dien Bien Phu area, the defenders will suffer as much as the attackers. If the communication lines to China are attacked, there is a risk of general war. In either case, the garrison at Dien Bien Phu, far from receiving help, will find itself in greater danger."[24]

Comments of Anthony Eden on Events of April 25, 1954

While the Cabinet was in session, other moves were being made. During the afternoon, the French Ambassador, M. Massigli, came to tell me that Mr. Dulles' letter had been delivered to the French Government. He also informed me that the United States Government were now proposing that an immediate declaration should be made on behalf of the Governments of the United States, the United Kingdom, France, the Philippines and the Associated States, proclaiming their common will to check the expansion of communism in South-East Asia and to use "eventual military means" for this purpose. Once President Eisenhower had been assured that the United Kingdom would participate in this declaration, he would be prepared to seek Congressional approval for intervention. United States naval aircraft would go into action at Dien Bien Phu on April 28. The French Government had been urged by the Americans to persuade us to agree to this course.

This was a new development, so the Cabinet met once more in emergency session at 4 P.M. on the same afternoon to discuss it. I was surprised at the American tactic of approaching us on a major issue by way of the French instead of through our own Ambassador in Washington, who had not been consulted in any way. If the United Kingdom acceded to this latest American proposal, we should be supporting direct United States intervention in the Indo-China war and, probably, later American action against the Chinese mainland. Her Majesty's Government consequently decided to reject the American proposal, and I was asked to inform Mr. Dulles and M. Bidault of our decision, on my way to Geneva.[25]

Comments of French Prime Minister, Joseph Laniel

On April 24, I received Mr. Foster Dulles at the Hotel Matignon. The Secretary of State, while he regretted not being able to reach a solution more rapidly, expressed the need, according to him, of working together with other allied countries. . . .

Operation *Vautour* (Vulture), which our military chiefs had worked out in agreement with the chiefs of the American air force, would have brought into action 300 fighters, bombers, and 60 heavy bombers. Their effectiveness, the experts said, might have been quite considerable, especially on enemy communication routes. I am convinced that without enlarging the conflict, it would have altered the fate of Dien Bien Phu.

I am not undertaking here to establish the relative importance of the causes which checked our negotiations. There is no doubt that very rapidly a disagreement developed between the Pentagon

---

[24]Bidault, *op. cit.*, p. 198.

[25]Eden, *op. cit.*, p. 119.

and Washington. The attitude of certain French circles undoubtedly contributed to our allies' restraining their zeal. In any case, on April 28, at Washington, where a meeting of several powers had been called by Mr. Dulles, our old ally England, faithful to her policy of "wait and see," preferred to await the results of the Geneva Conference, thus not recognizing that the evolution of the military situation would have its own influence.[26]

Comments of President Eisenhower, Referring to Events of April 24–25, 1954

That evening I telephoned Bedell Smith about the French request for direct intervention, and agreed that Foster's position should stand unchanged. There would be no intervention without allies.

In Paris, Foster decided to bring the British position into the clear. In a conference with Anthony Eden, Foster told

[26]Laniel, op. cit., pp. 85–88.

him, unequivocally, that major combat action by United States forces in Indochina would need the consent of Congress, but that Congress would be more amenable if assured that Britain agreed to participate in unified action. Admiral Radford had convinced Eden in another meeting that day that the United States military chiefs took a gloomier view of the situation than the French had given the British most recently. That evening Eden flew back to London, for a Cabinet meeting on Sunday, April 25. The Churchill government decided, once and for all, that unified action must wait until all possibility of settlement by negotiation had been tried and failed. This ended for the time being our efforts to find any satisfactory method of Allied intervention. I was disappointed but such was my confidence in Prime Minister Churchill and the British government that I accepted their decision in the confidence that it was honestly made, and reflected their best judgment of what was best for Britain and, from their viewpoint, for the Free World.[27]

[27]Eisenhower, op. cit., p. 351.

By April 28, when it had become clear that there would be no American intervention, the situation at Dien Bien Phu had become catastrophic. The garrison was finally overrun on May 7.

Comments of Bernard Fall

Like Stalingrad, Dienbienphu slowly starved on its airlift tonnage. When the siege began, it had about eight days' worth of supplies on hand and required 200 tons a day to maintain minimum levels. The sheer magnitude of preparing that mass of supplies for parachuting was solved only by superhuman feats of the airborne supply units on the outside—efforts more than matched by the heroism of the soldiers inside the valley, who had

to crawl into the open, under fire, to collect the containers.

But as the position shrunk every day (it finally was the size of a ball park), the bulk of the supplies fell into Communist hands. Even de Castries's general's stars, dropped to him by General Cogny with a bottle of champagne, landed in enemy territory.

The airdrops were a harrowing experience in that narrow valley which permitted only straight approaches. Communist antiaircraft artillery played havoc among the lumbering transport planes as they slowly disgorged their loads. A few figures tell how murderous the air war around Dienbienphu was: of a total of 420 aircraft available in all of Indochina then, sixty-two were lost in connection with Dienbienphu and 167 sustained hits. Some of the American civilian pilots who flew the run said that Vietminh flak was as dense as anything encountered during World War II over the Ruhr.

When the battle ended, the 82,926 parachutes expended in supplying the fortress covered the battlefield like freshly fallen snow. Or like a burial shroud. . . .

On May 7, 1954, the struggle for Indochina was almost over for France. As a French colonel looked out over the battlefield from a slit trench near his command post, a small white flag, probably a handkerchief, appeared on top of a rifle hardly fifty feet away from him, followed by the flat-helmeted head of a Vietminh soldier.

"You're not going to shoot anymore?" said the Vietminh in French.

"No, I'm not going to shoot anymore," said the colonel.

"C'est fini?" said the Vietminh.

"Oui, c'est fini," said the colonel.

And all around them, as on some gruesome Judgment Day, soldiers, French and enemy alike, began to crawl out of their trenches and stand erect for the first time in 54 days, as firing ceased everywhere. The sudden silence was deafening.[28]

General Giap's Replies to Questions for Article in Revolution Africaine, May, 1963

QUESTION: *Could you, please, tell whether there was an important American aid to the French Expeditionary Corps during the Dien Bien Phu campaign?*

ANSWER: Since the first years of our patriotic resistance, the American imperialists had closely colluded with the French colonialists, supplied them with weapons, munitions, planes, gunboats to massacre the Vietnamese people.

After their rout from the Chinese mainland and their shameful defeat in Korea, the American imperialists stepped up their intervention in Vietnam, taking advantage of the difficulties facing the French to kick the latter out of Indo-China. In fact they had taken the command of the war in Indo-China since 1953, witness the Navarre Plan.

Since 1951 American aid and weapons poured into Indo-China had increased with every passing day.

From 119 million dollars in 1951, it rose to 800 million in 1954.

American weapons introduced in Indo-China averaged 6,000 tons monthly in 1952, rose to over 20,000 tons in 1953, and at times to nearly 100,000 tons in 1954, especially during the Dien Bien Phu campaign.

Ever since the day when the French colonialists dropped paratroops on Dien Bien Phu and began building the Dien Bien Phu fortified entrenched camp (11-1953) the American imperialists had established a number of airlifts to supply weapons and foodstuffs to the French, then sent aircraft carriers of the Seventh Fleet to Bac Bo Gulf and despatched American pilots directly to man American planes flying French colours to massacre the Vietnamese people.

The realities of the aggressive war in Vietnam as well as in the Dien Bien Phu campaign have shown that for the French imperialists and colonialists this is a dirty war waged by the French soldiers and a contingent of other mercenaries with dollars and weaponry of the American imperialists.[29]

---

[28]Bernard Fall, "Dienbienphu: a Battle to Remember," *The New York Times Magazine*, May 3, 1964. © 1964 by The New York Times Company. Reprinted by permission.

[29]Giap, *op. cit.*, pp. 250–51.

On May 8, the day following Dien Bien Phu's collapse, French Foreign Minister Bidault grappled with the unenviable task of introducing proposals before the Geneva Conference to end the Vietnam hostilities. For a month the negotiations went on, and finally bogged down early in June. Dulles, who wanted a Southeast Asian pact to emerge, became more and more inclined to boycott the meeting. Soviet Foreign Minister Molotov hinted that Russian goodwill could be obtained at the expense of the embryonic European Defense Community, which Bidault was committed to uphold.

On June 12, the Laniel government fell, and Pierre Mendès-France obtained the French parliament's enthusiastic support when he guaranteed a settlement in Indochina within 30 days. Anthony Eden here describes his efforts to develop an Anglo-American proposal which he hoped might break the deadlock.

Comments of Anthony Eden

During a further conversation with Mr. Dulles on June 29, we agreed on the text of a joint communication to the French Government, stating the willingness of the United States and the United Kingdom to respect an armistice agreement on Indo-China which:

1. Preserves the integrity and independence of Laos and Cambodia and assures the withdrawal of Vietminh forces therefrom.

2. Preserves at least the southern half of Vietnam, and if possible an enclave in the delta; in this connection we would be unwilling to see the line of division of responsibility drawn further south than a line running generally west from Dong Hoi.

3. Does not impose on Laos, Cambodia, or retained Vietnam any restrictions materially impairing their capacity to maintain stable non-Communist regimes; and especially restrictions impairing their right to maintain adequate forces for internal security, to import arms and to employ foreign advisers.

4. Does not contain political provisions which would risk loss of the retained area to Communist control.

5. Does not exclude the possibility of the ultimate reunification of Vietnam by peaceful means.

6. Provides for the peaceful and humane transfer, under international supervision, of those people desiring to be moved from one zone to another of Vietnam; and

7. Provides effective machinery for international supervision of the agreement.[30]

---

[30]Eden, *op. cit.*, p. 149.

Time was running out. The French forces in Vietnam were falling back. On July 12, discussions at Geneva resumed, with Mendès-France working frantically to meet his deadline. The following documents refer to the Conference's conclusion.

FOR CONSIDERATION   The Final Declaration of the Conference was not formally signed, but each delegate made a statement concerning it. Of the great powers, France, Great Britain, Russia, and China indicated their approval; the United States did not approve but made a separate statement indicating it would not "disturb" the arrangements, and would view any violation of them "with grave concern." The U.S. preferred elections supervised by the U.N. rather than by the International Supervisory Commission, and did not accept paragraph 13.

Comments of Anthony Eden

I held conversations with Mr. Molotov and Mr. Chou En-lai in turn, immediately after my arrival. As a result of these, I reckoned that we had an even chance of agreement, provided that we could persuade the Americans to join us in a final all-out diplomatic effort. With this thought in mind, I flew to Paris the next day for discussions with M. Mendès-France and with Mr. Dulles, who had just arrived from America.

M. Mendès-France's main purpose in these conversations, which he pursued with drive and skill, was to dispel Mr. Dulles' suspicion that there would inevitably be some departure by France from the seven points on which we had agreed in Washington. He described to us his negotiations with the Vietminh on the question of the demarcation line in Vietnam and effectively demonstrated that at no point had his position diverged from the minimum terms which had been defined by the Americans and ourselves.

Our combined arguments at first produced no impression. Mr. Dulles told us that after discussion with the President it had been agreed that he should not return to Geneva. He reiterated his fears that, in the event, France would be compelled to depart from the seven points, and the United States would then have to dissociate herself from the resulting agreement. He said that even if the settlement adhered to the seven points faithfully, the United States still could not guarantee it. American public opinion would never tolerate "the guaranteeing of the subjection of millions of Vietnamese to Communist rule." Dulles concluded by saying that

he did not want to put himself in the position of having to say no in public. To this Mendès-France replied that the United States would not escape the dilemma by refusing to appear at Geneva. Since they were already represented at the Conference, they would have to make a decision in any case. He repeatedly emphasized that Dulles' suspicions about a departure from the "seven points" were wholly unjustified; it was precisely because he wished to secure them that he was anxious for Dulles to come to Geneva. In the end, Mr. Dulles told us that he would give us his final answer on the following day. M. Mendès-France's courage and persistence were rewarded. . . .

A conference followed at the Quai d'Orsay, where Mr. Dulles announced that Mr. Bedell Smith would be returning to Geneva in the very near future to share in the work of the Conference.

. . . . .

The first indication that the Conference might at least be on the verge of success came on the afternoon of July 18, when Chou En-lai proposed to me that the supervisory commission should consist of India, Canada and Poland. After all the argument, this was a definite step towards us and the proposal was accepted by all three Western powers. From that moment the tangled ends of the negotiations began to sort themselves out. On the afternoon of the 20th, after frantic activity at all levels, M. Mendès-France and the Vietminh delegate were able to announce that they had reached agreement on a demarcation line, which was to be a river just south of the 17th parallel. M. Mendès-France had also persuaded the Vietminh to agree that elections should not be held until July 1956. By nine o'clock that evening, the armistice agreements for both Vietnam and Laos were almost complete. The Cambodians skilfully held out till last, when we were exhausted. Molotov and I, as joint chairmen, together with Mendès-France, held a long meeting with them and the Vietminh. It was a gruelling session. At two o'clock on the morning of the 21st, after hard bargaining and some surprising last-minute concessions by Molotov, we succeeded in resolving the remaining differences between them. As we were concluding our meeting, news arrived that the armistice agreements for Laos and Vietnam had been signed by military representatives of the two commands. The Cambodian agreement followed shortly after noon. The pattern of the final settlement was now complete.[31]

Excerpts from the Final Declaration of the Geneva Conference, July 21, 1954

1. The Conference takes note of the agreements ending hostilities in Cambodia, Laos and Viet Nam and organising international control and the supervision of the execution of the provisions of these agreements.

.   .   .   .   .

4. The Conference takes note of the clauses in the agreement on the cessation of hostilities in Viet Nam prohibiting the introduction into Viet Nam of foreign troops and military personnel as well as of all kinds of arms and munitions. . . .

5. The Conference takes note of the clauses in the agreement on the cessation of hostilities in Viet Nam to the effect that no military base under the control of a foreign State may be established in the regrouping zones of the two parties, the latter having the obligation to see that the

zones allotted to them shall not constitute part of any military alliance and shall not be utilised for the resumption of hostilities or in the service of an aggressive policy. . . .

6. The Conference recognises that the essential purpose of the agreement relating to Viet Nam is to settle military questions with a view to ending hostilities and that the military demarcation line is provisional and should not in any way be interpreted as constituting a political or territorial boundary. . . .

7. The Conference declares that, so far as Viet Nam is concerned, the settlement of political problems, effected on the basis of respect for the principles of independence, unity and territorial integrity, shall permit the Vietnamese people to enjoy the fundamental freedoms, guaranteed by democratic institutions established as a result of free general elections by secret ballot. In order to ensure that sufficient progress in the restoration of peace has been made, and that all the necessary conditions obtain for free expression of the national will, general elections shall be held in July 1956, under the supervision of an international commission composed of representatives of the Member States of the International Supervisory Commission, referred to in the agreement on the cessation of hostilities. Consultations will be held on this subject between the competent representative authorities of the two zones from July 20, 1955, onwards.

8. The provisions of the agreements on the cessation of hostilities intended to ensure the protection of individuals and of property must be most strictly applied and must, in particular, allow everyone in Viet Nam to decide freely in which zone he wishes to live.

9. The competent representative authorities of the Northern and Southern zones of Viet Nam, as well as the authorities of Laos and Cambodia, must not permit any individual or collective reprisals against persons who have collaborated in

31*Ibid.*, pp. 156–59.

any way with one of the parties during the war, or against members of such persons' families.

10. The Conference takes note of the declaration of the Government of the French Republic to the effect that it is ready to withdraw its troops. . . .

.   .   .   .   .

13. The members of the Conference agree to consult one another on any question which may be referred to them by the International Supervisory Commission, in order to study such measures as may prove necessary to ensure that the agreements on the cessation of hostilities in Cambodia, Laos and Viet Nam are respected.[32]

---

[32]*Further Documents relating to the discussion of Indo-China at the Geneva Conference,* Cmd. 9239 (London: Her Majesty's Stationery Office, 1954), pp. 9–10. Quoted by permission of the Controller of Her Britannic Majesty's Stationery Office.

The Geneva Agreement permitted the French to withdraw from Vietnam and ended what Bernard Fall refers to as the First Indochina War. A new political phase under the leadership of Ngo Dinh Diem, the American-supported Catholic who had become premier in Bao Dai's south Vietnam government on July 7, 1954, was beginning. Some of the implications of the post-Geneva period are here suggested by Bernard Fall. (Mr. Fall, one of the most dedicated and expert students of Vietnam, was killed there by a land mine explosion in 1967.)

FOR CONSIDERATION   Whether or not Mendès-France made a deal with Molotov is an interesting question. It is a fact, in any case, that when the EDC pact came up for consideration in August, Mendès-France entangled it with so many amendments that it was never passed.

A month later, on September 8, 1954, the Southeast Asia agreement (SEATO) was signed.

Comments of Bernard Fall

In Viet-Nam itself, the state of affairs which resulted from the Geneva settlement was grim: 860,000 refugees—more than 500,000 of them Catholics—began to pour into what was now rapidly becoming "South Viet-Nam"—i.e., Viet-Nam south of the new demarcation line at the 17th Parallel. North of the line, stolid-faced Viet-Minh regulars began to occupy the cities and towns left behind by withdrawing French troops.

Some 190,000 Franco-Vietnamese troops moved south of the demarcation line, although many of the Vietnamese whose home villages were in the North preferred to desert in order not to be separated from their families. In the South, it is now admitted (though it was carefully hushed up at the time), perhaps as many as 80,000 local guerrillas and regulars and their dependents, including almost 10,000 mountain tribesmen, went northward.

Perhaps another 5,000 to 6,000 local hard-core guerrillas—probably the élite of the Viet-Minh's military and political operators in the South—simply went underground. They hid their weapons and radio equipment and became anonymous villagers—at least for a while. In the cities, others, such as the Viet-Cong's present leader, Nguyen Huu Tho, created "legal struggle" organizations with the aim of propagating the new catch-phrase of "peace and reunification in two years." They, however, were soon disbanded or arrested by the Saigon police.

In Saigon, the fledgling Diem regime was trying to cope both with the administrative chaos resulting from partition and the influx of refugees, and with the challenges against its survival from various political and religious groups and sects. The government's chances of surviving even as long as the two-year election deadline were rated as poor. President Eisenhower summed up the situation in his memoirs:

I have never talked or corresponded with a person knowledgeable in Indochinese affairs who did not agree that had elections been held as of the time of the fighting, possibly 80 per cent of the population would have voted for the Communist Ho Chi Minh as their leader, rather than Chief of State Bao Dai.

Since the North controlled a population of more than 15 million and the South fewer than 12 million, and since the North could be trusted to "deliver" its electorate in overwhelming numbers, such an election would beyond a doubt have resulted in a peaceful take-over of all of Viet-Nam by Ho Chi Minh in July, 1956. It is worth noting that Diem disposed of Bao Dai by a rigged plebiscite, held in 1955. Diem got 98.8 per cent of the vote. Diem was overthrown and assassinated in a coup in 1963; Bao Dai is now living in France.) . . .

As for the elections, the deadline passed without a ballot or undue incident. Both North Viet-Nam and the Soviet Union made protests against this apparent violation of the Geneva Agreements, but both South Viet-Nam and the United States—the latter in a statement by Walter S. Robertson, then Assistant Secretary of State, on June 1, 1956—argued that North

Viet-Nam already had violated the cease-fire provisions with regard to increases in troops and equipment, as well as with regard to the freedom-of-movement provisions. Indeed, in a diplomatic note sent in April, 1956, by Britain to the Soviet Government, as co-chairman of the Geneva Conference, London pointed out that North Vietnamese regular units had increased from seven to twenty divisions.

In the South, difficulties arose over such matters as the entry and departure of military equipment and American advisers, about whose exact numbers there were disagreements from the start. The I.C.S.C. complained, in its January, 1957, report, that "While the commission has experienced difficulties in North Viet-Nam, the major part of its difficulties has arisen in South Viet-Nam."

As for the North Vietnamese, the passage of the July, 1956, election deadline was the signal that South Viet-Nam would not come to terms willingly. As long as there was even a remote chance of peaceful reunification, Hanoi—as well as the guerrilla stay-behinds inside South Viet-Nam—had presented to the outside world a picture of sweet reasonableness: After all, there was hardly any point in risking international good will, as well as valuable cadres, to hasten what was assumed to be an orderly take-over.

But within a few months after the deadline had passed in 1956, the killing of village chiefs in South Viet-Nam began—by stay-behind guerrillas, not the "outside aggressors" of 1959–60 cited by the recent State Department white paper. By the time the South Viet-Nam problem had become a military challenge to the United States late in 1961, the second Indochina war had been under way for almost five years.[33]

---

[33]Bernard Fall, "How the French Got out of Viet-Nam," in Marcus G. Raskin and Bernard B. Fall, *The Viet-Nam Reader* (New York: Vintage Books, 1965), pp. 88–91.

BIBLIOGRAPHY

SOURCES USED IN THIS PROBLEM

1. *Collections and Official Documents*

COLE, ALLAN B. (ed.). *Conflict in Indo-China and International Repercussions.* Ithaca, N.Y.: Cornell University Press, 1956.

Further Documents relating to the discussion of Indo-China at the Geneva Conference, Cmd. 9239. London: Her Majesty's Stationery Office, 1954.

Journal Officiel, Débats. Paris: Imprimerie nationale.

Life (periodical).

The New York Times Magazine.

RASKIN, MARCUS G. and FALL, BERNARD B. *The Viet-Nam Reader.* New York: Vintage Books, 1965.

The Reporter (periodical).

2. *Others*

BIDAULT, GEORGES. *D'une résistance à l'autre.* Paris: Les Presses du Siècle, 1965.

CATROUX, GENERAL GEORGES. *Deau actes du drame indochinois.* Paris: Librairie Plon, 1959.

EDEN, ANTHONY. *Full Circle.* Boston: Houghton Mifflin, 1960.

EISENHOWER, DWIGHT D. *The White House Years.* Vol. I, *Mandate for Change 1953–56.* Garden City, N.Y.: Doubleday, 1963.

ELY, PAUL. *Mémoires.* Vol. I, *L'Indochine dans la tourmente.* Paris: Librairie Plon, 1964.

FALL, BERNARD B. *Hell in a Very Small Place.* Philadelphia: J. B. Lippincott, 1966.

GIAP, GENERAL VO NGUYEN. *Dien Bien Phu.* Hanoi: Foreign Languages Publishing House, 1964.

ISAACS, HAROLD R. *No Peace for Asia.* New York: Macmillan, 1947; Cambridge, Mass.: MIT Press, 1967.

LANIEL, JOSEPH. *Le Drame indochinois.* Paris: Librairie Plon, 1957.

NAVARRE, HENRI. *Agonie de l'Indochine.* Paris: Librairie Plon, 1956.

NEWMAN, BERNARD. *Background to Vietnam.* New York: Roy Publishers, Inc., 1965.

RIDGWAY, GENERAL MATTHEW B. *Soldier: The Memoirs of Matthew B. Ridgway* (as told to HAROLD W. MARTIN). New York: Harper, 1956.

SELECT LIST OF BOOKS RECOMMENDED FOR FURTHER READING

ARON, RAYMOND and LERNER, DAVID. *France Defeats EDC.* New York: Praeger, 1957.

BODARD, LUCIEN. *The Quicksand War: Prelude to Vietnam.* Boston: Little Brown, 1967.

BURCHETT, WILFRED G. *Vietnam: Inside Story of the Guerrilla War.* New York: International Publishers, 1965.

BUTTINGER, JOSEPH. *The Smaller Dragon: A Political History of Vietnam.* New York: Praeger, 1958.

BUTTINGER, JOSEPH. *Vietnam: A Dragon Embattled.* 2 vols. New York: Praeger, 1967.

FALL, BERNARD B. *Street without Joy: Indochina at War, 1946–1954.* Harrisburg, Pa.: Stockpole (2d ed.), 1964.

FALL, BERNARD B. *The Two Vietnams.* New York: Praeger (2d ed.), 1967.

FALL, BERNARD B. *Viet Nam—Witness 1953–66.* New York: Praeger, 1966.

FALL, BERNARD B. *Ho Chi Minh on Revolution 1920–1966.* New York: Praeger, 1967.

GIAP, GENERAL VO NGUYEN. *People's War, People's Army.* New York: Praeger, 1962.

GRAUWIN, PAUL. *Doctor at Dien Bien Phu.* New York: Praeger, 1955.

GURTOV, MELVIN. *The First Vietnam Crisis.* New York: Columbia University Press, 1967.

HAMMER, ELLEN. *The Struggle for Indochina.* Stanford, Calif.: Stanford University Press, 1954.

HOANG-VAN-CHI. *From Colonialism to Communism: A Case History of North Vietnam.* New York: Praeger, 1964.

HO CHI MINH. *Selected Works.* 4 vols. Hanoi: Foreign Languages Publishing House, 1960–62.

KAHIN, GEORGE MCTURNAN (ed.). *Government and Politics of Southeast Asia.* Ithaca, N.Y.: Cornell University Press, 1964.

LACOUTURE, JEAN and DEVILLERS, PHILLIPPE. *La fin d'une guerre: Indochine, 1954.* Paris: Seuil, 1960.

LANCASTER, DONALD. *The Emancipation of French Indochina.* Royal Institute of International Affairs. London: Oxford University Press, 1961.

RAY, SIBNARAYAN (ed.). *Vietnam Seen from East and West: An International Symposium.* New York: Praeger, 1966.

ROY, JULES. *The Battle of Dienbienphu.* New York: Harper, 1965.

SALISBURY-JONES, SIR G. *So Full a Glory: De Lattre de Tassigny.* London: Weidenfeld & Nicolson, 1954.

SHAPLEN, ROBERT. *The Lost Revolution: The Story of Twenty Years of Neglected Opportunities in Vietnam.* New York: Harper & Row, 1965.

TANHAM, GEORGE K. *Communist Revolutionary Warfare: The Vietminh in Indochina.* New York: Praeger, 1961.

THE SUEZ CRISIS

Big-power conflicts in the

Middle East, 1955-56

The Suez Crisis of 1956 was far more than a local conflict in the eastern Mediterranean. It involved the rights of newly independent countries, and it brought into focus the various interests of big powers in giving military and economic aid to Israelis and Arabs. The crisis split the NATO alliance, and provided Russia with an opportunity to extend its influence into the Middle East. It precipitated a reappraisal of the means whereby strategic oil can be shipped from Arabia and Iraq to the West. In France, Charles de Gaulle observed events from the sidelines and could not help but be confirmed in his conviction that his country must never be dependent on Anglo-American resources. The crisis provided a delicate test case for the United Nations, whose Security Council could not place sanctions against major powers. Out of this impotency came an increased significance for the General Assembly (and by extension, Afro-Asian influence), for it enabled the Assembly to bring into existence, for the first time, an implementing arm, the UN Emergency Force.

Certain basic elements must be understood: (1) the status of the Suez Canal; (2) the Israeli-Arab rivalry for the procurement of weapons; and (3) the importance of Middle Eastern oil. The following documents set forth some of the fundamentals.

FOR CONSIDERATION   Notice that between 1948 and 1955 the amount of oil shipped via the Mediterranean had more than tripled. Notice also the proportionate amount transported by pipelines as against tankers. If Egypt could close the Canal, Iraq, Syria, or Lebanon could shut down the pipelines any time they wished. This would not necessarily involve violence, because merely cutting the lines would prevent the flow of oil.

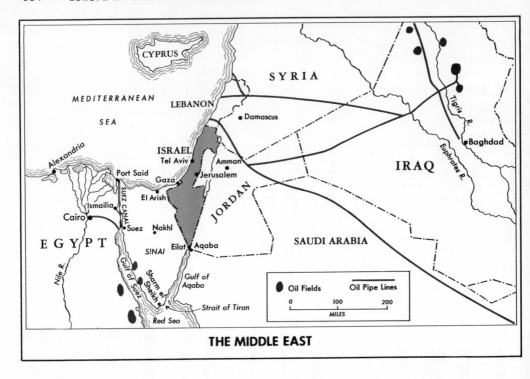

THE MIDDLE EAST

Convention between Great Britain, Austria-Hungary, France, Germany, Italy, the Netherlands, Russia, Spain, and Turkey, Respecting the Free Navigation of the Suez Maritime Canal, October 29, 1888

Art. I. The Suez Maritime Canal shall always be free and open, in time of war as in time of peace, to every vessel of commerce or of war, without distinction of flag.

The Canal shall never be subject to the exercise of the right of blockade.

·   ·   ·   ·   ·

Art. VIII. The Agents in Egypt of the Signatory Powers of the present Treaty shall be charged to see that it is carried out. In any circumstance threatening the security and free passage of the Canal, they shall meet at the summons of three of them and under the presidency of their Doyen, to make the necessary verifications. . . .

·   ·   ·   ·   ·

Art. XII. The High Contracting Par-

ties, by application of the principle of equality as regards free use of the Canal, a principle which forms one of the bases of the present Treaty, agree that none of them shall seek, with respect to the Canal, territorial or commercial advantages or privileges in any international arrangements that may be concluded. . . .[1]

Tripartite Declaration of France, Great Britain, and the United States on Arms to the Middle East, Released May 25, 1950

·   ·   ·   ·   ·

1. The three Governments recognize that the Arab states and Israel all need to maintain a certain level of armed forces for the purposes of assuring their internal security and their legitimate self-defense and to permit them to play their

---

[1] *The Suez Canal Problem,* Department of State Publication No. 6392 (Washington, D.C.: U.S. Government Printing Office, October, 1956), pp. 16–19.

part in the defense of the area as a whole. All applications for arms or war material for these countries will be considered in the light of these principles. . . .

2. The three Governments declare that assurances have been received from all the states in question, to which they permit arms to be supplied from their countries, that the purchasing state does not intend to undertake any act of aggression against any other state. . . .

3. . . . The three Governments, should they find that any of these states was preparing to violate frontiers or armistice lines, would, consistently with their obligations as members of the United Nations, immediately take action, both within and outside the United Nations, to prevent such violation.[2]

Consequences of Closing the Suez Canal and Cutting the Syrian Pipeline, Described by George Lenczowski

Translated into absolute figures the situation was as follows: Both the Suez oil traffic, representing 77 million tons a year and the Syrian pipeline transit amounting to 25 million tons a year came to a complete stop. Together this constituted 102 million tons a year or 2.04 million barrels a day, of which 87.5 million tons a year or 1.75 million barrels a day went to Europe. In 1956 Europe was importing oil at the rate of 125 million tons a year or 2.5 million barrels a day. In the postinvasion period therefore Europe was deprived of 70 per cent of its usual oil supplies. True enough, the oil which normally went through the Suez

[2]*Department of State Bulletin*, June 5, 1950, p. 886.

Canal could be shipped around the Cape. But this meant a delay of at least two weeks. Because of the longer time needed for tankers to make the journey, supplies via the Cape could amount to barely 60 per cent of the oil directed through Suez. Thus Europe was bound to be short about 45 per cent of its normal supplies. Even this figure is based on the assumption that all the tankers hitherto using the Canal would go to Europe instead of being divided between European (80 per cent) and the Western Hemisphere (20 per cent) destinations, as was the case before the blocking of the Canal.[3]

Exports of Middle Eastern Petroleum through Mediterranean Pipelines, Suez Canal, and Indian Ocean

	Millions of Barrels			
Year	Suez Canal	Eastern Mediterranean Pipelines	Indian Ocean	Total
1938	39	30	31	100
1948	214	26	151	391
1949	273	28	173	474
1950	352	55	199	606
1951	317	166	203	686
1952	340	228	174	742
1953	366	292	197	855
1954	422	303	242	967
1955	495	305	335	1,135
1956	487	280	443	1,210
1957	400	211	631	1,242
1958	699	305	493	1,497
1959	730	326	544	1,600
1960	847	343	634	1,824

SOURCE: Charles Issawi and Mohammed Yeganeh, *The Economics of Middle Eastern Oil* (New York: Frederick A. Praeger, Inc., 1962), p. 21.

[3]George Lenczowski, *Oil and State in the Middle East* (Ithaca, N.Y.: Cornell University Press, 1960), pp. 326–27. © 1960 by Cornell University. Used by permission of Cornell University Press.

In Egypt, following the Egyptian withdrawal from Israel after 1949, events developed rapidly, pressured by British defense requirements and by Egyptian nationalism. Since 1936 the British maintained forces in the

Canal area, and in 1951, countering Egyptian efforts to gain control of the Sudan, they increased their forces and militarized the Canal.

In the following year Egyptian nationalists, led by General Naguib and a young colonel named Gamal Abdel Nasser, overthrew the corrupt government of King Farouk, and proclaimed the revolution. Shortly after the uprising, Nasser put in writing some of his thoughts about revolution and its implications for the future.

Excerpt from Nasser's "Philosophy of Revolution" (of July 23, 1952), Written in 1952

Our revolution must be sustained by our having the courage to embark on whatever is deemed necessary, no matter what loss of popularity and applause and cheers such action may cost us. Otherwise we will have failed in our trust as leaders of the revolution.

Frequently people come to me and say: "But you are arousing certain people's resentment." To which I always reply: "The resentment of certain people is not the important factor. The real question is always: is what they resent good for the nation, or bad for themselves?" ...

This is our role as determined for us by the history of our nation. There is no choice, no matter what the price we may have to pay. We are under no illusion concerning the task we are to achieve, or the nature of the duties imposed upon us. We removed the former king without consulting anyone because he was an obstacle in the clear way of our caravan. We began our plans for expelling the English

from Egypt because their presence here weighs upon us and our progress, and leads many among us off the right track and into emotional detours.

There are the steps that had to be taken in correcting the legacy of the past. We have proceeded on the way and borne all the responsibility for everything.

But when the time came that the future of our country was to be discussed and fashioned, we said that it was no right of ours alone. To make secure the political life of our country in the future, we sought leaders of opinion from different classes and beliefs....

There are no limits beyond which we will not go. Our task is the removal of rocks and obstacles from off the way. This is our only duty. The future and all its challenge is work that is open to all patriots with ideas and experience. This is a duty and a privilege demanded of them....[4]

[4]Gamal Abdul Nasser, *Egypt's Liberation: The Philosophy of Revolution* (Washington, D.C.: Public Affairs Press, 1955), pp. 74–77.

Naguib did not remain for long as head of the Revolutionary Council, and real power was obtained by Nasser when in February, 1954, he became Prime Minister. (In 1956 he was elected President.) A few months later, on October 19, 1954, he successfully negotiated an agreement whereby British troops would leave the Suez Canal. Prime Minister Churchill had reluctantly concluded that against a Russian atomic threat the obsolete defenses would be useless. And to say that he was under strong pressure from the United States would be an understatement.

Britain's agreement to withdraw drastically altered Egypt's relations with Israel, for there was no longer a buffer between the two hostile states. After 1954 border incidents became more frequent.

Meanwhile, Nasser's stature was growing. After the Bandung Conference in 1955, he developed closer relations with the Soviet Union. During the summer of 1955, this led to the shipment of Russian (ostensibly Czech) weapons to Egypt. The arms deal was defiantly made public by Nasser in a speech, part of which is here reproduced.

FOR CONSIDERATION   Egypt obtained around 100 MIG15 fighters, 50 bombers, and several hundred tanks from Russia and Czechoslovakia. The French wondered to what extent these weapons would reach rebel forces in Algeria.

Speech of Nasser, Sept. 27, 1955

Now, what was the tale of Britain? Britain told us that she was prepared to supply us with weapons, and we answered that we learned this thankfully. But what was the result? It was that Britain supplied us with quantities of arms that did not accord with our revolution's objectives. And what did this entail, my brothers? The enemy army was being supplied with arms by several nations; the Israeli army was receiving weapons from Britain, France, Belgium, Canada, and several other countries. . . . France kept back arms from us as a result of our feelings about North Africa. When we learned this, when we saw this arbitrary decision, this biased use of in-

fluence, we decided to ask every nation in the world to supply us with arms unconditionally. I made this request, and in doing so emphasized that the weapons would be used not for aggression, but for defence. We harbour no aggressive intentions; our aims are only peaceful. . . .

When we received a reply to our request from the Government of Czechoslovakia declaring its readiness to supply us with weapons in accordance with the Egyptian army's needs and on a purely commercial basis, and stating that the transaction would be regarded as any other commercial one, we accepted immediately.[5]

   [5]Royal Institute of International Affairs, *Documents on International Affairs, 1955* (London: Oxford University Press, 1958), pp. 370-71.

During 1955 Nasser was also negotiating for the Aswan Dam loan. The "High Dam" project made sense to the West, and especially to the United States, which hoped that economic aid to Arab countries would balance out the assistance given Israel. Tentative arrangements for financing through the World Bank were concluded on December 16, 1955. It should be realized, of course, that without State Department approval, a final commitment for the loan could not be made.

During early 1956, Secretary of State John Foster Dulles became increasingly disenchanted with Nasser, whose wooing of the Communist bloc showed no signs of diminishing. Irked by Nasser's attitude, Dulles scheduled a meeting with the Egyptian Ambassador.

A Reconstruction of the Meeting between Dulles and Egyptian Ambassador Hussein, July 19, 1956, by Herman Finer

On July 19, 1956, Dulles was in the office at work, as usual, at shortly after 8:00 A.M. He repeated his consultation with the President, the issue not closed. At about 11:00 his phone rang and he was told that Ambassador Hussein was on his way up to the office. Two very high State Department career officials were present in the room with Dulles. The Ambassador entered with his aide. He himself was a not unwelcome figure. He had held his position since long before Nasser's deposition of Naguib and, according to some State Department officials, was not an idolator of Nasser. Indeed, he was said to be rather inclined toward the Western point of view in the struggle for mastery in the Middle East and the world in general. Dulles did not dislike him personally.

Dulles began to explain the many difficulties he was encountering in clinching the loan. This took him a little time, as he always spoke very carefully, in rather pedantic language and syntax.

The Ambassador began to advance questions on certain matters. The Aswan Dam scheme, if it was to be helped, was, as the Ambassador had long known, to follow on an agreement between Egypt and the Sudan whereby Sudan's share of the upper waters of the Nile would be assigned satisfactorily to that country. But this had not yet been concluded? He was anxious about this. Dulles in each case put the other point of view. It seemed that Hussein, by the proper demeanor and rhetoric, might have an indefinite postponement or an alibi, rather than a complete refusal.

Then, as Dulles appeared to be bringing the various reasons against the loan to a head, all in tones rather sad and firm, the Ambassador became excited. He was sitting on the divan near the coffee table, while Dulles was sitting just on the other side of that same table in an armchair with his legs stretched out onto the table. At a certain point, Ambassador Hussein, perhaps remembering the instructions received in Cairo, became worried and agitated. He leaned forward over the table, gesticulating. "Don't please say," he blurted out, "you are going to withdraw the offer, because . . ." (and he pointed to his pocket) "we have the Russian offer to finance the Dam right here in my pocket!"

No nerve was so raw in all of Dulles's sensitive composition as Russia. He at once retorted, "Well, as you have the money already, you don't need any from us! My offer is withdrawn!" The Egyptian Ambassador left, terribly unhappy, and at once the press services became extremely active. Serious things began to happen—irreversible deeds, deeds with widespread and disastrous repercussions.[6]

Comments of Robert D. Murphy, Undersecretary of State for Political Affairs

Those of us who worked with Dulles were never told explicitly why he acted so abruptly. We surmised that perhaps the main reason was because Nasser was scheduled to make a trip to Moscow early in August. If the United States would agree to the Aswan Dam financing, the Egyptian President could then concentrate in Moscow on concluding his second big arms deal with the Russians, thus getting the best of both worlds. Dulles guessed accurately that Nasser would not journey to Moscow at all if the Aswan Dam offer were rescinded, because that would compel the Egyptian to go hat-in-hand not only with regard to the High Dam project but on the arms deal as well.

[6]Herman Finer, *Dulles over Suez* (Chicago: Quadrangle Books, 1964), pp. 47–48.

But the effects of summarily withdrawing the Aswan offer had not been weighed carefully in advance. Although aware for several days of the Soviet arms deal, Dulles had summoned no staff meeting to discuss this new development. I was working with him at the time on related Middle Eastern problems, but he did not mention the Aswan matter to me. Even President Eisenhower was not consulted until the morning of Hussein's visit. There also was regrettable lack of adequate notice to the partners in the consortium, especially Britain which was chiefly affected. . . . As Prime Minister Eden later said: "Her Majesty's Government were informed but were not consulted."[7]

Secretary of State Dulles to President Eisenhower, September 15, 1956

You asked whether our withdrawal from the Aswan Dam project could properly be deemed "abrupt."

I think not, at least so far as Egypt was concerned. For several months we had left unanswered an Egyptian memorandum on this subject, and the Egyptians knew full well the reasons why. Telephone conversations of which we learned indicated that the Egyptian Government knew that when they came, as they did, to get a definitive reply it would be negative.

There had for some time been mounting Congressional opposition. The Senate Appropriations Committee had already passed a resolution directing that there should be no support for the Aswan Dam without the approval of the Committee— an action which, while it was probably not Constitutional, indicated a Congressional attitude, in the face of which it would have been impossible to finance the Dam. If I had not announced our withdrawal when I did, the Congress would certainly have imposed it on us, almost unanimously. As it was, we retained some flexibility.

Of course Egypt, in its flirtations with the Soviet Union, had itself consciously jeopardized our sharing in this project, and they had tried to bluff us by pretending to [accept] Soviet "offers."

The outcome was not in fact anything in the nature of a "shock" or "surprise" to the Egyptians.[8]

[7]Robert D. Murphy, *Diplomat among Warriors* (Garden City, N.Y.: Doubleday & Company, Inc., 1964), p. 377. Copyright © 1964 by Robert Murphy. Reprinted by permission of Doubleday & Co., Inc.

[8]Dwight D. Eisenhower, *The White House Years*, Vol. II, *Waging Peace, 1956–1961* (Garden City, N.Y.: Doubleday & Company, Inc., 1965), p. 33. Copyright © 1965 by Dwight D. Eisenhower. Reproduced by permission of Doubleday & Co., Inc.

Nasser's reaction was swift. Within a week he decided to nationalize the Suez Canal. This was announced on July 26.

FOR CONSIDERATION   Was Nasser's move an impetuous one or had he planned it in advance? The "plot theory" has been advanced by some (see, for example, Erskine Childer's *The Road to Suez*), but is discounted by an authoritative scholar of the crisis, Herman Finer.[9] It is true, however, that Nasser had initiated surveys of the Canal's operations as early as 1954.

[9]Finer, *op. cit.*, pp. 517–18.

An Eyewitness Account of Nasser's Speech Nationalizing the Canal, July 26, 1956

At about seven o'clock that evening, as night began to fall on the huge Mohamed Ali Square, the great crowd was well contained by powerful detachments of police. A wonderful breeze literally revived all those who, like ourselves, had just survived one of the most stifling weeks Cairo had ever experienced. . . . Nasser passed close by us as he made for the rostrum. . . . He took the microphone in his hand and started his speech on a rather odd note. Whence this *baladi* language, this rather colloquial and slangy form of Egyptian? The entranced crowd reacted to every inflection in this jesting harangue. We came expecting to hear a tragic monologue, and instead he was giving us a humorous account of what had happened.

"Now I'll give you the dope about my adventures with the American diplomats . . ." There was the austere Gamal Nasser, former Staff College instructor, posing as a kind of Hyde Park orator and couching his message in the lingo of the East End. The crowd roared. "An American diplomat came and told me, 'If Mr. Allen passes you a message from the State Department about Czech armaments, just you chuck him out of your office. But if he goes back without having given it you, then Mr. Dulles will chuck him out.' . . .

What's to be done for poor Mr. Allen?" . . .

But now the tone began to change. Telling of his difficulties with the president of the International Bank, Eugene Black, Nasser suddenly said, strangely, "Mr. Black suddenly reminded me of Ferdinand de Lesseps . . ." He pronounced the name "de Lissipse" [sic], with a kind of hissing tone. This unleashed an unbroken denunciation—bitter, violent, finally furious—against what he called "mortgage colonialism." . . . On the rostrum as well as in the "pit" people began to clap their hands in surprise, to say the least. "And I can announce that at the very moment when I am speaking to you, the government Journal is publishing a new Law nationalizing the Suez Company, and at this very moment our Government agents are taking over the Company's premises!" There was uproar all around us. Journalists whom we knew to be sceptical of the government were standing on their chairs, shouting enthusiastically, while Nasser—suddenly seized with a fit of laughing at his own cheek—continued, "Well, the Canal will pay for the Dam. Four years ago today King Faruk fled from Egypt. Today, in the name of the people, I am taking over the Company. Tonight our Egyptian canal will be run by Egyptians. Egyptians!" . . .[10]

[10]Jean and Simone Lacouture, *Egypt in Transition*, trans. Frances Scarfe (New York: Criterion Books, Inc., 1958), pp. 471–73.

The reaction among the Western powers was immediate. Anthony Eden, who had succeeded Churchill as Prime Minister, saw the ultimate need of force. Eisenhower and Dulles, equally persuaded that peaceful solutions could be found, sent the State Department's experienced troubleshooter Robert D. Murphy to London "to hold the fort." Dulles soon followed and persuaded the British and French to hold a conference.

FOR CONSIDERATION   Eden has been criticized for agreeing to the conference. Did the conference weaken the Anglo-French position? Could the problem have been handled by NATO? Could it have been brought immediately before the UN?

Prime Minister Anthony Eden to President Eisenhower, July 27, 1956

This morning I have reviewed the whole position with my Cabinet colleagues and Chiefs of Staff. We are all agreed that we cannot afford to allow Nasser to seize control of the canal in this way, in defiance of international agreements. If we take a firm stand over this now we shall have the support of all the maritime powers. If we do not, our influence and yours throughout the Middle East will, we are all convinced, be finally destroyed. . . .

My colleagues and I are convinced that we must be ready, in the last resort, to use force to bring Nasser to his senses. For our part we are prepared to do so. I have this morning instructed our Chiefs of Staff to prepare a military plan accordingly.

However, the first step must be for you and us and France to exchange views, align our policies and concert together how we can best bring the maximum pressure to bear on the Egyptian Government.[11]

President Eisenhower to Prime Minister Eden, July 31, 1956

. . . early this morning I received the messages, communicated to me through Murphy from you and Harold Macmillan, telling me on a most secret basis of your decision to employ force without delay or attempting any intermediate and less drastic steps.

For my part, I cannot over-emphasize the strength of my conviction that some such method must be attempted before action such as you contemplate should be undertaken. If unfortunately the situation can finally be resolved only by drastic means, there should be no grounds for be-

lief anywhere that corrective measures were undertaken merely to protect national or individual investors, or the legal rights of a sovereign nation were ruthlessly flouted. A conference, at the very least, should have a great educational effect throughout the world. . . .[12]

Comments of French Foreign Minister Christian Pineau in the Chamber of Deputies, August 3, 1956

. . . the French Government has taken, in relations to its Allies, the strongest possible position. It cannot, in any way, or in any form, accept the decision taken by the Egyptian Government and it will use all the means necessary to block its success.

On the effectiveness of our action depends not only the international traffic through the canal, but the situation in all of North Africa.

No matter what the bonds of friendship that we may wish to maintain with the Egyptian people and the Muslim world, we will not accept the law of a dictator who is less concerned with his people's interests than with his own prestige and his personal ambition. (*Applaud on the Left, Center, and Right.*) . . .

Parliament can place confidence in the Government. It has not wavered and it will not waver before this menace. It will go to the end along the route it has taken, without abandoning either its composure or its resolution. (*Applaud on the Left, Center, and Right.*)[13]

Excerpts from the Three Power Declaration of France, Great Britain, and the United States, August 2, 1956

. . . The present action involves far more than a simple act of nationalisation. It involves the arbitrary and unilateral

---

[11]Anthony Eden, *Full Circle* (Boston: Houghton Mifflin Company, 1960), pp. 476–77.

[12]Eisenhower, *op. cit.*, p. 664.
[13]*Journal Officiel, Assemblée, Débats,* August 4, 1956, p. 3873.

seizure by one nation of an international agency which has the responsibility to maintain and to operate the Suez Canal so that all the signatories to, and beneficiaries of, the Treaty of 1888 can effectively enjoy the use of an international waterway upon which the economy, commerce, and security of much of the world depends. This seizure is the more serious in its implications because it avowedly was made for the purpose of enabling the Government of Egypt to make the Canal serve the purely national purposes of the Egyptian Government, rather than the international purpose established by the Convention of 1888.

. . . . .

The Governments of France, the United Kingdom and the United States . . . consider that steps should be taken

to establish operating arrangements under an international system designed to assure the continuity of operation of the Canal as guaranteed by the Convention of 29th October, 1888, consistently with legitimate Egyptian interests.

To this end they propose that a conference should promptly be held of parties to the Convention and other nations largely concerned with the use of the Canal. The invitations to such a conference, to be held in London, on August 16, 1956, will be extended by the Government of the United Kingdom. . . . The Governments of France and the United States are ready to take part in the conference.[14]

---

[14]Royal Institute of International Affairs, *Documents on International Affairs, 1956* (London: Oxford University Press, 1959), pp. 138–39.

The United States, France, and England froze Egyptian credits pending the outcome of the proposed London conference. Against this move, Nasser undertook to demonstrate his good faith by efficiently moving vessels through the canal, but on August 12 announced that Egypt would boycott the meeting.

In the United States, Eisenhower and Dulles saw that the crisis was not easing. Even though the Democratic Convention was then in session (it should not be forgotten that 1956 was an election year), they decided to consult with congressional leaders.

Eyewitness Account of White House Briefing of August 12, 1956, by Presidential Assistant Sherman Adams

On a Sunday, August 12, four days before the start of the conference in London, Eisenhower called a bipartisan meeting of the Congressional leaders at the White House for a full discussion of the Suez crisis. The Democrats willingly interrupted their deliberations at the Democratic national convention in Chicago in order to attend it. Gathering in the Cabinet Room, talking among themselves about party politics, which was the

topic of the hour, the Senators and the Representatives looked up as the meeting was called to order and saw facing them a serious President and a grim Secretary of State. . . .

The Secretary of State told the Congressmen that he had been forced to make his fast trip to London after the seizure of the canal because the British and the French were ready at that time to attack Egypt. It had taken considerable persuasion to get them to agree to hold a Suez Canal conference at all. . . .

Sam Rayburn wanted to know how much provocation would be needed to make the British and the French take action against Egypt. Dulles stared through his glasses at Rayburn with surprise.

"They think there has been sufficient provocation already," the Secretary said. "They have only agreed to bide their time until the conference. They call Nasser a wild man brandishing an ax." . . .

Closing the meeting, Eisenhower tried to express some of his usual optimism by telling the Congressmen that he had been greatly encouraged by the stand taken in England by Hugh Gaitskell in opposing the use of military force against Nasser until all possible attempts to reach a peaceful settlement had been exhausted. "There are so many possibilities involved that I shudder to think of them," the President said. "The most important thing is that we must explore every peaceful means of getting to a settlement and the world must know that we are doing so."[15]

---

[15]Sherman Adams, *Firsthand Report: The Story of the Eisenhower Administration* (New York: Harper & Row, 1961), pp. 250-53. Reprinted by permission of Harper & Row, Publishers.

Twenty-two countries finally sent representatives to London for the conference. The United States made a proposal which with minor modifications was finally adopted. The strongest opponent, taking Nasser's part, was the Russian delegate, Foreign Minister Shepolov. The following documents reveal various attitudes toward the conference.

Remarks of Foreign Minister Shepolov, August 21, 1956

We should also bear in mind that colonialism formerly endeavoured to prevent the peoples of the East from achieving political independence. Now that this independence has already been won by the majority of nations, colonialism is manoeuvring and asserting that its actions are, so to speak, far removed from politics.

For that reason, particular caution is required every time we have to consider matters relating to the interests of the nations of the East, so that the old colonial policy may not be pursued under the guise of "non-political" steps.

It is asserted that the American draft is motivated by a desire to guarantee freedom of navigation through the Suez Canal. But that draft, apparently, proceeds from the assumption that force is the only reliable guarantee in relations among nations. It is not by chance that the draft directly provides for "effective sanctions". We are convinced that far more importance should be attached to international obligations that are assumed voluntarily and to the willingness of nations to co-operate in the interests of peace and of developing international economic ties. . . .

The proposed solution is an expression of the old policy. Instead of the Suez Canal being dominated by one power— and in the past that power was in fact Britain—it is now suggested that the canal be dominated by several foreign powers.

However, a proposal of that kind is unreal because it ignores the substantial changes that have taken place in the East during the last decades. . . .

These are, in the main, the reasons why the Soviet delegation cannot agree to the draft submitted by the United States delegation.[16]

---

[16]*Documents on International Affairs, 1956,* pp. 180-81.

Excerpt from the United States Proposal, as Adopted by the London Conference, August 21, 1956

. . . There should be established by a Convention to be negotiated with Egypt:

Institutional arrangements for co-operation between Egypt and other interested nations in the operation, maintenance and development of the Canal and for harmonising and safeguarding their respective interests in the Canal. To this end, operating, maintaining and developing the Canal and enlarging it so as to increase the volume of traffic in the interest of the world trade and of Egypt, would be the responsibility of a Suez Canal Board. Egypt would grant this Board all rights and facilities appropriate to its functioning as here outlined. The status of the Board would be defined in the above-mentioned Convention.

The members of the Board, in addition to Egypt, would be other States chosen in a manner to be agreed upon from among the States parties to the Convention with due re-

Illingworth in the Daily Mail *(London)*

"Imports for the Holy Land" – a British View.

gard to use, pattern of trade and geographical distribution.[17]

[17]*Ibid.*, p. 176.

While France and England were willing to attend conferences on Suez, they lost no time in preparing for a military operation against Egypt. On August 11, 1956, Eden appointed General Sir Charles Keightly as Supreme Commander, to plan an operation against Egypt. The following accounts clarify aspects of the military question. The statements quoted from Terence Robertson's book *Crisis* were obtained by Mr. Robertson from the individuals concerned.

FOR CONSIDERATION Eisenhower and Dulles have maintained that the British and French acted unilaterally, that the United States was uninformed about their intentions. Would it not seem probable, from the evidence, that Anglo-French *intentions* were clear? Is there a difference between "intention," and the final decision to carry out what is intended?

Preparations for Operation "Musketeer," as Described by A. J. Barker

Following the appointment of the Supreme Commander, the joint staffs' work began in earnest and by the middle of August the first tentative plan had taken

shape. The operation was to be known as "Hamilcar"—an esoteric reference to the Carthaginian general who had had a record of successful invasions. It had been estimated that at least six weeks' preparation were needed to mount an operation and as two of these had already elapsed everything should be ready for an attack about the middle of September. In preparation for a move to Egypt, troops assembling in Cyprus and Malta were ordered to paint a single, large, white letter "H" denoting "Hamilcar" across the bonnets and roofs of vehicles as aircraft recognition signs—an action which in itself revealed one of the peculiar differences which militated against British and French integration. The British painted "H" ("H" for "Hegypt" according to the British troops!), the French, whose spelling of the name is "Amilcar", painted "A". The paint was hardly dry, when a new plan was christened "Musketeer"—supposedly at the instigation of General Stockwell, who had a weakness for Dumas's dashing characters.

"Musketeer", like its predecessor "Hamilcar", was based on the combined British and American methods used in the Mediterranean landings of the last war. First, air superiority was to be attained by a series of strikes at Egyptian airfields; airborne landings would then precede a seaborne assault designed to seize the base through which men and material could be poured in; the whole operation would be supported by the guns and aircraft of the combined fleets. . . .

The forces finally allocated to General Keightley for the Egyptian expedition consisted on the British side of about 45,000 men, 12,000 vehicles, 300 aircraft and 100 warships of the Royal Navy, including 3 conventional aircraft carriers, 2 obsolete carriers converted as helicopter-carrying troopships and 3 cruisers; on the French side, about 34,000 men (not including Marines and Air Force personnel), 9,000 vehicles, 200 aircraft and about 30 warships, including 2 aircraft carriers, a battleship and 3 cruisers. . . .[18]

---

[18]A. J. Barker, *Suez: the Seven Days' War* (London: Faber & Faber, Ltd., 1965), pp. 34–35.

Comments of Israeli Prime Minister Ben Gurion Regarding French Arms Shipments

The Government of Israel . . . regarded it as its central and most vital task at that moment to obtain defensive arms no lower in quality than the offensive arms that continued to flow to Egypt.

These efforts continued without respite since the beginning of the Czech-Egyptian arms deal, and they were finally crowned with success at the beginning of the second half of 1956, when M. Guy Mollet, the French Socialist, was Prime Minister, and M. Bourgès-Maunoury, of the Radical Party, was his Minister of Defence.

The way was opened wide for the acquisition of modern arms of superior quality—planes, tanks, artillery and so forth, though under unusual conditions, which amounted to conditions of secrecy. Arms ships used to arrive in the dead of night "somewhere" on our Mediterranean coast and were unloaded at top speed by our devoted soldiers in a short space of time; the ships would return immediately under cover of darkness to the country they came from, and the arms would be transported without delay to their destinations in the army camps, without anyone in Israel or abroad, except for the French officers and seamen who brought the arms and the Israeli officers and men who received them, being aware of what was happening, until all the arms ordered had been delivered. . . .[19]

From an Account by French Minister of Defense Bourges-Maunoury, as Recorded by Terence Robertson

The first meetings between myself and Mr. Peres [Israeli Director General of Defence] took place more than a year before

---

[19]David Ben Gurion, "Israel's Security and Her International Position," *Israel Government Yearbook 1959/60* (Tel Aviv: Israel Government Printing Press, n.d.), pp. 26, 28.

the war, in the autumn of 1955, when I was Minister of the Interior. But they developed seriously in January 1956 when I became Defence Minister in M. Mollet's government. We reached complete understanding on Franco-Israeli co-operation in the struggle against the Arabs during March and April. After the nationalisation of the Suez Canal, Britain came into the picture, and it was our policy not to undertake any form of military operation without British partnership.

It has not been made public before, but British planning was so long and slow that I had to send General Challe of our General Staff to see Prime Minister Eden to hurry things up. Mr. Eden had assumed complete charge of British planning, but it was only later, when Mr. Head became Defence Minister, that we began to shorten the time required for the operation. The principal British reason for caution was that they had played a large part in training the Egyptian army and they believed it was a good army when, in fact, it was not good at all. There was also the difficulty that the British were pro-Arab and anti-Israel, whereas we were anti-Arab and pro-Israel.

Once our own preparations were under way and the Israelis decided when to attack, our assistance programme was speeded up and I had to consult with the Americans to get spare parts and items of equipment we lacked. The Americans knew just about everything that was going on in Paris. I saw Ambassador Dillon about once every two weeks to request further supplies from the United States, and in my opinion he was quite aware that they were destined for Cyprus, from where a proportion was sent on to Israel. It was Ambassador Dillon who told me that the British were also asking United States Ambassador Aldrich in London for equipment and supplies from the United States. In total, we asked for and received ninety different items of arms equipment, and the British received a hundred and

sixty-seven different types. It is quite pointless for the Americans to continue to say they were kept in the dark about our plans. Certainly Mr. Dillon was a clever man, and not likely to be deceived. . . .

The United States military were also kept informed through the Chief of Staff in Washington, with whom I sometimes had to be in touch to iron out delivery schedules, and through the Central Intelligence Agency. It is sometimes customary in such circumstances to allow information to pass through secret channels rather than formally through normal diplomatic exchanges. Of course, there is always the possibility that President Eisenhower, facing an election, was not informed until it was too late.[20]

Comment of CIA Director Allen Dulles

. . . Intelligence was well alerted as to what Israel and then Britain and then France were likely to do. The public received the impression, however, that there had been an intelligence failure; statements were issued by U.S. officials to the effect that the country had not been given advance warning of the action. Our officials, of course, intended to imply only that the British and French and Israelis had failed to tell us what they were doing. In fact, United States intelligence had kept the government informed but, as usual, did not advertise its achievement.[21]

Appendix to a Memorandum for the Record, Made by President Eisenhower, October 15, 1956

It is believed that one of the recent

---

[20]From *Crisis: The Inside Story of the Suez Conspiracy* by Terence Robertson. Copyright © 1964 by Terence Robertson. Reprinted by permission of Atheneum Publishers.

[21]Allen Dulles, *The Craft of Intelligence* (New York: Harper & Row, Publishers, 1963), p. 168. Reprinted by permission of Harper & Row, Publishers.

Israeli raids against Jordan involved two or three battalions of infantry, artillery, and jet airplanes. Incidentally, our high-flying reconnaissance planes have shown that Israel had obtained some 60 of the French Mystère pursuit planes, when there had been reported the transfer of only 24. Jordan has no aviation.[22]

---

[22]Eisenhower, *op. cit.*, p. 677.

Following the London Conference a Committee of Five, with Australian Prime Minister R. G. Menzies as chairman, was authorized to attempt to get Nasser's approval of an association to run the canal. Mr. Menzies' efforts failed, but until the outcome of his negotiations was known, it did not seem advisable to try other solutions.

Excerpt from Prime Minister Menzies' Comments on His Mission to Nasser, as Reported to Prime Minister Eden

I was told that Nasser was a man of great personal charm who might beguile me into believing something foreign to my own thought. This is not so. He is in some ways quite a likeable fellow but so far from being charming he is rather *gauche*, with some irritating mannerisms, such as rolling his eyes up to the ceiling when he is talking to you and producing a quick, quite evanescent grin when he can think of nothing else to do. I would say that he was a man of considerable but immature intelligence. . . . His logic does not travel very far; that is to say, he will produce a perfectly accurate major premise and sometimes an accurate minor premise, but his deduction will be astonishing. I will give you a powerful example of this which I think you might usefully have in mind. I will put it in the form of a substantially verbatim account of one passage in one of the arguments which I had with him.

NASSER: You say in your proposals that you are "concerned by the grave situation regarding the Suez Canal." I agree that there is. But who created it? We didn't create it, for all we did was to nationalize the Suez Canal Company and this was a matter which we had a perfect legal right to do. Therefore that action of ours could not have created the grave situation. It was the subsequent threats of Great Britain and France which created the grave situation.

MENZIES: But don't you see that the critical atmosphere in the world began at the very moment that you nationalized? It was that announcement which brought me back from America to the United Kingdom. It was that announcement which took Dulles from the United States to London. It was that announcement which brought the representatives of twenty-two nations to London. What you are overlooking is that the actual thing you did was to repudiate (and I use that expression because plain language will be appreciated) a concession which had twelve years to run.

NASSER: But how could anybody complain about that, if it was within our power?

MENZIES: I don't concede it was within your power. In fact, I think it was not. But can't you see that if your attitude is that merely because it was within your power you can repudiate a contract binding upon you, this, in one hit, destroys the confidence that the world has in your contractual word?

NASSER: I don't understand this. The concession would have expired in twelve years anyhow and then I suppose the same uproar would have occurred, if you are right.

MENZIES: Not at all. If you had not interfered with the concession, I have no doubt that the company itself would have quite soon begun negotiations with you for some future organization for the canal. But those negotiations would have been conducted in an atmosphere which was not one of crisis, and sensible and fair conclusions might well have been arrived at without the heated exchanges on such matters as "sovereignty."

NASSER: But this ignores the fact that we had the right to do what we did, and if we have the right to do something we can't understand how people can take exception to it.

This will explain the kind of logical mess which exists in his mind.[23]

[23]Eden, op. cit., pp. 526–27.

F aced with the failure of the Menzies' mission, France and England finally agreed, on September 12, to turn the problem over to the United Nations. At the same time, a plan for a Suez Canal Users' Association went ahead, and was supported by an 18-nation conference held at London from September 18 to 21. But Nasser would have none of it, and made his position clear in a speech on September 16.

Excerpt from a Speech Given by Nasser at Bilbeis, September 16, 1956

If the big powers are using threats to derogate from our independence we will have them know we happen to believe in this independence and that what we have done is purely within our sovereign rights. What users of the canal have a right to is free passage through the canal and this we guarantee.

They are threatening to use force against us. But we are fully determined never to surrender any of our rights. We shall resist any aggression and fight against those who attempt to derogate from our sovereignty.

By stating that, by succeeding, Abdel Nasser would weaken Britain's stand against Arab nationalism, Eden is in fact admitting his real objective is not Abdel Nasser as such but rather to defeat Arab nationalism and crush its cause. Eden speaks and finds his own answer. A month ago he let out the cry that he was after Abdel Nasser. Today the Egyptian people are fully conscious of their sovereign rights and Arab nationalism is fully awakened to its new destiny.

Then they claim they wish to apply such and such clauses of the 1888 convention. But Egypt has been executing provisions of the 1888 convention throughout past years till the present day. Between 1888 and 1956 ships have been sailing through the canal and paying dues to a body responsible for its administration. Ships had always abided by measures and regulations imposed by the canal company.

Of 8,000,000 Algerians, 10,000 are fighting half a million French soldiers. We have arms sufficient to equip those who can fight. We shall fight aggressors.

Those who attack Egypt will never leave Egypt alive. We shall fight a regular war, a total war, a guerrilla war. Those who attack Egypt will soon realize they brought disaster upon themselves. He who attacks Egypt attacks the whole Arab world. They say in their papers the whole thing will be over in forty-eight hours. They do not know how strong we really are.[24]

Declaration of Second London Conference, September 21, 1956

I. The Members of the Suez Canal Users Association (SCUA) shall be those nations which have participated in the

[24]The Suez Canal Problem, pp. 348–49.

second London Suez Conference and which subscribe to the present Declaration, and any other adhering nations which conform to criteria to be laid down hereafter by the association.

II. SCUA shall have the following purposes;

(1) to facilitate any steps which may lead to a final or provisional solution of the Suez Canal problem and to assist the members in the exercise of their rights as users of the Suez Canal in consonance with the 1888 Convention, wtih due regard for the rights of Egypt;

(2) to promote safe, orderly, efficient and economical transit of the Canal by vessels of any member nation desiring to avail themselves of the facilities of SCUA and to seek the co-operation of the competent Egyptian authorities for this purpose;

(3) to extend its facilities to vessels of non-member nations which desire to use them;

(4) To receive, hold and disburse the revenues accruing from dues and other sums which any user of the Canal may pay to SCUA, without prejudice to existing rights, pending a final settlement;

(5) to consider and report to Members regarding any significant developments affecting the use or non-use of the Canal; . . .[25]

Comments of Secretary of State Dulles at a Press Conference, October 2, 1956

As far as the formula for the users association is concerned, there is no detectable change, at least not detectable to me, between what it now is and what was planned, at least as far as the United States is concerned, and as we made known to the British and the French be-fore the project was launched in any way. . . . There is talk about the "teeth" being pulled out of it. There were never "teeth" in it, if that means the use of force. . . .

There are . . . problems where our approach is not always identical. For example, there is in Asia and Africa the so-called problem of colonialism. Now there the United States plays a somewhat independent role. . . . I suspect that the United States will find that its role, not only today but in the coming years, will be to try to aid that process [from colonialism to independence], without identifying itself 100 percent either with the so-called colonial powers or with the powers which are primarily and uniquely concerned with the problem of getting their independence as rapidly as possible.[26]

Reaction of Prime Minister Eden to Dulles' Remarks of October 2, 1956

The representatives of the Users' Association countries were then assembled in London confidently awaiting the United States decision to pay the canal dues to their organization. These were the teeth. Mr. Dulles' statement was in conflict with the users' understanding of the United States Government's intentions. Our representative on the committee, Lord John Hope, reported exasperation and dismay in their ranks. The dispute over Nasser's seizure of the canal had, of course, nothing to do with colonialism, but was concerned with international rights. If the United States had to defend her treaty rights in the Panama Canal, she would not regard such action as colonialism; neither would I. Yet her rights in Panama are those of one nation, not of many nations, as at Suez.[27]

---

[25]*The Suez Canal Problem,* pp. 365-66.

[26]*Department of State Bulletin,* October 15, 1956, p. 577.

[27]Eden, *op. cit.,* p. 557.

Comments of Robert D. Murphy

If John Foster Dulles ever was actually convinced of the possibility of organizing a Canal Users Association to operate the Suez Canal, I was not aware of it. Perhaps he considered the idea useful as a negotiating device. Probably he thought that a legal case could be made, sound enough to be upheld in any tribunal, which could demonstrate the good faith of the Association in keeping the Canal operating and in paying tolls to maintain it. A practical effect would be to divert tolls from Egyptian hands until a settlement and compensation for nationalization could be arranged. But Dulles did not spell this out and it seemed to me that he was skillfully working for time in the hope that public opinion in western Europe would harden against a military adventure. He recognized that it would be almost impossible to arouse Americans to join in defense of the Canal Company, especially considering the history of the original Suez concession and its long profitable enjoyment from 1888 to 1956.

It is true, as Eden reported, that Dulles once declared: "A way must be found to make Nasser disgorge what he is attempting to swallow!" But one never could be quite sure of the thoughts in the innermost recesses of the Dulles mind.[28]

[28]Murphy, *op. cit.*, p. 386.

If the British were dismayed at the negative wind that seemed to blow from Washington, the French and Israelis were even more concerned.

FOR CONSIDERATION　　It should not be forgotten that France was carrying out military operations against Algerian nationalists, who they realized received aid from Nasser and the U.S.S.R. Franco-Israeli interests were therefore somewhat different from British objectives.

General Moshe Dayan had distinguished himself in the 1948–49 war against the Arabs, and was highly regarded by Prime Minister Ben Gurion. Note that the objective of Operation "Kadesh" is to *capture* the Straits of Tiran, but only to *advance* toward the Suez Canal.

Comments of French Foreign Minister Christian Pineau, as Recorded by Terence Robertson

We arrived at the middle of September without anything useful having been done about Nasser. We were at a dead halt. Peaceful negotiations had failed. Dulles was an interesting personality in every sense, evidently motivated by preoccupations completely different from ours. They were of an order more metaphysical than political. I recall the words of someone who was quite unkind on this subject. He said: "Dulles is indeed an average American, but he has his eyes turned to the sky and his feet planted in oil."

I will admit that on a personal level his users' club was utterly disagreeable to me. It convinced some members of the French government that we were operating on a private plan in the interests of the old Suez Company and its shareholders—of whom there were more than two hundred thousand in France. This was not the case. While one cannot ignore entirely the element of justice in respect of suitable indemnity for shareholders, this was not the factor that led me to insist so forcibly on common action.

I felt that if we did not do something we would put ourselves in an inferior position in Algeria, that we would give the FLN rebels a major trump. Also, we would discourage every kind of aid to underdeveloped countries by allowing a manifest violation of international law. I saw no other course but common action, and by that I mean action by NATO, not users of the canal. I insist strongly therefore today, as I did then, that in the mind of the French government it was really a question of great principles, and a question of providing for the future by making it clear that international agreements should be binding, and that nations with greedy and ambitious objectives would not be permitted to get away with criminal action. . . .[29]

General Moshe Dayan Describes His Trip to Paris (with Shimon Peres) October 1, 1956

This morning we met with the French Chief of Staff, General Ely. The meeting was held at the home of our friend Louis Mangin, political adviser to the French Minister of Defence, Maurice Bourges-Maunoury. Participants from the Israel delegation were myself and officers of our Military Attaché's staff. With General Ely were his deputy for Air Force affairs, General Maurice Challe; General Martin, second-in-command to Challe; Colonel Simon, of Operations Branch of the General Staff; a Naval officer; and Louis Mangin. The purpose of our meeting was an exchange of information and the clarification of technical matters. General Ely opened by asking the strength of Egypt's forces, and we told him what we knew. Our information seems to tally with his own intelligence reports. He then turned to our security problems, asking me how I saw

[29]Robertson, op. cit., pp. 129–30.

developments in the Middle East and in what way France could help us.

His initial questions were already indicative of his attitude. General Ely was anxious to be helpful to us but he was not disposed to talk about French plans for the Suez Canal. My efforts to get him to discuss these plans proved fruitless.

Towards the end of our meeting, General Ely asked what equipment we wanted from France.

General Ely looked through the list and said that he would try and satisfy our request; but he has difficulties: the Army in Algeria puts up a constant cry for more equipment; and he is also reluctant to reduce the quantities earmarked for his units in Cyprus assigned to the Suez operations.[30]

Operation "Kadesh" October 5, 1956

MOST SECRET
Operations Branch/GHQ
5 October 1956

"Kadesh"
Planning Order No. 1

INFORMATION

1. See intelligence summary.

INTENTION

2. Forces of the IDF (Israel Defence Forces) will capture Northern Sinai, establish a defence line on the east bank of the Suez Canal, and give protection to the State on its other sectors.

METHOD

3. *General*

a. The conquest of Northern Sinai will

[30]Major General Moshe Dayan, *Diary of the Sinai Campaign* (New York: Harper & Row, Publishers, 1966), pp. 30–31. Copyright © by Moshe Dayan. English translation © 1966 by George Weidenfeld & Nicolson Ltd. Reprinted by permission of Harper & Row, Publishers.

be carried out by Southern Command with a force of 6 infantry brigades and 3 armoured brigades.

b. Northern and Central Commands will defend their regions. . . .

c. 202nd Paratroop Infantry Brigade will capture El Arish in a parachute landing.

d. 2 infantry brigades will serve as GHQ reserves.

e. Phases:

i. Capture of Northern Sinai up to El Arish-Jebel Livni-Bir Hassna-Nakhl line, and continuance of advance. (D-day to D plus 1.)

ii. Advance towards the Suez Canal and completion of clearance of Gaza Strip. (D plus 1 to D plus 3.)

iii. Capture of Straits of Tiran.[31]

---

[31] *Ibid.*, p. 209.

During the first two weeks of October, the Secretary-General in the United Nations, Dag Hammarskjold, had worked ceaselessly to find some formula which could satisfy not only Egypt but the veto-holding powers in the Security Council. Working closely with the Foreign Ministers concerned, he evolved six principles which by their reasonableness seemed susceptible of acceptance by all parties. These principles were discussed by British Foreign Secretary Selwyn Lloyd, French Foreign Minister Pineau, and Dr. Fawzi, the Egyptian representative. But Fawzi objected to one part of the Resolution, and when it came up for vote in the Security Council, on October 13, it was vetoed by Russia. The first of the following documents is a résumé made by Hammarskjold of closed discussions among Lloyd, Pineau, and Fawzi.

UN Secretary-General Hammarskjold's Summary of Conversations, October 10–12, 1956

OCTOBER 10

LLOYD: What is Egypt's basis for negotiation?

FAWZI: Egypt will set aside an agreed percentage of revenues for canal development; accept an agreement on tolls for a fixed number of years; recognize an association of users; accept a system of combined meetings of the association and Egyptian board; accept an arbitration tribunal to settle disputes consisting of one user, one Egyptian and a United Nations chairman.

PINEAU: Will the users' association employ its own pilots?

FAWZI: It is not impossible to come to some arrangement on this. The Egyptian board will have to be satisfied as to the technical competence of the pilots.

LLOYD: Will Egypt accept the principle of insulating the canal from the politics of any one country?

FAWZI: Yes, of course.

OCTOBER 11

Hammarskjold produced a piece of paper containing his impressions of what had been said the previous day. It caused such prolonged, acrimonious argument that he was instructed to tear it up.

LLOYD: Vague promises from Dr. Fawzi are not enough. Will Egypt give reality to insulation of the canal from the politics of any one country?

FAWZI: I have said so yesterday. Egypt accepts this principle without qualification.

PINEAU: Will Egypt guarantee free and open transit through the canal to all users?

FAWZI: Yes. We will propose a new treaty to replace the 1888 Convention.

LLOYD: Will Egypt accept the users' association as already being formed?

FAWZI: The users can organize themselves as they wish. Does this association of yours exist, or was it stillborn?

LLOYD: It will live. There must be a collateral agreement regarding tolls, as these will be applicable to all users of the canal, not merely to those who join the association.

PINEAU: Will you persist in refusing passage to ships wearing the flag of Israel?

FAWZI: Israel will have the same rights it had under the 1888 Convention.

OCTOBER 12

Lloyd described the main areas of accommodation while the Secretary General made notes. Hammarskjold produced from these the six principles which later convinced delegates that the Middle East was at long last teetering on the brink of peace. The principles were:

1. There should be free and open transit through the canal without discrimination, overt or covert;
2. The sovereignty of Egypt should be respected;
3. The operation of the Canal should be insulated from the politics of any one country;
4. The manner of fixing tolls and charges should be decided by agreement between Egypt and the users;
5. A fair proportion of the dues should be allotted to development;
6. In case of disputes, unresolved questions between the Suez Canal Company and the Egyptian government should be settled by arbitration, with suitable terms of reference and suitable provisions for the payment of sums found to be due.[32]

Comments by Robert D. Murphy

At first we did not understand why the British and French were so opposed to recourse to the UN, but realized later that they knew their military schedule would be disarranged if they became entangled in drawn-out procedures in New York. But one British official said to me in August that a bow probably would have to be made to the UN sooner or later, and the courtesy gesture was made on October 13 when a resolution providing for free and open transit in the Canal was voted upon by the Security Council. As Dulles had foreseen, the action of the Council ended in a Soviet veto, thus leaving the Egyptians with a clearer international position regarding their seizure of the Canal.[33]

[32]Robertson, *op. cit.*, pp. 142–43.
[33]Murphy, *op. cit.*, p. 388.

With the Soviet veto of October 13, no alternatives appeared to the French and Israeli except to press on with their military plans. The British also continued, working closely with the French.

FOR CONSIDERATION   The treaty referred to in the passage by Terence Robertson is not mentioned in Eden's *Memoirs*, and in spite of accusations from the Opposition, the Conservative government maintained that it lacked specific information about Israeli plans.[34] Mr. Robertson interviewed many of the participants, and his account was read by Pineau. It agrees in essence with other accounts, such as those of Tournoux, Randolph Churchill, Thomas, and Finer. The "official denial" is a problem for the contemporary historian, who through interviews and inference may be convinced of the truth but does not have the documents to prove it.

Reconstruction of French-Israeli-British Negotiations at Sèvres (Near Paris) October 23–24, 1956 by Terence Robertson

Next morning an inconspicuous car pulled up in the driveway, Mollet stepped out, and Pineau introduced the Prime Minister of France to the Prime Minister of Israel.

The conference, devoid of formality, began with the three Israeli and the two French leaders facing each other across a dining-room table.

Ben-Gurion spoke first, ranging widely over the problems of nation-building, the fears of fewer than two million Jews surrounded by more than forty million hostile Arabs, and the responsibilities of a government faced with an external threat of overwhelming proportions. . . .

"Bombardment of Tel Aviv, Haifa, Jaffa, and Jerusalem will result in a death toll we, as a small nation, cannot accept," he said. "An invasion high up on our coast would place an enemy force in our heart. We are condemned to death unless we fight. M. Mollet, you are a member of the Resistance, a Socialist, and a democrat. You cannot allow us to perish. Israel's existence is at stake here today."

Mollet had no intention at the outset of the conference to commit France beyond the supply of additional arms and the loan of more instructors if Israel needed them. At this point he had only the haziest notion of how extensively Bourgès-

Maunoury and Abel Thomas had involved the French forces in Israeli defence arrangements. . . .

Appalled by the prospect of another mass extermination, so vividly portrayed by Ben-Gurion's eloquence, he instinctively answered: "I shall not let these things happen."

By lunchtime they reached formal agreement that the French air force would provide cover for Israel's major cities, that French warships would patrol its coastline, and that France would use these forces to protect Israel from any belligerent Arab state, as well as from Egypt. . . .

In the afternoon another aircraft, this one wearing the markings of the Royal Air Force, landed at Villa Coublay, where the tireless Mangin was already waiting. When he delivered the new arrivals to the villa at Sèvres for the second session of the conference, Britain, according to Pineau's account, was represented by Selwyn Lloyd and Patrick Dean, an under-secretary of state at the Foreign Office and a political intelligence coordinator. . . .

Pineau, who appreciated the elderly statesman's keenly prophetic wisdom without ever allowing himself to be wholly seduced to the Israeli cause, has since said: "We discussed British intervention very seriously and very frankly. I was struck by the fact that the English sought above all else a method of justifying their action in the eyes of the Arabs and before world opinion. I thought it would be much simpler to say that the Egyptians had taken over the canal illegally, that this was an aggression under international

[34]See *Parliamentary Debates, Commons*, December 4–6, 1956 (London: Her Majesty's Stationery Office, 1957).

law, and that we were acting purely and simply to recover it. That was not sufficient for the English. So our discussions ended in a rather complex agreement. . . .

Mollet drove back to Paris that night, Pineau flew to London with Lloyd to discuss their decisions with Eden, and Patrick Dean stayed at the villa with Ben-Gurion, Peres, and Dayan. Mangin, their unobtrusive host, also remained, but Dayan's staff officers were taken to Paris to begin drafting a detailed schedule with the French Chiefs of Staff.

Pineau returned to Sèvres early the next morning, October 24, with Eden's consent to the agreement, and the conference resumed without Mollet and Lloyd for the drafting of a formal three-power treaty. Several hours later the text was unanimously approved and a copy dispatched to London for Eden's final approval. . . .

"When we received Eden's approval of the text," said Pineau, "it was incorporated into a formal document signed that afternoon by Patrick Dean for Britain, Ben-Gurion for Israel, and myself for France. I believe three copies were made, one for each government, and we decided that the agreement should never be published." . . .

Ben-Gurion landed in Israel on October 25 with a severe cold, a high temperature, and his "piece of paper." He informed the Israeli Cabinet that as the new Arab military alliance placed Israel in "direct and immediate danger," he was preparing an order for general mobilisation. The stage was being set less than twenty-four hours after signing the Treaty of Sèvres.[35]

Comments of Prime Minister Eden

On October 25 the Cabinet discussed the specific possibility of conflict between Israel and Egypt and decided in principle how it would react if this occurred.

[35]Robertson, *op. cit.*, pp. 158–63.

The Governments of France and the United Kingdom should, it considered, at once call on both parties to stop hostilities and withdraw their forces to a distance from either bank of the canal. It one or both failed to comply within a definite period, then British and French forces would intervene as a temporary measure to separate the combatants. To ensure this being effective, they would have to occupy key positions at Port Said, Ismailia and Suez. Our purpose was to safeguard free passage through the canal, if it were threatened with becoming a zone of warfare, and to arrest the spread of fighting in the Middle East.

To realize this we would put into operation the plan for occupation of the Suez Canal zone, prepared by the joint Anglo-French military staff which had been studying the problem since the end of July. An advantage of this course was that we did not need to recast our military preparations. The same plan that had been intended to deal with Nasser's seizure of the canal fitted equally well with our new objective.[36]

From an Account by French Prime Minister Guy Mollet, as Recorded by Terence Robertson

I did not know a lot about Israel. I had met its leaders first as members of the Socialist International. Ben-Gurion was Secretary General of the Socialist party there, as I am here in France. The only thing I knew was that a democratic country, in some way trying to find a socialist solution to its problem, was in danger.

One day I received a visit from their leaders, who explained to me quite clearly that they were condemned to disappear, that they would be attacked very soon. They had information that Nasser

[36]Eden, *op. cit.*, p. 584.

had received Soviet MIGs and bombers, so naturally when they asked for help, I gave it to them by having French arms sent to Israel.

My reasons were that when a free country is menaced, all the free countries of the world must protect it. I do not mean we should make war on the régimes of Hungary and Poland to bring liberty to their peoples. You cannot bring freedom with arms to a state that is not free.

But when a country is free, you cannot allow dictators anywhere to make this country disappear. I gave a great deal of help to Israel, because this was my purpose. Then other questions came up, problems of oil supplies, the Suez Canal, and Algeria. My British allies in this did not have the same purpose. They did not think so much about the freedom of Israel as they did about the canal.[37]

[37]Robertson, *op. cit.*, pp. 154–55.

On October 29, Israel attacked Egypt. On the following day came the Anglo-French ultimatum calling for a cease-fire in 12 hours. When the time was up, bombing attacks (but no landings) began on Egyptian installations.

FOR CONSIDERATION   Events seemed to follow the timetable set out by General Dayan on October 25, particularly in regard to item 4, which assumes the ultimatum will be disregarded.

Diary of General Moshe Dayan, Entry of October 25, 1956

After numerous internal conferences, and contacts and clarifications with people overseas, which started about two months ago, we can sum up the situation today as follows:

1. The Prime Minister and Minister of Defence, David Ben Gurion, has given approval in principle to the campaign and its aims.
2. Our forces will go into action at dusk on 29 October 1956, and we must complete the capture of the Sinai Peninsula within seven to ten days.
3. The decision on the campaign and its planning are based on the assumption that British and French forces are about to take action against Egypt.
4. According to information in our possession, the Anglo-French forces propose to launch their operations on 31 October 1956.

Their aim is to secure control of the Suez Canal Zone, and for this they will need to effect a sea landing or an air drop with, no doubt, suitable air cover.

At 13.45 I met with the senior officers of Operation Branch. For this meeting I prepared directives for the operational order (Appendix 2) which replaces those in the previous order, "Kadesh"-1 (Appendix 1) of 5 October 1956. Apart from the time-table, which lays down the day and hour of the start of the action, today's order contains several changes from the previous order. The first occurs in the paragraph on aims. Stress is now placed on the creation of a threat to the Suez Canal, and only after that come the basic purposes of the campaign—capture of the Straits of Tiran (Sharm e-Sheikh and the islands of Tiran and Sanapir) and defeat of the Egyptian forces.[38]

[38]Dayan, *op. cit.*, pp. 60–61.

The Outbreak of War, as Described by Israeli Prime Minister Ben Gurion

At the Cabinet meeting on October 28, 1956, the Prime Minister and Minister of Defence proposed that the Israel Defence Forces be authorized to carry out an extensive operation in all parts of the Sinai Desert and in the Gaza Strip, with the aim of demolishing the bases of the *fedayin* and the Egyptian Army in these areas, and occupying the shore of the Gulf of Akaba to safeguard freedom of navigation to and from Eilat via the Red Sea and the Indian Ocean. This offensive would require a large force, for Egypt maintained large military forces and military airfields in Sinai and the Gaza Strip. The offensive was to begin in the evening of October 29 and to be limited to the Sinai area, without crossing the Suez Canal or touching the territory of Egypt. . . .

When the Prime Minister was asked what would be the fate of Sinai if our offensive should succeed in destroying all the enemy forces in the area, he said: "I do not know what will be the fate of Sinai. We are interested first of all in the shore of Eilat and the Straits. . . ."

The discussion at this meeting was really no more than formal, for the Prime Minister had submitted the proposal and the plan of the offensive to all the members of the Cabinet, one party at a time, the day before.[39]

Comments of Robert Murphy

A few more days passed quietly and then the State Department received a cablegram from the military attaché of the American Embassy at Tel Aviv conveying information which he had obtained confidentially regarding Israeli

mobilization. That Israel might be preparing for action seemed plausible. . . .

Yet, when I read the cablegram from our military attaché, I found it hard to believe that Israeli mobilization could be taking place in isolation. It seemed that France and Britain must have some intimation, however informally, of such activity. But we had no evidence that they did. Pineau had not so much as hinted of any French military arrangements with Israeli leaders. Eden did not suggest this even at official conferences with Ambassador Aldrich, and this deception of the American Ambassador may have been a factor in President Eisenhower's indignation later. Macmillan was very frank about all Anglo-French plans—except French encouragement to Israel. This never was revealed to any American, privately or otherwise.[40]

The Anglo-French "Ultimatum," October 30, 1956 (Similar Note to Israel)

The Governments of the United Kingdom and France have taken note of the outbreak of hostilities between Israel and Egypt. This event threatens to disrupt the freedom of navigation through the Suez Canal, on which the economic life of many nations depends. The Governments of the United Kingdom and France are resolved to do all in their power to bring about the early cessation of hostilities and to safeguard the free passage of the Canal. They accordingly request the Government of Egypt:

(a) to stop all warlike action on land, sea and air forthwith;

(b) to withdraw all Egyptian military forces to a distance of ten miles from the Canal; and

(c) in order to guarantee freedom of

---

[39]Ben Gurion, *loc. cit.*, pp. 30–31.

[40]Murphy, *op. cit.*, pp. 388–89.

transit through the Canal by the ships of all nations and in order to separate the belligerents, to accept the temporary occupation by Anglo-French forces of key positions at Port Said, Ismailia and Suez.

The United Kingdom and French Governments request an answer to this communication within twelve hours. If at the expiration of that time one or both

Governments have not undertaken to comply with the above requirements, United Kingdom and French forces will intervene in whatever strength may be necessary to secure compliance.

A similar communication has been sent to the Government of Israel.[41]

---

[41]*Documents on International Affairs, 1956,* p. 261.

A̲ll reports agree that Eisenhower seethed with indignation when he learned of the Israeli attack and the Anglo-French ultimatum. An American resolution in the Security Council was vetoed by France and England, providing an anomalous situation in which the United States and the Soviet Union found themselves voting together.

Excerpt from Radio and Television Speech of President Eisenhower, October 31, 1956

The United States was not consulted in any way about any phase of these actions. Nor were we informed of them in advance.

As it is the manifest right of any of these nations to take such decisions and actions, it is likewise our right—if our judgment so dictates—to dissent. We believe these actions to have been taken in error. For we do not accept the use of force as a wise or proper instrument for the settlement of international disputes.

.   .   .   .   .

The present fact, nonetheless, seems clear: The actions taken can scarcely be reconciled with the principles and pur-

poses of the United Nations to which we have all subscribed. And, beyond this, we are forced to doubt even if resort to war will for long serve the permanent interests of the attacking nations.

Now we must look to the future.

In the circumstances I have described there will be no United States involvement in these present hostilities. I therefore have no plan to call the Congress in special session. Of course, we shall continue to keep in contact with congressional leaders of both parties. At the same time it is—and it will remain—the dedicated purpose of your Government to do all in its power to localize the fighting and to end the conflict.[42]

---

[42]*Department of State Bulletin,* November 12, 1956, pp. 743–45.

W̲ith action in the Security Council barred, Secretary of State Dulles supported a parliamentary move whereby the General Assembly, unaffected by the veto, might take action. At this juncture the astute Canadian Secretary for External Affairs, Lester Pearson, concluded that the United

Nations should invoke force, and, for the first time, carry out a police action in a developing emergency. By abstaining from an American resolution, the Canadian delegation was free to initiate a novel proposal. But time was of the essence. The French and British were bombing Egypt but their landings had not yet been accomplished.

Comments of Lester Pearson, as Reported by Terence Robertson

There was only one course—to do our best to ensure that the British and French action was not examined by itself under a spotlight narrowly focused on recent events alone. I felt it should be examined in the fullest possible perspective against the situation that had led to the intervention, and against the past records of both countries. It was clear even then that if they had suffered considerable provocation at the hands of Egypt, they had endured too the frustrating sequels to what undoubtedly comprised the worst chapter in Dulles's diplomatic career. I regretted they thought it necessary to take the keeping of peace into their own hands, but it was equally obvious that the peace needed keeping in the Middle East.

That was principally because members of the United Nations had failed to discharge their collective responsibility. They had failed to protect life on both sides of the Arab-Israeli borders, failed for five years to enforce their own resolution that the canal should be kept open to traffic of all nations. All members, ourselves included, were to blame for these failures, and none of us had the right to act the accuser or to throw the first stone.[43]

[43]Robertson, *op. cit.*, p. 180.

U.S. Resolution of November 2, 1956, Passed by the UN General Assembly with Canada Abstaining

The General Assembly,

Noting the disregard on many occasions by parties to the Israel-Arab armistice agreements of 1949 of the terms of such agreements, and that the armed forces of Israel have penetrated deeply into Egyptian territory in violation of the General Armistice Agreement between Egypt and Israel of 24 February 1949,

Noting that armed forces of France and the United Kingdom of Great Britain and Northern Ireland are conducting military operations against Egyptian territory,

Noting that traffic through the Suez Canal is now interrupted to the serious prejudice of many nations,

Expressing its grave concern over these developments,

1. *Urges* as a matter of priority that all parties now involved in hostilities in the area agree to an immediate cease-fire and, as part thereof, halt the movement of military forces and arms into the area. . . .[44]

[44]*Documents on International Affairs, 1956,* pp. 270–71.

A race developed between the wagers of peace and the wagers of war. The brilliant Israeli victory, summarized here by Prime Minister Ben Gurion, brought about a practical cease-fire, if not an official one, by November 3.

If Israeli-Egyptian hostilities ended, it would be difficult to justify Anglo-French intervention. Yet the Anglo-French landings, requiring ships steaming from Malta, were not scheduled for three more days, before which time the UN resolution for an Emergency Force might be passed. General Keightly could not advance the long-planned ship movements, but it might be possible to bring paratroopers in earlier. The material which follows deals with this problem.

FOR CONSIDERATION   The quick trip of Defense Minister Head to Cyprus has provoked some controversy. Prime Minister Eden was already vacillating between an acceleration or a postponement of the landings, and was gravely affected by American pressure. But in this decision to advance the attack, French influence prevailed.

Israeli Military Action in the Sinai Peninsula, October 29–November 5, 1956, Described by Prime Minister Ben Gurion

On the first night of the action Kuntilla, Ras en-Nakb, opposite Eilat, and Kuseima were occupied. The next day, on October 30, Thamad, El-Bassup and El-Ufrad in the heart of Sinai were taken. On 31 October Bir Hasna was occupied without resistance and Abu Ageila after fierce fighting. On November 1, all the posts at the approaches to Rafah, El Gafgafa (on the Nitzana–Ismailia road), and the first post on the approaches to El-Arish, were captured. On November 2, El-Arish was taken after bitter resistance, and three hours later Gaza surrendered without opposition. The strongest resistance was shown at Khan Yunis.

On November 3, several important posts on the western shore of the Gulf of Aqaba, including Dahab and Ras Nasrani, were occupied. The entire Sinai Peninsula was then in effect in our hands, except for a small bay in the Straits, opposite Tiran, which had been very strongly fortified by Egypt, and also had a military airfield.[45]

---

[45]Ben Gurion, *loc. cit.*, p. 32.

Advance of the Time Schedule, November 3, 1956

On the 31st October, the French Government, via the medium of Admiral Barjot, suggested that the Israeli advance and the Allied air programme now proposed might make it desirable to move much more quickly than the existing plan provided for. . . . [A new plan was made and] was called "Omelette"—an apt name perhaps, because Port Said might well have suffered considerable damage in the action.

Although preparations went ahead for the "Omelette" plan to be put into effect, nothing came of it, and on 2nd November, Admiral Barjot sought out General Beaufre. Pressed by his Government to get the Allied operation under way, the Admiral told his compatriot at about 1600 hours that day, that "Paris" were of the opinion that the political situation warranted troops being landed in Egypt "within two hours"! . . .

That night (2nd November) Beaufre put forward the idea of a British parachute drop on Gamil, a French drop to replace the helicopter assault on the bridges, and a second French drop to the south of Port Fuad. . . . If this revised

"Omelette" plan—later referred to as "Telescope"—was agreed, it ought to be possible for the action to start by the morning of the 4th. By 1100 hours the next day, Saturday, 3rd November, the plan had been approved, with the exception of the second French drop south of Port Fuad, and Monday (5th) was fixed as "D" day for the assault. Subsequently, on Monday afternoon the operation was going so well that it was decided to include the only feature of Beaufre's plan which had been omitted, and French "Paras" were dropped just outside Port Fuad. . . .

The effect of Beaufre's "Telescope" plan was to advance the parachute attack by twenty-four hours.[46]

Levine in The New York Review of Books

British Minister of Defence Antony Head's Trip to Cyprus, as Reported by Randolph Churchill

At the same time [Nov. 3] Mr. Antony Head, the Minister of Defence, was dispatched to Cyprus on a seventeen-hour round trip. His object was to assure himself, and so the Cabinet, that the Anglo-French plans had been perfectly concerted. On the air-strip at Akrotiri early on Sunday morning, Head spoke to General Keightley, the Allied C.-in-C., and Vice-Admiral Barjot, his deputy. He accepted the final plan for a paratroop descent on Port Said the following day, and returned home.

When Mr. Head arrived at 10 Downing Street later that afternoon, he found there M. Pineau, who had flown over from Paris that morning, bringing with him, for the first time, M. Bourgès-Maunoury, the French Defence Minister. To them and to the assembled Cabinet Mr. Head reported in reassuring terms what he had seen and heard in Cyprus.[47]

Minister of Defence Head's Comments on Trip to Cyprus, November 3–4, 1956

What was the next aspect of the plan? It was said that there should be an assault on Port Said, with minimum damage. An assault on a defended port is not an entirely easy matter, and everybody felt and said that this must be an example of what the Air Force could do towards the capture of the place with the minimum damage. I went to see General Keightley, not for the reasons reported by that very fine imaginative writer Mr. Randolph Churchill—who can be bracketed with Edgar Allan Poe for imagination—but to see whether the airborne drop could be made earlier to overcome the beach defences and eliminate the naval bombardment, which would inevitably cause more destruction at Port Said. That was done and the airborne drop went absolutely without a hitch, and was 100 per cent successful. The landing went in exactly on time and the objective was seized as planned.[48]

---

[46]Barker, *op. cit.*, pp. 114–16.

[47]Randolph Churchill, *The Rise and Fall of Anthony Eden* (New York: G. P. Putnam's Sons,

1959), p. 282. Copyright 1959 by Randolph S. Churchill. Reprinted by permission of G. P. Putnam's Sons.

[48]Parliamentary Debates, Commons, December 16, 1958 (London: Her Majesty's Stationery Office, 1959) p. 1074.

E den hoped that if the UN authorized an emergency force, it might just as well designate the Anglo-French detachment, which was in the area but not yet ashore, as representing the UN. The communication from Hammarskjold on November 4 clarified the UN position on that matter. At the same time Pearson was performing prodigies in lining up votes for the Canadian proposal. At 2:00 A.M., on the morning of November 5, the General Assembly approved. For these labors during the Suez crisis, Lester Pearson was later awarded the Nobel Peace Prize.

Hammarskjold to British Foreign Secretary Selwyn Lloyd and French Foreign Minister Pineau, November 4, 1956

. . . The statements made prior to the adoption of the resolution on the United Nations Force made it clear that it was a widespread view that none of the parties engaged in the present operations in the area should participate in the Force. This has a direct and obvious bearing on any possibility of stationing Anglo-French troops between the combatants, pending the establishment of a United Nations Force. I must assume the decision in question to have been taken on the basis of an interpretation which if maintained would exclude such an arrangement as a possible condition for a cease-fire.

.   .   .   .   .

I wish to draw to your attention that the Government of Israel has accepted the cease-fire on the condition of reciprocal acceptance by Egypt, while Egypt has accepted the cease-fire provided that military actions against Egypt are stopped. With the stands thus taken by Israel and Egypt, it is obvious that the position of your Government and the Government of France will determine whether or not it will be possible to achieve a cease-fire between Egypt and Israel.[49]

UN General Assembly Resolution, Session of November 4, 1956 (Actually Passed at 2:00 A.M. November 5.)

The General Assembly,

Bearing in mind the urgent necessity of facilitating compliance with its resolution 997 (ES-I) of 2 November 1956,

Requests, as a matter of priority, the Secretary-General to submit to it within forty-eight hours a plan for the setting up, with the consent of the nations concerned, of an emergency international United Nations Force to secure and supervise the cessation of hostilities in accordance with all the terms of the aforementioned resolution.[50]

---

[49]*Documents on International Affairs, 1956,* pp. 277–78.
[50]*Ibid.,* p. 275.

U p to this moment the Soviet Union, preoccupied with its own crisis in Hungary, had protested but had not taken action. After an awkward proposal for joint Soviet–U.S. reprisals was rejected, Chairman Bulganin wrote to Mollet and Eden.

FOR CONSIDERATION   There is a threat of missile and nuclear attack in the Soviet message. Was Russia bluffing? Did the threat of the Hungarian uprising, which had broken out on October 22, prevent her from taking more definite steps in the eastern Mediterranean? Which was more important to Russia, Egypt or Hungary?

If Churchill and de Gaulle had been in the shoes of Eden and Mollet, would they have stopped? In any case, the pressures were too great for Eden and on November 6, at midnight, the attack was called to a halt, short of its objectives. Mollet was unwilling to go ahead without the British.

Soviet Chairman Bulganin to Prime Minister Eden, November 5, 1956

.   .   .   .   .

The Suez Canal issue was only a pretext for British and French aggression, which has other and far-reaching aims. It cannot be concealed that in actual fact an aggressive predatory war is now unfolding against the Arab peoples with the object of destroying the national independence of the states of the Near and Middle East and of re-establishing the régime of colonial slavery rejected by the peoples.

There is no justification for the fact that the armed forces of Britain and France, two great powers that are permanent members of the Security Council, have attacked a country which only recently acquired its national independence and which does not possess adequate means for self-defence.

In what situation would Britain find herself if she were attacked by stronger states, possessing all types of modern destructive weapons? And such countries could, at the present time, refrain from sending naval or air forces to the shores of Britain and use other means—for instance, rocket weapons. Were rocket weapons used against Britain and France, you would, most probably, call this a barbarous action. But how does the inhuman attack launched by the armed forces of Britain and France against a practically defenceless Egypt differ from this?

With deep anxiety over the developments in the Near and Middle East, and guided by the interests of the maintenance of universal peace, we think that the government of Britain should listen to the voice of reason and put an end to the war in Egypt. We call upon you, upon Parliament, upon the Labour Party, the trade unions, upon the whole of the British people: Put an end to the armed aggression; stop the bloodshed. The war in Egypt can spread to other countries and turn into a third world war.

The Soviet government has already addressed the United Nations and the President of the United States of America with the proposal to resort, jointly with other United Nations member-states, to the use of naval and air forces in order to end the war in Egypt and to curb aggression. We are fully determined to crush the aggressors by the use of force and to restore peace in the East.

We hope that at this critical moment you will show due common sense and draw the appropriate conclusions.[51]

Comments of CIA Director Allen Dulles

General Charles P. Cabell, Deputy Director of the CIA . . . read to me a Soviet

---

[51]*Documents on International Affairs, 1956*, p. 289.

note that had just come over the wires. Bulganin was threatening London and Paris with missile attacks unless the British and French forces withdrew from Egypt. I asked General Cabell to call a meeting of the intelligence community, and immediately flew back to Washington. The USIB [United States Intelligence Board] met throughout the night, and early on election morning I took to President Eisenhower our agreed estimate of Soviet intentions and probable courses of action in this crisis.[52]

Prime Minister Eden to President Eisenhower, November 6, 1956

If we drew back now chaos will not be avoided. Everything will go up in flames in the Middle East. You will realize, with all your experience, that we cannot have a military vacuum while a United Nations force is being constituted and is being transported to the spot. That is why we feel we must go on to hold the position until we can hand over responsibility to the United Nations.[53]

Eisenhower's Report of a Telephone Conversation with Eden, November 6, 1956

"I hope that you will now go along with the United Nations resolutions without imposing any conditions," I said. "This I think would be highly advisable so as to deny Russia any opportunity to create trouble. The United Nations is making preparation for the concentration of a caretaking force."

Anthony felt that the size of that force would have to be considerable.

"I hope you [the Americans] will be

there," he said. "Are we all going to go?"

"What I want to do is this," I replied. "I would like to see none of the great nations in it." My thought was that if any of the large nations provided troop contingents the Soviets would try to provide the largest. I told Anthony we should put the matter in Mr. Hammarskjold's hands and say to him, "When we see you coming with enough troops to take over, we'll leave."

If anyone then made an aggressive move, I said, the attack would be a challenge to the whole United Nations. This, I felt, no one would want to make.[54]

The Situation around Noon, November 6, 1956, as Described by Terence Robertson

At Downing Street, Macmillan was summoned from the cabinet room to take a telephone call from Washington. He was told in effect that a United States loan of $1,000 million would be immediately available if Britain and France agreed to cease fire at midnight. Aid while Britain was fighting despite United Nations recommendations might be misinterpreted in other countries.

The ethical, moral, political, and legal issues no longer predominated. With the unanimous consent of the full Cabinet Eden placed his call to Paris. . . . Pineau waited in silence while Mollet listened to Eden's plea for understanding and cooperation. According to the French version of the conversation, Eden said in effect: "My dear friend, I am overwhelmed by all kinds of pressures. The Labour Party has divided the country, two of my colleagues have resigned, and other ministers are threatening to follow suit. I cannot count upon the full support of the Conservative party any longer. There are pressures too from the Commonwealth and from the President of the

---

[52]Dulles, *op. cit.*, p. 159.
[53]Eden, *op. cit.*, p. 617.

[54]Eisenhower, *op. cit.*, p. 92.

United States. Nehru may sever relations . . . and Canada is not with us. I cannot go on alone without the United States, that is impossible. We must stop this afternoon."

Mollet, shocked by the grave implications of the British decision, replied: "But that is absolutely impossible. We cannot stop so quickly. If we wait a little longer our troops will reach Suez. I strongly urge that you reconsider."

"I cannot wait," said Eden. "I am under pressure here to bring hostilities to an end today. The best I can do is to postpone it until tonight. We must stop at midnight."[55]

---

[55]Robertson, *op. cit.*, p. 263.

W ith strong American support, the Suez police action might have succeeded. For the fiasco, Eden blamed Washington, and both Eisenhower and Dulles were indignant at Eden's unilateral action. Here are two views.

Robert D. Murphy's Evaluation of the Roles of Eden, Eisenhower and Dulles

Eden's greatest miscalculation was that he was unable to enlist the support of Eisenhower. In fact the President made his displeasure very apparent. From his point of view the attack on Egypt in the final days of October was calamitous timing. Nationwide elections in the United States were to be held the first Tuesday in November, Eisenhower himself was running for re-election, and he was confronted with a situation in which three friendly nations, two of them allies, had decided to wage war without a word of consultation with him. That alone would be sufficient explanation for his attitude, but Eisenhower's wrath went further than that. The President already had made it very clear that he thoroughly disapproved of what he regarded as eighteenth-century tactics instead of recourse to diplomacy and United Nations procedures. . . .

Many British newspapers blamed the American Secretary of State for the Suez fiasco, but their bitter comments did not bother Dulles. In fact, he seemed to enjoy their attitude. If they wanted to assign to him, rather than to Eisenhower, the dominant role in our Suez policy, that did not displease Dulles. And gradually, largely as reaction to this Suez criticism, Dulles' reputation grew in stature.[56]

Prime Minister Eden's Reaction to the U.S. Position (after the Cease-Fire)

It might have been thought that, however much angered, the United States Government would wish to get the best possible results out of the situation for the future of Western Europe, whose economic security was at stake. This was not so. The attitude was rather that the President had been slighted because the allies had acted without permission. The allies must pay for it, and pay they did. The many warnings, both public and private, which had been given by the allies over the waiting months did not help to assuage official American opinion. On the contrary, they irritated it. If an individual has been warned by his friend that the friend will take some action, and has not heeded the warning, and his friend then takes action, the individual is likely to feel sore. His own error of judgment only

---

[56]Murphy, *op. cit.*, pp. 392–93.

increases his exasperation. So it can be with countries. . . .

The United States Administration seemed to be dominated at this time by one thought only, to harry their allies. Mr. Dulles, who was still recovering from an operation, deplored to the Foreign Sec- retary that we had not managed to bring Nasser down and declared that he must be prevented from getting away with it. The actions of the United States Government had exactly the opposite result.[57]

---

[57]Eden, *op. cit.*, pp. 634–35.

The consequences of the Suez crisis have been grave. With ships blocking the canal, tankers were forced into a long detour. Egypt's ally Syria had blown up the pipeline pumping stations, which were not repaired for months. A new peace-keeping arrangement, the UNEF (United Nations Emergency Force), had been brought into existence, and with the first detachments under General E. L. M. Burns arriving on November 15 an uneasy respite was introduced into a troubled area. And Israel achieved one important objective: access to the Red Sea via the Gulf of Aqaba. If this route could be kept open, guaranteed by the Great Powers, Israel could develop trade and have access to oil without the Suez Canal. The following documents make significant comment on these matters.

An Economic Consequence of Middle East Tension

Increase in the clearing capacity of the Suez Canal presented a complicated problem inasmuch as it involved not only the arduous technical task of deepening and widening the navigable channel but also of settling the issue of political control. By mid-1956 the Suez Canal was capable of handling vessels with a maximum draught of 35 feet. A program of improvements prepared by the Suez Canal Company was aiming at an increase of the permissible draught to 36 feet in the first stage, to be followed by an increase to 40 feet in the succeeding phase. With a draught of about 36 feet the Canal could accommodate fully loaded tankers of up to slightly under 40,000 dead-weight tons. Larger tankers would have to pass only partly loaded, and passage of those above 65,000 tons would have to be subjected to strict limitations on account of the wash and suction effects on the banks of the Canal. . . . Because of both eco- nomic considerations and political un- certainties, the trend is now toward the construction of supertankers of 80,000 tons or more. . . .[58]

U.S. Aide-Memoire, Secretary of State Dulles to Ambassador Abba Eban, February 11, 1957

With respect to the Gulf of Aqaba and access thereto—the United States believes that the Gulf comprehends international waters and that no nation has the right to prevent free and innocent passage in the Gulf and through the Straits giving access thereto. We have in mind not only commercial usage, but the passage of pilgrims on religious missions, which should be fully respected.

The United States recalls that on January 28, 1950, the Egyptian Ministry of Foreign Affairs informed the United States that the Egyptian occupation of the two islands of Tiran and Sanafir at the

---

[58]Lenczowski, *op. cit.*, p. 32.

entrance of the Gulf of Aqaba was only to protect the islands themselves against "possible damage or violation" and that "this occupation being in no way conceived in a spirit of obstructing in any way innocent passage through the stretch of water separating these two islands from the Egyptian coast of Sinai, it follows that this passage, the only practicable one, will remain free as in the past, in conformity with international practice and recognized principles of the law of nations."

In the absence of some overriding decision to the contrary, as by the International Court of Justice, the United States, on behalf of vessels of United States registry, is prepared to exercise the right of free and innocent passage and to join with others to secure general recognition of this right. . . . [59]

Comments of General Burns, Commander UNEF, 1961

This chapter was first written in the early months of 1959, and was revised in the spring of 1961. There has been no basic change in the intervening two years. Are the prospects for peace between Israel and her Arab neighbours any better now than at any time during the four and a half years covered by this narrative? I do not believe that they are. To the extent that there have been no serious hostilities since 1956 and consequently no inflammation of passions, there has been opportunity for a calm approach to a negotiated settlement. But if there have been any such approaches, they have been shrouded in diplomatic secrecy, and so far apparent results have been nil. There has been no modification of the positions of Arabs or Israelis which would promise progress towards a negotiated peace. The power of Western nations alone to maintain peace in the Middle East until a peaceful solution is reached has declined. There is a nexus of cold-war hostility between the United States and Russia in this area, with all that implies of danger of a local conflict's getting out of hand, and even setting off a third world war.[60]

---

[59]*Department of State Bulletin*, March 11, 1957, p. 393.

[60]Edson L. M. Burns, *Between Arab and Israeli* (Toronto: Clarke, Irwin, & Co., Ltd., 1962), p. 282. Reprinted by permission.

BIBLIOGRAPHY

SOURCES USED IN THIS PROBLEM

1. *Collections and Official Documents*

Department of State Bulletin.

Documents on International Affairs. 1955. 1956. Royal Institute of International Affairs. London: Oxford University Press, 1958, 1959.

Israel Government Yearbook. 1959–60. Tel Aviv: Israel Government Printing Press.

Journal Officiel. Assemblée, Débats. Paris.

Parliamentary Debates. Commons. London: Her Majesty's Stationery Office.

The Suez Canal Problem. Department of State Publication No. 6292. Washington, D.C.: U.S. Government Printing Office, 1956.

2. *Others*

ADAMS, SHERMAN. *Firsthand Report: The Story of the Eisenhower Administration.* New York: Harper, 1961.

BARKER, A. J. *Suez: The Seven Days' War*. London: Faber & Faber, 1965.

BURNS, EDSON L. M. *Between Arab and Israeli*. Toronto: Clarke, Irwin & Co., Ltd., 1962.

CAMPBELL, JOHN C. *Defense of the Middle East*. New York: Harper, 1958.

CHURCHILL, RANDOLPH. *The Rise and Fall of Anthony Eden*. New York: Putnam's, 1959.

DAYAN, GENERAL MOSHE. *Diary of the Sinai Campaign*. New York: Harper & Row, 1966.

DULLES, ALLEN. *The Craft of Intelligence*. New York: Harper & Row, 1963.

EDEN, ANTHONY. *Full Circle*. Boston: Houghton Mifflin, 1960. Excerpts published as: *The Suez Crisis of 1956* (Boston: Beacon Press, 1968).

EISENHOWER, DWIGHT D. *The White House Years*, Vol. II, *Waging Peace, 1956–1961*. Garden City, N.Y.: Doubleday, 1965.

FINER, HERMAN. *Dulles over Suez*. Chicago: Quadrangle Books, 1964.

ISSAWI, CHARLES and YEGANEH, MOHAMMED. *The Economics of Middle Eastern Oil*. New York: Praeger, 1962.

LACOUTURE, JEAN and SIMONE. *Egypt in Transition*. Tr. by FRANCES SCARFE. New York: Criterion Books, 1958.

LENCZOWSKI, GEORGE. *Oil and State in the Middle East*. Ithaca, N.Y.: Cornell University Press, 1960.

MURPHY, ROBERT D. *Diplomat among Warriors*. Garden City, N.Y.: Doubleday, 1964.

NASSER, GAMAL ABDUL. *Egypt's Liberation: The Philosophy of Revolution*. Washington, D.C.: Public Affairs Press, 1955.

ROBERTSON, TERENCE. *Crisis: The Inside Story of the Suez Conspiracy*. New York: Atheneum, 1956.

SELECT LIST OF BOOKS RECOMMENDED FOR FURTHER READING

AZEAU, HENRI. *Le Piège de Suez*. Paris: Laffont, 1964.

BLOOMFIELD, LINCOLN P. *The United Nations and U.S. Foreign Policy*. Boston: Little Brown, 1967.

BLAXLAND, GREGORY. *Egypt and Sinai: Eternal Battleground*. New York: Funk and Wagnalls, 1968.

BROMBERGER, MERRY and SERGE. *Secrets of Suez*. London: Sidgwick and Jackson, 1957.

CALVOCORESSI, PETER. *Suez: Ten Years After*. New York: Pantheon, 1967.

CAMPBELL, JOHN C. *Defense of the Middle East*. New York: Harper, 1960.

CHILDERS, ERSKINE. *The Road to Suez*. London: MacGibbon and Kee, 1960.

DONOVAN, ROBERT J. *Eisenhower: The Inside Story*. New York: Harper, 1956.

DRUMMOND, ROSCOE, and COBLE, GASTON. *Duel at the Brink: John Foster Dulles' Command of American Power*. New York: Doubleday, 1960.

EDELMAN, MAURICE. *Ben Gurion: a Political Biography*. London: Hodder and Stoughton, 1964.

EPSTEIN, LEON DAVID. *British Politics in the Suez Crisis*. Urbana, Ill.: University of Illinois Press, 1964.

HENRIQUES, ROBERT. *A Hundred Hours to Suez: An Account of Israel's Campaign in the Sinai Peninsula*. New York: Viking, 1957.

HUGHES, EMMET JOHN. *The Ordeal of Power: A Political Memoir of the Eisenhower Years*. New York: Atheneum, 1963.

HUSSEIN.   *Uneasy Lies the Head.* New York: Random House, 1962.

KEIGHTLEY, SIR CHARLES.   *Operations in Egypt. London Gazette (Supplement)*, September 10, 1957.

LAQUEUR, WALTER Z.   *The Soviet Union and the Middle East.* New York: Praeger, 1959.

LEEMAN, WAYNE.   *The Price of Middle East Oil.* Ithaca, N.Y.: Cornell University Press, 1962.

NUTTING, ANTHONY.   *No End of a Lesson: the Story of Suez.* London: Constable, 1967.

RIVLIN, B. and SZYLIOWICZ, J. S. (eds.).   *The Contemporary Middle East.* New York: Random House, 1965.

THOMAS, HUGH.   *Suez.* New York: Harper & Row, 1967.

WYNN, WILTON.   *Nasser of Egypt: the Search for Dignity.* Cambridge, Mass.: Arlington Books, 1959.

SECTION VII

Issues of the Nuclear World

FRANCE'S PLACE IN THE POSTWAR WORLD

Charles de Gaulle, NATO, and the French striking force, 1958-66

France in the early 1940's and the late 1950's meant Charles de Gaulle. With the same consciousness with which Louis XIV could say "L'état c'est moi," de Gaulle has felt with unswerving conviction that he personally epitomized 20th-century France. And in spite of the record—France ignominiously defeated in 1940 and France a second-rate power in the 1960's—de Gaulle has managed to profess his country's grandeur so effectively that France has regained a considerable amount of the prestige it lost in defeat and during the *immobilisme* of the Fourth Republic. Between 1946 and 1958, de Gaulle held no official position, and by 1954 he seemed to have no future in French politics. Thus he remained on the sidelines during the Dien Bien Phu episode in Indochina; he had no say in France's joining the European Defense Community, or in its participation in NATO; he was not consulted about the Suez crisis; nor could he guide France's position in the United Nations. He was not responsible for France's atomic program, which began to develop seriously after 1955 when the French Atomic Energy Commissariat was authorized to develop an experimental bomb. The first French atomic explosion had not been made, however, when de Gaulle returned to power in 1958.

De Gaulle has been called intransigent, haughty, difficult to get along with. His policies have been described as unreasonable, narrow, and inspired by his personal dislike of the "Anglo-Saxons," for whom he developed a resentment when, during World War II, he was excluded from high policy decisions regarding France. Yet de Gaulle has in fact been astonishingly consistent, and the position he maintained in 1932 established a pattern from which he has not deviated. This is emphasized by passages from the book he published in that year.

Excerpts from Charles de Gaulle's
Le fil de l'épée (*The Edge of the Sword*),
1932

But, hope though we may, what reason have we for thinking that passion and self-interest, the root cause of armed conflict in men and in nations, will cease to operate; that anyone will willingly surrender what he has or not try to get what he wants; in short, that human nature will ever become something other than it is? Is it really likely that the present balance of power will remain unchanged so long as the small want to become great, the strong to dominate the weak, the old to live on? How are frontiers to be stabilized, how is power to be controlled if evolution continues along the same lines as hitherto? . . .

Is it possible to conceive of life without force? Only if children cease to be born, only if minds are sterilized, feelings frozen, men's needs anaesthetized, only if the world is reduced to immobility, can it be banished. Otherwise, in some form or another, it will remain indispensable, for, without it, thought would have no driving power, action no strength. It is the prerequisite of movement and the midwife of progress. Whether as the bulwark of authority, the defender of thrones, the motive-power of revolution, we owe to it, turn and turn about, both order and liberty. Force has watched over civilizations in the cradle: force has ruled empires, and dug the grave of decadence: force gives laws to the peoples and controls their destinies.

.   .   .   .   .

What, above all else, we look for in a leader is the power to dominate events, to leave his mark on them, and to assume responsibility for the consequences of his actions. The setting up of one man over his fellows can be justified only if he can bring to the common task the drive and certainty which comes of character. But why, for that matter, should a man be granted, free gratis and for nothing, the privilege of domination, the right to issue orders, the pride of seeing them obeyed, the thousand and one tokens of respect, unquestioning obedience and loyalty which surround the seat of power? To him goes the greater part of the honour and glory. But that is fair enough, for he makes the best repayment that he can by shouldering the risks. Obedience would be intolerable if he who demands it did not use it to produce effective results, and how can he do so if he does not possess the qualities of daring, decision and initiative?

.   .   .   .   .

It is the task of political leaders to dominate opinion: that of the monarch, of the council, of the people, since it is from these that they draw their authority. They have no value, and can do nothing, except in the name of the sovereign power. But their abilities matter less than their skill in pleasing, and promises are more effective than arguments. The statesman, therefore, must concentrate all his efforts on captivating men's minds. He must know when to dissemble, when to be frank. He must pose as the servant of the public in order to become its master. He must outbid his rivals in self-confidence, and only after a thousand intrigues and solemn undertakings will he find himself entrusted with full power. Even when he has it in his grasp, he can never be completely open in his dealings, for he must still be concerned to please, to know how to convince Prince or Parliament, how to gratify popular passions and soothe the anxieties of vested interests. His authority, no matter how unquestioned, is precarious. Public Opinion, that inconstant mistress, follows his lead with a capricious step, ready to stop dead should he race too far ahead, to take giant strides when he thinks it advisable to move with caution. . . . Great or small, historic figure or colourless politician, he comes and goes between power and powerlessness, between prestige and public ingratitude. The whole of his life and the sum total of his work are marked by instability, restlessness and storm, and so are very different from those of the soldier. The soldier's profession is that of arms, but the power they give him has to be strictly organized. From the moment that he embarks upon it he becomes the slave to a body of regulations, and so remains all through his active life. The army is generous but jealous. . . . As a man he suffers much from its demands, for he must renounce his personal liberty, his chances of making money and, sometimes, sacrifice his life, and what greater offering could there be? But at this high cost it opens the door for him to the empire of armed might. That is why, though he often grumbles at his slavery, he clings to it: nay, more, he loves it, and glories in the price he has to pay. "It is my honour!" he says.[1]

_____

[1]Charles de Gaulle, *The Edge of the Sword*, trans. Gerard Hopkins (London: Faber & Faber, Ltd., 1960), pp. 12–13, 58, 96–97.

There is truth in the allegation that de Gaulle was left out of high-level strategic decisions during World War II. Whether or not Roosevelt and Churchill had strong personal feelings about de Gaulle, neither they nor Stalin would permit consultation with a leader whose country lacked the perquisites of power. De Gaulle dedicated himself as a result of his wartime experience to a policy which would give France equal standing at the council table. His major criticism of his country's role in the Suez episode attacked the arrangement which gave military control to Britain.

FOR CONSIDERATION   This interview was given two years before de Gaulle returned to power. At that time he had virtually retired from politics. Is it likely that he ever discounted the possibility of a return?

Comments of J. R. Tournoux, 1956

I was given an interview by de Gaulle at this time.

"What do you think of the Suez incident?" I asked.

It started out all right. For once they were doing something! But the operation was very difficult. It needed perfect preparation on both the political and military level.

We left all the organization to the British. Why did we leave them all the commands? They commanded on sea, on land, in the air!

When I speak of political preparation, I think we should warn the Americans and tell them: "Here is what we intend to do. If you don't approve . . ."

De Gaulle finished his sentence, but, because of his return to power and his diplomatic responsibilities, we don't feel we have the right to report what he actually said.

The General continued: "And the Americans would have accepted it. Now, they threaten to cut off our gasoline. All right! I would tell them . . ."[2]

_____

[2]J. R. Tournoux, *Secrets d'État* (Paris: Librairie Plon, 1960), p. 177; all rights reserved.

Once France had withdrawn its forces from Indochina, it was in a better position to hold down the incipient independence movement in Algeria. But the war there deteriorated and the disaffected military and civil leaders threatened open insurrection against the state. Throughout the crisis, Charles de Gaulle worked on his memoirs in the semiretirement of his home at Colombey-les-deux-églises, keeping in touch with all factions. In May, 1958, the gravity of the situation brought him back to power and he began to direct his energies to the task of restoring order in North Africa.

In Washington and in London, President Eisenhower and Prime Minister Macmillan speculated as to what the new French regime would do. Both Eisenhower and Macmillan had known de Gaulle personally in 1943 in Algiers, when Macmillan was British adviser on Eisenhower's staff, and de Gaulle was chairman of the French Committee of National Liberation. For immediate consideration with the new French government were three "A's:" atomic power, the Atlantic Community, and Algeria, as well as the threat of a new crisis, developing in the Middle East as a result of revolution in Iraq. It was decided that Secretary of State Dulles should consult with de Gaulle as soon as feasible. This meeting was arranged in July.

David Schoenbrun was CBS correspondent in Paris. Dulles gave him details of his meeting with de Gaulle in several "off-the-record" conversations.

Secretary of State Dulles' Meeting with President de Gaulle, July 5, 1958, as Described by David Schoenbrun

Dulles told de Gaulle at once that there would "very unlikely have to be military action in the Levant." He said that the United States held the view that it would be in the best interest of France and all concerned if the French would decide not to participate in that intervention. He offered to explain the reasons behind this thinking if the President of France requested it.

President de Gaulle thanked Secretary Dulles for his courtesy. He did not request any explanation. He simply stated, "If it becomes necessary to defend Western interests in the Levant, France will not be found absent."

De Gaulle and Dulles agreed that it was necessary for the two governments to keep in close touch with each other and with the British in this fluid situation.

Secretary Dulles said that there was nothing more important than being fully informed in all areas of concern to each of the allies and, since they were allies, the concern of each was always the concern of all. With this careful, respectful qualification, the Secretary asked President de Gaulle to evaluate the over-all French situation in the wake of "recent events" in North Africa. (The "recent events" were the uprisings in Algiers that had brought down the Fourth Republic and brought back de Gaulle.)

General de Gaulle said that the present was one of the most critical moments in French history. The recent events in Algiers he considered to be symptoms of a deeply inflamed wound. The French people had suffered greatly in body and in spirit as a result of what had happened in Indochina. There was a real danger that the spirit might falter unless the morale of the people was preserved and strengthened in order to face the new trials ahead. De Gaulle said that there was a danger that the country might disintegrate under the strain of liquidating the French Empire in Africa if the people saw it as another defeat instead of the great new construction of a French-led "community of peoples." "That is why at this crucial moment there is nothing more important for the French people than to be made to believe again that France is a great power," de Gaulle told Dulles. He explained that "grandeur" is not a romantic notion; it is a reality, a tangible factor in a nation's efforts. The French "have the need to believe in themselves and the right to believe in themselves."

Dulles said he understood the need for the French to think of their country as the great nation it has been for so long and that this was in the highest interest of all France's allies. "The spirit of France is the spirit of Western civilization," said Dulles, adding, "It is certainly in our interest that this spirit be kept strong." He went on to warn, however, that there might well be a clash of wills if France, striving to maintain the status of a great power, were to appear to be setting herself up separately and above Germany and Italy. The Secretary pointed out that the Germans and Italians had their serious emotional and political problems; that they might misunderstand French motives and become mistrustful, and thereby severely strain the entire Atlantic Alliance.[3]

---

[3]From *The Three Lives of Charles De Gaulle* by David Schoenbrun. Copyright © 1965 by David Schoenbrun. Reprinted by permission of Atheneum Publishers.

O ut of the meeting with Dulles developed a concept close to de Gaulle's heart, that of an Anglo-French-American "triumvirate" which would in a sense supersede NATO as the basic Western strategic entity. De Gaulle sounded out Rome and Bonn, and then sent a letter to Eisenhower (and Macmillan) outlining his proposal.

A summary of de Gaulle's letter and the text of Eisenhower's reply is given here.

FOR CONSIDERATION   Would it have been possible for de Gaulle's proposition to have been accepted? Would a modified acceptance have been possible? Would such an acceptance have reduced de Gaulle's hostility toward the "Anglo-Saxons"?

Summary of General de Gaulle's Letter to President Eisenhower, September 17, 1958, as Given in a State Department Memorandum

General de Gaulle . . . wrote to President Eisenhower on September 17, 1958, to indicate that NATO in its present form no longer met the needs of French security. He noted that France had responsibilities not only in the North Atlantic, but in Africa, the Indian Ocean, and the Pacific, as did the United Kingdom and the United States. He considered that the world situation no longer justified delegating to the United States the power to make decisions concerning free world defense. He therefore called for a tripartite organization on the level of world policy and strategy, to take joint decisions on political questions affecting world security and to establish and put into effect strategic plans of action, notably with regard to the employment of nuclear weapons. He thought it would also be possible to foresee and organize, among the three governments, eventual theaters of operation and subordinate theaters. Such a security organization was considered indispensable by General de Gaulle. He declared that France would henceforth subordinate to its achievement any development of French participation in NATO, and would if necessary propose a revision of the North Atlantic Treaty. He called for tripartite consultations on this proposal.[4]

President Eisenhower to General de Gaulle, October 20, 1958

I have given considerable thought to the views expressed in your letter of September 17. You have posed serious questions which require earnest thinking and careful study.

The central problem you raise—the organization of the free world's defense—is very much on my mind also. I agree that we should constantly seek means for making that organization more effective.

We are, I believe, in full agreement that the threat we face is global and that our policies should be adapted to deal with the worldwide nature of the threat. Although recognizing that more needs to be done, we believe that our policies have

to an extent already been adapted to this end. It is in recognition of the need to deal with the worldwide threat that the United States has joined with its allies in establishing elements of strength throughout the world. The United States and France are closely associated in certain of these groupings, such as NATO and SEATO. The United States has also associated itself with many other countries, in both multilateral and bilateral arrangements, all directed toward the same general purpose. We have also sought to give recognition to the fact that the threat is more than military through our economic, financial, and technical assistance programs designed to aid nations throughout the world to resist subversion.

As for the Atlantic Alliance itself, I believe there has been a significant evolution in NATO over the past 2 years. Consultation in NATO has in fact been extended well beyond the confines of the European area. We, for example, have sought to use the NATO Council to inform or consult with our allies on the threat facing the free world in the Far East and the Middle East. We have also sought to use the Council to develop common policies toward the Soviet bloc. We feel that this "habit of consultation" among the NATO nations must be still further broadened but that this cannot be forced. I do not believe that we can afford to lose any of this developing intimacy among all the members of NATO and the closer bonds it forges.

As for the means for dealing with the problem which you propose, our present procedures for organizing the defense of the free world clearly require the willing cooperation of many other nations, both within and outside NATO. We cannot afford to adopt any system which would give to our other allies, or other free world countries, the impression that basic decisions affecting their own vital interests are being made without their participation. As regards NATO itself, I must in all

---

[4]*The Atlantic Alliance,* Hearings before the U.S. Senate Subcommittee on National Security, Part 7, Supplement, August 15, 1966 (Washington, D.C.: U.S. Government Printing Office, 1966), p. 228.

frankness say that I see very serious problems, both within and outside NATO, in any effort to amend the North Atlantic Treaty so as to extend its coverage beyond the areas presently covered.

All this having been said, I must add that I recognize that a community associa-tion to live must constantly evolve and find means to make itself more useful in the face of changing conditions. I am quite prepared to explore this aspect of the matter in appropriate ways.[5]

_____

[5]*Ibid.*, pp. 230–31.

During the fall and winter of 1958, de Gaulle had to face enormous problems: the referendum on the new constitution which would inaugurate the Fifth French Republic; the continuing agitation in Algeria; a thorough-going reform of the entire military establishment which would result in the ordinance of January 7, 1959. Under the new constitution and military ordinance, de Gaulle, as President of the Republic, would be commander in chief of the armed forces. Well aware of the progress France was making in atomic research, he pressed his bid for acceptance by the nuclear powers. In December, 1958, de Gaulle again consulted with Dulles.

Comments of David Schoenbrun

Secretary Dulles, upon his return to Paris for the December meeting of NATO, went to see de Gaulle for a second time. He was particularly anxious to find out whether de Gaulle's use of expressions like "joint decisions" did specifically mean a veto power, in the sense that a "joint deci-sion" can only come about if all parties concur. Under such definition, France, by withholding agreement, could prevent *joint allied* decision, thereby paralyzing the Anglo-Saxons. This was the kind of subtle legalism that appealed to Dulles and that he was well trained to spot in any contract or agreement.

After his talk with de Gaulle, the Sec-retary looked grim and glum. I had a chance to ask him about this "veto" issue shortly after he saw de Gaulle. Dulles was deeply distressed. He felt that de Gaulle had made an impossible demand and that there was no hope of an allied agreement. Soon after seeing Dulles, I interviewed French Foreign Minister Maurice Couve de Murville. He further confirmed de Gaulle's demand: "Yes, in effect, it does amount to a veto on the use of nuclear weapons anywhere in the world." The Foreign Minister explained: "If China at-tacks Taiwan, America may have to strike back with atomic weapons. This could lead to world war if Russia reacts. As your allies we would be plunged into war with you, without ever having been consulted or having participated in the chain of events. Do you think this is reasonable?"[6]

_____

[6]Schoenbrun, *op. cit.*, p. 300.

Although some tripartite meetings at diplomatic and military levels took place in 1959, de Gaulle was not satisfied with their course and in charac-teristic fashion began to place pressure on England and the United States.

He denied the storage of nuclear warheads in France, and he withdrew French naval units from the NATO Mediterranean forces. Questioned about this, he replied in a press conference. Included with this document is testimony made later (in 1966) by Robert Murphy. Murphy was at the time Deputy Undersecretary of State and the American delegate to the tripartite conferences.

President de Gaulle's Comments on Withdrawal of French Naval Forces, Press Conference of March 25, 1959

The zone of possible NATO action does not extend south of the Mediterranean. The Middle East, North Africa, Black Africa, the Red Sea, etc. are not a part of it. Who can deny that France may possibly find herself obliged to act in these different areas? She would therefore have to act independently of NATO. But how could she do so if her fleet were not available? Without her fleet, how could she carry on any type of action in the regions that I have just referred to?

I observe, furthermore, that the two other great world powers of the Atlantic Alliance—the United States and Great Britain—have taken steps to prevent the greater part of their naval forces from being integrated in NATO. I add that Americans and British have kept in their hands alone the principal element of their strength, their atomic bombers.

The fact that France has resumed the power to dispose of her own fleet certainly would not prevent her from using it, should the occasion arise, in a common battle in the Mediterranean. Thus there is nothing in this change that might weaken the Alliance. Quite the contrary. Indeed, I believe that the Alliance will be all the more vital and strong as the great powers unite on the basis of a cooperation in which each carries his own load, rather than on the basis of an integration in which peoples and governments find themselves more or less deprived of their

roles and responsibilities in the domain of their own defense.[7]

Comments of Robert D. Murphy

I would like to address myself to the proximate cause of the present crisis—De Gaulle's policy. Having been in contact with him during the war days in North Africa, I have followed with interest the trend of his policy vis-a-vis NATO since he came to power for the second time in 1958. Then I worked in the State Department and presided over the tripartite conversations we had with French and British representatives regarding De Gaulle's proposal to establish a form of triumvirate consisting of himself, Prime Minister Macmillan, and President Eisenhower for the determination of global policy. When that proposal was found unacceptable both to the British and to ourselves, there began a series of French decisions affecting France's participation in NATO, the elimination of the French Mediterranean naval units from NATO command; later the elimination of similar units from the Channel command; the refusal of bomber bases in France; the refusal to stockpile nuclear weapons, and other matters. These actions were taken in De Gaulle's typical leisurely chopping away which seems to characterize the phase when his plan or policy is in the making. In past dealings with

[7] *Major Addresses, Statements and Press Conferences of General Charles de Gaulle,* May 19, 1958-January 31, 1964 (New York: French Embassy, 1964), p. 49.

other questions, De Gaulle has concealed his ultimate intention or real goal until he is in a tactical position to achieve it. Algeria is a good example. When possible, he operates according to plan. There may be a lengthy period of quiet preparation allowing time for events to occur. With a good sense of timing, he eventually comes to a phase of realization, after appropriate orchestration, where the action may be swift or even violent. Thus, his planning

for NATO with a beginning in 1958 hesitated through the Kennedy administration with gentle efforts to take under his fatherly wing our young President, but becoming more pointed after Mr. Johnson came to power. . . .[8]

[8]*The Crisis in NATO,* Report of the Subcommittee on Europe of the House Committee on Foreign Affairs, August, 1966 (Washington, D.C.: U.S. Government Printing Office, 1966), p. 199.

The conversations did not meet de Gaulle's desires, but some advantage for France came out of the American-French discussions. The United States agreed on May 7, 1959, to sell France up to 986 pounds of enriched uranium to use as fuel in development of a land-based prototype of an atomic submarine power plant.

Several months later, with news of the American-Soviet *détente* which would lead to Khrushchev-Eisenhower meetings, de Gaulle had to admit that his bid to enter the atomic club saw little chance of acceptance. Eisenhower made a quick round of European capitals and conferred with de Gaulle at Rambouillet on September 2.

Eisenhower has described this meeting in his memoirs (*The White House Years,* Vol. II, *Waging Peace,* p. 427), but a much more revealing interpretation is found in the interview he granted to David Schoenbrun.

Two additional views are given here, one American and one French. Thomas K. Finletter had been American Ambassador to NATO, and René Pleven, a former Prime Minister, had at one time been a member of de Gaulle's wartime Committee of National Liberation.

President Eisenhower's Comments on His Relations with de Gaulle, as Told to David Schoenbrun

I could have reached a satisfactory agreement with de Gaulle on the atom thing except for the law. I told de Gaulle time and again. I said, look, Mr. President, I'll go as far as I can today and I'm going to try to get Congress to change some of the provisions in the atomic-energy law. He believed me and I did do it. I changed the law twice, but we never did get all we

needed. The atomic-energy act ought to be repealed, because it's a futile thing—those restrictions on the president. But there's a joint committee down there in Washington, a very powerful one, and it became an emotional issue. . . .

De Gaulle knew where I stood on this question of being a loyal ally and good friend, so he did not doubt my motives when I disagreed with him on the big pitch he made for a three-power directorate, or triumvirate of the West. He knew I was sincere and not just being well, selfish or trying to monopolize power, because he knew I was trying to help him on atomic power. But the three-power thing—I just couldn't see it. . . . Our biggest argument as presidents came out of this idea he was sold on, to have a publicly proclaimed triumvirate. You've got that right in your book, that tripartite business and public recognition of France as a great power. That is exactly what he wanted.

I would say to him, look, I'll do everything else. I'll consult you as you request. I'll promise to make no move and neither will the British unless we've all agreed that we'll do this thing by study, but let's don't proclaim it publicly as a three-power directorate. But de Gaulle would have none of it, nothing less than his demands. I'd say to de Gaulle, now, Mr. President, this is trouble. I can't do it. I'd say that I believe that in the long run we've got to have the support of West Germany, of Italy and of the rest of western Europe, as well as France. Now, Mr. President, if we are going to just tell them that they are going to have to do such and such—while we are going to do so and so—why, pretty soon they are going to say, now hold on there, you are making us second-class citizens and then they will desert us. . . .

He finally made his biggest pitch for it when we were alone together—at Rambouillet, it was, in September 1959. Just the two of us and one interpreter—nobody else. That's when he took up all the world issues, you know, Vietnam, Laos and so forth, and French interests and influence there, and how we really needed to work out tactics and strategy together and how he could help us there, too, because we were going to have a big problem there. . . . I worried more about the French and helped them more than I did for the British. There was never any special English-speaking favoritism, and de Gaulle should know that. And then, much later in NATO, we set up the Standing Group of the French, British and American military advisors meeting in Washington. We brought them in. But I do admit that, no matter what we did, de Gaulle had this fixed misconception and he would never forget it. But he's wrong and I told him so, over and over again.

You can't just have two or three pals acting as a self-contained unit in the diplomatic and strategic world without just losing all your other friends, and that's all there is to it. And I just couldn't go along with this plan of his for joint global strategy—what you call in your articles here his veto on our strategic air power. You're right, that's what joint planning as de Gaulle requested would amount to—a veto. Why, he said we wouldn't use our nuclear weapon anywhere in the world without consulting him, and his sharing in the policy decisions. Now, he must know we couldn't do that. Why, the British haven't got any such kind of deal. That's where I stood on this business and I told him so as often as he brought it up.

I was willing to recognize de Gaulle as an important world figure, but he didn't have any means of exercising real world power. He had no real air force, he had no fleet, he had nothing else, so when we were trying to defend ourselves in Formosa, in Korea, Vietnam, or carrying out things all around the world, I wasn't going to be saying to my commanders: Are you going to consult now with these people and wait for them to do something. Good gracious, if you try to conduct our United States foreign policy and defense policies on the basis of not being able to do anything until you went and consulted everybody and said, here now, they've got to agree before we do it, well, you'd be in an awful lot of trouble, I'll tell you that. But short of just delivering our initiatives over to him and submitting ourselves to his judgments, well, short of that, I really did try to meet his desire and need for some kind of world position and prestige.[9]

---

[9]Schoenbrun, *op. cit.*, pp. 335–39.

**Comments of Thomas K. Finletter,
Testifying before the House Committee
on *The Crisis in NATO*, 1966**

MR. ZABLOCKI: Let me pose this question. For the sake of unity and of keeping France within NATO, and keeping it vitalized, should we have shared our secrets with them—possibly at the expense of our own security?

MR. FINLETTER: At the expense of our own security?

MR. ZABLOCKI: At an increase in the risk of having these secrets relayed to one of the Communist monoliths.

MR. FINLETTER: It all depends on the facts, Mr. Zablocki. I would find it hard to reconstruct the various developments in atomic weapons and weapons carriers. To answer your question as to, first of all, how great was the security risk, how much more would it have been increased by telling all the allies, and what difference that would have made, I can attest to a certain feeling that sometimes these secrets are not as secret as they are supposed to be and certainly not for as long as they are supposed to be, but undoubtedly it is true you have to keep secrets up to a certain point, and it is no doubt true our secrets were not widespread throughout the alliance.

As to whether or not it would have been wise to have reversed that policy, I don't feel competent now to answer. I think it would have been desirable to have handled it more equally, let's put it that way.

MR. ZABLOCKI: In your opinion, Mr. Ambassador, would that have preserved the unity?

MR. FINLETTER: Not at all. I want to make clear my belief that these views of General de Gaulle's are deep convictions of his and are not to be bartered away.

NATO and the North Atlantic Alliance were set up when he was not President of France. He found NATO on his doorstep when he got there, and he never supported it from the time he was President of France for the second time. One of his opening moves was the letter to President Eisenhower in which he was virtually saying let us get rid of the alliance and let the three of us run the show.

All this about secrets and the rest in my opinion has nothing to do with the basic fact of what the general believes.[10]

**Comments of Former French Prime
Minister René Pleven**

The French proposal of September 1958 immediately caused misunderstandings. One assertion was that France was seeking to establish a sort of directorate of three in NATO. I think this is a mistaken interpretation, for certainly the French Government is aware that an attempt of that sort would drive the other members into opposition to France and would ultimately break up the organization. What France was trying to do was simply to get the United States to realize how important it is that the nations of the West stand together against the Soviet challenge and that they be so organized that they cannot be taken by surprise whenever and wherever that challenge is presented. The French thesis is that the surprises which the Soviet Union is adept at producing in all parts of the world may at any moment directly affect the territories of the French Community; and that in view of this it would be both logical and useful to allow France to participate in the formulation of global defense plans, since these must make provision for any and all eventualities. It wants permanent co-operation with the United States and Great Britain along these lines, whether through NATO or otherwise. In the event that a sudden threat arises outside the geographical limits of NATO, France does not want to find herself confronted with

[10]*The Crisis in NATO*, pp. 138–39.

a *fait accompli,* unable to do anything but agree to the implementation of plans which have been drawn up by others and which in this nuclear age may have incalculable consequences.

·   ·   ·   ·   ·

Another aspect of France's relations with NATO which has dissatisfied the present French Government is the distribution of commands. . . .

It should be remembered that every French Government since the time NATO was established has opposed a certain concept of military integration favored by the Anglo-Saxon countries. Under this concept each member country would have had to specialize in its military contribution. The United States, for example, would have put at NATO's disposal its nuclear weapons and strategic bombers, Great Britain would have been primarily responsible for providing tactical and defense aircraft, and the major part of the ground forces would have been provided by the continental countries, particularly France.

Our governments always countered this theory with the argument that every major power should have a balanced military establishment and that each of the principal members of NATO should accordingly furnish a part of each kind of equipment required, whether atomic weapons, aircraft, infantry or tanks. . . .

This French argument, consistently upheld since the establishment of NATO, has now been expanded to include other considerations to which the President attaches great importance.[11]

---

[11]René Pleven, "France in the Atlantic Community," *Foreign Affairs,* October, 1959, pp. 22–23, 27–28.

By the end of 1959, rebuffed by London and Washington, de Gaulle saw no alternative than to go ahead with his own military plans. The atomic testing center in the Reggan region of the Sahara was nearing completion and the first tests were scheduled for early 1960. In no uncertain terms de Gaulle pronounced his policy in a speech to army officers.

Address of President de Gaulle to Officers at the French War College (Ecole de Guerre), November 3, 1959

. . . The defense of France must be French. That is a necessity which has not always been too well understood in recent years. I know this. It is absolutely essential that it become recognized once more. With a country like France, if war should come, then that war must be her war. Its effort must be her effort. If it were otherwise, our country would be acting counter to everything it has been since its origins—to its role, to its self-respect, to its very soul. Naturally, should the occasion arise, French defense would be joined with that of other countries. That is in the nature of things. But it is indispensable that our defense belong to us, that France defend herself by herself, for herself and in her own way.

If it should be otherwise, if France's defense were long allowed to remain outside the national framework or to become an integral part of, or mingled with, something else, then it would not be possible for us to maintain a State. In any period of history, the government's *raison d'être* is to defend the independence and the integrity of the territory. It arises from this necessity. Especially in France, all our regimes have been based on their ability to do so. . . .

It goes without saying that our defense, the mobilization of our means, the way in which the conduct of war is conceived— all this must be combined for us with what exists in other countries. Our strategy must be joined with the strategy of others. On the battlefields, there is every probability that we would find ourselves side by side with our allies. But let each one have a share that is all his own.

This is a fundamental point which I ask you to reflect upon. The concept of a defense of France and of the Community which would be a French defense—that is a concept which ought to underlie the philosophy of your centers and schools.

Obviously the consequence of this is that we must know how, during the next few years, to provide ourselves with a force capable of acting in our behalf, with what is commonly called a "striking force," capable of being deployed at any time and any place. It goes without saying that the basis of this force will be atomic weapons, which—whether we manufacture them or whether we buy them—must belong to us; and since—should the circumstances arise—France could be destroyed from any point in the world, our force must be ready to act anywhere on earth.[12]

[12]Service de Presse et d'Information (New York: French Embassy).

No one can tell what might have happened had the Summit Conference scheduled for Paris early in 1960 taken place. But the U-2 crisis temporarily blasted hopes for such a meeting.

Meanwhile France had become an atomic power, exploding its first nuclear device on February 13, and a second one on April 1, 1960. A series of exchanges between Eisenhower and de Gaulle continued through the summer of 1960, but the differences remained essentially the same. De Gaulle's comments regarding NATO at his press conference in September suggested that he would be taking more drastic steps. The press conference terminated the negotiations between de Gaulle and President Eisenhower, whose days in office were drawing to a close.

FOR CONSIDERATION   De Gaulle had a great deal on his mind besides France's position in NATO. Having returned to power over Algeria, he had not only the Algerian problem but the problem of all colonial French Africa to dispose of. In Europe he was confronted with Britain's growing interest in joining the Common Market and with the challenge of Germany's escalated prosperity.

This press conference, it has been said, ended an introductory and exploratory phase of de Gaulle's foreign policy. What evidence can be invoked that after 1960 he felt less dependent on the United States?

Comments of President de Gaulle at his Press Conference, September 5, 1960

With regard to France, there are at least two points on which the treaty must be revised. Moreover, you know that when the Treaty of the North Atlantic Organization was drawn up, its text specified that it could be revised at the end of ten years, and the ten years have elapsed.

What are the two essential points for France? The first, as I have indicated, is the limitation of the Alliance to the single area of Europe. We feel that, at least among the world powers of the West, there must be something organized— where the Alliance is concerned—as to their political conduct and, should the occasion arise, their strategic conduct outside Europe, especially in the Middle East, and in Africa, where these three powers are constantly involved. Furthermore, if there is no agreement among the principal members of the Atlantic Alliance on matters other than Europe, how can the Alliance be indefinitely maintained in Europe? This must be remedied.

The second point on which France thinks there should be a change is that of integration in the defense of Europe. It seems to us that the defense of a country, while being of course combined with that of other countries, must have a national character. How indeed in the long run could a Government, a Parliament, a people give their money and their services with all their heart in time of peace, and make their sacrifices in time of war, for a system in which they are not responsible for their own defense? That is why from this point of view as well, a revival of the Alliance seems indispensable to us. Moreover, as you know, we have already taken a few steps in this direction. That is why, for example, France keeps her fleet directly under her own orders. For exactly what is a fleet? It is a means of distant action. And how could it be imagined that France would leave this means of distant action to the discretion of an exclusively European organization which has nothing to do with Africa, while she herself, through her interests and her responsibilities, is continually involved in Africa?

Furthermore, France feels that if atomic weapons are to be stockpiled on her territory, these weapons should be in her own hands. Given the nature of these weapons and the possible consequences of their use, France obviously can not leave her own destiny and even her own life to the discretion of others.[13]

---

[13]*Major Addresses, Statements and Press Conferences of General Charles de Gaulle*, p. 96.

The positions of the United States and France did not change by reason of John Kennedy's inauguration as President in 1961. The two Presidents met in June, 1961, and promised to consult together frequently. (They never did, although it was later reported that Kennedy studied French so that he could communicate more fluently with de Gaulle.) In spite of several efforts on de Gaulle's part (he wrote the American President in August, 1961, and again in January, 1962), there would be no fundamental change in American policy.[14]

In France, General de Gaulle's strategic concept of a nuclear striking force—the *Force de Frappe*— was by no means hailed with enthusiasm on all sides. The issue was vigorously debated in the French Parliament during the winter of 1960, and it continued to be argued thereafter. An official statement of the military position in 1964 is here followed by two typical opposing arguments. General Pierre Gallois, although not officially representing de Gaulle, argues the Government's case. A dissenting

---

[14]The documents reproduced here concentrate on the French side of the controversy. A student interested in the American side might profitably examine books like Henry A. Kissinger's *The Troubled Partnership* (Anchor edition, 1966), pp. 31–41, or John W. Spanier's *World Politics in an Age of Revolution* (New York: Frederick A. Praeger, Inc., 1967), Chap. VIII.

opinion is expressed by Raymond Aron, France's most distinguished political commentator.

FOR CONSIDERATION   In 1962 President Kennedy launched his concept of a "Grand Design" that would bind the United States to an integrated Europe. Did de Gaulle insist on a French nuclear program as a means of thwarting the Kennedy proposal? If the "Grand Design" had come into being, what role would France have played?

French Government Statement on Status of Its "Force de Frappe" in 1964

PRESENT FORMATION OF THE STRATEGIC NUCLEAR FORCE

The strategic nuclear force is currently equipped with the Mach 2+ Mirage IV bomber powered by two Atar jet engines. The airframes and powerplants are designed and produced in France. The Mirage IV carries a Cyrano II radar system providing precise location of targets and allowing contour flying without visibility. Electronic countermeasures protect it against enemy defense.

The Mirage IV can deliver the French 60-kiloton nuclear weapon (three times the power of the Hiroshima bomb), in production since the middle of 1963. The aircraft's range is 1,550 miles without refueling and nearly 3,000 miles with inflight refueling by American-built KC-135F tanker plane. The first preseries of three Mirage IV's was delivered at the end of 1963, to be followed by 50 production aircraft from then through the end of 1966.

The French Navy's carrier-based Etendard IV aircraft also has a nuclear capability. Its speed is Mach 1 and its range is 600 nautical miles, which can be extended with inflight refueling.

The French strategic nuclear force is independent, although in wartime it can operate within the framework of the Atlantic Alliance. The aircraft are dispersed over a dozen airfields, with logistical support and maintenance in the rear, to reduce the strategic force's vulnerability.

Many of the aircraft will be placed on ground alert while the others will be used for pilot training.[15]

Excerpts from an Interview with General Pierre Gallois in *Der Spiegel* (Hamburg)

Then you believe that it is impossible to wage a conventional war when atomic arms are available?

All the studies we have made, both in the NATO Supreme Command and in the national general staffs, show that conventional and atomic warfare cannot be waged simultaneously. Conventional defense demands a concentration of men and matériel as well as a far-flung supply network. It rests on operations that take time to develop, on possibilities that take time to exploit, on time to rally both human and industrial reserves. A nuclear war does not require a concentration of either men or matériel and would probably soon be fought to a finish.

Still, during a war, it is possible to move from one stage to the other, even if the first stage—the conventional—is quite short.

It is impossible to employ one mode of warfare right after the other on the same territory. Either you prepare for atomic conflict and deploy your forces accordingly, or you strike with conventional weapons and use the organization suited to that type of warfare. In Western Europe, particularly its central area, no ra-

[15]*France and Its Armed Forces* (New York: French Embassy, 1964), pp. 8–9.

tional person can believe the Soviets will choose traditional warfare if it entails any risk of forced withdrawal. These are the only alternatives, either the Russians win with their conventional forces and we are lost, or we stop the Russians with our conventional arms, whereupon they resort to their nuclear weapons. And since the same logic applies to both sides, Russia knows she has only two options: the peaceful status quo or nuclear attack.

Then, according to your reasoning, every war in Europe must immediately lead to a great nuclear conflict?

What I am saying is that reliance on conventional weapons alone may eliminate the deterrent, for if the enemy knows from the very beginning that he faces an atomic war, he must take into account the risk that such a war implies. And this is too great. If we accept the strategy of a conventional-arms "interlude," we may diminish the risk but we encourage aggression. The foe will conquer Hamburg and then offer to negotiate. No one will want to refuse, because that would entail starting a nuclear war for the sake of a Hamburg that had already fallen to the enemy. Two such "interludes" and Germany is lost.

You do not believe that conventional fighting forces constitute a deterrent?

Of course such forces are needed to check local attacks; in order to achieve complete deterrence, however, they must also lend credence to the idea that atomic weapons will be used if necessary. But what return do we get for the billions poured into strong conventional forces when the defense system they have built crumbles in a few hours? In addition, such forces invite the danger of nuclear attack because of their extreme vulnerability to atomic weapons.

.   .   .   .   .

We believe that it may very well be in the interest of both the country attacked and its population not to use atomic weapons.

But in each case you must decide at what point you will engage in nuclear warfare. And the enemy must know that you are ready to use nuclear weapons if you are unable to beat off his attack with your limited conventional forces. Thus the need for atomic war would be diminished, not increased. The enemy must be prevented from concentrating his troops. He cannot simultaneously achieve tactical superiority by conventional means and disperse his forces to avoid atomic annihilation.

In this connection it is surprising that you consider the force de frappe *a tactical atomic instrument. It was our impression that the French military nuclear force was intended to be purely retaliatory, to be employed against cities and industrial centers.*

The *force de frappe* is a flexible instrument. In its "first generation" (stage of development), when planes are still the vehicles of delivery, it will obviously play a tactical role in a time of crisis. It will pose a threat to any aggressor who contemplates sending strong conventional forces to our frontiers. The enemy's general staff will have to reckon with the *force de frappe.* Consequently, he will have to follow the strategy of nuclear warfare and disperse his units.

If France believes the United States may not defend Europe with nuclear arms, the question arises as to whether the force de frappe *really represents the required minimum of deterrent power.*

This is important. Both the Americans and the Russians are intent on making their "second-strike" retaliatory missiles invulnerable. Assume the Americans will soon have 1,200 intercontinental missiles "hardened" in underground silos. A simple calculation shows that with the accuracy and reliability of present-day missiles, the Russians need ten operational missiles for every one the Americans have in order to launch a preventive strike and knock the latter out of commission. This means the Russians need 12,000 missiles. But that is completely out of the question, since they have barely more than 150. Yet even if they had the 12,000, they would still have to figure on 10 percent of the American striking force —120 missiles—remaining intact. But this is more than twice the number required to destroy the forty-eight Russian cities in which, according to American studies, 90 percent of the Russian ruling elite and 50 percent of the population are concentrated. In other words, a Russian nuclear attack on America is sheer insanity and the reverse is equally true. In this sense both countries are a kind of "sanctuary" and cannot fire their missiles at each other. When the Americans tell us that the *force de frappe* is absurd because it represents only 1 percent of the American potential—actually they should say one thousandth of 1 percent—I am always tempted to reply: "Perhaps, but 90 percent of your potential is superfluous."

Will the force de frappe *suffice to defend the French "sanctuary" and deter the Russians? In case of a preventive Soviet strike French security will certainly depend on the readiness of American nuclear weapons to deliver a counterblow.*

A Russian nuclear attack on Europe would bring British as well as French nuclear forces into play. Besides, what good would it do the Russians to have all of Europe and part of the Soviet Union destroyed without a simultaneous attack on the United States?[16]

Comments of Raymond Aron

In Europe, the French force is of necessity complementary to the American deterrent, and the scope of its contribution

[16]Reprinted from *Atlas*, January, 1965, pp. 10–12. Translated from *Der Spiegel* (Hamburg), November 4, 1964.

to security must therefore be measured by the extent to which it would be capable of deterring the Soviet Union from acts of aggression that the combined (Anglo-American) force had failed to inhibit. I must confess that I find such a situation between now and 1970 hard to imagine.

Whether it is a matter of massive conventional attacks or limited atomic actions, the Soviet Union (assuming that it would contemplate either, which under present world conditions is highly improbable) would be deterred far more effectively by the combined Atlantic organization than by the French force alone. This, therefore, leaves local aggression, conducted with conventional arms, which the Americans would be unable to deter but which the existence of a small French force would stop the Kremlin from committing. The argument may not be entirely devoid of merit—who can ever be absolutely sure of anything, in speculations of this sort? But once again, it rather strains the imagination.

By taking the initiative and sending all available Mirage IV bombers—about thirty at the most, since some will always be out of commission at any given time— against Soviet cities, the French Government would deliberately accept in advance the doom of the entire French nation, the inevitable response to whatever damage may have been inflicted by the A-bombs dropped from these planes. And how many planes would actually be able to penetrate Soviet defenses? That question may be left for the experts to argue about, while we confine ourselves to the fact that the principal Soviet cities are ringed by numerous ground-to-air missiles installations, that the Sam III has a good chance of detecting and downing even low-flying bombers, that furthermore the Mirage IV with a ceiling of about 50,000 feet is not made for hedgehopping and that few, if any, would be likely to return from their mission. Given these facts, Soviet leaders would find it very hard to believe that the government of a country so transparently vulnerable, and without even a trace of civil defense, would deliberately choose to unleash the holocaust in full awareness of the vast discrepancy between what it could inflict and what in turn would be inflicted upon it. A French government trying with this sort of force to deter Soviet leaders from actions from which American power would not deter them would be able to convey to them nothing but a convincing impression of its own insanity. In other words, the deterrence would be effective only within the framework of the so-called "rationality of the irrational." A chief of state with a small nuclear force at his disposal could manifest such blind intransigence, such manifest indifference to danger and to the voice of reason alike, such obstinate determination, that in the end both enemies and friends might uneasily come to believe him capable of bringing down the ultimate catastrophe on all of them. Is General de Gaulle the man able to play this particular role? In any case no successor now in sight could hope to fill his shoes and aspire to the same sort of rather equivocal glory.

. . . . .

The first problem, in fact, raised by the second-generation deterrent is one of cost and of the extent to which this cost is compatible with even the most minimal modernization of the armed forces. Plans call for the completion by 1972–73 of three nuclear submarines, each equipped with a battery of missiles comparable to the Polaris (of which there are sixteen in every American nuclear submarine). But

some five years before we ever finish our three submarines, the Americans will have forty-one. One would really have to have an exceedingly low estimate of American determination and at the same time be unduly impressed by French willingness to commit suicide in order to believe that her own three submarines will offer France a greater security than that provided by forty-one American vessels. No one can predict exactly how much these submarines and missiles are going to cost. According to Peyrefitte, each Polaris-equipped submarine comes to 800 million new francs, or $160,000,000. But even if we accept this as the figure given in the budget or as the price at which these ships would be sold to the allies, it still remains difficult accurately to estimate the past, present, and future cost of research, development, and maintenance. It is equally rash to quote a 12-million-dollar figure for Polaris missiles, because the proportion of design and development cost included in the price is not known. Even according to present estimates the second-generation French deterrent will absorb about 25 per cent of the French budget from 1964 to 1969, and there is nothing to indicate that this fraction will actually prove sufficient to permit construction of three nuclear submarines as well as of Polaris-type missiles and the miniaturized nuclear warheads adaptable to them.[17]

---

[17] Raymond Aron, *The Great Debate: Theories of Nuclear Strategy,* trans. Ernst Pawel (Garden City, N.Y.: Doubleday & Company, Inc., 1965), pp. 106–07, 114–15. Copyright © by Doubleday & Co., Inc. Reprinted by permission of the publisher.

D e Gaulle persisted in straining French resources so that the "first generation" of planes for nuclear strikes could be developed. In the course of 1962 his position became more and more firm. He declared that France "must help build Western Europe into an organized union of States," but he baulked at the thought that such a union would exist under American hegemony. De Gaulle's talks with Prime Minister Macmillan about Britain's entry into the Common Market limped along during the summer but attained to no concrete result. In the fall of 1962 Kennedy was faced with the Cuban crisis, and in December met with Macmillan at Nassau, where he agreed to deliver Polaris missiles to Great Britain.

These events had considerable impact on de Gaulle. At his annual press conference in January, 1963, he blocked British hopes regarding the Common Market, and he clarified French policy.

Comments of President de Gaulle at his Press Conference, January 14, 1963

We are in the atomic age and we are a country that can be destroyed at any moment unless the aggressor is deterred from the undertaking by the certainty that he too will suffer frightful destruction. This justifies both alliance and independence. The Americans, our allies and our friends, have for a long time, alone, possessed a nuclear arsenal. So long as they alone had such an arsenal and so long as they showed their will to use it immediately if Europe were attacked—for at that time Europe alone could be attacked—the Americans acted in such a way that for France the question of an invasion hardly arose, since an attack was beyond all probability. . . .

Since then the Soviets have also acquired a nuclear arsenal, and that arsenal is powerful enough to endanger the very life of America. Naturally, I am not making an evaluation—if indeed it is possible to find a relation between the degree of one death and the degree of another—but the new and gigantic fact is there. From then on, the Americans found and are finding themselves confronted with the possibility of direct destruction. Thus the immediate defense, and one can say privileged defense of Europe, and the military participation of the Europeans, which were once basic factors of their strategy, moved by the force of circumstances into second place. We have just witnessed this during the Cuban affair.

The Americans, finding themselves exposed to a direct atomic attack from the Caribbean, acted in such a way as to rid themselves of that menace and, if it had been necessary, to crush it without its having occurred either to them or to anyone else that the game would necessarily be played in Europe and without recourse to the direct assistance of the Europeans. Moreover, the means which they immediately decided to employ in order to counter a direct attack, whether it came from Cuba only or was combined with another originating elsewhere, these means were automatically set aside for something other than the defense of Europe, even if Europe had been attacked in its turn. . . .

Thus principles and realities combine to lead France to equip herself with an atomic force of her own. . . .

Then, in the Bahamas, America and Britain concluded an agreement and we were asked to subscribe to it ourselves. Of course, I am only speaking of this proposal and agreement because they have been published and because their content is known. It is a question of constituting a so-called multilateral atomic force, in which Britain would turn over the weapons it has and will have and in which the Americans would place a few of their own. This multilateral force is assigned to the defense of Europe and is under the American NATO command. It is nevertheless understood that the British retain the possibility of withdrawing their atomic weapons for their own use should supreme national interest seem to them to demand it.

As for the bulk of American nuclear weapons, it remains outside the multilateral force and under the direct orders of the President of the United States. Furthermore and in a way by compensation, Britain may purchase from America, if it so desires, Polaris missiles which are, as you know, launched from submarines specially built for that purpose and which carry the thermonuclear warheads adapted to them for a distance of 1,100–2,000 miles. To build these submarines and warheads, the British receive privileged assistance from the Americans. You know—I say this in passing—that this assistance was never offered to us and you should know, despite what some report, that we have never asked for it.

France has taken note of the Anglo-American Nassau agreement. As it was conceived, undoubtedly no one will be surprised that we cannot subscribe to it. It truly would not be useful for us to buy Polaris missiles when we have neither the submarines to launch them nor the thermonuclear warheads to arm them. Doubtless the day will come when we will have these submarines and these warheads. But that day will be long in coming. . . .

But also, it does not meet with the principle about which I just spoke and which consists of disposing in our own right of our deterrent force. To turn over our weapons to a multilateral force, under a foreign command, would be to act contrary to that principle of our defense and our policy. . . .

In sum, we will adhere to the decision we have made: to construct and, if necessary, to employ our atomic force ourselves. And that without refusing, of course, cooperation, be it technological or strategic, if this cooperation is, on the other hand, desired by our allies.[18]

18*Major Addresses, Statements and Press Conferences of General de Gaulle*, pp. 216–19.

Several new lines of policy developed in 1963. Under the guidance of Adenauer and de Gaulle, West Germany and France drew closer together. Washington reacted by pressing for the Nassau strategy of a multilateral force (MLF) which would provide NATO members with nuclear warheads. Later in the spring, Khrushchev broke the stalemate in atomic test-ban negotiations and in July, they were resumed in Moscow.

Dirk Stikker, whose comments follow, was a former foreign minister of the Netherlands, later Ambassador to NATO, and finally Secretary General of NATO.

FOR CONSIDERATION   If Germany obtained nuclear warheads under the MLF policy, would de Gaulle's *Force de Frappe* be outclassed? Would a *détente* between Washington and Moscow, from de Gaulle's point of view, be useful to France? Kennedy suggested to de Gaulle that the United States would assist France's atomic program if France would concur in the test-ban treaty.

Comments of NATO Secretary-General Dirk Stikker

In the course of our March, 1963, discussions the President [Kennedy], reviewing recent events and the situation confronting the Alliance, commented that after years of difficulties France was finally back again in a position of power and prosperity, but that, even so, de Gaulle's focus was entirely on France and not on Europe. De Gaulle, the President remarked, talked only about a French, not a European nuclear force, and the logical end of de Gaulle's reasoning was a situation where each country would want its own national deterrent, with all the dangers this would entail for Europe as a whole.

I then recounted to the President a significant passage from my conversation with de Gaulle. The French President had asked me, "Do you really believe the United States would ever use the bomb purely for the defense of Europe?" I had answered, "Yes, and not only because they have repeatedly said so since the creation of NATO, but also because it is in the direct interest of the United States that Europe remain free." De Gaulle did not agree. "They will use the bomb purely for their own interests," he said. "That is the reason why France must have a bomb of its own." To this I responded with a question of my own. "When you have the bomb," I asked de Gaulle, "will you use it for Europe?" The answer was unequivocal. "Just as the United States," said de Gaulle, "we will use the bomb for our own interests."

President Kennedy's reaction to this was the observation that there was a widespread myth in America that there was a single entity called Europe and that de Gaulle spoke for it. I told him that this was, of course, totally wrong. Europe would not accept such a situation. . . .

President Kennedy noted specifically the low level of France's military contribution to the Alliance. Here my own views were mixed. On the one hand, I was disturbed, as I told the President, by de Gaulle's comments to me about military integration. De Gaulle had asked me whether I believed in integration, and I had replied, "Undoubtedly modern war or defense is no longer possible without integration." De Gaulle disagreed. "Since the insurrection in Algiers," he explained to me, "I cannot rely on my generals and

officers. That has to be changed, but loyalty can only be restored if the Army and the officers know what they are fighting for, that is, for France. They cannot fight for, or be loyal to, some philosophical concept like NATO, and they cannot be loyal to some unknown American general or admiral."[19]

Comments of President de Gaulle at His Press Conference, July 29, 1963

As for a draft nonaggression pact—which, we are told, was discussed in Moscow—between the States belonging to NATO and the leaders of the countries subjected to the Kremlin's yoke, I must say right away that France does not appreciate this assimilation between the Atlantic Alliance and Communist servitude. And then, moreover, there is no need for a pact in order for France to declare that she will never be the first to attack, it being understood that she will defend herself with whatever means she may have against whomsoever would attack either her or her allies. But today France solemnly declares through the voice of the President of the Republic that there will never be any French aggression. And consequently our eventual participation in a nonaggression pact no longer has any kind of purpose.

But it remains that what happened in Moscow shows that the course followed by the policy of the United States is not identical with ours. With regard to defense, until recently the Americans, thanks to their nuclear weapons, were in a position to assure the free world almost complete protection, but they have lost this monopoly, while continuing at great expense to strengthen their power. Owing to the fact that the Russians also now have

---

[19]Dirk U. Stikker, *Men of Responsibility* (New York: Harper & Row, Publishers, 1966), pp. 375–76. Reprinted by permission of Harper & Row, Publishers.

the wherewithal to destroy the world and particularly the new continent, it is quite natural that America is seeing its own survival as the principal objective in a possible conflict and is not considering the time, degree, terms and conditions of its nuclear intervention for the defense of other regions, particularly Europe, except in relation to this natural and primary necessity. This, moreover, is one of the reasons that France is equipping herself with her own atomic weapons. The result of this is that, as far as the French Government is concerned, important modifications are necessary with regard to the terms and conditions of our participation in the Alliance, since this organization has been built on the basis of integration, which today is no longer valid for us.[20]

[20]*Major Addresses, Statements and Press Conferences of General Charles de Gaulle*, pp. 235–36.

The Test-Ban Treaty was signed on August 5, 1963, but France, determined to go her own way, did not become a signatory. The United States, in November, 1964, tried to reduce France's nuclear capacity by terminating the uranium deliveries that had been agreed on in 1959. But in spite of continuing protests by some Frenchmen who opposed de Gaulle, prosperity in France permitted a step-up in the nuclear and military programs.

Paul Reynaud had been Prime Minister of France in 1940, when the country was overrun by Germany.

Comments of Former Prime Minister, Paul Reynaud

The nuclear race between the two great powers is a hellish one. Tomorrow they will be able to stop the enemy's rockets, and the day after tomorrow they will send satellites into space capable of carrying nuclear warheads which can be exploded at any given point on the earth.

Does de Gaulle really believe that, in the throes of this race, Khruschev is going to sit down at the roadside and wait for us? We shall always lag behind. Admittedly, the modern weapon is the nuclear weapon, but it can only be employed by those powers which have sufficient waste spaces in which to perfect their weapons and all the resources of a great continent. To give an example: our air alert system is directly dependent on NATO, so not even on this crucial point can we pretend to be independent.

Certain people are surprised that today, having always wanted France to assume leadership, I reject the nuclear weapon for the French Army. Isn't an army without nuclear weapons hopelessly old-fashioned? The situation could be contrasted, so the argument might run, with 1940, when the army was accused of being deficient—both in armoured divisions and in assault aircraft.

I want to explain myself clearly. France must have chairs of science and she must have laboratories. She must produce nuclear energy for her industries. Her scientists must continue research in the nuclear field.

. . . Europe lives today under the terrible threat (even if improbable) of total destruction. So a bucket brigade must be formed, as at a fire. The United States now has a nuclear force superior in certain respects to that of the Soviet Union. She has more than 2000 nuclear stockpiles, according to the statement made by Mr McNamara on December 17th, 1963, to the Council of NATO ministers. Our own contribution to the Atlantic community in this field would be insignificant compared with American nuclear power, nor could we make it for some years to come. These are the facts.

Now what would a striking force cost us? The third Pierrelatte factory, which is exclusively engaged at present in manufacturing the hydrogen bomb, will cost us more than 500,000 million old francs, and 50,000 million annually in running costs.

But I must stress again that it is not enough to make the bomb. We have to be able to deliver it on target. Hence the offer of the American Polaris, accepted in principle by Germany and Britain but refused by us. We should fight, therefore, with bomb-carrying aircraft against rockets!

Will the effort be worth-while? No! For compared with the stockpiles accumulated by the United States, our contribution to the Community will be practically nil, as we have seen.

De Gaulle boasted in one of his press conferences that France could despatch them to any part of the globe.

This ability is of dubious practical value.

. . . . .

WHY HAVE THERE BEEN SO MANY MISTAKES?

Why impede the progress towards the United Europe which Robert Schuman and then the Treaty of Rome got under way?

Why this refusal to participate loyally in the defence of Europe, within the framework of NATO?

Why scoff at the United Nations?

Why this obstinate refusal to speak to Mr Khruschev, talking all the while about "Europe from the Atlantic to the Urals"?

Why this affront to Great Britain, whose courage in the war saved us, after we had signed an armistice which lost our entire fleet to the allied cause?

Why this mistrust, this hostility, this malice towards the United States to whom we owe our very freedom?

What is the meaning of a solemn treaty with Germany, if our policy is directly opposed to hers on all major issues?

Why was the Constitution first twisted and later violated, the Council of State threatened and a tribunal dissolved because the judges proved intractable?

De Gaulle constantly repeats that France needs continuity. Alas, France has continuity today but of what a kind!

There are reasons for so many grave mistakes.

The first and deepest, of course, is General de Gaulle's brand of patriotism: "France in the front rank"—an illusion which breeds further illusions.

But of course there are other reasons as well. One can be a great man without being a statesman. A real statesman must be familiar with the facts about the world in which he lives. We have seen that de Gaulle is uninformed on many essentials. But is this his fault? He forged a brilliant career for himself in the army. Could he possibly have supplemented it with the training provided by a long parliamentary career? Compare the development of de Gaulle with that of Churchill, who entered the House of Commons at the beginning of the century, who learned about public affairs as President of the Board of Trade, Home Secretary, Chancellor of the Exchequer and First Lord of the Admiralty—to mention only a few of his early government posts. To have taken part for so many years in so many debates, on so many different subjects, to have been subjected to a host of diametrically opposed views both in the House and in the lobbies—is not all this more valuable equipment for a politician than a keen military mind?

This is the reason for de Gaulle's failure

to appreciate the realities of world politics today.

Politics is a difficult art.

But, it might be argued, he could be informed by his colleagues. Very true, but is he prepared to accept their advice? When I think of him I always recall the words of Fenelon concerning Louis XIV: "The gap around the throne terrifies me."

.   .   .   .   .

If de Gaulle continues to make mistakes it is because no one has the power to enlighten him by contradicting him. His greatest enemy is his prestige—abroad as well as in France. . . .

Alas, de Gaulle's personal tragedy is also the tragedy of France. For France is the victim of all these mistakes.[21]

Major Goals of the French "Second Program" Law, December, 1964

The second military program law was passed by Parliament in December 1964. Like its forerunner, it deals exclusively with military studies and equipment of major importance financed under Title V,

---

[21]Reprinted by permission from Paul Reynaud, *The Foreign Policy of Charles de Gaulle* (New York: The Odyssey Press, Inc.; London: Paul Hamlyn, 1964), pp. 56–57, 147–49. © Copyright 1964 by Rene Juilliard. English translation © by Paul Hamlyn Limited.

i.e., the essential part of the investment expenses in the annual military budget.

For strategic weapons systems, the projects covered are the completion of the strategic nuclear air force, whose weapon is the nuclear bomb and whose vehicle is the Mirage IV; the maintenance of the deterrence level with 12 additional Mirage IV's and then with strategic surface-to-surface ballistic missiles with a range of about 2,000 miles; preparations for the delivery at the end of the plan of the first nuclear submarine, armed with strategic sea-to-surface ballistic missiles with thermonuclear warheads, and the beginning of work on two other nuclear submarines; and studies on a more highly developed weapons system in connection with the space program.

For tactical nuclear weapons, the second program law provides for the development and production of smaller bombs for the Mirage III and Etendard IV and continued studies on missiles for aircraft such as the SS-37 and Aramis (with Great Britain), the Pluton weapons system for the Army, the Roland anti-aircraft missile (with Federal Germany) and the Acra antitank missile which should be operational in 1968–69. The three Services will be fully armed with nuclear weapons by 1972–73, regardless of the priority given to any one of these weapons systems.[22]

---

[22]*France and Its Armed Forces,* pp. 53–54.

By the end of 1965 President de Gaulle had decided to make implicit the move which he had prepared since he first came back to power. The following documents refer to France's withdrawal from NATO.

FOR CONSIDERATION   It should not be overlooked that de Gaulle had other means at his disposal to counter British and American policies. The principal devices which he continued to employ were economic: keeping Britain out of the Common Market and insisting on gold payments in international trade.

President de Gaulle's Press Conference, as Described by David Schoenbrun

On September 9, 1965, at exactly 3 P.M., two ushers, formally attired in white tie and tails, stepped through red velvet curtains and held them apart to clear the way to the stage for General de Gaulle, President of the French Republic. Wearing a dark-gray double-breasted suit and suntan makeup on his face—a recent concession both to television and to age—the President blinked briefly in the glare of the lights, acknowledged the presence of one thousand reporters gathered in the ornate Hall of Festivals of the Elysée Palace, waved them to their seats and began his ritual performance with a word of thanks for their attendance at his conference. It was the twelfth "news conference" by General de Gaulle since he took office as president in January 1959. In every respect save one it was identical in spirit and substance to all the others. The one difference made it a special occasion: it was the last news conference of his presidential term, which would end in December.

Reporters had learned that General de Gaulle used his conferences to announce major policy decisions. They were carefully stage-managed to get maximum world attention. History had been made at these press performances: in 1963 General de Gaulle used the conference platform to announce his veto of Britain's entry into the Common Market; in 1964 he further startled and dismayed his allies by announcing his decision to establish diplomatic relations with Communist China; in January 1965, in the opening semi-annual session of the last year of his presidency, General de Gaulle called for a return to the gold-exchange standard for world trade and finance to replace the dollar as the universal currency. Everyone in the Hall of Festivals on September 9, 1965, knew that General de Gaulle would have

something very special to say in the last performance of his term of office.

The audience was not disappointed. General de Gaulle put on one of his best, or worst, performances, depending on the point of view of the observer.[23]

Statement of President de Gaulle at His Press Conference of September 9, 1965

France's capabilities, what she does, what she wants to do, are at this time arousing an attention and a consideration that sharply contrast with the indifference or the commiseration which, in the past, too often surrounded her. In short, we can, and consequently we must, have a policy that is our own.

Which policy? Above all, it is a question of keeping ourselves free of any vassalage. It is true that, in many areas, we have the best reasons for associating with others. But on condition of retaining our self-determination. Thus, so long as the solidarity of the Western peoples appears to us necessary for the eventual defense of Europe, our country will remain the ally of her allies but, upon the expiration of the commitments formerly taken—that is, in 1969 by the latest—the subordination known as "integration" which is provided for by NATO and which hands our fate over to foreign authority shall cease, as far as we are concerned.[24]

Excerpt from President de Gaulle's Handwritten Letter to President Johnson, March 7, 1966

. . . France intends to recover, in her territory, the full exercise of her sovereignty, now impaired by the permanent presence of Allied military elements or by the

---

[23]Schoenbrun, *op. cit.*, pp. 344–45.
[24]*Speeches and Press Conferences*, No. 228 (New York: French Embassy), p. 7.

habitual use being made of its air space, to terminate her participation in the "integrated" commands, and no longer to place forces at the disposal of NATO. It goes without saying that, in order to implement these decisions, she is prepared to make arrangements with the Allied Governments, and in particular with the Government of the United States, regarding the practical measures that concern them. Furthermore, she is prepared to reach agreement with them regarding the military facilities to be accorded on a mutual basis in the event of a conflict in which she would join battle at their side, and regarding the conditions governing the cooperation between her forces and theirs in the event of joint action, especially in Germany.

And so, Mr. President, my Government will get in touch with yours regarding all these points. However, in order to act in the spirit of friendly candor that should inspire the relations between our two countries, and, allow me to add, between you and me, I have sought, first of all, to let you know personally, for what reasons, to what end, and within what limits France believes that she must, for her part, change the form of our alliance without altering its substance.[25]

Excerpt from President Johnson's Reply to President de Gaulle, March 22, 1966

. . . . . .

I am puzzled by your view that the presence of allied military forces on French soil impairs the sovereignty of France. Those forces have been there at French invitation pursuant to a common plan to help insure the security of France and her allies. I have always viewed their presence as a wise and far-seeing exercise of French sovereignty.

For our part, we continue to believe that if the Treaty is to have force and reality, members of the Alliance should prepare the command structure, the strategic and tactical plans, the forces in being, and their designation to NATO in advance of any crisis and for use in time of crisis. NATO arrangements should reflect the technological and strategic imperatives of our age. Readiness to fight instantly under agreed plans and procedures, worked out and practiced in peacetime, adds immeasurably to our common strength. We will continue our past policy of full participation and cooperation in NATO. We believe the member nations, working within the Alliance with one another, should adapt to whatever organizational arrangements the needs of the hour may require.

I do not consider that such participation and cooperation involves any impairment of our own sovereignty—or that of any of our allies. In my judgment it reflects the exercise of sovereignty according to the highest traditions of responsible self-interest. . . .

The other fourteen member nations of NATO do not take the same view of their interests as that taken at this moment by the Government of France. The United States is determined to join with them in preserving the deterrent system of NATO —indeed, in strengthening it in support of the vital common purposes of the West. We do not intend to ignore the experience of the past twenty years.

Indeed, we find it difficult to believe that France, which has made a unique contribution to Western security and development, will long remain withdrawn from the common affairs and responsibilities of the Atlantic. As our old friend and ally her place will await France whenever she decides to resume her leading role.[26]

---

[25]*The Crisis in NATO*, p. 60.

[26]*Ibid.*, p. 61.

A full-fledged member of the atomic club, France transferred its atomic testing from the Sahara to the South Pacific where, on Mururoa Atoll, 745 miles from Tahiti, it constructed a new testing facility. General de Gaulle, completing a world tour, presided at a spectacular nuclear explosion there on October 2, 1966.

Faced with France's unilateral decision, NATO closed down its operations in France by April, 1967.

What had happened? The American House of Representatives Committee on Foreign Affairs asked the same question and made an inquiry. The last document in this series consists of excerpts from the Subcommittee's conclusions.

Excerpts from the Report of the House Committee on the Crisis in NATO, August, 1966

. . . . .

5. *The new climate of prosperity, self-confidence, and ostensible security was conducive to the revival of nationalism in Europe. The countries of that continent began to focus on their traditional sectional, national and European issues and interests.*

In France, General de Gaulle moved to implement his political philosophy which regards the nation-state as the only valid and enduring collective entity in mankind's progress through history. Desirous of assuring France the position of leadership in Europe, he embarked upon an independent course of action on the international scene. He ended the Algerian war, restored political stability to France, revived the flagging economy of his country and, while cooperating to some extent with the Common Market and NATO, refused to join in any actions which could lead to economic, political or military integration and which he felt could impair his independence of action and the sovereignty of France. His withdrawal from NATO's military structure represents a step in the implementation of his political thought. . . .

6. *One other factor warrants mention in this brief summary of developments and attitudes which came to characterize the new Europe: the return of prosperity and self-confidence rekindled the old feeling that Europe is Europe and that its interests do not necessarily coincide with those of the United States. . . .*

7. *Until recently, NATO has remained virtually untouched by the complex and far-reaching developments which have transpired in Europe during the past 20 years. . . .*

8. *In time, NATO's imperviousness to change became an anachronism which began to vex some members of the alliance.*

While the war-deterring value of the Organization continues to command substantial respect, dissatisfaction with the Organization began to focus on three issues: American domination of NATO; apprehension that the continued existence of the Organization as presently constituted may inhibit the solution of Europe's basic political problems; and concern that U.S. policies and actions in other parts of the world may embroil the remaining members of the alliance in conflicts in which they do not wish to become involved.

9. *The United States must shoulder a part of the responsibility for this disaffection with NATO and, ultimately, with our own policies.*

Admittedly, there is no easy way to reconcile the various aspirations and concerns of more than a dozen sovereign nations. It is even more difficult to achieve the subordination of national interests required to produce unity and effective action. Furthermore, the great power which the United States wields in the world arena tends by its very existence to antagonize some people—even those whose freedom and security may depend on the exercise of such power.

With these things said, we nevertheless believe that the record of the U.S. Government's performance with respect to the problems which have come to trouble NATO has been less than inspiring. On various occasions, we have displayed insensitivity to the changes which have taken place on the Continent. Apparently unable to shed habits acquired during the time of the great emergency, we have tended to dictate rather than to lead. Until very recently, our efforts to bring the other members of NATO into a meaningful partnership have been sporadic, inadequate, and marked by inconsistencies. We made unilateral declarations and entered into bilateral agreements instead of trying to arrive at joint decisions on issues which affect the security of the entire North Atlantic community. And we have devoted less than our best effort to the task of promoting the mutual understanding which is vital to the achievement of unity within the North Atlantic community.

.   .   .   .   .

12. *The subcommittee does not have any readymade solution for curing the disarray in the North Atlantic alliance. We believe, however, that the necessary reappraisal must begin with a reference to the basic purpose of NATO.*

We must ask ourselves, "What is the basic purpose of the Organization?" And, "Is this purpose valid in the light of the circumstances which obtain today?" After we answer these questions, we can proceed to examine other issues relevant to the current status and future prospects of the Organization.

13. *The basic purpose of NATO is to provide the 15 members of the alliance with a joint military capability sufficient to deter—or, if necessary, to repel—Communist aggression against the territory of any one, or all, of its members. . . .*

14. *Does a Communist military threat to Western Europe exist today? Has the nature of that threat changed significantly in recent years—perhaps to the point of obviating the need for the complex, time-consuming and expensive defense arrangements embodied in NATO?*

For nearly 3 months, in consultation with private and governmental experts, this subcommittee has sought answers to these questions. And we considered first the evidence regarding the Communist military *capability* in eastern and central Europe.

The subcommittte found that the Warsaw Pact countries continue to maintain nearly 3 million men in arms. There are more than 100 Communist divisions stationed in east and central Europe. This vast concentration of military manpower is augmented by several thousand military aircraft and a substantial array of missiles targeted on Western Europe. . . .

The conclusion is inescapable, therefore, that there exists today in eastern and central Europe a tremendous military force, fully capable of launching and sustaining a large-scale offensive against the Western half of the European continent.

15. *In spite of this fact, some Europeans appear to feel that the nature of the Soviet military threat has changed appreciably in recent times and that the*

danger of Communist aggression has receded.

These assumptions are not supported by the stark reality of the Communist military capability. They are based on wishful thinking and speculation: speculation regarding Soviet intentions and the deterrent effect of the U.S. nuclear capability. We do not believe that such speculation provides a proper foundation for the security of the North Atlantic community. . . .

16. *Two additional considerations argue in favor of Western European military preparedness and the maintenance of unity within the North Atlantic community. The first relates to the issue of Soviet intentions toward Western Europe.*

It is this: If, as some Europeans maintain, their continent is the checkerboard in a power contest between the Soviet Union and the United States, it is also the prize which may decide the ultimate outcome of that contest. Control of the magnificent resources of Europe—some 350 million highly skilled people equipped with an industrial establishment and material resources which rival those of the United States—could help the Soviet Union attain the position of primacy in world affairs. . . .

17. *The second consideration relates to Communist China and the distinct possibility that that country's rise to power may increase the military threat to Western Europe.*

A nation of some 700 million people, led by an aggressive totalitarian regime, and within an arm's reach of possessing nuclear weapons, Communist China promises to exert an unsettling influence on world affairs for some time to come. Today, the Communist regimes of China and of the Soviet Union control the destiny of nearly one-third of the human race. Further, in spite of their ideological and tactical differences, the two regimes are united in their determination to bring to an end the age of capitalism. Common-

sense suggests, therefore, that we should not let our guard down—and that we give added thought to the prospect that, in the long run, disunity may increase the risks which confront us today.

18. *We must now turn to the central issue of this report: If the realities of our age and our self-interest argue for the retention of NATO, how can that organization be transformed to become a force for the unity—as well as the security—of the North Atlantic community? . . .*

19. *In the first instance, it seems to us that NATO needs a much broader charter than its present constitution.*

As matters stand today, the security of Europe depends not only on what the Soviet Union may do in Europe, but also on what Communist China and the Soviet Union may do on other continents. It would appear logical, therefore, that the alliance concern itself with the security requirements of other areas. . . .

20. *Second, the remodeled Organization should become the forum for the discussion, initiation, and coordination of actions designed to enlarge the areas of peaceful cooperation between the East and the West. . . .*

21. *Third, in any discussion dealing with the reorganization of NATO, the issue of nuclear sharing should receive the most thorough attention. . . .*

22. *Fourth, it seems to us that France's withdrawal from the military structure of NATO makes necessary a reappraisal of the conventional military capability of the Organization and of the policies which have governed NATO's operations for a considerable period of time. . . .*

23. *Finally, we again wish to underline our conviction that the tasks of collective security are no longer sufficient to keep the alliance together and that we must seek closer cooperation with Europe in other areas in order to maintain unity. . . .*[27]

---

[27]*Ibid.*, pp. 2–9.

BIBLIOGRAPHY

Sources Used in This Problem

1. *Collections and Official Documents*

The Atlantic Alliance. Hearings before the U.S. Senate Subcommittee on National Security, Part 7, Supplement, August 15, 1966. Washington, D.C.: U.S. Government Printing Office, 1966.

Atlas (periodical).

The Crisis in NATO. Report of the Subcommittee on Europe of the House Committee on Foreign Affairs, August, 1966. Washington, D.C.: U.S. Government Printing Office, 1966.

Foreign Affairs (periodical).

France and Its Armed Forces. New York: French Embassy, 1964.

Major Addresses, Statements, and Press Conferences of General Charles De Gaulle, May 19, 1958–January 31, 1964. New York: French Embassy, 1964.

Speeches and Press Conferences. New York: French Embassy.

2. *Others*

ARON, RAYMOND. *The Great Debate: Theories of Nuclear Strategy.* Trans. by ERNST PAWEL. Garden City, N.Y.: Doubleday, 1965.

DE GAULLE, CHARLES. *The Edge of the Sword (Le fil de l'Epée).* Trans. by GERARD HOPKINS. London: Faber & Faber, 1960.

REYNAUD, PAUL. *The Foreign Policy of Charles de Gaulle.* New York: Odyssey Press; London: Paul Hamlyn, 1964.

SCHOENBRUN, DAVID. *The Three Lives of Charles de Gaulle.* New York: Atheneum, 1966.

STIKKER, DIRK V. *Men of Responsibility.* New York: Harper & Row, 1966.

TOURNOUX, J. R. *Secrets d'État.* Paris: Librairie Plon, 1960.

Select List of Books Recommended for Further Reading

AMBLER, J. S. *The French Army in Politics.* Columbus, Ohio: Ohio State University Press, 1966.

BARNET, RICHARD J. and RASKIN, MARCUS G. *After Twenty Years: Alternatives to the Cold War in Europe.* New York: Random House, 1965.

BEATON, L. and MADDOX, J. *The Spread of Nuclear Weapons.* London: Chatto and Windus for the Institute for Strategic Studies, 1962.

BEAUFRE, ANDRÉ. *NATO and Europe.* New York: Knopf, 1966.

BUCHAN, ALASTAIR. *NATO in the 1960's: The Implications of Interdependence.* New York: Praeger, 1963.

CALLEO, DAVID P. *Europe's Future: the Grand Alternatives.* New York: Horizon, 1965.

CALVOCORESSI, PETER. *International Politics since 1945.* New York: Praeger, 1967.

COTTRELL, A. J. and DOUGHERTY, J. F. *The Politics of the Atlantic Alliance.* New York: Praeger, 1964.

DELMAS, CLAUDE, CARPENTIER, GENERAL, GALLOIS, GENERAL and FAURE, MAURICE. *L'avenir de l'alliance atlantique.* Paris: Editions Berger-Levrault, 1961.

FREYMOND, JACQUES. *Western Europe since the War.* New York: Praeger, 1963.

FURNISS, EDGAR S. *France, Troubled Ally: De Gaulle's Heritage and Prospects.* New York: Praeger, 1960.

FURNISS, EDGAR S. *The Western Alliance: Its Status and Prospects.* Columbus, Ohio: Ohio State University Press, 1965.

GROSSER, ALFRED. *Foreign Policy under De Gaulle.* Boston: Little, Brown, 1966.

HOFFMAN, STANLEY. *The State of War: Essays in the Theory and Practice.* New York: Praeger, 1965.

KISSINGER, HENRY A. *The Necessity for Choice.* New York: Harper & Row, 1961.

KISSINGER, HENRY A. *The Troubled Partnership: A Re-Appraisal of the Atlantic Alliance.* New York: McGraw-Hill, 1965.

KLEIMAN, ROBERT. *Atlantic Crisis.* New York: W. W. Norton, 1964.

KULSKI, W. W. *De Gaulle and the World.* Syracuse, N.Y.: Syracuse University Press, 1966.

LACOUTURE, JEAN. *De Gaulle.* Trans. by FRANCIS K. PRICE. New York: New American Library, 1966.

MARSHALL, CHARLES BURTON. *The Exercise of Sovereignty.* Baltimore: Johns Hopkins Press, 1965.

MIDDLETON, DREW. *The Atlantic Community: a Study in Unity and Disunity.* New York: McKay, 1965.

OSGOOD, ROBERT E. *NATO: The Entangling Alliance.* Chicago: University of Chicago Press, 1962.

PICKLES, DOROTHY. *The Fifth French Republic.* 3rd ed. New York: Praeger, 1966.

PICKLES, DOROTHY. *The Uneasy Entente.* London: Oxford University Press, 1966.

SPANIER, JOHN W. *World Politics in an Age of Revolution.* New York: Praeger, 1967.

STANLEY, TIMOTHY. *NATO in Transition: the Future of the Atlantic Alliance.* New York: Praeger, 1965.

STEEL, RONALD. *The End of Alliance: America and the Future of Europe.* New York: Viking, 1964.

STOESINGER, J. G. and WESTIN, A. F. (eds.). *Power and Order.* New York: Harcourt, Brace, 1964.

TAYLOR, MAXWELL D. *The Uncertain Trumpet.* New York: Harper, 1960.

WERTH, ALEXANDER. *De Gaulle: A Political Biography.* New York: Simon and Schuster, 1965.

WILCOX, F. O. and HAVILAND, H. F. (eds.). *The Atlantic Community: Progress and Prospects.* New York: Praeger, 1963.

WILLIS, F. ROY. *France, Germany and the New Europe, 1945–63.* Stanford, Calif.: Stanford University Press, 1965.

WOLFERS, ARNOLD (ed.). *Changing East-West Relations and the Unity of the West.* Baltimore: Johns Hopkins Press, 1964.

PROBLEM 14

THE SOVIET UNION AND
COMMUNIST CHINA

Friction in the Communist world, from the rise of Mao to the fall of Khrushchev, 1950-64

Although relations between Russia and China have a history extending back to the middle ages, they entered a new phase after 1949 when Mao Tse-tung consolidated Communist control of the mainland. Stalin had been allied, during World War II, with Chiang Kai-shek, and after Japan's defeat the Soviet Union had obtained advantageous positions in Manchuria, where control of Port Arthur had long been a Russian aim. Moscow hailed the great Communist victory in China. But potentialities for disagreement and conflict were present: a 2,000-mile frontier with large areas in dispute; a Chinese population double that of Russia; and a leader, in the person of Mao, who did not consider himself, by any means, a subservient puppet waiting for someone in Moscow to give him orders.

The first relations between the giant Communist states were outwardly warm and friendly. In the interest of developing comradely ties, Moscow relinquished its special positions in Manchuria, and signed a mutual aid agreement early in 1950.

Excerpts from the Treaty between the U.S.S.R. and China, February 14, 1950

(A) THE TREATY

Article I

Both High Contracting Parties under-take jointly to take all the necessary measures at their disposal for the purpose of preventing a repetition of aggression and violation of peace on the part of Japan or any other State which should unite with Japan, directly or indirectly, in acts of aggression. . . .

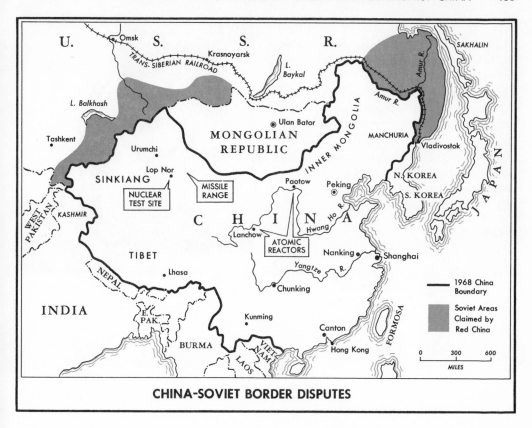

CHINA-SOVIET BORDER DISPUTES

Article II

Both the High Contracting Parties undertake by means of mutual agreement to strive for the earliest conclusion of a peace treaty with Japan, jointly with the other Powers which were allies during the Second World War.

Article III

Both High Contracting Parties undertake not to conclude any alliance directed against the other High Contracting Party, and not to take part in any coalition or in actions or measures directed against the other High Contracting Party.

Article IV

Both High Contracting Parties will consult each other in regard to all important international problems affecting the common interests of the Soviet Union and China, being guided by the interests of the consolidation of peace and universal security. . . .

(B) AN AGREEMENT ON THE CHINESE CHANGCHUN RAILWAY, PORT ARTHUR, AND DALNY

. . . . .

Article I

Both High Contracting Parties have agreed that the Soviet Government transfers gratis to the Government of the People's Republic of China all its rights in the joint administration of the Chinese Changchun Railway, with all the property belonging to the Railway. The transfer will be effected immediately upon the conclusion of a peace treaty with Japan, but not later than the end of 1952. . . .

Article II

Both High Contracting Parties have agreed that Soviet troops will be withdrawn from the jointly utilized naval base of Port Arthur and that the installations in this area will be handed over to the Government of the People's Republic of China immediately upon the conclusion of a peace treaty with Japan, but not later than the end of 1952, with the Government of the People's Republic of China compensating the Soviet Union for expenses incurred in the restoration and construction of installations affected by the Soviet Union since 1945. . . .

Article III

Both High Contracting Parties have agreed that the question of Port Dalny must be further considered upon the conclusion of a peace treaty with Japan.

As regards the administration in Dalny, it fully belongs to the Government of the People's Republic of China. . . .

(c) An Agreement on the Granting of Credits by the U.S.S.R. to China

. . . . .

Article I

The Government of the Union of Soviet Socialist Republics grants the Central People's Government of the People's Republic of China credits, calculated in dollars, amounting to 300 million American dollars, taking 35 American dollars to one ounce of fine gold.

In view of the extreme devastation of China as a result of prolonged hostilities on its territory, the Soviet Government has agreed to grant credits on favorable terms of 1 per cent annual interest.

Article II

The credits mentioned in Article I will be granted in the course of five years, as from January 1, 1950. . . .

Article III

The Central People's Government of the People's Republic of China repays the

Costello in The Bristol Virginia-Tennessean

"Rogue's New Robe."

credits mentioned in Article I, as well as interest on them, with deliveries of raw materials, tea, gold, American dollars.[1]

Excerpt from a Soviet-Chinese Communiqué

In 1950 and in 1951, according to an agreement between the Soviet and Chinese Governments, four mixed Soviet-Chinese companies were set up on a basis of parity; a company for the mining of nonferrous and rare metals in Sinkiang Province of the Chinese People's Republic; a company for the extraction and refining of oil in this province; a company for the building and repair of ships in the town of Dairen, and a company for the organization and exploitation of civil airlines. . . .[2]

----

[1]*Tass,* February 14, 1950. Complete text may be found in Max Beloff, *Soviet Policy in the Far East* (London: Oxford University Press, 1953), pp. 260–64.

[2]*New York Times,* October 12, 1954. © 1954 by the New York Times Company. Reprinted by permission.

No serious differences developed during the first few years of the alliance. The Chinese Communists were much involved in consolidating their revolution, and were embroiled in the Korean conflict. Stalin's death in March, 1953, brought no change in policy, and the new leaders (Khrushchev, Mikoyan, and Bulganin) made a state visit to Peking in October, 1954. At this time the Soviet government appeared to be willing to extend aid in all areas, especially economic and scientific, and to reduce its military forces in vital areas.

As a result of the various pacts, thousands of Russian teachers and technicians descended on China. The Soviet Union made plans and specifications for factories and machinery available, and generous credits helped to restore and improve Chinese industry.

Excerpts from Communiqués Released October 11, 1954, Relating to Soviet-Chinese Agreements

COMMUNIQUÉ ON THE EVACUATION OF SOVIET MILITARY UNITS

. . . The Governments of the Soviet Union and the Chinese People's Republic . . . have agreed that Soviet military units are to be evacuated from the jointly used naval base of Port Arthur and the installations in that area are to be transferred without compensation to the Government of the Chinese People's Republic. . . .

The evacuation of the Soviet troops and the transfer of the installations to the Government of the Chinese People's Republic in the Port Arthur Naval Base Area will be completed by May 31, 1955. . . .

COMMUNIQUÉ ON THE TRANSFER OF MIXED COMPANIES

. . . The Governments of the U.S.S.R. and of the Chinese People's Republic have reached agreement that the Soviet share of participation in the mixed Soviet-Chinese companies will be transferred entirely to the Chinese People's Republic on Jan. 1, 1955. The value of this share will be compensated over a number of years by supplying to the Soviet Union goods

which are items of usual export from the Chinese People's Republic. . . .

COMMUNIQUÉ ON SCIENTIFIC-TECHNICAL COOPERATION

Talks on Soviet-Chinese scientific-technical cooperation have been held in Moscow and Peiping between the Governments of the U.S.S.R. and the Chinese People's Republic. The talks, which were conducted in a sincere and friendly atmosphere, ended in the signing on October 11 in Peiping of an agreement on scientific-technical cooperation between the U.S.S.R. and the Chinese People's Republic. . . . In accordance with the agreement, the two Governments agree on the implementation of scientific-technical cooperation. . . . Both sides will hand over to each other technical documents, will exchange appropriate information, and will also commission specialists to give technical assistance and to acquaint themselves with the achievements of both countries in scientific-technical fields. . . .

COMMUNIQUÉ ON THE BUILDING OF A RAILWAY

With the purpose of strengthening mutual economic and cultural relations, the Governments of the U.S.S.R. and of the

Chinese People's Republic have agreed that both sides, in the nearest future, should begin the building of a railway line from Lanchow through Urumchi, on Chinese territory, to Alma Ata on Soviet territory. . . .[3]

----
[3]*Ibid.*

If there was cooperation regarding Soviet aid in China, other problems were developing in terms of world leadership. By 1956, the Kremlin had concluded that a head-on clash with the West should be avoided. From these considerations developed the policy of De-Stalinization (see Khrushchev speech in Problem 7), and of Peaceful Co-existence. Excerpts from some of the basic documents are given here, together with Chinese reactions.

FOR CONSIDERATION   Notice that some Chinese attacks came several years after the Russian pronouncement. If differences were developing under the surface, so far as the general public knew, friendship and unity was still, in 1956, the party line.

In Communist documents, Communist Party of the Soviet Union is abbreviated CPSU; Communist Party of China, CPC; Central Committee, CC. Communist jargon is a study in itself, and the following excerpt from Brzezinski and Dallin's brilliant exposition of "Issues and Methods" should help the neophyte in his review of Communist polemics. A serious student should read the entire essay. It should be borne in mind that many Communist speeches and "open letters" run to 50 pages or more; therefore the excerpts in this collection serve to provide only the flavor of the complete document.

Excerpts from Zbigniew Brzezinski and Alexander Dallin's "Introduction: Issues and Methods," in *Diversity in International Communism*

Communist leaders themselves acknowledge that they read documents with an eye to such tell-tale indicators of loyalty, nonconformity, unity, and disagreement. Especially in the post-Stalin era, differences in the public utterances of Communist leaders and organs cannot be taken to be the result of diabolically clever stage management and central manipulation. Hence it may be useful to point out some examples of the use of symbols and phrases that an analyst of Communist documents may wish to watch out for.

When Khrushchev, at a CPSU congress, attacks the Albanian leadership, the "antiparty group" (a characteristic label for what should be called the "anti-Khrushchev group"), and the "personality cult" (a circumlocution for Stalinism), all delegations of foreign Communist parties are expected to express their solidarity with the Soviet position by making similarly unambiguous statements about the objects of the Soviet attack. Any omission is suspicious; silence regarding the Albanian crisis—the issue with most obvious international overtones, greatest drama, and most overt aspects of a "loyalty test" for other Communist parties—may be taken to indicate divergence from the Moscow line.

. . . . .

Indirection, the essence of the esoteric argument, is often used to avoid identifying precisely the target of a given comment. In many cases the pattern of circumlocution is quite distinct and easily pierced. "Some comrades" may be translated as "the Soviet leadership" when the Chinese or Albanian Communists use the term, or as "the Chinese Communist leadership" when Moscow uses the term. "Sectarian," "dogmatist," and "adventurist" are used to identify the more radical and militant wing of the movement; "revisionist" or "opportunist" for their opponents. Gradations of disapproval may extend through such terms as "reformism" and "petty bourgeois" to charges of "objectively" aiding the imperialist camp.

A related technique has been the use of "proxies." While various parties have criticized both the Soviet and the Chinese leaders or policies, Moscow and Peking did not *publicly* trade charges and accusations identifying the other side. Instead, the Soviet press, until December, 1962, extensively republished Italian, Bulgarian, Iraqi, Polish, and other Communist press attacks which directly identified the Chinese.

. . . . .

The particular code used often corresponds to the level of the debate. Thus the surprisingly numerous gradations of conflict may be exemplified by the following stages: (1) two or more organs separately promoting divergent lines; without taking explicit cognizance of the differences; (2) the use of references to "classics" of Marxism-Leninism and other noncontemporary proxies, such as discussions of Lenin's *Left-Wing Communism*, to Kautsky, Bernstein, and the Second International; (3) indirect allusions which indicate dissent but camouflage the target, down to the references to "some comrades" and to "modern revisionists"; (4) references to individual proxies, such as the use of Tito and Hoxha by Peking and

Moscow in referring to each other; (5) explicit disagreement attributed to others, such as *Pravda's* publication of quotations from Togliatti, Thorez, and Novotny about the Chinese Communists in December, 1962; (6) full identification of target and issues, such as Hoxha's speech of November, 1961, and the exchange of letters between the Soviet and Chinese parties' Central Committees in February, 1963.

Adherence to certain variants in terminology often indicates substantive differences as well. Thus, reference to the XX CPSU Congress has become a "shorthand" way of suggesting the essence of the Khrushchev policy and the binding nature of Soviet decisions for other parties. Gomulka's statements are scrutinized to see whether he refers to the Soviet Union and the CPSU as "first" in seniority (and in power) or as the "vanguard" of, but not as "guiding" or "leading," the Communist world. "National roads to communism" are permissible but "national communism" is not: the former implies diversity in unity, the latter disunity.

Other such variations in the apparent minutiae of phrase or stereotype can be revealing. It is significant whether "peaceful coexistence" or "struggle against imperialism" comes first in a listing of Communist objectives. Whether the Albanian leaders are still called "comrades" or not (and reciprocate in kind) is a clue to a given individual's or party's position in the dispute. While Moscow may equivocate as to whether Albania or Yugoslavia is a *bona fide* "socialist" state, the Indonesian Communists find Albania to be socialist by definition (or by objective criteria) and draw inferences critical of the Moscow line. The Dutch Communist leader is even more roundabout: by labeling Cuba the "thirteenth" socialist state he implies that in his view Albania is still one of the other twelve.

On the other hand, similar terminology does not always indicate identical views. There are taboos and ritual phrases which no Communist party is likely to tamper with. All parties will ordinarily support "unity," endorse "Leninist principles," condemn "fractionalism," and depict themselves as stalwart champions of "class struggle" and "revolution," advocates of "peace" and "progress," and foes of "imperialism."[4]

Excerpts from Report of Khrushchev to the Twentieth Congress of the Communist Party of the Soviet Union, February, 1956

THE PEACEFUL COEXISTENCE OF THE TWO SYSTEMS

The Leninist principle of peaceful coexistence of states with different social systems has always been and remains the general line of our country's foreign policy.

It has been alleged that the Soviet Union puts forward the principle of peaceful coexistence merely out of tactical considerations, considerations of expediency. Yet it is common knowledge that we have always, from the very first years of Soviet power, stood with equal firmness for peaceful coexistence. Hence, it is not a tactical move, but a fundamental principle of Soviet foreign policy.

. . . . .

THE POSSIBILITY OF PREVENTING WAR IN THE PRESENT ERA

Millions of people all over the world are asking whether another war is really inevitable, whether mankind, which has already experienced two devastating world wars, must still go through a third one? Marxists must answer this question, taking into consideration the epoch-making changes of the last decades.

There is, of course, a Marxist-Leninist proposition that wars are inevitable as

long as imperialism exists. This proposition was evolved at a time when (i) imperialism was an all-embracing world system, and (ii) the social and political forces which did not want war were weak, poorly organised, and hence unable to compel the imperialists to renounce war.

People usually take only one aspect of the question and examine only the economic basis of wars under imperialism. This is not enough. War is not only an economic phenomenon. Whether there is to be a war or not depends in large measure on the correlation of class, political forces, the degree of organisation and the awareness and determination of the people. . . .

In that period this precept was absolutely correct. At the present time, however, the situation has changed radically. Now there is a world camp of socialism, which has become a mighty force. In this camp the peace forces find not only the moral, but also the material means to prevent aggression. Moreover, there is a large group of other countries with a population running into many hundreds of millions which are actively working to avert war. The labour movement in the capitalist countries has today become a tremendous force. The movement of peace supporters has sprung up and developed into a powerful factor. . . .

As long as capitalism survives in the world, the reactionary forces representing the interests of the capitalist monopolies will continue their drive towards military gambles and aggression, and may try to unleash war. *But war is not fatalistically inevitable.*

. . . . .

FORMS OF TRANSITION TO SOCIALISM IN DIFFERENT COUNTRIES

In connexion with the radical changes in the world arena new prospects are also opening up as regards the transition of countries and nations to socialism.

Alongside the Soviet form of recon-

---

[4]Alexander Dallin *et al.* (eds.), *Diversity in International Communism* (New York: Columbia University Press, 1963), pp. xxxviii–xliii.

structing society on socialist lines, we now have the form of people's democracy.

In Poland, Bulgaria, Czechoslovakia, Albania and the other European people's democracies, this form sprang up and is being utilised in conformity with the concrete historical, social and economic conditions and peculiarities of each of these countries. It has been thoroughly tried and tested in the course of ten years and has fully proved its worth.

Much that is unique in socialist construction is being contributed by the People's Republic of China, whose economy prior to the victory of the revolution was exceedingly backward, semi-feudal and semi-colonial in character. Having taken over the decisive commanding positions, the people's democratic state is using them in the social revolution to implement a policy of peaceful reorganisation of private industry and trade and their gradual transformation into a component of socialist economy.

The leadership of the great cause of socialist reconstruction by the Communist Party of China and the Communist and Workers' parties of the other people's democracies, exercised in keeping with the peculiarities and specific features of each country, is creative Marxism in action.

In the Federal People's Republic of Yugoslavia, where state power belongs to the working people, and society is founded on public ownership of the means of production, specific concrete forms of economic management and organisation of the state apparatus are arising in the process of socialist construction.

It is probable that more forms of transition to socialism will appear. Moreover, the implementation of these forms need not be associated with civil war under all circumstances. . . . The forms of social revolution vary. It is not true that we regard violence and civil war as the only way to remake society. . . .

Whatever the form of transition to socialism, the decisive and indispensable factor is the political leadership of the working class headed by its vanguard. Without this there can be no transition to socialism.[5]

Chinese Reaction to the Attack on Stalin, Expressed in "The Origin and Development of the Differences between the Leadership of the CPSU and Ourselves," by the Editorial Departments of the *Jen-min Jih-pao* and the *Red Flag*, September 6, 1963

The truth is that the whole series of differences of principle in the international communist movement began more than seven years ago.

To be specific, it began with the 20th Congress of the CPSU in 1956.

The 20th Congress of the CPSU was the first step along the road of revisionism taken by the leadership of the CPSU. From the 20th Congress to the present, the revisionist line of the leadership of the CPSU has gone through the process of emergence, formation, growth and systematisation. And by a gradual process, too, people have come to understand more and more deeply the revisionist line of the CPSU leadership.

From the very outset we held that a number of views advanced at the 20th Congress concerning the contemporary international struggle and the international Communist movement were wrong, were violations of Marxism-Leninism. In particular, the complete negation of Stalin on the pretext of "combating the personality cult" and the thesis of peaceful transition to Socialism by "the parliamentary road" are gross errors of principle.

---

[5]*Soviet News Booklet No. 4* (London: Soviet Embassy), quoted in David Floyd, *Mao against Khrushchev: A Short History of the Sino-Soviet Conflict* (New York: Frederick A. Praeger, Inc., 1963), pp. 228–30.

The criticism of Stalin at the 20th Congress of the CPSU was wrong both in principle and in method. . . .

In completely negating Stalin at the 20th Congress of the CPSU, Khrushchov in effect negated the dictatorship of the proletariat and the fundamental theories of Marxism-Leninism which Stalin defended and developed. It was at that congress that Khrushchov, in his summary report, began the repudiation of Marxism-Leninism on a number of questions of principle.

In his report to the 20th Congress, under the pretext that "radical changes" had taken place in the world situation, Khrushchov put forward the thesis of "peaceful transition." He said that the road of the October Revolution was "the only correct road in those historical conditions," but that as the situation had changed, it had become possible to effect the transition from capitalism to Socialism "through the parliamentary road." In essence, this erroneous thesis is a clear revision of the Marxist-Leninist teachings on the state and revolution and a clear denial of the universal significance of the road of the October Revolution.

In his report, under the same pretext that "radical changes" had taken place in the world situation, Khrushchov also questioned the continued validity of Lenin's teachings on imperialism and on war and peace, and in fact tampered with Lenin's teachings.

Khrushchov pictured the U.S. Government and its head as people resisting the forces of war, and not as representatives of the imperialist forces of war. He said, ". . . the advocates of settling outstanding issues by means of war still hold strong positions there (in the United States), and . . . they continue to exert big pressure on the President and the Administration." He went on to say that the imperialists were beginning to admit that the positions-of-strength policy had failed and that "symptoms of a certain sobering up are appearing" among them. It was as much as saying that it was possible for the U.S. Government and its head not to represent the interests of U.S. monopoly capital and for them to abandon their policies of war and aggression and that they had become forces defending peace.[6]

------

[6]*New China News Agency*, Peking, September 6, 1963, as quoted in American Consulate General, Hong Kong, *Current Background*, No. 714 (September 12, 1963), pp. 3-5.

During 1957, outward appearances indicated that no important differences had developed between Peking and Moscow. Chou En-lai had visited Moscow early in the year, to be followed by Mao in November. In that month representatives of the 12 leading Communist Parties subscribed to a position that China seemed to accept. At that time Mao publicly stated: "The socialist camp must have a leader, and this leader is the Soviet Union."

Points of the Moscow Declaration, which became a basic paper in Sino-Soviet relations, are given here.

The Moscow Declaration of November, 1957

1. The main content of our epoch is the transition from capitalism to socialism which was begun by the great October socialist revolution in Russia. . . .

The world socialist system, which is growing and becoming stronger, is exerting ever greater influence upon the international situation in the interests of peace and progress and the freedom of the peoples.

The policy of certain aggressive groups in the United States is aimed at rallying around them all the reactionary forces of the capitalist world. Acting in this way they are becoming the centre of world reaction, the sworn enemies of the people. By this policy these anti-popular, aggressive imperialist forces are courting their own ruin, creating their own grave-diggers.

So long as imperialism exists there will always be soil for aggressive wars. . . .

The question of war or peaceful coexistence is now the crucial question of world policy. All the nations must display the utmost vigilance in regard to the war danger created by imperialism.

At present the forces of peace have so grown that there is a real possibility of averting wars as was demonstrated by the collapse of the imperialist designs in Egypt. The imperialist plan to use the counter-revolutionary forces for the overthrow of the People's Democratic system in Hungary failed as well. . . .

The Communist and Workers' parties taking part in the meeting declare that the Leninist principles of peaceful coexistence of the two systems, which has been further developed and brought up to date in the decisions of the Twentieth Congress of the CPSU is the sound basis of the foreign policy of the socialist countries and the dependable pillar of peace and friendship among the peoples. . . .

2. The meeting considers that in the present situation the strengthening of the unity and fraternal co-operation of the socialist countries, the Communist and Workers' parties and the solidarity of the international working-class, national liberation and democratic movements acquire special significance.

The working class, the democratic forces and the working people everywhere are interested in tirelessly strength-

ening fraternal contacts for the sake of the common cause, in safeguarding from enemy encroachments the historical, political and social gains effected in the Soviet Union—the first and mightiest socialist power—in the Chinese People's Republic and in all the socialist countries in seeing these gains extended and consolidated.

The socialist countries base their relations on principles of complete equality, respect for territorial integrity, state independence and sovereignty and non-interference in one another's affairs. These are vital principles. However, they do not exhaust the essence of relations between them. Fraternal mutual aid is part and parcel of these relations. This aid is a striking expression of socialist internationalism. . . .

3. The meeting confirmed the identity of views of the Communist and Workers' parties on the cardinal problems of the socialist revolution and socialist construction. The experience of the Soviet Union and the other socialist countries has fully borne out the correctness of the Marxist-Leninist proposition that the processes of the socialist revolution and the building of socialism are governed by a number of basic laws applicable in all countries embarking on a socialist course. These laws manifest themselves everywhere, alongside a great variety of historic national peculiarities and traditions which must by all means be taken into account.

Of vital importance in the present stage is intensified struggle against opportunist trends in the working class and Communist movement. The meeting underlines the necessity of resolutely overcoming revisionism and dogmatism in the ranks of the Communist and Workers' parties. . . .

In condemning dogmatism, the Communist parties believe that the main danger at present is revisionism or, in other words, right-wing opportunism, which as a manifestation of bourgeois ideology paralyses the revolutionary energy of the working class and demands the preservation or restoration of capitalism. However, dogmatism and sectarianism can also be the main danger at different phases of development in one party or another. It is for each Communist party to decide what danger threatens it more at a given time.

4. The Communist and Workers' parties are faced with great historic tasks. The carrying out of these tasks necessitates closer unity not only of the Communist and Workers' parties, but of the entire working class, necessitates cementing the alliance of the working class and peasantry, rallying the working people and progressive mankind, the freedom and peace-loving forces of the world.

The defence of peace is the most important world-wide task of the day. . . .

After exchanging views, the participants in the meeting arrived at the conclusion that in present conditions it is expedient besides bilateral meetings of leading personnel and exchange of information, to hold, as the need arises, more representative conferences of Communist and Workers' parties to discuss current problems, share experience, study each other's views and attitudes and concert action in the joint struggle for the common goals—peace, democracy and socialism.[7]

[7]*New China News Agency*, November 22, 1957, as quoted in Floyd, *op. cit.*, pp. 247–50.

A source of friction between Russia and China existed in their respective attitudes toward India. Nehru had been trying consistently to maintain neutrality between East and West, but he could not accept Chinese claims to mountainous territory in the Ladakh area between Sinkiang and Kashmir. Even though the Chinese had virtually occupied large areas by 1959, Nehru played down the border incidents. The Soviet Union feared that open warfare (which did break out in 1962) would place it in the embarrassing dilemma of having to back one of the contestants. A *Tass* statement, after a border incident in 1959, revealed the Russian position.

FOR CONSIDERATION   In 1963, when the Sino-Soviet break had become more violent, this article in *Tass* was denounced by the Chinese who accused Moscow of violating security.

Statement in *Tass*, September 9, 1959

Certain political circles and the press in Western countries have recently worked up a noisy campaign around an incident which took place not long ago on the Sino-Indian frontier in the region of the Himalayas. This campaign was obviously aimed at driving a wedge in between the two largest states of Asia—the Chinese People's Republic and the Republic of India, whose friendship has great significance for ensuring peace and international collaboration in Asia and throughout the world. . . .

One cannot fail to express regret at the fact that the incident on the Sino-Indian frontier took place. The Soviet Union is in friendly relations both with the Chinese People's Republic and the Republic of India. The Chinese and Soviet people are linked by indestructible bonds of fraternal friendship, based on the great principles of socialist internationalism. . . .

In Soviet ruling circles the assurance is being expressed that the government of the Chinese Peoples' Republic and the government of the Republic of India will not permit this incident to give comfort to those forces who do not want an im-

provement of the international situation but its worsening, and who are trying not to admit the planned slackening of international tension in relations between states. In the same circles *the assurance is being expressed that both governments will adjust the misunderstanding that has arisen*, taking account of their mutual interests in the spirit of the traditional friendship between the peoples of China and India. This will also contribute to the strengthening of the forces working for peace and international collaboration.[8]

------

[8]Quoted in Floyd, *op. cit.*, pp. 261–62.

Affter 1958, when China's five-year plan, "The Great Leap Forward," undertook to develop communes which were to improve the organization of labor, Mao became increasingly involved in economic problems. Unfortunately, so far as Soviet aid was concerned, Moscow began to taper off its technical assistance and finally withdrew its advisers. Trade between the two countries declined, and in spite of a Trade Agreement signed on March 29, 1960, exchange of goods in 1961 fell to one half of what it had been in 1959.

S. Chandrasekhar, an Indian sociologist, visited China in 1959, and Robert Guillain, a journalist associated with *Le Monde*, toured China in 1964.

Comments of S. Chandrasekhar, 1959

We drove to the Heavy Machine Tool Plant, a huge factory rather neatly laid out. The Deputy Director, an engineer (the Director, who was a Party man, was away), received us at the entrance and took us to the reception room, which looked exactly like all the other reception rooms I had seen across the length and breadth of China. . . .

He told me that the Wuhan Heavy Machine Tool Plant produces a large variety of machine tools. The construction of the plant started in April, 1956, and was completed in July, 1958, which was, as usual, one year and a half ahead of schedule. . . .

The plant covers, the Deputy Director said, an area of 500,000 square meters and it houses nine workshops, including the forging shop, the first machine assembling shop, the second machine assembling shop, the material-preparing shop, the foundry shop, and the tool-repairing shop.

There were some 2,000 machines in all, half of which were imported from the Soviet Union and other Communist countries. There were a planer four meters in width and three hundred and sixty tons in weight and a vertical lathe with a bench five meters long, and other heavy machines. . . . There were some 5,000 workers in the plant, and the average wage was about fifty-six *yuan* a month.

The plant produced vertical lathes, planers, milling machines, horizontal boring machines, gear hobbing machines, and seventy other types of machinery. The plant is capable of producing a 2,000-ton lathe, if the domestic market needed such a lathe.

With his introduction over, the Deputy Director took me around the factory. . . .

As I did not notice a single Russian expert anywhere in the huge factory, I asked the Deputy Director whether there were any Soviet technicians around.

"Only a few are left here now, and they are in the offices," he said. "Once they have trained a few Chinese, their role is over. The Soviet-trained Chinese have now trained all the workers in the factory. This way we have solved the language problem."

The fact that Russians are not to be seen in factories and offices is true not only of Wuhan but of China as a whole. For though I did meet Russians in hotels and theatres, and at art shows and exhibi-

tions, and on trains and planes, I never ran across a single one working in a factory or instructing Chinese workers, much less ordering Chinese about. The Russian technicians were all apparently well behind the scenes, their presence as inconspicuous as their aid was impressive.[9]

_____

[9]S. Chandrasekhar, Red China: An Asian View (New York: Frederick A. Praeger, Inc., 1961), pp. 62–63.

Sino-Soviet Trade

Year	In Million Rubles		
	Soviet Exports (Chinese Imports)	Soviet Imports (Chinese Exports)	Soviet Imports (Chinese Exports) Surplus (+)
1950................	350	172	−178
1951................	431	298	−133
1952................	499	373	−126
1953................	628	428	−200
1954................	684	521	−163
1955................	674	579	−94
1956................	660	688	+28
1957................	490	664	+174
1958................	571	793	+223
1959................	859	990	+131
1960................	735	763	+28
1961................	331	496	+166
1962................	210	465	+255
1963................	169	372	+203

Note: All data in *new* rubles. Data for 1959 and earlier have been converted to new rubles at the rate of 1 old ruble = 0.225 new ruble.

SOURCE: U.S.S.R., *Vneshniaia Torgovlia*, Statistical Supplements (Moscow, 1950-63), as reproduced in Yuan-li Wu, *The Economy of Communist China* (New York: Frederick A. Praeger, Inc., 1965), p. 176.

Soviet Technical Aid to China, 1950–1963, as Reported by Mikhail Suslov

More than 10,000 Soviet specialists were sent to the People's Republic of China for varying terms between 1950 and 1960. Some 10,000 Chinese engineers, technicians and skilled workers, and about 1,000 scientists, were taught and trained in the USSR between 1951 and 1962. More than 11,000 students and post-graduates graduated from Soviet higher educational establishments in this period.

Soviet-Chinese cooperation reached its peak after 1953, when elements of inequality in the relations between our

countries imposed during the Stalin personality cult, were removed on the initiative of the CC CPSU and Comrade N. S. Khrushchov. "In the Chinese question," Mao Tse-tung said in 1957, "the credit for removing the disagreeable and the extraneous belongs to N. S. Khrushchov."

In 1959 the proportions of Soviet-Chinese economic contacts were nearly double those of 1953, while deliveries for the building projects increased in that period as much as eightfold. Between 1954 and 1963 the Soviet Union turned over to China more than 24,000 sets of scientific and technical documents, including 1,400 projects of large industrial enterprises.

These documents contained the vast experience accumulated by the Soviet people, by its scientists and technicians. In effect, all these scientific and technical documents were turned over to China gratuitously.

The Soviet Union granted the People's Republic of China long-term credits totaling 1,816 million roubles on favourable terms. . . .

Although the Soviet Government was aware that this course of the Chinese leaders would harm Soviet-Chinese friendship and cooperation, it had no choice but to consent to it. As a result, the total volume of economic cooperation between the Soviet Union and the CPR (including trade and technical assistance) dropped in 1962 to 36.5 per cent of what it was in 1959, while deliveries of sets of equipment and materials decreased 40-fold. In 1963 economic cooperation and trade continued to drop.[10]

Report from *Agence France Presse*, August 13, 1960

The departures of Soviet technicians and their families from Peking and from the industrial provinces have increased at such a rate since the end of July that they are now coming to be spoken of openly in diplomatic circles in the Chinese capital as a veritable exodus.

These departures, which appeared to be normal until May, since they coincided with the return to China of Chinese technicians trained in the Soviet Union and the other socialist countries as well as with an increase in the number of students leaving Chinese schools, have now assumed such proportions that it would be difficult not to give them a political significance.

It appears that the 'ideological' discussion which has been going on for some weeks between the Russians and the Chinese Communists is at the root of this exodus which, if it continues, could leave a gap in the Chinese economy and endanger the progress so far made. . . .

The exodus affects at present only the Soviet experts and not those from the people's democracies.[11]

Comments of French Journalist, Robert Guillain

It is certain that China's animosity against the Moscow "revisionists" is equalled only by Russia's loathing of the Peking "dogmatists." This is something that can be checked on right in Peking. The Soviet Embassy is still there and wide open. There are a great many Russian correspondents (from *Tass*, *Pravda* and *Isvestia*, Soviet Radio, etc.) as well as correspondents from the other Iron Curtain countries, and Yugoslavia. . . .

These men told me the Russian version of the withdrawal of Russian technicians and aid in July, 1960. Far from being a surprise and a stab in the back from Khrushchev personally, as the Chinese claim, the break had been expected for a long time and had become inevitable—given the actions of the Chinese. What happened was this: over the years the Chinese became less and less docile disciples of their Russian teachers and finally became absolutely unmanageable.

"The Great Leap Forward went to their heads," a Russian told me. "Having decided on a breakneck speedup of production, they thought that they knew better than we did what the necessary precautions and technical norms were. They drove the machinery too hard, built plants in a slipshod fashion, even sacrificed human lives stupidly.

"For instance. We asked forty hours per pilot to train them for a certain model we were delivering. The Chinese said that was

---

[10]*Pravda*, April 3, 1964, as quoted in Basil Dmytryshyn, *USSR: A Concise History* (New York: Charles Scribner's Sons, 1965), pp. 561–62.

[11]Quoted in Floyd, *op. cit.*, pp. 284–85.

too much time. Chinese pilots could learn as much in twenty hours. It was no use protesting. We explained that the results would be catastrophic. Nothing helped. They wasted an incredible number of lives and amount of material. All right, they said, we'll try twenty-five hours. Further protests, further obstinancy—and the same disastrous results. And do you know what they came and said? 'We will *compromise* on thirty hours.' There was no way of convincing them that forty hours had been arrived at scientifically and that a Chinese is like anybody else!"

Analogous forcing had occurred in every domain, the Russians said, and in every sort of factory and shop. They cited a hydroelectric installation where thousands of tons of rock caved in, another where the cofferdams broke simply because Russian experts were not listened to—there were many casualties in both cases. As soon as the Great Leap was under way many Russian technicians found that they were no longer being listened to, many that they were being avoided. When they got to work they found posters on their doors or walls inscribed "Conservatives! Rightists! Revisionists!" They were handed pamphlets directed against their own regime. They were even expected to join with the Chinese against their own government's position on Marxism and the international situation! And

Long *of* The Minneapolis Tribune

"Comrades."

the exhaustion of machinery and personnel continued, the Russians say, due to the Chinese philosophy that given revolutionary ardor such as theirs and leadership such as that of the Chinese Communist Party no miracle would remain impossible. . . .[12]

---

[12]Robert Guillain, *When China Wakes* (New York: Walker & Company, 1966), pp. 172–74.

Peking became increasingly bitter at the cold shoulder which resulted from Khrushchev's "co-existence" policy. Russian verbal attacks on the United States quieted down, and Moscow seemed prepared to write off the attacks on Quemoy, which had started in 1958, as a Chinese failure. As the final stamp on the new attitude, Khrushchev visited the United States in the fall of 1959, and at the end of his stay enjoyed those personal exchanges with President Eisenhower which promoted the short-lived "spirit of Camp David."

To Chinese Communists, who saw themselves in the early stages of Marxist revolution, Russia had abandoned the basic precepts of Lenin to accept compromises with the decadent and imperialist West. On the

90th anniversary of Lenin's birth, they released a long ideological manifesto, which summarized their position. It is a basic document in the propaganda war between China and the Soviet Union.

Excerpt from Letter of the Chinese Communist Party, "Long Live Leninism," April 16, 1960

We believe in the absolute correctness of Lenin's thinking: War is an inevitable outcome of systems of exploitation and the source of modern wars is the imperialist system. Until the imperialist system and the exploiting classes come to an end, wars of one kind or another will always occur. They may be wars among the imperialists for redivision of the world, or wars of aggression and anti-aggression between the imperialists and the oppressed nations, or civil wars of revolution and counter-revolution between the exploited and exploiting classes in the imperialist countries, or, of course, wars in which the imperialists attack the socialist countries and the socialist countries are forced to defend themselves. All these kinds of wars represent the continuation of the policies of definite classes. . . .

Peaceful coexistence of nations and people's revolutions in various countries are in themselves two different things, not one and the same thing; two different concepts, not one; two different kinds of question, and not one and the same kind of question.

Peaceful coexistence refers to relations between nations, revolution means the overthrow of the oppressors as a class by the oppressed people within each country, while in the case of the colonial and semi-colonial countries, it is first and foremost a question of overthrowing alien oppressors, namely, the imperialists.

· · · · · ·

So, contrary to the modern revisionists who seek to paralyse the revolutionary will of the people by empty talk about peaceful transition, Marxist-Leninists hold that the question of possible peaceful transition to socialism can be raised only in the light of the specific conditions in each country at a particular time. The proletariat must never allow itself to one-sidedly and groundlessly base its thinking, policy and its whole work on the calculation that the bourgeoisie is willing to accept peaceful transformation. It must, at the same time, prepare for alternatives: one for the peaceful development of the revolution and the other for the non-peaceful development of the revolution. Whether the transition will be carried out through armed uprising or by peaceful means is a question that is fundamentally separate from that of peaceful coexistence between the socialist and capitalist countries; it is an internal affair of each country, one to be determined only by the relation of classes in that country in a given period, a matter to be decided only by the Communists of that country themselves. . . .

"Peace" in the mouths of modern revisionists is intended to whitewash the war preparations of the imperialists, to play again the tune of "ultra-imperialism" of the old opportunists, which was long since refuted by Lenin, and to distort our Communist policy concerning peaceful coexistence of countries with two different systems into elimination of the people's revolution in various countries. It was that old revisionist Bernstein who made this shameful and notorious statement: The movement is everything, the final aim is nothing. The modern revisionists have a similar statement: The peace movement is everything, the aim is nothing. Therefore, the "peace" they talk about is in practice limited to the "peace" which may be acceptable to the imperialists under certain historical conditions. It attempts to lower the revolutionary standards of the peoples of various countries and destroy their revolutionary will.

We Communists are struggling in defence of world peace, for the realisation of the policy of peaceful coexistence. At the same time we support the revolutionary wars of the oppressed nations against imperialism. We support the revolutionary wars of the oppressed people for their own liberation and social progress because all these revolutionary wars are just wars. Naturally, we must continue to explain to the masses Lenin's thesis concerning the capitalist-imperialist system as the source of modern war; we must continue to explain to the masses the Marxist-Leninist thesis on the replacement of capitalist imperialism by socialism and Communism as the final goal of our struggle. We must not hide our principles before the masses. . . .

Marching in the forefront of all the socialist countries and of the whole socialist camp is the great Soviet Union, the first socialist state created by the workers and peasants led by Lenin and their Communist Party. Lenin's ideals have been realised in the Soviet Union: socialism has long since built. Now, under the leadership of the Central Committee of the Communist Party of the Soviet Union and the Soviet government headed by Comrade Khrushchev, a great period of extensive building of Communism is already beginning. The valiant and enormously talented Soviet workers, peasants and intellectuals have brought about a great new labour upsurge in their struggle for the grand goal of building Communism.

We, the Chinese Communists and the Chinese people, cheer every new achievement of the Soviet Union, the native land of Leninism. The Chinese Communist Party, integrating the universal truths of Marxism-Leninism with the concrete practice of the Chinese revolution, has led the people of the entire country in winning great victories in the people's revolution, marching along the broad common road of socialist revolution and socialist construction charted by Lenin, carrying the socialist revolution to full completion and it has already begun to win great victories on the various fronts of socialist construction. The Central Committee of the Chinese Communist Party creatively set down for the Chinese people, in accordance with Lenin's principles and in the light of conditions in China, the correct principles of the general line for building socialism, the big leap forward and the people's communes, which have inspired the initiative and revolutionary spirit of the masses throughout the country and are thus day after day bringing about new changes in the face of our country. . . .

Leninism is the complete and integrated revolutionary teaching of the proletariat, it is a complete and integrated revolutionary outlook which, following Marx and Engels, continues to express the thinking of the proletariat. This complete and integrated revolutionary teaching and revolutionary outlook must not be distorted or carved up. We hold the view that the attempts of the modern revisionists to distort and carve up Leninism are nothing but a manifestation of the last ditch struggle of the imperialists facing their doom. In face of continuous victories in building Communism in the Soviet Union, in face of continuous victories in building socialism in the socialist countries, in face of constant strengthening of the unity of the socialist camp headed by the Soviet Union and of the steadfast and valiant struggles being waged by the increasingly awakened peoples of the world seeking to free themselves from the shackles of capitalist imperialism, the revisionist endeavours of Tito and his ilk are completely futile.

Long live great Leninism![13]

[13]Red Flag, No. 8 (April 16, 1960), English version in Peking Review, No. 17 (1960), as quoted in Floyd, op. cit., pp. 266–71.

Shortly after "Long Live Leninism" appeared, the American U-2 was shot down over the Soviet Union. With the cancellation of a summit conference and general worsening of Soviet relations with the West, Peking could gloat that its warnings had been justified. But cracks in the Communist bloc, noticeable at the Rumanian Party Congress in June, became more marked at the large conference, attended by delegates of 81 Communist Parties, which took place in Moscow toward the end of 1960. This meeting saw Albania and China drawing closer together, with a clear, open split between Moscow and Peking. The position of the Chinese delegation is outlined here by members of the Belgian group. The Manifesto of December 6, 1960, represented a compromise view.

FOR CONSIDERATION   Up to this time there had been given little publicity to Soviet-Chinese differences, and Khrushchev had prefered to obscure his attacks by saying "Albania" when he meant "China." But the Chinese representative, Teng Hsiao-ping, had shocked many delegates at the meeting by his sharp, vituperative defiance of Moscow.

The Chinese Position at the Moscow Conference of 81, as Reported by the Belgian Delegation, November, 1960

First Thesis. We must stop referring to the Twentieth Congress of the CPSU as though its teachings were valid for the whole of the world Communist movement. In the opinion of the Chinese delegation it is from the time of the Twentieth Congress that the CPSU has been leading the majority of the Communist parties along the road of capitulation to imperialism. The Albanian Communist Party made this argument more precise by accusing the CPSU of having gone over to revisionism.

Here we have our finger on the key point of difference; they deny altogether the validity and usefulness of the criticism of the cult of personality, they object to the idea that it is possible and useful to prevent the outbreak of a third world conflict, they question the political value of the application of the various paths to socialism, they describe as utopian the theory that the working class in certain countries and certain conditions may take power without bloodshed. Moreover, the essential unity of the working-class movement against the dictatorship of the monopoly capitalists and of militarist forces is relegated to the second place in importance to make room for the verbal denunciation of the socialist democrat leaders and their mistakes.

Second Thesis. The struggle for peaceful coexistence can be regarded only as a tactical move, a means of morally disarming the peoples of the capitalist countries and materially disarming the countries themselves. World disarmament and lasting peaceful coexistence will be not possible in practice until there are only socialist countries left in the world. The whole gravity of this sort of attitude is apparent. In the first place it leads to thinking that a third world conflict is inevitable and that the first duty is to prepare to win it at no matter what price in human lives and devastation. From this several theories develop logically. There is the theory that "local wars" are essentially inoffensive and without risk as far as world peace is concerned. There is the theory of the futility of efforts made by many Communist parties in the capitalist countries to work out plans of action aimed at developing democracy, restricting the power of the monopolies and changing substantially the policy of their countries. There is the theory which describes as "revisionist" the work of the second Rome conference of the 17 Communist parties of the capitalist countries.

In fact all these theories rest on a deep distrust of the working-class movement of the non-socialist countries and of its advance-guard parties, the Communist parties. The latter are regarded purely and simply as supernumerary forces and not as organisations enjoying full responsibility before the working-class of their own countries and the world working-class. They thus arrive finally at the anti-Marxist conception of "exported revolution" and it was not by accident that Maurice Thorez had to remind the Chinese comrades that the people do not like "booted missionaries."

Third Thesis. In the world Communist movement the minority does not have to take account of the general political line adopted by the whole movement. It has the right to embark on continuous fractional activity with no restrictions whatsoever.

In this connexion the debates assumed a certain bitterness. All the more so since at the Moscow conference the Chinese and Albanian delegations, while opposing

the principle of fraternal equality between the parties, clung determinedly to the mistaken concept of the "leading party", the latter being for the time being the CPSU. It is well said: for the time being. Actually from the moment that one considers that the "leading party" is mistaken ideologically and politically one is raising the question of its replacement and, consequently, submitting a candidate.[14]

Preamble to Manifesto of the Moscow Conference, December 6, 1960

Representatives of the Communist and Workers' parties have discussed at this meeting urgent problems of the present international situation and of the further struggle for peace, national independence, democracy and socialism.

The meeting has shown unity of views among the participants on the issues discussed. The Communist and Workers' parties have unanimously reaffirmed their allegiance to the Declaration and Peace Manifesto adopted in 1957. These programme documents of creative Marxism-Leninism determined the fundamental positions of the international Communist movement on the more important issues of our time and contributed in great measure toward uniting the efforts of the Communist and Workers' parties in the struggle to achieve common goals. They remain the banner and guide to action for the whole of the international Communist movement.

The course of events in the past three years has demonstrated the correctness of the analysis of the international situation and the outlook for world development as given in the Declaration and Peace Manifesto, and the great scientific force and effective role of creative Marxism-Leninism.

The chief result of these years is the rapid growth of the might and interna-

---

[14]*Le Drapeau Rouge,* February 22, 1962, as quoted in Floyd, *op. cit.,* pp. 287–88.

tional influence of the world socialist system, the vigorous process of disintegration of the colonial system under the impact of the national-liberation movement, the intensification of class struggles in the *capitalist world, and the continued decline and decay of the world capitalist system.[15]*

---

[15]As quoted in Floyd, *op. cit.,* p. 296.

In spite of the sporadic efforts on both sides to patch up areas of difference, neither China nor the Soviet Union would alter their basic positions.

In October, 1961, the Twenty-Second Congress of the Soviet Communist Party was held. This was the first Congress since the De-Stalinization Congress in 1956. Chou En-lai spoke with Khrushchev without useful results and when Khrushchev denounced Albania—China by inference—Chou En-lai walked out of the meeting. Before he left Moscow, Chou pointedly laid a wreath on Stalin's tomb.

FOR CONSIDERATION   To what extent was Khrushchev's posture toward China determined by developments in the West? John F. Kennedy had been inaugurated in January, 1961, and Khrushchev had sounded him out in Vienna the following June. Two months later the Berlin Wall was built. How strong an anti-West position could Khrushchev take with a hostile China on his back?

Excerpt from Khrushchev's Remarks at the Twenty-Second Congress of the CPSU, October 27, 1961

Clearly, the Central Committee of our party could not fail to tell the Congress the whole truth about the reprehensible stand taken by the leadership of the Albanian Party of Labor. Had we not done so, they would have gone on claiming that the Central Committee of the Communist Party of the Soviet Union was afraid to let the Party know of its differences with the leadership of the Albanian Party of Labor. Our party and the Soviet people should know how the Albanian leaders have been acting. And let the Congress, which is empowered to speak for the whole Party, state its attitude on this matter, pronounce its authoritative opinion.

It has been emphasized at our Congress that we are prepared to normalize relations with the Albanian Party of Labor

on the basis of Marxist-Leninist principles. How have the Albanian leaders responded to this? They have lashed out at our party and its Central Committee with a blatant, mud-slinging statement.

Comrade Chou En-lai, head of the delegation of the Communist Party of China, voiced concern in his speech over our having openly raised the issue of Albanian-Soviet relations at the Congress. As far as we can see, his statement primarily reflects alarm lest the present state of our relations with the Albanian Party of Labor affect the solidarity of the socialist camp.

We share the anxiety of our Chinese friends and appreciate their concern for the strengthening of unity. If the Chinese comrades wish to apply their efforts to normalizing the Albanian Party of Labor's relations with the fraternal parties, it is doubtful whether there is anyone better able to facilitate accomplishment of this purpose than the Communist Party of

China. This would really redound to the benefit of the Albanian Party of Labor and accord with the interests of the entire commonwealth of socialist countries. (*Prolonged applause.*) . . .

Comrades! Our party will continue to combat revisionists of all shades as it has in the past. Steadfastly conforming to the principles of the Declaration and the Statement of the conferences of Marxist-Leninist parties, we have exposed and shall continue unremittingly to expose the revisionism that has found expression in the Program of the Yugoslav League of Communists. We shall also constantly combat dogmatism and all other deviations from Marxism-Leninism. (*Applause.*)[16]

---

[16]*Pravda*, October 29, 1961, as quoted in Dallin *et al.*, *Diversity in International Communism*, pp. 74-75, 78.

While theoretical polemics have a basic significance in Communist politics, just as patristic writings provided a doctrinal foundation for early Christianity, the realistic Westerner cannot help but inquire into the practical and power aspects of Sino-Soviet tension. Little information has come out concerning the boundary disputes in the long frontier that runs from the Himalayas to the Sea of Japan, but what is known suggests that the issue is one of paramount significance.

The dangers inherent in the boundary problems were pointed out in 1954 in a provocative thesis formulated by Dr. Wilhelm Starlinger. Whether or not facts are available to support the theory, which is questioned in a study of John Tashjean, the population pressures in central Asia provide a potential source of conflict which cannot be ignored.

Outer Mongolia is a vast enclave which cuts into China's "natural" border along the Amur River. Harrison Salisbury, an American journalist, is one of the few Westerners to visit this remote area. His trip was made in 1957.

FOR CONSIDERATION   The disputed area along the upper Amur borders Sinkiang, where Chinese nuclear test sites and missile ranges have been developed. Could disputes in this region have provided a justification for a Russian attack on Chinese atomic installations? The Republic of Outer Mongolia has been developing close ties with the Soviet Union, but would be extremely vulnerable to Chinese attack from the south. If a complete break with China meant loss of Mongolia to Soviet interests, it might be that Russia would not gain by the conflict. It has been suggested that Khrushchev's hard line on the border issue brought him into disfavor with Brezhnev and others who preferred to safeguard the Soviet position in Outer Mongolia.

Summary of the Starlinger Thesis by John E. Tashjean

China has much territory, but even today this territory does not suffice to meet the demands of its peasantry. What will happen when, "in a few years," a nation of 700 million is short of land? No matter how much Mao Tse-tung may speed up industrialization, it can never by itself match the population increase. Emigration to the south has been going on for a long time, and with notable results. Even if, from now on, such emigration is supported by a powerful China, it can never amount to very much because the neighbors of China to the south and southwest are themselves overpopulated. In fact, their population pressure is so great that it has made itself felt as far away as the east coast of Africa, where it will overcome restrictions on immigration sooner or later. Australia, on the other hand, will be unattainable to China for a long time.

What will be the result? Since the beginning of history, it has never been possible to stabilize permanently a quickly increasing differential of population pressure in reciprocal quantities of space. The best intentions of the two governments cannot alter this fact, even if they began by sharing the same ideology. Given the unalterable conditions, China can expand only to the north and the northwest, and expand it must. In the 1930's China was weak and a strong Japan ruled Manchukuo, but Chinese moved into that area in very large numbers. Now that China is stronger it appears all the more likely that the process which took place in Manchuria may repeat itself first in Mongolia, then on the Amur and finally in all the lands on the Chinese side of Lake Baikal. The process will be peaceful if Russia gives in, as it has given in in Sinkiang, Manchuria, North Korea, and Tibet. If Russia remains adamant, blood will be shed for the control of soil.[17]

Excerpt from Chinese Comment on Soviet Open Letter, September 6, 1963

In April and May 1962 the leaders of the CPSU used their organs and personnel in Sinkiang, China, to carry out large-scale subversive activities in the Ili region and enticed and coerced several tens of thousands of Chinese citizens into going to the Soviet Union. The Chinese Government lodged repeated protests and made repeated representations, but the Soviet Government refused to repatriate these Chinese citizens on the pretext of the "sense of Soviet legality" and "humanitarianism." To this day this incident remains unsettled. This is indeed an astounding event, unheard of in the relations between socialist countries.[18]

Article in *New York Times*, September 7, 1963

Specialists in China affairs say the "citizens" referred to are without doubt Kazakhs, Uighurs and Uzbeks who went voluntarily to the Soviet Union to escape from Communist persecution. Opposition of these minority peoples—all predominantly Moslems—to Peking's Communist decrees has flared into uprisings on a number of occasions during the last few years. . . .

Earlier this year, White Russian refugees who crossed China from Sinkiang to Hong Kong reported that Kazakhs, Uighurs, and Uzbeks in the towns of Kuldja and Thacheng near the Soviet border had marched on the Soviet consulate in Kuldja and asked for arms "with which to drive out the Chinese."

The Soviet consul is reported to have turned down their request and advised them to submit it to local Chinese authorities.

Many fled to the Soviet Union. Shortly after the incident, the Soviet Consulate in Sinkiang was reported to have been closed at the request of the Chinese.[19]

---

[17]Summary of pp. 116 ff. of Wilhelm Starlinger's *Grenzen der Sowjetmacht* (1954) in John E. Tashjean, *Where China Meets Russia: An Analysis of Dr. Starlinger's Theory* (Washington, D.C.: Central Asian Collecteana, No. 2, 1959), p. 14.

[18]*New China News Agency*, Peking, September 6, 1963, as quoted in American Consulate General, Hong Kong, *Current Background*, No. 714 (September 12, 1963, p. 20.

[19]*New York Times*, September 7, 1963.

Reference to Border Incidents in a Report (1964) by Mikhail Suslov

We also consider it necessary to tell the Plenum about the violations of the Soviet-Chinese border, occasioned through the fault of the Chinese side. This has already been mentioned in the documents of the CPSU and the Soviet Government. In 1962 and 1963 violations of the Soviet border kept occurring continuously, often assuming the form of crude provocations.

The Soviet Government has come forward with the initiative of holding consultations in order to specify the border line between the USSR and the CPR at certain of its points. We do so in the belief that no territorial issues exist between the USSR and the CPR, that the Soviet-Chinese border took shape historically, and that the issue can concern only some sections of the border, to make them more precise wherever necessary.[20]

Comments of American Journalist Harrison E. Salisbury regarding Outer Mongolia, 1957

. . . the generous Communist Chinese Government . . . not only was providing the labor. It was also paying the wages of the labor crews, taking care of their shelter and food, providing the supplies and equipment. So far as I could learn, all the Mongol government had to do was to tell the Chinese what they wanted built.

These were not spindly, beaten slaves. They were fine, husky, muscular young men. They carried their heads high and their shoulders squared. I saw them in the early morning drizzle doing calisthenics on the sandy banks of the Tola. I saw them working under their great straw hats in blazing sun while the Mongols slept in the shade of buildings or the thickets of willows along the river. I watched them pedaling briskly on their bicycles across

the Tola River bridge at the end of the day.

It was not only in Ulan Bator that the blue ants were busy. We found them training the Mongols to run a glass factory they had built for them, and they were erecting an addition to it. We found them working under arc lights far in the interior to build a new bridge to replace one which floods had swept away. We found them digging irrigation works on new collective farm tracts.

They were installing the machinery in the fine new textile plant in Ulan Bator. They also were putting in the looms and the spindles—and every bit of the equipment had been purchased through the Chinese National Sales Corporation. There was nothing but the finest and newest English machinery from Platts, William Whiteley & Sons, Smith and Steels, and Metropolitan Vickers.

Even the repairs to the great Gandan monastery were being made by Chinese workmen. . . .

How many of them were there? I could not find out precisely. Mr. Lotchin said he thought there were ten thousand. Premier Tsedenbal said twenty thousand. My own guess was that the number was substantially greater. Almost every construction project in the country was dependent upon Chinese labor. Russian technicians were helping on some factories. But the labor was Chinese. The blue ants were the first and possibly the most dramatic evidence that struck my eye of the struggle between the giants of the world of Communism, Russia and China, over which was to control the future of Mongolia.

If the steady influx of skilled, able, aggressive Chinese continued, it was apparent that they would acquire an influence far out of proportion to their numbers; for they were culturally, technologically, and even physically far more advanced than the descendants of Genghis Khan's horse cavalry. And, by agreement with the Mon-

---

[20]*Pravda*, April 3, 1964, as quoted in Dmytryshyn, *op. cit.*, p. 566.

gol government, the Chinese had the right to opt for Mongol citizenship and stay permanently in the country—a Trojan horse of formidable size.

Nor was this the only string to Peking's bow. The Chinese obviously did not expect to win over the faithful among Moscow's trained top leaders. But they were concentrating on the second level: the young Mongols who would be the leaders of the next generation—the young men who had graduated in the last few years from the Ulan Bator State University, the young doctors and teachers, the engineers just back from courses in Prague and Budapest.

This level of the Mongol intelligentsia, small in numbers but strong in leadership potential, was being taken to China on excursions, trips, and study courses. They were being shown the way of the China revolution—how an Asian land was advancing with giant strides to world power, lifting itself by its own bootstraps. For the China slogan was: "Do It Alone. Do not rely on the West." And "West" in Ulan Bator means Russia, not America. Indeed, I even had the curious experience a time or two of hearing young Mongols referring to "Western countries like Russia and America."[21]

---

[21]Harrison E. Salisbury, *To Moscow—And Beyond* (New York: Harper & Row, Publishers, 1959), pp. 228–29, 235. Copyright © 1959, 1960 by Harrison E. Salisbury. Reprinted by permission of Harper & Row, Publishers.

In the fall of 1962, Khrushchev embarked on the construction of the Cuban missile sites which, if successfully completed, would have posed a constant threat to the United States. Kennedy's prompt and vigorous action in October forced the Soviet Union to back down. Khrushchev was undoubtedly impressed by the American President's quick response, and he also had to assess a counterthreat in the Multilateral Force (MLF) program which, early in 1963, would have provided West Germany with nuclear warheads. Khrushchev lost no time in suggesting to Kennedy that he was prepared to talk.

FOR CONSIDERATION   What were Khrushchev's alternatives? Could he have patched up his differences, still not widely publicized, with China? The price of amelioration in Sino-Soviet relations would probably have meant, among other things, assistance to China's atomic program and support of China's invasion of India. Would such backing have been to Russia's interest?

Excerpt from Soviet Note to the United States, Great Britain and West Germany, April 8, 1963

If the United States, Britain and France were to take the path of spreading nuclear weapons, the Soviet Government would, of course, be compelled to draw the appropriate conclusions and, in view of the new situation, to take measures which would ensure the maintenance at a proper level of the security of the Soviet Union, its friends and allies. . . .

The representatives of the United States present the case as though the alternative to a NATO multinational and multilateral nuclear force would be for the Federal Republic of Germany to create its own nuclear potential. Well then, the inference is that the United States and its allies are even now not in a position to control the course of the arming of the Federal Republic of Germany and to resist the pressure and blackmail emanating from that country. . . .

The Soviet Government urges the Government of the United States to contribute likewise to the settlement of the aforementioned problems and to make joint efforts to stop the nuclear missile armaments race. The Soviet Government is in favour of settling at a conference table the questions that have been brought to the fore by the development of international relations.[22]

[22]*American Foreign Policy: Current Documents 1963* (Washington, D.C.: U.S. Government Printing Office, 1967), p. 400.

Krushchev Statement to Editors of *Pravda* and *Izvestia*, June 15, 1963

What do we lack today? We lack the desire of the Western powers to reach an agreement and to abandon playing at negotiations. In regard to the Soviet Union, we are ready to sign an agreement on the discontinuation of all nuclear tests even today. It is up to the West. We agreed to a meeting between the representatives of the three powers in Moscow to try once again to reach an agreement on this question. But the success of this meeting will depend on the luggage the United States and British representatives bring with them to our country.[23]

[23]*Ibid.,* p. 974.

Meanwhile, some of the most vituperative ideological exchanges took place. The Soviet Communist Party put out a long letter on March 30, 1963, and the Chinese replied on June 14. To this the Russians countered with the Open Letter of July 14, a sampling of which is given here.

FOR CONSIDERATION   It should be borne in mind that, as a typical Communist polemic can run to 20,000 words or more, the excerpts reproduced touch on only a few of the arguments offered. The student who wishes more detail is referred to William E. Griffith's *The Sino-Soviet Rift* (Cambridge, Mass.: The M.I.T. Press, 1964), where texts of 16 exchanges of 1963 cover 250 pages.

Excerpts from the Soviet CP's "Open Letter to Party Organizations and Party Members," July 14, 1963

The Central Committee of the CPSU deems it necessary to address this open letter to you in order to set out our position on the fundamental questions of the international communist movement in connection with the letter of the Central Committee of the Communist Party of China of June 14, 1963.

The Soviet people are well aware that our Party and government, expressing as they do the will of the entire Soviet peo-

ple, spare no effort to strengthen fraternal friendship with the peoples of all socialist countries, with the Chinese people. We are united by a common struggle for the victory of communism, we have the same aim, the same aspirations and hopes.

For many years the relations between our parties were good. But *some time ago, serious differences came to light between the CPC on the one hand and the CPSU and other fraternal parties on the other. At the present time the Central Committee of the CPSU feels increasingly concerned over statements and actions by the leader-*

ship of the Communist Party of China which undermine the cohesion of our parties, the friendship of our peoples.

· · · · ·

The Chinese comrades allege that in the period of the Caribbean crisis we made an "adventurist" mistake by introducing rockets into Cuba and then, "capitulated" to American imperialism when we removed the rockets from Cuba. . . .

Inasmuch as the point in question was not simply a conflict between the United States and Cuba, but a clash between two nuclear powers, the crisis in the area of the Caribbean Sea would have turned from a local into a world one. A real danger of thermonuclear world war arose.

There were two alternatives in the prevailing situation: Either to follow in the wake of the "madmen" (that is how the most aggressive and reactionary representatives of American imperialism are called) and embark upon the road of unleashing a world thermonuclear war or, using the opportunities offered by the delivery of missiles, to take all measures to reach agreement on the peaceful solution of the crisis and to prevent aggression against the Republic of Cuba.

We have chosen, as is known, the second road and are convinced that we have done the right thing. We are confident that all our people are unanimous on this score. The Soviet people have proved more than once that they know how to stand up for themselves, how to defend the cause of the revolution, the cause of socialism. And nobody knows better than they do how much sorrow and sufferings a war brings, what difficulties and sacrifices it costs to the peoples.

Agreement on the removal of missile weapons in reply to the United States government's commitment not to invade Cuba and to keep its allies from doing this, the heroic struggle of the Cuban people, the support rendered to them by the peace-loving nations, have made possible the frustration of the plans of the extreme adventuristic circles of American imperialism, which were ready to go the whole hog. As a result it was possible to defend revolutionary Cuba and save peace.

The Chinese comrades regard as "embellishment of imperialism" our statement that the Kennedy government has also displayed definite reasonableness, a realistic approach in the course of the crisis around Cuba. Do they really think that all bourgeois governments lack all reason in everything they do?

Thanks to the courageous and far-sighted position of the USSR, the staunchness and restraint of the heroic Cuban people, their government, the forces of socialism and peace have proved that they are able to curb the aggressive forces of imperialism, to impose peace on the war advocates. This was a major victory of the policy of reason, of the forces of peace and socialism; this was a defeat of the forces of imperialism, of the policy of military ventures.

· · · · ·

We are living in an epoch when there are two worlds, two systems: socialism and imperialism. *It would be absurd to think that all the questions inevitably arising in relations among the countries of these two systems must be solved only by force of arms, ruling out all talks and agreements. Wars would never end then. We are against such an approach.*

The Chinese comrades argue that the imperialists cannot be trusted in anything, that they are bound to cheat. But this is not a case of faith, but rather a case of sober calculation. *Eight months have passed since the liquidation of the crisis in the Caribbean Sea area, and the United States Government is keeping its word— there is no invasion of Cuba. We have also assumed a commitment to remove our missiles from Cuba and we have fulfilled it.*

· · · · ·

If one is to extract the genuine content

of all this mass of pseudotheoretical discourses contained in the letter of the CPC Central Committee on these questions, it boils down to the following: the Chinese comrades come out against the line of the CPSU aimed at developing socialist democracy, that was proclaimed with such force in the decisions of the 20th, 21st and 22nd Congresses of our Party. In the CPSU program, it is not fortuitous that nowhere in their long letter did they find place even for a mere mentioning of the development of democracy in conditions of socialism, in conditions of construction of Communism.

It is difficult to judge in full measure about the motives the Chinese comrades guide themselves by when upholding the personality cult. Actually, for the first time in the history of the International Communist Movement we encounter an open exaltation of the personality cult. It must be said that even during the period when the personality cult flourished in our country, Stalin himself was forced, at least in words, to refuse to have anything to do with this petty bourgeois theory and said that it came from the social revolutionaries.

The attempts to use Marx and Lenin to defend the ideology of the personality cult can evoke nothing but surprise. Can it really be true that the Chinese comrades do not know that Lenin, as far back as during the birth of our Party, waged a gigantic struggle against the Narodniks' theories about the heroes and the masses, that genuinely collective methods of leadership were implemented under Lenin in the Central Committee of our Party and the Soviet state, that Lenin was extremely modest and mercilessly lashed out at the slightest manifestations of toadyism and servility to his person.

Of course, struggle against the personality cult was never regarded by our Party, or the other Marxist-Leninist parties, as negation of the authority of Party and government leaders. The CPSU stressed time and again, including at the 20th and 22nd Congresses, that the Party cherishes the authority of its leadership, that while debunking the personality cult and fighting against its consequences the Party puts high the leaders who really express the interests of the people and give all their strength to struggle for the victory of communism, and for this reason enjoy deserved prestige.

.   .   .   .   .

A meeting of the delegations of the CPSU and the CPC is being held in Moscow at present. *Unfortunately, the CPC representatives at the meeting continue to aggravate the situation. Despite this, the delegation of the CPSU display the utmost patience and self-control, working for a successful outcome of the negotiations. The nearest future will show whether the Chinese comrades agree to build our relations on the basis of what unites us, and not what divides us, on the basis of the principles of Marxism-Leninism.*

Our enemies build their calculations on deepening the contradictions between the CPC and the CPSU. They are now looking for something to profit by. The American *Daily News* wrote recently: Let us set Red Russia and Red China against each other so that they tear each other to pieces. We communists should never forget these insidious plans of the imperialists.

Aware of its responsibility to the international communist movement, to the peoples of the world, our Party urges the Chinese comrades to take to the road of resolving the differences and strengthening the genuine unity of our parties on the principles of Marxism-Leninism and proletarian internationalism.[24]

---

[24]*New China News Agency*, Peking, July 20, 1963, as quoted in American Consulate General, Hong Kong, *Current Background*, No. 709 (July 29, 1963), pp. 3, 13, 14, 21, 32.

The West accepted Khrushchev's invitation to resume talks to limit atomic explosions, and on July 25, 1963, the three powers came to an agreement. China and France refused to accept the treaty (China's reaction is given here), and de Gaulle shortly broke with Western policy when he resumed diplomatic relations with mainland China in the following year.

FOR CONSIDERATION   Had Khrushchev ever defied Peking so blatantly in any previous move? It seems clear that Khrushchev, thwarted in Berlin and in Cuba, unsuccessful in many domestic programs, fearful of a developing China, was increasingly anxious to develop a *détente* with the West. The United States responded and, even though President Kennedy was assassinated in November, 1963, his successor did not press the MLF program.

Excerpt from the Test-Ban Treaty, Signed by the Soviet Union, Great Britain, and the United States, August 5, 1963

1. Each of the Parties to this Treaty undertakes to prohibit, to prevent, and not to carry out any nuclear weapon test explosion, or any other nuclear explosion, at any place under its jurisdiction or control:

(*a*) in the atmosphere; beyond its limits, including outer space; or underwater, including territorial waters or high seas; or

(*b*) in any other environment if such explosion causes radioactive debris to be present outside the territorial limits of the State under whose jurisdiction or control such explosion is conducted. It is understood in this connection that the provisions of this subparagraph are without prejudice to the conclusion of a treaty resulting in the permanent banning of all nuclear test explosions, including all such explosions underground, the conclusion of which, as the Parties have stated in the Preamble to this Treaty, they seek to achieve.

2. Each of the Parties to this Treaty undertakes furthermore to refrain from causing, encouraging, or in any way participating in, the carrying out of any nuclear weapon test explosion.[25]

Statement of Chinese Government, July 31, 1963

A treaty on the partial halting of nuclear tests was initialled by the representatives of the United States, Britain and the Soviet Union in Moscow on July 25.

This is a treaty signed by three nuclear powers. By this treaty they attempt to consolidate their nuclear monopoly and bind the hands of all the peace-loving countries subjected to the nuclear threat.

This treaty signed in Moscow is a big fraud to fool the people of the world. It runs diametrically counter to the wishes of the peace-loving people of the world.

The people of the world demand a genuine peace; this treaty provides them with a fake peace.

The people of the world demand general disarmament and a complete ban on nuclear weapons; this treaty completely divorces the cessation of nuclear tests

---

[25]*American Foreign Policy: Current Documents 1963*, p. 1032.

from the total prohibition of nuclear weapons, legalizes the continued manufacture, stockpiling and use of nuclear weapons by the three nuclear powers, and runs counter to disarmament.

The people of the world demand the complete cessation of nuclear tests; this treaty leaves out the prohibition of underground nuclear tests, an omission which is particularly advantageous for the further development of nuclear weapons by U.S. imperialism.

The people of the world demand the defense of world peace and the elimination of the threat of nuclear war; this treaty actually strengthens the position of nuclear powers for nuclear blackmail and increases the danger of imperialism launching a nuclear war and a world war.

If this fraud is not exposed, it can do even greater harm. It is unthinkable for the Chinese Government to be a party to this dirty fraud. The Chinese Government regards it as its unshirkable and sacred duty to thoroughly expose this fraud. . . .[26]

[26]New China News Agency, Peking, July 31, 1963, as quoted in American Consulate General, Hong Kong, Survey of China Mainland Press, No. 3032 (August 2, 1963), p. 31.

It is difficult to assess how grave Soviet and Chinese leaders considered the frontier questions that affected both countries. It is known that the two governments held discussions on border issues in February, 1964, but that the conversations broke down in May.[27] When Mao Tse-tung granted an interview to a group of Japanese socialists on July 10, he made it clear that the issue remained a serious one.

FOR CONSIDERATION   Is it possible that Moscow and Peking were content to keep the border issue alive? Such conflicts have often been used as justification for action when more fundamental but less tangible objectives were at stake.

Mao Tse-tung's Interview with Japanese Socialists, July 10, 1964

Tetsuo Ara, leader of the delegation of the Hokkaido headquarters of the Socialist Party, asked: "Behind our backs the Kuril Islands were taken away from us under the Yalta agreement and Potsdam declaration. We demand that they be returned to us, and would like to hear the opinion of Chairman Mao on this score."

The reply was as follows:

There are too many places occupied by the Soviet Union. According to the Yalta

[27]In 1966, these conversations were referred to as not having been resumed (Keesing's Contemporary Archives [1966], p. 21633).

agreement, the Soviet Union, under the pretext of guaranteeing the independence of Mongolia has actually placed that country under its domination. Mongolia occupies a much larger area than the Kuril Islands. In 1954, when Khrushchov and Bulganin came to China, we raised this question, but they refused to talk with us. They appropriated part of Rumania. They separated part of East Germany, and expelled the local inhabitants to the western part. . . . They have separated everything that could be separated. Some people have stated that the Sinkiang area and the territories north of the River Amur should be incorporated into the Soviet Union. The USSR is concentrating troops on its border.

The Soviet Union occupies an area of 22 million square kilometres, and its population is only 200 million people. It is time it stopped the partition. Japan occupies an area of 370,000 square kilometres, and its population is 100 million people. About a hundred years ago the area east of Baikal became Russian territory, and since then Vladivostok, Khabarovsk, Kamchatka and other points have been the territory of the Soviet Union. We have not yet asked for a settlement of this account. As for the Kuril Islands, this question is clear for us. They must be returned to Japan. . . .

Naturally, a war in Southeast Asia would not be so bad, after all. The situation there is like a cancerous growth. When it begins to grow it must be removed. It must be cut out. Thus, it would not be so bad after all if the situation were to be cleared up. Here you have our aggressive talk, as they say in Washington and of which our friend Khrushchov is always speaking.[28]

[28]*Pravda*, September 2, 1964, in *Information Bulletin: Documents of the Communist and Workers Parties, Articles and Speeches*, Vol. 21 (Prague: Peace and Socialism Publishers, 1964), pp. 1188–89.

The breakdown of the Sino-Soviet border discussions may have confirmed Khrushchev in his conviction that he must improve Russian relations with the West in spite of those Communists who saw in such a *détente* a crumbling of the Communist bloc. When West German Chancellor Erhard visited President Johnson in December, 1963, the President had suggested that the Federal Republic improve its relations with Russia. Publicity was given this suggestion when it appeared in the German magazine *Quick*, which in April, 1964, published an interview with Johnson. In July, Khrushchev's son-in-law, Alexeis Adzhubei, visited Bonn to make arrangements for the Soviet leader's visit. In September, it was announced that Khrushchev would plan to visit West Germany if an invitation was forthcoming.

When Mikhail Suslov, the fourth-ranking Soviet Communist, gave a long report to the Plenary Session of the Central Committee on February 14, 1964, he summarized the differences existing between Russia and China. His pointed references to West Germany may have prepared the way for a *rapprochement*.

FOR CONSIDERATION   Suslov had been chosen in 1963 to negotiate with the Chinese, and was under some attack from Khrushchev. At the time of the Suslov report (which runs to over 60 pages), Khrushchev's ouster was only seven months away.

Excerpt from Speech of Mikhail Suslov at the Plenary Meeting of the Central Committee of the CPSU, February 14, 1964

Hysterically attacking the Moscow partial test ban treaty of July 31, 1963 and thereby finding themselves aligned with the most aggressive circles of imperialism, the Chinese leaders still further exposed themselves as opponents of the policy of peace and peaceful coexistence of states with different social systems. The enemies rejoiced over their actions and friends could not but condemn them. . . .

It is well known that the CPC leaders insistently sought to obtain the atomic bomb from the Soviet Union. They expressed their deep mortification when our country did not give them samples of nuclear weapons.

The CC, CPSU and the Soviet Government have already explained why we consider it inexpedient to help China produce nuclear weapons. The inevitable reaction to this would be the nuclear arming of powers of the imperialist camp, in particular, West Germany and Japan. Having a higher level of economic, scientific and technological development they could undoubtedly produce more bombs than China and build up a nuclear potential much faster. It should be borne in mind that revanchist aspirations are particularly strong in these countries. These are the countries which in the past were the main hotbeds of military threats and militarism.

The Soviet Union's atomic weapon is a reliable guarantee of the defence not only of our country but also of the entire socialist camp, including China. The leaders of the CPC are well aware of this fact. Nonetheless, they want to acquire the nuclear weapon at all costs. . . .

Everyone knows the sharply negative reaction of the Chinese leaders to the efforts the Soviet Union and other socialist countries are making to normalise and improve economic and other relations with the capitalist countries, including the United States of America. Why, one involuntarily asks, does any normalisation of relations between the USSR and the USA, the two great nuclear powers on whose efforts a relaxation of international tension largely depends, evoke such opposition from the Chinese government? With a persistence worthy of better application, the Chinese leaders are doing their utmost to hinder an improvement of US-Soviet relations, portraying it as a "conspiracy with the imperialists". At the same time the CPR Government is making feverish efforts to establish better relations with Britain, France, Japan, West Germany and Italy. All the indications are that they would not be averse to an improvement in relations with the USA if the opportunity presented itself. . . .

We know that peace is a true ally of socialism. The situation created by peaceful coexistence also favourably influences the development of the national liberation movement and the revolutionary struggle of the working class in the capitalist countries. . . .

The efforts of the working class and all working people to avert the threat of another world war help to educate the peoples in a spirit of international solidarity because under present-day conditions the struggle for peace is, as never before, essentially an international struggle.

What, for example, does it mean to work for peace in a country like the Federal Republic of Germany? It means, first and foremost, active opposition to the big monopolies, which are hatching ideas of revenge, opposition to their offensive against the vital rights and political freedoms of the working people. By participating in this struggle, the revolutionary working class, far from "dissolving" in the mass democratic movement, as the Chinese leaders maintain, gets a schooling in revolutionary organisation and discipline, unites its ranks and wins greater influence among the masses.[29]

---

[29]*Pravda*, April 3, 1964, as quoted in Dmytryshyn, *op. cit.*, pp. 548–51.

B etween October 12 and 15, 1964, those secret maneuvers which forced Khrushchev from power took place. The pressures against Khrushchev were complex, and certainly not limited to disagreement exclusively with his foreign policy. An enigmatic comment in *Pravda*, reproduced here, contained the gist of what Soviet officialdom was willing to reveal.

On October 16, China exploded her first atomic device.

FOR CONSIDERATION   The coincidence of the two events, Khrushchev's fall and China's bomb, has given rise to some speculation. Certainly Khrushchev was working toward closer relations with Germany. Was that the "harebrained scheme" referred to by *Pravda?* Or did he have some project concerning China? It was known that he had been planning a great Party conference for December 15, 1964. Had he planned to read China out of the international Communist movement? Could he have planned an attack on Chinese atomic installations? These are all interesting speculations.[30]

Excerpt from Editorial in *Pravda*, October 17, 1964

The Leninist party is an enemy of subjectivism and drifting in Communist construction, harebrained scheming, immature conclusions and hasty decisions and actions divorced from reality. Bragging and phrase-mongering, commandism, unwillingness to take into account the achievements of science and practical experience are alien to it.[31]

[30]See Harold C. Hinton, *Communist China in World Politics* (Boston: Houghton Mifflin Company, 1966), pp. 469–88; Edward Crankshaw, *Khrushchev: A Career* (Avon Discus edition, 1967), p. 290.

[31]*Facts on File*, Vol. XXIV, No. 1251 (October 15–21, 1964), p. 357.

AFTERWORD   Khrushchev's fall was hailed with delight in Peking, but in due time it appeared that the policies of Brezhnev and Kosygin could not alter fundamental differences. Chinese Communists came to deplore what they called "Khrushchevism without Khrushchev," and an added irritant developed with diverse attitudes toward the Vietnamese War.

China's atomic program pushed ahead at a rate no Western observer had anticipated: one detonation in 1965, three in 1966, and the first hydrogen bomb on June 17, 1967.

This series of documents terminates with an interview given in 1966 by Chinese Foreign Minister Chen Yi, the vituperative old marshal who had been at Mao's side since the early days of the Revolution.

FOR CONSIDERATION   How inevitable was the struggle between China and the Soviet Union? Can one pinpoint the real issues? Can the conflict be compared, in its combination of ideological and political issues, to the schism between Rome and Constantinople which split the medieval Catholic Church?

**Excerpt from an Interview with
Marshal Chen Yi, Chinese Deputy
Premier and Foreign Minister,
by Carlos María Guttiérrez**

.   .   .   .   .

I asked a question: Has China considered the final consequences of this intransigent position? Chen Yi began to talk and suddenly there was a great silence; even the whispers of the pines in the garden were hushed, for the old man had closed his eyes and was saying terrible things. His words conveyed at one and the same time how the almost academic subject of nuclear war is viewed as a distinct possibility here in China and how painfully aware these men are of the game they have chosen to play: "China is hated by both the reactionaries and the revisionists. We have to run the risk. Perhaps one day they will destroy Peking with their bomb. North Americans and Japanese will land in China and wipe us out. I cannot stop thinking of that. The generals in the Pentagon have said it openly: they want to attack the Chinese atomic installations. The last stage of the escalation is China. The leaders of China have studied this problem. And the conclusion was that we have to run this risk. The coastal cities will probably be destroyed. We estimate that hundreds of millions of people will be sacrificed. We shall fight for maybe thirty more years. . . ." He paused, and added pensively, as though he had forgotten I was there: "Russian missiles may some day fly from Moscow to Peking. Peking is already an atomic target . . ." What sort of a question would add anything, when the foreign minister of a world power has said things like that and has admitted that he anticipates a nuclear holocaust? Chen finished his declaration: "We are as brave as Stalin who let the Germans go all the way to the gates of Moscow. We can no longer turn back. To retreat would be to capitulate. This is not a matter of propaganda. It is possible that the earth may soon reach the boiling point and that everything will be delayed for many years."

From outside of China, it is possible to believe in the futility of the polemic about revisionism. The documents we see only give the theoretical arguments and thus, to the outside observer, everything is reduced to a mere grievance which can be kept apart from the real political struggle.

Chen's statements, on the other hand, give us another yardstick. Chen spoke of the U.S.S.R. as the enemy; the split has been completed although the ambassadors still continue at their posts. Once placed in its role as an atomic target, China defined its friends and enemies, possibly with a Manichaeanism brought on by the danger of death, but also with cold conviction. Three years ago there were thousands of Soviet advisers living there, associating with the Chinese. The traces remain: most vehicles are Russian, and there are whole sections full of Russian texts in all the book stores, although the readers for whom they were intended are no longer there. This country, so close to the Chinese for a half century, is now regarded as the nuclear enemy. There is no better proof of their complete alienation than the vehement words of the Foreign Minister. Nevertheless, the condemnation of the U.S.S.R. does not keep the Chinese from studying its supposed heresy, trying to analyze it. There is an element of self-defense in this: "Before," said Chen, "the U.S.S.R. was an example for China. It is now too. It is, in the words of Comrade Mao, 'a teacher in the negative sense.' "[32]

---

[32]Carlos María Gutiérrez in *Marcha* (Montevideo, May 20, 1966), published in *Atlas* (October, 1966), pp. 10–12.

BIBLIOGRAPHY

Sources Used in This Problem

1. Collections and Official Documents

American Foreign Policy: Current Documents 1963. Washington, D.C.: U.S. Government Printing Office, 1967.

Atlas.

Current Background. Hong Kong: American Consulate General.

Facts on File.

Information Bulletin. Documents of the Communist and Workers Parties, Articles and Speeches, Vol. 21. Prague: Peace and Socialism Publishers, 1964.

Keesing's Contemporary Archives.

New York Times.

Peking Review.

Soviet News.

Survey of China Mainland Press. Hong Kong: American Consulate General, 1963.

2. Others

Beloff, Max. *Soviet Policy in the Far East.* London: Oxford University Press, 1953.

Chandrasekhar, S. *Red China: An Asian View.* New York: Praeger, 1961.

Dallin, Alexander, et al. (eds.). *Diversity in International Communism.* New York: Columbia University Press, 1963.

Dmytryshyn, Basil. *USSR: A Concise History.* New York: Scribner's, 1965.

Floyd, David. *Mao against Khrushchev: A Short History of the Sino-Soviet Conflict.* New York: Praeger, 1963.

Guillain, Robert. *When China Wakes.* New York: Walker & Co., 1966.

Salisbury, Harrison E. *To Moscow—and Beyond.* New York: Harper, 1959.

Tashjean, John E. *Where China Meets Russia: An Analysis of Dr. Starlinger's Theory.* Washington, D.C.: Central Asian Collecteana, 1959.

Wu Yuan-li. *The Economy of Communist China.* New York: Praeger, 1965.

Select List of Books Recommended for Further Reading

Barnett, A. Doak. *China after Mao.* Princeton, N.J.: Princeton University Press, 1967.

Beaton, L. and Maddox, J. *The Spread of Nuclear Weapons.* London: Chatto and Windus for the Institute of Strategic Studies, 1962.

Bloomfield, Lincoln P., et al. *Khrushchev and the Arms Race: Soviet Interests in Arms Control and Disarmament, 1954–1964.* Cambridge, Mass.: MIT Press, 1966.

Brzezinski, Zbigniew K. *The Soviet Bloc: Unity and Conflict.* Rev. ed. Cambridge, Mass.: Harvard University Press, 1967.

Chang, Tien-fong. *A History of Sino-Russian Relations.* Washington, D.C.: Public Affairs Press, 1957.

Crankshaw, Edward. *Khrushchev: A Career.* New York: Viking, 1966.

Crankshaw, Edward. *The New Cold War: Moscow vs Peking.* Baltimore: Penguin, 1963.

DALLIN, ALEXANDER, et al. *The Soviet Union and Disarmament.* New York: Praeger, 1964.

DALLIN, DAVID J. *Soviet Foreign Policy.* Philadelphia: J. P. Lippincott, 1961.

DALLIN, DAVID J. *Soviet Russia and the Far East.* New Haven, Conn.: Yale University Press, 1948.

DUTT, V. P. *China and the World.* New York: Praeger, 1966.

ECKSTEIN, ALEXANDER. *Communist China's Economic Growth.* New York: McGraw-Hill, 1966.

GITTINGS, JOHN (ed.). *The Sino-Soviet Dispute: Extracts from Recent Documents.* Royal Institute of International Affairs. London: Oxford University Press, 1964.

GRIFFITH, WILLIAM E. *Albania and the Sino-Soviet Rift.* Cambridge, Mass.: The M.I.T. Press, 1963.

GRIFFITH, WILLIAM E. *The Sino-Soviet Rift.* Cambridge, Mass.: M.I.T. Press, 1964.

GUILLAIN, ROBERT. *600 Million Chinese.* New York: Criterion Books, 1957.

HALPERIN, MORTON H. *China and the Bomb.* New York: Praeger, 1965.

HALPERIN, MORTON H. and PERKINS, DWIGHT H. *Communist China and Arms Control.* New York: Praeger, 1965.

HINTON, HAROLD C. *Communist China in World Politics.* Boston: Houghton Mifflin, 1966.

HORELICK, ARNOLD L. and RUSH, MYRON. *Strategic Power and Soviet Foreign Policy.* Chicago: University of Chicago Press, 1966.

HSIEH, ALICE LANGLEY. *Communist China's Strategy in the Nuclear Era.* Englewood Cliffs, N.J.: Prentice-Hall, 1962.

HUDSON, G. H., LOWENTHAL, RICHARD and MacFARQUHAR, RODERICK (eds.). *The Sino-Soviet Dispute.* New York: Praeger, 1961.

LAQUEUR, WALTER Z. *Russia and Germany: A Century of Conflict.* Boston: Little Brown, 1965.

LINDEN, CARL A. *Khrushchev and the Soviet Leadership 1957–1964.* Baltimore: Johns Hopkins Press, 1966.

LONDON, KURT (ed.). *Unity and Contradiction: Major Aspects of Sino-Soviet Relations.* New York: Praeger, 1962.

LOWENTHAL, RICHARD. *World Communism: The Disintegration of a Secular Faith.* New York: Oxford University Press, 1964.

McKINTOSH, JOHN M. *Strategy and Tactics of Soviet Foreign Policy.* New York: Oxford University Press, 1962.

MEHNERT, KLAUS. *Peking and Moscow.* New York: Putnam's, 1963.

MOSELY, PHILIP E. (ed.). *The Soviet Union, 1922–1962.* New York: Praeger, 1963.

NORTH, ROBERT C. *Moscow and Chinese Communists.* Stanford, Calif.: Stanford University Press, 1963.

PENTONY, DeVERE E. (ed.). *Red World in Tumult.* San Francisco: Chandler Press, 1962.

RUBENSTEIN, ALVIN Z. *The Foreign Policy of the Soviet Union.* 2d ed. New York: Random House, 1966.

RUPEN, ROBERT A. *The Mongolian People's Republic.* Stanford, Calif.: Stanford University Press, 1966.

SALISBURY, HARRISON E. *Orbit of China.* New York: Harper and Row, 1967.

SENN, ALFRED E. *Readings in Russian Political and Diplomatic History.* Vol. II, *The Soviet Period.* Homewood, Ill.: The Dorsey Press, 1966.

SKILLING, H. GORDON. *Communism National and International: Eastern Europe after Stalin.* Toronto: University of Toronto Press, 1964.

WINT, GUY. *Communist China's Crusade: Mao's Road to Power and the New Campaign for World Revolution.* New York: Praeger, 1965.

ZAGORIA, DONALD S. *The Sino-Soviet Conflict, 1956–61.* Princeton, N.J.: Princeton University Press, 1962.

ZAGORIA, DONALD S. *Vietnam Triangle: Moscow, Peking, Hanoi.* New York: Pegasus, 1967.